Readings on Financial Institutions and Markets

Readings on Financial Institutions and Markets

Fourth Edition

Edited by

Donald R. Fraser
Peter S. Rose
both of
Texas A&M University

IRWIN

Homewood, IL 60430
Boston, MA 02116

Previous editions of this text were published under the title,
FINANCIAL INSTITUTIONS AND MARKETS IN A
CHANGING WORLD

© RICHARD D. IRWIN, INC., 1980, 1984, 1987, and 1990

Sponsoring editor: Michael W. Junior
Project editor: Lynne Basler
Production manager: Bette K. Ittersagen
Designer: Robyn Basquin
Compositor: Better Graphics, Inc.
Printer: Malloy Lithographing, Inc.

Library of Congress Cataloging-in-Publication Data

Readings on financial institutions and markets/edited by Donald R.
    Fraser and Peter S. Rose—4th ed.
        p.   cm.
    Rev. ed. of: Financial institutions and markets in a changing
    world. 3rd ed. 1987.
    ISBN 0-256-08339-8
    1. Financial institutions—United States.   2. Finance—United
States.   I. Fraser, Donald R.   II. Rose, Peter S.   III. Title:
Financial institutions and markets in a changing world.
  HG181.F633   1990
  332.1′0973—dc20   89–39285
                                                                CIP

Printed in the United States of America
1 2 3 4 5 6 7 8 9 0 ML 6 5 4 3 2 1 0 9

Preface

The operation and regulation of financial institutions and markets faces significant changes and substantial problems. The challenges to managers and regulators stem from a variety of interrelated factors that include the following:

The introduction of a vast group of new financial instruments.

The breakdown of the traditional specialization of function among individual financial institutions.

Legislative and regulatory deregulation.

The globalization of the operations of both financial markets and institutions.

The development of new technology that has increased the immediacy of financial transactions and lowered their costs.

The increased instability of interest rates and exchange rates as well as financial distress within some sectors, such as energy and agriculture, and in some of the less developed countries (LDCs) also play a role. The net result of these developments is to obsolete information on these topics at an ever-increasing rate. As a result, traditional textbooks that survey financial markets and institutions find it virtually impossible to provide up-to-date analysis of the significant issues and problems in this important subject area.

This compilation of readings on financial institutions and markets is designed to fill the void created by the accelerated pace of change. It complements existing texts by covering topics whose importance has only recently become obvious, and it provides an analysis of innovations in financial instruments, markets, and institutions that are too recent to be captured in textbooks. Finally, the readings allow for more in-depth treatment of selected topics than is possible within a textbook setting.

The specific readings included in this book have been carefully selected with three principal criteria: *immediacy, relevance,* and *readability*. The readings must be current if the goal of filling the void caused by rapid change is to be accomplished. In fact, the articles selected are very current: almost one half of the articles were published in 1989, and almost three quarters were published either in 1988 or 1989. The readings must be relevant to the important policy issues of the day. In that regard, we have selected a number of readings that relate to the bank failure problem, the thrift crisis, and the Bush plan. An article is also included that analyzes the implications of Europe 1992 for the U.S. economy and especially for U.S. financial institutions. The articles must be readable if they are to accomplish their task of conveying useful information. In that regard, we have made a conscious effort to select readings that have a minimum amount of technical jargon, that are short and to-the-point, and that present their ideas in an organized way. The brevity of many of the articles contributes to this goal; the mean length of an article included in the set of readings is about 10 pages.

The 38 readings are divided into seven sections that span the topics generally covered in courses in financial institutions and markets, financial institutions, or money and banking. Part One—Financial Institutions: Management and Regulation deals with some of the important innovations in the operation and regulation of commercial banks and other depository institutions, including risk-based capital and new types of organizational strategies and types of lending. Part Two—Regulatory

Reform for Financial Institutions focuses on the problem of failed and failing banks and savings and loans and deals with various alternative strategies for reforming the regulatory structure (including deposit insurance reform) to handle what is truly a massive problem.

Part Three—Determination of Interest Rates and Stock Prices concentrates on the equity market, with an article on the topic of stock market efficiency and another on the relationship between inflation and stock prices. There are also two articles on interest rates, both of which adopt an international perspective. Part Four—Instruments of the Money and Capital Markets focuses on some of the important innovations in these markets, including interest rate swaps, low-grade or "junk" bonds, stripped securities, and Eurocommerical paper.

Part Five—International Finance includes not only an article on Europe 1992, but also articles dealing with international policy coordination, nontariff barriers to trade, and credit risk to U.S. banks through their foreign lending. These five articles in the "International Finance" section are not, however, the only ones related to the subject. The growing internationalization of financial markets makes it impossible to compartmentalize the topic. In fact, there are six other articles scattered throughout the book that deal with international finance topics.

Part Six—Macroeconomics and Financial Policy focuses on some of the important issues dealing with the formulation and implementation of monetary and fiscal policy. It includes a review article on the effects of money on inflation and one on the effects of deficit spending. The last selection—Financial Innovation covers some of the more important recent changes in financial markets, including stock index futures, market index deposits, securitization, home-equity loans, mortgage-backed securities, and off–balance sheet banking.

Part Seven—Financial Innovation concentrates on the major new financial instruments that have dramatically altered the flow of funds in the financial system. Participants in the financial arena have created new types of financial packages that better meet the risk and return preferences of borrowers and lenders. These include the stock index futures (and the use of these index futures in program trading), market-index deposits and home-equity loans. Particularly significant is the securitization phenomenon that has turned billions of dollars of nonmarketable assets into securities traded in well-developed secondary markets, though the prepayment risk involved in securitized home mortgages is a significant factor to market participants. Risk is also an important feature in the use of off–balance sheet contingent obligations that have been created by commercial banks in their attempt to deal with the challenging environment they faced in the 1980s.

We believe that this book is suitable for a wide variety of courses in economics and finance. It has particular application to courses dealing with money and banking, financial institutions, the money and capital markets, and commercial bank management. In addition, practitioners in industry and other individuals who desire to update their knowledge of recent innovations and policy issues in the financial sector will find the book a useful guide.

We wish to express our deep gratitude to those who wrote the articles included in this edition. We hope their thoughts and ideas will reach an even larger audience through the medium of this book. In addition, we would like to acknowledge the cooperation of the publishers of the articles included, whose support made this book possible. A special thanks is due to our families who, as before, endured the demands of time and the not-infrequent frustration involved in putting this new edition together. Without their encouragement and understanding this project could not have been completed.

Donald R. Fraser
Peter S. Rose

Acknowledgments

Article 1: "Managing Interest Rate Risk with Interest Rate Futures," Charles S. Morris, Federal Reserve Bank of Kansas City *Economic Review*, March 1989, pp. 3–20.

Article 2: "Economics of Scale and Scope at Depository Financial Institutions: A Review of the Literature," Jeffrey A. Clark, Federal Reserve Bank of Kansas City *Economic Review*, September/October 1988, p. 16–33.

Article 3: "The Risk-Based Capital Agreement: A Further Step towards Policy Convergence," Jeffrey Bardos, Federal Reserve Bank of New York *Quarterly Review*, Winter 1987–88, pp. 26–34.

Article 4: "Joint Ventures: Meeting the Competition in Banking," Paul Calem, Federal Reserve Bank of Philadelphia *Business Review*, May/June 1988, pp. 13–21.

Article 5: "The Bank Credit-Card Boom: Some Explanations and Consequences," Paul R. Watro, Federal Reserve Bank of Cleveland *Economic Commentary*, March 1, 1988, pp. 1–6.

Article 6: "Bank Lending to LBOs: Risks and Supervisory Response," James B. Thomson, Federal Reserve Bank of Cleveland *Economic Commentary*, February 15, 1989, pp. 1–4.

Article 7: "Can Regulatory Reform Prevent the Impending Disaster in Financial Markets?" Franklin R. Edwards, Federal Reserve Bank of Kansas City *Economic Review*, January 1988, pp. 29–39.

Article 8: "Bank Runs, Deposit Insurance, and Bank Regulation," Charles T. Carlstrom, Federal Reserve Bank of Cleveland *Economic Commentary*, Part I, February 1, 1989; Part II, February 15, 1989.

Article 9: "Troubled Banks and Thrifts," Michael C. Keeley, Federal Reserve Bank of San Francisco *Weekly Letter*, January 29, 1988, pp. 1–3.

Article 10: "Reforming Deposit Insurance," Michael C. Keeley, Federal Reserve Bank of San Francisco *Weekly Letter*, April 21, 1989, pp. 1–3.

Article 11: "The Thrift Insurance Crisis," Michael Keeley and Jonathan Neuberger, Federal Reserve Bank of San Francisco *Weekly Letter*, March 31, 1989, pp. 1–3.

Article 12: "The FSLIC Bailout and the Economy," Fred Furlong, Federal Reserve Bank of San Francisco *Weekly Letter*, May 12, 1989, pp. 1–3.

Article 13: "Challenges to the Concept Of Stock Market Efficiency," Douglas K. Pearce, Federal Reserve Bank of Kansas City *Economic Review*, September/October 1987, pp. 18–33.

Article 14: "The Stock Market and Inflation: A Synthesis of the Theory and Evidence," David P. Ely and Kenneth J. Robinson, Federal Reserve Bank of Dallas *Economic Review*, March 1989, pp. 17–29.

Article 15: "Interest Rates and Exchange Rates—What Is the Relationship?" Craig S. Hakkio, Federal Reserve Bank of Kansas City *Economic Review*, November 1986, pp. 33–43.

Article 16: "Interest Rate Divergences among the Major Industrial Nations," Bruce Kasman and Charles Pigott, Federal Reserve Bank of New York *Quarterly Review*, Autumn 1988, pp. 28–44.

Article 17: "Federal Funds: Instruments Of Federal Reserve Policy," Marvin Good-friend and William Whelpley, Federal Reserve Bank of Richmond *Economic Review*, September/October 1986, pp. 3–11.

Article 18: "Repurchase And Reverse Repurchase Agreements," Stephen A. Lumpkin, Federal Reserve Bank of Richmond *Economic Review*, January/February 1987, pp. 15–23.

Article 19: "Interest Rate Swaps: A Review of the Issues," Larry D. Wall and John J. Pringle, Federal Reserve Bank of Atlanta *Economic Review*, November/December 1988, pp. 22–40.

Article 20: "The Role of Stripped Securities in Portfolio Management," Sean Becketti, Federal Reserve Bank of Kansas City *Economic Review*, May 1988, pp. 20–31.

Article 21: "Low-Grade Bonds: A Growing Source of Corporate Funding," Jan Loeys, Federal Reserve Bank of Philadelphia *Business Review*, November/December 1986, pp. 3–12.

Article 22: "Eurocommerical Paper and U.S. Commercial Paper: Converging Money Markets?" Robert N. McCauley and Lauren A. Hargraves, Federal Reserve Bank of New York *Quarterly Review*, Autumn 1987, pp. 24–25.

Article 23: "Europe 1992: Implications for U.S. Firms," Thomas Bennett and Craig S. Hakkio, Federal Reserve Bank of Kansas City *Economic Review*, April 1989, pp. 3–17.

Article 24: "International Policy Cooperation: Building a Sound Foundation," Brian J. Cody, Federal Reserve Bank of Philadelphia *Business Review*, March/April 1989, pp. 3–12.

Article 25: "An Introduction to Non-Tariff Barriers to Trade," Cletus C. Coughlin and Geoffrey E. Wood, Federal Reserve Bank of St. Louis *Review*, January/February 1989, pp. 32–46.

Article 26: "U.S. Banks' Exposure to Developing Countries: An Examination of Recent Trends," Barbara A. Bennett and Gary C. Zimmerman, Federal Reserve Bank of San Francisco *Economic Review*, Spring 1988, pp. 14–29.

Article 27: "The Costs of Default and International Lending," Chien Nan Wang, Federal Reserve Bank of Cleveland *Economic Commentary*, March 1, 1989, pp. 1–4.

Article 28: "Monetary Aggregates: A User's Guide," John R. Walter, Federal Reserve Bank of Richmond *Economic Review*, January/February 1989, pp. 1–4.

Article 29: "Money and Inflation in a Deregulated Financial Environment: An Overview," W. Michael Cox and Harvey Roseblum, Federal Reserve Bank of Dallas *Economic Review*, May 1989, pp. 1–20.

Article 30: "Reserve Requirements, the Monetary Base, and Economic Activity," Joseph H. Haslag and Scott E. Hein, Federal Reserve Bank of Dallas *Economic Review*, March 1989, pp. 1–15.

Article 31: "The Macroeconomic Effects of Deficit Spending: A Review," K. Alec Chrystal and Daniel L. Thornton, Federal Reserve Bank of St. Louis *Review*, November/December 1988, pp. 48–60.

Article 32: "Should We Intervene in Exchange Markets?" Owen F. Humpage, Federal Reserve Bank of Cleveland *Economic Commentary*, February 1, 1987, pp. 1–4.

Article 33: "Fact and Fantasy about Stock Index Futures Program Trading," John J. Merrick, Jr., Federal Reserve Bank of Philadelphia *Business Review*, September/October 1987, pp. 13–25.

Article 34: "The Pricing and Hedging of Market Index Deposits," Stephen R. King and Eli M. Remolona, Federal Reserve Bank of New York *Quarterly Review*, Summer 1987, pp. 9–20.

Article 35: "Home Equity Lending: Boon or Bane?" Randall Johnston Pozdena, Federal Reserve Bank of San Francisco *Weekly Letter,* June 2, 1989, pp. 1–3.

Article 36: "The Economics of Securitization," Christine Cumming, Federal Reserve Bank of New York *Quarterly Review,* Autumn 1987, pp. 11–23.

Article 37: "The Prepayment Risk of Mortgage-Backed Securities," Sean Becketti, Federal Reserve Bank of Kansas City *Economic Review,* February 1989, pp. 43–57.

Article 38: "Off Balance Sheet Risk in Banking: The Case of Standby Letters of Credit," Barbara Bennett, Federal Reserve Bank of San Francisco *Economic Review,* Winter 1986, no. 1, pp. 19–29.

Contents

Part One

Financial Institutions:
Management and Regulation

The six articles included in Part One cover a variety of topics related to the management and regulation of commercial banks. While the topics appear diverse, they all relate to the adaptation of commercial banks to the new economic, competitive, and regulatory environment that they have confronted during the 1980s. Extremely volatile interest rates have made asset/liability management of great importance and fostered the development of new techniques, such as swaps and futures. At the same time, the bank regulatory authorities have increased the minimum capital ratios required of commercial banks and most recently have adopted risk-based capital standards to apply on an international level. In this competitive environment, survival is difficult and is possible only for those institutions that take full advantage of the potential for economies of scale and scope in the production of financial services. Banks have also sought to respond to the competitive challenge by innovative new production strategies, such as using joint ventures, seeking out new types of lending, making credit available to finance leveraged buyouts, and also by placing greater emphasis on credit card operations.

In "Managing Interest Rate Risk with Interest Rate Futures," Charles Morris explains the benefits and costs to financial institutions (and others) of using financial futures to hedge against interest rate fluctuations. As Morris points out, the volatility of interest rates on 1-year and 10-year Treasury securities increased dramatically during the 1980s. Interest rate futures are a useful (though not the only) vehicle for hedging this risk because they have low transaction costs and their prices are highly correlated with cash market prices. Yet banks using these vehicles to hedge interest rate risk must be aware of the potential hazards that accompany them.

In the second article in this section, "Economies of Scale and Scope at Depository Financial Institutions: A Review of the Literature," Jeffrey A. Clark reviews the extensive literature devoted to measuring the extent of production cost economies at commercial banks and other depository institutions. The existence (or lack) of production economies at financial service firms fundamentally determines the ability of different size firms to survive and prosper. As Clark points out, the existing evidence suggests these cost economies are relatively small.

The third article in this section, "The Risk-based Capital Agreement: A Further Step towards Policy Convergence," by Jeffrey Bardos, deals with a regulatory issue: the definition of capital and the regulations governing the minimum amount of capital held by banks. These regulations affect the competitive position of U.S. banks versus their domestic nonbank competitors and also versus international banks. As Bardos points out, the major central banks have agreed on a common capital standard internationally and on one for which required capital is related to risk. With this agreement, the major central banks have not only attempted to establish a "level playing field" internationally, but also have designed a system that would restrain banking risk-taking.

In the fourth article in this section, Paul Calem, in "Joint Ventures: Meeting the Competition in Banking," deals with one of the new production devices banks are experimenting with as they attempt to meet increased competition. These joint ventures allow banks to participate in some activities they could not do so legally by themselves and also allow them to lower their costs in producing other financial services. It appears that joint ventures may be one of many organizational structures used by banks to deliver financial services in the future.

Paul Watro, in "The Bank Credit-Card Boom: Some Explanations and Consequences," (the fifth article in the section), points out that bank credit card lending has exploded in the 1980s. This expansion reflects a great increase in consumer demand and attractive earnings available on this financial product. Yet there are important issues concerning the potential effects of rising charge-offs on these loans that are relevant both to bankers and regulators.

The final article in this section, "Bank Lending to LBOs: Risks and Supervisory Response," by James Thomson, deals with a type of financial transaction that banks have recently participated in and that has grown dramatically. Yet bank participation in leveraged buyout (LBO) financing is the subject of considerable controversy, not only because of the potentially high risk to the lender but also due to the possible effects of LBOs on the entire U.S. economy.

Article 1

Managing Interest Rate Risk with Interest Rate Futures

By Charles S. Morris

Increased interest rate volatility in the 1970s and 1980s has led to greater volatility in the returns on bonds and other fixed income assets. Consequently, investors in bonds and financial institutions with fixed income assets and liabilities on their balance sheets are now exposed to much greater risks from capital gains and losses. The problem is compounded because managing risks caused by interest rate volatility has traditionally been difficult and costly.

During the last 15 years, however, many new financial instruments have been developed to help investors manage risks caused by increased interest rate volatility. One of the most popular types of instruments is interest rate futures contracts. Interest rate futures allow investors to protect the value of their fixed income invest-

ments by providing a hedge against interest rate changes. Interest rate futures are now an important tool for investors who want to protect themselves from interest rate volatility.

This article explains how interest rate futures, when properly used in a hedging strategy, allow investors to manage interest rate risk. The first section of the article defines interest rate risk, examines its impact on investors and institutions, and discusses how interest rate risk can be managed. The second section provides an introduction to interest rate futures and discusses why they are good assets for hedging interest rate risk. The third section shows how investors and institutions can use interest rate futures to manage interest rate risk and discusses some of the other risks involved in using interest rate futures.

Interest rate risk and interest rate risk management

Bonds and other fixed income assets have become riskier investments in recent years.

Charles S. Morris is a senior economist at the Federal Reserve Bank of Kansas City. Julia Reigel, a research associate at the bank, assisted in the preparation of this article.

These assets are riskier, not because issuers are more likely to default on their obligations, but because interest rates have become more volatile. This section explains why increased interest rate volatility has increased the risk of fixed income assets, provides some examples of investors and institutions affected by greater interest rate volatility, and discusses methods of managing interest rate risk.

What is interest rate risk?

Investments in fixed income assets, such as bonds, are risky because the volatility of their prices can lead to unexpected capital gains and losses. The risk of an asset can be measured by the volatility of its returns, which is the sum of the income flows from the asset plus any changes in its price. Since the income flows from a fixed income asset, such as the coupon payments and maturity value of a coupon bond, are fixed, the riskiness of the asset depends only on its price volatility. For example, as the volatility of a bond's price rises, the bond's riskiness rises because unexpected capital gains or losses are more likely.

The primary cause of volatility in the price of a fixed income asset is interest rate volatility.[1] Indeed, the volatility in prices due to interest rate changes is commonly termed "interest rate risk." For example, when interest rates fall, the price of a bond rises; when interest rates rise, the price of a bond falls. The sensitivity of a fixed income asset's price to interest rates, that is, the degree of interest rate risk, depends largely on the asset's maturity. The longer to maturity, the larger the change in price due to a change in interest rates.[2]

Interest rate volatility has risen sharply in recent years. Chart 1 shows the volatility of interest rates on 1-year and 10-year Treasury securities from 1955 to 1988. Interest rate volatility in each year is measured by the standard deviation of the monthly interest rates during that year. The average standard deviation of 1-year interest rates over the 1979-88 period was more than twice that of the 1955-78 period, rising from 0.5 percent per month over the 1955-78 period to 1.2 percent over the 1979-88 period. The relative increase in the volatility of 10-year rates was even sharper. The average standard deviation of 10-year interest rates over the 1979-88 period was more than three times higher than that over the 1955-78 period, rising from 0.25 percent to 0.8 percent. The rise in interest rate volatility over those periods is not limited to 1-year and 10-year rates, but is typical of the volatility of interest rates at all maturities.

Who is affected by rising interest rate volatility?

Many investors and business firms are exposed to greater risks because of the increase in interest rate volatility in recent years. Examples include individual and institutional

---

[1] The riskiness of a fixed income asset also depends on the volatility of other factors that affect its price, such as the creditworthiness of the issuer and the liquidity of the asset.

[2] This assumes a uniform change in rates on all maturities. The interest rate sensitivity of a fixed income asset also depends on other factors, such as the size of the coupon payments and the dates the coupon payments are received.

CHART 1
Interest rate volatility

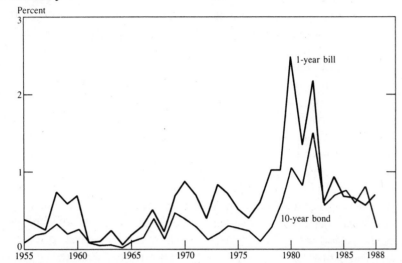

Note: Annual standard deviations of monthly constant maturity rates for 1-year U.S. Treasury bills and 10-year U.S. Treasury bonds.

Source: Board of Governors of the Federal Reserve System.

CHART 2
Bond market volatility

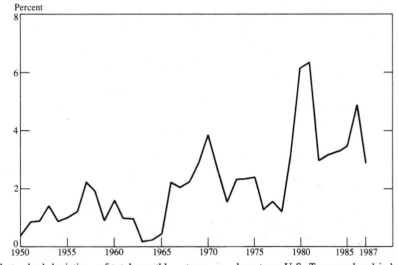

Note: Annual standard deviations of total monthly returns on a long-term U.S. Treasury bond index.

Source: Center for Research in Stock Prices.

investors in government and corporate bonds, depository institutions such as banks and savings and loans, securities dealers, mortgage banks, and life insurance companies to name a few.

One group of investors exposed to greater risks is investors in bonds. The rising risk of holding bonds is clear from Chart 2, which shows the volatility of returns on U.S. Treasury bonds from 1950 to 1987. Bond market volatility in each year is measured by the standard deviation of the monthly percentage returns on a long-term U.S. Treasury bond index during that year.[3] Bond market volatility rose from an average annual standard deviation of 1 percent per month over the period from 1950 to 1965 to 2.25 percent over the period from 1966 to 1978. Bond market volatility rose further from 1979 to 1987, averaging 4.1 percent per month.

Rising interest rate volatility has also increased the risk exposure of depository institutions, such as banks and S&Ls. When interest rates rise, the market value of their net worth generally falls; when interest rates fall, the market value of their net worth generally rises. The market value of an institution's net worth is the difference between the market values of its assets and liabilities. The effect of a change in interest rates on the market value of a firm's net worth depends on the relative interest rate sensitivities of its assets and liabilities, which primarily depend on their relative maturities.

Because the assets of banks and S&Ls generally take longer to mature than do their liabilities, the value of their assets is more sensitive to changes in interest rates than the value of their liabilities. As a result, when interest rates rise, for example, the net worth of a depository institution falls because the value of its assets falls more than the value of its liabilities.

Securities dealers are also exposed to greater risks due to rising interest rate volatility. When interest rates rise, securities dealers suffer losses like other bondholders because the value of the bonds they are holding in inventory falls.[4] Securities dealers can also suffer losses when interest rates fall, however, because they often commit themselves to delivering bonds at a future date for a fixed price when they do not have the bonds in inventory or the funds to purchase them immediately. If interest rates fall before a dealer purchases the bonds, he will suffer a loss because the price he has to pay for the bonds he has to deliver will be higher than he had expected when he made the initial commitment.

Mortgage banks are also exposed to greater interest rate volatility. A mortgage bank originates mortgages and then sells them to other investors. In general, mortgage banks hold very few mortgages on their balance sheet. They can suffer losses if interest rates rise, however, because they typically commit to a mortgage

---

[3] Although the volatility of total returns is the same as price volatility for a given bond, the volatilities are not the same when the composition of a bond portfolio changes over time because the coupon payments change. Since the composition of the portfolio that underlies the index in Chart 2 changes, the volatility of total returns is shown.

[4] Securities dealers make a profit on their bonds when interest rates fall. Indeed, all investors in fixed income assets make a profit when interest rates move in one direction and suffer a loss when interest rates move in the other direction. In the remaining examples, the discussion will focus on how a change in interest rates in only one direction affects an investor. The direction of the change in interest rates that is used is the one that produces a loss for the investor.

rate before the mortgage is actually closed and sold. If interest rates rise between the time they commit to a rate and the time the mortgage is sold, the value of the mortgage will fall; and mortgage banks will get a lower price than they had expected when they made the initial commitment.

A final example of a group of firms exposed to greater risks due to rising interest rate volatility is life insurance companies. For example, changes in interest rates affect life insurance companies because when interest rates fall the spread earned on Guaranteed Interest Contract (GIC) commitments falls. In recent years, life insurance companies have become heavy issuers of GICs, which are securities that guarantee a fixed interest rate on invested funds over a several-year period. GICs are generally purchased by long-term investors, such as pension funds and company thrift plans. Often, a life insurance company will commit to a rate on a GIC for a short time period before it receives the funds. Life insurance companies can suffer losses if interest rates fall during the commitment period because when they receive the funds from the GIC, they will have to invest the funds at a lower rate than they had expected when they committed to the GIC rate. As a result, the spread earned on the GIC falls.[5]

What is risk management and hedging?

Investors and business firms manage risk by

_____

[5] Viewed another way, a GIC commitment is a fixed rate liability that is not matched by an asset. When interest rates fall, the value of the GIC commitment rises, but there is no asset whose value also rises. Therefore, the insurance company's net worth falls when interest rates fall.

choosing the amount of risk to which they want to be exposed. The choice of how much risk to bear varies with every investor. For example, some investors will choose to accept the increased price volatility of fixed income investments of recent years, while others will take actions to reduce the riskiness of their fixed income investments. In general, though, investors will not choose to minimize risk because there are costs to reducing risk. The most important cost is that the expected return on their investment also falls when risk is reduced.

Traditionally, investors have found it difficult and costly to reduce risks caused by interest rate volatility. Investors in bonds, for example, typically could reduce interest rate risk only by selling some of their bonds and buying short-term money market instruments. Financial institutions exposed to interest rate risk had to rely on balance sheet restructuring to reduce the mismatch between the maturities of their assets and liabilities.

In recent years new financial instruments—such as interest rate futures, options on interest rate futures, and interest rate swaps—have been developed that allow investors in fixed income assets to manage interest rate risk at a relatively low cost by hedging. In general, hedging is a risk management strategy in which investors choose assets such that changes in the prices of the assets systematically offset each other. Fixed income investors can hedge the interest rate risk of an asset, such as a Treasury bond, by buying or selling hedging assets whose values change in the opposite direction to the value of the Treasury bond when interest rates change. The interest rate riskiness of a hedged Treasury bond is lower than the interest rate riskiness of the unhedged bond because the change in the value of the hedging asset due to a change in interest rates offsets at least some of the change in the value of the bond. It is important to realize, however, that hedging reduces price volatility because it offsets increases as well as decreases in the price of the Treasury bond.

For any given fixed income asset, the best hedging instrument for reducing interest rate risk is the one whose price is most closely related to the price of the asset when interest rates change. The more closely the prices are related, the larger the reduction in risk that is possible because changes in the price of the hedging asset are more likely to offset changes in the price of the asset being hedged.

While hedging can reduce risk, it generally cannot completely eliminate risk. Hedging will completely eliminate risk only if the values of the portfolio and hedging asset are perfectly related. However, the prices of the assets being hedged and the hedging asset are rarely perfectly related because of differences in factors such as credit quality, liquidity, maturity, and call or prepayment options. Thus, as a practical matter, hedging is an activity that permits investors to manage, but not eliminate, risk.[6]

---

[6] The risk that remains after a portfolio has been hedged is called *basis risk*. If the riskiness of a portfolio is measured by the standard deviation of the change in its value, the minimum level of basis risk that can be achieved through hedging is

$$\sigma_h = \sigma_p \sqrt{(1 - \varrho^2)},$$

where σ_p is the standard deviation of the change in the value of the unhedged portfolio, and ϱ is the correlation coefficient between the changes in the values of the portfolio and the hedging asset. The maximum percentage reduction in risk is

$$100(\sigma_p - \sigma_h)/\sigma_p = 100(1 - \sqrt{(1 - \varrho^2)}),$$

which depends only on ϱ, and risk will be completely eliminated only if ϱ equals 1 or -1.

An introduction to interest rate futures

Of the variety of financial instruments used to hedge interest rate risk, one of the most popular is interest rate futures. This section describes interest rate futures, discusses the types of interest rate futures available, and explains why they are good hedging instruments.

What are interest rate futures?

An interest rate futures contract is an agreement between two parties to buy or sell a fixed income asset, such as a Treasury bond or Treasury bill, at a given time in the future for a predetermined price. For example, if in January a person buys March Treasury bond futures, he is simply agreeing to buy Treasury bonds in March. On the other hand, if in January he sells March Treasury bond futures, he is simply agreeing to sell Treasury bonds in March. Nothing is exchanged when the futures contract is written because it is only an agreement to make an exchange at a future date. The price of a futures contract is the price the buyer agrees to pay the seller for the asset when it is delivered.[7]

---

[7] The delivery dates for most interest rate futures are in March, June, September, and December. The actual delivery date varies with the contract. For example, the seller of a Treasury bond contract at the Chicago Board of Trade can deliver Treasury bonds on any day in the contract month, although the last trading day is seven business days prior to the last business day of the month. Although some interest rate futures have contract months that extend out to three years, most of the contracts traded are contracts with the nearest delivery month.

Delivery of the asset in a futures contract rarely occurs, however. The reason is futures traders can always close out the contracts they have bought or sold by taking an offsetting position in the same futures contract before delivery occurs. For example, rather than taking delivery, a buyer of ten March Treasury bond futures can settle his position by selling ten March Treasury bond futures. Similarly, a seller of ten March Treasury bond futures can settle his position by buying ten March Treasury bond futures. In 1988, Treasury bonds were delivered in less than 0.1 percent of all Treasury bond futures traded at the Chicago Board of Trade, which are one of the most widely traded interest rate futures.[8]

Since a futures trader who has settled an initial position has both bought and sold futures, his profit depends on the prices of the futures he has bought and sold. Just like any other trader, futures traders make a profit when they buy futures at a price lower than they sell futures, and they suffer a loss when they buy futures at a price higher than they sell futures. Whether a person makes a profit or suffers a loss, therefore, depends on two conditions: first, whether he initially bought or sold futures, and second, whether the price of the futures rises or falls between the time he enters the initial contract and the time he takes an offsetting position.

A buyer of futures makes a profit when the futures price rises and suffers a loss when the

futures price falls. Suppose, for example, on January 10 a person buys a March Treasury bond futures contract for $95 per $100 face value of Treasury bonds, and on February 15 he settles his position by selling a March Treasury bond futures contract for $97. Under these circumstances, the person would make a profit of $2 per $100 face value of Treasury bonds because he has one agreement to buy Treasury bonds in March for $95 and another agreement to sell Treasury bonds in March for $97. On the other hand, if the price falls to $92 on February 15, he would lose $3 per $100 because he has one agreement to buy Treasury bonds for $95 and another agreement to sell Treasury bonds for $92.

In contrast, a seller of futures suffers a loss when the futures price rises and makes a profit when the futures price falls. This time, suppose on January 10 a person sells a March Treasury bond futures contract for $95, and on February 15 he settles his position by buying a March Treasury bond futures for $97. The person would suffer a loss of $2 because he has one agreement to sell Treasury bonds in March for $95 and another agreement to buy Treasury bonds in March for $97. On the other hand, if the price falls to $92 on February 15, he would make a profit of $3 because he has one agreement to sell Treasury bonds for $95 and another agreement to buy Treasury bonds for $92.

Interest rate futures are relatively new financial instruments. While futures on commodities have been trading on organized exchanges in the United States since the latter half of the 1860s, the first interest rate futures contract did not start trading until October 1975, when the Chicago Board of Trade (CBT) introduced futures on Government National Mortgage

---

[8] For some interest rate futures, such as the Eurodollar time deposit futures on the International Monetary Market exchange, all contracts must be settled by taking an offsetting position. That is, delivery of the underlying instrument is not allowed.

Association (GNMA) certificates.[9] Since then, futures on many different fixed income assets have been developed. However, there are still many fixed income assets, such as corporate bonds, on which no futures are traded.

The assets on which interest rate futures are traded span the maturity spectrum—interest rate futures on short-term, medium-term, and long-term assets are traded on several futures exchanges in the United States and abroad. The first futures contract on a short-term asset was the Treasury bill futures contract, which was introduced on the International Monetary Market (IMM) exchange in 1976. Since then, interest rate futures on other short-term assets, such as Eurodollar time deposits and 30-day interest rates, have begun trading on several exchanges, with the IMM Eurodollar futures being the most popular.[10] Interest rate futures on medium-term assets, such as Treasury notes, are also traded on several exchanges.[11] Finally, there are interest rate futures on long-term assets, such as Treasury bonds and a municipal bond index, with the CBT Treasury bond futures being the most popular.[12]

The success of interest rate futures is shown in Chart 3. One measure of activity in a futures market is a contract's open interest—the number of contracts not yet offset by opposite transactions or delivery. Chart 3 shows the open interest in the CBT Treasury bond futures contract from 1978 to 1988. Although open interest in Treasury bond futures is fairly volatile, the trend is clearly upward. Chart 3 also shows open interest rose sharply in 1980 and 1981—the two peak years in bond market volatility (Chart 2)—suggesting that investors took advantage of the futures market for managing risk.

Why are interest rate futures good hedging assets?

Interest rate futures are good hedging assets for two reasons. First, the transaction costs of buying and selling them are relatively low. Second, interest rate futures prices are closely related to the prices of many fixed income assets when interest rates change.

The transaction costs of establishing a futures position are low because nothing is really being bought or sold—the contract is just an agreement to make a trade at a future date. When a position is established, the only outlays are broker fees and commissions and an initial margin deposit with the broker.[13] The fees paid to brokers and traders are quite small. For example, the cost of establishing and settling a position in a CBT Treasury bond futures con-

---

[9] Although the GNMA futures contract was initially successful, it stopped trading in December 1984.

[10] Treasury bill futures are also traded on the MidAmerica Commodity Exchange in Chicago. Eurodollar futures are also traded on the London International Financial Futures Exchange. The 30-day interest rate futures contract is traded at the Chicago Board of Trade.

[11] Treasury note futures are traded on the Chicago Board of Trade exchange, the MidAmerica Commodity Exchange in Chicago, and the Financial Instrument Exchange, a division of the New York Cotton Exchange.

[12] Treasury bond futures are also traded on the MidAmerica Commodity Exchange in Chicago and the London International Financial Futures Exchange. Futures on the municipal bond index are traded at the Chicago Board of Trade.

---

[13] The margin on a futures contract is ''good faith'' money deposited with a broker to assure him that losses can be covered in the event of adverse price movements.

CHART 3

Treasury bond futures open interest

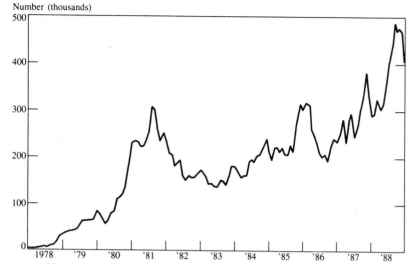

Number (thousands)

Note: Values are monthly averages of daily open interest in the nearest Chicago Board of Trade Treasury bond futures contract with at least one month until expiration.

Source: Data Resources Inc.

tract, which is based on $100,000 face value of bonds, is about $41.[14] The initial margin is also very small—the margin on a CBT Treasury bond futures used for hedging purposes is $2,000—and the margin generally earns a market rate of interest.[15]

Interest rate futures hedge the interest rate risk of many fixed income assets successfully because interest rate futures prices are closely related to the prices of many fixed income assets. The prices are closely related because interest rate futures prices are sensitive to changes in interest rates just like fixed income asset prices. The price of any futures contract—whether it is an interest rate, exchange rate, commodity, or any other type of futures contract—is always very closely related to the

[14] See Arnold Kling, "Futures Markets and Transaction Costs," in Myron L. Kwast, ed., *Financial Futures and Options in the U.S. Economy: A Study by the Staff of the Federal Reserve System* (Washington, D.C.: Board of Governors of the Federal Reserve System, 1986), pp. 41-54.

[15] The minimum initial margin a person must deposit when establishing an open position in a futures contract and the minimum level that must be maintained is set by the exchanges and is changed from time to time. The margin level depends on factors such as the volatility of the price of the underlying instrument and the maximum daily change in the futures price the exchange allows. Margins also may

depend on whether a person is just buying or selling futures alone or is buying or selling futures to establish a hedge. The margin on an outright purchase or sale of CBT Treasury bond futures is $2,500. Although interest is generally paid on the initial margin, interest is not paid on additions to the margin account because additions represent losses that have been transferred to the accounts of parties that have gained from price movements.

price of the underlying asset.[16] Since interest rate futures are based on fixed income assets and the prices of these assets move in the opposite direction of interest rates, interest rate futures prices move in the opposite direction of interest rates.

Like any other hedging asset, though, the extent to which a given interest rate futures contract will provide an effective hedge for a fixed income asset depends on how closely the futures price is related to the price of the asset being hedged. Chart 4, for example, shows that the prices of a 30-year Treasury bond and the CBT Treasury bond futures are nearly identical.[17] The small differences that do exist are shown at the bottom of the chart. Because of this close relationship, Treasury bond futures should be very effective at hedging Treasury bonds against interest rate volatility.

In contrast, the price of the CBT Treasury bond futures is not as closely related to the price of a 30-year corporate bond as to the price of the 30-year Treasury bond (Chart 5). The difference between the corporate bond price and the futures price is clearly more variable than the difference between the Treasury bond price and the futures price.

The prices of corporate bonds and Treasury bond futures are less closely related because corporate bond prices can change for a variety of reasons other than changes in the general level of interest rates. For example, the price of a corporate bond would fall if the issuer's credit rating fell or if adverse general economic conditions led investors to believe the chances of default were more likely. The price of a corporate bond could also fall if a large investor decided to sell his share of an issue. Since these factors would not affect the price of a Treasury bond, a Treasury bond futures contract would not hedge an investor against these price changes. As a result, Treasury bond futures should be a less effective hedge for a corporate bond than for a Treasury bond.[18]

---

16 The relationship between the price of a futures contract and the price of its underlying asset is most easily seen on the last day of trading for a particular contract, at which time the two prices must be exactly equal. In general, if there are no transaction costs and capital markets are perfect, the difference between a futures price and the price of the underlying asset can be no larger than the net cost of holding the underlying asset in inventory—inventory costs less income flows from the asset—until the futures contract expires. This relationship between the price of a futures contract and the price of its underlying asset is known as the cost of carry theory of futures prices. Prices do deviate slightly from cost of carry, though, because of transaction costs and capital market imperfections. For a detailed discussion of the relationship between interest rate futures prices and bond prices, see James M. Little, "What are Financial Futures?" in Nancy H. Rothstein and James M. Little, eds. *The Handbook of Financial Futures* (New York: McGraw-Hill Book Company, 1984), pp. 35-66.

17 The closeness of these two prices should not be surprising. The CBT Treasury bond futures price should be very closely related to the price of its underlying asset, which is an 8 percent 20-year Treasury bond. Since 30-year Treasury bond prices and 20-year Treasury bond prices are closely related, the futures price, and the bond price in Chart 4 are closely related.

18 Viewed another way, Treasury bond futures are less effective in hedging the *total* risk of a corporate bond than a Treasury bond because (1) Treasury bond futures only hedge interest rate risk, and (2) interest rate risk accounts for a smaller share of the total risk of a corporate bond than of a Treasury bond. In terms of hedging only the interest rate risk of a corporate bond—that is, changes in the price of the corporate bond due to changes in interest rates—Treasury bond futures should be fairly effective.

CHART 4

Treasury bond futures price and treasury bond price

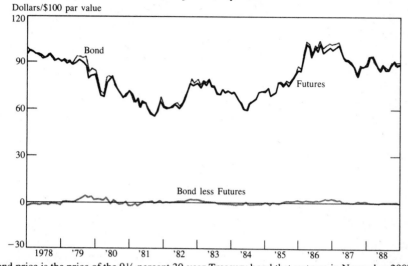

Note: The bond price is the price of the 9¼ percent 30-year Treasury bond that matures in November 2007. The futures price is the price of the nearest Chicago Board of Trade Treasury bond future with at least one month until expiration.

Source: Data Resources Inc.

CHART 5

Treasury bond futures price and corporate bond price

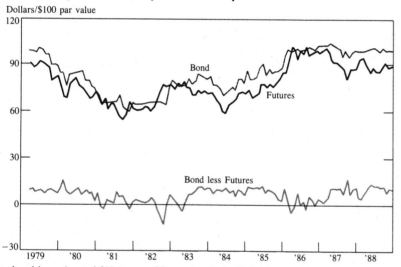

Note: Corporate bond is an A-rated 9½ percent 30-year bond of a U.S. industrial firm. The futures price is the price of the nearest Chicago Board of Trade Treasury bond future with at least one month until expiration.

Source: Data Resources Inc.

Managing interest rate risk with interest rate futures

Businesses and investors use interest rate futures in a variety of ways to manage interest rate risk. Hedging strategies can be complex, however, and this can expose investors to new risks. This section provides some specific examples of how interest rate futures are used to hedge interest rate risk and then discusses some of the other risks involved in hedging with interest rate futures.

Hedging interest rate risk with interest rate futures

Investors can hedge interest rate risk by selling or buying interest rate futures. Whether an investor sells or buys futures depends on how changes in interest rates affect the value of his portfolio.

In general, an investor who suffers losses on his investment portfolio when interest rates *rise* hedges interest rate risk by *selling* interest rate futures.[19] When interest rates rise, interest rate futures prices fall. If an investor loses money on his portfolio when interest rates rise, then, he needs to make a profit from falling futures prices. That is, he needs the gain on his futures contract to offset the loss on his original investment portfolio. Since sellers of futures make a profit when futures prices fall, the investor would hedge by selling futures. Similarly, when interest rates fall, the losses on the futures off-set the profits on the original investment portfolio.

Conversely, an investor who suffers losses on his portfolio when interest rates *fall* hedges by *buying* interest rate futures. When interest rates fall, interest rate futures prices rise. If an investor loses money on his portfolio when interest rates fall, he needs to make a profit from rising futures prices. Since buyers of futures make a profit when futures prices rise, the investor would hedge by buying futures. Similarly, when interest rates rise, the losses on the futures offset the profits on the portfolio.

Hedging a Treasury bond portfolio. Treasury bond prices fall when interest rates rise, so an investor in Treasury bonds would hedge his portfolio against changes in interest rates by selling interest rate futures. In this way, a gain or loss on the Treasury bonds would be offset by a loss or gain on the futures contracts.

An example of the reduction in price volatility that can be achieved by hedging is shown in Chart 6. This chart shows the price of a portfolio of unhedged Treasury bonds and the price of a hedged portfolio. The unhedged portfolio contains 30-year and 10-year U.S. Treasury bonds. The bonds are hedged using the CBT Treasury bond futures.[20] The value of the

---

19 Of course, an equivalent statement of this rule is that an investor who makes profits on his investment portfolio when interest rates fall hedges interest rate risk by selling interest rate futures.

20 This example assumes the investor wants to minimize risk. For simplicity, the value of the hedged portfolio ignores the effects of margin requirements, transaction costs, taxation, accounting practices, and regulatory requirements, all of which could affect the value of the hedge and the hedging strategy. The prices are end-of-month data, and the futures price is on the nearest contract with at least one month until expiration.

The example does not account for the possibility that risk could be reduced further by (1) using futures with contract months that are farther out, and (2) estimating the number of contracts to sell over shorter time periods and then

CHART 6
Hedging treasury bonds

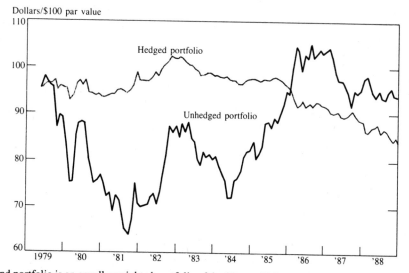

Note: The bond portfolio is an equally weighted portfolio of the 30-year U.S. Treasury bond that matures in November 2007 and the 10-year U.S. Treasury bond that matures in May 1989. The hedged price is the price of the minimum risk hedged portfolio of bonds using the nearest futures contract with at least one month until expiration.

Source: Data Resources Inc.

hedged portfolio of bonds is clearly less variable than the value of the unhedged portfolio. The volatility of the price of the hedged portfolio, measured by the standard deviation of the change in price, is 60 percent lower than the volatility of the price of the unhedged portfolio.

Hedging a corporate bond. An investor in corporate bonds would hedge his portfolio against changes in interest rates by selling interest rate futures because corporate bond prices fall when interest rates rise. Corporate

bond futures do not exist, so the investor would use Treasury bond futures as a hedge. Treasury bond futures should be a less effective hedge for corporate bonds than for Treasury bonds, however, because Treasury bond futures prices are not as closely related to corporate bond prices as to Treasury bond prices.

An example of the reduction in the price volatility of a corporate bond that can be achieved by hedging is shown in Chart 7. This chart shows the prices of an A-rated 9-1/2 percent 30-year bond of a U.S. industrial company and the value of the hedged bond.[21]

---

adjusting the number of contracts to account for the changes. On the other hand, the example could be overstating the degree of risk reduction because the number of contracts sold is estimated from actual price data over the hedging period, whereas investors must estimate the number of contracts using data from periods prior to the hedging period.

---

[21] The qualifications and assumptions that applied to the hedge of the Treasury bond portfolio also apply to this example (see footnote 20).

CHART 7
Hedging corporate bonds

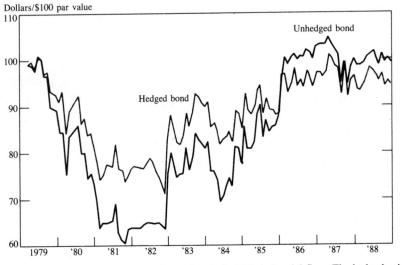

Note: Corporate bond is an A-rated 9½ percent 30-year bond of a U.S. industrial firm. The hedged price is the price of the minimum risk hedged bond using the nearest futures contract with at least one month until expiration.

Source: Data Resources Inc.

The value of the hedged bond is still quite variable, but less variable than the unhedged portfolio. The standard deviation of the change in the value of the hedged bond is 8 percent lower than that of the unhedged portfolio. As expected, Treasury bond futures are a less effective hedge for corporate bonds than for Treasury bonds.[22]

Depository institutions. Depository institutions, such as banks and S&Ls, would hedge net worth against changes in interest rates by selling interest rate futures because their net worth generally falls when interest rates rise.[23]

_____

22 Although Treasury bond futures did not provide a good hedge for a single corporate bond, they should provide a better hedge for a portfolio of corporate bonds. The corporate bond in this example had an A rating, which suggests that credit risk is at least partly responsible for the relatively poor relationship between the bond price and the futures price. A diversified portfolio of corporate bonds, however, would be exposed to less credit risk, and therefore its price would be more closely related to the futures price.

23 The best futures contract for hedging a depository institution's net worth is one whose price sensitivity to interest rate changes is as close as possible to the sensitivity of the institution's net worth to interest rate changes. The sensitivity of the institution's net worth to interest rate changes rises with the extent to which its asset and liability maturities are mismatched. Thus, institutions whose maturity structure is only slightly mismatched would choose futures contracts based on short-term assets, such as Treasury bills or Eurodollar time deposits. On the other hand, institutions whose maturity structure is highly mismatched would choose futures contracts based on longer term assets, such as Treasury bond and note futures.

When interest rates rise, the net worth of a typical depository institution falls because the value of its assets falls by more than the value of its liabilities. For example, suppose an S&L has assets with a market value of $100 million and liabilities with a market value of $90 million, resulting in a net worth of $10 million. If interest rates rise, the value of the assets might fall by, say, $5 million to $95 million. Since the liabilities have shorter maturities, their value would fall by only, say, $4 million to $86 million, resulting in a net worth of $9 million. But interest rate futures prices also fall when interest rates rise. So if the S&L sells interest rate futures, the gain on the futures when interest rates rise would offset some of the $1 million decline in net worth due to the rise in interest rates.[24]

Securities dealers. Securities dealers hedge interest rate risk by selling interest rate futures sometimes and buying them at other times. Securities dealers would hedge the bonds they have in inventory against changes in interest rates like any other bondholder by selling interest rate futures. On the other hand, securities dealers would hedge bonds they are committed to deliver at a future date for a predetermined price against changes in interest rates by buying interest rate futures.

To understand when securities dealers would buy futures, consider the following example. Suppose a securities dealer has agreed to deliver $10 million face value of Treasury bonds for $90.00 per $100 face value of bonds in two months, and the current price of the bonds is $89.50 per $100. If the dealer had the bonds in inventory or the funds to buy them, he would make a profit of $0.50 per $100, or $50,000. If not, though, he faces the risk that interest rates will fall and bond prices will rise. For example, if interest rates fall and bond prices rise $0.25, he would have to pay $89.75 per $100 for the bonds, and the profit on the commitment would fall 50 percent to $25,000. However, if interest rates fall, the futures price should rise. Since a person who buys a futures contract makes a profit when its price rises, the profit on the futures should offset much of the decrease in the profit on the commitment when interest rates fall.

Mortgage banks. Because the value of mortgage commitments falls when interest rates rise, mortgage bankers would hedge mortgage commitments against changes in interest rates by selling interest rate futures. For example, suppose a mortgage banker commits to a 10 percent interest rate on a $100,000 mortgage. If the mortgage closes in two months and interest rates do not change, the mortgage banker could sell the mortgage for $100,000. However, if interest rates rise, the value of the mortgage will fall. If, for example, the mortgage value falls to $98,000, the value of the mortgage commitment would fall $2,000. But since interest rates rose, interest rate futures prices would have fallen. Therefore, if the mortgage banker sells interest rate futures, the profit on the futures he sold would offset the loss on the mortgage commitment when interest rates rise.

---

[24] Of course, when interest rates fall, the value of the S&L's assets will rise more than the value of its liabilities, but the gain in net worth will be offset by a loss on the futures. In other words, like any other hedging asset, futures offset capital gains as well as capital losses. In the remaining examples, the discussion will focus on how hedging with futures offsets capital losses, but it is important to remember that futures hedges also offset capital gains.

Life insurance companies. Life insurance companies would hedge GIC commitments against changes in interest rates by buying interest rate futures. For example, suppose a life insurance company commits to a 10 percent interest rate on a GIC but will not receive the funds for two months. In addition, suppose the life insurance company expects to invest the funds in an 11 percent corporate bond. If interest rates do not change in the two-month period, the life insurance company would earn a spread of one percentage point. But if interest rates fall and the corporate bond rate falls to, say, 10.5 percent, the spread earned on the GIC would fall 50 percent to 0.5 percentage points. When interest rates fall, though, interest rate futures prices rise. Therefore, by buying futures, life insurance companies can offset declines in the spread on GIC commitments when interest rates fall.[25]

The risks of hedging with interest rate futures

Although hedging with interest rate futures allows investors to reduce interest rate risk, it generally cannot completely eliminate risk. All hedges generally contain some residual, or basis, risk. Moreover, hedging also introduces some new risks. Some of those risks are credit risk, marking to market risk, and managerial risk.

Basis risk. The risk that remains after an investor hedges his portfolio is called basis risk. An investor who hedges his portfolio with interest rate futures bears basis risk because, when interest rates change, the change in the price of the futures contract does not perfectly offset the change in the price of the asset being hedged. Fixed income asset prices can change for reasons other than changes in interest rates. As a result, the basis risk in a hedge will be relatively high when factors other than interest rates are an important source of the changes in the price of the asset being hedged.

For example, an asset's price will fall if the issuer's credit rating falls or if the asset is relatively illiquid and a large amount is sold. Since these factors would not affect the prices of interest rate futures, such as Treasury bond futures, interest rate futures cannot offset price changes caused by such factors. In fact, that is why Treasury bond futures proved to be a less effective hedging instrument for the corporate bond than for the Treasury bond portfolio in the examples used in the preceding section.

Credit risk. The credit risk in an interest rate futures hedge is not that the opposite party in the futures contract will default, but that the opposite party in the asset being hedged will default. Individuals do not have to be concerned about the opposite party defaulting on a futures contract because every futures exchange has a clearing organization that is a party to every futures contract in order to guarantee the integrity of the contract.[26] That is, the clearing house is the seller in every contract bought

---

[25] Recall that a GIC commitment is a fixed rate liability that is not matched by an asset. Therefore, net worth falls when interest rates fall because the increase in the value of the GIC commitment is not offset by an increase in the value of an asset. Since net worth falls when interest rates fall, the GIC commitment can be hedged against changes in interest rates by buying interest rate futures.

[26] The exchanges are also protected because many exchanges have limits on the amount a futures price can change within a day. The limits are equal to the minimum margin deposit that individuals must have on deposit with their broker.

and the buyer in every contract sold. But the risk remains that an investor will end up with an unhedged open futures position if there is a default on the asset being hedged.

For example, suppose an investor in corporate bonds hedges his portfolio against changes in interest rates by selling interest rate futures. If interest rates fall, the prices of the bond and futures will rise. Since futures were sold, the investor would suffer losses on the futures, but those losses would be offset by the gains on the bonds. If the bond issuer defaults, though, the investor would have the losses on his futures position but no gains to offset the losses.

Marking to market risk. Marking to market risk is the risk investors will have to cover futures losses when the contract is marked to market at the end of each day. All futures exchanges require every unsettled futures position to be marked to market every night and settled daily. That is, at the end of each day, funds are transferred from individuals who lose on their contracts to individuals who gain on their contracts so that buyers and sellers actually realize the gains and losses from daily price changes as they occur. A problem could occur for those who suffer losses on their futures position, though, because they must make immediate cash outlays. Although losses on futures contracts are generally offset by gains on the asset being hedged, investors usually do not receive those gains as they occur. Therefore, investors would either have to liquidate other investments and lose the associated income flows or pay interest on borrowed funds to cover their futures losses as they occur.

Managerial risk. Managerial risk, broadly defined, is the risk futures will be used inappropriately and result in greater, rather than less, risk. This is really a "catch all" category

that accounts for anything else that can go wrong with a hedging program. One major reason managerial risk arises is interest rate futures can be used for speculative purposes. In addition to being good assets for hedging, futures are also good assets for speculating on price movements for two reasons. First, it costs very little to open a futures position, and second, an open unhedged futures position is as risky as the underlying asset. While speculators play an important and useful role in futures markets, an institution that wants to hedge with futures must have internal controls to make sure those responsible for hedging are not speculating.

Managerial risk also arises because futures hedging strategies are complicated. Because they are complicated, it is possible for managers to make incorrect decisions that significantly lower a firm's value. For example, suppose a manager wants to minimize the interest rate risk of his bond portfolio, but he overhedges by selling too many futures contracts. If interest rates were to fall, the losses on the futures position could be much greater than the gains on the bonds. Thus, when overhedged, the riskiness of a portfolio is greater than the minimum level of risk and the return is less than that associated with the minimum level of risk. In fact, the riskiness of an overhedged portfolio can be even greater than the riskiness of the unhedged portfolio. To control this risk, it is important that managers understand the complexities of hedging with interest rate futures, the capabilities and limitations of a hedging program, and the need to continually monitor hedging programs.

Conclusion

The riskiness of investments in bonds and

other fixed income assets has increased in recent years because of increased interest rate volatility. The lack of traditional low-cost methods for managing this increase in interest rate risk led to the development of many new financial instruments that can be used to hedge interest rate risk. One of the most popular types of instruments is interest rate futures contracts. Interest rate futures are now trading on exchanges around the world, and they have become an important part of virtually every portfolio manager's tool kit for managing interest rate risk.

This article showed how interest rate futures can be used to manage interest rate risk. In many cases, interest rate risk can be substantially reduced. It must be remembered, though, that hedging with interest rate futures can be complex, and investors must thoroughly examine all aspects of interest rate futures and hedging techniques before implementing a hedging strategy.

Economies of Scale and Scope At Depository Financial Institutions: A Review of the Literature

By Jeffrey A. Clark

In recent years, changes in laws and regulations have greatly increased the opportunities for commercial banks and other depository financial institutions to expand their operations. Restrictions on interstate banking and intrastate branching have been liberalized in many states. In addition, limitations have been narrowed on the types of services depository institutions can offer.

While these changes have created new opportunities for individual depository institutions to grow, they have raised questions about the future structure of the banking industry. As some institutions expand and others fall prey to competitive pressures and decline or disappear, the industry's structure might come to be dominated by a small number of large diversified institutions. The market power of these institutions might allow them to keep loan rates too high and deposit rates too low, resulting in a misallocation of the

Jeffrey A. Clark is associate professor of finance at Florida State University and a visiting scholar at the Federal Reserve Bank of Kansas City. The views expressed in this article are those of the author and do not necessarily represent those of the Federal Reserve Bank of Kansas City or the Federal Reserve System.

nation's financial resources. The potential for resource misallocation would likely be attenuated by competitive pressures from nondepository financial institutions and from nonfinancial firms. Nevertheless, the evolving structure of the banking industry remains a source of interest and potential concern for industry observers, regulatory agencies, and policymakers.

The industry's evolving structure will depend on what types of depository institutions can remain profitable over time. Among the primary determinants of profitability will be the extent that production economies and resultant cost reductions can be achieved as firms expand their operations. If extensive cost reductions are possible, large diversified firms will potentially be more profitable than small specialized institutions.

By studying production and cost conditions that have prevailed in the past, some insight can be gained into whether the increased opportunities for growth will allow cost reduction to be achieved. This article reviews the recent literature and concludes that, in general, large diversified depository institutions have not enjoyed a large cost advantage over smaller, more specialized institutions. The article's first section discusses production economies and their role in influencing industry structure. The second section reviews the empirical literature on production economies at depository financial institutions. Several important issues and problems that arise in the estimation of production economies are examined in the third section. The last section summarizes the article and describes several policy implications that may be drawn from this literature.

Production economies

Two types of production economies may be achieved by individual firms in any industry—economies of scale, which are associated with firm size, and economies of scope, which relate to the joint production of two or more products.[1] Firms in an industry realize economies of scale if technology allows production costs to rise proportionately less than output when output increases. That is, economies of scale exist if per-unit or average production costs decline as output rises. Conversely, if average costs rise with output, diseconomies of scale are present. Economies of scope arise if two or more products can be jointly produced at a lower cost than is incurred in their independent production. Diseconomies of scope are present if joint production is more costly than independent production.

Industry structure is greatly influenced by the nature of production economies. If an industry's technology allows for both economies of scale and economies of scope, the industry will tend to be made up of large diversified firms.[2] These firms will be able to produce at lower per-unit costs than smaller specialized firms and can potentially use this cost advantage to gain market share. Alternatively, if technology allows neither economies of scale nor scope, small specialized firms will tend to dominate the industry. A mixture of larger diversified firms and smaller specialized firms will develop in the absence of significant economies of scale and scope.

Economies of scale

There are two kinds of economies of scale. Economies that arise from increases in the production of individual products are called product-specific economies of scale. Economies associated with increases in all of a firm's outputs are referred to as overall economies of scale.

While the two types are synonymous for a single-product firm, both types of scale economies may be present for firms that produce more than one product. For multiproduct firms, overall economies of scale occur if total costs increase proportionately less than output when there is a simultaneous and equal percentage increase in each of the firm's products. With overall economies of scale, average costs decline as the firm expands production while maintaining a constant product mix.

Product-specific economies of scale are present if a decline in the per-unit cost of producing a specific product occurs as the output of that product increases. In principle, product-specific economies of scale for each product should be measured independently from the other products in the product mix. However, in practice such a measure is not meaningful since, under joint

---

[1] For an extensive discussion of economies of scale, see Scherer (1980).

[2] In the economics literature, these institutions would be termed competitively viable. More formally, a firm is defined as competitively viable if, in the long run, no other firm can produce a given product, or product mix, at a lower per-unit cost. To an economist the concept of cost means opportunity cost. Thus, the definition of competitive viability is inclusive of all revenue

and cost streams generated by alternative uses of the firm's assets. That is, if a firm's long-run costs are not at a minimum, there will be an incentive to increase profit by altering the level and/or mix of firm output.

production, it is generally impossible to change the output of one product while holding constant the output of the other products.[3] In spite of this problem, an approximate measure of product-specific economies of scale has been proposed and used in the empirical literature. This measure is discussed in the box on page 27.

Economies of scope

There are two types of economies of scope, global and product-specific. To define global economies of scope, it is necessary to compare the costs of both joint production and separate production, assuming a given scale for each product. For a given product mix, if the total costs from joint production of all products in the product mix are less than the sum of the costs of producing each product independently, global economies of scope are present.

Product-specific economies of scope refer to economies that arise from the joint production of a particular product with other products. If production efficiency can be enhanced by adding a particular product to a given product mix, then product-specific economies of scope exist. That is, if the cost of producing a product independently from the other products in the product mix exceeds the cost of producing it jointly, product-specific economies of scope can be realized from joint production.

Product-specific economies of scope for a given product may result from joint production efficiencies with one or a large number of products in the mix. To determine which product pairs share jointness in production, cost complementarities between all pairs of products can be computed.

---

[3] For expanded discussion of this problem, see Fuss and Waverman (1981).

A cost complementarity exists between two products if the marginal cost of producing one product declines when it is produced jointly with the other.

Sources of production economies at depository institutions

The literature on the theory of the firm has hypothesized numerous ways in which economies of scale and scope might arise in production. Making better use of specialized labor and capital and spreading fixed costs over large levels of output are usually cited as the predominant sources of economies of scale. Most economies of scope are thought to arise from the joint usage of a fixed resource.

Consistent with the theory of the firm, research on production by depository institutions often points to these important sources of both economies of scale and scope: specialized labor, computer and telecommunications technology, and information. For example, at small depository institutions, labor is unlikely to perform specialized functions. Tellers and loan officers probably process a variety of loan and deposit accounts since they are likely to be underutilized in handling specialized products. Their unspecialized labor is then a fixed input that can be shared in the production of a number of products, with the potential to create economies of scope. As these smaller institutions grow, they may be able to fully employ more specialized labor in producing some or all of their products. If the expertise of specialized tellers and loan officers results in the processing of a greater volume of deposit and loan accounts per unit of labor, then per-unit labor costs can be reduced through increased specialization. In this example, increased size may result in production efficiencies through the substitution of economies of scale for economies of scope.

The adoption of computer and telecommunications equipment can provide another basis for both economies of scale and scope at depository institutions. Despite the large set-up costs required, computer and other electronic funds transfer equipment can process a large volume of transactions at a small additional cost per transaction. As depository institutions increase the number of transactions of all types that can be performed by this equipment, it may be possible to reduce the per-unit cost of the firm as a whole as well as for individual products. Embracing this technology may provide a basis for both overall and product-specific economies of scale. In addition, any excess capacity of the equipment could be used to process other types of accounts at a small additional cost per transaction, thus realizing economies of scope.

Economies of scale and scope may also accompany information production. Before lending decisions can be made, credit information must be gathered and analyzed. Once gathered, however, this information can be reused in other lending decisions. Where the cost of reusing information is less than the independent cost of its production, reuse can help reduce the incremental costs of extending additional credit. If the information is reused to make similar loans to the same customer or to other customers in the same region or industry, it will provide a source of economies of scale. Alternatively, if the information can be used to make unrelated types of loans to the institution's customers, it may serve as a source of economies of scope.

A review of the empirical literature

Most of the evidence about the existence and extent of production economies at depository institutions comes from the empirical estimation of statistical cost functions. In developing these functions, researchers begin with the microeconomic principle that production costs depend on input prices and the level and composition of output.[4] After defining these variables, the researcher selects a statistical function to explicitly relate production costs to outputs and input prices. The most frequently selected statistical function is the transcendental logarithmic or translog function. This function is usually selected because it is flexible enough to yield both economies and diseconomies of scale at different output levels and to provide information on scope economies by incorporating interdependencies between products.[5]

Once the statistical function is selected and specified, the researcher estimates the parameters of the function using sample data. The estimated parameters and sample data are then used to construct empirical measures of the various types of scale and scope economies discussed in the previous section. A discussion of the most frequently used empirical measures is presented in the box on page 27. Technical statements of each measure are presented in Appendix B.

Empirical evidence

The 13 studies reviewed in this article attempted to estimate economies of scale and scope for credit unions, savings and loan associations, or commercial banks. Each study used a translog statistical cost function and employed similar measures of economies of scale and scope. The studies' results suggest four broad conclusions: First, overall economies of scale appear to exist

---

[4] This functional relationship follows from the property of duality between the production and cost functions. When the statistical cost function is being estimated with cross-sectional data, it may be necessary to include other variables that may induce interfirm variation in cost. Among the variables most commonly included are the number of branches and affiliation with a holding company.

[5] An example of the general form taken by the translog function appears in Appendix B.

only at low levels of output with diseconomies of scale at large output levels. Second, there is no consistent evidence of global economies of scope. Third, there is some evidence of cost complementarities (product-specific economies of scope) in production. Finally, these results appear to be generally robust across the three types of institutions, as well as across different data sets and product and cost definitions.

Twelve of the 13 studies report significant overall economies of scale at relatively low levels of output (Table 1, column 2). Only Mester fails to find any evidence of scale economies, and then only for savings and loan associations below $100 million of deposits.[6] Only two studies, however, find significant overall economies of scale above $100 million of deposits (Table 1, column 3). Moreover, the authors of one of these—Goldstein, McNulty, and Verbrugge—do not directly control for potential scope economies, and the authors of the other study—Benston, Hanweck, and Humphrey—report scale economies only for large branch banking organizations.[7] Several authors report greater economies of scale among branch banking institutions, but when an augmented measure of overall economies of scale is employed to control for the interdependency between the number of offices and the number of accounts serviced, the cost advantage of branch banks seems to disappear.[8]

As already noted, it is not conceptually possible to measure product-specific economies of scale without ambiguities, so it may not be surprising that only four of the 13 studies report evidence on this type of production economy.[9] The results presented in these four studies do not support a conclusion of widespread product-specific economies of scale (Table 1, column 4). Both H.Y. Kim and Mester report product specific economies of scale for mortgage loans. However, H.Y. Kim and Gilligan, Smirlock and Marshall also report product specific diseconomies of scale for several products.[10] Benston, Berger, Hanweck, and Humphrey report estimates of the marginal cost of production for five products by size class. However, they acknowledge that the negative marginal costs reported for some products are "implausible" and most likely indicate some type of estimation problem.[11]

Eleven of the studies compute a measure of global economies of scope. However, only three report evidence of statistical significance for their measure. Further, in two of the three studies that report statistically significant global economies of scope, the statistical cost function that was estimated contained only two broadly defined products.[12] Only M. Kim reported statistically

---

[6] See Mester (1987).

[7] See Goldstein, McNulty, and Verbrugge (1987); and Benston, Hanweck, and Humphrey (1982).

[8] See Appendix B for a presentation of the augmented measure of overall economies of scale used to control for the relationship between the number of offices and the number of accounts.

---

[9] Appendix B presents several methods proposed by these authors for measuring product-specific economies of scale.

[10] These products include nonmortgage loans, investment services, total loans and total deposits.

[11] The authors suggest that the most likely estimation problems are the presence of multicollinearity and the loss of degrees of freedom, both resulting from the large number of parameters that must be estimated when the translog function is used. See Benston et al. (1983).

[12] Gilligan, Smirlock, and Marshall (1984) include total deposit accounts and total loan accounts as the only two products in the cost function they estimate. Gilligan and Smirlock (1984) estimate two statistical cost functions, each with a pair of products. The product pairs employed in the two cost functions are, respectively, the total dollar amounts of demand and time deposits, and the total dollar amounts of total loans outstanding and total securities held.

TABLE 1

Summary of results of studies reviewed

Authors	Significant economies of scale			Significant economies of scope	
	Overall		Product specific	Global	Cost complementarities
	Below $100 million in deposits	Above $100 million in deposits			
Murray and White (1983)	yes	no	no measure	no	yes
H.Y. Kim (1987)	yes[c]	no	yes[o,j] no[p,j]	no[k]	no[k]
Mester (1987)	no	no	yes[o]	no	no
Goldstein, McNulty, & Verbrugge (1987)	yes[a]	yes[a]	no measure	no measure	no measure
LaCompte and Smith (1986)	yes[b]	no	no measure	no	yes(1978) no(1983)
Benston, Hanweck, & Humphrey (1982)	yes[d,f] no[e]	yes[d,f] no[e]	no measure	no measure[l]	no measure[l]
Benston, Berger, Hanweck, & Humphrey (1983)	yes	no	yes[r,j]	no	yes[j]
Gilligan and Smirlock (1984)	yes	no	no measure	yes[m]	no measure
Gilligan, Smirlock, & Marshall (1984)	yes	no	no[s,j]	yes[m]	no measure
M. Kim (1986)	yes	no	no measure	yes[n] no	yes[n] no
Lawrence and Shay (1986)	no[g]	no[h]	no measure	no[o]	yes[o]
Berger, Hanweck, & Humphrey (1987)	yes	no	no measure	no	yes
Kolari and Zardhooki (1987)	no[e] yes[d]	no[e] no[d,i]	no measure	no	yes

Notes:
a: Did not control for economies of scope.
b: Up to $50 million in total deposits.
c: Reports diseconomies of scale to nonmortgage lending.
d: Denotes branch banking.
e: Denotes unit banking.
f: Reports diseconomies of scale if an augmented global scale economies measure is utilized.
g: Reports increasing returns to scale in 1980 and 1981 only.
h: No diseconomies of scale found in the upper two quartiles as high as $2.5 billion in 1980 and 1981.
i: Up to $100 million in total deposits.
j: Provides no statistical tests.
k: Reports scope economies but without tests of statistical significance.
l: Employed Divisia Index for output.
m: Test of nonjointness restrictions used only one pair of outputs.
n: Denotes a no-aggregation model.
o: Diseconomies of scope found between loans and investments.
p: For mortgage loans only.
q: Reports diseconomies for nonmortgage lending and investment services.
r: Reports computed marginal costs for selected products and arbitrarily chosen deposit size classification.
s: Reports diseconomies of scale for total loans and total deposits.

significant global economies of scope for a more disaggregated product mix.[13] The last two columns of Table 1 summarize the estimates of global and product-specific (cost complementarities from joint production) economies of scope.

Although the empirical evidence does not support a conclusion of global economies of scope from joint production, many of the studies report some evidence of cost complementarities between pairs of products. When the translog function is estimated, evidence of a cost complementarity between any two products is given by a negative and statistically significant parameter estimate on the cross-product term between the two products. Table 2 lists all product pairs for which the estimated cross-product term is statistically significant. Inspection of this table indicates that some evidence of cost complementarities can be found in a number of studies and among a variety of different product pairs. The strongest evidence of cost complementarities occurs in the joint production of two product pairs: total loans and total deposits, and investments and mortgage loans.[14] However, diseconomies of joint production were also reported between two related product pairs: investments and total loans, and total loans and total deposits for branch banks with total deposits below $100 million.[15]

---

[13] In his study of Israeli banks, Kim (1986) defined several alternative product mixes as combinations of four distinct products: demand deposits, foreign currency, loans, and securities. His results indicate that global economies of scope only occur when the four products appear separately in the cost function. Kim reports an absence of global economies of scope for all other combinations of these four products.

[14] A cost complementarity between total loans and total deposits is reported in Berger, Hanweck, and Humphrey (1987); Gilligan, Smirlock, and Marshall (1984); and Lawrence and Shay (1986). A cost complementarity between investments and mortgage loans is reported in LaCompte and Smith (1986), and Mester (1987).

[15] The diseconomy of the first type is reported in Lawrence and Shay (1986). The second type of diseconomy is reported in

Issues and problems

Several issues and problems may have influenced the results discussed in the preceding section. These issues and problems are both conceptual and methodological in nature. The problems tend to limit, but not eliminate, the usefulness of the empirical conclusions in drawing policy implications.

Defining bank costs and output

The banking literature is divided over the conceptual issue of the appropriate definition of bank output, and consequently on the related issue of defining bank costs. In general, researchers take one of two approaches.[16] These alternative approaches are labeled the "intermediation approach" and the "production approach."[17] No consensus has developed favoring one of the definitions over the other, and reasonable arguments have been made for both approaches.

Under the intermediation approach, depository financial institutions are viewed as producers of services related directly to their role as an intermediator in financial markets. That is, they are viewed as collecting deposits and purchasing funds to be subsequently intermediated into loans and other assets. In this approach, deposits are treated as inputs along with capital and labor. Those authors who adopt this approach generally define the institution's various dollar volumes of earning assets as measures of output. Also con-

---

Berger, Hanweck, and Humphrey (1987). Lawrence and Shay report an additional diseconomy of joint production between nonbank activities and total deposits.

[16] The approaches taken in the 13 papers reviewed here appear in the second column of Appendix A.

[17] Discussions of these two approaches can be found in a number of recent papers including Humphrey (1987); Mester (1987a); and Berger, Hanweck, and Humphrey (1987).

TABLE 2
Significant cost complementarities

Output Pairs	Author(s)	Year(s)	Sign
Consumer and mortgage loans	LaCompte and Smith	1978	negative
Investments and total loans	Gilligan and Smirlock	1973-78	negative
	Lawrence and Shay	1982	positive
Nonbank activity and total loans	Lawrence and Shay	1982	negative
Total deposits and total loans	Lawrence and Shay	1982	negative
	Gilligan, Smirlock, & Marshall	1978	negative
	Berger, Hanweck, & Humphrey	1983	negative*
Investments and mortgage loans	Mester	1982	negative
	LaCompte and Smith	1978	negative
Nonbank activity and investments	Lawrence and Shay	1982	negative
Total deposits and investments	Lawrence and Shay	1982	negative
Nonbank activity and total deposits	Lawrence and Shay	1982	positive
Time deposits and demand deposits	Gilligan and Smirlock	1973-78	negative

* Negative for branch banks with deposits > $100 million in total deposits; positive for branch banks < $100 million in total deposits.

sistent with this approach, costs are defined to include both interest expense and total costs of production.

The production approach, on the other hand, views depository institutions as producers of services associated with individual loan and deposit accounts. These account services are produced using capital and labor. Under this approach, it follows that the number of accounts of each type are the appropriate definitions of outputs. Total costs are defined exclusive of interest costs.

Conceptually, the intermediation and production approaches are very different. In reviewing the literature, it is surprising that the empirical results do not appear to be sensitive to the approach taken in defining outputs and costs. Why this should be the case is unclear. However, one possibility is that other issues, as discussed below, are more important.

Data

One of two types of data has been employed in nearly all recent attempts at estimating statistical cost functions for depository institutions. The data are drawn either from Call Report and financial statement data (as reported to the Federal Deposit Insurance Corporation, the Federal Savings and Loan Insurance Corporation, and the National Credit Union Share Insurance Fund), or from the Functional Cost Analysis (FCA) program conducted by the Federal Reserve System.

Each of these two sources of data offers advantages and disadvantages. An advantage of the FCA data is that they are constructed using simple cost accounting techniques to allocate costs among several distinguishable banking functions. In addition, these data include information on the number and average size of a variety of deposit and loan products. However, the generalization of the results obtained using FCA data to all depository institutions may be inappropriate for several reasons. Because the FCA program is

voluntary, subscribing banks might be either high-cost institutions interested in identifying areas for cost reduction or low-cost firms that place greater emphasis on cost control. Further, the FCA data are heavily skewed toward small banks.[18] Finally, the procedures used to allocate costs are sometimes imprecise and may induce unknown bias in parameter estimates when the FCA data are used to estimate statistical cost functions.[19]

An advantage of Call Report and financial statement data is that they provide information on a much wider range of institutional size and impose uniform reporting requirements. The empirical results obtained using these data, therefore, should be more generally applicable. However, this source of data also imposes limitations. First, the absence of information on numbers of deposit and loan accounts and average account size make this source of data unsuitable for use under the production approach. Further, there is some evidence that the average account size and institution size are positively correlated. Thus, a failure to control for average account size under the intermediation approach may tend to overstate any finding of economies of scale. Second, data on some banking functions such as loan commitments, standby letters of credit, safety deposit and trust activity have only recently, if at all, been reported in these data. Finally, it is questionable whether financial statement data can be used to construct meaningful proxies for the input prices, given the high level of aggregation at which these data are reported.

---

[18] As of 1986, only 490 banks participated in the program. Of this number, 416 were under $200 million in total deposits.

[19] In some cases, the allocations are made according to the judgment of the participating banker (e.g., wages and salaries). In other instances, the allocations are performed by computer algorithms developed for a representative bank using "experience factors" that are derived from previous data. For additional discussion of the allocation rules, see the *Introduction to Functional Cost Analysis: 1986 Average Banks.*

Level of aggregation and limitations of the translog functional form

Two closely related issues arise in the estimation of scale and scope economies: the appropriate level of aggregation and the suitability of the translog functional form for use with data from depository institutions. Theoretically, a measure of each distinct product offered by depository institutions should be included in the estimated function. However, the feasibility of doing this is usually limited by the availability of data and the use of a translog functional form. The larger the number of distinct products that are defined, the greater the likelihood that institutions included in the sample do not produce some of the products. Since the translog function expresses each input price and the output of each product in logarithmic form, the values of these variables must be strictly greater than zero. If a high level of disaggregation is chosen to increase the ability to identify jointness in production, then smaller and more specialized depository institutions will need to be deleted from the sample. Alternatively, if the level of aggregation in defining products is high enough to provide positive values for the output of all defined products for all institutions in the sample, then much of the information on efficiencies from joint production may be lost.[20]

A second problem involving the level of disaggregation and the translog functional form arises in attempting to compute measures of product specific economies of scale and global economies of scope. The computation of these measures requires the assumption of a zero level of output for at least one of the products being produced. However, the translog cost function will always yield zero total costs whenever the output of even one product is zero. To circumvent this problem, most researchers compute total costs by choosing an arbitrarily small but nonzero value for use in place of zero. This procedure has two drawbacks. First, the arbitrarily chosen value is usually well outside the bounds of the data. As a consequence, the confidence intervals around any computed values for these measures will be extremely wide. Second, the conventional measure of global economies of scope can be made to yield scope diseconomies. This result can be insured by replacing all zero outputs with a sufficiently small nonzero value.[21]

A third source of problems involving the level of disaggregation and the translog function arises from the number of parameters that must be estimated. As more products are defined and included in the statistical cost function, the number of parameters that must be estimated increases disproportionately.[22] For depository institutions, the number of products that must be defined to yield any meaningful level of disaggregation is large. With the necessity of including linear, quadratic, and cross-product terms for all defined products and input prices, the likelihood of severe multicollinearity would appear to be high. In this case, it may not be possible to identify individual parameter estimates. Any statistical tests will be imprecise since the standard errors of the parameter estimates are likely to be large.[23]

---

[20] Kim (1986) reports evidence that suggests if product definitions are drawn too broadly, the resulting parameter estimates will be biased against the identification of significant economies of scope.

[21] A thorough discussion of this problem can be found in Benston et al. (1983).

[22] Mester (1987a) has noted that the addition of one input and one product to a translog function consisting of three inputs and three products increases the number of parameters that must be estimated from 28 to 45.

[23] The author of this article estimated a translog cost function with seven defined products using a sample of 190 commercial banks in the Denver SMSA in 1987. All of the included banks had nonzero values for each defined product. The products

Other incentives for joint production

The concept of cost in economics is synonymous with opportunity cost, not accounting cost. Thus, in principle, the measurement of economies of scale and scope using a statistical cost function should attempt to measure the total costs of production in terms of opportunity costs rather than accounting costs. While technology may provide opportunities for the sharing of inputs, the decision to add product lines will depend ultimately on whether the additional product will increase after-tax, risk-adjusted returns. The focus on accounting costs results in the exclusion of any revenue and tax-related incentives for adding product lines—such as a reduction in earnings volatility from increased diversification—that are not rooted in production efficiencies and may even increase per-unit accounting costs.[24]

appearing in the cost function included the dollar value of transactions deposits, time deposits, investments, real estate loans, installment loans, credit card loans, and commercial loans, respectively. Under the assumption that at the margin all banks in the market faced the same input prices, use of the translog cost function required the estimation of 36 parameters. The estimation of the translog cost function produced an adjusted R^2 of .9783 and an F-statistic of 245.782. However, of the 36 parameters only four were statistically significant at the 5 percent level of significance. The variance decomposition collinearity diagnostics provided in SAS produced "high" condition indices for all but five of the variables. Further, there were numerous instances in which variables with high condition indices contributed strongly (exhibited a variable proportion greater than 0.5) to the variances of two or more variables. These results are indicative of a severe multicollinearity problem.

[24] Other incentives may include greater use of off-balance sheet activities to avoid regulatory taxes imposed by risk-based capital requirements and deposit insurance premiums, and joint customer demand for banking services that arise from a desire to reduce transactions costs. See Baer and Pavel (1988) for a recent analysis of the regulatory tax imposed by minimum capital requirements and deposit insurance premiums.

Summary

Care should be exercised in attempting to use the existing empirical literature as a sole basis for policy. At present, no systematic attempts have been made at conducting a sensitivity analysis of the empirical results to the issues and problems discussed above. Further, it is difficult to assess the severity of these problems by examining the existing literature because differences among studies are sufficiently large to prevent drawing conclusions on specific issues.

Finally, the studies reviewed in this article predate the granting of new securities, insurance, mutual funds, and other powers to depository institutions and therefore cannot be used to draw inferences about their likely impact on costs. This is particularly true since the size of any impact will depend importantly upon whether the new powers are granted directly to institutions or can be offered only through affiliates of bank holding companies.

Conclusions and policy implications

A review of the empirical evidence presented in 13 separate studies of economies of joint production for depository institutions yields several tentative results. First, the empirical evidence appears to support a conclusion of significant overall economies of scale only for depository institutions of relatively small size—less than $100 million in total deposits. Second, the empirical evidence does not appear to support a conclusion of global economies of scope. Third, there appears to be some evidence of economies in joint production among specific pairs of products that might be offered by depository institutions.

The three results listed above suggest several tentative policy conclusions. Taken together, the evidence implies that the smallest, most specialized of depository institutions may be at a cost disadvantage relative to larger, more diversified institutions. These smaller institutions are likely to be faced with the necessity of increasing both the scale and scope of their operations to remain cost competitive. Failure to achieve sufficient growth and to exploit available cost complementarities may drive these depository institutions from the market or cause them to be absorbed by other more cost-efficient institutions. However, the evidence also suggests that once overall scale economies have been exhausted, there will still be opportunities for the smaller, less diversified depository institutions. The absence of strong global economies of scope, combined with evidence of several cost complementarities, will probably provide a number of market niches for these smaller institutions.

From a policy perspective, the absence of a cost advantage for the largest, most diversified depository institutions appears to minimize any concern that the banking industry will be dominated by a few large depository financial institutions. The

lifting of restrictions on interstate banking and intrastate branching might help consolidate resources in states that have prohibited or severely limited branch banking by permitting small banks to achieve a more efficient scale of production. The absence of significant scope economies suggests, however, that the lifting of these restrictions is unlikely to require significant adjustment in product mix.

In light of the issues and problems raised in this article, there is ample room for more research. Future efforts should address questions like these: Is there a better statistical function for use in measuring economies of scale and scope than the translog cost function? What is the appropriate level for the disaggregation of output for depository institutions? What is the best way to broaden the focus to include incentives for joint production? And, as new powers are granted to depository institutions, how will this affect their production efficiencies?

Empirical Measures of Production Economies

Researchers have developed empirical measures for both economies of scale and economies of scope. Overall economies of scale are typically measured by computing the sum of the output cost elasticities of individual products. The output cost elasticity for a product is the percentage change in production costs that occurs for a given percentage change in the output of the product. And, the sum of the individual output cost elasticities is equivalent to the percentage change in costs that results from an equal percentage change in the output of all products. When this measure of overall economies of scale is equal to one at a given level of overall output, there are constant returns to scale. Thus, no additional production efficiencies can be achieved in this range of production. If this measure of overall scale economies

is significantly less than one, then there are increasing returns to scale and production efficiencies will be realized in this range of production. Conversely, if this measure is significantly greater than one, there are decreasing returns to scale and production inefficiencies will be realized.

While product-specific economies of scale cannot be measured without ambiguities, an approximate measure has been proposed and utilized in several cost studies. This measure makes use of the theoretical relationship between the marginal cost, average cost, and economies of scale. Where the marginal cost of producing a product is less than average cost at a given level of output, average cost is declining in that range of output, implying economies of scale. Conversely, when marginal cost is greater than average cost, average cost is increasing, implying diseconomies of scale. To approximate this relationship in a multi-product setting, a new cost concept labeled "average incremental cost" (AIC) is utilized. AIC is defined as the addition to total cost of producing a specific level of a product as opposed to not producing it at all, divided by the level of output of the product. Then the AIC can be expressed as a ratio to the marginal cost of producing this level of output. If this ratio is greater than one, this is viewed as evidence of product-specific economies of scale for the range of output levels between zero and the level at which AIC and MC are evaluated, since it implies that average costs are declining. If the ratio is less than one, product-specific diseconomies of scale is implied.

Global economies of scope are measured by computing the cost differential that would arise between the independent and joint production of specific output levels of all products. This cost differential is then generally scaled by dividing by the total costs of joint production. This measure will have a value greater than zero when there are global economies of scope, and a negative value when diseconomies are present.

As an alternative to computing the preceding measure, researchers have demonstrated that a sufficient condition for global economies of scope is the existence of cost complementarities among all pairs of products in the product mix. A cost complementarity occurs when the marginal cost of producing one product declines with an increase in the level of production of another.

Product-specific economies of scope are measured in several alternative ways. One common measure is to compute the cost increase or decrease that arises from producing a specific product both independently from, and jointly with, the remaining product mix and expressing it as a percentage of the costs of joint production. If this ratio is greater than one, product-specific economies of scope are implied. If the ratio is less than one, diseconomies of scope exist.

Other alternative ways of identifying a cost complementarity between any two products in the product mix involve an assessment of how joint production of two products affects the marginal cost of producing each product. When parameter estimates from a translog statistical cost function are used, it can be shown that a necessary condition for the marginal cost of producing a product to decline with an increase in the production of a second product, referred to here as a pairwise cost complementarity, requires their cross-product term to be negative and statistically different from zero. However, while a negative cross-product term is consistent with the existence of a cost complementarity, it is not sufficient. Any reduction in marginal costs from the joint production of the two products may be offset by rapidly rising marginal costs from one or both of the two products. When the translog function is estimated, it can be shown that a sufficient condition for a cost complementarity between two products requires that the cross-product term not only be negative but also greater in absolute value than the product of the output elasticities of the two products being considered. A statistical test of this condition (test of nonjointness) is carried out by testing the parameter restrictions that would be required for nonjointness in the production of the two products.

Appendix A
Summary of Studies Reviewed

Authors	Approach	Data	Outputs	ECSCA*	ECSCO*
Murray and White (1983)	Intermediation	61 Canadian Credit Unions (1976-77)	y_1, y_2, y_{14}	OSA(1)	PSSO(2)
H. Y. Kim (1986)	Intermediation	61 Canadian Credit Unions (1976-77)	y_1, y_2, y_{14}	OSA(1) PSSA(1)	GSO(1) GSO(2) PSSO(4)
Mester (1987)	Intermediation	149 Calif. S&Ls (1982)	y_1, y_3, y_{14}	OSA(1)	GSO(1) PSSO(1)
Goldstein, McNulty, & Verbrugge (1987)	Production	FSLIC Insured S&Ls (1978-81)	y_{13}	OSA(1)** OSA(2)**	No measure
LaCompte & Smith (1986)	Intermediation	S&Ls Ninth Dist. FHLBB (1978-83)	y_1, y_2, y_3	OSA(1)	PSSO(2)
Benston, Hanweck & Humphrey (1982)	Production and Intermediation	FCA Data (1975-78)	Divisia Index	OSA(1)**	No measure
Benston, Berger, Hanweck & Humphrey (1983)	Production	FCA Data [deposits less than one billion] (1978)	y_4, y_5, y_6, y_7, y_8	OSA(1) OSA(2)	PSSO(3) PSSO(4)
Gilligan & Smirlock (1984)	Production	Financial Statement Data, 2700 banks (1973-78)	y_3, y_4, y_5, y_9	OSA(1)	PSSO(3)
Gilligan, Smirlock, & Marshall (1984)	Production	FCA Data (1978)	y_9, y_{10}	PSSA(2)	PSSO(3)
M. Kim (1986)	Intermediation	17 Israeli Banks (1979-82)	y_3, y_4, y_9, y_{11}	OSA(1) OSA(2)	GSO(1) PSSO(1)
Lawrence & Shay (1986)	Intermediation	FCA Data (1979-82)	y_3, y_4, y_9, y_{12}	OSA(1)	PSSO(4)
Berger, Hanweck & Humphrey (1987)	Production	FCA Data (1983)	y_4, y_5, y_6, y_7, y_8	OSA(1) EPSA	GSO(1) EPSUB
Kolari & Zardhooki (1987)	Production	FCA Data (1979-1983)	$y_3, y_4, y_5, y_9, y_{10}$	OSA(1)	GSO(1) PSSO(2)

Notes: *See Appendices A and B for definitions of the abbreviations for the measures of economies of scale and scope employed in this table.

** indicates the use of a Divisia Index for output. Other outputs are denoted as follows: y_1 = mortgage loans; y_2 = consumer loans; y_3 = investments; y_4 = demand deposits; y_5 = time deposits; y_6 = real estate loans; y_7 = commercial loans; y_8 = installment loans; y_9 = total loans; y_{10} = total deposits; y_{11} = foreign currency; y_{12} = nonbank activities; y_{13} = total assets; and y_{14} = other loans.

Appendix B
Empirical Measures of Economies of Scale and Scope

I. TRANSLOG STATISTICAL COST FUNCTION

$$lnTC = B_o + \sum_i B_i lny_i + \sum_k C_k lnp_k + (1/2)\sum_i \sum_j D_{ij} lny_i lny_j;$$

$$+ (1/2)\sum_k \sum_l E_{kl} lnp_k lnp_l + \sum_i \sum_k F_{ik} lny_i lnp_k + e,$$

where ln denotes the logarithm; $y_i(i=1,\ldots,m)$ denotes the ith output; $p_k(k=1,\ldots,n)$ denotes the kth input price; B_o, B_i, C_k, D_{ij}, E_{kl}, F_{ik} are the parameters to be estimated and e represents the random error term.

II. OVERALL ECONOMIES OF SCALE

A. Overall or Plant Economies of Scale

$$OSA(1) = \sum_i \frac{\partial lnTC}{\partial lny_i} = \sum_i \epsilon_i, \text{ where } \epsilon_i$$

is the output cost elasticity for product i. $OSA(1) < 1$ indicates overall economies of scale. $OSA(1) > 1$ indicates overall diseconomies of scale.

B. Augmented or Firm Economies of Scale

$$OSA(2) = \sum_i \frac{\partial lnTC}{\partial lny_i} + \frac{\partial lnTC}{\partial lnB} \times \frac{\partial lnB}{\partial lny_i},$$

where B is the number of branches operated by the depository institution. $OSA(2) < 1$ indicates overall economies of scale. $OSA(2) > 1$ indicates overall diseconomies of scale.

III. PRODUCT-SPECIFIC ECONOMIES OF SCALE

A. Average Incremental Costs

$$PSSA(1) = [(IC_i/TC)/\epsilon_i], \text{ where } \epsilon_i = \frac{\partial lnTC}{\partial lny_i}$$

$TC = C(y_i,\ldots,y_m)$ and $IC_i = [C(y_i,\ldots,y_m) - C(y_1,\ldots,y_{i-1}, 0, y_{i+1},\ldots,y_m)]$. $PSSA(1) > 0$ indicates product-specific economies of scale for product y_i. $PSSA(1) < 0$ indicates product-specific diseconomies of scale for product y_i.

B. Declining Marginal Cost

$$PSSA(2) = \frac{\partial^2 TC}{\partial y_i^2} = (\frac{TC}{y_i^2})[\frac{\partial lnTC}{\partial lny_i^2} + (\frac{\partial lnTC}{\partial lny_i})(\frac{\partial lnTC}{\partial lny_i} - 1)].$$

If $PSSA(2) < 0$ then marginal costs of product y_i are declining. This implies product-specific economies of scale for product y_i. $PSSA(2) > 0$ implies increasing marginal costs and product-specific diseconomies of scale for product y_i.

IV. EXPANSION PATH SCALE ECONOMIES

$$EPSA = \{\sum_i [((y_i^B - y_i^A)/y_i^B)(C(y_i^B) - C(y_i^A)/C(y_i^B))] \times \frac{\partial lnTC^B}{\partial lny_i}\},$$

where y_i denotes the level of output of product i produced by small Firm A or large Firm B. $C(\ )$ denotes the total cost of producing level y_i of product i by each type of firm. If $EPSA < 1$ this implies economies of scale along an expansion path including firms A and B. If $EPSA > 1$ this implies diseconomies of scale along this expansion path.

V. GLOBAL ECONOMIES OF SCOPE

A. Global Economies of Scope

$$GSO(1) = \{[C(y_1,o,\ldots,o) + \ldots + C(o,\ldots,o,y_m)] - C(y_1,\ldots,y_m)\}/C(y_1,\ldots,y_m),$$

where $C(\ )$ denotes the total costs of production. If $GSO(1) > 0$ then there are global economies of scope. If $GSO(1) < 0$ there are global diseconomies of scope.

B. Disjoint-Group Economies of Scope

$$GSO(2) = \{[C(y_1,\ldots,y_j) + C(y_{j+1},\ldots,y_m)] - C(y_1,\ldots,y_m)\}/C(y_1,\ldots,y_m), \text{ where}$$

$C(\ )$ denotes the total costs of production. $GSO(2) > 0$ denotes economies of scope in production. $GSO(2) < 0$ denotes diseconomies of scope.

VI. PRODUCT-SPECIFIC ECONOMIES OF SCOPE

A. Product-Specific Economies of Scope

$$PSSO(1) = \{[C(y_1,\ldots,y_{i-1},o,y_{i+1},\ldots,y_m) + C(o,\ldots,o,y_1,o,\ldots,o)] - C(y_1,\ldots,y_m)\}/C(y_1,\ldots,y_m)$$

where $C(\ )$ denotes the total costs of production. $PSSO(1) > 0$ implies product-specific economies of scope. $PSSO(1) < 0$ implies product-specific diseconomies of scope.

B. Cost Complementarities

$$PSSO(2) = \frac{\partial^2 TC}{\partial y_i \partial y_k} = \left(\frac{TC}{y_i y_k}\right)\left[\frac{\partial^2 \ln TC}{\partial \ln y_i \partial \ln y_k} + \left(\frac{\partial \ln TC}{\partial \ln y_i}\right)\left(\frac{\partial \ln TC}{\partial \ln y_k}\right)\right]$$

$PSSO(2) < 0$ implies that an increase in the level of production of product y_k reduces the marginal cost of producing product y_i. Thus $PSSO(2) < 0$ implies product-specific economies of scope between products y_i *and* y_k. Conversely, $PSSO(2) > 0$ implies product-specific diseconomies of scope between products y_i and y_k.

C. Test of Nonjointness

From $PSSO(2)$, nonjointness implies $(\partial^2 TC / \partial y_i \partial y_k) = 0$. At any nonzero level of production of y_i and y_k, $(TC/y_i y_k) > 0$. Therefore, nonjointness requires

$$PSSA(3) = \left[\frac{\partial \ln TC}{\partial \ln y_i \partial \ln y_k} + \left(\frac{\partial \ln TC}{\partial \ln y_i}\right)\left(\frac{\partial \ln TC}{\partial \ln y_k}\right)\right]^5 0.$$

From the translog this implies the restrictions that

$$[D_{ij} + \epsilon_i \times \epsilon_k] = 0, \text{ where}$$

$$\epsilon_i = \frac{\partial \ln TC}{\partial \ln y_i} = B_i + \sum_j D_{ij} \ln y_j + \sum_k F_{ik} \ln p_k.$$

The parameter restrictions can be imposed and a likelihood ratio test of the restrictions can be conducted.

D. Pairwise Cost Complementarities

A necessary condition for $(\partial^2 TC / \partial y_i \partial y_k) < 0$, is that the value of $(\partial \ln TC / \partial \ln y_i \partial \ln y_k) < 0$. This follows because, as in $PSSO(3)$, $(TC/y_i y_k) > 0$. Further, from theory, $MC_i = (\partial TC / \partial y_i) > 0$, so that $(\partial \ln TC / \partial \ln y_i) = (\partial TC / \partial y_i)(y_i / TC) > 0$. Therefore, a necessary condition for the existence of a cost complementarity between products y_i and y_k, when estimating the translog cost function, is

$$PSSO(4) = \frac{\partial^2 \ln TC}{\partial \ln y_i \partial \ln y_k} = D_{ik} < 0.$$

VII. EXPANSION PATH SUBADDITIVITY

$$EPSUB = \{[C(Y^A) + C(Y^D) - C(Y^B)]/C(Y^B)\},$$

where $Y^A = (y_1^A, y_2^A, \ldots, y_m^A)$ is the product-mix of small firm A, $Y^B = (y_1^B, y_2^B, \ldots, y_m^B)$ is the product-mix of large firm B, and $Y^D = (Y^B - Y^A)$; $y_i^B \geq y_i^A \geq 0$ $\forall i$. $EPSUB > 0$ implies a cost advantage for large firm A.

References

Baer, Herbert L. and Christie A. Pavel. "Does Deregulation Drive Innovation?" *Economic Perspectives.* Federal Reserve Bank of Chicago, March/April 1988, 3-16.

Bailey, Elizabeth E. and Ann F. Friedlaender. "Market Structure and Multiproduct Industries." *Journal of Economic Literature.* September 20, 1982, 1024-1048.

Baumol, William J., John C. Panzar, and Robert D. Willig. *Contestable Markets and Industry Structure.* New York, Harcourt Brace Jovanovich, Inc., 1982.

Benston, George J., Gerald A. Hanweck, and David Humphrey. "Scale Economies in Banking." *Journal of Money, Credit, and Banking,* 14, Part 1, November 1982, 435-456.

Benston, George J., Allen N. Berger, Gerald A. Hanweck, and David Humphrey. "Economies of Scale and Scope." *Proceedings of a Conference on Bank Structure and Competition.* Chicago, Federal Reserve Bank of Chicago, 1983.

Berger, Allen N., Gerald A. Hanweck, and David B. Humphrey. "Competitive Viability in Banking." *Journal of Monetary Economics,* 20, 1987, 501-520.

Functional Cost Analysis: 1986 Average Banks. Federal Reserve Banks, 1986.

Gilligan, Thomas W. and Michael L. Smirlock. "An Empirical Study of Joint Production and Scale Economies in Commercial Banking." *Journal of Banking and Finance,* 8, 1984, 67-77.

Gilligan, Thomas W., Michael Smirlock, and William Marshall. "Scale and Scope Economies in the Multi-Product Banking Firm." *Journal of Monetary Economics,* 13, 1984, 393-405.

Goldstein, Steven J., James E. McNulty, and James Verbrugge. "Scale Economies in the Savings and Loan Industry Before Diversification." *Journal of Economics and Business,* 1987, 199-207.

Humphrey, David B. "Cost Dispersion and the Measurement of Economies in Banking." *Economic Review,* Federal Reserve Bank of Richmond, May/June 1987, 24-38.

Kim, H. Youn. "Economies of Scale and Scope in Multiproduct Financial Institutions: Further Evidence from Credit Unions." *Journal of Money, Credit, and Banking,* 18, May 1986, 220-226.

Kim, Moshe. "Banking Technology and the Existence of a Consistent Output Aggregate." *Journal of Monetary Economics,* 18, 1986, 181-195.

Kolari, James and Asghar Zardhooki. *Bank Cost, Structure, and Performance.* Lexington, Mass., D.C. Heath, 1987.

LaCompte, Richard L.B. and Stephen D. Smith. "The Impact of Regulation on Cost Structures: The Case of the Savings and Loan Industry." Unpublished manuscript, September 1986.

Lawrence, Colin and Robert Shay. "Technology and Financial Intermediation in a Multiproduct Banking Firm: An Econometric Study of U.S. Banks, 1979-82." C. Lawrence and R. Shay, eds., *Technological Innovation, Regulation, and the Monetary Economy.* Cambridge, Mass., Ballinger, 1986.

Mester, Loretta J. "Efficient Production of Financial Services: Scale and Scope." *Business Review,* Federal Reserve Bank of Philadelphia, January/February 1987a, 15-25.

Mester, Loretta J. "A Multiproduct Cost Study of Savings and Loans." *Journal of Finance,* 42, June 1987, 423-445.

Murray, John D. and Robert W. White. "Economies of Scale and Economies of Scope in Multiproduct Financial Institutions: A Study of British Columbia Credit Unions." *Journal of Finance,* 38, June 1983, 887-901.

Scherer, F.M. *Industrial Market Performance and Economic Performance.* Chicago, Rand McNally, 2nd edition, 1980.

Article 3

The Risk-based Capital Agreement: A Further Step towards Policy Convergence

On December 10, 1987, the central banks of the major industrial countries published for comment a framework for assessing the capital adequacy of international banking organizations. The central banks negotiated this agreement as part of a continuing effort to coordinate bank supervisory policies, with the ultimate objective of strengthening the international banking system and alleviating competitive inequities. The convergence process, which has focused on the development of an internationally accepted definition of regulatory capital and a common risk-weighting system, reflects the desire and ability of national bank supervisors to adapt to a changing international financial environment. This article highlights the chief developments in the negotiations that led to the international agreement and explains several of the major issues that had to be resolved in designing the proposed capital standard.[1]

Background

Over the past decade or so, various events have had a major effect on the business of banking and the nature of competition in the banking industry, both in the United States and abroad. These events include the disintermediation of short-term corporate lending, the transformation of excess international liquidity into loans to less developed countries, substantial growth in products not accounted for on the balance sheet, and technological advancements enabling instantaneous global communications and twenty-four-hour trading. As

[1]This article does not provide a detailed analysis of the risk-based capital proposal. For an extensive technical description of the framework, see the recently released *Federal Register* notice on the subject.

a by-product, the business mix in which banks now engage is more diverse, and the risk characteristics of many of the newer financial instruments are more complex than the risks associated with instruments prevalent a decade ago.

In the United States, the effort to develop a risk-based capital measure began in 1985 as a response to the changes in banking activities and an attempt to move U.S. capital standards more closely in line with the standards used in many other industrial countries. Of particular concern in the United States were the rapidly growing risk exposures of certain U.S. banks stemming from off-balance sheet activities. For example, standby letters of credit issued by the 10 largest banking organizations had grown from 7.6 percent of total assets at year-end 1981 to 11.6 percent by mid-year 1985, even as total assets increased. Similarly, the ten largest banks' interest rate swaps, first introduced in 1981, had increased to 14 percent of total assets as of June 30, 1985, based on notional values (which are not directly comparable to asset values). Finally, the same banks' foreign exchange contracts had risen to 105 percent of total assets over this period, again based simply on notional values. None of these activities is systematically factored into existing U.S. capital guidelines, which focus on the level of capital relative to total balance sheet assets. While a multitude of factors have influenced the growth in off-balance sheet activities, the lack of quantitative capital requirements to support these activities most likely had a positive impact on their growth.

Another change in banking risk profiles addressed by the risk-based capital measure relates to balance sheet activities. By some measures, U.S. banks' investments in relatively low-risk liquid assets had declined during the early 1980s in relation to total assets. The current capital guidelines do not distinguish between higher- and lower-risk assets and thus require banks to hold the same amount of capital against lower-yielding U.S. government securities as against higher-yielding private sector loans. This treatment may have tempered many banks' desires to hold low-risk, relatively liquid assets.

The effort by U.S. bank regulatory authorities to develop a risk-based capital measure also reflected a recognition of the growing divergence between U.S. capital standards and the risk-related capital adequacy measures introduced by other major industrial countries. For example, France introduced a risk-related capital standard in 1979; the Bank of England adopted a formal risk-based approach in 1980; and German capital measures, set out in the Banking Act (as amended in 1985), recognize certain credit risk and interest rate risk distinctions.

Thus, in the summer of 1985, in an attempt to address the growing inadequacies of the existing capital-to-assets guidelines and to bring U.S. capital policies more closely in line with those used in other industrial countries, the three Federal bank supervisory authorities—the Office of the Comptroller of the Currency (OCC), the Federal Deposit Insurance Corporation, and the Federal Reserve—began working together to develop a risk-based capital measure for U.S. banking organizations. In January 1986, the original U.S. proposal was issued for public comment.[2]

A majority of the comments from banks and other market participants expressed general support—at least in principle—for the original proposal. However, many of the respondents asserted that, without similar requirements for foreign bank competitors, the proposed requirements would put U.S. banks at a competitive disadvantage both at home and abroad, particularly in the area of off-balance sheet products, which generally are not incorporated in capital standards abroad. At a minimum, foreign banks competing in the United States but not subject to comparable minimum capital standards might be able to underprice domestic banks. Concern was also voiced that capital standards applied to commercial and standby letters of credit would force domestic commercial banks to raise their prices relative to the prices charged by foreign bank competitors, eroding the ability of U.S. banks to compete in those markets.

[2]The first proposal assigned risk weights to assets and certain off-balance sheet activities according to broad gradations of risk. U.S. supervisors envisioned that this risk-weighted measure of exposure would be used as an additional tool in assessing an organization's capital adequacy.

During the summer of 1986, the U.S. supervisory authorities reviewed and revised their capital proposal in light of the comments received from the public and the further analyses pursued as a result of those comments. During the process, however, it became clear that an opportunity to move toward more explicit international convergence of supervisory policies was at hand. The United Kingdom's system of risk-weighting assets was conceptually similar to the U.S. proposal, and the U.K. authorities were in the process of revising their system to incorporate a wider range of off-balance sheet activities. Banking supervisors in both countries felt that, in light of the importance of New York and London as international banking centers, agreement on a single risk-based capital framework to be applied in both the United States and the United Kingdom would indeed represent a major step forward in international convergence.

As a result, in the fall of 1986, the U.S. authorities deferred action on their own proposal to work with the Bank of England on the development of a common approach to assessing capital adequacy. Significantly, this effort required a fundamental rethinking of the appropriate definition of capital, since each country brought its own definition to the negotiations. In fact, an important aspect of the ultimate agreement between the two countries was its two-tiered definition of total capital. "Base capital," consisting of specified capital elements, would be included in the measure of regulatory capital on an unlimited basis, while "limited capital," consisting of other types of capital instruments, would be restricted to the amount of base capital held by a banking organization.

Shortly after negotiations began, the two countries agreed to introduce the credit risk exposures stemming from interest rate and foreign exchange contracts in the capital adequacy framework. During the preceding twelve months or so, the Bank of England had investigated such a step in the course of reviewing and revising its own capital standards. In contrast, U.S. supervisory authorities had begun work on this aspect of risk-based capital only a few months before the bilateral negotiations started. Given the relative complexity of measuring rate contract credit risk, a special task force comprising representatives of the Bank of England, the Federal Reserve and the OCC was established to develop a measure acceptable to both countries.

In January 1987, a modified proposal, the United States/United Kingdom Agreement (U.S./U.K. Agreement), was announced simultaneously in the two countries. However, the task force assigned to address interest rate and foreign exchange contracts had not yet agreed on the appropriate measure of rate contract credit risk. Consequently, a supplemental agreement on rate contracts was issued somewhat later, in March 1987.

Multilateral convergence efforts

Even as the negotiators were developing the U.S./U.K. Agreement, they were giving consideration to expanding participation to achieve a multilateral agreement. Senior Japanese officials had indicated both publicly and privately their commitment to maintaining and strengthening the financial condition of international banking organizations, in part through increased cooperation among supervisory authorities. Consequently, it seemed possible that a trilateral agreement encompassing the world's three major financial centers might be achievable. Toward that end, the U.S. and U.K. supervisory authorities began discussions in late 1986 with the Japanese banking authorities.

When Japan entered the negotiations, the issues surrounding the appropriate definition of regulatory bank capital became even more complicated. Japanese banks maintain sizable unrealized gains on their securities (largely equity) positions, and these unrealized gains have traditionally been realized when necessary to offset losses. The Japanese bank supervisory authorities, in fact, had recently introduced capital guidelines that explicitly recognized these gains—called "hidden reserves"—as a form of capital. Those guidelines defined capital for Japanese-based international banks as equity plus 70 percent of hidden reserves. In contrast, U.S. and U.K. capital standards did not recognize hidden reserves, thus further complicating the task of developing a uniform definition of capital.

During the spring of 1987, after the U.S./U.K. Agreement had been published, the potential scope for convergence expanded once again. At an April meeting, the Cooke Committee, sponsored by the Bank for International Settlements (BIS), took the U.S./U.K. Agreement under consideration and addressed the possibility of expanding the agreement to include all of the countries represented on the committee (the G-10 countries and Luxembourg).[3] The Cooke Committee had been working for several years to develop a common measure of capital and, more recently, a risk-based capital model. The agreement reached by two of its members—the

[3] The committee comprises representatives of the central banks and supervisory authorities of the Group of Ten countries (Belgium, Canada, France, Germany, Italy, Japan, Netherlands, Sweden, Switzerland, United Kingdom, United States), and Luxembourg. Although its official name is the Committee on Banking Regulations and Supervisory Practices, it is often called the "Cooke Committee," after Peter Cooke of the Bank of England, its current chairman. More recently, the Committee has also been referred to as the "Basle Committee" after Basle, Switzerland, the city in which the BIS is located.

United States and the United Kingdom—and the negotiations being held with a third member—Japan—provided the impetus to accelerate the pace of these deliberations. On December 10, 1987, the outcome of the committee's efforts was published and has become known as the "Basle Agreement."

The issues

While the original U.S. proposal paid relatively little attention to the definition of regulatory bank capital, the definition of capital became an increasingly important issue as the negotiations expanded to include more countries. In fact, the appropriate definition of capital was perhaps the most difficult issue confronted by the Cooke Committee in negotiating the multilateral agreement. Nevertheless, a variety of other issues relating to the appropriate treatment of certain assets and off-balance sheet instruments presented the committee with significant difficulties as well. The most important of these were (1) the extent to which transfer risk distinctions would be incorporated in the capital framework, (2) the types of collateral to be recognized in the proposal, (3) the appropriate treatment of interest rate risk stemming from holdings of government securities, (4) the appropriate treatment of loan commitments, and (5) the measurement of credit risk exposure associated with interest rate and foreign exchange contracts.

Defining capital

At least in hindsight, the complexity of designing an internationally acceptable capital definition is not surprising. Each country involved in the Basle Agreement has its own definition of regulatory capital, and each of these definitions reflects a different set of country-specific accounting practices, banking activities, and supervisory philosophies. Furthermore, a change in the definition of capital can greatly affect measured capital ratios within a banking system and thus alter the market's perception of the financial strength of the banking organizations in that system. Consequently, a key element in achieving the multilateral agreement was to design a definition of capital that would be uniform across countries yet accommodate the many different components of capital as currently defined in the twelve different banking systems.

Reserves. A significant complicating factor in the negotiations was the differential treatment of reserves across countries. The various types of reserves, which differ in their financial and accounting features as well as their ability to absorb losses, had traditionally been viewed as regulatory capital in certain of the member countries. Reserves, including loan loss reserves, hidden reserves, and property revaluation reserves, hold varying degrees of importance in member countries' existing capital regulations. For example, although the loan loss reserve is a significant component of regulatory capital for U.S. banks, it is a less important component of capital for Japanese banks.

Efforts to achieve a compromise on the capital definition were influenced by actions taken by major banking organizations during 1987 when large LDC-related provisions were made to loan loss reserves. The banking supervisors represented on the Cooke Committee hold differing views regarding the degree to which these reserves are available to absorb credit losses generally—that is, the degree to which these reserves are "unencumbered." Conceptually, the loan loss reserve, to be included in regulatory capital, should be unallocated and thus available to absorb anticipated, but as yet unidentified, credit losses. To the extent that reserves are clearly allocated against specific assets, they should not be considered eligible for inclusion in capital. Because of the practical difficulties in defining "unencumbered reserves," the member countries have agreed to further discussions regarding the extent to which loan loss reserves should be included in capital.

Another type of banking "reserves" not universally recognized by supervisory authorities on the Cooke Committee is hidden reserves. These reserves, which are especially important for Japanese banks, are measured as the difference between the book value (usually cost) and market value of debt and equity securities. As their name suggests, hidden reserves are not disclosed in banks' financial statements. Consequently, only the home country supervisory authorities and the banks themselves know the size of hidden reserves available to absorb losses. Perhaps more importantly, because the market values of securities fluctuate over time, the current market value of securities may not represent the future realizable value of these securities. For example, Japanese supervisory authorities have recognized the uncertainty of future realizable values by applying a 30 percent discount to hidden reserves and including the remainder in capital. Within the context of the multilateral discussions, however, the appropriate size of the discount to be applied to hidden reserves was the subject of much debate.

A third type of banking reserves, asset revaluation reserves, are also included in bank capital in some countries (most notably the United Kingdom) but not in others. Asset revaluation reserves are generated when a bank revalues certain specified assets—usually real estate—at current market values. The difference between historical and current market values is recorded as a reserve that is part of the bank's capital. Like the size of hidden reserves, the size of asset revaluation reserves depends on current market values and may not be indicative of future realizable gains.

Other capital instruments. In addition to the variety of reserve accounts included in regulatory capital, various forms of equity and debt instruments qualify as regulatory capital in some, but not all, member countries. These instruments include preferred stock, certain hybrid debt instruments (such as mandatory convertible debt in the United States), and term subordinated debt. The appropriate treatment of these instruments in a multinational definition of capital proved to be difficult to determine, given the disparate nature of the instruments.

First, the characteristics of preferred stock vary widely, even within individual countries. Preferred stock can be issued for limited maturities (limited-life) or in perpetuity (perpetual), and pricing can be fixed or floating. Limited-life preferred can in some countries (for example, France) be redeemed at the issuer's option. Dividend payments can be deferred in some countries, notably in the United States, but not eliminated altogether. Second, a group of instruments referred to in the proposal as hybrid debt/equity instruments encompasses an even broader range of capital instruments. Generally, eligible hybrid instruments have some characteristics of debt—for example, fixed and regular interest payments—and also some characteristics of equity—for example, interest payments that can be suspended without bringing the banking organization into default. Third, various types of long-term subordinated debt have been included in member countries' capital definitions provided that the debt meets certain criteria. The types of debt instruments in this category vary by maturity as well as by covenants attached to the debt. For most types of subordinated debt issues, breach of covenants can compel the issuing banks to accelerate repayment, possibly generating or exacerbating bank liquidity pressures.

The proposed definition. Amid this diversity of capital components, only common shareholders' equity was found to be acceptable as capital by all the bank supervisors on the Cooke Committee. This universal acceptance of common equity served as the foundation for the two-tiered definition of capital ultimately developed by the committee. In the proposed approach, the first tier of capital comprises common shareholders' equity, and the second tier allows for the inclusion of the wide range of capital components recognized in the twelve countries participating in the agreement. Thus, the Cooke Committee's definition of capital provides for uniformity across countries through the common equity requirement of tier one, while accommodating country-specific differences in banking traditions and practices through the diversity allowed in tier two.

In the treatment of reserves, the second tier incorporates certain limitations that seek to address the difficulties in measuring the degree to which various forms of reserves are, in reality, available to absorb losses. Hidden reserves arising from unrealized gains on securities are discounted to 45 percent of their current market value and then included in the supplemental tier of capital. In addition, general reserves against credit-related losses, which are allowable in the second tier, are limited to a certain percentage of total risk assets, although organizations are free to maintain reserves in excess of this limitation.

Deductions from capital

In addition to agreeing on a common set of capital instruments eligible for inclusion in total capital, both the U.S./U.K. and Basle proposals suggested that certain assets should be deducted from both the capital base and total risk-adjusted assets. Of particular note with regard to the multilateral negotiations are goodwill and investments in other banks' capital instruments.

Goodwill. While goodwill is deducted under both proposals, the Basle framework differs from the U.S./U.K. Agreement in its approach to deductions of other types of intangibles.[4] First, the bilateral proposal deducted *all* intangibles from the total capital base as then defined, whereas the Basle framework explicitly deducts only unidentifiable intangibles (goodwill) from core capital and total risk-adjusted assets.[5]

In their comments on the U.S./U.K. Agreement, many bankers were critical of the proposed deduction of intangibles. In their opinion, intangible assets have value and should only be deducted on a case-by-case basis. Moreover, some bankers were concerned about the competitive implications of the proposed treatment. Deduction of intangibles, especially goodwill, would in their view place banking organizations at a competitive disadvantage in prospective acquisitions relative to other less-regulated companies.

From a prudential perspective, however, the "realizable" value of goodwill is highly uncertain. In theory, goodwill represents the present value of *expected* future benefits to the buyer—value not reflected in the acquired firm's quantifiable net assets but expected to accrue to the buyer in the future. Consequently, the book value of goodwill does not necessarily reflect any precise economic value that will be realized with certainty. Moreover, since goodwill is purely an estimate of future benefits, the realizable value of goodwill may

---

[4]Under current Federal Reserve capital guidelines, goodwill is explicitly deducted at the bank level only, not at the bank holding company level. However, tangible capital ratios are considered as part of the overall assessment of capital adequacy.

[5]The Basle framework provides national supervisors some flexibility in the treatment of goodwill during a transitional period; subsequently, existing goodwill must be deducted from capital.

very well fall to zero for financially troubled banking organizations.

The Basle proposal, while maintaining the goodwill deduction, does not explicitly call for exclusion of other intangibles from the capital base. However, the Federal Reserve has frequently stressed the importance of maintaining strong tangible common equity ratios when undertaking expansions and retains for itself the flexibility to deduct identifiable intangibles on a case-by-case basis when assessing expansion proposals.

Holdings of other banking organizations' capital instruments. Bank supervisors in several industrial countries (for example, France and the United Kingdom) currently require the deduction of holdings of other banking organizations' capital instruments, presumably to inhibit artificial increases in banks' capital positions while improving the prospects for drawing new capital into the banking system. The Basle framework does not propose to require such an across-the-board deduction for at least two reasons: 1) to date, such holdings have been widely accepted in certain countries, and 2) many banking organizations in the U.S. hold equity positions in other banks in anticipation of the relaxation of interstate banking laws. Here also, the Basle framework provides for national flexibility in deducting such holdings. The Federal Reserve plans to review such holdings in the examination process and to deduct them from capital when deemed appropriate. Interbank holdings not deducted will receive a "standard" risk weight of 100 percent.

Transfer/country risk

In addition to defining capital, Cooke Committee members had to agree on an approach to the risk-weighting framework. Perhaps the most complex issue regarding assets and off-balance sheet items was whether to incorporate transfer risk distinctions. Transfer risk, or country risk, is the risk of credit losses stemming from the inability of a country and its private sector borrowers to raise the necessary foreign exchange to repay their external debt.

Before the LDC debt servicing problems of the early 1980s, commercial bank and supervisory systems designed to assess credit risk gave little attention to transfer risk. But by 1985, when the U.S. bank supervisory authorities were developing their original risk-based capital proposal, the importance of transfer risk in assessing the risk profiles of major banking organizations had become clear, and U.S. supervisors wanted to include at least some recognition of transfer risk in the measure. For this purpose, the original U.S. proposal divided countries into two groups: the International Monetary Fund's (IMF's) list of industrial market economies and all other countries. Claims on governments and banks in the former group were afforded lower risk weights. During the subsequent public comment period, the U.S. approach was criticized as being arbitrary, since the IMF list is based on structural development indicators rather than on indicators of debt-servicing ability. Since 1986, other lists of "low risk" countries have been considered—for example, a list consisting of members of the European Community (EC) and the G-10 countries, or a grouping of EC members and members of the Organization for Economic Cooperation and Development. All of the techniques considered for categorizing countries into relative transfer risk groups were fraught with difficulties, both analytical and political.

Some U.S. market participants argued that the relative transfer risk rankings assigned by the Interagency Country Exposure Review Committee (ICERC) should be used to reflect differences in transfer risk in a risk-based capital measure. Although ICERC ratings specifically address transfer risk exposures, they are confidential ratings used only by bank examiners in the United States. The public generally would not have access to the list of ICERC ratings of country debt and therefore would be constrained in their ability to replicate supervisory assessments of capital adequacy. Furthermore, the use of ICERC-type ratings might place unwarranted pressure on the process of assigning transfer risk ratings to country exposures and would require an internationalization of this process that would be, at best, complicated to administer and carry out.

Another approach suggested by some market participants entails grouping countries on the basis of whether they have recently experienced debt-servicing difficulties. This approach also suffers from several problems. First, historical performance on external debt-servicing requirements is not necessarily indicative of future performance. Indeed, some countries appear willing to sustain interest payments as long as possible, even in the face of deteriorating economic conditions. Consequently, countries with good payment records could in fact represent increasing transfer risk. Conversely, this type of grouping might place an official mark of weakness on certain countries, even if their potential debt servicing ability has improved significantly. By categorizing countries based on past performance, the measure could thus overstate or understate the transfer risk of certain countries. Furthermore, a distinction based on recent debt-servicing experience would run counter to the objective of supervisory capital adequacy requirements: to insure the capacity of bank capital to absorb *prospective* losses.

Because country risk assessments depend on qualitative judgments, any discrete grouping of countries in a relatively simple, quantitative capital framework is bound to be somewhat arbitrary. Recognizing the arbitrariness of these assessments and the political difficulties associated with the supervisory identification of high- and low-risk countries, the Cooke Committee decided to use a relatively simple approach to transfer risk in the published framework.[6] Although some members of the committee felt that ignoring entirely the material differences in the transfer risk associated with lending to different foreign borrowers might limit the usefulness of the risk-based capital framework, the committee was not able to achieve a consensus on this issue. Still, the absence of country-risk distinctions does not significantly weaken the approach since the proposed risk-adjusted capital measure is envisioned as only one of many analytical tools to be used by both bank supervisors and market analysts.

Finally, it should be noted that the Cooke Committee's effort to develop a risk-based capital measure has paralleled efforts within the EC to develop a similar measure, and that the EC is likely to decide, within the next several years, to treat all claims on EC member governments and banks similar to domestic institutions. Designation of a "domestic zone" comprised solely of EC countries would, of course, introduce an element of inconsistency across industrial countries in the assessment of capital adequacy. For example, under this approach, a French bank would slot a long-term claim on the German government in a lower risk category than would a U.S. bank with a similar claim. Consequently, the Cooke Committee most likely will find it necessary to return to this issue at some point.

Collateral

The Basle agreement's recognition of collateral expands on both the original U.S. proposal and the subsequent U.S./U.K. Agreement. In the original U.S. proposal, only loans to broker/dealers secured by cash, U.S. government and agency securities, or other marketable securities were slotted in a risk category below 100 percent. The U.S./U.K. Agreement broadened the recognition of collateral to all loans collateralized by securities issued by the central government and its agencies. Both domestically and internationally, it was difficult to reach consensus on the degree to which collateral could be reasonably incorporated into the risk-based capital measure.[7] In theory, the risk-reducing effects of many

[6] The Basle framework generally assigns claims on a bank's home-country central government to a low-risk category, while claims on foreign governments are assigned to the standard risk category, that is, weighted at 100 percent.

[7] The same degree of difficulty was encountered when deciding on the appropriate treatment of guarantees. In the final Basle proposal, recognition of guarantees has been expanded to include not only central government guarantees, but also guarantees of domestic banks, and those of states, counties, and municipalities.

types of collateral could have been incorporated; however, the cost would have been tremendous administrative complexity. Moreover, it would seem inappropriate to include in a general measure of this type forms of collateral that have highly uncertain value (either because of credit or market risks).

Some comments on the first U.S. proposal advocated an even broader recognition of collateral. Most notably, respondents called for a lower risk weighting on one- to four-family residential mortgages. This sentiment was shared by supervisors in Europe who noted that the historical losses on such exposures have been relatively low across most industrial countries. Thus, the multilateral agreement's recognition of collateral is the broadest of any of the three proposals that have been issued for public comment. In the Basle agreement, exposures collateralized by cash, domestic central government debt, and residential mortgages attract risk weights below the standard risk weight of 100 percent.

Although U.S. supervisors have some sympathy for the arguments regarding residential mortgages, they also feel that the nature of protection afforded by residential collateral varies widely across the United States, as experience has shown that real estate values can drop sharply in response to sectoral economic weaknesses. Also, U.S. supervisors are reluctant to favor within this framework one sector of the economy over another. For these reasons, the U.S. version of the risk-based capital proposal diverges from the Basle framework by slotting residential mortgages in the 100 percent risk category. However, although the proposed measure does not explicitly recognize a wider range of collateral, such treatment does not imply that other types of collateral will be ignored in the U.S. examination process or that banks should disregard their own internal collateral requirements.

Interest rate risk: U.S. government securities
Although a banking organization's capital base must be available to absorb all losses beyond credit-related losses, pragmatism restrained the broad inclusion of other banking risks such as foreign exchange risk, liquidity or funding risk, and interest rate risk in the Cooke Committee's measure of capital adequacy. One partial exception is the treatment of interest rate risk on securities that bear no credit risk.

The question whether interest rate risk should be incorporated in the risk-based capital framework was one of the more controversial issues throughout the entire negotiation process. It is not surprising, therefore, that the treatment of securities has undergone substantial change since the U.S. proposal was published in early 1986. That first proposal made a distinction between securities held in banks' investment accounts

and those held in trading accounts, and weighted all trading account assets at 30 percent. Investment account securities were segregated into short-term U.S. Treasuries (zero percent risk weight), long-term U.S. Treasuries and all Federal agency securities (30 percent), and all other investment securities (100 percent).

Respondents to the U.S. bank supervisors' initial request for comment on this issue were generally opposed to the inclusion of interest rate risk in the proposed risk-based capital framework. Many contended that a banking organization's exposure to interest rate fluctuations was a function of the entire range of its assets, liabilities, and off-balance sheet exposures. Moreover, many bankers argued that a relatively simple focus on the dollar amount of U.S. government securities held by banks would not be indicative of the degree of interest rate risk facing those banks. A number of respondents advocated no capital charge for government securities, arguing that the examination process was a more appropriate vehicle for evaluating interest rate exposures.

At the multilateral level, the treatment of interest rate risk stemming from government securities positions was once again challenged. Several members of the Cooke Committee argued that the proposed treatment might not accurately reflect a banking organization's interest rate risk profile. Some national supervisors contended that, although the inclusion of interest rate risk might be desirable, any incorporation of this risk should be postponed until more refined approaches could be developed. Thus, the multinational agreement provides national supervisory authorities with the flexibility to apply low risk weights (10 or 20 percent) to securities issued by the domestic central government to reflect the "investment risk" associated with holding these securities, or to apply a zero risk weighting to these securities, thereby excluding them from the risk-asset measure.

In the Federal Reserve's proposal, short-term (91 days or less remaining maturity) U.S. government and agency securities are assigned to the zero percent category, while a 10 percent weight is attached to all other U.S. government and agency securities.[*] The three U.S. Federal bank supervisors are committed, however, to undertaking further research on a more comprehensive supervisory approach to measuring interest rate risk that might be incorporated in the Basle framework at some later date.

Loan commitments
The debate over how to incorporate unused lending commitments in a risk-based capital framework also

[*]U.S. government-sponsored agency securities are slotted in the 20 percent risk category.

began with the issuance of the original U.S. proposal in which most commercial and consumer commitments were effectively converted to balance sheet equivalent amounts at 30 percent of their notional principal values. The major issues raised in the letters commenting on this proposal and the subsequent U.S./U.K. Agreement included the proposed use of original maturity in determining conversion factors, the degree of protection against loss provided by "material adverse change" (MAC) clauses, and the appropriateness of incorporating consumer commitments in this framework.

While the U.S. proposal did not include a maturity distinction, the U.S./U.K. Agreement assigned credit conversion factors based on the original maturity of the commitment, that is, the length of time before a bank can, at its option, unconditionally cancel its commitment to the borrower. This approach was intended to be a proxy for the risks associated with various types of commitments. The industry criticized this approach, arguing that it was arbitrary and would not accurately reflect banks' credit exposures on these commitments. Many commented that, if a maturity approach was to be used, remaining maturity was a better indicator of credit risk. In fact, U.S. bankers maintained that remaining maturity is widely used in internal reports and that the focus on original maturity would represent a significant reporting burden.

Despite these criticisms, some members of the Cooke Committee strongly supported the use of original maturity. They viewed this relatively simple technique as a useful means of distinguishing among a variety of instrument types within the context of the proposal without increasing the complexity of the calculation. Thus, in the end, the use of original maturity was retained in the Basle framework.

The U.S./U.K. Agreement also addressed the issue of MAC clauses by explicitly including commitments with such clauses in the risk asset framework. Although many of the comment letters expressed the view that these clauses provided effective protection against deterioration in the creditworthiness of a prospective borrower, contrasting arguments prevailed in favor of excluding consideration of MAC clauses from this framework.

MAC clauses are generally more effective under conditions of rapid deterioration in the credit quality of an obligor than in other situations. In cases of more gradual decline in the customer's financial condition, the criteria contained in MAC clauses might be insufficiently specific to afford the lender any significant degree of protection. Furthermore, a borrower is likely to anticipate his own problems before the lender becomes aware of them, by which time the drawdown could have occurred.

Even in situations where MAC clauses are adequately worded to allow protection, banks may nonetheless be reluctant to exercise their right to deny lending. Refusing to lend funds in any but the most extreme cases might damage other customers' perceptions of both the bank and the value of their own credit lines. Bank managements may also be concerned about their potential exposure to lender liability suits.

The treatment of consumer loan commitments has varied widely among the three versions of the risk-based capital framework. Such commitments were not explicitly addressed in the original U.S. proposal, and the proposal's lack of specificity in this regard raised questions by market participants. The U.S./U.K. Agreement clarified the issue by explicitly including consumer loan commitments and applying the same credit conversion factors to these commitments as to other loan commitments. This proposed treatment of consumer commitments in turn evoked strong criticism, especially from banking organizations competing heavily in the consumer credit card market. These bankers argued that many types of consumer commitments (for example, credit card lines and overdraft facilities) are unconditionally cancelable at any time, for any reason, and therefore do not require capital support. Partly in response to this argument, the Basle framework treats consumer commitments as short-term commitments.

Interest rate and foreign exchange contracts

The original U.S. proposal did not include interest rate and foreign exchange contracts (rate contracts) in its measure of risk-adjusted assets. These rate contracts clearly expose banks to credit risk, but by late 1985, U.S. bank regulators had not yet developed a practical way to incorporate a measure of this risk in the risk-based capital framework.

The March 1987 supplement to the U.S./U.K. Agreement, which set out an approach to measuring rate contract credit exposure, proposed two measures: one for interest rate contracts and one for foreign exchange contracts. Both measures consisted of the current market value of contracts and an "add-on" factor intended to capture future potential credit risk exposure.

The comments received by the Federal Reserve on the supplemental proposal offered general support for the basic approach to measuring rate contract credit exposure but were often critical of many of the specifics of the proposal. In particular, most of the market participants commenting on the proposal argued that the amount of capital that banks would have to hold to support rate contracts would be excessive. Market participants provided detailed analyses of the underlying methodology used by the regulators to calculate the proposed add-on factors. In virtually every case, these analyses concluded that specific aspects of the regulators' methodology produced overly conservative estimates of the degree of credit risk exposure stemming from rate contracts.

Further, a number of commercial and investment bankers argued that the proposed risk weightings to be applied to rate contract credit exposure were too high. These bankers asserted that the counterparties to interest rate and foreign exchange contracts are, on average, more creditworthy than bank customers more generally. Consequently, they argued, it would not be reasonable to assign the same risk weight to rate contract credit exposure as that assigned to, say, a bank's loan portfolio credit exposure.

In the context of the multilateral discussions on the appropriate measure for rate contract credit risk, several of the European members of the Cooke Committee contended that the proposed U.S./U.K. approach was unduly complex, especially for banks with relatively minor involvement in these activities. Furthermore, a minority of the committee members did not favor the use of a mark-to-market approach for determining capital requirements on rate contracts.

Reflecting these divergent views, the Cooke Committee was not able to agree on a single measure of rate contract credit exposure that could be used by all member countries. Ultimately, a compromise was reached allowing each member country to use one or both of two approximately equivalent measures of credit exposure.

The first of these proposed measures, the "current exposure" measure, retains the basic structure of the original measure, which combined current market exposure and an add-on for future potential exposure. This measure was developed by refining the original U.S./U.K. methodology to incorporate suggestions made by market participants and by simplifying the measure in response to the general feeling that the original proposal was too complex.

The alternative measure proposed in the Basle agreement was based on "original exposure." It was developed to provide an even simpler measure of credit exposure that would still result in approximately the same amount of required capital as the current exposure approach for similar rate contract portfolios. Using the original exposure approach, a bank would not have to mark its rate contracts to market. Instead, the notional principal amounts of a bank's rate contracts would be multiplied by specified conversion factors to calculate an estimate of its credit exposure.

The Cooke Committee proposed that, regardless of the approach used,[9] credit exposure on rate contracts would be assigned a risk weight based on the broad categories of obligors used elsewhere in the proposed

[9] U.S. bank supervisors are proposing to use the "current exposure" approach.

capital framework. However, most committee members believe that a maximum risk weight of 50 percent should be used because of the relatively high quality of rate contract counterparties.

Going forward

Most of the issues that the Cooke Committee confronted were replete with technical, analytical, and political complexities. In addressing each issue, members of the committee had to weigh several competing factors. Simplicity in approach had to be balanced against precise risk measurement. More generally, the desire for a broad-based agreement that would strengthen the international banking system had to be weighed against country-specific practices and policies. In the end, the agreement on risk-based capital encompasses a considerable range of banking activities and sets uniform minimum target capital ratios for all banking organizations active in international financial markets.

In reaching the Basle Agreement, the banking authorities in the participating countries had to make significant compromises. Each member of the committee had to strike a balance between achieving the goal of a "more level playing field" through more uniform global supervision of banking organizations' capital levels on the one hand, and accommodating country-specific institutional structures on the other. For this reason, the proposal embodies a number of compromises that, taken in isolation, may not be optimal. But viewed within the broader context of an international agreement that encompasses the major industrial countries, these compromises reflect the desire of the international supervisory community to overcome national differences and to respond in a coordinated fashion to the changing international banking environment. In this context, the agreement represents a milestone in international bank supervisory cooperation.

Convergence is not, however, a discrete set of events consisting of major multinational agreements; rather, convergence is an ongoing process involving dialogue and the sharing of information among the various supervisors of financial institutions. In the United States, the increasingly ambiguous division between banking organizations and other financial services firms is providing a steady impetus to the domestic supervisory communication and convergence process. Moreover, the changing nature of the global financial services industry will necessitate continuing cooperation among the national supervisory authorities that together regulate the global financial marketplace. Significantly, the negotiation of the risk-based capital agreement may provide a model for this ongoing effort towards supervisory policy convergence.

Jeffrey Bardos

Article 4

Joint Ventures:
Meeting the Competition in Banking

*Paul Calem**

In recent years, banks have grown less content to be simply "banks." Faced with increasing competition in their traditional product markets, banks have sought to broaden the range of their activities. They have introduced new products, such as securities backed by consumer loans. They have pressed successfully for permission to engage in activities that were once legally off-limits, such as discount brokerage and investment advice. And they have proceeded to exploit various loopholes in the legal and regulatory structure. For instance, the Federal Reserve permits bank holding companies to underwrite and deal in some securities deemed ineligible under the Glass-Steagall Act so long as they do so through a subsidiary that is not "principally engaged" in those activities. As a result, a number of bank holding companies now underwrite and deal in commercial paper, mortgage-backed securities, municipal revenue bonds and consumer-related receivables through such subsidiaries.

One way banking organizations expand is

*Paul Calem is a Senior Economist in the Banking Section of the Research Department of the Federal Reserve Bank of Philadelphia.

through "joint ventures" with other banks or with a nonbanking firm. Indeed, the trend towards greater product variety in banking has generated an increase in joint venture activity. Between 1971 and 1982, joint ventures among financial service firms were not very common, with, on average, about three joint subsidiaries formed per year. But in 1983, 36 joint subsidiaries were formed, signaling the start of the new trend. Bank holding companies, in particular, became more active in forming joint subsidiaries at about that time, going from about two per year between 1971 and 1982 to 12 in 1983 and 12 again in 1984. Joint ventures not involving the creation of a joint subsidiary have also become more common. For instance, many banking organizations are now offering mutual funds to their customers by participating in joint ventures with mutual fund companies.[1]

If deregulation proceeds and banks are allowed to engage in a wider range of nonbanking activities, joint venture activity is likely to continue at a robust pace. Although some banking organizations have used joint ventures as a way around regulatory restrictions, others have found them the least costly, most efficient way to expand into permissible activities.

What lies behind the recent upsurge in joint venture activity? What advantages do joint ventures have over other expansion strategies? What are some of the potential pitfalls of joint ventures? Little has been written on how these issues pertain to banking organizations, and the time is ripe to begin investigating these questions.

WHAT IS A JOINT VENTURE?

A joint venture between two firms differs sharply from a mere producer-supplier relationship. A correspondent bank and its commercial bank customer do not have a joint venture—the commercial bank simply "produces" checking accounts by buying check-processing services from a correspondent bank. In a joint venture, however, the firms share ownership at some stage of the production process.

In a vertical joint venture, the partners share supply or distribution facilities, but their products retain distinct identities. A check-printing shop that is jointly owned by two banks is a shared supply facility. Automated teller machines (ATMs), when jointly owned by a group of banks, are shared distribution facilities. ATMs give a retail customer access to his bank account without altering the identity of that account as a product of the customer's bank. The bank retains control over account fees and services; ATM access is simply a service provided in conjunction with an account. Frequently, vertical joint ventures serve to make banks' supply or distribution more efficient.

Banks often engage in horizontal joint ventures in order to expand a product line or customer base. In a horizontal joint venture, the firms create a distinct, joint product. Each firm contributes labor, materials, expertise, or assets to the venture, and the firms share ownership of the final product.

One kind of horizontal joint venture is a jointly owned subsidiary providing a special product or service. A trust company owned by two banks is a case in point. But horizontal joint ventures can involve other types of arrangements as well. For instance, banks and mutual fund companies have cooperated to offer investment packages that include both mutual funds and time deposits.

---

[1]These figures come from Kathryn R. Harrigan, "Joint Ventures and Competitive Strategy," First Boston Working Paper Series, Columbia University School of Business, (December 1984); *Bank Expansion Reporter* (December 19, 1983) pp. 16-18 and (June 3, 1985) pp.16-17; and "Rising Number of Banks Offer Mutual Funds to Customers," *American Banker* (October 28, 1986) pp. 31ff. According to the *American Banker* article, about seven out of ten banks now offer mutual funds to their customers. The article states that close to 40 percent of these banks make mutual funds available through "their investment area (23 percent), trust department (9 percent), or retail department (7 percent)," with the rest simply providing access to mutual funds through a discount brokerage service or self-directed IRA. Those banks making mutual funds available through their investment, trust, or retail departments are probably engaged in joint ventures with mutual fund companies.

Banks that offer mutual funds to their customers through cooperative ventures with mutual fund companies are, in a sense, circumventing regulations that prohibit them from sponsoring mutual funds. Sometimes, cooperating with another financial firm in a joint venture is the only legal way a bank could participate in a restricted activity, of which there are many. For example, Federal Reserve member banks are prohibited by the Glass-Steagall Act, enacted in 1933, from underwriting and dealing in stocks, corporate bonds, or stock and bond funds. Also, the insurance activities of member banks are limited by the Bank Holding Company Act of 1956 and by the Garn-St. Germain Act of 1982. For state-chartered banks, which need not be members of the Federal Reserve, each state has its own restrictions on their nonbanking activities. In addition, the Bank Holding Company Act of 1956, as amended in 1970, permits a bank holding company to engage only in those activities that are "closely related to banking." Once a nonbanking activity is shown to be closely related to banking, the expected public benefits from a bank holding company engaging in that activity must then be shown to outweigh any possible adverse effects. In most cases, the Board of Governors of the Federal Reserve determines which activities are permissible according to these criteria.

Bank holding companies have used horizontal joint ventures to expand into various permissible activities. The Fed's Regulation Y lists commercial financing, leasing, financial planning, investment advice, and various other activities as generally permissible for bank holding companies. The Glass-Steagall Act authorizes banks to engage in certain municipal bond financing activities. Forming a joint subsidiary to pursue these activities, however, must be approved by the Federal Reserve Board. If two banking organizations wish to form a joint subsidiary, the Board takes into account the financial strength of the organizations, as well as the potential for adverse competitive effects. If a bank holding company and a nonbanking firm wish to form a joint sub-sidiary, the Board also takes into account the degree of separation between the joint subsidiary and the nonbanking firm.[2]

COMPETITION HAS MADE JOINT VENTURES MORE ATTRACTIVE

The push by banks to expand into new activities stems from stiffer competition, both from outside the banking industry and within it. From outside, competitors have made inroads into banks' traditional base of deposit and loan customers. On the lending side, securities firms that offer commercial paper and commercial bond financing have become increasingly sophisticated and aggressive.[3] On the deposit side, mutual fund companies compete by offering stock and bond funds as well as money market funds that provide checking and debit card services. Since the Garn-St. Germain Act of 1982 liberalized regulation of the thrift industry, thrifts have competed with banks on both fronts, in the market for commercial loans, as well as for demand deposits. Perhaps the greatest threat comes from the "financial supermarkets," commercial firms such as Sears, K Mart, and J. C. Penney that provide various kinds of banking services packaged with insurance and discount brokerage.

Within the banking industry, new technology and deregulation have tightened competition. The development of ATM networks and electronic payments systems has greatly enhanced customer access to bank services. As a result, just about any bank faces competition from within a larger geographic area. Deposit rate deregula-

---

[2]For a discussion of Federal Reserve policy towards joint ventures, see William J. Sweet, Jr. and John D. Hawke, Jr., "Joint Ventures Provide Vehicle for Nonbanking Activities," *Issues in Bank Regulation* (Spring 1984) pp. 25-36. For a discussion of antitrust issues related to joint ventures, see Steven D. Felgran, "Shared ATM Networks: Market Structure and Public Policy," *New England Economic Review*, Federal Reserve Bank of Boston (January/February 1984) pp. 23-38.

[3]For details concerning the growth of the commercial bond market, see Jan Loeys, "Low-Grade Bonds: A Growing Source of Corporate Funding," this *Business Review* (November/December 1986) pp. 3-12.

tion has also been an important factor. Regulatory ceilings on deposit interest rates were gradually removed over the period 1982-1986. To the extent that these ceilings were binding, banks must now pay more competitive rates on deposits. Geographic deregulation has further enhanced competition in banking. In the last few years, most states opened their borders to entry by out-of-state bank holding companies. Large regional and money center banking organizations are now moving into new markets nationwide, increasing the competitive pressures on banks in those markets.[4]

Horizontal joint ventures are one way that banks have gone forth and met the competitive challenge. Through joint ventures, banks have expanded the variety of products they offer to their customers, strengthening customer ties against the pull of competition. Also through joint ventures, banks have found new sources of revenue, easing competitive pressures on their profitability.

HOW JOINT VENTURES WORK

One of the most common types of joint ventures is between a bank and an insurance company, a partnership which enables a bank to offer its customers a convenient package of banking and insurance products. The bank is thus able to counter the competitive threat posed by financial supermarkets that offer "one-stop financial shopping." At the same time, a bank engaged in an insurance joint venture generally earns some rental income.

In an insurance joint venture, an insurance company sets up shop in the bank's lobby and pays the bank either a flat rental rate or a rate that is tied to the number of insurance sales originated there. In addition, the bank may provide for automatic payment of insurance premiums out of customer accounts. In most cases, federal or state regulations curtail the bank's insurance marketing activities. What is permissible, however, is for the bank to place the insurance sales staff in a prominent spot, and to include an advertisement from its venture partner in its customer mailings. The John Hancock Mutual Life Insurance Company took a creative approach in 1986 in a joint venture with Wilbur National Bank, a small bank in upstate New York. The bank leased space in its main branch in Oneonta to the insurance company to set up an office to sell life and disability insurance products. The office is conveniently located, accessible both from the bank's lobby and through a separate, external entrance, enabling the insurance agents to keep separate hours from those of the bank. In addition to advertising through the mail to bank customers, Hancock tries to attract customers by offering basic financial planning services free of charge. The Hancock agents generate some referrals for the bank's products when counseling customers, but they do not receive commissions.[5]

Many banks are engaged in joint ventures with mutual fund companies. By making stock and bond funds available to its customers, a bank can retain the loyalty of depositors who might otherwise abandon the bank in favor of a mutual fund company. In addition, the bank can earn substantial fee income. Most commonly, a bank acts as a sales agent for a mutual fund sponsor; since it neither sponsors nor underwrites the fund itself, it does not violate the Glass-Steagall Act. Chase Manhattan Bank took a more unusual approach when it teamed up with The Dreyfus Corporation in 1985. Chase acts as the organizer and manager of the "Park Avenue Funds," while Dreyfus acts as the sponsor and distributor of these funds. Chase informs its bank and Visa Card customers in statement stuffers that these funds are available through

---

[4]For an analysis of how interstate banking is affecting competition in banking markets, see Paul Calem, "Interstate Bank Mergers and Competition in Banking," this *Business Review* (January/February 1987) pp. 3-14.

[5]Details on this joint venture are found in "One Bank/Insurer Venture that Works," *ABA Banking Journal* (February, 1987) p. 84.

Dreyfus. In announcing the venture, the chairman of Chase said it "will provide our customers with a convenient means of obtaining the benefits of mutual fund investments." [6] The arrangement also enhances the bank's prestige, since the bank is providing its own original mutual fund.

Strengthening customer relationships is only one of several reasons that banks have turned to joint ventures. As banks have faced more competitive conditions in their traditional markets, and have watched their profit margins decline, they have sought out new sources of revenue. Sometimes banks have used joint ventures to expand into new, specialized kinds of lending or assets, such as municipal bond guarantees. In other cases, they have sought to expand geographically or broaden their customer base, as when a U.S. bank holding company teams up with an automobile manufacturer to form a motor vehicle financing subsidiary. (For details on these arrangements, see HORIZONTAL JOINT VENTURES: TWO CASE STUDIES.)

ADVANTAGES OF JOINT VENTURES...

Although joint ventures may be the only legal route to expansion into restricted activities like insurance and mutual funds, banks have found them a useful way to engage in permissible activities as well. But they are not the only way. Bank holding companies also have responded to changing competitive conditions by acquisition or merger, by developing new products on their

---

[6]This joint venture was reported in "Dreyfus and Chase Join Forces on Mutual Funds," *American Banker*, (November 13, 1984) p. 32.

Horizontal Joint Ventures: Two Case Studies

A Motor Vehicle Financing Joint Venture: On December 9, 1987, the Federal Reserve Board Approved the formation of a joint subsidiary by Marine Midland Bank and Subaru. The subsidiary, Marine Midland Automotive Financial Corporation, will offer various kinds of financing and leasing services to Subaru dealers and their customers, including retail financing for Subaru purchasers and inventory financing for Subaru dealers. Since the joint venture puts Marine Midland in direct contact with Subaru dealers and their customers, it will enable the bank to expand its automobile financing and leasing activities. Subaru stands to benefit from Marine Midland's experience and know-how in the area of motor vehicle financing, and from the bank's ability to supply funds for the subsidiary's activities.[a]

A Municipal Bond Insurance Venture: In 1984, Bankers Trust New York Corporation, Xerox Credit Corporation, Phibro-Salomon Inc. and American International Group Inc. formed a joint insurance subsidiary specializing in municipal bond insurance. The venture, Bond Investors Guarantee Insurance Company, guarantees the timely payment of principal and interest on newly issued municipal bonds and bond portfolios. What apparently attracted Bankers Trust to this venture was the rapidly expanding market for municipal bond insurance and the expectation of generating substantial premiums. According to one industry analyst, "demand for this coverage has widely outstripped the supply."

Each of the venture partners has some experience in areas related to municipal bond coverage. Bankers Trust and Phibro-Salomon are both major municipal bond underwriters. AIG underwrites and sells various kinds of financial guarantee insurance, including, on occasion, municipal bond insurance. Xerox Corp., through certain subsidiaries, has been involved in insuring hospital municipal bonds as well as packaging municipal unit trusts. In addition, Bankers Trust brings to the venture its credit analysis skills. In the words of one insurance expert, "municipal bond insurance is a form of financial guarantee and basically involves a credit analysis decision."[b]

---

[a]Details on this joint venture are found in "Marine Midland Teams Up With Subaru," *Bank Expansion Reporter* (January 4, 1988) pp. 15–16.

[b]This joint venture is reported in "Bankers Trust Joins Venture in Thriving Municipals Market," *American Banker* (July 20, 1984) pp. 3ff.

own, and by introducing new products that are obtained from a wholesaler. So why is a joint venture sometimes preferred to these expansion strategies?

...Compared to Internal Expansion... Risk and financing considerations can make a joint venture a more attractive option than internal expansion. The parties to a joint venture share whatever risks are involved, while internal expansion requires a firm to face those risks alone. A joint venture may also offer financing advantages. A single organization, especially a small or moderate-sized one, may not have access to the capital needed for expansion. Internal financing may be unavailable, and raising outside capital may be too expensive. Outside investors will require an unnecessarily high risk premium if they cannot adequately evaluate the organization's ability to expand.[7] Moreover, obtaining a loan or floating a new stock issue involves transactions costs, such as the costs of finding, negotiating with, and paying an underwriter. These costs are present regardless of whether the amount of funds raised is large or small. By engaging in a joint venture, individual companies can pool their resources. Thus, the partners to a venture may be able to provide their own financing, or at least provide enough collateral to reduce the risk premium required by outside investors. Moreover, a joint venture may be able to reach a larger market than its partners would reach individually, resulting in comparatively large scale operations and financing needs. Outside financing will then involve a comparatively small transactions cost per unit of funds raised. The joint venture will thus achieve economies of scale in raising capital.[8]

A joint venture may achieve other kinds of scale economies as well. Consider a mortgage banking joint venture, in which the venture partners find themselves serving a fairly large market. The venture can improve its productivity by hiring highly trained mortgage banking specialists, because the large scale of the enterprise ensures that their talents will be fully used.[9]

Another advantage a joint venture might have over internal expansion is the ability to use complementary technology, skills, or information. A U.S. bank holding company familiar with the products of American exporters might team up with a Japanese bank familiar with the needs of Japanese firms to form an export trading company. Or a Texas bank holding company familiar with the regional real estate market might pool its skills with an investment banking firm experienced in the area of investment advice to form a real estate investment advisory firm.

While a bank may be able to achieve any or all of these advantages through merging with or acquiring the venture partner, those options may be ruled out for some activities by regulation. The Bank Holding Company Act would prohibit a bank holding company from acquiring a commercial firm, and interstate banking restrictions could prevent a merger between bank holding companies located in different parts of the country. But even when a merger or acquisition is feasible, a joint venture may be the more attractive option.

...Compared to Mergers or Acquisitions... An agreement regarding a joint venture might be quick and easy to achieve as compared with a merger or acquisition, where negotiations can be costly and time-consuming. Also, a joint venture is relatively easy to dissolve. Hence, it may be preferred by banks that wish to achieve a short-term objective, or engage in activities of uncertain profitability.

---

[7]As compensation for the perceived riskiness of a security, investors require a risk premium, that is, a discount on the purchase price of the security. There is some statistical evidence that higher risk premiums are associated with smaller firms. See F. M. Scherer, *Industrial Market Structure and Economic Performance* (Boston: Houghton Mifflin Company, 1980) pp. 104-108.

[8]A joint venture may also have relatively more bargaining power with a prospective lender or underwriter, since the lender is dealing with more than one corporation.

---

[9]For a full discussion of economies of scale in banking, see Loretta Mester, "Efficient Production of Financial Services: Scale and Scope Economies," this *Business Review* (January/February 1987) pp. 15-25.

Also, two banks may prefer a joint venture to a merger if they complement each other in ways specific to the venture, while in other respects the two organizations are incompatible. The Japanese bank in the above example may be highly decentralized, with individual departments operating fairly independently, while the U.S. bank holding company may be far more hierarchical, with the bank president and other top officers exercising considerable control. One organization may be more aggressive, accustomed to making riskier investments for the sake of a higher return, and the other may be more conservative. Or the organizations may have very different procedures for handling employee relations and business practices. Eliminating such conflicts subsequent to a merger could require costly restructuring of the combined organization.

...Compared to Franchising. A practical expansion strategy for a bank holding company is to package and sell a product obtained from a wholesale provider. For instance, many banking organizations have introduced discount brokerage by linking into the franchise services provided by companies such as Fidelity Brokerage Services and INVEST.[10] If insurance agency activities become permissible for bank holding companies, conceivably some banks would sell insurance as part of such a franchise network. However, not all products and services a bank might wish to provide can be obtained through a wholesale distribution network. Hence, an organization limiting itself to this strategy might pass up some profitable opportunities for product expansion.

The more customized a product, the less likely that it will be available wholesale. When a bank is trying to fill a customer's special needs with a tailored product, wholesale distribution will be inappropriate. Investment advice is a product that is often customized. An individual investor is likely to have unique needs and a special relationship with her bank; face-to-face discussions and a working relationship between the investor and a specialist may provide the best framework for evaluating her investment needs.[11]

Suppose that "Fourth National Bank of the Rockies" wants to advise individual and institutional investors on real estate investment opportunities in the west. Because a franchise arrangement would be inappropriate, the bank might set up an internal operation. Alternatively, the bank might engage in a joint venture with an established investment counseling firm. A joint venture may be chosen over internal expansion for any one of the reasons discussed earlier. For instance, while Fourth National may be quite familiar with the western real estate market, its customer base may be too narrow to justify setting up its own specialized subsidiary.

While joint ventures can offer some distinct advantages over other expansion strategies, they are not without problems of their own. Generally speaking, the aspect of joint ventures that is most likely to be troublesome is the relationship between the venture partners.

JOINT VENTURES AND THE CONTRACTING PROBLEM

A joint venture is like any other contractual relationship: it can be disrupted by disagreements, misunderstandings, conflicts of interest, or opportunistic behavior. These problems arise when it is not possible to write a con-

---

[10]Details concerning such franchise networks are found in Steven D. Felgran, "Bank Entry into Securities Brokerage: Competitive and Legal Aspects," *New England Economic Review,"* Federal Reserve Bank of Boston (November/December 1984) pp. 12-33, and "Networking in Retail Financial Services," *TransDataCorp Deposits and Credits Advisor* (November 1986).

[11]Of course, a bank can offer limited investment advice through a franchise arrangement. The bank can provide a standard form for customers to fill out and mail to the wholesaler, who evaluates the customers and provides recommendations. However, truly customized investment advice cannot be provided in this way.

tract that allocates specific rights and responsibilities, or specifies actions to be taken, under all possible contingencies. One of the main problems is when both parties have different information. Suppose the parties to a joint venture want the revenues to be divided according to each party's share of the costs. The parties cannot enforce such a contract unless they know a lot about each other's costs. Unlike people who split the cost of a lottery ticket, and can divide their winnings proportionately, it is difficult if not impossible for two firms who produce a joint product to verify each other's costs.

Problems also arise when future contingencies cannot all be anticipated, or when the appropriate contract terms are not evident until a particular contingency arises. Consider, for instance, a joint venture in municipal bond underwriting. It is virtually impossible for the venture partners to write a contract specifying all future bond offerings they will be willing to bid on.

Individuals and firms interacting in a marketplace, and workers and managers interacting within a firm, rely on various institutional mechanisms to minimize contracting problems. In repeated market transactions, contracting problems are made manageable by the use of standardized, legal contracts, and by the need of contracting parties to maintain a reputation for reliability. The use of a standardized contract reduces ambiguity and discourages bickering over the interpretation of contract terms. When a contingency arises that is not covered in the standard contract, a party that behaves "unreasonably" would see his reputation tarnished. Within a single organization, transaction costs are minimized by such institutional structures as the division of a firm into profit centers and cost centers and hierarchical control. For instance, division managers have a certain amount of authority to determine their division's response to unforeseen contingencies, but they must defer to their superiors on major decisions.[12]

The parties to a joint venture are not engaged in a series of "arm's length" interactions in a marketplace. Nor are they integrated into a single organization; they retain their independence. As a result, the parties to a joint venture are less able to rely on institutional mechanisms to reduce contracting problems, so they are especially vulnerable. Opportunistic behavior or haggling over rights and responsibilities may bring a joint venture to a screeching halt, or may keep it from getting started in the first place. The parties to a joint venture have to reconcile differing goals and expectations and build mutual confidence, trust, and understanding in order to succeed. Indeed, just as clashing corporate cultures can make a merger difficult to accomplish, it can cause instability in a joint venture.

Consider a joint venture between a bank and a mutual fund company. The bank may have a simple objective—making mutual funds available to its customers. It might make a minimal effort to market the funds, which are competitive with the bank's traditional products. The mutual fund company may expect the bank to make more of an effort to market the funds. Interpreting the bank's passivity as a breach of understanding, it may pull out of the relationship.

Or consider a joint venture by several banks in municipal securities underwriting. At some point, one of the banks may wish to bid independently to underwrite a security; the issuer of the security could be a longtime client of the bank, so the bank is willing to accept a lower margin of profit on the security than its partners want. The other partners may consider such independent bidding a breach of the joint venture agreement.

The relative instability of joint ventures is the primary reason why they are less common than alternative expansion strategies, such as mergers or acquisitions. Parties deciding whether or not

---

[12]For an examination of contracting problems and the mechanisms that have evolved to deal with them, see Oliver

Williamson, "Transaction Cost Economics: The Governance of Contractual Relations," *The Journal of Law and Economics* 22 (October 1979) pp. 233-261.

to engage in a joint venture weigh the expected advantages against the potential for instability. A joint venture agreement between a bank and mutual fund company could carefully spell out how the bank will go about marketing mutual funds. Similarly, the agreement governing an underwriting joint venture could delineate circumstances under which independent bidding would be allowed. To some extent, then, the threat of instability can be reduced through foresight and ingenuity when a joint venture agreement is fashioned.

CONCLUSION

Faced with increasing competition from outside the banking industry and from within, banks have sought to strengthen customer ties and generate new sources of revenue through product expansion. To these ends, joint ventures involving banking organizations and other financial firms have grown substantially in number. Through horizontal joint ventures, banking organizations have participated in some activities they could not legally engage in on their own. But banking organizations have also taken the joint venture route to expand into permissible activities, because joint ventures can offer various advantages over other expansion strategies. Thus, joint ventures are likely to remain an important expansion strategy even if deregulation makes securities, insurance, and other activities permissible for bank holding companies.

In contrast to internal expansion, a joint venture might allow for firms to share risks and to achieve greater economies of scale. And a joint venture is often easier to arrange than a full-scale merger or acquisition, which may be encumbered by a clash of corporate cultures or long, drawn-out negotiations. But while joint ventures may offer some distinct advantages, they also are particularly vulnerable to disputes over rights and responsibilities and other such contracting problems. The parties to a joint venture have to overcome conflicting goals and develop confidence in their relationship in order to succeed.

Article 5

The Bank Credit-Card Boom: Some Explanations and Consequences

by Paul R. Watro

In financial activities, there is a trade-off between risk and return. The higher the risk, the greater the required return.

This fundamental principle helps explain why credit-card interest rates are still in the 17-18 percent range, even though rates on most other kinds of bank loans have fallen significantly since the early 1980s.

Credit-card loans have higher interest rates because they generally lack collateral and involve more risk. If such loans are not repaid, banks often must charge them off and suffer a loss.

In the last three years, the rate of such charge-offs has more than doubled, indicating a decline in credit quality. In spite of this, however, strong consumer demand and attractive profit margins have led to greater credit-card lending by banks.

This increased lending comes at a time when fewer potential customers are without credit cards and when banks are using market segmentation to combat the more intense competition, which has made growth in credit-card operations more expensive.

In view of the expense, the risk, and the higher rate of charge-offs, are banks acting irrationally when they try to increase their credit-card lending business? The answer depends on the trade-off between risk and return.

In this article, we discuss factors behind the surge in credit-card lending, and identify factors related to risk-taking that help explain why some banks have higher charge-off rates than others.

■ Consumer Demand

Consumer spending has propelled economic growth, particularly in the early years of the current economic expansion, which began in November 1982.[1] Rising income levels and improved wealth positions have contributed to increased consumer spending. Consumers have also been borrowing more. For instance, consumer installment debt as a percentage of disposable personal income rose from 14 percent in 1982 to over 18 percent in the last year or two.

Credit cards have been the fastest-growing form of consumer credit. In the last five years, credit-card balances have more than doubled and now account for nearly 25 percent of all consumer installment debt, compared

What is behind the surge in credit-card lending and the sharp rise in credit-card charge-off rates at banks? Factors related to risk-taking help explain why some banks have higher charge-off rates than others.

to 20 percent in 1982. This growth has occurred even though lenders charge higher rates on credit-card loans than on other consumer loans, such as auto loans. One reason for the higher rates is that credit-card credit has no collateral.[2] If the cardholder defaults, the credit-card issuer is without recourse against the merchandise purchased with the card.

The growing popularity of credit cards may be attributed to many factors. From a user standpoint, acceptance, convenience, safety, and flexibility have encouraged consumers to make greater use of charge cards. Credit-card transactions provide users with a convenient way to maintain records for tax and other purposes and a way to minimize the risk and financial cost of carrying large cash balances. Credit cards might even be superior to checks or cash for some transactions, such as those in foreign countries and those over the telephone and through the mail.

■ Banks' Role

Spurred by growing consumer demand, high returns, and declining commercial lending profits, many banks have placed greater emphasis on consumer lending, especially on credit-card lending. As a percentage of total bank loans, credit-card receivables jumped from 3 percent in 1982 to over 5 percent by year-end 1986. Banks now hold close to two-thirds of the credit-card outstanding balances, up from just over one-half in 1982.

Technological advances, economies of scale, deregulation, and favorable market conditions have encouraged lenders to mass-market credit on a nationwide basis. Banks issuing credit cards face sizable volume requirements in order to achieve profitability because of high operating costs. This is why many banks that offer credit cards participate with larger banks or organizations that actually issue cards and determine their rates, fees, and service features.[3] Because of economies of scale in credit-card operations, banks have an incentive to expand and become the low-cost issuers.[4]

When the cost of money fell significantly in the mid-1980s, banks generally sought to expand credit-card lending through mass-mailing solicitations with preapproved credit. Banks have largely relied on credit-card availability and services rather than on price in issuing cards.

Credit-card issuers generally have increased credit limits, have provided a wider range of enticements, and have offered credit to riskier groups of consumers who were previously unable to obtain credit cards. The spreads between funding costs and credit-card interest rates enable banks to buffer the expected higher credit losses associated with lending to riskier customers.

Credit-card accounts may be more valuable than their direct dollar return if they provide banks with useful marketing and credit information. For instance, banks could judge the creditworthiness of cardholders for larger loans based on their payment history. Some banks, such as Citibank, have apparently used credit-card customers as target groups for selling insurance products and for penetrating out-of-state markets. Moreover, banks typically include advertisements in monthly bill statements in an effort to sell other banking services to credit-card customers.

Perhaps earnings have been the underlying force behind the rapid expansion in credit-card operations at banks. Chart 1 shows that credit-card profit margins have improved sharply and have been better than those from other types of lending in recent years.[5] From 1984 through 1986, the annual pretax net returns on bank credit-card balances averaged 3.6 percent. In the same period, banks earned 2.4 percent on real estate mortgages, 2.7 percent on consumer installment debt and 1.4 percent on commercial and other loans. Bank credit-card returns have benefited not only from the robust consumer demand, but also from the removal or relaxation of state usury laws in the early 1980s and from the large decline in funding costs from those years.

Over a longer period, however, credit-card profits look quite different. Credit-card issuers experienced a severe profit squeeze in the 1979-81 period because of historically high interest rates and binding usury laws. Credit-card earnings were generally more volatile and lower than earnings from other loans. Greater volatility may have reflected a combination of factors, including changes in the cost of funds, binding usury ceilings, and the higher degree of default risk in credit-card lending.

Credit-card performance was also quite poor during the developing stages of bank credit-card systems.[6] In addition to operating problems, banks underestimated the burden of controlling credit losses. In an effort to grow and to gain market acceptance, banks turned to mass mailing of unsolicited credit cards during the late 1960s. This marketing strategy led to large-scale credit and fraud losses, that, in turn, led to legislation prohibiting the unsolicited distribution of credit cards.[7]

Despite a shaky track record, the recent prosperity in credit-card earnings has spurred new entrants and more intense competition in the credit-card business. A few years ago Sears introduced the Discover Card, which has not become profitable yet.[8] American Express also introduced the Optima card, which offers a revolving credit line with a lower interest rate than most bank cards.[9]

With greater competition and fewer consumers without credit cards, however, large-scale expansion is probably becoming more expensive and more risky. Nevertheless, mass solicitations with preapproved credit lines, waived annual fees, and other enticements continue to be common among large issuers.

In an effort to build consumer loyalty, many banks have sought to tie credit cards to affinity groups such as airlines, hotel chains and alma maters during the past year or two. The sponsoring organization typically endorses the bank's card for financial compensation based on members' acceptance and use of the card. While aggressive marketing and liberal credit policies have promoted credit-card growth, some of the expansion came at the expense of loan quality.

CHART 1   NET PRETAX PROFIT MARGINS ON VARIOUS TYPES OF BANK CREDIT

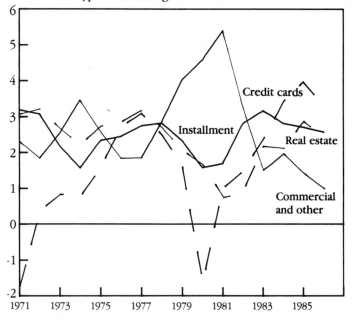

Percent credit type outstanding

NOTE: Based on annual data from the Federal Reserve System's Functional Cost Analysis.

CHART 2   NET CHARGE-OFFS ON BANK CREDIT CARDS (AS A PERCENT OF CREDIT-CARD AVERAGE BALANCES)

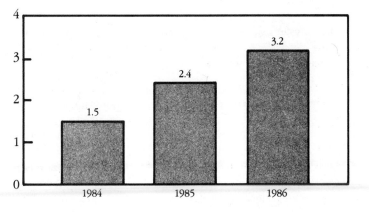

NOTE: Based on data from reports of income and condition for all banks.

■ **Credit Quality**

One widely used measure of loan quality is net charge-offs.[10] These are loans judged to be uncollectable in a given year, minus any recoveries of loans previously charged off. Banks generally write off unsecured loans, such as credit-card receivables, faster than well-secured loans like home mortgage loans.

Chart 2 shows that bank credit-card quality has deteriorated. Net charge-offs as a percentage of credit-card balances have more than doubled, jumping from 1.5 percent in 1984 to 3.2 percent in 1986. The deterioration reflects many factors, some and perhaps the most important of which have no relation to the business cycle.

In our study, we examine 148 large banking organizations to identify the level and variability of credit-card charge-off rates among individual banks. We look at banking organizations as a unit rather than as individual banks because some organizations have shifted credit-card balances among subsidiary banks. In fact, more than 20 bank holding companies operate special banks dealing primarily in credit-card accounts.[11]

Our sample included all bank holding companies established before 1982 that have a subsidiary bank with assets over $1 billion and that have total credit-card receivables of more than $25 million. These banking organizations hold 80 percent of bank credit-card receivables and accounted for nearly 85 percent of credit-card charge-offs at banks in 1986.

Credit-card charge-off rates varied considerably among our bank sample. Net charge-offs as a percentage of credit-card balances ranged from -0.6 to 8.9 percent and averaged 2.2 percent for 1986.[12] Charge-off differences could be due to numerous factors including differences in luck, economic conditions, and risk-taking.

TABLE 1   BANK CHARGE-OFF DIFFERENCES ON CREDIT CARDS

	High-Charge-off Group	Low-Charge-off Group	Difference
Credit-card balances/ total loans	7.9%	3.7%	4.2%[a]
Change in credit-card balances/ total loans (1983 to 1985)	2.5	-1.0	3.5[a]
Loans/assets	63.9	60.8	3.1
Revenues from credit-cards/ average credit-card balances	19.3	14.9	4.4[a]
Credit-card balances (billions)	$1.8	$0.1	$1.7[b]
Assets (billions)	27.8	5.0	22.8[b]

a. Denotes statistical significance at the 1 percent level.
b. Denotes statistical significance at the 5 percent level.
NOTE: Data are as of year-end 1986, unless otherwise noted.
SOURCE: Federal Financial Institutions Examination Council's Reports of Income and Condition for banks.

We examine credit-card growth, specialization, volume, revenue, loan-to-asset ratio and organizational size as potential explanatory factors for interbank charge-off differences. Each of these factors is related to risk-taking in one way or another.

Banks that experience faster credit-card growth might be expected to incur higher charge-offs because a trade-off may exist between credit growth and credit quality. Lenders that specialize in or devote more resources to a certain type of lending may also be more aggressive and extend riskier lines of credit in those areas. Alternatively, those banks may be better at managing risk. Specialization is measured by the current share of loans held in credit-card receivables and growth is measured by the change in this ratio over the two previous years.

There is a positive relationship between risk and returns. Lenders charge higher rates or require higher revenues for riskier loans. Accordingly, one would expect to find higher credit-card charge-offs at banks that generate higher revenues per dollar of credit-card balances. We also examined loan-to-asset ratios as a measure of an organization's overall attitude towards risk. Higher ratios are thought to reflect greater risk-taking since loans are usually riskier than other assets, such as government securities.

Product and geographical diversification helps to reduce risk. The largest credit-card issuers with a nationwide customer base should have more geographically diversified portfolios that could lower charge-off rates. On the other hand, the largest banking organizations might choose to have lower credit standards for issuing credit cards because of potentially lower risk levels from greater product and loan diversification.

We use two common tests to ascertain whether or not credit-card growth, specialization, volume, revenue, loan-to-asset ratios, and organizational size had any influence on charge-off rates. First, we compare the sample extremes—those with the highest and lowest charge-off rates. The high group included those with charge-off rates greater than 4.0 percent and the low group included those with charge-off rates less than 1.0 percent. For each variable, average values were computed for both groups and the difference was tested for statistical significance. Second, to explain differences in charge-off rates for the whole sample, we use a statistical technique that isolates the effects of one variable while taking into account other factors.

Our analysis, as expected, revealed that the 18 banking organizations in the high-charge-off group differed significantly from 21 banking organizations in the low-charge-off group. The table shows that the high-charge-off banks were much larger, placed greater emphasis on credit-card lending, and charged higher prices. The high-charge-off organizations experienced much faster credit-card growth and, on average, they held $1.8 billion in credit-card receivables, which accounted for nearly 8 percent of their loans. Average credit-card revenues generated by the high-charge-off group were 4.4 percent higher than the low-charge-off group.

Although we do not know if higher revenues were sufficient to offset higher default costs, this finding suggests that banks are taking credit risk into account at least to some degree when pricing credit cards. Higher

CHART 3 CREDIT-CARD REVENUE BY CHARGE-OFF GROUPS
(AS A PERCENT OF CREDIT-CARD AVERAGE BALANCES)

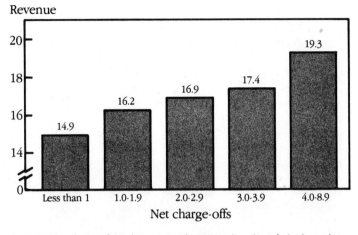

Revenue

NOTE: Based on 1986 data from reports of income and condition for bank sample.

charge-offs, therefore, do not necessarily imply inferior performance or cause for immediate concern, as long as lenders are being adequately compensated for credit risk.

The strong positive relationship between revenues and charge-offs is also depicted in chart 3. The chart shows average credit-card revenues for the whole bank sample broken out into five groups according to the level of credit-card charge-offs. Banks in the higher charge-off groups progressively earned higher revenues, suggesting that they charge higher rates and fees but lend to riskier customers.

However, the loan-quality/revenue relationship could be spurious, that is, other factors could be causing it. When we isolated the influence of individual factors while taking into account other factors, such as asset size and the percentage of loans in credit-card balances, we still found that banking organizations with higher credit-card charge-offs had significantly higher credit-card revenues.

Other results were also similar to the findings listed in the table.[13] One important exception was that credit-card balances were found to be negatively related to charge-off rates when asset size was taken into account. This finding, although statistically insignificant, is consistent with the view that larger portfolios are generally more diversified and carry less risk than smaller portfolios.

■ Conclusion

Bank credit-card lending has increased rapidly since the early 1980s. This increase has been fueled by a range of factors, including robust consumer demand, improved technology, removal or relaxation of state usury laws, economies of scale, cross-selling potential, substantial decline in funding cost and attractive profit margins. Higher credit-card earnings have attracted new competitors, more aggressive marketing and more liberal credit standards that, in turn, led to a sharp rise in credit-card losses.

Credit-card charge-offs varied considerably among issuers. Banks with higher propensities to take risk incurred higher charge-off rates. As long as issuers receive adequate compensation for credit risk, however, charge-offs are not necessarily a problem. Also, the potential impact of high credit-card charge-offs on the financial condition of banks is reduced by the fact that even the most aggressive banks in credit-card lending still have relatively small portions of their assets and loans in credit-card receivables.

Paul R. Watro is an economist at the Federal Reserve Bank of Cleveland. The author would like to thank John M. Davis, Mark S. Sniderman, and James B. Thomson for helpful comments. Research assistance was provided by John N. McElravey and Daniel J. Martin.

The views stated herein are those of the author and not necessarily those of the Federal Reserve Bank of Cleveland or of the Board of Governors of the Federal Reserve System.

■ Footnotes

1. See K. J. Kowalewski, "Is the Consumer Overextended?," *Economic Commentary,* Federal Reserve Bank of Cleveland, November 1986.

2. However, this does not necessarily explain why credit-card rates have not fallen in tandem with other loan rates.

3. There are approximately 3,000 banks and other institutions that issue credit cards. "Interest Rate Controls on Credit Cards — An Economic Analysis," Lexicon, Inc., October 1985.

4. See Christine Pavel and Paula Binkley, "Costs and Competition in Bank Credit Cards," *Economic Perspectives.* Federal Reserve Bank of Chicago, March-April 1987, pp. 3-13. The authors found economies of scale in credit-card operations for a sample of small- and medium-size banks.

5. Figures are based on data provided by banks participating in the Functional Cost Analysis of the Federal Reserve System. For a discussion of credit-card profitability, see Glenn Canner and James Fergus, "The Effects on Consumers and Creditors of Proposed Ceilings on Credit Card Interest Rates," Staff Study 154, Board of Governors of the Federal Reserve System, October 1987.

6. Peter S. Rose, "The Promise and the Peril," *The Canadian Banker & ICB Review,* Volume 85, November 6, December 1978, pp. 64-65, and Joel P. Friedman, "Golden Goose or Ugly Duckling?," *ABA Banking Journal,* September 1986, pp. 73-77.

7. The Consumer Protection Act (October 1970) also limited the cardholder's legal liability for unauthorized use of the card to a maximum of $50.

8. "Sears Is Discovering Discover Credit Card Isn't Hitting Pay Dirt," *Wall Street Journal,* February 10, 1988, p. 1.

9. Kathleen Hawk, "Plastic Warfare," *U.S. Banker,* June 1987, p. 40.

10. Delinquencies, or past due loans, are another measure of loan quality, but some of these figures are treated as confidential by bank regulations.

11. A list of so-called credit-card banks is provided by the *American Banker,* January 4, 1988, p. 15.

12. The weighted average net charge-off rate was 3.4 percent for the sample.

13. Credit-card charge-off rates were regressed on the six variables listed in the table. Each of the variables except credit-card balances was positively and statistically related to credit-card charge-offs at least at the 5 percent level of significance. The variables collectively explained 40 percent of the variance in the credit-card charge-off rates across the 148 banking organizations that were examined.

Article 6

Bank Lending to LBOs: Risks and Supervisory Response

by James B. Thomson

An increased use of debt financing has been a hallmark of the financial restructuring of corporate America that has taken place in the mid- and late 1980s. An organization that develops from a corporate reorganization now commonly has 80 to 90 percent of its financing in the form of debt, in contrast to the 30-percent debt-to-assets ratio that prevailed in the previous two decades. Because of the high degree of leverage employed in these deals, they are often referred to as leveraged buyouts (LBOs), a form of highly leveraged financings.

The news media, Congress, and the regulatory community have all focused considerable attention on LBOs in recent months, largely because of the use of this financing arrangement to fund corporate takeovers. Media interest has been heightened by the size and volume of recent deals, particularly the reported $25.3 billion that the firm of Kohlberg, Kravis & Roberts paid for RJR Nabisco. The total volume of LBO deals for 1988 exceeded $98 billion.

Congressional attention concerns the use of LBOs in takeover deals that involve a major restructuring of the acquired company. The result in such deals may be layoffs and plant closings in communities where the acquired firm is the major, and sometimes only, employer. Some members of Congress are also wary of the LBO market's potential effect on consumer and small-business credit and on the stability of the financial system itself. Furthermore, because the tax code makes debt financing relatively less expensive than equity financing, Congress is concerned that tax considerations alone may be a major motivation behind many of the LBO deals. The LBO situation is so important that only the $100 billion thrift-industry bailout and deposit-insurance reform take precedence over it on the 101st Congress's agenda for regulatory reform in the financial sector.

Bank regulators are becoming increasingly interested in bank participation in LBO lending because of the dramatic increase in LBO credits on bank portfolios. The Comptroller of the Currency estimates that of the $150 billion to $180 billion in LBO debt outstanding, $80 billion is held by U.S. banks.[1] Most of this exposure has been accumulated in recent years. In fact, estimates of total bank lending for LBOs in 1988 may exceed $48 billion (excluding $15 billion in bank loans to RJR Nabisco).

Leveraged buyouts (LBOs), a popular method of corporate restructuring in the past decade, have attracted significant attention among the news media, Congress, and bank regulators. The huge size of recent takeover deals and the dramatic increase in LBO credits on bank portfolios have raised concerns about the risks of LBO financing. This article examines these risks and discusses the current response of bank supervisory authorities to the increased use of funding by leveraged buyouts.

In addition, analysts estimate that LBO credits on bank portfolios equal 18 percent of the total dollar volume of commercial and industrial loans and 50 percent of bank capital.[2] Concentration of LBO exposure is uneven; one published estimate of LBO exposure for the 10 most active banks in the LBO market cites a range from 40 to 140 percent of equity capital.[3]

Bank regulators are concerned about the impact of increased LBO exposure on bank soundness and, ultimately, on the regulatory safety net. High levels of leverage are thought to be associated with both increased risk and larger expected returns than most loans to less-leveraged customers. Assuming the current system of federal deposit insurance remains intact, federal deposit guarantees may cause banks to underprice the risk of LBO credits and to book more LBO loans for their portfolios than they would in the absence of deposit guarantees.[4] Because of these incentives, it is likely that LBO-related credits will be a point of exposure in the banking system.

This *Economic Commentary* looks at the risks associated with LBO lending and the current response of federal bank regulators to banks' increasing participation in this market. First, we will provide a brief overview of LBOs. Then we will examine the risks associated with lending to these highly leveraged companies. Finally, we will outline the current response of federal bank regulators to the increased participation of banks and bank holding companies in funding LBOs.

■ **A Brief Primer on LBOs**
What degree of leverage must a firm have in order for its financial restructuring to be defined as an LBO? There seems to be no consensus: Bankers Trust defines a firm as highly leveraged if it has 70 percent debt financing, while the Federal Reserve System is now using 75 percent debt financing as a general examination guideline.[5]

The degree of leverage that constitutes a highly leveraged firm is a relative concept. For example, the J.P. Morgan deal that created U.S. Steel in 1901 was considered to be highly leveraged because it resulted in a debt-to-assets ratio of 35 percent.[6] Although a debt-to-assets ratio of 80 percent is not uncommon in a country like Japan, a U.S. firm with this ratio is considered to be highly leveraged.

Even though the transactions that have drawn the majority of attention lately are the multibillion-dollar deals like RJR Nabisco, the data presented in table 1 show that the bulk of the $98.3 billion of LBO deals last year were relatively small. Of the 304 deals in 1988 identified as LBOs by Venture Economics, Inc., roughly 88 percent had a transaction price under $500 million, 19 deals were between $500 million and $1 billion, and 17 deals exceeded $1 billion. The average size of LBO transactions in 1988 was $327 million. The multibillion-dollar deals dominated the market in terms of total dollar lending, however, accounting for nearly 57 percent of the $98.3 billion in total transactions.[7]

Making loans to highly leveraged firms is not a new activity for banks. Banks have lent to highly leveraged firms in the middle market (deals under $500 million) for years. Most loans guaranteed by the Small Business Administration can be defined as highly leveraged financings. However, the syndication of loans for leveraged buyouts of national and multinational companies is a more recent phenomenon.

LBOs typically have three tiers of financing. The first tier is senior debt, which makes up 50 to 60 percent of the total and mainly consists of secured bank loans. The second tier is mezzanine financing, which consists of unsecured debt and makes up roughly 30 percent of the total. These debentures are considered highly speculative investments (junk bonds). The last tier of financing is equity, which usually makes up 10 to 20 percent of total financing. Some of the equity in the reorganized firm may be held by non-bank subsidiaries of bank holding companies.

■ **Risks Associated with LBO Credits**
LBO financing is a natural market for banks. Loans to support LBO transactions carry many of the same risks of more traditional commercial loans, so banks should be in an excellent position to assess and assume these risks. However, the larger degree of leverage in LBO financing accentuates the risk of default, because there is less equity in the firm to absorb unexpected earnings losses. It is therefore essential that the lender conduct a sufficient analysis of the proposed transaction and of the creditor, and that it appropriately price the risks of these loans.

TABLE 1 LEVERAGED BUYOUTS IN 1988 BY TRANSACTION SIZE[a]

Transaction Size	Number of Buyouts	Percent of Total	Dollar Volume[b]	Percent of Total $
Under $50 million	105	34.5%	$2,206.6	2.2%
$50 million - $99.9 million	58	19.1%	4,086.8	4.2%
$100 million - $499.9 million	105	34.5%	22,334.0	22.7%
$500 million - $999.9 million	19	6.3%	13,961.0	14.2%
Over $1 billion	17	5.6%	55,687.0	56.7%
Totals	304	100.0%	$98,275.4	100.0%

a. Deals announced or consummated in 1988.
b. Millions of dollars.
SOURCE: *Buyouts*, vol. 2, issue 1, Venture Economics, Inc., January 11, 1989, page 2.

Lending analysis should be focused primarily on reasonable projections of cash flows and secondarily on collateral values. Recent experience with real-estate lending in Texas and with agricultural loans in the Midwest illustrates the problems that can arise when lending is based on inflated asset values and not on accurately projected cash flows.

However, the valuation of collateral and cash flows may be difficult, as the value of a firm's stock may double or triple when a takeover deal is announced. Furthermore, cash-flow projections are often based on a radically reorganized firm and on overly optimistic assumptions about cost-cutting measures and asset sales. These uncertainties make it difficult to use historical cash flows to project future cash flows.

The recent expansion of lending to highly leveraged firms has occurred during the relatively stable macroeconomic environment of the mid-1980s. Although banks' loss experience on LBO-related loans is not materially higher than for more traditional commercial loans, it is unclear how LBO credits will perform in a less stable macroeconomy. How much can interest rates rise before some highly leveraged firms can no longer meet their debt payments? What effects would an economic downturn (especially a prolonged recession) have on many highly leveraged firms' abilities to service their debt from operating income? A large part of a bank's LBO portfolio could conceivably go under if interest rates rise dramatically or if there is a severe economic downturn. The concern is that a bank may not be able to adequately hedge against macroeconomic risks in its LBO-related loan portfolio.

Although macroeconomic risk may not be mitigated by diversifying the LBO portfolio, diversification is important. Even in a robust macroeconomy, regional- or industry-specific problems can affect the ability of an LBO firm to service its debt. Through diversification, the impact of these problems on the bank's LBO portfolio is minimized.

■ Current Supervisory Response

Currently, federal bank authorities both supervise and regulate risks posed to the banking system from the LBO portfolios of banks. Because no additional restrictions have been imposed on the activities of banks participating in the LBO market, only the existing regulations for bank lending pertain to LBO loans.[8] Moreover, much like the approach taken to reign in daylight overdrafts in the payments system, banks are being asked to define, manage, and impose internal limits on their own LBO risk exposure.[9] Regulators, using their supervisory authority, would take action against a bank only if its internal procedures were deemed inadequate. Federal supervisors would emphasize management skills and portfolio composition in evaluating a bank or bank holding company's LBO exposure.

In their evaluation, bank examiners look for an internal definition of an LBO credit: can the bank identify its LBO portfolio and LBO loan exposure? In addition, are there procedures in place for evaluating the risk of LBO loans? Does management have the ability to evaluate the target company's management and operating controls?

Banks are also expected to have in place specific procedures to deal with defaults, including procedures to monitor their risk exposure to both individual and aggregate LBO credits. In addition, the banks must have established policies, procedures and documentation to handle the special legal problems associated with LBO lending.[10] Finally, the adequacy of internal controls will be examined. For instance, has management established prudent and reasonable limits on the total amount of exposure and the type of exposure to LBO credits (on both a bank and a consolidated holding company basis)?

In conjunction with their evaluation of management, bank examiners will pay particular attention to the composition of the LBO portfolio. Specifically, they will look at the quality of the credits and the overall diversification, as well as the bank's total capital exposure to the LBO portfolio, on both a firm and industry basis. In the context of the overall asset portfolio, total LBO loans may be treated as a specific concentration of credit.

Another concern of bank regulators is the syndicated loans in a bank's LBO portfolio. To the extent that the lead banks in the LBO loan syndicate primarily perform an investment banking function and retain only a small percentage of the loans on their books, the banks purchasing the loans must conduct their own independent evaluation of the loan. Examiners will scrutinize this part of the portfolio to determine the adequacy of internal procedures for evaluating and managing the risks of the syndicated loans. In addition, examiners are concerned with banks' potential higher risk of obtaining liens on collateral and participating in any debt renegotiation.

■ LBO Loans and Risk-Based Capital Standards

Bank regulators view capital as the last line of defense between unexpected earnings losses on a bank's portfolio and both uninsured bank depositors and the regulatory safety net. The traditional approach to capital regulation has been to set a uniform capital-to-assets ratio for all banks, regardless of their risk, and to control portfolio risk through supervision and regulation. This approach has been criticized for two reasons. First, regulators do not know with much precision how much capital an individual bank (let alone *all* banks) needs to hold to protect against insolvency. Second, the amount of capital required to protect the federal deposit insurance funds and uninsured depositors from loss varies from bank to bank depending on risk. In response to the second criticism, bank regulators in the United States and in the other major developed countries have recently announced new international capital standards for banks.[11] These new standards require banks to hold a level of capital that corresponds to the credit risk in their portfolio.

The new capital standards partition a bank's asset portfolio into four risk categories according to perceived default risk. The amount of capital a bank must hold against a particular asset (or activity) is then determined by its risk category. The premise behind this approach is that banks should be allowed to choose the risk of their portfolio without regulatory interference, so long as increased risk to depositors and to the federal deposit insurance funds is offset by increased capital protection.

Critics of the new capital guidelines claim that they do not explicitly recognize the increased risk associated with LBO-related loans. Under the current risk-based capital standards, loans to highly leveraged companies are placed into the same risk category as more traditional commercial and industrial loans. This means that a bank must hold the same amount of capital to back up an LBO-related credit as it would a similar credit to a less-leveraged firm.

Admittedly, the standards are not perfect because they do not take into account all risks. However, risk distinctions beyond those contained in the regulatory framework are difficult to define with precision. Additionally, regulating risk runs the danger of introducing unwanted effects on credit allocation. More important, the risk-based ratio is only a first step in assessing capital adequacy. As is the case with other loans, the quality of LBO-related loans and investments must also be taken into account.

Moreover, the final risk-based capital guidelines are the result of negotiation and compromise between bank regulators in the nations adopting the new capital standards. Given the differences in capital structure for non-financial firms across countries (as noted earlier, Japanese firms tend to be much more leveraged than U.S. firms), it would be difficult to gain a consensus among nations to adopt capital guidelines that differentiate among loans according to the leverage of the borrower. Consequently, it is unlikely that LBO-related loans will be assigned their own risk class under the international capital guidelines.

■ Conclusion

LBO financing is a natural market for banks to engage in, and they are in an excellent position to assess and assume this risk. With returns on LBO loans as much as four percentage points higher than those available on more traditional commercial loans, it appears that the higher risk may currently be offset by higher expected returns.[12]

The high debt-to-equity ratio in the resulting firm leaves little or no margin for error when evaluating and pricing these loans, however. Lenders therefore need to adopt adequate controls and procedures for evaluating, pricing, and managing the risks of this type of lending activity. As long as banks adopt appropriate internal controls, bank regulators should reasonably expect that supervision—not regulation—is the appropriate approach to LBO-related lending.

■ Footnotes

1. See Barbara A. Rehm, "Regulators Mull Changes in Fees on LBO Loans: Bank Exposure to Firms in Debt Raises Concerns," *American Banker*, January 31, 1989, page 1.

2. See Nancy J. Needham, "Son of LDCs: Banks Are Borrowing Trouble with Loans to LBOs," *Barron's*, December 26, 1988, page 13.

3. See Sarah Bartlett, "Bankers Defend Buyout Loans But Investors Fret," *The New York Times*, October 28, 1988, page D1.

4. As I discussed in an earlier article, the current system of federal deposit guarantees subsidizes risk-taking behavior by banks. The value of the subsidy increases with the risk of the bank. Therefore, banks will tend to hold riskier portfolios than they would if there were no deposit insurance subsidy. See James B. Thomson, "Equity, Efficiency, and Mispriced Deposit Guarantees," *Economic Commentary*, Federal Reserve Bank of Cleveland, July 15, 1986.

5. However, not all loans to companies with 75 percent debt financing are classified as LBOs by the Federal Reserve. In addition to the leverage criteria, the loans must be for the purpose of acquiring or reorganizing the firm to be considered as LBO credits by the Federal Reserve System.

6. See George Anders, "Shades of U.S. Steel: J.P. Morgan Paved the Way for LBOs: Bidding for RJR Nabisco Has Precedents Dating Back to the Turn of the Century," *The Wall Street Journal,* Midwest Edition, November 15, 1989, page A1.

7. See *Buyouts*, vol. 2, issue 1, Venture Economics, Inc., January 11, 1989.

8. Additional reporting requirements for LBO loans may be required. The Y-9 report for bank holding companies may include a line item for LBOs in the near future. Furthermore, the federal bank regulators may change the accounting treatment of fees on LBO credits. See Barbara A. Rehm, op. cit.

9. For a discussion of the payments system and daylight overdrafts, see E.J. Stevens, "Reducing Risk in Wire Transfer Systems," *Economic Review,* Federal Reserve Bank of Cleveland, Quarter 2 1986, pages 17-22; and E.J. Stevens, "Pricing Daylight Overdrafts," *Working Paper* 8816, Federal Reserve Bank of Cleveland, December 1988.

10. Unique legal problems can arise during the first year of an LBO loan, mostly concerning fraudulent conveyance, equitable subordination, and state bulk transfer laws.

11. For a more detailed discussion of the new capital guidelines, see Janice M. Moulton, "New Guidelines for Capital: An Attempt to Reflect Risk," *Business Review,* Federal Reserve Bank of Philadelphia, July/August 1987, pages 19-33.

12. See Stan Hinden, "Executive Urges LBO Loan Curbs: Moody's Official Sees History as a Warning," *The Washington Post,* February 2, 1989, page F2.

James B. Thomson is an assistant vice president and economist at the Federal Reserve Bank of Cleveland. The author would like to thank Lawrence Cuy, William Osterberg, and Mark Sniderman for helpful comments.

The views stated herein are those of the author and not necessarily those of the Federal Reserve Bank of Cleveland or of the Board of Governors of the Federal Reserve System.

Part Two

Regulatory Reform for
Financial Institutions

The six articles in this section have one common theme—the financial problems that have affected commercial banks and savings and loans in the 1980s and the appropriate regulatory response to those problems. The number of commercial bank and savings and loan failures has increased dramatically. To a considerable degree, the sharp increase in the number of failed institutions reflects the instability in interest rates and in the economy, especially in the "oil patch" and farm states. The deregulation associated with the Depository Institutions Deregulation and Monetary Control Act of 1980 and the Garn–St Germain Depository Institutions Act of 1980 may also play a role. But whatever the causes, the problem of reforming the regulatory structure remains.

In the first article in this section, "Can Regulatory Reform Prevent the Impending Disaster in Financial Markets?" Franklin Edwards provides a useful overview and a plea for action to deal with the problem. Professor Edwards provides a discussion of existing myths that must be confronted as a part of regulatory reform including "Myth 1: Deposit Insurance Is Necessary for Financial Stability" and "Myth 2: Bank Failures and Financial Instability Are the Same."

The second article in the section also deals with bank failures and deposit insurance. In "Bank Runs, Deposit Insurance, and Bank Regulation," Charles Carlstrom discusses bank runs and the important issue of whether deposit insurance is necessary to prevent such runs and a collapse of the banking system. He also discusses the costs and benefits of providing deposit insurance. In Part II of the article, the author discusses why bank runs may be contagious and examines some of the ways in which private clearinghouses are protected against widespread bank failure. He concludes that the argument that federal deposit insurance is necessary to prevent bank runs may not be valid.

The third article in this section, "Troubled Banks and Thrifts," by Michael Keeley, deals with another aspect of the problems created by distressed banks and savings and loans, that of capital forbearance. This policy allows troubled institutions to continue in operation despite inadequate (and sometimes even negative) equity capital positions. Keeley examines the advantages and disadvantages of such a policy as well as alternative approaches to the same problem.

The fourth article, "Reforming Deposit Insurance," also by Michael Keeley, focuses on the alternatives to the existing system of fixed-rate deposit insurance. As recognition has grown that traditional fixed-rate deposit insurance is incompatible with a deregulated financial system, analysts have searched for alternatives. Keeley discusses a variety of these alternatives, including eliminating deposit insurance, risk-based premiums, and market-value capital.

The last two articles focus on the thrift crisis and its consequences. This problem has been growing throughout the 1980s and it exploded as a political issue in late 1988 and early 1989. Although precise estimates are difficult to make with any degree of validity, many analysts have suggested that the thrift crisis could cost over $200 billion to solve. In "The Thrift Insurance Crisis," Michael Keeley and Jonathan Neuberger discuss the dimensions of the thrift crisis and alternative solutions to it. They provide information on the Bush plan that was proposed in February 1989 and discuss the importance of taking steps to prevent a repetition of the crisis. The last article in this section, "The FSLIC Bailout and the Economy," by Fred Furlong, explores the implications of the Bush plan for the entire economy, including alternative ways of financing the FSLIC bailout. An important issue in the discussion is whether the debt created in the bailout should be put in the federal budget and added to the federal budget deficit.

Article 7

Can Regulatory Reform Prevent the Impending Disaster in Financial Markets?

By Franklin R. Edwards

Introduction: an aura of uneasiness

A deep current of unrest flows through financial markets these days, carrying with it a feeling that things are, in some way, out of kilter. While no one is quite certain of the precise reasons for it, there is a general uneasiness about whether the fabric that binds and solidifies our financial system is coming unraveled. In recent years, we have witnessed spectacular bank failures (such as the Continental Illinois Bank), seen the collapse of two state deposit insurance systems, and been told that the prestigious Federal Savings and Loan Insurance Corporation (FSLIC) is in the red by some $30 billion. Newspapers carry daily stories of the billions of dollars of loans made by banks to third-world countries that

Franklin Edwards is a professor at Columbia University. The article is based on a paper given at a symposium on "Restructuring the Financial System," sponsored by the Federal Reserve Bank of Kansas City at Jackson Hole, Wyoming, August 20-22, 1987. The views expressed in this article are those of the author and do not necessarily reflect the views of the Federal Reserve Bank of Kansas City.

will never be repaid, but will have to be written off as bad debts. Banks and thrifts located in areas dependent upon the health of the energy and farm sectors are in deep trouble; many will fail. The total number of bank failures this year has already surpassed historical annual highs. Even the future of the mighty Bank of America is in doubt.

Intertwined with this shaken financial structure is the world of glittering high finance, where the successful (and the dishonest) amass large fortunes in only a few months or, at most, years, and where success is expected to come early to the best of our university graduates. A seemingly endless stream of innovations—swaps, coupon-stripping, futures, options, leveraged-buyouts, and so forth—occupy the attention and the resources of our best institutions. In this world, internationalization, global capital markets, and 24-hour trading are the vogue. In the lowly world of banks and thrift institutions we are still debating the feasibility of permitting Citibank to operate in New Jersey, or Illinois, or Texas, knowing full well that it already operates in every major country of the world. In high finance, anything is possible and nothing seems prohibited, while in the other world banks and traditional financial institutions seem entrapped in a static environment encumbered by archaic regulation. It is little wonder that these inconsistencies and the resulting pervasive bickering among financial market participants and regulators have begun to make us question the logic of the current financial structure and to ponder whether regulators are still playing a constructive role in guiding market developments.

Concern about the stability of the financial system is also being reinforced by persistent macroeconomic disequilibria. A continuing government budget deficit threatens us with uncertainty about debt markets and interest rates, and persistent trade imbalances have wrought currency instability and a threat to free-trade relationships. The recent behavior of the stock and bond markets is testimony to this unrest. More volatile than at any time in recent history, these markets epitomize the fragile nature of expectations about the future. We seem to be balancing on a knife-edge of stability, ready to be toppled one way or the other by economic or political news that either reinforces or shakes our view of the future.

The world is changing around us, in spite of us, and there is no clear path or end in sight. We have a financial system born in the 1930s in the depths of our greatest economic catastrophe, formulated and promoted as the fail-safe system of the future. Pictures of bank failures and bank runs, with their long lines of dispirited and desperate people, provide a vivid reminder of the intimate relationship between our economic health and the soundness of our financial institutions. More than 50 years have gone by since the collapse of the 1930s, years of relative calm and prosperity. During those years, our financial system, while buffeted by occasional shocks and imbalances, performed admirably. Financial institutions

of every type blossomed.

The idea that this system may in some way be seriously flawed is an alien thought. The notion that it should be drastically changed shocks us. "If it works, don't change it" is a philosophy that needs no proselytizing. But the world is changing, and our financial system is no longer working well. Worse, it is failing in ways that are not immediately obvious, giving us a false sense of comfort. The seeds of change, planted in the 1960s, have long ago sent their shoots into every corner of the financial landscape. Institutions are being entangled and will eventually be smothered unless the financial system is restructured to accommodate these changes.

Change, of course, is never easy, and changing something that has been almost sacrosanct for more than 50 years is an intimidating prospect. With longevity and prosperity come strong private-interest groups. We have done our best to nurture a system of heterogeneous institutions, insulating and protecting them from one another with the heavy hand of regulators. Institutions have responded predictably: where similar interests are at stake, they have banded together to form powerful special-interest groups, besieging Congress and regulators either for special privileges or to block intrusions into their preserves. Special-interest groups are the natural predators of change. When threatened by it, they erect still more formidable barriers to contain it.

This political-economic process is presently playing itself out, to the detriment of the entire country. The winds of change embracing us are seeping through the hastily erected barriers faster than they can be built. Once breached these barriers will crumble with electrifying speed, taking with them in a crash many institutions that appear sound today but are in reality teetering on the edge of instability.

It is important that we not allow this to happen; that we orchestrate this change, and not allow it to crash down upon us with unpredictable consequences. We have a governmentally-constructed and regulatory-maintained financial edifice, one that is not the product of natural market forces. It is a system neither prepared nor capable of coping with the market changes inundating us. We cannot close our eyes to its fate without serious risk.

The time has come for us to reach a consensus. We must determine the financial system of the future and put in place a compatible regulatory system. Barriers that prevent us from achieving these goals, or that threaten present stability, must be quickly dismantled, and regulations needed to assure financial soundness either retained or developed. There must also be provisions made for transitional problems that will be encountered in moving from an old to a new system.

A key to accomplishing this is to identify and discard myths that have been a continual obstacle to the restructuring of the financial system. Another critical step is to agree on fundamental goals of financial regulation and on the nature of government intervention that is needed to achieve these goals. Finally, we need to commit to a financial system that provides for the maximum degree of free-market discipline for our financial institutions, consistent with a stable financial environment.

These objectives may seem like a tall order to those of us who have long been enmeshed in the complex maze of financial regulation, but I believe there is more agreement among us than is commonly either realized or acknowledged. A first step is, therefore, to identify key principles and concepts on which we agree or disagree. Such an understanding is fundamental to establishing a firm foundation upon which to construct a new regulatory structure.

Why we must act

We must act soon. We are sitting on a ticking time-bomb with an uncertain timing device. Most of you will find this declaration startling, even unbelievable. Things do not seem that bad! True, some institutions are going bankrupt, but most are operating in the black. How can conditions be that threatening?

The situation today is similar to the rotting frame of an old house. Each piece of supporting timber has rotted from the inside. From casual observation, it is impossible to determine whether the supports are sound. A few probes with a sharp instrument, however, quickly reveals that the timber has rotted, its ability to support the house gone. Despite this enfeebled condition, the house miraculously stands, until one day a brief but intense gust of wind takes it down with a crash.

Is this an alarmist analogy? Yes. Does it misrepresent the current situation? I do not think so. The reason appearances today do not reflect reality is due to a combination of deposit insurance, fictitious accounting, and regulatory procrastination.

The deposit insurance crisis, and that is what it is, is increasing with every passing month. It is not a secret: almost everybody knows, even Congress. But its resolution is not a simple matter.

The insurance crisis is gathering in force because the numbers are getting larger.[1] We already know that the FSLIC is some $30 billion short. Were it to close only those thrift institutions it knows to be already insolvent and to repay depositors, it would need at least $30 billion more than it now has. Its solution, therefore, has been not to close these institutions, but to pretend that they are not insolvent.

This is not a neutral policy. It does not simply maintain the status quo; it makes things worse. The managements of the insolvent institutions have almost nothing more to lose. They have already lost their institutions, for all practical pur-

---

[1] Edward J. Kane, *The Gathering Crisis in Federal Deposit Insurance*, Cambridge: MIT Press, 1985.

poses. But they still have some of the deposits of their customers, and the hope that a miracle will revive them. It is a small step for them to try to help this miracle along by their taking a last, desperate gamble with their depositors' funds.

Football fans call this the "long-bomb" phenomenon. In a football game, with time running out, the team that is hopelessly behind begins to resort to the high-risk, seldom successful play—a long pass into the opponent's end zone. There is always a small chance that it may work!

In a football game, the failure of this "long-bomb" strategy is of little consequence: they would have lost the game anyway. It is there that the analogy with today's thrift crisis ends. The consequences of a failing thrift institution unsuccessfully pursuing such a high-risk strategy are serious: the institution goes deeper under water and its depositors are at greater risk. The institution's assets shrink even more, making the imbalance between its assets and liabilities greater. When the institution is finally declared insolvent, the FSLIC has an even bigger bill to pay. It must refund insured depositors their monies, using more of its own (and taxpayers') resources to do it.

Why would depositors leave their funds with insolvent institutions and be vulnerable to "long-bomb" risk-taking? Because, of course, they are insured by the government, and are confident that whatever the outcome they will be repaid by the government.

Thus, we have the makings of an escalating crisis. FSLIC, without adequate resources, is unable to close already insolvent institutions, but at the same time is unable to control risk-taking by these institutions. In addition, these institutions have every incentive to take even more risk, and ultimately, to fall deeper into debt. FSLIC's debt is steadily mounting. It is a matter of time before thrift depositors understand this too and begin to wonder about either the ability or the resolve of the government to stand by its guarantees. When this happens you have the classic "bank-run": depositors will indiscriminately remove their funds from solvent as well as insolvent thrifts, since they will not be able to distinguish one from the other.

This threat may extend to banks as well, and not only to thrift institutions. Those with deposits at banks look to the Federal Deposit Insurance Corporation (FDIC), just as thrift depositors look to the FSLIC. How good is the FDIC if the FSLIC has been let fail? Past decisions by depositors and other investors have been made on the basis of our present financial and regulatory structure. Deposit insurance and government guarantees are an integral part of this structure. Any loss of confidence in these guarantees risks serious repercussions for all institutions.

Congress is fiddling while risk is mounting. At best, it will eventually bail out our insurance funds, imposing a tremendous cost on taxpayers. At worst, it will do nothing until we have a panic on our hands. In either case, it will be acting irresponsibly late.

The growing insurance crisis is exacerbated by our antiquated accounting conventions and by the present regulatory policy of increasing "forbearance." The health of many financial institutions today is illusory. Their asset values reflect inflated historical values and not actual current market values. Their equity values are commensurately overstated. There is little doubt that were we to restate assets and liabilities on the basis of sensible market-value accounting principles, many financial institutions would become insolvent overnight.

The absence of realistic accounting conventions also causes regulators to defer acting even when they know they should. Instead of closing institutions early, when losses to the insurance fund (and taxpayers) are minimal, they defer action, hoping either for a miraculous recovery or that such action may be postponed until they are no longer in office. Were the balance sheets of institutions to reflect realistically their weakened condition, regulators would undoubtedly be under greater public and congressional pressure to act. Even depositors, despite the insurance guarantee, might begin to view with a jaundiced eye the wisdom of lending funds to insolvent entities. Better accounting means better information, and with better information the rot would be discovered and remedied before it could threaten the safety of the entire house.

The current policy of increasing regulatory forbearance (or forgiveness) is ill-advised. While its equity objectives are understandable, perhaps even laudable, it is dangerous and doomed to failure. The basic assumption underlying this policy is that future changes in the economy will occur that will rescue troubled institutions. Energy-troubled banks will return to good health when energy prices go back up, making the energy sector prosperous again; or, farm-troubled institutions will recover when farming does. In the meantime, losses are mounting.

Regulatory forbearance can work, and sometimes has worked, but it will not work this time. While some of our current problems are of a cyclical nature, the most critical ones are not. They are the result of structural changes in financial markets. These changes will be permanent features of the future financial landscape. They are not ephemeral fissures in the existing structure.

A major change has been the erosion of barriers to competition, which separated financial institutions and markets from each other. Deposit insurance, instituted during the 1930s as a supplement to the Federal Reserve, was directed at protecting small depositors, preventing bank runs, and protecting the payments system from disruption. In return for this federal guarantee and as a safeguard to the federal deposit insurance system, depository institutions were wrapped in protective regulation, which they accepted as a necessary component of the system. It was, if you will, a regulatory (or government) fostered cartel, complete with rigid entry barriers and regulations to prevent "destructive" competition. (An example was the interest rate ceilings imposed on deposit accounts.)

The result was to create an artificial financial structure characterized by thousands of small disparate financial institutions. We had institutions specializing in only mortgage loans, or consumer loans, or business finance, or trust services, and so forth. We had banks with thousands of branch offices, while others were prohibited from opening an office across the street from their main office. We had thousands of tiny institutions operating in insulated local markets, where competitors were unable to go, together with giant institutions operating in distant cities, like they were on different planets of the solar system. We had U.S. institutions doing in London and Frankfurt what they were prohibited from doing in New York and Chicago, and foreign banks doing in New York and Chicago what U.S. banks could not do in the United States. It was a regulatory-created and nurtured edifice, not the child of natural market phenomenon, and it could only be sustained by protective regulation.

Economics, technology, and competitive developments combined to tear down these protections. What is left is deposit insurance and government guarantees without the regulatory safeguards designed to support them. High and volatile interest rates (and therefore funding costs), sharply reduced information and communication costs, and the globalization of capital markets together with intense international competition have all played a role in eliminating competitive barriers. Interest rate ceilings on deposits have been removed, opening up competition for funds; the geographical operations of institutions has widened substantially; there has been a frantic search for new sources of earnings and ways of diversifying, which has led to U.S. banks going off-shore and to the development of the Euro-dollar market and foreign financial centers. Most of all, the new world of open competition has destroyed the cartel-like world of old, threatening the viability of many of the formerly insulated financial institutions.

Discarding old myths

A first step in moving to a new and more sustainable system is to discard certain myths that have prevented us from undertaking significant regulatory changes. These are false beliefs about what are necessary features of a financial system, about the role of government intervention, about regulation and its costs and effectiveness, and about what are necessary safeguards against a costly financial collapse.

Myth 1: Deposit insurance is necessary for financial stability.

Deposit insurance will undoubtedly be a central element of any new financial structure. It has occupied such a position for the last 50 years, and is understandably viewed as essential to a well-functioning and stable financial system.

Deposit insurance has had twin goals: to protect small depositors and to prevent bank runs. Its role as preventor of bank runs is seen as being integral to financial stability. Without it, what would prevent depositors, fearful of bank insolvencies, from engaging in the wholesale withdrawal of funds from the banking system? This view has led in recent years to the continued expansion of *de facto* (if not *de jure*) deposit insurance coverage, to where today such coverage may be as great as 100 percent of a bank's liabilities.

It is a falsehood that deposit insurance is necessary for financial stability. Indeed, under certain conditions, such as we have at present, it may even contribute to instability. Proof that deposit insurance is unnecessary is everywhere: many countries, both today and historically, have enjoyed financial stability without having a system of deposit insurance. While it is true that the financial structures of many countries are quite different from ours, the point remains valid: as a general proposition, deposit insurance is not required for stability. There is, in addition, little evidence to indicate that under normal market conditions a bank failure (or failures) will precipitate a run on depository institutions.

The primary safeguard against bank runs and financial panics is, and has always been, the central bank, with its unlimited lender-of-last-resort capability. Used intelligently and judiciously, this power is all that is needed to protect us against irrational and episodic financial panics. Deposit insurance is superfluous.[2]

As a country, we turned to deposit insurance out of distrust of the Federal Reserve. The Federal Reserve failed us miserably in the 1930s and, as a consequence, deposit insurance was adopted as the panacea. Deposit insurance would presumably remove the human element: we would not have to rely on the discretionary judgment of central bankers but could depend instead upon a failsafe institutional structure.

In reality, we substituted one set of regulators for another. We put our trust in regulators assigned to administer and protect the deposit insurance system, rather than in central bankers, and these regulators are failing us in the 1980s just as the Federal Reserve did in the 1930s. By failing to act and by following an expanding policy of regulatory forbearance, regulators are failing to protect our insurance system and are sowing the seeds of a financial disaster. In the end, it will be the Federal Reserve on which we must rely.

---

[2] Anna J. Schwartz, "Financial Stability and the Federal Safety Net," unpublished, prepared for the American Enterprise Institute's project on Financial Services Regulation, 1987.

If there is a role for deposit insurance in the future it is as a guarantor of small depositors. The rationale for such a role is one of "social justice" rather than "economic efficiency." We might want to consider retaining some deposit insurance for this purpose, as long as its coverage can be kept narrow. For the purpose of financial stability, however, deposit insurance should be discarded in favor of a more pervasive central bank role as lender-of-last-resort. Once this is done, a number of promising avenues for financial reform will be open to us.

A lender-of-last-resort policy also will not be subject to the same moral hazard problem that has undermined deposit insurance. The primary objective of the central bank should not be to rescue individual institutions but to provide market liquidity (through, for example, open market operations). If institutions are in general solvent, the provision of ample market liquidity should be adequate to prevent bank runs. The task of assuring institutional solvency should not fall to either the central bank or deposit insurance, but rather should be the result of a soundly conceived and maintained financial and regulatory structure. If there is pervasive institutional insolvency, not even the Federal Reserve can help.

If direct central bank lending to individual institutions were to become necessary, it also would not carry with it the same predictable and dependable subsidies as has deposit insurance. It would not, for example, result in a continuous divergence between what institutions pay for funds and what they should pay. Managers could not as easily internalize in everyday decisions the mere possibility that central bank funds might be forthcoming as they can the deposit subsidies on their funds.

Myth 2: Bank failures and financial instability are the same.

It is often thought that bank failures cannot be permitted without endangering the entire financial system. Similarly, bank failures are equated with high social costs. These are inhibiting notions. They keep regulators from closing banks when it would be prudent to do so.

Bank failures need not mean market disruption, or even customer disruption.[3] They can very often be accomplished by simply replacing old owners with new owners, where the losses are borne by the old owners. This is possible if regulators close banks in a timely manner, or before the market value of their equity is less than zero. The longer regulators wait to act, the more difficult it is to find new owners, and the higher the social costs.[4]

Bank failures (as well as the failure of other financial institutions) should be expected. They are an essential part of a competitive world. Competition without failure is anomalous. Failures are part of the engine that makes competition work. They must be anticipated and planned for. When that is done, bank failures and financial instability are not synonymous.

Myth 3: Effective monetary policy requires narrowly-defined banks.

An old obstacle to restructuring the financial system is the view that monetary policy cannot work unless the payments system is controlled by narrowly-defined banks. The argument is sometimes couched in terms of the uniqueness of the money supply and the necessity of regulatory-mandated minimum reserve requirements. In recent years, there has been a blurring of what constitutes "money" (or "transaction" balances),

---

[3] George Benston and George Kaufman, "Risk and Failures in Banking: Overview, History, and Evaluation," in George Kaufman and Roger Kormendi, eds., *Deregulating Financial Services*, Cambridge: Ballinger, 1986.

[4] George Benston and George Kaufman, "Risk and Solvency Regulation of Depository Institutions," unpublished, prepared for the American Enterprise Institute's project on Financial Services Regulation, 1987.

and of which institutions are providing (or should provide) such balances. The fear is that if these balances are not concentrated in "banks", or other commensurately regulated entities, the Federal Reserve will no longer be able to control the "money supply."

This fear is unfounded. The Federal Reserve is capable of controlling the monetary base, whatever the financial structure. The need for mandated reserve requirements is also questionable, although in principle they could be imposed on any institution (not only banks). Finally, there is no clear association between different types of financial structures and either the stability of the money supply or a central bank's ability to control money. In addition, there is evidence that the maintenance of artificial (or regulatory-induced) capital market barriers between different kinds of financial institutions and markets may inhibit effective monetary control. Our experiences with Regulation Q taught us this lesson well.

Thus, monetary policy can be effective even if "banks" are not the only providers of "money." The goal of effective monetary control cannot be used to justify a regulatory policy that mandates narrowly-defined banks.[5]

Myth 4: The separation of banking and securities activities is necessary for financial stability.

There are many arguments about why banking and securities activities should or should not be mixed. Some of these should be taken seriously; some should not. One that should not is that the mixing together of such activities will undermine the soundness of our financial system.

There is little dispute that, in principle, mixing banking and securities activities provides financial firms with greater diversification opportunities, which should enhance profitability and risk management. This should contribute to greater financial stability, not less. The empirical evidence that we have on banks suggests that greater diversification is valuable. Similarly, there may be economies of scale and scope that can add to profitability.

The major arguments against mixing banking and securities activities are potential abuses related to perceived conflicts of interests and to the "upstreaming" (or transferring) of profits or assets from the bank to associated entities, thereby weakening the bank. These arguments are related more to the corporate form employed—the holding company entity—than to the mixing of banking and securities activities. There is nothing inevitable about the holding company form of organization. It is also not obvious that abusive "upstreaming" practices by holding companies cannot be controlled.

Stripped of this controversy, there is nothing unique, or intrinsic, to securities activities that make them inherently dangerous for banks. They are not, for example, more risky. Nor do they pose conflicts of interest problems more severe than already exist in many banking and securities firms. Further, by permitting more open competition among banks and securities firms there should be less abuse of conflict situations in the future.[6] Finally, other major countries have permitted the mixing of banking and securities activities without undermining the soundness of their financial systems. Indeed, our own banks have done a securities business abroad for years without adverse consequences.

Myth 5: The payments system requires the separation of banking from commerce.

Some have argued that unless banks are kept

---

[5] Marvin Goodfriend and Robert King, "Private and Central Bank Provisions of Liquidity," *Ibid.*, 1987.

[6] Anthony Saunders, "Bank Holding Companies: Structure, Performance and Reform," *Ibid.*, 1987.

"pure," free of the risk associated with commercial activities, there will be an unacceptable risk of "settlement failure" in our payments system. This argument largely reflects concern about the private "wire transfer" segment of the payments system and, in particular, about CHIPS. CHIPS is an electronically linked network of over 130 large banks that processes about 90 percent of the international interbank dollar transfers.

It is feared that the failure of a single CHIPS bank to settle at the end of the day may generate a systemic risk of widespread failure, with a result similar to a bank run. A settlement failure may have a chain reaction, rendering some banks temporarily illiquid and others possibly even insolvent (which may occur if creditor banks are ultimately not able to collect a substantial percentage of what they are owed from the bankrupt institution). Such systemic risk is not present to the same degree in the Fedwire system because the Federal Reserve guarantees transfers when the receiving bank is notified of payment.

Settlement failures in wire transfers are logically quite similar to other credit risks that banks face. The only distinction is that daylight overdraft risks are concentrated among only the largest banks. There is, therefore, no "payments system risk" separate and distinct from the general issue of financial institution soundness. If mixing banking and commerce is in general unsound, it is also unsound from a payment system risk perspective. If such activity is not unsound, there is no special payment system risk problem. The only issue is the soundness of financial institutions.[7]

Myth 6: Small is "best."

The present financial structure is populated with thousands of small banks and financial institutions. Possibly as a result, it is sometimes thought that a system characterized by large financial institutions is not desirable.

Two fallacies underlie this view. First, the structure we now have is artificial: it is the child of regulation. It is a structure nurtured and preserved by restrictive regulation. Both geographic restrictions (such as branching prohibitions) and product restrictions (for example, banking versus securities activities) fostered and maintained this structure. Without them, it is doubtful that the financial structure would look anything like it does today. A quick glance at foreign countries confirms this: they have far fewer and relatively larger financial institutions. In addition, the current erosion of regulatory barriers to competition has had the predictable effect: reducing the number of institutions and increasing the size of those remaining.

Second, there is no evidence that a system with fewer and larger institutions is inferior. With fewer regulatory barriers, the general level of competition will increase, and not diminish, as is sometimes feared. Cost studies indicate that large banks are no less efficient than small banks, and there is no reason to think large banks pose a greater soundness problem. There is, finally, no reason to believe that a structure of fewer and larger banks (or financial institutions) creates additional problems with respect to conflicts of interest, the allocation of credit, or the exercise of political influence.

There is, therefore, no convincing reason to prevent market forces from working to alter our financial structure (governed, of course, by the enforcement of the antitrust laws). If the result is fewer and larger institutions, this may be "best." A structure of small, artificially protected, institutions is definitely not optimal.[8]

---

[7] Mark Flannery, "Public Policy Aspects of the U.S. Payments System," *Ibid.,* 1987.

[8] Franklin Edwards, "Consolidation, Concentration, and Competition Policy in Financial Markets: in Past and the Future," *Ibid.,* 1987.

Fundamentals of a new financial system

Discarding these myths does not by itself delineate the contours of a new financial system. It does free us to consider a broader range of possibilities. All of these alternatives, however, must satisfy, or be consistent with, a number of fundamental goals. Identifying these goals is essential to designing a new system and to defining the proper scope of government involvement.

There are four goals that any new financial structure should satisfy:
- A sound and stable financial system
- The most competitive system consistent with soundness and stability
- Equal (or fair) treatment of all customers
- Protection for the small and unsophisticated depositor

While it is beyond the scope of this paper to describe all of the features of a new financial system, a number of potential facets of such a system deserve consideration.

1. Deposit insurance should be restricted to protecting only small depositors. It should not be so pervasive as to insulate depository institutions from the forces of market discipline. A broad-based deposit insurance system should be avoided because it entails an unmanageable moral hazard.

2. The chief protection against bank runs and other systemic risk should be the Federal Reserve. It should use its lender-of-last-resort capability to prevent systemic problems due to illiquidity.

3. Competition should be encouraged by the removal of barriers preventing competition. In particular, nationwide branching should be adopted and financial institutions should be permitted to undertake a wide range of financial activities, including securities activities.

4. The general antitrust laws should be applied to financial institutions to prevent monopolization and unfair competitive behavior and should constitute the only competitive standard applicable to financial markets.

5. Efforts should be made to impose greater market discipline on financial institutions. The adoption of market-value based accounting principles is a first step, along with the public disclosure of an institution's performance.

6. Regulation to protect the safety and soundness of the financial system should be backed primarily by minimum capital requirements and by a "closure policy" that closes institutions before they have zero or negative (market-value) net worth. Insolvent institutions should not be permitted to exist.

If these features were adopted as the centerpiece of a new system, it would be relatively simple to fill in the required additional elements.

Conclusion

This paper is a plea for action—an appeal to end the political paralysis that now immobilizes Congress and regulators. Twenty percent of all thrift institutions are now unprofitable, and more than 450 are already technically insolvent. It has been estimated that the FSLIC, which insures $900 billion in thrift deposits, is some $30 to $50 billion in the red, and every day it does nothing taxpayers potentially lose another $10 million.

The banking situation is also deteriorating. About 200 banks are expected to fail in 1987, and the FDIC's list of problem banks has soared to 1,600, up from 218 in 1980. Intense competition from both bank and nonbank sources, and depressed conditions in certain economic sectors, such as energy and agriculture, threaten an even greater number. Large banks, finally, are faced with a steady erosion of earnings over future years by having to write off an increasing amount of the $300 billion owed to them by third-world debtor countries. The ability of even the FDIC to meet its potential future obligations is by no means assured.

If nothing is done, the situation will continue

to worsen. At some point, public confidence in our financial structure will collapse with potentially devastating effects. To do nothing is to challenge fate. Such a course is politically and economically irresponsible.

There are a number of long-standing myths about what are essential characteristics or components of a sound financial structure that must be debunked before we can hope to reform our financial system. These are, as you would expect, time-honored postulates, but ones that nevertheless must be confronted before we can move forward. By focusing debate on these general concepts, we can avoid much of the myopic political infighting that unfortunately dominates all discussions of financial reform. This paper sets forth a number of mythical postulates that I regard as serious obstacles to reform. My intention, clearly, is to center debate on these longer-run principles rather than on more obvious turf-threatening conflicts.

A companion effort must also be made to agree on and to adopt general goals for regulation. These goals are often lost sight of in our effort to respond to current exigencies and to shore up troubled institutions. Without having them to guide us, however, we are like a sailor without a compass: doomed to tacking back and forth aimlessly with only the slightest hope of finding the safety of solid land. I sketch out a number of general goals that I believe must guide our restructuring of the financial system.

In the coming months and years, Congress, regulators, and even the courts will be called upon to make decisions that will have far-reaching implications for the financial system and our economy. They must begin to develop a general blueprint to guide their way. Through debate, research, and discussion, such a blueprint can hopefully to be fleshed out to form a core of principles to guide us in creating a long-lasting, efficient, and sound financial structure.

Article 8

Bank Runs, Deposit Insurance, and Bank Regulation, Part I

by Charles T. Carlstrom

As long as there have been banks, there have been bank runs. Unlike the failure of mom-and-pop grocery stores (or Lockheed, for that matter), bank failures are frequently viewed as contagious—able to cause other bank runs and lead to failures of otherwise solvent banks.

A rumor or a hunch that a bank is in trouble can lead to its demise. Thus, the fear that a bank "might" be in trouble can be a self-fulfilling prophecy.

Haunted by the contagion of bank failures that occurred during the Great Depression, regulators are still wary of letting banks fail. Large banks in particular are a cause of concern, because the potential spillover effects are thought to be excessive.

Along with other bank regulators, the Federal Deposit Insurance Corporation (FDIC) has an implicit mandate to maintain confidence in, and provide stability to, the commercial banking system. A principal method of achieving this mandate is by insuring depositors for losses up to a current maximum of $100,000.[1]

The justification for FDIC insurance is simply that insured depositors will no longer have an incentive to pull their money out of a bank that is merely rumored to be insolvent. Unfortunately, federal deposit insurance provides little incentive for insured depositors to withdraw their funds from a bank that actually is insolvent.

For nearly 50 years after its inception in 1934, the FDIC was considered successful in fulfilling its mandate. The banking system grew rapidly with few bank failures, and none widespread enough to threaten the entire system. Since 1981, however, the number of bank failures has increased sharply. In 1987 there were 184 bank closings, and an additional 19 required FDIC assistance to stay afloat.[2] Bank failures are currently at their highest level since the Great Depression.

This *Economic Commentary,* presented in two parts, discusses whether federally provided deposit insurance is necessary to prevent widespread bank runs by exploring some of the myths and folklore associated with bank runs. Adam Smith argued that the invisible hand of self-interest leads men to effectually promote the interests of society. We attempt to analyze whether this invisible hand extends into the banking industry by examining both the causes and cures of bank runs.

Widespread bank failures are often thought to be a possible consequence of a banking system without federal deposit insurance. This article considers whether federal deposit insurance is necessary to prevent bank runs. Part I describes some of the costs of providing deposit insurance and then introduces its justification and benefits. Part II, presented in the upcoming February 15 *Economic Commentary,* concludes with an examination of contagious bank runs and a discussion of how the market handled banking panics prior to the Federal Reserve System and the Federal Deposit Insurance Corporation.

■ **The Nature of Bank Runs**
A bank run can occur when some of a bank's depositors perceive the bank to be insolvent or expect insolvency to occur.

If banks are like other businesses, then a bank run would be quite acceptable as a source of market discipline. For example, if the public thought that a bank's manager had embezzled a substantial portion of the bank's capital, depositors would have an incentive to withdraw their money. If a substantial portion of a bank's deposits were withdrawn, the bank would then be forced to close.

The threat of being run on and closed down provides the incentive for stockholders to spend the necessary resources to monitor their employees. The potential for bank runs also creates the incentive necessary to stop banks from undertaking excessively risky investments: those in which there is a high probability of failure as well as success.[3]

■ The Costs of Providing Deposit Insurance

Deposit insurance circumvents the market discipline of insured depositors. Because their funds are guaranteed, insured depositors (those with deposits less than or equal to $100,000) have little incentive to place their money in a safe, well-managed bank. Similarly, if they discover that a bank is not financially viable, they have no incentive to withdraw their money from the bank. Therefore, unless regulators promptly close insolvent institutions, it is up to the shareholders and the uninsured depositors to impose discipline on troubled banks.

The role of uninsured depositors may be quite small under the present system, however. Since a depositor can have several accounts of $100,000, the de facto maximum of deposit insurance is many times greater than the stated legal limit of $100,000. And, because of the failure-resolution policies that have been applied to some large banks (for example, Continental Illinois, First City, and First Republic), the perception exists that some banks are too big to fail and that all depositors in these banks are, in effect, insured.[4] Both of these factors work to reduce the disciplinary action of depositors.

Deposit insurance provides banks with a no-risk source of funding. Without the threat of bank runs, stockholders and senior management in the existing regulatory environment have reduced incentive to monitor their employees to minimize insider dealing, bank fraud, and simple incompetence.

It may not be a surprise that fraud and embezzlement have been the primary causes of bank failures.[5] According to a recent study by the Office of the Comptroller of the Currency, since 1979 "poor management, either by the bank officers, the board of directors, or both, played a significant role in 89 percent of the failures."[6]

Deposit insurance also reduces the amount of capital a bank chooses to maintain. A higher capital-to-asset ratio enables a bank to borrow money more easily in case of financial difficulty. By guaranteeing insured depositors against losses, the risk of bank runs, as well as the amount of capital that is necessary to protect a bank from withdrawals, is lessened.

At the turn of the century, capital-to-asset ratios were 20 percent; by the 1930s, they had declined to about 15 percent. Today the capital-to-asset ratio is approximately 7 percent—substantially less than the capital ratios of other industries.[7] Concern about the decrease in bank profitability and the increase in bank failures during the 1970s led to increased concern about capital adequacy and, in 1983, to enactment of a law that provided bank regulators with the legal authority to enforce minimum capital standards.

Along with limited liability, deposit insurance creates an incentive for banks to hold more risky investment portfolios. Bank owners reap the rewards when a bank's investment succeeds, but because of limited liability, the FDIC—and perhaps the taxpayers as well—shares in the losses when an investment fails.

Deposit insurance further reduces the incentives for banks to avoid risky investments, because a bank does not have to compensate its depositors (by paying them a higher interest rate) when it undertakes substantial risks. This problem is aggravated by the recent failure-resolution policies applied to some large banks. Such policies have served to erode the market's discipline further and to subsidize these banks just because they are large.

■ Bank Regulation and Deposit Insurance

Bank regulators are aware of these problems. Not only can regulators impose minimum capital requirements on banks, but they are empowered to close down banks that are not solvent and to assist banks that are becoming insolvent.

Traditionally, bank regulators did not have the power to close a bank when its market value reached zero. Instead, they could close a bank only after its book value became negative.[8] Even then, however, a bank was not necessarily closed down, as the recent FDIC-assisted merger of Alaska Mutual and United Bankcorporation of Alaska indicates.[9] With the Competitive Equality Banking Act of 1987, chartering authorities can now close a bank when book insolvency appears imminent.

This forbearance occurs even though the FDIC may spend more money later to bail out such banks. While it is true that an insolvent bank may later become financially viable, the Alaskan situation illustrates that financial health may not be regained.[10]

The incentive to take on more risk is especially prevalent for a bank that is close to being shut down. The threat that regulators might close a bank can lead a bank's manager to make investments that have a small chance of a large payoff and a larger chance of expected loss. In the outside chance that the gamble pays off, the manager saves the bank and hence his job; if the gamble fails, the bank goes out with a bang instead of a whimper. Although this scenario is not firmly established in banking, the precedent has been set in the thrift industry.

The longer the FDIC waits to close a bank, the greater the incentive for the bank to undertake risky investments. If an insolvent bank is not closed promptly, then the losses to shareholders are postponed. Because a dollar in the future is worth less than a dollar today, postponing shareholders' losses provides an extra indirect subsidy.

Besides closing banks when they first become insolvent, another way to lessen the negative aspects of deposit insurance is for regulators to charge banks an insurance premium based on the riskiness of their portfolios. Risk-taking would be punished by requiring the bank to pay higher premiums. However, Congress has long been opposed to any plan that would allow the FDIC to charge different premiums to different banks.

Absent these measures, the best ways to strengthen market discipline are to sharply reduce the legal limit of deposit insurance, to limit insurance to one account per person, to assist only insured depositors, and to send a signal to the market that no banks are too large to let fail.

■ **The Case for Deposit Insurance**
Supporters of the current deposit insurance and regulatory system generally respond to these criticisms on two fronts. First, while the FDIC is interested in economic efficiency, it is also interested in equity considerations, that is, in protecting the interests of the small or less-informed depositor. Second, while inefficiencies and moral hazards are the costs of providing deposit insurance, the benefits of deposit insurance are even

greater than the costs, because a bank is unlike other forms of business.

Unfortunately, using deposit insurance to protect the less-informed diminishes the incentives for them to become informed. If the objective is to protect the small depositors, one might question the need to insure depositors up to a current maximum of $100,000, to extend coverage to more than one account, or to protect uninsured depositors.

Society should ask itself not only whether it wants to protect certain depositors who lose money in bank runs, but also how much protection to provide in the most cost-effective way. For example, the federal government could allow an income tax credit so that depositors could deduct their losses, up to a legislated maximum.

Justifying deposit insurance because depositors lost money due to bank failures prior to the FDIC is also tenuous, because these losses were generally small. From 1930 to 1933, depositors of failed banks lost only 0.81 percent on average. During noncrisis years, losses to depositors averaged only 0.07 percent.[11]

Losses have typically been small because rational depositors run on a bank when they first perceive it to be insolvent. Given that depositors in failed institutions generally receive more than 99 cents on the dollar even during bad times, one might well question whether deposit insurance is necessary to protect the vast majority of depositors.

The most important argument in support of deposit insurance is that banks are not like other businesses. They are potentially special because 1) bank failures can cause undue economic hardship in a community, 2) the economy depends on the safety and security of the banking system, which could potentially be upset

if some larger banks were to fail, and 3) bank failures can be contagious and can cause otherwise solvent banks to fail.

The first argument, that banks are special because bank failures could impose a hardship in a particular geographical area, is not unique to banking. The closing of a mill in a one-mill town would be at least as devastating as the closing of the town's only bank.

In the absence of laws against branch banking, a bank failure would typically result in the transfer of ownership from a poorly managed banking firm to a banking company that is potentially better managed. It is the presence of regulations against branch banking and the restrictive policies of bank chartering agencies that can cause economic hardships when a bank closes in a small town.

Another potential reason for protecting banks is the argument that a well-functioning market economy depends on the security of the banking system. Because banks facilitate savings and investment, a large number of bank failures can have real effects.

The potential for a series of bank runs to threaten the banking system is limited, however, because the failure of a few banks would tend to strengthen the remaining banks. This is because large depositors who have a high opportunity cost of holding their assets in cash would redeposit their money in sound banks.[12] The exception to this rule is when a bank failure causes a run on otherwise sound banks.

A series of bank runs may also hamper economic activity because widespread bank failures can cause a significant drop in the money supply. The money supply contracted during the Great Depression because individuals decided to hold their money in currency instead of depositing it in banks. Because such a reduction in the money supply can be offset by supplying additional reserves to the banking system, justifying deposit insurance to eliminate a bank-run-induced multiple contraction of the money supply is not warranted.

In order to justify deposit insurance, one must understand not only the costs associated with its administration, but also the benefits of having deposit insurance. The preceding discussion indicates that an analysis of contagious bank failures is necessary in order to understand these benefits.

Part II of this article, presented in the upcoming February 15 *Economic Commentary*, concludes with an examination of contagious bank runs and a discussion of how the banking system prior to the Federal Reserve System handled such problems.

Charles T. Carlstrom is an economist at the Federal Reserve Bank of Cleveland. The author wishes to thank Walker Todd, James Thomson, John Scadding, William Gavin, and Mark Sniderman for their helpful comments.

The views stated herein are those of the author and not necessarily those of the Federal Reserve Bank of Cleveland or of the Board of Governors of the Federal Reserve System.

■ Footnotes

1. In 1934, the first year the FDIC operated, depositors were insured up to a maximum of $2,500 (which amounts to approximately $22,000 today). This maximum increased slowly until 1982, when it increased from $40,000 to its current level of $100,000.

2. See "1987 Bank Failures Set Post-Depression Record," *The Washington Post,* January 6, 1988.

3. See George G. Kaufman, "The Truth About Bank Runs," Staff Memoranda SM-87-3, Federal Reserve Bank of Chicago, April 1987.

4. See Daria B. Caliguire and James B. Thomson, "FDIC Policies for Dealing with Failed and Troubled Institutions," *Economic Commentary,* Federal Reserve Bank of Cleveland, October 1, 1987.

5. See George J. Benston, Robert A. Eisenbeis, Paul M. Horvitz, Edward J. Kane, and George G. Kaufman, *Perspectives on Safe and Sound Banking: Past, Present, and Future,* Cambridge, MA: The MIT Press, 1986, pp. 1-4.

6. See "Study Says Bad Management Had Key Role in Bank Failures," *The Washington Post,* January 21, 1988.

7. See George J. Benston and George G. Kaufman, "Risk and Solvency Regulation of Depository Institutions: Past Policies and Current Options," Staff Memoranda SM-88-1, Federal Reserve Bank of Chicago, 1988. This is not meant to imply that deposit insurance is the only reason for the decline in banks' capital-to-asset ratios.

8. See Edward J. Kane, *The Gathering Crisis in Federal Deposit Insurance,* Cambridge, MA: The MIT Press, 1985, p. 20.

9. See "Two Big Alaska Banks Unveil Rescue Plan," *The American Banker,* October 8, 1987.

10. In fact, in the thrift industry, financial health is usually not regained. See "Thrift Industry: Forbearance for Troubled Institutions, 1982-1986," U.S. General Accounting Office Briefing Report, May 1987.

11. See Benston, et al., op. cit., p. 64. Some investors did not receive their money until years later. If capital markets are efficient, however, depositors would have been able to borrow against a portion of their likely settlement.

12. This same argument has been used to contend that deposit insurance should cover deposits only up to a maximum of $5,000 to $10,000.

Article 8

Bank Runs, Deposit Insurance, and Bank Regulation, Part II

by Charles T. Carlstrom

Contagious bank failures are often thought to be a possible consequence of a banking system without federal deposit insurance. This article considers whether federal deposit insurance is necessary to prevent these types of bank runs.

Part I, which was presented in the February 1 *Economic Commentary*, described some of the costs and benefits of providing deposit insurance and concluded that an analysis of contagious bank failures is necessary in order to understand these benefits.

Part II continues with an examination of contagious bank runs and a discussion of how the market handled banking panics prior to the Federal Reserve System and the Federal Deposit Insurance Corporation.

■ Contagious Bank Failures
The last apparent difference between banks and other businesses is the possibility for a rumor or a failure of another bank to ignite bank runs and cause the failure of financially sound banks.

These types of bank failures are termed "sunspots" because, if depositors truly believe that a bank's solvency depends on events unrelated to market funda-

mentals—such as the amount of solar activity—a bank's solvency would, in fact, depend on the amount of solar activity. In the typical example, a sunspot is the failure of one bank or a group of banks, which ignites rumors that other banks might also fail.

It would seem irrational for depositors to run on a solvent bank. However, because a bank's liquidity and solvency depend in part on the number of depositors wishing to withdraw money, it is rational for each depositor to queue up if he expects other depositors also to stand on line.[1]

Sunspot bank runs are also said to be "bubble" phenomena. One of the most famous examples of a bubble involved tulip bulbs in Holland during the seventeenth century. Investors frantically bought tulip bulbs, expecting their price to rise, which in turn caused their price to rise.[2]

Sunspot bank runs are like bubbles in that they are self-fulfilling prophecies. To determine the correct regulatory response to this apparent market failure, one must first inquire empirically how frequently bank failures are caused by sunspots and then ask what is special about banking that allows these types of phenomena to arise.

Part I of this article, presented in the February 1 *Economic Commentary*, described some of the costs and benefits of providing federal deposit insurance. The major benefit of providing deposit insurance is the prevention of contagious bank runs—a bank failure that spreads to solvent banks. Part II, presented here, discusses why bank runs may be contagious and examines some of the ways in which private clearinghouses protected against widespread bank failures. The article concludes that federally provided deposit insurance may not be necessary in order to protect against such bank runs.

Determining how often bank runs are caused by sunspots—extraneous events—is difficult to do with any degree of statistical accuracy. However, we can examine whether bank failures were the products of the same type of deposit and withdrawal behavior during both panics and nonpanics.

Gorton tests this hypothesis for bank failures during the U.S. National Banking Era (1863 to 1914) and shows that the factors affecting deposits and withdrawals were similar in periods of widespread bank failures and in periods when banking failures were not widespread. His results suggest that "banking panics during the National Banking Era were systematic responses by depositors to changing perceptions of risk."[3]

Corroborating evidence that extraneous events did not seem to cause a substantial number of bank failures prior to the Great Depression is given by Benston, et al. They show that the average annual rate of bank failures for the 1875 to 1919 period was 0.82 percent, versus 1.01 percent for non-financial firms.[4] If banks are like other firms except for the possibility of contagious bank runs, one would expect the failure rate of banks to be at least as great as it is for other kinds of businesses.

Most bank runs do not seem to be of the type pictured in textbooks (or in the Frank Capra movie *American Madness*): banks falling like dominoes, with mass hysteria as depositors line up for blocks hoping to withdraw their money. Instead, the evidence indicates that bank runs have primarily been rational responses to changes in the financial worth of a bank. Even the recent runs on the Ohio and Maryland savings and loans seem to have been based on market fundamentals.[5]

Since the evidence against contagious bank failures is indirect, one should not completely dismiss the possibility that a contagion of sunspot bank runs might arise in an unregulated environment. However, this type of bank run does not appear to be as widespread as typically thought, so the regulatory response to this possibility should be tempered by our current state of knowledge.

■ Why Bank Runs Can Be Contagious

The possibility for extraneous events leading to bank runs arises from two elements of banking structure: the first-come, first-served aspect of banking deposits, and the illiquidity of many bank assets. The former is necessary in order for runs to exist. If the amount in a depositor's account fluctuated with the market value of the assets and liabilities of the bank (as it does in a mutual fund), bank runs would typically not occur. However, as discussed earlier, the threat of bank runs imposes a necessary discipline on banks.

A bank asset is said to be illiquid if the bank cannot sell it in a short amount of time without incurring a substantial loss. Illiquidity results from the asymmetry between the bank's perception of the value of its assets and the market's (depositor's) perception of the value of those assets. This difference arises because information that a bank learns at the time a loan is made (such as a borrower's credit history, assets, and liabilities) and information that a bank learns during the life of a loan (such as timing and receipt of payments) cannot be costlessly acquired by other financial firms.

The fire-sale value of an asset is the price that can be received for an asset on short notice. Asymmetric information explains why the fire-sale value of a government security (in which all investors have the same information about its quality) is nearly 100 percent of its longer-run market price. Similarly, the fire-sale value of a corporate bond is much closer to its longer-run value than the fire-sale value of a personal loan.

Banks will tend to first sell off assets that might look good to purchasers but that the banks know are of poor quality. Because the marketplace anticipates this, asymmetric information causes some of a bank's assets to

sell at a large discount.[6] Therefore, when a bank run occurs, a financially sound but illiquid bank can conceivably become insolvent. A bank may be forced to sell off a high-quality asset in order to get quick cash, which may bring a low fire-sale value since information about the quality of the asset is not made public.

■ Cures for Contagious Bank Runs

The two principal methods the federal government uses to eliminate bank runs based on extraneous events are federal deposit insurance and discount lending by Federal Reserve Banks.

FDIC insurance has eliminated the need for most depositors to run on a bank, whether the run is caused by sunspots or by information that the bank has become insolvent. Federal Reserve Bank lending can minimize such runs because the Fed stands willing to provide "adjustment" or even extended credit to a solvent but troubled bank, so that it does not have to liquidate its assets at fire-sale prices.

Before the Federal Reserve Act, the pre-1914 banking industry was organized by a system of regional clearinghouses, whose powers and functions resembled those of a central bank. In many ways the Federal Reserve System was simply the nationalization of the private clearinghouses.

A study by Gorton indicates that the New York Clearing House was also a private deposit insurance company. It "taxed" sound banks in order to pay off depositors at a troubled bank.[7] The New York Clearing House also maintained capital requirements and reserve requirements and required banks to publish their balance sheet items. In addition, it could effectively shut down an insolvent bank.

These practices are similar to current proposals to allow private insurance companies or mutual insurance funds to insure banks. Critics of this approach argue that the insurance companies could fail with a contagion of bank runs, as were experienced during the Great Depression. However, branch banking, to some extent, enables a bank to insure itself. During the Great Depression, only one bank in California failed, and no banks in Canada failed—both areas in which branch banking was allowed.

How broad a role private insurance could play in our banking system is an open question. The recent crisis with the Ohio thrifts, in particular, seems to cast doubt on the ability of a private insurance system to protect against bank runs. In spring 1985, runs occurred on thrifts insured by the Ohio Deposit Guarantee Fund (ODGF) after the fund was depleted by the failure of the Home State Savings Bank.

Any viable private insurance scheme, however, would have to give the insurance company the right to cancel a contract or the right to close a bank. That is, it would have to resemble the functions of the private clearinghouses. The ODGF did not have the right to close its member thrifts when they became insolvent, however. Consequently, institutions like Home State Savings were not closed promptly.

Another way the New York Clearing House helped eliminate contagious bank runs was by suspending convertibility of deposits into specie or currency: a bank would stay open and make payments, but temporarily would not honor cash withdrawals. Although suspending convertibility was technically illegal, it was allowed to occur on at least eight occasions during the nineteenth and early twentieth centuries.

Gorton argues that "such accommodating behavior arose because suspension was part of a mutually beneficial arrangement." He maintains that by

suspending convertibility, banks signaled to depositors that further liquidation of the bank's assets was not in their best interests.[8] The ability to temporarily suspend convertibility not only helped to quell existing bank runs, but it also reduced the chance that a run based on extraneous information, or sunspots, could occur.

■ **Bank Runs During the Great Depression**

Another lesson can be learned by examining bank failures during the Great Depression. With the inception of the Federal Reserve System, suspension of convertibility did not occur (except for the government-imposed banking holidays). Friedman and Schwartz argue that "if the pre-Federal Reserve banking system had been in effect ... restriction (suspending convertibility) would have almost certainly taken place in September 1931 and very likely would have prevented at least the subsequent failures.[9]

Instead, the total suspension that eventually took place aggravated the situation. The haphazard ways in which states declared banking holidays in 1932 and 1933 further worsened the runs as depositors in open states rushed to get their money after neighboring states imposed holidays.[10]

Ironically, at its inception, the Federal Reserve System instituted a discount window in order to prevent banking panics. As argued earlier, discount lending lessens the incentives for banks to hold liquid assets, making banks more vulnerable to runs. Instead of lowering the discount rate in order to provide liquidity during the panics, the Federal Reserve raised the discount rate in September 1931 and again in February 1933.

Although the level of discount lending increased during the Great Depression, banks also had to dump

assets on the market to try to meet depositors' withdrawals.[11] The Federal Reserve System aggravated the situation by not actively pursuing open market operations in order to prevent a multiple contraction of the money supply.

■ **Conclusion**

Many agree that reform of the current banking structure is overdue. To their credit, bank regulators allowed nearly 200 insolvent banks to fail in 1987. Unfortunately, they may not be letting enough insolvent banks fail, and even when regulators close a bank, the FDIC sometimes employs a rescue procedure that protects the "uninsured" depositors.

Although reform of the present banking system may be desirable, a growing body of evidence indicates that many of the current financial problems in banking are at least partly the result of the incentive structure created by deposit insurance and by the way deposit insurance is administered.

Regulators contemplating reform of the banking system should consider the costs associated with federal deposit insurance. Left on its own, the private system provided many of the current safeguards considered necessary for a well-functioning banking system.

Charles T. Carlstrom is an economist at the Federal Reserve Bank of Cleveland. The author wishes to thank Walker Todd, James Thomson, John Scadding, William Gavin, and Mark Sniderman for their helpful comments.

The views stated herein are those of the author and not necessarily those of the Federal Reserve Bank of Cleveland or of the Board of Governors of the Federal Reserve System.

■ Footnotes

1. For a formal treatment of these types of bank runs, see Douglas W. Diamond and Philip H. Dybvig, "Bank Runs, Deposit Insurance, and Liquidity," *Journal of Political Economy,* vol. 91, no. 3 (June 1983), pp. 401-419.

2. See Charles Mackay, *Extraordinary Popular Delusions and the Madness of Crowds,* London: Richard Bentley, 1841. For a dissenting opinion to this popular belief, see Peter Garber, "Digging for the Roots of Tulipmania," *The Wall Street Journal,* January 4, 1988. He argues that the "tulip bubble" was not a bubble but in fact is explainable by market fundamentals.

3. See Gary Gorton, "Banking Panics and Business Cycles," Working Paper No. 86-9, Federal Reserve Bank of Philadelphia, March 1986.

4. See George J. Benston, Robert A. Eisenbeis, Paul M. Horvitz, Edward J. Kane, and George G. Kaufman, *Perspectives on Safe and Sound Banking: Past, Present, and Future,* Cambridge, MA: The MIT Press, 1986, p. 64.

5. See J. Huston McCulloch, "The Ohio S&L Crisis in Retrospect: Implications for the Current Federal Deposit Insurance Crisis," and Edward Kane, "Who Should Learn What from the Failure and Delayed Bailout of the ODGF?" in *Merging Commercial and Investment Banking: Proceedings of A Conference on Bank Structure and Competition,* Federal Reserve Bank of Chicago, May 1987.

6. That is, of a group of assets that seem identical, banks will sell off the least desirable of the assets first. In the case of a run, the bank will want to minimize the costs of getting quick cash and will first sell assets with no informational problems (such as government securities) and will then sell highly rated corporate bonds.

7. See Gary Gorton, "Clearinghouses and the Origin of Central Banking in the United States," *Journal of Economic History,* vol. 45, no. 2 (June 1985), pp. 277-284.

8. See Gary Gorton, "Bank Suspension of Convertibility," *Journal of Monetary Economics,* vol. 15, no. 2 (March 1985), pp. 177-194.

9. See Milton Friedman and Anna Jacobson Schwartz, *A Monetary History of the United States, 1867-1960,* Princeton, NJ: Princeton University Press, 1963, p. 316.

10. See Benston, et al., op. cit., p. 64.

11. See Friedman and Schwartz, op. cit., p. 318.

Article 9 _____

Troubled Banks and Thrifts

Our financial system has had many difficulties in recent years. Banks and thrifts have failed in record high numbers since the Great Depression; the Federal Savings and Loan Insurance Corporation faces financial troubles; and troubled institutions still are operating.

"Troubled" (insolvent or near-insolvent) institutions appear to be most prevalent in the thrift industry, but the banking sector is far from free of similar institutions. There are about 1,600 banks on the Federal Deposit Insurance Corporation's problem bank list. Moreover, since many institutions' book values exceed their market values, current book value accounting practices most likely understate the number of institutions that are insolvent on a market value basis.

This *Letter* examines the consequences of allowing troubled institutions to continue in operation — a policy known as capital forbearance. It argues that the best policy would be to require such institutions to bolster their capital and, if they were unable to do so, to sell or close those institutions. However, should such a policy be politically unfeasible, the second-best policy would be to limit the damage such institutions can inflict on the economy.

Underpriced deposit insurance
In a world of fixed-rate deposit insurance, under which a bank's or thrift's cost of insured deposits is independent of its risk-taking, regulation is needed to limit the exposure of the insurance fund. The reason is that an insured institution would earn profits on successful investment outcomes while the insurance fund would absorb losses that exceeded the institution's capital on unsuccessful ones.

In a system of full insurance coverage, insured institutions could earn virtually unlimited profits by attracting funds at a risk-free rate and investing them in higher yielding risky projects. That is, without regulation and under our current deposit insurance system (which underprices risk), insured financial institutions would expand at the expense of their uninsured competitors.

Market value closure
One way to contain such risk-taking is to require or induce insured institutions to hold sufficient capital, depending on their asset risk (credit and interest rate risk) and the length of time between supervisory examinations. Sufficient capital ensures that the institutions' equityholders, and not the insurance fund, bear the full risk of any loss. This principle underlies the current proposals for risk-based capital that would require banks with riskier asset portfolios to hold more capital. For example, if an institution can be closed before the market value of its net worth falls below zero, that institution's equityholders would bear the full consequences of its risk-taking.

Moreover, if institutions know with certainty that they will be sold or closed with a positive (market value) net worth (say, one percent of assets), and thus lose their capital in the process, they would have an incentive voluntarily to hold sufficient capital relative to the asset risk of their portfolios to avoid such regulatory "bankruptcy" costs. Even if this closure policy could not be implemented in such a way that banks always were closed before their net worth fell below zero, requiring more capital would still reduce the incentive of insured institutions to increase asset risk.

Such a system might have been able to forestall the severe difficulties our financial system faces today. But now, after the kind of trauma our depository industry has experienced over the last 15 years, it may be politically impossible to implement. What, then, should be done, and, in particular, how should weak or insolvent institutions be handled? Is it possible to move toward a market value closure rule without closing large numbers of institutions?

Insolvent institutions
Those insured institutions that are insolvent on a market value basis but are still operating pose the greatest risk to the deposit insurance funds, to solvent banks and thrifts, and to the stability of the entire financial system. To see why, consider the incentives of the owners of such institutions.

First, such institutions have very strong incentives to increase the riskiness of their asset portfolios. Since they stand to gain from profitable investments and loans but have no equity to lose if the investments and loans prove unprofitable, they will seek large payoffs that occur with low probabilities. Unfortunately, such "bet the bank" strategies are all too common. Moreover, such institutions will even undertake investments where the average return is less than the cost of their funds, as long as there is a chance of a payoff that exceeds the cost of their funds.

Second, such institutions have a strong incentive to expand assets funded with insured deposits. The reason is that a larger asset base increases their gain when investments are profitable. But, there is no countervailing loss when the investments are not profitable, as there would be for an uninsured institution. Moreover, insured institutions would be willing and able to pay above market rates for insured deposits in order to grow as rapidly as possible. This strategy of trying to "grow" out of past mistakes also is all too common.

The risks of these strategies for the deposit insurance funds are evident. Absent efforts to contain the risk-taking and expansionary behavior of insolvent institutions, only good luck will prevent the insurance funds themselves from facing ever-increasing losses.

Competing institutions

Less well-recognized are the implications of such behavior for solvent banks and thrifts competing with insolvent institutions. It is very difficult for solvent institutions that have positive capital to compete with insolvent ones that in effect are operating with no capital. Absent regulation, on the liability side, insolvent institutions will outbid solvent institutions to achieve rapid asset growth. Similarly, on the asset side, insolvent institutions will underbid solvent competitors by underpricing loans and other investments.

Since, under certain circumstances, insolvent institutions left unchecked would expand even when the expected return on their loans and investments is less than their cost of funds, solvent institutions themselves eventually may even be driven toward insolvency as they face market-determined asset returns that are too low to cover the cost of their liabilities.

As mentioned above, the best solution to these problems would be to sell or close insolvent institutions promptly. Doing so would not only contain the damage they can do to the financial system, but also provide a greater incentive for solvent institutions voluntarily to hold asset portfolios that are prudent in relation to their capital positions (to lessen the risk they would be sold or closed).

There is no economic benefit to protecting the owners of insolvent institutions. An institution is insolvent on a market value basis by definition only when its discounted expected cash payments (to depositors and other liability holders) exceed its expected discounted cash receipts (from loans and investments). Only an unexpected event will return such an institution to solvency.

As mentioned above, it may be politically impossible after-the-fact, to close a large number of institutions. The time for a strict closure policy is before institutions get into trouble, so that massive closures are not needed. Nevertheless, to contain the adverse effects such institutions can have, it is important that they be highly regulated.

Needed regulations

To keep troubled institutions from imposing even larger losses on the insurance funds and driving solvent competitors toward insolvency, they should not be permitted to grow or be allowed to increase the riskiness of their assets. One way to limit their potential harm would be to prohibit them from acquiring any new assets or issuing new insured liabilities. Although such a policy of "freezing" their assets and liabilities probably would force many of them to die a slow death as their loans matured, a slow death that contained losses is preferable to the potentially much larger losses that could occur absent asset growth and risk-taking restrictions.

Since the owners of such moribund institutions would have little incentive to run them efficiently, such stop-gap measures should be temporary while a buyer for the institution is sought. Although other policies, such as deposit rate ceilings for insured deposits (at the rate for comparable Treasury instruments, for example) and/or requiring additional capital for new growth, may be partly successful in containing the tendency of these institutions to grow, stringent asset portfolio risk restrictions still would be needed to contain the risk exposure of the deposit insurance system.

Troubled but still solvent

Although institutions that are insolvent on a market value basis pose the gravest threat to the insurance funds and the financial system, institutions near insolvency also pose a similar threat. For example, an institution with capital insufficient to protect the deposit insurance fund from losses in the event the institution's assets produce low returns has incentives similar to an insolvent institution. In fact, any institution that can shift potential losses onto the insurance agency (in excess of its deposit insurance premium) has incentives to grow and increase asset risk.

To reduce or eliminate these incentives for damaging behavior, weak institutions should be required to bolster their capital-to-asset ratios by an amount dependent on the riskiness of their asset portfolios.

Institutions could increase their capital ratios either by issuing new equity or perpetual subordinated debt, by selling assets and retiring insured deposits with the proceeds, or by retaining earnings (if available). From a regulatory perspective, an institution that refuses to bolster its capital or that cannot do so, should be treated just like an insolvent institution (i.e., ideally, it should be sold or closed; failing that, it should not be permitted to acquire any new assets).

It might be noted that increasing deposit insurance premium assessments of solvent institutions to bail out insolvent ones (for example, by raising the deposit insurance premium uniformly across all institutions) will not solve the basic problems discussed. Higher premiums unrelated to risk alone do nothing to contain the socially damaging risk-taking incentives of value-maximizing insolvent institutions. Moreover, higher premiums applied to only one sector of the industry, such as the current higher deposit insurance premium for thrifts, would cause that sector to shrink relative to sectors paying lower premiums, all other things equal.

Although solvent institutions should support policies such as those discussed above that limit destructive competition, weak or insolvent institutions may resist such policy actions because the actions reduce their shareholders' wealth. One way to lessen this resistance is to compensate shareholders at least partially by offering to enhance the franchise values of the institutions involved. For example, an expanded range of powers — such as investment banking, insurance sales and underwriting, and real estate investment and brokerage — could be allowed for firms that complied with more stringent capital and closure requirements. In fact, the proposed repeal of Glass-Steagall seems to be a step in this direction, although expanded powers under the proposal do not appear to be tied to more stringent capital regulation or closure policy.

Summary and conclusions

Solving the financial problems of some of our insured depository institutions will not be easy. With the advantage of hindsight, it is easy to see that such policies as market value closure and risk-based capital requirements, if they had been in place a number of years ago would have reduced the severity of today's problems.

Nevertheless, there are still measures that can be taken with regard to troubled institutions to ensure that problems do not worsen in the future. For one, troubled institutions should be required to bolster their (market value) capital ratios in relation to the risk of their portfolios (both credit and interest rate risk). If this is not possible, they should ideally be sold or closed, or at the very least not permitted to acquire new assets or insured deposits.

Institutions still operating even though they are insolvent on a market value basis pose a grave threat both to the solvency of the deposit insurance funds and to the stability and competitiveness of the rest of the depository industry. If left unchecked, such institutions, will expand and increase asset risk, conceivably even driving solvent institutions toward insolvency. Without strict regulation and supervision, solvent institutions that are weak in capital pose a similar threat.

The steps proposed here would go a long way toward containing the losses already incurred, and would allow the industry to make the transition to a new structure better able to deal with risk.

Michael C. Keeley

Reforming Deposit Insurance

The deposit insurance system is facing a crisis of historic proportions. The Federal Savings and Loan Insurance Corporation (FSLIC) is insolvent to the extent of at least $90 billion; bank and thrift failures are at record highs; the Federal Deposit Insurance Corporation (FDIC) just experienced its first-ever decline in reserves; and some economists think the FDIC's reserves may be inadequate.

Many blame these problems on adverse economic conditions, such as high and volatile interest rates and troubles in the farm belt and the oil patch. Others argue that unscrupulous bank and thrift management and inadequate supervision and regulation are to blame. And some fault deregulation, expansion of powers, and increases in the ceiling for deposit insurance coverage. All of these factors may have hastened the deterioration of the deposit insurance funds. They also may be partly responsible for the timing and intensity of the problem.

But economists have long argued that at the root of the current problem is an inherently flawed deposit insurance system. By employing a flat-rate pricing system that does not relate the insurance premium to the risks that are being insured, deposit insurance provides an incentive for excessive risk taking. This is the so-called "moral hazard" of deposit insurance.

This *Letter* evaluates ways to reform the deposit insurance and regulatory systems to eliminate this moral hazard. Such reform is vital to ensure that problems similar to those we are facing today do not recur.

Resolving current insolvencies
The obvious and necessary first step towards deposit insurance reform is to deal with the institutions that currently are insolvent or near-insolvent. Insolvencies should be resolved as quickly as possible, through liquidations or through acquisitions by strongly capitalized firms, whichever is least costly. And institutions near insolvency should be required to raise additional capital as soon as possible.

Although resolving current insolvencies quickly will help to limit the costs of the current problem, it will do little to ensure that similar problems do not recur. Thus, it is desirable to move beyond current difficulties to design a system that has desirable long-run properties.

A variety of reforms have been proposed. In general, these proposals fall into one of two main categories. The first involves enhancing depositor surveillance of institutions' risk taking. The second focuses on providing bank capital holders with appropriate incentives to control risk taking. Because enhanced depositor surveillance might reduce banking system stability, I argue that it would be better to strengthen bank capital and ensure that banks maintain sufficient capital over time to absorb losses.

Depositor surveillance
Depositor surveillance of bank and thrift risk taking could be enhanced in many different ways. For example, the ceiling for insurance coverage could be lowered from $100,000 to $40,000, or even $20,000. Alternatively, co-insurance could be instituted, whereby each deposit account would be only partially insured. Or insurance coverage could be limited to deposits used to fund risk-free assets such as Treasury securities. This last approach, known as the "narrow banking" proposal, would in effect shift the saving-lending intermediation functions banks now perform to uninsured institutions.

There is no doubt that such measures would induce at least some depositors to monitor carefully the health of banks and thrifts and thus would penalize those institutions that undertake excessive risks by requiring them to pay higher deposit rates. However, almost by definition, increased depositor surveillance also means that institutions will be exposed to an increased risk of depositor runs. Not only would the probability of runs on individual institutions increase, but perhaps the entire banking *system* would become less stable. Even under the narrow bank proposal banking stability could be threatened since "wide banks," where the actual saving-lending intermediation would take place, would have no deposit insurance. A less stable banking system could, in turn, lead to a less stable financial system and economy.

Some proponents of diminished depositor protection argue that scaling back deposit insurance coverage would cause only a *little* more banking instability, and that a little more instability would be a small price to pay for reducing the moral hazard for excessive risk taking. But it is questionable whether there is such a thing as just a little instability—partial coverage might lead to nearly the same degree of instability as no coverage.

Eliminate deposit insurance?
Others go even further and argue that a run on an individual bank would *not* lead to runs on other banks. They argue that since an increased likelihood of runs would not lead to an unstable banking *system* or an unstable economy, there is no fundamental economic reason for deposit insurance. Moreover, eliminating deposit insurance altogether has the advantage that it eliminates the incentive for excessive risk taking, whereas proposals to merely scale back coverage do not.

The notion that government deposit insurance is not necessary to ensure banking system stability is not universally accepted, even among free-market economists. And there is contrary theoretical and empirical evidence in support of a centralized deposit insurance system. Thus, it seems unlikely that the debate over whether deposit insurance performs a vital economic function will be resolved any time soon.

Perhaps even more important, proposals to eliminate deposit insurance do not seem to have much popular appeal. The public has grown used to a system in which bank runs do not occur. Neither the public nor the Congress is likely to embrace proposals that solve the deposit insurance problem by increasing the likelihood of runs. This is especially so in light of the history of banking panics and runs in the U.S. prior to the advent of deposit insurance.

In lieu of increased depositor surveillance of institutions' risk taking, some have advocated stronger direct limitations on risk taking. But most economists argue that such an approach is ineffective when there are strong countervailing economic incentives. It usually is more effective to alter the underlying incentives. In essence, this means that appropriate incentives must be given to those providing non-deposit sources of funds —either equity holders, other liability holders, or both—to police risk taking.

Market-value capital
One way to change underlying incentives would be to institute risk-based insurance premia. While sound in principle, most economists believe such an approach is currently not feasible. An alternative would be to provide insured institutions with incentive to maintain strong market-value capital positions. Capital provides a buffer to depositors and the insurance funds against fluctuations in the values of bank and thrift portfolios. The more capital, the greater the protection against loss. And higher capital actually *reduces* banks' incentives to increase asset risk. With more of their own capital at risk, bank and thrift owners will be more concerned about potential losses from the risks they take. In contrast, the owners of an institution with very little capital have strong incentives to engage in bet-the-bank, go-for-broke strategies since they enjoy all the gains if their investments fare well, but only a fraction of the losses if their investments perform poorly.

For capital regulations to be fully effective, it is essential that capital be measured on a current, or market-value, basis, not on the historical cost, or book-value, basis used now. Market-value capital is the difference between the market values of an institution's assets and liabilities. In essence, this means that regulators need to mark down (or up) the values of an institution's assets and liabilities to reflect changes in interest rates and/or credit risk. Marking institutions' assets and liabilities to their current values is essential because it is the current value, not the past value, that determines the insurer's exposure and influences an institution's risk-taking incentives. Market-value capital has the added advantage that it cannot be manipulated to disguise institutions' true financial health as easily as book-value measures can.

A market test
To provide depository institutions with incentives

to maintain sufficient market-value capital ratios, institutions whose capital fell below some predetermined amount, say, 10 percent, would be subjected to a market test of their solvency. An institution with capital below 10 percent would be required to bring its capital ratio back up to standard within a short time. A market-value solvent institution should have no trouble raising its capital ratio, either by issuing new capital securities or by selling assets and using the proceeds to retire liabilities. Moreover, the possibility that the market might misjudge an institution's true solvency would give it an incentive to hold more capital in the first place.

If the institution could not raise its market-value capital ratio, this would be *prima facie* evidence that it was market-value insolvent, and regulators would need to take prompt action to liquidate or sell it. There is little economic rationale for allowing insured institutions that are unable to maintain their capital ratios above some prudent level to continue in operation. In fact, allowing them to do so can greatly increase the risk exposure of the insurance fund.

A number of objections have been raised to this type of proposal. However, each of these objections can be addressed. First, many argue that market value capital regulation simply is not feasible, primarily because many of banks' assets are loans for which there are not readily ascertainable market values. However, market participants routinely evaluate the values of banks' portfolios when they purchase and sell bank equity, subordinated debt, and other securities. Thus, while market-value accounting may never be perfect, it need not be so for market-value capital regulation to be effective, as the behavior of private investors in bank and thrift securities seems to attest.

Second, some argue that there may be ethical or even legal problems with giving regulators the authority to close institutions that are not book-value insolvent. An alternative would be to grant the insuring agency authority to promptly remove a poorly-capitalized institution's insurance guarantee, giving existing insured depositors a reasonable chance to withdraw their deposits if they so desired. In fact, the FDIC has requested such

authority in its reform proposal. Although such an approach probably would force insolvent (and possibly even some marginally solvent) institutions into bankruptcy, it would not precipitate runs since deposit insurance would remain in force for existing depositors.

Third, it is argued that equity capital is a far more costly source of funds than insured deposits. Consequently, heavy reliance on equity capital could cause the banking industry to become less profitable and shrink. But one of the reasons that equity capital now appears to be more costly is that deposit insurance is underpriced, at least for institutions that are financially weak. And even if equity capital were *truly* more expensive, it is possible to permit institutions to count long-term subordinated debt (which cannot run) as regulatory capital.

A final problem is ensuring that bank and thrift regulators have the incentive and the wherewithal (in the form of adequate reserves) to strictly enforce market-value capital standards. If the current incentives are not deemed sufficient, regulators could be subjected to specific penalties for failure to strictly enforce capital requirements and/or provides specific rewards for strict enforcement.

Credible commitment

Strengthening capital requirements and subjecting banks and thrifts to market tests of solvency would provide insured institutions with incentives to maintain strong capital ratios. Such an approach has considerable appeal as a way to reduce the moral hazard of deposit insurance. However, for this or any other reform to succeed, it is essential that bank and thrift regulators credibly commit themselves to strictly follow a policy that alters the risk-taking behavior of bank and thrift managers. Regulatory reform cannot succeed if bank and thrift executives know that they can pursue high-risk strategies and then invoke special exceptions or expect forbearance. In fact, it was just such forbearance that got us into the mess we are in today.

Michael C. Keeley
Research Officer

Article 11

The Thrift Insurance Crisis

Since its founding in 1934, the Federal Savings and Loan Insurance Corporation (FSLIC) has helped to prevent depositor runs and panics at the thrift institutions it insures. Beginning in the early 1980s, however, the FSLIC has faced a growing threat to its ability to perform this function. Indeed, with the number of thrift failures and insolvencies at unheard-of levels, the FSLIC is now insolvent to the extent of about $90 billion, according to Treasury Department estimates. This *Letter* discusses why we are faced with a problem of this magnitude and how we might pay for its resolution.

Thrift failures

The large, unexpected rise in interest rates from late 1979 through 1981 was the catalyst for the crisis the thrift industry and the FSLIC now face (although the rise in interest rates through the entire latter half of the 1970s left the industry in a vulnerable position). During this period, the cost of many thrifts' deposits exceeded the yield on the long-term fixed-rate mortgages they held. This negative interest spread meant that the market value of these institutions' assets had fallen below that of their liabilities. Thus, except for the thrifts with large equity capital cushions, much of the rest of the industry was insolvent on a market-value basis in 1981, even though the book, or historical, values of assets and liabilities tended to camouflage the problem. Moreover, if the FSLIC had tried at this point to liquidate all the market-value insolvent thrifts, it would have been bankrupt as well.

These weak and insolvent thrifts faced enormous incentives to pursue high-risk strategies. With little or none of their own money at stake any longer, owners of these institutions faced a "heads-I-win, tails-you-lose" situation. If their high-risk, high-return investments panned out, they stood to profit handsomely. And if their investments fared poorly, the burden fell on the FSLIC. At the same time, the FSLIC itself was also market-value insolvent and lacked the resources to resolve the problems quickly. Thus, a policy of capital forbearance was pursued in the hope that interest rates would decline and the industry

would be restored to solvency. This approach enabled weakened institutions to continue to operate and take even greater risks. Also, Congress relaxed restrictions on thrift activities, thereby providing new opportunities for risk-taking in activities that regulators were unaccustomed to monitoring. These factors all increased the risk exposure of the already weakened insurance fund.

To make matters worse, during this period the thrift industry also faced stiffer competition from banks and even nonbank financial firms that became major providers of home mortgages. This reduced thrifts' interest margins and profitability, which, in turn, further eroded thrifts' capital base, thus providing an additional incentive for risk taking.

This confluence of economic and regulatory events exposed a fatal flaw in the deposit insurance system. By charging insurance premiums unrelated to risk, deposit insurance provides an incentive for excessive risk taking. This incentive grows larger as institutions approach insolvency. Thus, once the FSLIC no longer had sufficient resources to close insolvent institutions, it was no surprise that weak and insolvent institutions created a large and growing problem.

How big is the problem?

Until recently, thrift industry spokesmen tended to play down the extent of the problem. But others argued that thrift losses were substantial. These divergent estimates tended to confuse policymakers and the public. Although Congress authorized a $10.8 billion increase in FSLIC borrowing in 1987 to resolve thrift insolvencies, that amount proved, in hindsight, woefully inadequate.

Currently, the estimates are converging at about $90 to $100 billion—staggering figures by any measure. Still, some economists argue the costs could be as high as $200 billion. The ultimate tally depends on the number of market-value insolvent thrifts and the extent to which they are insolvent. Although the number of book-value insolvencies and book-value net worth are available, the FSLIC's cost when it liquidates or reorganizes a failed thrift is equal to the difference between the prices the institution's assets and liabilities can be sold for on the open market. Book accounting values have little relevance in a liquidation.

Through the end of 1988, the FSLIC had resolved over 200 savings and loan insolvencies, at an estimated total cost of approximately $40 billion. A small number of these resolutions entailed liquidations but the majority involved merger, reorganization, or purchase-of-asset and assumption-of-liability arrangements. In a liquidation, the FSLIC generally liquidates the thrift's assets and pays off the insured depositors, thereby incurring costs equal to the difference between the market values of the assets and liabilities. Alternatively, when the FSLIC reorganizes an ailing thrift or arranges for another institution to take control, it typically provides funds to bring the acquired thrift's market-value net worth close to zero as a necessary inducement to the acquirer. Also, the FSLIC may make guarantees to protect the acquirer against potential future losses, which can result in additional future costs to the FSLIC.

The Bush plan
In the plan recently presented by the Bush Administration, officials estimate that an additional $50 billion is needed to resolve the remaining involvencies. This figure brings the total cost to more than $90 billion. This amount is in line with several other estimates, including that of the FDIC, and is a reasonable benchmark measure of the current size of the FSLIC insolvency (that is, the aggregate negative net worth of insolvent institutions).

It is essential to distinguish between the current size of the insolvency and the stream of funds that might finance a solution to that problem over time. There are several ways this $90 billion could be financed. For example, the entire amount could be funded through the issuance of 30-year, 10 percent bonds. $9 billion per year would be needed to cover interest costs. If the $90 billion principal on these bonds were not amortized, it would be due in 30 years. One way to meet that obligation would be to purchase 30-year, zero-coupon bonds, as the Administration has proposed. In this case, an additional $5.2

billion would be needed to purchase the zero-coupon bonds, which, at an interest rate of 10 percent, would be worth $90 billion in 30 years.

Thrift industry resources
It is frequently argued that the savings and loan industry holds the primary responsibility for the current crisis and, therefore, should bear the burden of resolving the problem. Even if this is so, the industry's resources are inadequate.

As of mid-year 1988, thrifts that were solvent according to generally accepted accounting principles (GAAP) had a net worth of only $34 billion excluding goodwill. Taking this as an estimate of market-value net worth (even though regulatory incentives result in book net worth that generally overstates market-value net worth), the $34 billion would cover only a fraction of the estimated cost of the FSLIC bailout. Thus, even if all the net worth in the thrift industry could be taxed, the proceeds would be inadequate. And it is unreasonable to suppose such a draconian tax could be imposed while still preserving the industry.

A similar conclusion holds when one considers the thrift industry's ability to bear the financing costs. The Administration's plan to raise the insurance premium thrifts pay to 23 cents per $100 of total liabilities would yield about $2.9 billion per year, based on the industry's total liability base as of June 1988. Even if all this premium income could be used to service the bonds, $2.9 billion is a far cry from the $9 billion annual funding needed.

And even these premium figures are optimistic because they assume no loss of deposits at thrift institutions. Recent evidence is inconsistent with this assumption. In December 1988, there was an outflow of deposit liabilities at insured thrifts of about $8 billion. Similarly, in January and February, deposits fell by $10.7 billion and $8–9 billion, respectively. And this drawdown of deposits continues apace in March. Moreover, it will be extremely hard for thrifts to maintain their deposit base in the long run since banks would be paying a much lower premium of 15 cents per hundred, to say nothing of nondepository competitors that pay no insurance premium. In any event, it probably will not be possible to use all the premium income to service the interest cost of the bonds since some will be needed to resolve future thrift failures. Also it would be prudent to set some aside to build a reserve fund, as the Bush plan proposes.

Some have proposed tapping the net worth of the Federal Home Loan Banks to raise additional funds. Since the Home Loan Banks are owned by the thrift industry, this would reduce the net worth of thrifts commensurately. Tapping the Home Loan Banks' net worth or retained earnings is a viable way to tax the thrifts' net worth, but the Banks are not an independent source of funds.

Who else might pay?
It is obvious that the thrift industry itself does not have sufficient resources to pay the total cost of resolving the FSLIC's insolvency. Some have argued that insurance premiums paid by commercial banks to their insuring agency, the Federal Deposit Insurance Corporation (FDIC), might be an appropriate source of funds. Domestic deposits of all FDIC-insured banks in the United States were approximately $2 trillion as of the middle of 1988. At the proposed premium of 15 cents per $100 of deposits, these deposits would produce about $3 billion in premium income each year.

Even if the banks' entire $3 billion premium income *could* be used for this purpose, the combined bank and thrift premium income still would not pay the $9 billion annual interest on the bonds used to resolve current thrift insolvencies. Moreover, the Bush plan calls for using the larger bank insurance premium only to increase the reserves of the FDIC. This is appropriate, considering that the number of bank failures is at a record high and the FDIC's reserves per deposit dollar are near an all-time low.

It might be conceivable to raise sufficient revenues for the FSLIC problem by subjecting the banking industry to further taxes. However, such taxes would impose a tremendous burden on the industry. Banks would face a large competitive disadvantage relative to money market funds and other financial firms that could offer bank-like services without the regulatory burden of the additional tax. Moreover, from equity considerations, there seems little reason to single out the banking industry now and in the future to pay for past thrift insolvencies.

In the final analysis, if the deposit insurance guarantees are to be honored, several billion dollars of additional funds per year must be obtained from another source, presumably general taxpayers. It is important to allocate sufficient funds to resolve current thrift insolvencies quickly. Delay will increase the ultimate cost since the longer insolvent and near-insolvent thrifts continue in operation, the greater will be their losses from excessive risk taking.

Never again
Equally important is the need to ensure that *future* thrift insolvencies will not require the use of general taxpayers' funds. The Administration proposal takes several important steps in this direction, mainly by imposing more stringent capital adequacy and regulatory standards on thrifts. Moreover, it proposes a detailed study of long-term deposit insurance reform.

The goal of such long-term reform should be to eliminate the incentives the bank and thrift insurance funds provide for excessive risk taking. Many approaches to reform are possible. The main issue is to ensure that if banks and thrifts choose to take risks, their owners' funds are on the line, and not the taxpayers'.

Michael Keeley
Research Officer

Jonathan Neuberger
Economist

Monetary Policy Objectives for 1989
Federal Reserve Chairman Alan Greenspan presented a report to the Congress on the Federal Reserve's monetary policy objectives for 1989 on February 21. The report includes a summary of the Federal Reserve's monetary policy plans along with a review of economic and financial developments in 1988 and the economic outlook in 1989. Single or multiple copies of the report can be obtained upon request from the Public Information Department, Federal Reserve Bank of San Francisco, P.O. Box 7702, San Francisco, CA 94120; phone (415) 974-2246.

Article 12

The FSLIC Bailout and the Economy

The Bush Administration's proposal for raising the funds to cover deposit liabilities at hundreds of insolvent thrifts is gathering momentum in the Congress. One provision would raise $50 billion "off budget" through bonds issued by a federally-sponsored agency. (That debt would add to the nearly $40 billion in liabilities already amassed by the Federal Savings and Loan Insurance Corporation—FSLIC—in handling insolvent institutions prior to this year.) The principal on the bonds issued by the federal agency would be covered by zero coupon bonds that would be purchased with resources from the thrift industry. However, the Treasury would be responsible for most of the interest. (See *Letter* of March 31, 1989.)

This raises a question: if the cost of servicing this debt really is the Treasury's obligation, shouldn't the liability be "booked," that is, put on the federal budget and added to the federal budget deficit? On this question, Martin Feldstein recently argued that this debt legitimately belongs off budget since debt financing of FSLIC expenses will not affect aggregate demand, raise interest rates, nor crowd out private investment.

This *Letter* shows that this argument is true only in a narrow context. The actual issuance of agency bonds merely would "book" government debt that, in effect, already has been incurred. However, in a broader context, because the method of financing government spending seems to affect saving and spending decisions, government debt incurred in connection with deposit insurance liabilities *does* have macroeconomic consequences. Accordingly, steps should be taken to ensure that in the future changes in the expected expenses of the deposit insurance system are not ignored in the federal budget process.

Redistribution of losses

Thrifts become insolvent when the value of their assets falls below that of their liabilities. To society as a whole, such a decline in value represents a loss of wealth, which in itself should have a negative effect on aggregate demand. Deposit insurance cannot diminish the size of this loss. But the existence of deposit insurance and the method used to finance it may affect the incidence of the loss, by protecting depositors of failed institutions and placing the burden on others in the economy.

Payouts by the deposit insurance fund, then, can be viewed as transfer payments to depositors. When the reserves of the deposit insurance fund are inadequate to cover these payouts, as in the case of the FSLIC currently, funds have to be raised from other sources. To the extent that the solvent portion of the industry cannot raise the needed funds, taxpayers may be called on to bear a share of the losses in order to honor the deposit guarantees.

Raising taxes

Such a transfer would mean that depositors as a group would be better off than if they were not insured, but current taxpayers generally would be worse off. With no net change in wealth, this transfer should not have any *additional* effect on aggregate spending and interest rates, assuming depositors' tastes regarding spending and saving broadly reflected those of society as a whole. This argument suggests that although the actual loss in wealth has an effect on the economy, shifting the burden of that loss from one group (depositors) to another (taxpayers) should not have an impact.

A simple numerical example can help illustrate the economic consequences of financing FSLIC expenses through taxation. Consider first the case where no deposit insurance is provided. Starting with a healthy thrift industry that holds $100 million in loans funded by $90 million in deposits and $10 million in capital, household wealth is $100 million (since deposits and thrift stock are both assets). If an economic catastrophe were to reduce the value of the thrift industry's loans by $30 million, the industry would be insolvent and household wealth would decline by $30 million. Without deposit insurance, depositors would absorb $20 million of losses and equity holders would absorb $10 million.

When deposit insurance costs are financed through current taxes, the outcome in terms of private credit and household wealth is identical to that for the case of no deposit insurance. To make depositors whole, the government would pay out $20 million, increasing taxes by an equal amount to cover the liability. Thus, household wealth would decline by $30 million: $10 million from the loss in the value of the thrift industry's stock and $20 million associated with the increase in taxes. The thrift industry would hold $70 million in loans and total deposits would equal $70 million. Thus, the volume of private credit and household wealth would be unaffected by deposit insurance when it is financed through current taxes. As a consequence, an FSLIC bailout financed through taxes should not affect the economy.

Debt financing

How does this scenario change when the FSLIC shortfall is covered by issuing government debt? Some have argued that budget deficits have the same economic consequences as raising taxes. When faced with a future tax liability associated with an increase in government borrowing today, so this argument goes, rational households will increase their current saving to generate sufficient resources to cover the higher future tax liability. As a result, spending will be curtailed by the same amount as if current taxes had been raised. The bonds held by households would not increase wealth since there would be an offsetting increase in future tax liabilities. Thus, using debt to finance the FSLIC bailout would not be stimulative.

An extension of the earlier example will help to illustrate this point. Instead of raising taxes by $20 million to cover the loss to depositors, assume that the government issues $20 million in bonds and gives these bonds directly to the thrifts. In this case, deposit liabilities would total $90 million and assets would total $90 million—$70 million in loans and $20 million in government bonds. As in the case of tax-financed deposit insurance, household net wealth would decline by the $10 million capital loss and by the $20 million future tax liability that the bonds represent.

Changing the example so that the government sells the bonds to the public does not alter these results. For example, households could purchase the $20 million in government bonds and the government then would inject cash into the thrift industry to make up the loss to depositors. Assuming households draw down their holdings of deposits to purchase the bonds, the net result would be that the thrift industry would have $70 million in loans and the public would have $70 million in deposits. The $20 million in bonds held as assets by households would be balanced by a future tax liability of $20 million. Thus, household wealth still would decline by $30 million.

However, other economists have argued that households may not perceive their net worth as declining by the full $30 million, particularly if some of this future tax burden falls on future generations and current households place a higher value on their own spending than they do on the spending of future generations. In this case, households probably will not increase their saving to compensate fully for higher future taxes. As a result, government budget deficits would transfer wealth from future generations to the current generation.

In the two debt-financing examples above, if current households ignore entirely the liability created by the government debt, the effective decline in wealth for current households would be only $10 million, the value of the thrift stock, rather than $30 million. The $20 million in government bonds would be perceived as adding to current household wealth since the expected rise in taxes in the future would not be perceived as a liability. In the near term, this smaller decline in household wealth would mean higher aggregate demand and interest rates than if current taxes had been increased.

The examples show that depositors and thrift stockholders are not any better or any worse off when insurance costs are financed through government debt rather than through taxes. The difference between the two methods of financing deposit insurance lies in the way current taxpayers view the future tax liability connected with the $20 million in government debt. On the one hand, if current taxpayers treat the future taxes as a current liability, there will be no difference between tax-financed and debt-financed deposit insurance. On the other, if current taxpayers do not view themselves as liable for the future tax burden, debt financing can affect current wealth, inducing more current spending and less future spending. In the near term, this would be stimulative and would boost interest rates relative to the levels that would have prevailed if deposit insurance were financed through current taxes.

The experience in the 1980s suggests that households do not adjust saving fully to compensate for an increase in future tax liabilities. Since 1982, the federal budget deficit has increased very sharply, but the U.S. saving rate has continued to decline. This evidence suggests that an increase in government borrowing *does* affect aggregate demand over and above the effects on demand from an increase in government spending.

Booking the debt
Thus, government debt incurred in covering the deposits of insolvent thrifts does have economic consequences. This does not mean, however, that the *act* of issuing the $50 billion in bonds to assist the FSLIC will have an impact. Since most of the problem thrifts have been insolvent for some time, the expenses and government debt *already* have been incurred as far as their economic consequences are concerned. Executing the plan to assist the FSLIC merely would book the debt, and should have no additional impact unless the amount of debt issued is materially different from that expected.

Treasury or agency?
Part of the debate in the Congress concerns using a federal agency rather than the Treasury to issue the $50 billion in bonds. By using a federal agency to issue the debt, the proceeds from the bonds would be treated as revenue that offsets FSLIC's expenses. Although federal agency debt is somewhat more costly than direct Treasury debt, the practical appeal of this approach is that it would be easier to meet the Gramm-Rudman-Hollings targets for the federal budget deficit.

The use of agency, or off-budget, debt also has been rationalized on the grounds that the "new" debt has no economic consequences. Although this argument technically is true in the sense that booking debt that already has been incurred should have no further consequences, it fails to acknowledge the real economic impact of this previously unbooked liability. Thus, if there is an economic rationale for issuing the bonds on an off-budget basis, it is merely that two wrongs do not make a right. That is, it was wrong to exclude the unbooked expenses of the FSLIC from past budgets. That wrong cannot be corrected by increasing budget deficits in the immediate future to reflect *past* losses.

Fundamental problem
The more fundamental problem with the argument that using debt to finance FSLIC expenses does not have economic consequences is that it provides erroneous guidance concerning how *future* "unbooked" deposit insurance liabilities should be handled. This argument implies that since debt incurred by the government (or the FSLIC) does not have economic consequences, it is okay in the budget process to ignore unbooked expenses incurred by the FSLIC in the future. The analysis in this *Letter* suggests the opposite; debt financing (whether implicit or explicit) *does* affect the economy and should be taken into consideration.

In principle, then, any increase in the expected cost to the deposit insurance system of resolving problems in the future should be included in the federal budget as a current expense, in accordance with generally accepted accounting practices. Alternatively, regular deposit insurance premia should not be counted as future federal revenues since, in theory, such premia merely reflect the change in the value of the future unbooked liabilities of the deposit insurance system. However, in its estimates of the budget effects of the Administration's proposal to assist the FSLIC, the Office of Management and Budget includes *future* deposit insurance premia from both banks and thrifts as revenue that offsets FSLIC expenses in resolving *current* problem thrift cases. Such treatment of these insurance premia means that the true macroeconomic impact of changes in deposit insurance liabilities will not be reflected in future federal budgets.

Fred Furlong
Research Officer

Part Three

Determination of Interest Rates and Stock Prices

One of the most challenging tasks faced by business managers and households is to anticipate changes in interest rates and changes in the value of stocks, bonds, and other securities in order to make informed decisions about saving and borrowing money. The challenge is even greater for managers of financial institutions because changing interest rates and security prices profoundly affect the value of institutional assets as well as the income of all financial institutions. Clearly, the ability to successfully *predict* interest rate and security price changes would be of incalculable value. Businesses and consumers would know exactly when to borrow to minimize their borrowing costs. Individual investors and financial institutions would know exactly when to sell their holdings of stocks, bonds, and other financial instruments and when to add new securities to their portfolios.

Unfortunately, predicting interest rates and stock prices is treacherous business. Most financial analysts are convinced today that the best most investors and borrowers can do is to anticipate the near-term *direction* (but not the magnitude) of interest rate and security price changes. Hedging instruments (such as financial futures contracts) can then be used to protect against loss in case rates and prices move in an unexpected direction or change by a far greater magnitude than originally anticipated. However, to successfully predict at least the direction of interest rate and security price movements, we must know more about the fundamental forces that shape conditions in the financial markets where securities are traded and loans are made. This is the purpose of Part Three and the articles it contains.

The opening reading, "Challenges to the Concept of Stock Market Efficiency," contains an excellent review of the literature on what forces seem to affect stock prices. This first article, by Douglas Pearce, focuses on a perennial issue: Is the stock market really efficient? Certainly this is a vitally important question because stock prices affect the ability of business firms to expand plant and equipment. Stock prices also send out important signals to savers about the potential rewards from supplying savings to the credit markets so the economy can grow and produce more in the future. However, there is continuing dispute over whether stock price movements conform to the "efficient markets" model in which all available information is used to value stocks and other securities, and security prices are assumed to respond almost instantaneously to *new* information. If the stock market is truly "efficient" in this sense, then investors can expect to earn no more, on average, than a normal rate of return given the amount of risk exposure they face. Pearce finds that the weight of evidence, after many years of research, *does* tend to support the assumptions and conclusions of the efficient markets model.

In the second article, the possible linkages between the stock market and inflation are explored in depth by two economists, David P. Ely and Kenneth J. Robinson, writing for the Federal Reserve Bank of Dallas. *Inflation*, as economists understand the term today, refers to a rise in the average level of prices of all goods and services produced and traded in the economy. The fundamental issue pursued by Ely and Robinson in "The Stock Market and Inflation: A Synthesis of the Theory and Evidence," is why stock prices often decline or display little growth during periods of inflation. Because a share of stock represents a claim against the income and real assets of a corporation, we might expect that stock prices would rise along with rising asset prices and corporate incomes that *are* sensitive to inflation. However, there is much evidence from several countries that stock prices are not necessarily good inflation hedges. Economists Ely and Robinson examine two possible reasons for this unexpected result—the burden of tax laws and the money and credit policies of modern governments.

For example, price inflation may also inflate corporate profits because the depreciation of equipment and the cost of business inventories is usually based on historical cost rather than current market prices. Thus, these two important sources of business expense become understated in periods of inflation and profits become overstated, increasing the amount of income taxes owed by the individual firm. Then, too, government efforts to tighten credit in inflationary periods and to issue greater amounts of public debt that may be *monetized* by the central bank also may depress stock prices even as inflationary pressures are growing.

Craig Hakkio of the Federal Reserve Bank of Kansas City turns our attention to yet another key issue for public policy, business managers, and private investors today. His article, "Interest Rates and Exchange Rates—What Is the Relationship?" looks carefully at the correlation between interest rate movements and the value of the dollar in international markets, searching for the underlying factors that influence both currency prices and market interest rates. This issue is particularly puzzling because interest rates and currency prices were negatively correlated during much of the 1970s, only to become positively correlated through much of the 1980s. Hakkio concludes that inflation and real interest rates influence both nominal (published) interest rates and currency prices. Moreover, the relative importance of these two factors appears to have changed over time. Inflationary shocks seem to have been dominant in the 1970s, while real interest-rate movements appear to have played the leading role over the past decade, shifting the correlation between loan rates and currency values.

Finally, a related article by Bruce Kasman and Charles Pigott, writing for the Federal Reserve Bank of New York, helps to broaden our understanding of interest rate movements by focusing on the relative interest rates prevailing in leading industrial countries, including the United States, Canada, Germany, Japan, and the United Kingdom. Recent globalization of financial markets suggests that differences in interest rates between countries should be narrowing. To the contrary, however, interest-rate differences have not declined and, in some cases, are larger than before. Economists Kasman and Pigott believe that expected changes in currency prices explain much of the discrepancy in interest rates from country to country. The risk of adverse currency price movements has risen recently in an era of more flexible exchange rates even as another key factor in interest-rate determination—government regulation—has declined in relative importance. In the future the spread between interest rates from nation to nation will depend heavily on how effectively the world's leading countries can coordinate their domestic economic policies.

Article 13

Challenges to the Concept Of Stock Market Efficiency

By Douglas K. Pearce

Stock prices have risen about 75 percent since the end of 1984. The tremendous surge in the average price of stocks has been accompanied by large daily fluctuations and historically high trading volumes. Not surprisingly, such activity has spurred new interest in the question of what underlies these movements in stock prices. In particular, are stock price movements quick and appropriate responses to new information about economic conditions? This question is often phrased: Is the stock market efficient? Despite some apparent anomalies, this article concludes that the preponderance of evidence supports the view that the stock market is efficient.

The issue of the efficiency of the stock market has significant consequences for the economy. Since stock price movements affect the cost of financing capital expansion and give managers of firms a direct evaluation of their performance,

stock prices are thought to be important signals for the efficient allocation of a country's savings. Faith in the appropriateness of signals from the stock market is based on the belief that stock prices reflect the well-informed opinions of investors about the future profitability of businesses. As economist William Baumol has stated:

> If security prices were divorced from earnings potential, the stock market could not be expected to serve as an effective disciplinary force capable of pressing management to maintain the efficiency of company operations.[1]

The belief that stock prices depend on investors' expectations of profits is generally referred to as the "fundamental model" or "intrinsic value model" of stock prices. According to this model, stock prices equal the present or discounted value of future dividends.

The concept of stock market "efficiency" is also used in a different but related context.

Douglas K. Pearce is an associate professor of economics and business at North Carolina State University. The views expressed in this article are those of the author and do not necessarily reflect the views of the Federal Reserve Bank of Kansas City or the Federal Reserve System.

[1] Baumol (1965), p. 36. For the full citation for this book and other studies cited in this article, see the list of references at the end of the article.

According to the "efficient markets" theory of stock prices, stock prices accurately reflect all information that is available about the future profitability of firms. When new information comes available, stock prices rapidly adjust to their new equilibrium levels. The basic implication of this model is that investors cannot use available information to generate expected returns in excess of a normal return on the risk they bear. It might be said that the efficient markets model is simply another version of the economic rule that there are no free lunches.

Many observers of the stock market scoff at the notion that the stock market is efficient. They argue that stock price movements reflect short-run speculative waves of optimism or pessimism that, at best, are weakly tied to forecasts of profits. The stock market is likened to a gambling parlor and stock price changes to the outcomes from a roulette wheel. These commentators often quote Keynes' famous remark that "when the capital development of a country becomes a by-product of the activities of a casino, the job is likely to be ill-done."[2] When the stock market is volatile, this argument is raised to support the need for an industrial policy in which the government plays a larger role in allocating capital.

Skepticism about the efficiency of the stock market has been bolstered by several recent challenges to the empirical validity of the efficient markets model. These challenges are of two kinds. First, some researchers report instances in which stock returns do not behave according to the predictions of the efficient markets theory because investors can use available information to earn "excess" profits. Second, other researchers argue that stock price movements are much too volatile to be compatible with the efficient markets model. It has even been suggested that if "excess volatility" characterizes stock prices,

the Federal Reserve should reduce volatility through open market operations in the stock market.[3]

This article reviews these recent challenges to the efficiency of the stock market. The first section reviews the fundamental model of stock prices and its relationship to the efficient markets model. The second section discusses the empirical implications of the efficient markets model and examines evidence that stock returns do not conform with these implications. The third section analyzes recent research on whether stock price fluctuations are excessively volatile.

The efficient markets model of stock prices

The fundamental or traditional model of stock prices starts with the assumption that stock prices depend on the anticipated profits of firms. The efficient markets model makes additional assumptions about what information investors use in forming their expectations.

The fundamental model of stock prices

The fundamental model of stock prices asserts that the price of a share of stock equals the present or discounted value of all expected dividends.[4]

---

[2] Keynes (1936), p. 159.

---

[3] See Fischer and Merton (1984).

[4] The fundamental model is expressed formally as:

$$P_o = \frac{E(D_1)}{(1+\delta)} + \frac{E(D_2)}{(1+\delta)^2} + \ldots + \frac{E(D_n)}{(1+\delta)^n}$$

where P_o is the current share price, $E(D_t)$ is the dividend per share expected to be paid at time t, δ is the rate of discount, and n is the number of periods into the future the stock is assumed to exist. The rate of discount can be thought of as the expected rate of return since δ can be expressed as:

$$\delta = \frac{E(P_1) - P_o}{P_o} + \frac{E(D_1)}{P_o}$$

Thus, δ is the expected capital gain (the first term) plus the expected dividend yield (the second term).

If this model is correct, stock prices change only if investors revise their expectations of future dividends or revise the rate at which they discount these dividends.

The rate that investors use to discount future dividends is the expected rate of return they require to be satisfied in holding that stock. It is usually assumed that investors are risk averse, which means that investors require a higher expected return for riskier stocks. Risk, however, is not simply the amount of variation in the stock's return. The Capital Asset Pricing Model (CAPM) is generally used in determining the expected rate of return. According to this model, investors realize that some of the risk of a stock can be eliminated by holding a diversified portfolio. Stock returns are assumed to change because of two kinds of shocks or unexpected events. The first kind of shock is specific to the individual stock. Each firm will be hit by a certain amount of random disturbance—luck that produces unexpectedly high returns or unexpectedly low returns. Investors can avoid this firm specific risk, however, by holding a portfolio of stocks so that good and bad luck averages out. The CAPM argues that investors will not be rewarded for bearing such firm specific, or unsystematic, risk.

The second kind of shock affecting stock returns can be thought of as economywide. Thus, to some extent, it is common to all stocks. An unexpected economic downturn, for example, is likely to depress the returns on most stocks. The uncertainty arising from these kinds of shocks is called systematic or undiversifiable risk because investors cannot eliminate this uncertainty by holding a portfolio of stocks. The CAPM states that the expected return on an individual stock depends on how sensitive the return is to such economywide shocks. A stock with a return that is expected to vary more than the average is considered riskier than average. As a result, its expected return should be higher. A stock with a return that varies less than the average is con-

sidered less risky. And as a result, its expected return should be less. The extent to which the return on a stock varies with the return on the stock market as a whole is called its *beta*. A *beta* higher than one indicates that the return on the stock has varied more than the market. A *beta* less than one indicates that the return on the stock has varied less than the market.[5] The larger the *beta*, the riskier is the stock and the higher its expected return should be. Thus, stock return data should show a positive relationship between a stock's *beta* and its average rate of return. The CAPM goes further by arguing that no other factor except *beta* need be considered in explaining the individual behavior of expected stock returns. This last assumption is critically important in tests of market efficiency because the usual measure of excess or abnormal returns is the difference between actual returns and the returns predicted by this model. If the CAPM is an inadequate model of expected returns, these tests could lead to incorrect inferences about market efficiency, since returns for bearing more risk might be mistaken for excess returns.

Information and efficiency

The fundamental model along with the CAPM predicts that stock prices and returns depend on investors' expectations of future profits of firms and the amount of undiversifiable risk attached to their expectations. The efficient markets model makes the additional assumption that investors are well-informed and that their expectations of future dividends are "rational." According to this

---

[5] For a derivation of the CAPM, see chapter 7 of Copeland and Weston (1983). The formal statement of the CAPM is:

$$E(R_{it} - R_{ft}) = \beta E(R_{mt} - R_{ft})$$

where R_{it} = return on i-th stock in period t
R_{ft} = return on a risk-free asset in period t
R_{mt} = return on the market portfolio of stocks in period t
β = Covariance (R_{it}, R_{mt}) / Variance (R_{mt}).

assumption, investors make the best forecasts of dividends that can be made from the available information. If some news changes these expectations, investors are assumed to bid the stock price up or down very quickly to its new equilibrium.

It is customary to distinguish between three types of stock market efficiency.[6] One, the stock market is said to be "weak-form" efficient if there is no pattern in past stock prices or stock returns that would allow investors to earn above-normal returns. Next, the market is said to be "semistrong-form" efficient if investors cannot use publicly available information to make above-normal profits. And three, the market is said to be "strong-form" efficient if no information can be used to make above-normal profits.

Empirical implications and evidence of market efficiency

Several strong empirical implications follow from the efficient markets model. Weak-form efficiency implies that there should be no discernible pattern to changes in stock prices and thus stock returns. Since only news causes prices to change and since news by definition means new, unforeseen information, stock returns should not be predictable from past returns. If, for example, an increase in stock prices of 1 percent today was likely to be followed by a further increase, investors would bid up the price today rather than wait. Charts of past price movements should be of no help in predicting subsequent changes. Stock prices should follow what is called a "random walk" in which the best guess of tomorrow's price is today's price.[7]

Semistrong-form efficiency implies that not just past stock prices but any information that is publicly available should be uncorrelated with subsequent movements in stock prices. As soon as news is announced, prices will move to reflect completely the impact that investors expect the news to have on the future profitability of businesses. If, for example, the government announced a new tax policy that was not expected, the stock market would react immediately and not over several days. Announcements of policies that had been fully anticipated should have no effect on stock prices. Thus, if Congress has debated a tax bill and investors know its provisions and that it will be passed, the actual passage will have no impact. Profit announcements by corporations will have an effect only if the announcement differs from expectations. Thus, a corporation may announce higher profits and see its stock price go down if investors view the announced profits as unexpectedly low.

Strong-form efficiency implies that no information, public or private, should help in predicting stock returns. The public information referred to in semi-strong efficiency can be thought of as essentially costless to investors. Private information is often equated with "insider" information—information that is known only to individuals with some connection with the company in question. Private information is assumed to be costly to collect or process. It has been pointed out, however, that if stock prices are to reflect

---

[6] The standard reference on types of efficiency is Fama (1970).

[7] The random walk prediction is only an approximation for most stocks. Because much of the total return on the average stock is in the form of capital gains, investors expect stock prices to rise over time by enough to provide the expected return. For example, if a stock pays no dividends and investors require a 10 percent annual rate of return to hold the stock, the stock price would be expected to rise an average of 0.026 percent per day. In this case, the efficient markets model predicts that the natural logarithm of the stock price follows a "random walk with drift." This means that the first difference of the logarithm of the stock price, which measures the rate of return, is a constant (0.026 percent) plus a random error term. The best guess of the rate of return is simply the constant or drift term (0.026 percent) because there is no systematic pattern in past returns.

all information, someone has to bear the costs of collecting and evaluating private information. If there was no expected return to this activity, investors who incurred the costs of assembling the information would be at a disadvantage to "uninformed" investors and would stop gathering information. How, then, could stock prices reflect all information?[8] Thus, strong-form efficiency is usually modified to say that the returns to using private, costly information are just enough for investors to earn a normal rate of profit on their information expenditures.

Tests of market efficiency generally look for evidence that investors could have earned excess returns by following some systematic pattern of buying or selling. Such "trading rules" should not exist if the stock market is efficient. A strategy of simply buying and holding stocks should yield higher average returns when the transactions costs of buying and selling are taken into account. Evidence generally supports weak and semistrong forms of efficiency but is more mixed with regard to strong-form efficiency.

Weak-form efficiency

Tests of weak-form efficiency restrict the trading rules to those based on past changes in stock prices. If there were any patterns, or serial correlation, in stock price changes, then investors could base their buying and selling on such patterns. Stock returns would be positively serially correlated, for example, if news was only slowly reflected in prices. Positive (negative) news would then cause prices to rise (fall) over several days so that a rise (fall) today would likely be followed by a rise (fall) tomorrow. Returns would be negatively serially correlated if the stock market overreacted to news so that a rise (fall) in price today would likely be followed by a fall (rise) tomor-

row. The efficient markets model asserts that any such pattern would be quickly recognized by the horde of financial analysts hunting for such regularities and their buying and selling would eliminate the pattern.

Empirical studies have generally found support for weak-form efficiency.[9] One way to assess the degree of serial correlation in stock returns is to estimate the relationship between current and past returns. If there is no statistically significant relationship, weak-form efficiency would be supported. Table 1 presents estimates of this relationship for daily and monthly returns on two measures of stock returns. One measure, VWT, is the rate of return on a portfolio of all stocks on the New York Stock Exchange and American Stock Exchange in which the return on each stock is value weighted by the size of the company. The other measure, EWT, is the rate of return on the same portfolio but with each stock being equally weighted. Hence VWT is dominated by larger firms while EWT is dominated by smaller firms.

The estimates in Table 1 indicate that for daily returns from 1966 to 1985 there is some evidence of serial correlation, although the fraction of variation in stock returns that can be explained by past variation (the R^2's) is small. That the EWT series shows more serial correlation may be due to the less frequent trading of smaller stocks rather than to serial correlation in individual stock returns.[10] If some stocks do not trade every day, the response of a portfolio of such stocks to any news may be spread over several days. Given the transactions costs of buying or selling daily, the small degree of serial correlation would be unlikely to allow investors to earn

---

[8] For a discussion of this issue, see Grossman and Stiglitz (1980).

[9] Support for weak-form efficiency is given in Fama (1970) and Berkman (1978).

[10] See Roll (1981) for a discussion of the possible effects of nonsynchronous trading. Atchison et al. (1987), however, suggest that this cannot explain all the serial correlation.

TABLE 1
Tests of weak-form efficiency

$$\text{Model: } r_t = b_0 + b_1 r_{t-1} + b_2 r_{t-2} + b_3 r_{t-3} + b_4 r_{t-4} + b_5 r_{t-5}$$

Return Series	b_1	b_2	b_3	b_4	b_5	R^2	F
Daily VWT 1966-85	0.245*	−0.046*	0.027	−0.003	0.006	0.057	60.97*
Daily EWT 1966-85	0.411*	−0.089*	0.095*	0.018	0.043	0.169	204.06*
Monthly VWT 1956-85	0.056	−0.050	0.030	0.081	0.087	0.022	1.59
Monthly EWT 1956-85	0.131*	−0.040	0.005	0.040	0.050	0.023	1.66

Notes: *indicates statistical significance at the 5 percent level.

F statistic is for the hypothesis that all the coefficients are jointly equal to zero.

VWT = value-weighted index of stock returns.

EWT = equally weighted index of stock returns.

Data are from the Center for Research in Security Prices at the Graduate School of Business, University of Chicago.

excess returns. The estimates for monthly data from 1956 to 1985 show no serial correlation for the VWT over that period and very slight serial correlation for the EWT series. Again, the amount of variation in monthly returns accounted for by past returns is small. When five-year subperiods are examined, the degree of serial correlation falls over time for both weekly and monthly data, indicating that the market has become more efficient.[11]

More sophisticated trading rules using past stock returns, usually called filter rules, look for such strategies as buying when stocks have risen by x percent and selling when they have fallen by y percent. Studies investigating such rules usually find that when transactions costs are taken into account the rules do not produce returns in excess of a buy-and-hold strategy.[12]

Several empirical papers have focused on two apparent anomalies to weak-form efficiency. One is referred to as the "weekend" effect. Researchers report that average stock returns have been lower on Mondays and higher on Fridays than on other days of the week. This difference is an anomaly, since the efficient markets model cannot account for this systematic effect. The model would predict, if anything, that returns should be higher on Mondays because Monday's return is for three days rather than for one. Part of the weekend effect may be due to the settlement practices of financial markets. When stocks are bought or sold, transactors have five business days to settle. Combined with a one-day check clearing delay, this practice produces higher returns on

---

[11] For the VWT daily stock returns, the coefficient on the first lagged return is 0.359 for 1966-70 and falls to 0.136 for 1981-85. For the EWT series, the coefficient falls from 0.467 to 0.290 for these subperiods. A similar pattern occurs in the monthly return series for ten-year subperiods.

[12] See Fama and Blume (1966).

TABLE 2
Tests of the weekend effect

Model: $r_t = c_0 + c_1 \text{TUE}_t + c_2 \text{WED}_t + c_3 \text{THUR}_t + c_4 \text{FRI}_t$

Return Series	c_0	c_1	c_2	c_3	c_4	R^2	F
Daily VWT 1966-85	−0.111*	0.131*	0.214*	0.172*	0.219*	0.066	14.74*
Daily EWT 1966-85	−0.121*	0.113*	0.255*	0.241*	0.350*	0.184	44.14*

Notes: All coefficients are multiplied by 100.

* indicates statistical significance at the 5 percent level.

F statistic is for the hypothesis that all days have the same average return.

Equations estimated by generalized least squares to correct for serial correlation.

TUE_t = 1 if day t is a Tuesday, = 0 otherwise and so on.

Fridays and lower returns on Mondays to compensate for the extra two days of interest accruing to buyers of stock on Friday.[13]

The presence of a pattern in daily stock returns can be investigated by estimating a model that allows the average stock return to depend on the day of the week. Table 2 reports estimates of such a model using VWT and EWT from 1966 to 1985. The constant term estimates the average return on Mondays, and its significantly negative values are evidence of low Monday returns. The positive coefficients for the other days of the week indicate that their mean returns are higher than that for Monday. Only for the EWT series, however, is there evidence of high returns on Fridays, casting some doubt on the settlement practices explanation. There is also evidence that the daily pattern of stock returns has weakened in recent years.[14]

The other anomaly is the "January" effect. Researchers find the return on holding stocks over January averages higher than for other months. This finding is often ascribed to investors selling stocks in December to realize capital losses for tax purposes and then rebuying stocks in January. Such a practice would lower stock prices in December and raise them in January so that calculated returns over January would be high. However, several problems with this explanation have been raised. Studies have shown that it is not optimal to wait until December to realize capital losses.[15] Moreover, the January effect appears to have existed before the imposition of income taxes in the United States.[16]

---

[13] French (1980) and Gibbons and Hess (1981) document the existence of the weekend effect. The settlement practices explanation is given in Lakonishok and Levi (1982), and criticized by Dyl and Martin (1985).

[14] For the VWT series, re-estimating the model over five-year subperiods indicates that the weekend effect disappears after 1975. For the EWT series, the effect remains but becomes less significant.

[15] See Constantinides (1984) for a discussion of the issues.

[16] See Jones et al. (1987).

The existence of the January effect can be examined by estimating a model that allows the average monthly stock return to depend on the month of the year. Table 3 reports estimates of such a model for the two return series from 1956 to 1985. The constant term in the model estimates the average return for January and the coefficients on the other variables estimate how the average returns in the other months differ from January's. If there is a January effect, the coefficients for the other months should be negative. For the VWT series, the coefficients on the monthly variables are individually and jointly equal to zero, which rejects the presence of a January effect. For the EWT series, however, all the non-January coefficients are negative and, with one exception, statistically different from zero, which indicates that returns average higher in January than other months. Since the EWT series gives more weight to small firms than does the VWT series, these results are consistent with other studies that find the January effect to be concentrated in the returns of small stocks. While the finding of high returns in January supports the tax selling argument, there is no evidence that December returns are abnormally low, contrary to the prediction of the tax selling theory. Splitting the sample into ten-year subperiods produced evidence that the January effect appears to have been reduced over time.[17]

In summary, the evidence suggests that weak-form efficiency is a reasonable characterization of historical stock returns. While there is some evidence of serial correlation in daily stock returns, it is of little value in predicting future returns. Similarly, although low returns on Mondays and high returns in January contradict weak-form efficiency, these deviations appear to be con-

TABLE 3
Tests of the January effect

Model: $r_t = d_0 + d_1 \text{February}_t + d_2 \text{March}_t$
$+ d_3 \text{April}_t + d_4 \text{May}_t + d_5 \text{June}_t + d_6 \text{July}_t$
$+ d_7 \text{August}_t + d_8 \text{September}_t + d_9 \text{October}_t$
$+ d_{10} \text{November}_t + d_{11} \text{December}_t$

	Return Series	
	VWT 1956-85	**EWT 1956-85**
d_0	0.014	0.046*
d_1	−0.012	−0.041*
d_2	−0.001	−0.030*
d_3	0.001	−0.034*
d_4	−0.016	−0.049*
d_5	−0.012	−0.046*
d_6	−0.007	−0.036*
d_7	−0.002	−0.033*
d_8	−0.020	−0.049*
d_9	−0.002	−0.044*
d_{10}	0.011	−0.019
d_{11}	0.001	−0.033*
R^2	0.042	0.067
F	1.37	2.29*

Notes: * indicates statistical significance at the 5 percent level.

F statistic is for the hypothesis that all months have the same average return.

$\text{February}_t = 1$ if month t is February, $= 0$ otherwise and so on.

centrated in the returns of small firms and to have declined over time.

Semistrong-form efficiency

Most studies support semistrong-form efficiency, but as with weak-form efficiency, there are some anomalous findings. Researchers have

---

[17] Over the period from 1976 to 1985, neither measure of stock returns exhibited a statistically significant January effect.

tested semistrong efficiency in the stock market mainly in two ways. One way is by seeing if trading rules based on publicly available information about the firms or the economy yield excess returns to investors. The other way, an "event" study, is by looking at the reaction of stock prices to announcements thought to be relevant to stock prices.

A trading rule is a decision rule that tells an investor when to buy or sell stock or which stocks to buy or sell. The first kind of trading rule uses economywide information to come up with the appropriate times to buy or sell. A trading rule would be profitable if it yielded higher returns, after considering transactions costs, than a buy-and-hold strategy. Several early studies asserted, for example, that investors could make abnormal profits by using a trading rule based on past movements in the money supply. The efficient markets hypothesis argues that no such trading rule exists because only contemporaneous, unexpected changes in the money supply could affect stock returns. Subsequent work has found evidence that knowledge of past money supply changes would not have allowed investors to earn abnormal profits.[18]

One test of whether money supply growth can be used to predict stock returns is to estimate the relationship between stock returns and past money growth rates. If the stock market is semistrong-form efficient, there should be no statistically significant association between stock returns and past money supply movements. Table 4 reports estimates of this relationship from 1966 to 1985 for both a narrow definition of money (M1) and a broader definition of money (M2). For neither money supply measure is there evidence of a systematic relationship between past money

growth and stock returns. These results do not imply, however, that there is no relationship between money growth and stock returns. If the current month's rate of growth of the money supply is included, there is evidence of a significantly positive relationship between contemporaneous money growth and stock returns as indicated in the last two columns of Table 4. This relationship does not allow investors to predict stock returns, however, because they do not know the current month's money growth.[19]

A second kind of trading rule is based on publicly available information about individual firms or groups of firms. Again, the efficient markets model asserts that no such trading rule can be used to make abnormal profits. Recent studies, however, have provided several apparent exceptions to this rule. One exception is referred to as the small firm effect. Several researchers have documented that smaller firms have consistently earned higher returns than larger firms. In addition, these abnormal returns are concentrated in January returns. One interpretation of these findings is that smaller firms are riskier, and hence should earn a higher average return than the CAPM predicts. According to this interpretation, the CAPM inadequately adjusts for risk. While this explanation is a plausible reason for smaller stocks earning higher average returns, it does not account for the excess returns being concentrated in January.[20]

---

[18] Sprinkel (1964) and Homa and Jaffee (1971) report that money supply movements help predict stock prices. Rozeff (1974) and Davidson and Froyen (1982) reach the opposite conclusion.

---

[19] Care should be exercised in interpreting these results. The contemporaneous relationship could reflect feedback from the financial market to the money supply. In addition, the use of actual changes in the money supply in the model given in Table 4 reflects an implicit assumption that investors cannot accurately predict money growth.

[20] Banz (1981), Reinganum (1981), and Lustiq and Leinbach (1983) all find evidence of a small firm effect. Keim (1983) and Reinganum (1983) report that the higher returns for small firms occur in January.

TABLE 4
Stock returns and money supply growth, 1966-85

Model: $r_t = g_0 + g_1 M_t + g_2 M_{t-1} + \ldots + g_{12} M_{t-12}$

| | Money Supply Measures | | | |
	M1	M2	M1	M2
g_0	0.012	0.0004	0.001	−0.010
g_1			2.795*	4.356*
g_2	0.102	0.861	−0.722	−1.999
g_3	−0.077	0.291	˙0.181	0.918
g_4	0.410	0.737	−0.053	0.167
g_5	0.248	1.572	0.842	1.844
g_6	0.019	−0.339	−0.552	−1.091
g_7	−1.260*	−1.999	−1.120	−1.739
g_8	−0.319	−0.930	−0.462	−0.742
g_9	0.441	0.800	0.505	0.459
g_{10}	0.014	−0.183	−0.418	−0.740
g_{11}	0.330	0.262	0.699	0.982
g_{12}	−0.880	−0.050	−0.980	−0.001
g_{13}	−0.506	−0.459	−0.087	−0.411
R^2	0.051	0.076	0.150	0.170
F	1.01	1.56	3.06*	3.57*

Notes: * indicates statistical significance at the 5 percent level.

Stock returns measured by the percentage change in the New York Stock Exchange's index. M_{t-i} is the rate of growth in M in month t-i. All data are from the Citibase data bank.

F statistics are for the joint hypothesis that all coefficients are zero.

Higher January returns are consistent with the tax selling hypothesis. If smaller firms have more variable prices, these firms are more likely to have capital losses and, hence, their stocks are more likely to be sold at the end of the year to qualify for tax losses. Another interpretation is that there are higher transactions costs in buying or selling small stocks and that when these costs are taken into account the excess returns disappear. Again, however, this leaves the question of why the transactions costs are higher in January.[21]

A similarly puzzling empirical regularity is the finding that stocks with low (high) price-earnings ratios earn average returns above (below) what the CAPM would predict. This anomalous result appears to occur even after other factors, such as the size of the firm and the effects of taxation, are taken into account. Since last period's price-earnings ratio is public information, excess returns on portfolios chosen by picking stocks with low price-earnings ratios violate semistrong-form efficiency. Moreover, such a finding implies that investors overreact to news about a firm's earnings, being either too optimistic and bidding the price-earnings ratio too high or too pessimistic and causing the price-earnings ratio to fall too far.[22]

Still another puzzle is the "Value Line" anomaly. Semistrong-form efficiency implies that investment advice based on publicly available information should be worthless. The Value Line Investment Survey, the largest advisory firm in the United States, uses public information to rank stocks by expected returns. Thus, semistrong-form efficiency predicts that investors should not benefit from the Value Line recommendations. Several studies have documented, however, that investors following the Value Line recommendations would have earned abnormally high returns.[23]

The second method of testing market efficiency uses event studies to examine the responses of stock prices to announcements thought to be relevant to stock returns. Semistrong-form efficiency is supported if stock prices react only to the unexpected part of any announcement and react quickly. Most event studies find that the stock market conforms reasonably well to semistrong-form efficiency. One famous study investigated the responses of stock prices to announcements of stock splits. Stock prices are expected to rise after stock splits are announced because splits are usually reliable predictors of higher dividends. The study found this reaction was essentially immediate.[24] Support for semistrong-form efficiency has also come from studies of how the aggregate stock market reacts to announcements concerning monetary policy. Stock prices were found to respond quickly to the unexpected parts of weekly money supply reports and announcements of changes in the discount rate.[25]

The evidence from event studies is not unanimous, however, in support of the efficient markets model. Some studies have found evidence of stock price reactions to public announcements that last more than one day. Studies of the reaction of stock prices to earnings announcements of firms also have found responses which are spread over time rather than occurring immediately.[26]

---

[21] The transactions cost explanation is discussed in Stoll and Whaley (1983). For evidence that transactions costs do not fully account for the small firm effect, see Schultz (1983).

[22] Basu (1977, 1983) and Dowen and Bauman (1986) conclude that the price-earnings ratio has an independent effect on returns, while Reinganum (1981) argues that it is only firm size that matters. Evidence that stock prices overreact to news was reported by DeBondt and Thaler (1985). This study found that portfolios of stocks which were "losers" in the recent past subsequently earned substantially higher returns than portfolios of past "winners" over a three-year period. Contrary to the tax-loss selling hypothesis for high January returns, they report that the "loser" portfolios had high returns in January every year and not just the first year.

---

[23] Studies of the Value Line anomaly include Copeland and Mayers (1982), Holloway (1981), and Stekel (1985). These studies suggest that transactions costs incurred in frequent trading could eliminate the abnormally high returns.

[24] See Fama et al. (1969).

[25] See Pearce and Roley (1985) and Smirlock and Yawitz (1985).

[26] Slow responses to unexpected earnings announcements were found by Rendleman et al. (1982). Adjustments to stock analysts' recommendations published in the *Wall Street Journal* were found by Lloyd-Davies and Canes (1978) to persist beyond the first day.

Strong-form efficiency

Strong-form efficiency asserts that even investors with information that is not publicly available cannot earn abnormal returns. Researchers have tested for strong-form efficiency two ways, by examining the returns to insider trading and by evaluating the performance of mutual fund managers. These tests provide mixed results.

The evidence from studies of insider trading does not support the strong form of the efficient markets model. Legal insider trading consists of the buying or selling of a company's stock by an officer or director of the company. Such trading is legal as long as it is not motivated by specific news about the company's prospects that has not been announced to the public. Insider trading must be registered with the Securities and Exchange Commission and, therefore, is known to researchers. Studies that have examined the returns to legal insider trading have generally concluded that insiders make abnormal profits and, hence, that the stock market is not strong-form efficient. Moreover, it appears that a trading strategy based on the publicly announced insider trading activity can also earn abnormal profits, a finding that contradicts even semistrong-form efficiency.[27]

In contrast, tests that focus on the investment performance of mutual fund managers tend to support the strong form of the efficient markets model. These tests assume that fund managers are more likely to have access to private information or are better able to access the effects of information on stock returns. Thus, if certain funds consistently earn abnormal returns, that is, after accounting for the level of risk, this would be evidence against strong-form efficiency. However, studies comparing fund performance indicate no such violations of strong-form efficiency.[28]

In short, the evidence on market efficiency does not lend strong support for strong-form efficiency. The evidence, however, does tend to support weak-form and semistrong-form efficiency, which means that stock prices appear to reflect publicly available information but not all information.

Are stock prices too volatile?

Even without strong evidence that publicly available information can be used by investors to earn abnormal returns, this lack of evidence does not confirm that the efficient markets model explains the movements in stock prices. An alternative test of this model, proposed by Robert Shiller, examines whether the model can account for the historical variability of stock prices.[29] Applying this test to the history of stock prices in the United States, Shiller concludes that stock prices have been much more volatile than the fundamental model would predict. He argues that fads and mass psychology play an important role in the stock market. While this strong assertion has stimulated a lively and continuing literature, recent work suggests that the efficient markets model can account for the volatility of stock prices.

Shiller's argument runs as follows. Suppose investors had perfect foresight so that they could predict dividends without error. According to the fundamental model, the price investors would be willing to pay for a stock would be the present value of the known future dividends. Assuming

---

[27] Baesel and Stein (1979), Finnerty (1976), Givoly and Palmon (1985), and Lorie and Niederhoffer (1968) report evidence that insiders earned abnormally high returns.

[28] Jensen (1968) reports no evidence of superior performance while Kon and Jen (1979) find weaker evidence in favor of strong-form efficiency.

[29] See Shiller (1981a, 1981b, 1984). A similar approach for testing for excess volatility is LeRoy and Porter (1981).

CHART 1
Actual versus perfect foresight stock prices, 1926-85

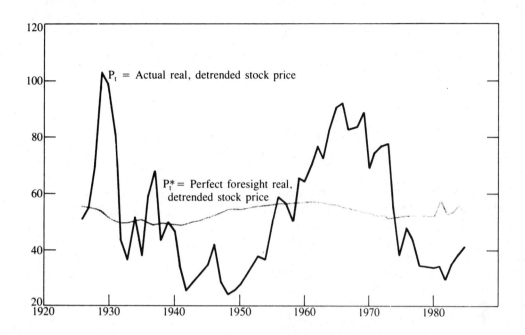

the rate at which investors discount future dividends is constant, Shiller constructs a series of stock prices, P*$_t$, that would have resulted under the assumption of perfect foresight. The efficient markets model does not assume that investors have perfect foresight, but rather that they make the best possible predictions based on the available information. If the discount rate investors use is constant, the model implies that actual stock prices, P$_t$, are the optimal forecasts that investors can make with their limited information of the perfect foresight prices. Shiller notes that optimal forecasts of economic variables should vary less than the variables themselves. He concludes from this that the actual variance of stock prices should be less than the estimated variance of the perfect foresight series he constructs. This condition is referred to as a "variance bounds restriction."[30]

Shiller tested this variance bounds restriction by constructing a measure of P*$_t$ and comparing its variability with the actual stock price series, P$_t$. He used a constant discount rate, actual dividends, and an assumption about the terminal stock price to compute the present value of actual dividends, after first deflating by the producer price index and eliminating trends. The startling result of this exercise is given in Chart 1. The dashed line is the constructed P*$_t$ series, and the solid line is the actual stock price series, P$_t$. As the chart illustrates, the P*$_t$ series is much smoother than the P$_t$ series. From this, Shiller concluded that stock prices vary too much to be the present value of expected dividends.

[30] See appendix for details on Shiller's approach.

Shiller's results have created considerable controversy, with several well-known economists referring to his results as evidence that the stock market is not likely to allocate capital efficiently.[31] In addition, because stock price fluctuations have substantial effects on the economy, such excess volatility suggests to some that the Federal Reserve should smooth these excessive swings through open market operations in equities as well as short-term government securities.[32]

Several researchers, however, have challenged the approach of Shiller. One exception taken to his approach is that the comparison of variances is inappropriate because it ignores the information available to investors. According to the efficient markets model, the current stock price is the present value of the best forecast of future dividends that can be made from current information. The appropriate comparison is between this forecast and any other forecast based on the same information. Since the variance of P^*_t depends on all actual future dividends whereas the variance of P_t depends only on information known at time t, there is no reason to conclude that Shiller's variance bounds test contradicts the efficient markets model. Indeed, one researcher has shown that figures such as Chart 1 can result even when the efficient markets model holds by construction.[33] The intuition behind this finding is that when dividends change in, say, period t, investors change their forecasts of all future dividends. If dividend changes tend to persist, an increase in dividends would increase the predicted dividends for many periods into the future. Thus,

the present value of these dividends, and hence P_t, may increase substantially. P^*_t, however, is based on the known future dividends and can only rise by enough to produce a return equal to the assumed constant discount rate. Hence P_t will appear much more volatile than P^*_t.

Related to this objection to Shiller's approach is work suggesting that dividends should not be treated as exogenous but rather as a choice made by managers of firms. Models of aggregate dividends that assume managers try to keep dividends payments smooth appear to fit the historical pattern of dividends quite well.[34] If managers smooth dividends rather than let dividends vary proportionately with profits, the observed dividends will vary little, and stock prices will appear much more volatile than the present value of the observed dividends.

A third objection to Shiller's variance bounds test is the assumption of a constant discount rate. If the discount rate changes substantially over time, stock prices could vary considerably, even if expected changes in dividends were small. If investors are risk averse, the rate of return they require to hold stocks will vary with the state of the economy. When incomes are high, investors are likely to save more and to accept a lower return. When incomes are low, investors would tend to sell their stocks to maintain their consumption and the required rate of return would have to rise. Thus, stock prices would be boosted by falling discount rates in good times and depressed by rising discount rates in bad times. The more risk averse investors are the more variation in discount rates. While Shiller and others suggest that this variation is insufficient to account for the

---

[31] See, for example, Arrow (1982), pp. 1-9, and Ackley (1983).

[32] See Fischer and Merton (1984).

[33] For a detailed discussion of these issues, see Kleidon (1986). A summary of problems with volatility tests is given by LeRoy (1984).

[34] See Marsh and Merton (1986, 1987). Much of the discussion about the dividend process centers on the question of whether the aggregate dividend series is nonstationary or whether it is stationary about a trend as assumed by Shiller.

volatility of stock prices, other work gives more support to this factor.[35]

The question of whether the historical volatility of stock prices is inconsistent with the efficient markets model is still an open question. While several objections have been raised to the original tests, which indicated excessive volatility, new tests that do not suffer from these drawbacks have also found evidence against the rational expectations, present value model.[36] It appears, however, that the assumptions of relatively smooth dividends and a fluctuating expected rate of return allow the efficient markets model to account for the apparent excess volatility of stock prices.

Summary and conclusions

For stock prices to serve as signals that lead to the efficient allocation of capital, they need to reflect the best forecasts of the future profitability of firms. According to the efficient markets model of stock price determination, this condition is met.

Investors are assumed to use all available information in predicting stock prices, which implies that stock prices quickly reflect any relevant news. Investors should expect to earn only a normal rate of return for the risk they bear.

Challenges to this notion of stock market efficiency have often been raised in the spirit of Keynes. Critics see stock prices as strongly influenced by changes in mass psychology in addition to news about future profits. Recent empirical challenges have taken two forms. First, studies have pointed out anomalies to the efficient markets model in which investors appear able to earn excess returns based on the use of available information. Second, recent work on the volatility of stock prices has claimed that this volatility cannot be explained by the efficient markets model.

After reviewing many studies on these two challenges, this article concludes that the evidence against the efficient markets model is not sufficient to reject the model. When transactions costs are taken into account, many of the apparent deviations from the predictions of the efficient markets model are too small to allow investors to earn excess returns. Moreover, these deviations are concentrated in the behavior of the stock prices of small firms, which suggests that the standard model of expected returns may not be adequate for small firms. Studies of excess volatility, while initially accepted as startling evidence against the efficient markets model, have been found to be flawed. More recent work suggests that the evidence of excess volatility is suspect and that the efficient markets model can account for the historical variability of stock prices.

---

[35] Allowing for a variable discount rate was found to be insufficient to account for the variation in stock prices in Grossman and Shiller (1981) and Shiller (June 1981). For a model allowing for an endogenously determined discount rate that is relatively successful in explaining stock returns, see Litzenberger and Ronn (1986). For discussions of the connection between risk aversion and the variable discount rates, see LeRoy and La Civita (1981) and Michener (1982).

[36] See Mankiw et al. (1985) and Scott (1985). While these tests appear insensitive to the issue of nonstationary dividend processes, they do assume a constant discount rate.

Appendix

Shiller's Volatility Test

The perfect foresight stock price, P^*_t, is defined as

$$(1) \quad P^*_t = \sum_{i=1}^{n} d^i D_{t+i}$$

where $d = (1/1+\delta)$

δ = discount rate (assumed constant)

D_t = dividends paid in period t.

The actual stock price, P_t, according to the fundamental model, is:

$$(2) \quad P_t = \sum_{i=1}^{n} d^i D^e_{t+i}$$

where D^e_t = expected dividends for period t.

Assuming a constant discount rate, P_t is a forecast of P^*_t so that

$$(3) \quad P^*_t = P_t + e_t$$

where e_t = forecast error.

Under the efficient markets model, P_t is the optimal forecast of P^*_t, which implies that e_t must be uncorrelated with P_t. Thus, taking variances of Equation 3,

$$(4) \quad \text{var}(P^*_t) = \text{var}(P_t) + \text{var}(e_t)$$

Since variances must always be positive, Equation 4 implies that the variance of the perfect foresight price, P^*_t, must exceed the variance of the actual price, P_t. This is the "variance bounds" restriction Shiller tests.

Shiller constructs P^*_t recursively. Let P^*_T be the terminal price at the end of the data set. P^*_{T-1} can then be calculated as follows:

$$P^*_{T-1} = (P^*_T + D_T)d$$

That is, P^*_{T-1} is the present value of the one-period-ahead price plus the one-period-ahead dividends. This calculation is then repeated recursively to obtain the entire series graphed in Chart 1. Following Shiller, the actual stock price series (the Standard & Poor's Composite) and the dividend series were deflated by the Wholesale Price Index and detrended. The discount rate was set at the ratio of average real, detrended dividends to average real, detrended price, which equaled 5.17 percent over 1926-85. The stock price and dividend data are from *Security Price Index Record,* Standard & Poor's Statistical Service, 1986.

References

Gardner Ackley, "Commodities and Capital: Prices and Quantities," *American Economic Review,* March 1983, pp. 1-16.

Kenneth J. Arrow, "Risk Perception in Psychology and Economics," *Economic Inquiry,* January 1982, pp. 1-9.

Michael D. Atchison, Kirt C. Butler, and Richard Simonds, "Nonsynchronous Trading and Market Index Autocorrelation," *Journal of Finance,* March 1987, pp. 111-118.

Jerome B. Baesel and Garry R. Stein, "The Value of Information: Inferences from the Predictability of Insider Trading," *Journal of Financial and Quantitative Analysis,* September 1979, pp. 553-571.

Rolf W. Banz, "The Relationship Between Return and Market Value of Common Stocks," *Journal of Financial Economics,* March 1981, pp. 3-18.

Sanjoy Basu, "Investment Performance of Common Stocks in Relation to Their Price-Earnings Ratios: A Test of the Efficient Market," *Journal of Finance*, June 1977, pp. 663-682.

Sanjoy Basu, "The Relationship Between Earnings' Yield, Market Value and Return for NYSE Common Stocks: Further Evidence," *Journal of Financial Economics*, June 1983, pp. 129-156.

William J. Baumol, *The Stock Market and Economic Efficiency*, Fordham University Press, New York, 1965.

Neil G. Berkman, "A Primer on Random Walks in the Stock Market," *New England Economic Review*, September/October 1978, pp. 32-50.

George M. Constantinides, "Optimal Stock Trading with Personal Taxes," *Journal of Financial Economics*, March 1984, pp. 65-89.

Thomas E. Copeland and David Mayers, "The Value Line Enigma (1965-1978): A Case Study of Performance Evaluation Issues," *Journal of Financial Economics*, November 1982, pp. 289-321.

Thomas E. Copeland and J. Fred Weston, *Financial Theory and Corporate Policy*, 2nd Edition, Addison-Wesley, Reading, Mass., 1983.

Lawrence S. Davidson and Richard T. Froyen, "Monetary Policy and Stock Returns: Are Stock Markets Efficient?" *Review*, Federal Reserve Bank of St. Louis, March 1982, pp. 3-12.

Werner F.M. DeBondt and Richard Thaler, "Does the Stock Market Overreact?" *Journal of Finance*, July 1985, pp. 793-805.

Richard J. Dowen and W. Scott Bauman, "The Relative Importance of Size, P/E, and Neglect," *Journal of Portfolio Management*, Spring 1986, pp. 30-34.

Edward A. Dyl and Stanley A. Martin, Jr., "Weekend Effects on Stock Returns: A Comment," *Journal of Finance*, March 1985, pp. 347-349.

Eugene F. Fama, "Efficient Capital Markets: A Review of Theory and Empirical Work," *Journal of Finance*, May 1970, pp. 383-417.

Eugene F. Fama and Marshall Blume, "Filter Rules and Stock Market Trading Profits," *Journal of Business*, January 1966, pp. 226-241.

Eugene F. Fama, Lawrence Fisher, Michael C. Jensen, and Richard Roll, "The Adjustment of Stock Prices to New Information," *International Economic Review*, February 1969, pp. 1-21.

Joseph E. Finnerty, "Insiders and Market Efficiency," *Journal of Finance*, September 1976, pp. 1141-1148.

Stanley Fischer and Robert C. Merton, "Macroeconomics and Finance: The Role of the Stock Market," *Essays on Macroeconomic Implications of Financial and Labor Markets and Political Processes*, Carnegie-Rochester Conference Series on Public Policy, Vol. 21, eds. Karl Brunner and Allan H. Meltzer, North-Holland, Amsterdam, 1984.

Kenneth R. French, "Stock Returns and the Weekend Effect," *Journal of Financial Economics*, March 1980, pp. 55-69.

Michael R. Gibbons and Patrick J. Hess, "Day of the Week Effects and Asset Returns," *Journal of Business*, October 1981, pp. 579-596.

Dan Givoly and Dan Palmon, "Insider Trading and the Exploitation of Inside Information: Some Empirical Evidence," *Journal of Business*, January 1985, pp. 69-87.

Sanford J. Grossman and Robert J. Shiller, "The Determinants of the Variability of Stock Market Prices," *American Economic Review*, May 1981, pp. 222-227.

Sanford J. Grossman and Joseph E. Stiglitz, "On the Impossibility of Informationally Efficient Markets," *American Economic Review*, June 1980, pp. 393-408.

Clark Holloway, "A Note on Testing an Aggressive Investment Strategy Using Value Line Ranks," *Journal of Finance*, June 1981, pp. 711-719.

Kenneth E. Homa and Dwight M. Jaffee, "The Supply of Money and Common Stock Prices," *Journal of Finance*, December 1971, pp. 1056-1066.

Michael C. Jensen, "The Performance of Mutual Funds in the Period 1945-64," *Journal of Finance*, May 1968, pp. 389-416.

Charles P. Jones, Douglas K. Pearce, and Jack W. Wilson, "Can Tax Loss Selling Explain the January Effect? A Note," *Journal of Finance*, June 1987, pp. 453-461.

Donald B. Keim, "Size-Related Anomalies and Stock Market Seasonality: Some Further Empirical Evidence," *Journal of Financial Economics*, June 1983, pp. 13-32.

John Maynard Keynes, *The General Theory of Employment, Interest, and Money*, Macmillan, London, 1936.

Allan W. Kleidon, "Variance Bounds Tests and Stock Market Valuation Models," *Journal of Political Economy*, October 1986, pp. 953-1001.

Stanley J. Kon and Frank C. Jen, "The Investment Performance of Mutual Funds: An Empirical Investigation of Timing, Selectivity, and Market Efficiency," *Journal of Business*, April 1979, pp. 263-289.

Josef Lakonishok and Maurice Levi, "Weekend Effects of Stock Returns: A Note," *Journal of Finance*, June 1982, pp. 883-889.

Stephen F. LeRoy, "Efficiency and the Variability of Stock Prices," *American Economic Review*, May 1984, pp. 183-187.

Stephen F. LeRoy and C. J. La Civita, "Risk Aversion and the Dispersion of Asset Prices," *Journal of Business*, October 1981, pp. 535-547.

Stephen F. LeRoy and Richard D. Porter, "The Present-Value Relation: Tests Based on Implied Variance Bounds," *Econometrica*, May 1981, pp. 555-574.

Robert H. Litzenberger and Ehud I. Ronn, "A Utility-Based Model of Common Stock Price Movements," *Journal of Finance*, March 1986, pp. 67-92.

Peter Lloyd-Davies and Michael Canes, "Stock Prices and the Publication of Second-hand Information," *Journal of Business*, January 1978, pp. 43-56.

James H. Lorie and Victor Niederhoffer, "Predictive and Statistical Properties of Insider Trading," *Journal of Law and Economics*, April 1968, pp. 35-53.

Ivan L. Lustiq and Philip A. Leinbach, "The Small Firm Effect," *Financial Analysts Journal*, May/June 1983, pp. 46-49.

N. Gregory Mankiw, David Romer, and Matthew D. Shapiro, "An Unbiased Reexamination of Stock Market Volatility," *Journal of Finance*, July 1985, pp. 677-689.

Terry A. Marsh and Robert C. Merton, "Dividend Variability and Variance Bounds Tests for the Rationality of Stock Prices," *American Economic Review,* June 1986, pp. 483-498.

Terry A. Marsh and Robert C. Merton, "Dividend Behavior for the Aggregate Stock Market," *Journal of Business,* January 1987, pp. 1-40.

Ronald W. Michener, "Variance Bounds in a Simple Model of Asset Pricing," *Journal of Political Economy,* February 1982, pp. 166-175.

Douglas K. Pearce and V. Vance Roley, "Stock Prices and Economic News," *Journal of Business,* January 1985, pp. 49-67.

Marc R. Reinganum, "Misspecification of Capital Asset Pricing: Empirical Anomalies Based on Earnings Yields and Market Value," *Journal of Financial Economics,* March 1981, pp. 19-46.

Marc R. Reinganum, "The Anomalous Stock Market Behavior of Small Firms in January," *Journal of Financial Economics,* June 1983, pp. 89-104.

Richard J. Rendleman, Jr., Charles P. Jones, and Henry A. Latane, "Empirical Anomalies Based on Unexpected Earnings and the Importance of Risk Adjustments," *Journal of Financial Economics,* November 1982, pp. 269-287.

Richard Roll, "A Possible Explanation of the Small Firm Effect," *Journal of Finance,* September 1981, pp. 879-888.

Richard Roll, "Vas Ist Das?" *Journal of Portfolio Management,* Winter 1983, pp. 18- 28.

Michael S. Rozeff, "Money and Stock Prices," *Journal of Financial Economics,* March 1984, pp. 65-89.

Michael S. Rozeff and William R. Kinney, Jr., "Capital Market Seasonality: The Case of Stock Returns," *Journal of Financial Economics,* October 1976, pp. 379-402.

Paul Schultz, "Transactions Costs and the Small Firm Effect," *Journal of Financial Economics,* June 1983, pp. 81-88.

Louis O. Scott, "The Present Value Model of Stock Prices: Regression Tests and Monte Carlo Results," *Review of Economics and Statistics,* November 1985, pp. 599-605.

Robert J. Shiller, "The Use of Volatility Measures in Assessing Market Efficiency," *Journal of Finance,* May 1981, pp. 291-304.

Robert J. Shiller, "Do Stock Prices Move Too Much to be Justified by Subsequent Changes in Dividends?" *American Economic Review,* June 1981, pp. 421-436.

Robert J. Shiller, "Stock Prices and Social Dynamics," *Brookings Papers on Economic Activity,* 2:1984, pp. 457-510.

Michael Smirlock and Jess Yawitz, "Asset Returns, Discount Rate Changes, and Market Efficiency," *Journal of Finance,* September 1985, pp. 1141-1158.

Beryl W. Sprinkel, *Money and Stock Prices,* Richard D. Irwin, Homewood, Ill., 1964. Scott E. Stickel, "The Effect of Value Line Investment Survey Rank Changes on Common Stock Prices," *Journal of Financial Economics,* March 1985, pp. 121-143.

Hans R. Stoll and Robert E. Whaley, "Transactions Costs and the Small Firm Effect," *Journal of Financial Economics,* June 1983, p. 57-79.

Article 14

David P. Ely
Assistant Professor
San Diego State University

Kenneth J. Robinson
Economist
Federal Reserve Bank of Dallas

The Stock Market and Inflation:
A Synthesis of the Theory and Evidence

One of the more puzzling anomalies found in financial markets is the poor perform- ance of the stock market during periods of infla- tion. The failure of equities to maintain their value during inflationary time periods is consid- ered anomalous as stocks, representing claims to *real* assets, should provide a good hedge against inflation. Moreover, if the so-called "Fisher" effect holds, stocks should be positively related to meas- ures of expected inflation as well.

As shown in Chart 1, during the rapid infla- tion years of the 1970s, movements in U.S. stock prices failed to keep pace with movements in the general level of prices. This pattern has also been found in a number of other countries. Table 1 contains correlation coefficients between real stock returns and inflation for the Group of Seven countries using monthly data over the period 1950–1986. As that table shows, a significant negative relationship holds during at least one extended subperiod for all except one of the countries listed. And a significant negative rela- tionship is found in four of the seven countries for the overall period of 1950–1986. Against this backdrop, it is not surprising that "inflation fears" were cited as a possible contributing factor to the stock market crash of October 1987.[1]

A number of studies have documented the inverse relationship between real common stock returns and various measures of both actual and expected inflation.[2] The literature is generally di- vided, however, over the reasons why equities might fail to maintain their value during periods of inflation. This paper surveys the two main arguments that have been advanced as possible explanations for this observed anomaly in the U.S. stock market. First, the so-called "tax-effect" hy-

pothesis is examined. This hypothesis focuses on the treatment of depreciation and the valuation of inventories in periods of inflation. Particularly, share prices fail to keep pace with inflation be- cause inflation increases corporate tax liabilities and thus reduces after-tax earnings. Here, infla- tion can be said, in an econometric sense, to "cause"—or more precisely to temporally pre- cede—movements in stock prices.

The "proxy-effect" hypothesis is the alterna- tive explanation for why real stock returns are negatively correlated with inflation. In its current form, this hypothesis involves two assumptions— one that cyclical variations in output and earnings growth are positively correlated, and the other that monetary policy is countercyclical. The cen- tral tenet here is that lower stock returns signal lower expected future output and earnings growth, which, in turn, initiates a countercyclical policy response by the central bank. Individuals anticipate the expansion in the money supply and thus anticipate future inflation, which leads to an increase in *current* inflation. So, when stock re-

The authors would like to thank Mike Cox, Joe Haslag and Scott Hein for helpful comments without implicating them in our conclusions.

[1] The Report of the Presidential Task Force on Market Mecha- nisms *(1988, p. I-13)* states that *"It is meaningless whether or not these inflation fears were justified, for it is clear that for as long as financial authorities were responding to the infla- tion threat—whether real or imagined..."* the equity market might suffer.

[2] See Bodie *(1976)*, Nelson *(1976)*, and Fama and Schwert *(1977)*.

Chart 1
Annual CPI and S&P 500
Common Stock Price Index

1970 = 100

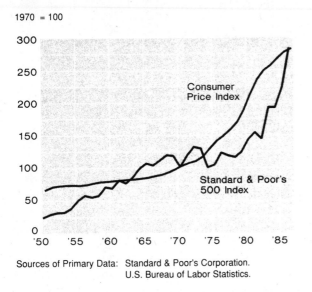

Sources of Primary Data: Standard & Poor's Corporation.
U.S. Bureau of Labor Statistics.

Table 1
Real Stock Returns and Inflation:
Various Periods

Country	1950-1959	1960-1969	1970-1979	1980-1986	1950-1986
United States	−0.05	−0.28*	−0.24*	−0.34*	−0.25*
Japan	−0.08	−0.21*	−0.33*	−0.26*	−0.20*
West Germany	−0.05	−0.19*	−0.02	−0.12	−0.09
France	−0.24*	−0.12	−0.005	−0.15	−−0.13*
United Kingdom	−0.02	−0.16	−0.06	−0.08	−0.04
Italy	−0.26*	−0.16	−0.29*	−0.09	−0.20*
Canada	−0.06	−0.12	−0.04	−0.26*	−0.03

* Significant at the 1-percent level.

turns fall, inflation increases. Although inflation in this case, is negatively correlated with stock returns, more precisely, stock returns temporally precede inflation. Thus, in an econometric sense, they are said to "cause" inflation.[3]

In the following analysis, a simple model of stock-price determination is offered. (*See the accompanying box for a description.*) This model can be used to highlight the role that inflation has played in determining both stock prices and stock returns in the U.S. economy. In the context of this model, the tax-effect hypothesis is first examined, with emphasis on particular features of the U.S. Tax Code that may have given rise to inflation's adverse effect on equity markets. This is followed by an exposition of the proxy-effect hypothesis, which shows how monetary policy may have historically contributed to the anomalous relationship between stock returns and inflation.

Tax-effect hypothesis: the firm's perspective

Adherents of the tax-effect hypothesis argue that the adverse effect of inflation on share prices stems primarily from two sources—inflation's effect on after-tax earnings of firms and inflation's effect on individuals' portfolio allocation. This section considers the first of these two sources.

From the standpoint of firms, inflation has a detrimental effect due primarily to two features of the U.S. Tax Code. The first of these features is the treatment of depreciation. Traditionally, the value of the depreciation deduction allowed for firms has been based on the original or "historic cost" of an asset, and *not* on its full replacement value. In a period of rising prices, then, the value of the depreciation allowance becomes inadequate and real corporate tax liabilities increase. In this way, inflation leads to a reduction in real after-tax earnings of firms and a consequent reduction in real dividends and stock prices.

Also contributing to the adverse effect of inflation on the firm is the treatment of inventory valuation under U.S. tax laws. When inventories are valued under FIFO (or first-in-first-out) accounting, inflation leads to an understatement of the costs of replacing these inventories. As is the case under the use of historic-cost accounting for depreciation charges, inflation raises the effective corporate tax burden, thus depressing net earn-

ings. Each of the above two factors—depreciation allowances and inventory valuation—acts to make inflation a penalty to firm profitability; consequently, inflation penalizes a firm's dividends and share prices.

There is, however, one potential *benefit* to firm profitability from rising prices. Namely, at higher rates of inflation, nominal interest rates are higher. And, since firms are allowed to deduct the full nominal interest payments on debt, accounting profits are in this regard reduced by inflation.

The net corporate tax burden caused by inflation thus depends on a comparison of the *penalty* arising from historic-cost accounting methods to the *benefit* arising from the deductibility of nominal interest payments on debt. Using simulation analysis, Hasbrouck (1983) finds that, under tax laws in effect through 1980, the loss due to historic-cost accounting outweighs the leverage gain at low inflation rates. Hasbrouck estimates that the corporate tax-maximizing inflation rate is in the range of 7–9 percent. Beyond these rates, inflation actually reduces the corporate tax burden since gains resulting from the use of debt financing outweigh the effects of historic-cost accounting.[4] It is worth noting that from 1973 to 1980, when real stock prices tended to fall, the rate of inflation averaged 9.2 percent per year. Interpreted in light of Hasbrouck's esti-

---

[3] *Modigliani and Cohn (1979) offer a third explanation. Investors commit two "major errors" in evaluating stocks during periods of inflation. First, investors are said to be unable to distinguish between real and nominal rates of return in the valuation of equities. Second, market participants fail to realize the gain that flows from a depreciation in the value of corporate debt outstanding in a time of inflation. In essence, Modigliani and Cohn argue that investors suffer from a form of "money illusion." This framework is ignored in the current analysis as it is outside the generally accepted paradigm of market efficiency and thus has not generated much interest.*

[4] *Maher and Nantell (1983) argue that there is no offset possible from debt usage as the premium that must be paid to bondholders in the face of inflation exceeds the tax advantages of debt financing. The crucial assumption for this result to hold is that the bondholder's marginal tax rate must exceed the corporate tax rate.*

A Model of Share Price Determination

This box outlines a simple model of stock-price determination helpful for illustrating the relationship between stock prices and inflation. In order to focus attention on the issues considered in this article—specifically, on the tax-effect hypothesis and on the proxy-effect hypothesis—certain simplifying assumptions are made.

In general, the price of a firm's stock today can be expressed as the present discounted value of expected future dividends (Brealey and Myers 1984, Chap. 4). That is,

$$(1) \qquad V_t = \sum_{i=1}^{\infty} \frac{DIV_{t+i}^e}{(1+R)^i}$$

where V_t equals the dollar price of the firm's stock today, DIV_{t+i}^e equals the firm's nominal expected future dividend (dividend in period $t+i$), and R represents the nominal rate (presumed constant over time) at which market participants discount these expected future cash flows (or the rate of return required by investors).

Consider first the numerator of this expression. There are essentially two ways that expected dividends can grow over time. One of these is through growth in expected *real* earnings, and the other is through inflation. That is, $DIV_{t+i}^e = div_{t+i}^e * P_{t+i}^e$, where div_{t+i}^e represents real earnings of the firm in period $t+i$ and P_{t+i}^e is the expected price level in period $t+i$. Since the purpose of this paper is to investigate the relationship between *inflation* and the stock market, both actual and expected real earnings will be provisionally treated as constant over time. This allows div_{t+i}^e to be expressed simply as div in all periods.

For simplicity, it is also assumed that inflation, π, is constant over time and fully anticipated. Under these assumptions, P_{t+i}^e can be rewritten simply as $P_t(1+\pi)^i$. This allows expected nominal dividends to be separated into its two components, real dividends and the general level of prices, so $DIV_{t+i}^e = div * P_t(1+\pi)^i$.

Turning now to the denominator of this expression, the nominal rate of discount can be separated into its two components—inflation and the (constant) real rate of discount (r)—by making use of the Fisher relationship. That is, $1+R$ equals $(1+r)(1+\pi)$.

With these simplifications, the value of the firm's stock can then be expressed as:

$$(2) \qquad V_t = \sum_{i=1}^{\infty} \frac{div * P_t (1+\Pi)^i}{(1+r)^i (1+\Pi)^i},$$

which, upon simplification, reduces to:

$$(3) \qquad V_t = \frac{div \cdot P_t}{r}$$

As equation 3 makes clear, stock prices will not increase proportionately with an increase in the general price level if inflation is associated with either (1) a reduction in real dividends of the firm, or (2) an increase in individuals' discount rate. Equation 3 is thus helpful in explaining both the tax-effect hypothesis and the proxy-effect hypothesis. The tax-effect hypothesis, for example, is represented in equation 3 as the case where either (1) div is reduced, or (2) r is increased due to an increase in P_t. The proxy-effect hypothesis, on the other hand, is represented as the case where an anticipated reduction in GNP growth causes a reduction in div and V_t, which is associated with an increase in P_t. In the text we will discuss more fully the underlying bases for each of these hypotheses.

mates, stock prices fell during a period in which inflation had risen to roughly its corporate tax-maximizing rate, indicating the possibility of an adverse tax-effect at work.

Tax-effect hypothesis: individuals' perspective

The foregoing discussion pertains to the adverse effect that inflation can have on stock prices due solely to its direct effect on firms' profitability. Inflation was shown to potentially lower firms' real dividends which, as seen from Equation 3, prevents stock prices from keeping pace with the general level of prices. Chart 2 illustrates this hypothesized link between inflation and stock prices.

There are, however, other methods by which taxes and inflation can interact to lower firms' stock prices. One of these methods, as outlined by Martin Feldstein (1980 a & b), pertains to the manner in which tax rules and inflation interact to raise individuals' effective rate of discount. Feldstein's argument relies principally on the assumption that individuals invest in a wide range of alternative assets (stocks, bonds, land, gold, owner-occupied housing, tax-free instruments, etc.). Furthermore, although inflation generally reduces firm profitability and thus reduces the rate of return on stocks, it tends to raise the relative return offered on a variety of other assets. (In fact, as Feldstein points out, individuals may actually experience an increase in their net real yield on some assets during inflation).

Therefore, since they: (1) must pay income tax on both dividends and capital gains; (2) must pay taxes on nominal interest income from corporate bonds; and (3) may invest in a much wider range of alternative investments, individuals will substitute out of corporate stocks and bonds in times of rising prices. The effect of this substitution is to increase the real cost to firms of raising capital or, viewed alternatively, to increase the real rate at which individuals discount their before-tax dividends received from firms (r). As seen in equation (3), this effect of inflation on individuals' rate of discount reinforces that outlined previously on firms' dividends, so that real stock prices would be further depressed in periods of inflation.[5] Chart 2 illustrates this added

effect of inflation on stock prices.

Tax-effect hypothesis: empirical evidence

While the theoretical justification for the tax-effect hypothesis is generally acknowledged, formal empirical evidence is more problematic. As shown previously, when firms' computation of taxes is based on historic-cost accounting methods for both depreciation and cost of goods sold, tax-deductible firm costs differ from the current costs of factors of production. It follows that real *aggregate* corporate tax liabilities, then, should vary directly with the rate of inflation. Following this line of reasoning, Gonedes (1981) attempts to assess the impact of both expected and unexpected inflation on various measures of the aggregate real corporate tax burden over the period 1929–1974. Contrary to expectations, Gonedes presents evidence that appears to be inconsistent with the tax-effect hypothesis.[6] Specifically, aggregate corporate tax liabilities over the period from 1929–1974 are found to be unrelated to various measures of inflation—-rather than positively affected by inflation—and thus not in support of the tax-effect hypothesis.

Gonedes attributes the lack of empirical verification of a tax effect at work to an implicit "indexing" that has occurred over the period 1929–1974. Indexing the tax code with respect to both depreciation and inventory charges would eliminate the effect of inflation on share prices. Gonedes argues that de facto indexation has been

---

[5] Friend and Hasbrouck (1982) criticize the ad hoc nature of Feldstein's approach to share-price determination. Using a model based on expected utility maximization, along with different values of the tax and risk parameters, Friend and Hasbrouck arrive at the same qualitative conclusions as Feldstein. That is, inflation places downward pressure on share prices due to tax effects, but the magnitude of the effect is discovered to be much smaller than what follows from Feldstein's model. Feldstein (1982) acknowledges the usefulness of deriving the price investors are willing to pay per share on the basis of expected utility maximization, but rejects as "implausible" some of the parameter values assumed by Friend and Hasbrouck.

[6] Gordon (1983) also finds little evidence in support of a tax effect at work.

Chart 2

Tax-Effect Hypothesis

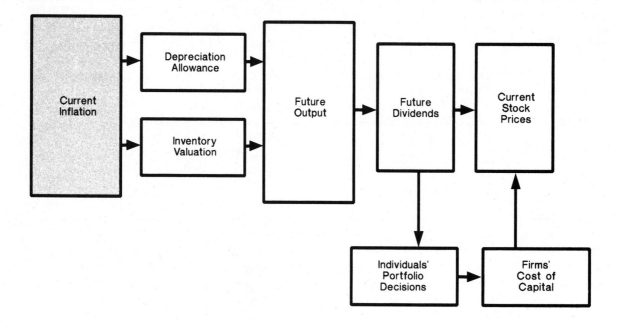

Proxy-Effect Hypothesis

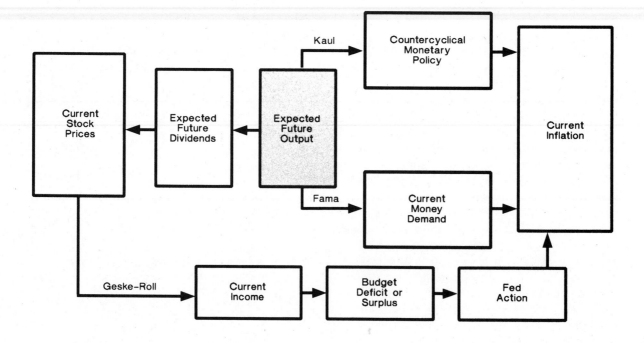

achieved through such factors as: (1) The implementation of accelerated depreciation schedules; (2) Various subsidies, such as the Investment Tax Credit; and (3) Decreasing the service lives on depreciable assets, all of which occurred simultaneously over the period 1929-1974.

Recall that, during times of inflation, the *net* corporate tax burden depends on both a penalty arising from historic-cost accounting methods and a benefit arising from the deductibility of nominal interest payments on corporate debt. If inflation is unanticipated, an additional benefit is available from the unforeseen decline in the real value of a firms'outstanding debt. Over the time period November 1977 through December 1982, Pearce and Roley (1988) examine the impact of unanticipated inflation on firms' share prices by considering these potential penalties and benefits. Historic-cost accounting of inventories is found to adversely affect stock prices. But, depreciation expenses are not a significant factor in explaining movements in share prices. Finally, the magnitude of a firms' outstanding debt is found to have a positive affect on share prices, indicating that inflation, in part, reduced the real value of firms' liabilities.

Tax-effects hypothesis: recapitulation of theory and evidence

The failure of changes in share prices to keep pace with movements in the overall level of prices could be attributed to certain features of the tax system. Particularly, the use of historic-cost accounting drives a wedge between tax-deductible costs and current costs of the factors of production. As a result, taxable profits increase at a faster pace than inflation, which puts downward pressure on equity prices. Empirical evidence of a tax effect at work is mixed and does not generally come out in support of the tax-effects hypothesis. Also, evidence that relies on simulation analysis is usually quite sensitive to the assumptions regarding the *effective* corporate tax burden.[7] Further, if it *is* the tax structure which is the driving force behind the seemingly anomalous relationship between inflation and stock prices in the U.S., then it is puzzling to observe (*see Table 1*) basically the same phenomenon across countries despite variation in tax laws.

An alternative framework: the proxy-effect hypothesis

In view of the criticisms of the tax-effect hypothesis, an alternative framework has developed to explain why inflation and stock values are inversely related. This explanation—known as the proxy-effect hypothesis—argues that expected future output growth and current inflation are inversely correlated. Inflation is said to be merely "proxying" for expected output or earnings growth in statistical tests of the relationship between stock returns and inflation. According to the proxy-effect hypothesis, any significant inverse relationship between these two variables is spurious, because it is induced by a *direct* relationship between stock returns and expected output growth together with an *inverse* relationship between expected future output growth and inflation. In contrast to the tax-effect hypothesis, the proxy-effect hypothesis claims that inflation has not been a causal factor in the performance of real stock prices but, rather, the relationship between inflation and stock prices is spurious.

Understanding the proxy-effect hypothesis requires exposition of the purported links in two contemporaneous chains of causality. Each chain begins with an increase or decrease in the rate of growth of expected future output. In one case this chain runs to expected future dividends and thus to current stock returns and in the other case, to expected future inflation and thus to current inflation. The link between expected future output growth and current stock returns is straightforward and requires little explanation. The purported link between expected future output growth and current inflation is not commonly acknowledged and requires further elaboration. In what follows, three explanations are reviewed to show how movements in expected future output may be related to current inflation.

---

[7] See the discussion in Friend and Hasbrouck (1982) *and* Feldstein (1982) for an example of the importance of assumed parameter values.

The proxy-effect hypothesis: linkage through money demand

The proxy-effect hypothesis was first introduced by Eugene Fama (1981). Fama's explanation for the inverse relationship between expected economic activity and current inflation follows from two key assumptions—(1) that individuals are "rational" in the sense of making use of all available current information relevant to their money and financial decisions, and (2) that individuals' current demand for money is related to future real economic activity and current interest rates.[8] Then, assuming that the money supply, real economic activity, and interest rates are exogenous, this demand for money, in effect, becomes a vehicle for the transmission of expected future inflation to current inflation.

In order to explain this more fully, consider the case where individuals' expectations of future output growth are revised downward. The lowering in expected future output growth leads to a lowering in expected future dividends and has the direct and immediate effect of reducing current stock returns. But also, the decline in expected future output growth leads to a decrease in money demand currently and thus an excess supply of money. Following Fama's assumption that interest rates and the money supply are exogenous, the excess supply of money is accompanied by an increase in the price level to restore monetary equilibrium. Essentially, the forward-looking nature of individuals' money demand generates an inverse relationship between current inflation and expected future growth in GNP. This enables a decrease in future output growth to cause *both* a decline in current stock returns and an increase in current inflation.

In terms of the model developed earlier, and summarized in equation 3, a reduction in expected future output and earnings growth lowers *div* with the direct effect of lowering V_t.[9] But also, the reduction in anticipated future output growth raises P_t. Chart 2 outlines this purported linkage of the proxy-effect hypothesis (identified as the Fama scenario). Any observed relation between stock returns and current or expected inflation then, according to this theory, is purely spurious, with no causal chain from inflation to stock returns.[10]

The proxy-effect hypothesis: linkage through debt monetization

Geske and Roll (1983), who relax the assumption of an exogenous money supply, have suggested an extension of Fama's argument. These authors posit, in fact, that a "reverse causality" actually drives the inverse relationship between stock returns and inflation. In contrast to earlier work which hypothesized a causative influence of inflation on stock returns (and in contrast to Fama's model in which inflation and stock returns are spuriously related), it is stock returns which "cause" inflation.[11]

Geske and Roll weave a sequence of events by which this reverse causality comes about. In order to illustrate the Geske-Roll hypothesis, consider the case where expectations regarding future GNP growth are lowered. Stock prices decrease in response to projections of slower growth which leads to a decline in both personal and corporate income. Government tax revenues then decline which leads to a deficit in government revenue. That is, Geske and Roll suggest that a decline in expected future economic activity should be fol-

---

[8] It should be pointed out that it is not common in economic models to assume that the demand for money currently is related to future economic activity, and, on this basis, Fama has been criticized. It is worth noting, however, that Fama's results could also be obtained in a more standard framework where, instead of Fama's assumption (2), current money demand is assumed to be related to current income and current interest rates, but with individuals being forward looking in decisions regarding interest rates. In this case, a decline in expected future output growth would lead to a perceived future excess supply of money and thus to a perceived increase in future inflation and interest rates (equivalently a decrease in future bond prices). Expecting such an increase in future interest rates, individuals may bid up interest rates today (bond prices fall) as they sell bonds in order to avoid a future capital loss. Again, the demand for money currently would fall leading to an excess supply of money and inflation.

[9] This application of the proxy-effect hypothesis assumes that the expected growth rate of future output was initially zero, so that a decline in the growth rate amounts to an anticipated contraction in GNP.

lowed both by a decline in government revenue *and* by an increase in the federal budget deficit. The next step in the Geske-Roll model involves the central bank. When deficits begin to grow, government debt outstanding increases. The central bank chooses to monetize a portion of this debt, thus leading to inflation. Since this debt monetization is anticipated by rational individuals, a decline in the stock market will cause an increase in expected future inflation. Therefore, stock returns are inversely correlated with expected future inflation.

Geske and Roll point out that changes in expected inflation tend to be highly correlated with unexpected inflation. This explains the negative association between stock returns and unexpected inflation which Fama (1981) found puzzling. Finally, through individuals' forward-looking behavior, the increase in expected future inflation is transmitted to current inflation as well. It is through this extended chain of causality, then, that lower current stock returns cause an increase in current inflation. In terms of the model developed earlier, *div* first falls (due to an anticipated cyclical contraction in output). The reduction in *div* drives V_t down, which ultimately leads to an increase in P_t. Chart 2 shows this hypothesized chain of events (identified as the Geske-Roll scenario).

The proxy-effect hypothesis: linkage through countercyclical monetary policy

The Fama model excludes any response by the monetary authority while Geske and Roll stress a policy response of debt monetization. An extension of these arguments is developed by Kaul (1987) who agrees that the relationship between stock returns and inflation is spurious. Following Fama, Kaul stresses the importance of the money demand linkage in his analysis but is also willing to incorporate a response of the monetary authorities. Unlike Geske and Roll, however, this response does not hinge exclusively on the practice of debt monetization. Rather, Kaul presumes that the central bank follows a *countercyclical* money supply process.

The full sequence of events as viewed by Kaul occurs as follows. First, expected future output declines which is signaled by a fall in stock prices. The Fed then responds with a countercyclical policy which results in an increase in the money supply. This causes both an increase in current inflation and an upward revision in inflation expectations. As a result, there is an observed inverse relationship between stock returns and both actual and expected inflation.

Kaul's version of the proxy effect hypothesis thus incorporates two commonly accepted effects of a perceived reduction in future GNP growth. For one, the anticipated slowing lowers current stock returns. For another, the anticipated slowing causes a current monetary expansion, and thus inflation. These two alone are sufficient to generate the inverse relationship often found between stock returns and inflation. The inverse relationship between expected future GNP growth and current inflation now is the result of the equilibrium process in the monetary sector. In terms of the model developed earlier, *div* first declines (due to an anticipated decline in GNP) which lowers V_t. But also, the decline in *div* stimulates a countercyclical response on the part of the monetary authorities which raises P_t. Chart 2 shows this hypothesized connection between stock prices and inflation (identified as the Kaul scenario).

[10] Benderly and Zwick (1985) agree with Fama that the relationship between stock returns and inflation is spurious. Unlike Fama though, Benderly and Zwick argue that the relationship runs from inflation to expected output growth. These authors base their conclusion on a real balance model of output in which changes in aggregate demand are related to lagged changes in real money balances.

[11] One should take note of the subtle distinction in Geske and Roll's use of the term "cause" here. Really, there is not reverse causality in the sense previously described for the tax-effect hypothesis because the sequence of events does not begin with stock prices. It begins with movements in expected future output. Actually, then, the relationship between current inflation and stock returns is here, too, spurious because both inflation and stock returns are ultimately driven by a decline in expectations of future GNP growth. Movements in stock prices, however, do precede movements in inflation and in this sense can be said to cause inflation.

Proxy-effect hypothesis:
the empirical evidence

Empirical evidence on the proxy-effect hypothesis is extensive and generally may be delineated into the categories outlined above in reviewing the theoretical linkages between stock returns and inflation. In what follows, we will review the empirical evidence on the proxy-effect hypothesis beginning with the evidence on the linkage through money demand, as theorized by Fama.

Recall that the key to the spurious relationship between inflation and stock returns in Fama's hypothesis is that movements in expected future economic activity cause movements in both expected and current inflation. Empirical evidence relating real stock returns to both expected and unexpected inflation reveal a significant negative relationship. However, in multiple tests which also include real expected output growth, expected inflation looses its significance in explaining stock returns. This evidence suggests a spurious relationship between expected future inflation and current stock returns. Note also that *unexpected* inflation remains significant in nearly all of Fama's tests (all but those using annual data), and the expected inflation term looses significance in explaining real stock returns only when the growth rate of the monetary base is added to the set of explanatory variables. Fama points out that his measure of expected inflation is highly correlated with monetary base growth. Therefore, it is possible that one proxy for expected inflation has simply replaced another and the puzzling relationship between stock returns and inflation remains.

Turning now to empirical evidence on other views of the proxy-effect hypothesis, recall that Geske and Roll view current stock prices as driving current inflation through a practice of debt monetization by the central bank. Geske and Roll offer as empirical evidence a series of "transfer-functions" which purport to establish the linkage between stock prices and inflation in their model. For the most crucial element of this linkage, however—the practice of debt monetization—Geske and Roll do not offer compelling evidence. Empirical verification of the existence of debt monetization by the Federal Reserve is mixed, at best.[12] Geske and Roll point out that "...the detectable effect of Federal Reserve System Treasury debt holdings on the Fed's issuance of base money is very small in estimated magnitude; however, it *is* significant." The failure to discover a very substantial degree of debt monetization is blamed on "the incredible short-term churning of the Fed's asset portfolio."[13]

Kaul (1987) presents empirical evidence for the United States, as well as for Canada, the United Kingdom and Germany, consistent with the central tenets of the proxy-effect hypothesis. Regression results indicate a positive relationship between stock returns and expected real activity. Inflation and expected real activity are found to be negatively related, Kaul argues, due to both a countercyclical monetary policy response and to the practice of debt monetization.

Just as Geske and Roll's results hinge on the practice of debt monetization, Kaul's conclusions rely on a consistent countercyclical policy response which is anticipated by individuals. In estimates of both base-growth and monetary-aggregate growth equations, Kaul includes the unemployment rate to capture this policy response. In the four countries analyzed, however, the unemployment rate is generally insignificant in explaining money growth.

Evidence of central bank behavior from reaction functions casts doubt about the consistency of Federal Reserve policymaking, making it difficult to derive a generally accepted model of central-bank behavior.[14] Moreover, throughout most of the 1970's, the Fed engaged in federal funds rate targeting, which tends to result in a *procyclical* policy. Also, the current procedure of targeting on borrowed reserves, in effect since the fall of 1982, represents a return to funds rate targeting.[15] Clearly, a procyclical policy results in either a *positive* relationship between stock re-

---

[12] See Allen and McCrickard (1988) and Joines (1988). For additional support of the inconclusive evidence of debt monetization, see the references in McMillin (1986).

[13] Geske and Roll (1983, p. 22)

[14] For a summary of the reaction function literature, see Barth Sickles and Wiest (1982).

[15] See Gilbert (1985) and Thornton (1988).

turns and inflation or, at best, no relationship. Yet there has been an inverse relationship between stock returns and inflation in the United States during the 1970's and 1980's, as Table 1 shows, despite evidence of a procyclical policy stance by the central bank. These findings cast further doubt on the validity of Kaul's hypothesis.

Summary and conclusions

Equities, representing claims to real assets, should prove to be good hedges against inflation. Moreover, if future inflation can be at all foreseen, stock-market returns should be positively related to expected inflation as well. During much of the post-war time period, however, a well-documented tendency exists for equities to perform poorly during periods of inflation. Two main schools of thought have arisen to explain this anomaly.

The first of these appeals to particular features of the tax code in the United States as the primary factor behind the failure of equities to maintain their value during inflation. Historic-cost accounting for both depreciation and inventories results in an overstatement of corporate profits during periods of inflation. As a result, real corporate tax liabilities increase, which decreases net earnings. A simple model of share price determination then predicts downward pressures on real equity values during periods of inflation. While theoretically valid, empirical evidence for a tax effect at work is inconclusive.

The second school of thought appeals to the monetary sector as a vehicle through which the inverse stock return-inflation relationship occurs. A combination of money demand effects, along with both the practice of debt monetization and countercyclical monetary policy responses by the central bank is said to give rise to an inverse relationship between stock returns and inflation. Again, empirical evidence for this model is problematic.

References

Allen, Stuart D., and Donald L. McCrickard, (1988), "Deficits and Money Growth in the United States: A Comment," *Journal of Monetary Economics* 21 (January): 143–153.

Barth, James, Robin Sickles, and Philip Wiest, (1982), "Assessing the Impact of Varying Economic Conditions on Federal Reserve Behavior," *Journal of Macroeconomics* 4 (Winter): 47–70.

Benderly, Jason, and Burton Zwick, (1985), "Inflation, Real Balances, Output, and Real Stock Returns," *American Economic Review* 75 (December): 1115–1123.

Bodie, Zvi (1976), "Common Stocks as a Hedge Against Inflation," *Journal of Finance* 31 (May): 459–470.

Brealey, Richard, and Stewart Myers (1984), *Principles of Corporate Finance* (New York: McGraw-Hill).

Fama, Eugene F. (1981), "Stock Returns, Real Activity, Inflation and Money," *American Economic Review* 71 (September): 545–565.

————— and G. William Schwert, (1977), "Asset Returns and Inflation," *Journal of Financial Economics* 5 (November): 115–146.

Feldstein, Martin (1980a), "Inflation, Tax Rules and the Stock Market," *Journal of Monetary Economics* 6 (July): 309–331.

————— (1980b), "Inflation and the Stock Market," *American Economic Review* 70 (December): 839-847.

————— (1982), "Inflation and the Stock Market: Reply," *American Economic Review* 72 (March): 243–246.

Friend, Irwin, and Joel Hasbrouck (1982), "Inflation and the Stock Market: Comment," *American Economic Review* 72 (March): 237–242.

Geske, Robert, and Richard Roll (1983), "The Fiscal and Monetary Linkage between Stock Returns and Inflation, "*Journal of Finance* 38 (March): 1–33.

Gilbert R. Alton, (1985), "Operating Procedures for Conducting Monetary Policy," Federal Reserve Bank of St. Louis *Review*, (February): 13–21.

Gonedes, Nicholas J. (1981), "Evidence on the 'Tax Effects' of Inflation under Historical Cost Accounting Methods, "*Journal of Business* 54 (April): 227–270.

Gordon, Myron G. (1983), "The Impact of Real Factors and Inflation on the Performance of the U.S. Stock Market from 1960-1980," *Journal of Finance* 38 (May): 553–563.

Hasbrouck, Joel (1983) "The Impact of Inflation Upon Corporate Taxation," *National Tax Journal* 36 (March): 65–81.

Joines, Douglas H. (1988), "Deficits and Money Growth in the United States: Reply, *Journal of Monetary Economics* 21 (January): 155–160.

Kaul, Gatam (1987), "Stock Returns and Inflation: The Role of the Monetary Sector," *Journal of Financial Economics* 18 (June): 253–276.

Maher, Michael, and Timothy J. Nantell (1983), "The Tax Effects of Inflation: Depreciation, Debt and Miller's Equilibrium Tax Rates," *Journal of Accounting Research* 21 (Spring): 329–340.

McMillin, W. Douglas (1986), "Federal Deficits, Macrostabilization Goals, and Federal Reserve Behavior," *Economic Inquiry* 24 (April): 257–269.

Modigliani, Franco, and Richard A. Cohn (1979), "Inflation, Rational Valuation and the Market," *Financial Analysts Journal* (March/April): 24–36.

Nelson, Charles R. (1976), "Inflation and Rates of Return on Common Stocks, *Journal of Finance* 31, no. 2, (May): 471–483.

Pearce, Douglas K., and V. Vance Roley (1988), "Firm Characteristics, Unanticipated Inflation, and Stock Returns," *Journal of Finance* 43 (September): 965–981

Report of The Presidential Task Force on Market Mechanisms (1988) (Washington, D.C.: Government Printing Office, January).

Thornton, Daniel L. (1988), "The Borrowed-Reserves Operating Procedure: Theory and Evidence," Federal Reserve Bank of St. Louis *Review*, (January/February): 30–54.

Article 15

Interest Rates and Exchange Rates— What is the Relationship?

By Craig S. Hakkio

During much of the 1970s, U.S. interest rates and the foreign exchange value of the dollar moved in opposite directions. This relationship was particularly pronounced from 1976 to 1979, when short-term interest rates doubled, while the trade-weighted value of the dollar fell 17 percent. In the 1980s, however, the relationship between interest rates and the exchange rate appears to be considerably different. Indeed, for much of this period, U.S. interest rates and the value of the dollar have been positively correlated.

A key question is whether the apparent change in the relationship between interest rates and exchange rates represents a significant structural change in their linkages or whether the change in the relationship can be explained by using standard economic models. The answer to this question has important implications for policymakers. Interest rates and exchange rates are crucial elements in the transmission of monetary and

Craig S. Hakkio is a senior economist at the Federal Reserve Bank of Kansas City. J. Gregg Whittaker, assistant economist at the bank, assisted in the preparation of the article.

fiscal policy actions to economic activity. If the channels through which policy actions affect the economy have been altered, policymakers may find the design of policy to be more difficult and the consequences of policy actions more unpredictable. Thus, models of interest rate and exchange rate linkages that worked well during the 1970s may not be appropriate in the 1980s.

This article argues that much of the apparent instability in the interest rate-exchange rate relationship can be readily explained in terms of standard economic models. The change from a negative correlation between interest rates and exchange rates in the 1970s to a positive correlation in the 1980s is due to changes in the relative importance of factors underlying interest rate and exchange rate movements. Thus, changes in inflation and expected inflation were the dominant influences causing high interest rates and a lower dollar in the 1970s. In the 1980s, in contrast, changes in real interest rates have been the dominant factor responsible for the positive correlation between interest rates and the dollar.

The article is divided into four sections. The first section briefly reviews recent interest rate and exchange rate movements. The next section discusses the fundamental determinants of interest rates and exchange rates. The third section reviews the linkages between interest rates and exchange rates and shows how they can be positively or negatively correlated. The final section applies this analysis to interpreting the behavior of interest rates and the dollar over the 1974-86 period.

Interest rates and exchange rates: the evidence since 1974

The changing relationship between interest rates and the value of the dollar is illustrated in Chart 1. The interest rate used in this chart is the 10-year constant maturity Treasury bond rate. The exchange rate is the effective exchange rate—a weighted average of ten bilateral exchange rates between the dollar and other major currencies. The data in the chart have been smoothed to remove the influence of short-run factors and to highlight basic trend behavior.[1]

As shown in Chart 1, interest rates and exchange rates appear to have been negatively correlated in the 1970s. From 1975 to 1977, for example, interest rates fell while the dollar rose. Then, from 1977 to 1980, while interest rates rose sharply, the value of the dollar declined.

---

[1] The exchange rate is the effective exchange rate—a weighted average of ten bilateral exchange rates with Germany, Japan, France, the United Kingdom, Canada, Italy, the Netherlands, Belgium, Sweden, and Switzerland. The long-term U.S. interest rate is the 10-year constant maturity U.S. Treasury bond rate. The data in Charts 1-5 have been smoothed, to reduce the influence of short-run factors. A six-month moving average was used to smooth the data: if x_t equals the original data, and s_t equals the smoothed data, then $s_t = (x_t + x_{t-1} + \ldots + x_{t-5})/6$. The discussion in the text refers to the smoothed data and not the original data. Smoothing the data usually causes the peaks and troughs to occur later than with the original data. In Chart 1, for example, the exchange rate peaks in June 1985, but in the original data the peak occurs in February 1985. Using the 3-month CD rate produces a similar chart.

The basic relationship between interest rates and the dollar appears to have changed in the 1980s, however. As the chart shows, during the 1980-81 period, interest rates and the dollar moved in the same direction rather than in opposite directions; interest rates and the dollar trended upward, after abstracting from the sharp movement in interest rates in 1980 due to credit controls. In 1982, however, the relationship reverted to the 1970s pattern, with a drop in interest rates associated with a rising dollar. Then, from 1983 to 1986, a positive correlation reappeared and interest rates and the dollar again moved up and down together.

Chart 1 shows that there is no simple relationship between interest rates and the dollar. This does not imply, however, that the relationship is unstable or that the structure of the relationship broke down in the 1980s. As argued in the following sections, much of the behavior of interest rates and exchange rates over the 1974-86 period can be explained by the behavior of their underlying determinants.

Determinants of interest rates and exchange rates

The interest rate and exchange rate shown in Chart 1 are rates quoted in financial markets, that is, they are nominal rates. To understand their behavior over the 1974-86 period, it is useful to distinguish between real and nominal interest rates and between real and nominal exchange rates. This section develops this distinction and identifies common factors affecting interest rates and exchange rates.

Real and nominal interest rates

The distinction between real and nominal interest rates has become familiar in analyses of inflation during the 1970s. While the nominal interest rate is the rate quoted by banks and the

CHART 1

U.S. long-term interest rate and the exchange rate

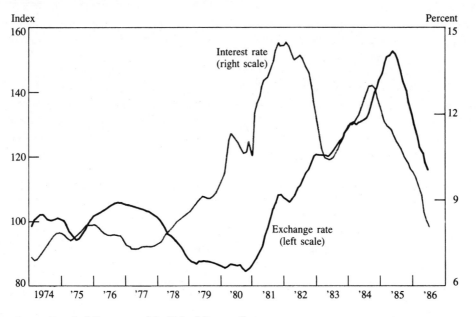

Source: Board of Governors of the Federal Reserve System

financial press, the real rate adjusts the nominal rate for the influence of inflation. According to the "Fisher equation," the nominal interest rate i is equal to the real interest rate r plus the expected rate of inflation p^e:

$$(1) \quad i = r + p^e.$$

Thus, for example, when a lender receives a 10 percent nominal interest rate but expected inflation is 7 percent, the real interest rate is only 3 percent.[2] Although the lender receives 10 percent more dollars, he can buy only 3 percent more goods and services because inflation has increased the price of goods and services.

In this framework, nominal interest rates

change either because of a change in the underlying real rate of interest or because of a change in expected inflation. For example, nominal interest rates could increase because of an increase in the real rate, with no change in expected inflation. Similarly, nominal interest rates could decline because of a decline in inflationary expectations, with no change in the real rate. A number of factors can cause variation in the underlying real rate or expected rate of inflation.

The real rate of interest is determined by the demand for and supply of funds in the economy. The supply of funds in the domestic economy comes from the saving of individuals and firms plus funds provided by the banking system. The demand for funds comes from firms making investment decisions, consumers borrowing in excess of current income, and government financing a budget deficit. In an open economy, other

---

[2] The tax deductibility of interest payments changes this statement slightly, but the basic concepts are the same.

countries may provide an additional net demand for or supply of funds.

The real interest rate tends to rise or fall as the demand for funds grows faster or slower than the supply of funds. The demand for funds increases, for example, if the government borrows to finance an increase in the deficit.[3] The government's increased demand for funds crowds out private investors, driving up the real interest rate. By paying a higher real interest rate, the government ensures that it, rather than others, obtains the funds it needs. In this way, an increase in the demand for funds puts upward pressure on the real interest rate.

Expectations of inflation can also change for several reasons. On the one hand, such special factors as one-time changes in the price of energy or food can have a temporary effect on the inflation rate. Since this shock may take several years to work its way through the economy, expectations of inflation can be affected for some time even though the shock has no permanent effect on the inflation rate. On the other hand, inflation expectations can change because of events leading to a continuously rising or falling price level. Such an effect might be associated with an excessive or deficient rate of money growth.

Real and nominal exchange rates

While the concept of the real interest rate has been widely discussed in recent years, the concept of a real exchange rate may be somewhat less familiar. As in the case of interest rates,

however, the distinction between a nominal exchange rate and a real exchange rate makes it possible to distinguish real or relative price effects from changes in the general price level.

The nominal exchange rate quoted in the financial press is the price of the dollar in terms of foreign currency. For example, the exchange rate between the dollar and the Japanese yen might be quoted as 160 yen per dollar. In contrast, the real exchange rate is not a rate of currency exchange. Rather, it is the relative price of U.S. goods in terms of foreign goods. As such, the real exchange rate reflects the underlying terms of trade between U.S. and foreign goods.

Equation 2 shows the relationship between the nominal exchange rate and the real exchange rate:

$$(2) \quad e = q \, P^*/P.$$

In this equation, e is the nominal exchange rate, q is the real exchange rate, P is the U.S. price level, and P^* is the foreign price level. The nominal exchange rate, e, can be viewed either as the price of the dollar in terms of foreign currency or, equivalently, as the foreign price of U.S. goods relative to the dollar price of U.S. goods.[4] In contrast, the real exchange rate, q, is the price of U.S. goods in terms of foreign goods. Rearranging equation 2, it can be shown that the real exchange rate is simply the nominal exchange rate deflated by the ratio of foreign to domestic prices ($q = e/[P^*/P]$).

From equation 2, it is clear that the nominal exchange rate can change either because of a change in the real exchange rate or because of a change in the general price levels in the United States or abroad. An increase in the real exchange

---

[3] Some have argued that the federal budget deficit also leads to an equal increase in the amount of savings, since individuals take into account the future tax liabilities associated with the budget deficit. Others, however, believe that the supply of funds does not increase equally, so that there is a net increase in the demand for funds. For a discussion of these arguments and a review of the empirical evidence, see Charles Webster, "The Effects of Deficits on Interest Rates," *Economic Review,* Federal Reserve Bank of Kansas City, May 1983, pp. 19-28.

---

[4] For further elaboration on the determinants of the nominal exchange rate, see Craig S. Hakkio, "Exchange Rate Volatility and Federal Reserve Policy," *Economic Review,* Federal Reserve Bank of Kansas City, July/August 1984, pp. 18-31.

rate or the foreign price level causes the nominal exchange rate to appreciate, while an increase in the domestic price level causes the nominal exchange rate to depreciate.

A variety of factors can cause the real exchange rate to change. For example, there may be a change in tastes away from domestically produced goods to foreign goods. Suppose that Japanese consumers decide to buy more U.S. goods rather than domestic products. This shift in demand will tend to raise the relative price of U.S. goods, leading to a rise in the real exchange rate. Then, if domestic and foreign price levels do not change, the nominal exchange rate will also rise. The reason is that since Japanese consumers need more dollars to purchase U.S. products, they will sell yen and buy dollars, causing the foreign exchange value of the dollar to increase.

Another reason for changes in real exchange rates comes from international investment and savings decisions. In addition to buying U.S. goods, Japanese investors might buy U.S. financial assets. A decision to buy more U.S. assets could result from the view that the real return on U.S. assets exceeds the real return on comparable Japanese assets. If Japanese investors buy more U.S. assets, the real exchange rate will rise. Since this decision requires the purchase of additional dollars in the foreign exchange market, the nominal exchange rate will also appreciate.

Changes in domestic and foreign price levels are the second factor influencing nominal exchange rates. Equation 2 shows that exchange rate movements are influenced by differences in foreign and domestic price levels. When prices in the United States rise faster than prices abroad, the nominal exchange rate depreciates because foreigners reduce their purchases of more expensive U.S. goods and thus reduce their demand for dollars in foreign exchange markets. In contrast, when foreign prices rise faster than U.S. prices, the nominal exchange rate appreciates because U.S. citizens tend to import fewer of the more expensive foreign goods. As a result, the demand for foreign currencies falls and the foreign exchange value of the dollar rises.

The linkages between interest rates and exchange rates

The preceding section identified key factors underlying the behavior of nominal interest rates and exchange rates. This section examines the channels linking interest rate and exchange rate movements and shows how changes in the relative importance of the underlying factors can result in patterns of positive or negative correlation between interest rates and exchange rates.

Inflation effects on interest rates and exchange rates

One simple channel linking interest rates and exchange rates is through the effects of inflation. Since nominal interest rates depend on expected inflation while nominal exchange rates depend on relative rates of foreign and domestic inflation, an inflation shock will affect both nominal interest rates and exchange rates.

Inflation shocks can usually be expected to lead to a negative correlation between nominal interest rates and exchange rates. Suppose, for example, that an increase in the price of energy or faster money growth leads to an increase in U.S. inflation. To the extent that higher inflation is built into inflation expectations, nominal interest rates in the United States will tend to rise. And, if U.S. inflation exceeds foreign inflation, the nominal exchange rate will tend to fall.

Similarly, disinflationary policy could lead to a negative relationship between interest rates and exchange rates. A reduction in U.S. inflation that led to lower inflation expectations would tend to reduce nominal interest rates in the United States. And, if the U.S. inflation rate is lower than foreign inflation rates, U.S. products would become more attractive in international markets and the dollar would tend to appreciate.

Real effects on interest rates and exchange rates

Nominal interest rates and exchange rates are also linked through movements in real interest rates. As discussion of the Fisher relationship showed, changes in real interest rates are translated directly into changes in nominal interest rates. In addition, changes in real interest rates, by altering the relative attractiveness of domestic and foreign investment opportunities, cause movements in real and nominal exchange rates.

To see the connection between real interest rates and the exchange rate, consider a foreign investor with a choice of investing in U.S. or domestic assets. The choice depends partly on a comparison of relative real interest rates. But because assets in different countries are denominated in different currencies, changes in the real exchange rate also affect the relative returns. Any expected appreciation of the real value of the dollar represents an expected capital gain and adds to the U.S. real return. Likewise, any expected depreciation of the real value of the dollar represents a capital loss and lowers the U.S. real return.

Generally, market forces should equalize the real returns to investment in the two countries. As a result, the real return to investment in the United States—the U.S. real interest rate plus the expected appreciation of the real exchange rate—should equal the foreign real interest rate:

(3) U.S. real + expected = foreign real
    interest   appreciation   interest
      rate   of real   rate
          exchange rate

That is, if the U.S. real interest rate is higher than the foreign real interest rate, the market must be expecting the real exchange rate to depreciate.

In this way, the expected depreciation of the real exchange rate offsets the higher U.S. real interest rate and the total U.S. real return equals the foreign real return. Viewed differently, the expected appreciation or depreciation of the dollar is directly related to the real interest rate differential in the two countries.

In this framework, an increase in the U.S. real interest rate will lead to an increase in the real exchange rate and the nominal exchange rate. A higher U.S. real interest rate increases the attractiveness of U.S. assets, leading to an increase in the demand for dollar-denominated assets and an appreciation of the real exchange rate. Then, for given price levels at home and abroad, the nominal exchange rate also tends to rise.

There is another way to see that an increase in the U.S. real interest rate leads to an increase in the real exchange rate. Because the total real return in the United States must equal the foreign real interest rate, as shown in equation 3, a rise in the U.S. real interest rate relative to the foreign real interest rate must lead to an expected depreciation of the real exchange rate. Therefore, if the real exchange rate is assumed to be constant in the long run, the only way for the market to expect the real exchange rate to depreciate in the future is for the real exchange rate to appreciate today. That is, an increase in the real interest rate leads to an increase in the current real exchange rate and an expected depreciation of the real exchange rate. As William Branson put it, "What must go down in the future [an expected depreciation], must go up today [the current real exchange rate]."[5]

---

[5] See William H. Branson, "Causes of Appreciation and Volatility of the Dollar," *The U.S. Dollar—Recent Developments, Outlook, and Policy Options,* proceedings of a conference sponsored by the Federal Reserve Bank of Kansas City, August 21-23, 1985, and Craig S. Hakkio and J. Gregg Whittaker, "The U.S. Dollar—Recent Developments, Outlook, and Policy Options," *Economic Review,* September/October 1985, Federal Reserve Bank of Kansas City, pp. 3-15.

Unlike inflation shocks, real interest rate shocks can be expected to result in a positive correlation between nominal interest rates and exchange rates. A rise in U.S. real interest rates resulting from higher budget deficits, for example, will directly cause a rise in nominal interest rates. In addition, the higher real interest rate in the United States will tend to raise both the real exchange rate and the nominal exchange rate. Similarly, a reduction in real rates in the United States will tend to lower nominal rates in the United States directly. And if the U.S. real interest rate falls relative to foreign real rates, there will be a corresponding fall in the real and nominal value of the dollar.

Interest rates and the exchange rate—explaining the evidence

Chart 1 showed that the relationship between nominal interest rates and the foreign exchange value of the dollar appeared to change in the 1980s. Interest rates and the exchange rate were negatively related until 1980. For most of the period since 1980, however, interest rates and the dollar have tended to move in the same direction.

The preceding section presented a theoretical framework in which inflation and real interest rate shocks can cause different patterns in the interest rate-exchange rate relationship. This section examines data on expected inflation, real interest rates, inflation differentials, and real interest rate differentials to see whether the theoretical framework provides a consistent explanation of the empirical evidence.

Interest rates and exchange rates: 1974 to 1979

According to the analysis presented in this article, the negative relationship between interest rates and the exchange rate during the 1970s, shown in Chart 1, is consistent with the view that inflation shocks dominated interest rate and exchange rate movements. Casual evidence supports this view. Oil and food prices increased dramatically in the early 1970s. After rising only 5 percent in 1972, food prices increased at an annual rate of 15 percent during the first three quarters of 1973. Then, as a result of OPEC, retail energy prices jumped 44 percent from the end of 1973 to the middle of 1974, after rising only 8 percent in the three previous quarters. Inflation rose again in the late 1970s, as food price increases in 1977-79 and oil price increases in 1978-79 occurred during a period of rapid growth in the money supply.

More direct evidence in support of an inflation explanation of interest rate and exchange rate movements can be obtained by looking at their underlying determinants. To the extent that inflation in the United States is built into inflation expectations, nominal interest rates will tend to rise and fall with inflation expectations. Thus, a high positive correlation between nominal interest rates and expected inflation supports the view that real factors were not an important determinant of nominal interest rate changes. If, in addition, there is a strong negative correlation between the dollar and the inflation differential in the United States and abroad, this supports an inflation explanation for exchange rate movements rather than a real explanation.

Chart 2, which plots the U.S. 3-month CD interest rate and a measure of expected inflation, shows that interest rates and expected inflation moved together from January 1974 to December 1979.[6] Both rose in the first three quarters of 1974, fell through the first quarter of 1977, and rose again until the end of 1979. Given the close

---

[6] The Board of Governors of the Federal Reserve System reports a real interest rate that is comparable with the 3-month CD interest rate. The expected rate of U.S. inflation is defined as the CD interest rate minus the real interest rate.

CHART 4
U.S. real and nominal interest rates

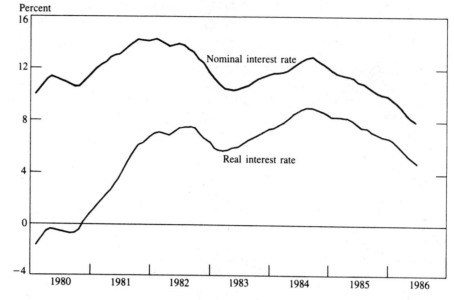

CHART 5
The exchange rate and real interest rate differential

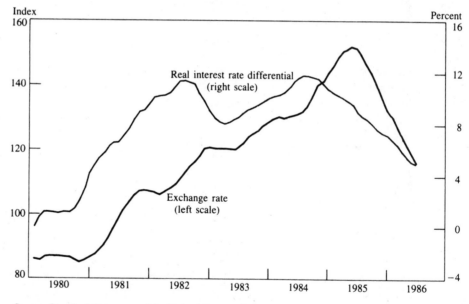

Source: Board of Governors of the Federal Reserve System

movement of nominal interest rates and expected inflation during this period, most of the changes in the nominal interest rate appear to be due to changes in expected inflation rather than to changes in real interest rates.

Chart 3, which plots the nominal exchange rate and the difference in U.S. and foreign inflation, supports the inflation explanation of exchange rate movements for the period from January 1974 to December 1979.[7] During the 1974-79 period, the nominal exchange rate and the inflation differential moved in opposite directions and were highly correlated. In 1975 and 1976, the inflation differential fell as foreign inflation exceeded U.S. inflation. During this period the dollar rose. Then, from 1977 to 1979, the inflation differential rose as U.S. inflation exceeded foreign inflation and the dollar fell. Thus, inflation factors appear to have dominated real factors in explaining exchange rate movements during this period.

Interest rates and exchange rates: 1980 to 1986

Nominal interest rates and the dollar have been positively correlated during much of the 1980s, as shown in Chart 1. Such a relationship is consistent with the dominance of real rather than inflationary shocks to the economy. At first glance, this dominance might seem puzzling. After all, the 1980s have generally been a period of disinflation, with inflation declining from double-digit rates in the late 1970s to the 3 to 4 percent range in the mid-1980s.

Real factors have been important, however. Real interest rates have been significantly higher in the 1980s than at any other time in the postwar period. The rise in real rates has been attributed to a number of factors: restrictive monetary policy in the 1980-82 period, major changes in tax laws affecting investment spending, an apparent decline in the personal savings rate, and record federal budget deficits.[8]

Again, evidence in support of a real explanation of interest rate and exchange rate movements during the 1980s can be obtained by looking at their underlying determinants. If real factors are important in explaining nominal interest rate movements, real interest rates should have a significant positive correlation with nominal interest rates. Similarly, if real factors are of primary importance in explaining exchange rate movements, there should be a strong positive correlation between the nominal exchange rate and the difference between real interest rates in the United States and abroad.

Chart 4, by plotting the real and nominal 10-year constant maturity bond rate from January 1980 to December 1985, shows that there is a clear positive relationship between nominal and real interest rates over this period.[9] Moreover, since expected inflation declined during most of this period, nominal interest rates should have declined if inflationary factors were dominant.

Movements in the nominal exchange rate and the real interest rate differential, as shown in Chart 5, also tend to support the real explanation of exchange rate movements. From 1980 to mid-1982, the real interest rate differential rose

[7] The Board of Governors reports a foreign weighted average CPI. The foreign rate of inflation equals the percentage change in the foreign weighted average CPI; the U.S. rate of inflation equals the percentage change in the U.S. CPI; the inflation differential equals the U.S. rate of inflation minus the foreign rate of inflation (and is a 12-month moving average).

[8] See Stephen Cecchetti, "High Real Interest Rates: Can They Be Explained?" *Economic Review,* Federal Reserve Bank of Kansas City, September/October 1986, for a discussion of the determinants of real interest rates and an analysis of recent movements in U.S. real interest rates.

[9] The Board of Governors of the Federal Reserve System reports a long-term U.S. and foreign real interest rate. The foreign real interest rate is a weighted average of ten corresponding foreign rates.

CHART 2
U.S. interest rates and expected inflation

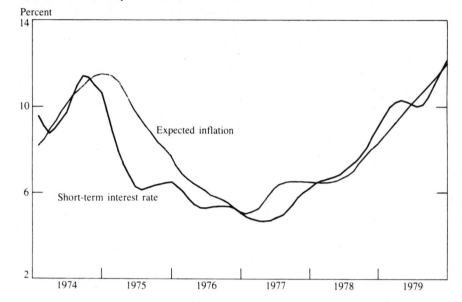

CHART 3
Exchange rate and inflation differential

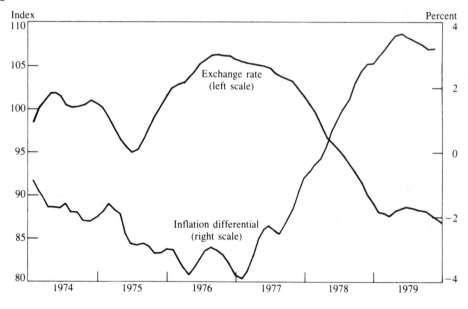

Source: Board of Governors of the Federal Reserve System

as the dollar appreciated. Then, from mid-1983 to late 1984, both the exchange rate and the real interest rate differential increased together. Finally, from mid-1985 to mid-1986, the dollar and the real interest rate differential moved lower. Thus, for most of the 1980-86 period, movements in the real interest rate differential provide a sensible explanation for exchange rate movements.

During two subperiods, however, real factors do not provide a good explanation for exchange rate movements. From July 1982 to March 1983, the exchange rate rose while the real interest differential fell. During that time, however, the inflation differential declined as U.S. inflation fell faster than foreign inflation. Thus, inflation factors seem to provide a better explanation of exchange rate movements during this period. The second subperiod, from September 1984 to May 1985, however, is not easily explained in the framework of this article. During this period, the real interest differential fell while the inflation differential rose. Either of these factors should have caused the dollar to fall. Instead, the dollar rose. Thus, the behavior of the exchange rate during this period does not seem to fit either the real or inflation explanation of exchange rate movements.[10]

Conclusion

This article has sought to explain changes in the relationship between interest rates and exchange rates over the 1974-86 period. In the framework presented in this article, the negative correlation between nominal interest rates in the United States and the dollar during the 1970s is consistent with the view that inflation shocks dominated interest rates and exchange rate movements. In contrast, during the 1980s, the generally positive relationship between interest rates and the dollar is consistent with the view that changes in real interest rates were the dominant influence on nominal interest rates and the dollar.

---

[10] See, for example, Richard Meese and Kenneth Rogoff, "Was It Real? The Exchange Rate-Interest Differential Relation, 1973-1974," International Finance Discussion Paper No. 268, Board of Governors of the Federal Reserve System, August 1985.

Article 16

Interest Rate Divergences among the Major Industrial Nations

The international integration of financial markets has increased dramatically during the last decade. Government-imposed barriers to international capital flows were gradually relaxed throughout the 1970s and by now have been substantially eliminated in the major industrial countries. More recently, the development and growth of currency and interest rate swaps, options, and other new financial instruments have further stimulated international financial integration by giving investors and borrowers a wider range of choices than that traditionally available from purely domestic channels. Distinctions between domestic and foreign financial markets are fading rapidly as major corporations can gain access to New York, London, and other international financial centers nearly as readily as their home markets.

It is widely presumed that financial integration reduces interest rate divergences among similar credit instruments and increases the degree to which yields in different markets move together over time. Historical experience with integration of domestic financial markets would seem to support this presumption. For example, the development of national money and capital markets in the United States during the latter part of the 19th century reduced regional disparities among interest rates and made the rates increasingly responsive to national, as opposed to purely local, conditions. This experience suggests that growing international financial integration should reduce interest differentials across countries and possibly limit the autonomy of national monetary authorities in controlling domestic financial yields. The actual record of the last two decades, however, raises doubts about these propositions. In particular, international interest divergences during much of the 1980s have been as great or greater than those observed during most of the 1960s and 1970s.

This article examines interest rate divergences among the United States and other major industrial countries from the 1960s through the present. As the next section shows, interest rate disparities among nations can arise from differences in currency denomination and national jurisdiction as well as from factors that cause yields to diverge domestically. Expected exchange rate changes and their associated risks, together with institutional barriers to financial flows across national borders, are potentially important sources of international interest disparities. The analysis also shows that increased financial integration unambiguously reduces one source of international interest rate divergences, that arising from institutional barriers. Whether integration actually leads to interest rate convergence, however, depends critically on the nature of other economic changes occurring at the same time and their effect upon currency expectations and risks.

These points are underscored by our empirical analysis of interest divergences. Neither nominal nor real interest rates have shown any systematic tendency toward convergence during the past 25 years. However, the factors underlying interest rate disparities apparently have changed significantly. Currency expectations and associated risks are now the primary sources of divergence, while the importance of overt barriers to capital mobility has declined markedly. These changes can be attributed to the historical association of increased financial integration with the shift from fixed to flexible exchange rates that has resulted in increased volatility in currency values.

Causes of interest divergences

In general, disparities among yields on alternative assets reflect differences in their underlying characteristics. Within a given nation, liquidity, credit risk, tax treatment, and other related attributes determine the relative yields on various instruments. Differences in these characteristics also contribute to interest variations across countries—indeed, the international diversity in these attributes is often greater than the diversity within any single nation. In a world composed of many countries, however, interest rates may also diverge because of currency distinctions and jurisdictional differences, the latter reflected largely in capital controls and other institutional barriers to financial flows across borders.

The existence of different national currencies is a fundamental source of international interest rate divergences. To compare yields on assets denominated in different currencies, an investor requires an estimate of their exchange rate at maturity. For example, the *dollar* return on an instrument denominated in German marks (DM) depends upon how much the DM is expected to appreciate (or depreciate) over the holding period. This means that yield differentials among assets denominated in different currencies implicitly reflect market forecasts of future exchange rate changes. In addition, investing in one currency as against another involves potential risks because exchange rates cannot be predicted exactly. This currency risk, resulting from uncertainty about future exchange rates, is also a potential source of interest divergences across countries.[1]

International interest divergences also reflect nationality distinctions arising from a variety of government policies and institutional imperfections that effectively impede financial flows across national jurisdictions. Until fairly recently, most industrial countries explicitly restricted or otherwise regulated international capital flows; these restrictions have been substantially removed in the United States, Canada, Japan, the United Kingdom, and Germany, but remain important in many other nations.[2] Interest divergences based on nationality can also arise from differences in tax systems or other

policies not explicitly aimed at capital flows, as well as from private market imperfections such as incomplete information or monopolistic restrictions on market access and pricing.

The effects of these various factors on interest divergences across countries can be summarized in the following identity:

$$\text{(i)} \quad i - i^* = \%s + DOM + CRISK + BAR,$$

where i and i^* are, respectively, the interest rates on U.S. assets and foreign-currency-denominated assets of a given maturity while $\%s$ is the expected (annualized) rate of dollar depreciation to maturity. The remaining terms represent the effects of "domestic" distinctions among the assets (DOM), currency risk factors (CRISK), and official and private barriers to capital flows (BAR).[3]

The difference in asset returns expressed in a common currency, that is, adjusted for expected exchange rate changes, is a reflection of these last three elements:[4]

$$\text{(ii)} \quad i - i^* - \%s = DOM + CRISK + BAR.$$

Furthermore, an investor can in some cases avoid the risk associated with uncertainty about future exchange rates by "hedging" (selling) the proceeds of a foreign currency investment in the appropriate forward market. The return differential on this hedged (or "covered") basis is simply the interest differential $(i - i^*)$ less the forward premium on the dollar (fp), defined as the annualized difference between its forward and spot values:

$$\text{(iii)} \quad i - i^* - fp = DOM + BAR.$$

The covered return differential is not (directly) affected by currency distinctions since it is adjusted for both the expected level and uncertainty of future exchange rates.[5] Thus, for assets that are comparable in terms of their domestic characteristics (DOM = 0), the covered differential is essentially a reflection of barriers to capital flows (BAR).

---

[1]Currency risk thus arises from the variances of the perceived distribution of exchange rates rather than their means. From a market perspective this risk reflects the potential loss to an investor in a currency from an unanticipated change in that currency's value

[2]Deregulation of capital flows generally has proceeded furthest in shorter-term markets. See M. A. Akhtar and Kenneth Weiller, "Developments in International Capital Mobility: A Perspective on the Underlying Forces and the Empirical Literature," Federal Reserve Bank of New York, Research Paper no. 8711, in *International Integration of Financial Markets and U.S. Monetary Policy*, December 1987. Note that even the prospect of the imposition of capital controls can affect interest rates. Risks arising from the possible inability to repatriate funds are generally referred to as "sovereign" and "political" risks.

[3]The substitutability of different countries' assets is essentially a function of the importance of the factors summarized by BAR and CRISK. In reality, the factors underlying these terms are often closely related, even if distinct in theory.

[4]The common currency differential as we have defined it is also known as the "uncovered" differential, denoting that the relative return is not hedged in the forward market.

[5]However, currency distinctions may be implicit in the covered differential when, for example, official regulations treat foreign currency investments differently from investments in domestic currencies (the effect would be captured in BAR). Generally, formal forward markets exist only for certain short-term assets, although recently developed currency swap facilities provide comparable arrangements for some longer-term assets.

It is also useful to express the yield differential in terms of the traditional expected inflation (%p) and real interest (r) components of nominal interest rates:

$$\text{(iv)} \quad i - i^* = (\%p - \%p^*) + (r - r^*).$$

Nominal interest divergences among countries also can be expressed as the sum of differences in expected inflation rates and in their real interest rates (where the real interest rate measures an asset's return in goods rather than money). Furthermore, the real interest differential is itself partly a reflection of expectations about the future *real* exchange rate (x), defined as the nominal rate deflated by the ratio of home to foreign prices (p and p*):

$$x \equiv s \div (p/p^*).$$

The real exchange rate effectively measures the value of a country's goods in terms of its foreign counterparts.[6] Using the last two expressions, we can write the real interest differential in terms analogous to relation (i) for the nominal difference,

$$\text{(v)} \quad r - r^* = \%x + CRISK + BAR + DOM.$$

To summarize, observed nominal interest divergences across countries can be accounted for by four sets of factors: expected changes in nominal exchange rates (which in turn reflect differences in anticipated inflation and expected changes in real exchange rates); currency risk; the effects of barriers to capital mobility; and domestic characteristics summarized in DOM. These factors are the proximate determinants of international interest differentials and will provide a useful framework for our later analysis of the actual behavior of interest rate divergences among the United States and other countries.

Fundamental determinants

These proximate sources are not, however, the most basic causes of international interest divergences, but rather the reflection of more fundamental exogenous economic conditions. In thinking about these fundamental causes, we can make a distinction between factors directly affecting particular financial markets and those determining the transmission of their effects among countries.

In principle, virtually any disturbance that affects one country's financial markets more than another's may lead to international interest rate differentials. Of particular importance historically have been divergent national inflation rates, which normally have been associated with disparate monetary policies. A country that has a higher inflation rate than abroad must generally maintain nominal interest rates above those of its trading partners in order to compensate for the decline in the value of its currency that typically results from the inflation.[7] Divergences in real as well as nominal interest rates have also resulted from shorter-term fluctuations in monetary policy that affect domestic liquidity, from disparities in fiscal policies, and even from commodity supply shocks such as the oil price increases of the 1970s.[8]

All of these conditions can create pressures for interest rates to diverge across countries. Nonetheless, the extent to which such divergences actually occur, as well as the way in which they are reflected in currency expectations and other proximate components, depends upon the nature and strength of the transmission of such disturbances from one country to another. Particularly critical to this transmission mechanism are the mobility of capital and the exchange rate regime.

In its broadest sense, capital mobility refers to the degree to which international financial flows tend to respond to changes in asset yields.[9] Key aspects of international capital mobility are the extent and severity of explicit official and private barriers to capital flows and the degree to which assets that are similar (DOM = 0) but issued in different countries or currencies are viewed as close substitutes by investors. Generally, the greater the mobility of capital, the larger the combined effect of a change in a country's interest rates on foreign interest rates and exchange rates. An increase

---

[6]The real exchange rate is essentially an extension of the "terms of trade" to include nontraded goods as well. Changes in the nominal exchange rate can be expressed as the sum of the change in the corresponding real exchange rate plus the inflation differential. The traditional theory known as "purchasing power parity" essentially asserts that real exchange rates are constant in the long run.

[7]To the extent that a rise in the inflation rate simply leads to a compensating increase in domestic interest rates and depreciation in the nominal exchange rate (leaving the real exchange rate unaltered), it need not lead to any further divergence in real interest rates or yields expressed in a common currency. Typically, however, inflation has indirect effects on real interest and exchange rates and may affect the BAR and CRISK components as well.

[8]For example, the mid-1970s oil price rise led to the following consequences in most importing countries: an acceleration of inflation, sharp increases in nominal and real interest rates, and a subsequent downturn in real economic activity. Because the magnitude and timing of these effects varied greatly across countries, depending on their reliance on oil imports and other factors, international interest divergences increased markedly during this episode.

[9]This is the traditional broad definition of capital mobility. Under a narrower definition, capital mobility refers only to the severity of explicit barriers and other market imperfections that impede international financial flows. Thus currency risk is a determinant of the degree of capital mobility under the broad definition but not necessarily under the narrower one.

in capital mobility can be thought of as a reduction in the average size and variability of the BAR and CRISK terms defined earlier. It follows that a given disturbance is apt to produce smaller divergences in asset yields expressed in a common currency when capital mobility is high than when it is low.

Equally important to the international transmission of interest rate changes, however, is the flexibility of exchange rates. Unlike a fixed rate regime where exchange rates (at least in principle) are not free to vary, a floating rate system allows changes in interest rates to affect present and future currency values. Consequently, for a given amount of capital mobility, a change in one country's interest rates will have more impact on actual and expected exchange rates (and possibly CRISK), and less on foreign interest rates, when exchange rates are flexible than when they are fixed. In this sense, the current flexible exchange rate regimes may allow greater scope for international interest rate divergences.

Implications of reduced barriers to capital mobility

International financial integration has risen considerably over the last two decades, in large part because of a dramatic reduction in overt barriers to capital flows among the major industrial nations. The discussion in the preceding section shows that this development, of itself, should reduce international interest rate divergences, whether expressed in national currencies, a common currency, or in real terms. Historically, however, changes in international financial integration have not occurred in isolation but have been accompanied by other complex economic changes, some with potential effects on interest rate determination. For this reason, the implications of increased financial integration are apt to be less clear-cut in an international context than within a single nation.

In a national market, the use of a single currency precludes variations in nominal exchange rates as well as any persistent disparities in inflation rates across regions. The domestic sources of interest divergences are therefore significantly fewer than the international sources; consequently, there is a fairly strong presumption that increased financial mobility and integration will lead to closer alignment of interest rates across markets.

In an international economy comprising many nations and currencies, however, whether increased capital mobility leads to convergence of interest rates depends upon the nature of the changes in exchange rate behavior and government policies that are occurring at the same time. During the postwar era, increased financial integration has been accompanied by a transition from fixed to highly variable exchange rates and, as documented in the next section, greater disparities in national inflation rates. In effect, as the importance of factors reflected in BAR has declined, the potential importance of currency expectations and risk factors may well have increased. Accordingly, interest rates have been subject to conflicting pressures: easing of restrictions on capital flows has tended to push the rates toward convergence, while greater exchange rate volatility and inflation disparities have increased pressures for the rates to diverge. As we show in the empirical analysis that follows, this configuration of economic changes over the last three decades has led to a fairly complex and variable pattern of interest rate divergences among the major industrial nations.

Evidence on interest rate divergences

We now examine the historical pattern of interest rate divergences and their proximate determinants for five major industrial countries—the United States, Germany, Japan, the United Kingdom, and Canada. Divergences among both short-term money market rates and longer-term government bond yields are considered.[10] We first show that these nations' nominal interest rates exhibit no consistent trend toward convergence over the last two decades, although the impact of barriers to capital mobility (BAR) has declined markedly. This implies that currency factors are now the main source of observed international interest rate divergences. We then go on to consider the extent to which expected exchange rate changes can account for interest differentials across countries, asking whether asset yields expressed in a common currency have converged over time. Finally, we examine the nature of the currency expectations themselves, in particular the degree to which they appear to be a reflection of anticipated inflation differentials or of fluctuations in real exchange rates.

Nominal interest rate divergence

Interest rate dispersion can, in principle, be measured in several ways. In most of the analysis below, we focus on an indicator of the aggregate level of interest rate divergence for the group as a whole—the average absolute deviation of individual rates from the group mean. This indicator measures the collective impact of the proximate sources of interest differentials identified earlier: expected exchange rate changes, currency risk,

[10]The short-term rates used in this study are: three-month certificate of deposit (CD) rate for the United States; three-month interbank rate for Germany; two- to three-month interbank (call) rate for Japan; the one-month financial paper rate for Canada; and the three-month interbank loan rate for the United Kingdom. The long term rates are government bond yields of greater than five-year maturities. These are generally the most comparable rates available for the entire period.

and barriers to capital mobility, as well as any domestic comparability distinctions among assets. For assets that are reasonably comparable, this measure indicates the degree to which international interest rates diverge in a given period and their tendency towards convergence over time.

Of course, the assets considered here are not perfectly comparable, and thus interest rate divergences need not disappear across countries even as currency and jurisdictional differences subside. Our analysis will suggest that domestic comparability distinctions are generally insignificant among short-term instruments. More important differences in average maturity and other characteristics are, however, reflected in long-term rates. Nonetheless, these distinctions have remained relatively stable and hence are unlikely to have had a substantial impact on changes in the pattern of interest rate dispersion over time. For this reason, a comparison of average levels of interest rate divergence across relevant periods should provide a reasonable indication of trends in their proximate determinants.

Further insight into the nature of international interest rate divergences is provided by examining bilateral interest rate relations. We present evidence concerning one important component of our aggregate dispersion measure, U.S.-foreign bilateral interest rate differentials. In addition, the tendency for U.S. and foreign interest rates to move together is analyzed in the accompanying Box. While not directly measuring the size of divergences, this analysis provides some indication of the strength of linkages between domestic and foreign asset markets during different historical periods.

Chart 1 presents our measure of the degree of dispersion of nominal interest rates from the 1960s onward. The chart shows clearly that nominal interest rates often have diverged widely. The average absolute deviation of short-term interest rates from the group mean has frequently exceeded 200 basis points and has only rarely fallen below 150 basis points during this decade. Long-term rates, although typically less widely dispersed than the short rates, have generally diverged by more than 150 basis points.

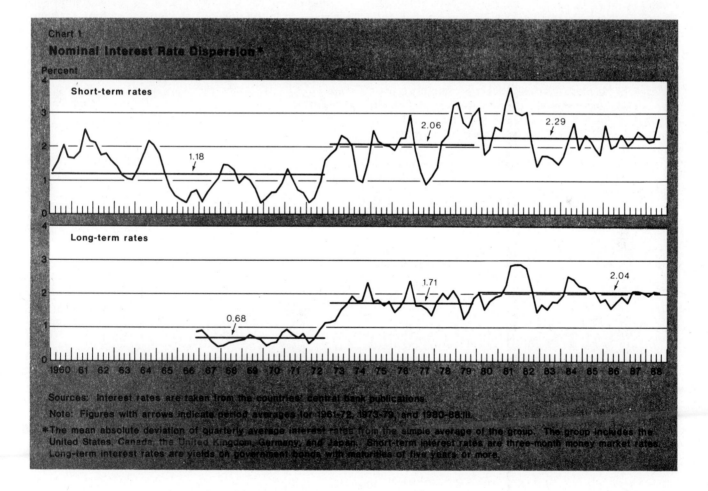

Chart 1
Nominal Interest Rate Dispersion*

Sources: Interest rates are taken from the countries' central bank publications.

Note: Figures with arrows indicate period averages for 1961-72, 1973-79, and 1980-88:III.

*The mean absolute deviation of quarterly average interest rates from the simple average of the group. The group includes the United States, Canada, the United Kingdom, Germany, and Japan. Short-term interest rates are three-month money market rates. Long-term interest rates are yields on government bonds with maturities of five years or more.

It is also apparent that the degree of nominal interest rate divergence has tended to increase over time. Interest rates were most closely aligned during the years 1966-71: both short- and long-term rates generally fell within 100 basis points of the group mean during this period. Since 1973, however, divergences among the rates have become increasingly pronounced. Average rate deviations over 1973-79 exceeded 200 basis points on short-term and 170 basis points on long-term rates, roughly double the levels of the 1960s and early 1970s. The dispersion of nominal interest rates reached its peak in 1981. Nonetheless, for the 1980s as a whole, interest rate divergence has exceeded that of the two preceding decades.

This trend towards greater nominal interest rate dispersion among industrial countries can also be observed in U.S.-foreign bilateral interest rate relations. The average absolute interest differential between U.S. rates and those abroad has risen steadily during the past two decades, increasing roughly by 100 basis points for both short- and long-term rates (Table 1). Underlying this trend have been particularly sharp increases in the size of U.S. interest differentials with Germany and Japan. U.S. rates, uniformly the lowest among industrial nations during the 1960s, began to rise relative to those in Germany and Japan during the 1970s; by the 1980s both short- and long-term U.S. interest rates had increased on average to more than 300 basis points above their German and Japanese counterparts. In contrast, the gap between U.S. interest rates and their typically higher Canadian and U.K. counterparts exhibits no systematic tendency to increase over time. In nearly all cases, however, the volatility of the U.S.-foreign interest differentials has been substantially higher since 1973 than earlier.

The impression that interest rates have not converged is further supported by evidence on the correlation of U.S. and foreign yields (see the accompanying Box). Specifically, the response of foreign interest rates to a given change in U.S. rates was generally *smaller* during the 1980s than the average response over the 1970s and 1960s.

These results are particularly striking in view of the clear evidence that the component of interest divergences attributable to explicit barriers to international capital flows (BAR) has declined markedly over time. These barriers were fairly stringent in Japan and Europe for much of the postwar period and effectively helped insulate domestic interest rates from changes in financial conditions abroad.[11] Beginning in the mid-1970s these impediments were largely removed in the major industrial countries as part of a larger move toward financial deregulation.

An indication of the effect of these changes can be seen from the fall in the dispersion of *covered* short-term interest rates shown in Chart 2.[12] The identity (iii) discussed in the previous section shows that, for com-

[11]The United States also imposed barriers to capital flows during parts of the 1960s and 1970s, although they were usually less restrictive than those imposed by other major industrial countries. An example is the interest equalization tax of the late 1960s.

[12]Because of limitations on forward rates and other required data, our analysis is largely confined to short-term interest rates over the 1970s and 1980s. To reduce comparability differences, we have used the Japanese Gensaki (bond repurchase) rate for this section and the appendix rather than the two- to three-month call rate referred to elsewhere in the article (and in all other charts and tables). The Gensaki rate is most comparable to the short rates for the other countries but was only available on a regular basis from the early 1970s on.

Table 1

U.S.-Foreign Bilateral Nominal Interest Differentials
(Period Average of Quarterly Observations in Percentage Points)

Period	Average Absolute Deviation†		Germany		Japan‡		Canada		United Kingdom‖	
	Short	Long	Short	Long	Short	Long	Short	Long	Short	Long
1960-72	1.78	1.19	0.60 (1.54)	−1.82 (0.82)	−2.86 (2.53)	−0.85 (0.75)	−0.66 (0.75)	−0.72 (0.37)	−1.95 (1.18)	−1.88 (0.52)
1973-79	2.57	2.16	1.32 (2.81)	−0.01 (2.01)	0.31 (3.38)	−0.04 (1.51)	−1.15 (1.53)	−0.62 (0.44)	−3.31 (2.26)	−4.93 (1.49)
1980-88§	2.81	2.17	3.23 (1.25)	3.03 (1.02)	3.68 (2.64)	3.77 (1.34)	−1.49 (1.09)	−0.71 (0.71)	−1.76 (2.56)	−0.72 (1.33)

Note: Figures in parentheses are standard deviations.
†Simple average of the four absolute bilateral interest differentials.
‡Japan's long-term interest rates begin in 1967.
‖United Kingdom's long-term interest rates begin in 1961.
§1988 data through third quarter.

Box: Foreign Responses to U.S. Interest Rate Changes

The analysis of interest rate dispersion presented in the text focuses on cumulative levels of interest rate divergence across countries. Our aggregate indicator—the average absolute deviation of rates from the group mean—provides a good summary measure of the overall size of interest rate divergences that arise from currency and jurisdictional differences. It is also useful, however, to examine whether the tendency for national interest rate movements to be associated with each other has been affected by financial integration. Accordingly, in this section we present evidence concerning the average response of foreign interest rates to movements in U.S. and German rates.

The correlation and average response measures in Table A identify the strength and magnitude of interest rate linkages between national asset markets, thus providing some indication of the nature of the transmission of disturbances from one country to another.† No clear relationship exists, however, between these measures of responsiveness and the degree of interest rate dispersion. An increase in the response of foreign to U.S. interest rate changes, for example, does not necessarily imply a narrowing of interest differentials or consequently our measure of rate divergence. The extent to which rates will diverge also depends upon the size of the original disturbance and its persistence over time.

An examination of Table A suggests that only Canadian interest rates respond in a consistent and strong manner to movements in U.S. rates. Responses of other foreign

†Like the dispersion indicator, these measures provide a purely statistical indication of the degree of association—in this case between changes in U.S. and foreign rates. They provide no direct measure of causal relations or the strength of interest rate transmission in any fundamental sense.

Table A

Transmission of Interest Rate Movements†

	Nominal						Real		
	Short-Term			Long-Term			Short-Term		
1960s	ρ	B_1	B_2	ρ	B_1	B_2	ρ	B_1	B_2
United States	—	—	0.10	—	—	0.27	—	—	0.00
Germany	0.25	0.64	—	0.35	0.45	—	0.20	0.01	—
Japan‡	0.01	0.02	0.08	NA	NA	NA	−0.07	−0.25	−0.06
Canada	0.60	0.88	0.13	0.63	0.91	0.26	0.15	0.17	0.11
United Kingdom§	0.25	0.47	0.86	−0.02	0.57	0.16	0.34	0.83	−0.26
1970s									
United States	—	—	0.45	—	—	0.34	—	—	0.31
Germany	0.50	0.56	—	0.41	0.52	—	0.34	0.38	—
Japan	0.28	0.21	0.16	0.15	0.16	0.47	−0.22	−0.26	−0.16
Canada	0.78	0.69	0.34	0.72	1.10	0.42	0.43	0.37	−0.11
United Kingdom	0.28	0.38	0.29	0.22	0.58	0.82	0.41	0.98	1.06
1980 to 1988-II									
United States	—	—	0.66	—	—	1.05	—	—	0.45
Germany	0.33	0.17	—	0.61	0.36	—	0.29	0.19	—
Japan	−0.36	−0.20	−0.10	0.42	0.21	0.40	−0.18	−0.13	−0.22
Canada	0.77	0.80	1.31	0.89	1.05	1.21	0.69	0.81	0.86
United Kingdom	0.14	0.12	0.01	0.47	0.41	0.65	0.13	0.17	0.09

†The column headings: ρ = correlation of U.S. with foreign interest rate.
B_1, B_2 = average response, in percentage points, of foreign interest rates associated with a one percent change in U.S. (B_1) and German (B_2) rates.
‡Japan's long-term interest rates begin in 1967.
§United Kingdom's long-term interest rates begin in 1961.

rates to U.S. yields have been much more variable and generally very modest. In addition, movements in German interest rates seem to elicit only a weak response from all countries.

Overall, these response measures support the conclusions in the text that financial integration has not been associated with a closer alignment of interest rates across countries. At the least, there appears to be no systematic tendency for foreign rates to become more responsive to U.S. yields over time; this result also applies generally to the responses of foreign rates to German yields. Indeed, a one percent change in U.S. nominal interest rates was generally associated with a smaller response

in corresponding European and Japanese rates during the 1980s than during the 1970s or 1960s.‡ Similarly, associations among short-term real interest rates were generally weaker for the 1980s as a whole than for the prior decade. Thus, statistical linkages among national interest rates do not seem to have become stronger over time—a pattern clearly consistent with the evidence cited earlier.

‡Correlations among long-term interest rates were somewhat greater during the 1980s than the 1970s. This finding is largely a reflection of the higher variability of interest rates in the latter period. Correlations, however, do not directly measure the quantitative change in one interest rate associated with a change in another.

---

parable assets (DOM = 0), the level of the covered U.S.-foreign yield differential—with asset proceeds hedged in the forward markets to compensate for expected exchange rate changes and currency risk factors—provides a direct measure of the contribution of nationality distinctions (BAR).

Divergences in covered yields clearly have become both substantially smaller and less variable over the past decade. Most notably, since 1982 the average (absolute) deviation of short-term covered interest rates from the group mean has fallen to roughly 25 basis points, a level representing only about 10 percent of the dispersion of short-term nominal interest rates. This reflects a sharp decline when compared to the 90 basis point dispersion in covered yields over the 1974-79 period, which represents more than 40 percent of the total dispersion of unadjusted rates during this period.

Further insight into this apparent decline in barriers to capital mobility is presented in the Appendix, where we consider the determinants of U.S.-foreign bilateral covered interest differentials. The analysis suggests that the closer alignment of covered yields during the 1980s is the result of a general dismantling of official barriers to capital flows—both abroad and in the United States—as well as other developments promoting the integration of short-term financial markets across industrial nations.[13]

[13]The extent of integration among longer-term markets (or its change over time) is much more difficult to gauge, in part because forward or other explicit mechanisms for hedging longer-maturity investments have not been available until the last several years. A recent analysis by Helen Popper ("Long-Term Covered Interest Parity: Two Tests Using Currency Swaps," unpublished paper, Department of Economics, University of California at Berkeley, August 1987) does suggest fairly close alignment of covered yields as calculated from

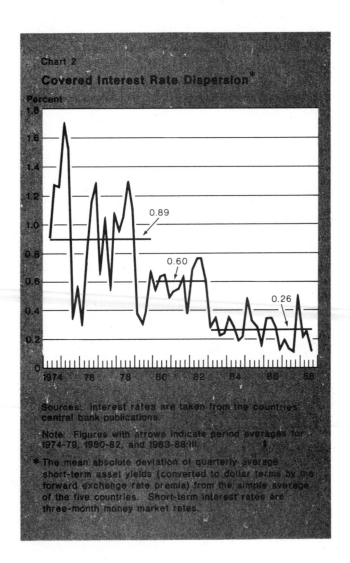

Chart 2
Covered Interest Rate Dispersion*

Differentials expressed in common currency

The fact that interest rates nave not converged even as barriers to capital mobility have fallen has one reasonably unambiguous implication: currency-related factors, as reflected in forward exchange premia, are now the primary source of international yield divergences. What then is the nature of these currency factors and, more specifically, how do we assess the relative importance of exchange rate expectations and currency risk?

One common view is that eliminating barriers to financial flows across countries necessarily means the near equalization of asset yields expressed in a common currency, that is, adjusted for expected exchange rate changes. This would imply that anticipated exchange rate movements are now the primary source of observed interest differentials across countries on comparable assets and that currency risks have a fairly limited role, at least at the margin. This view is implicit in several recent analyses that link the rise in U.S. interest rates above those abroad over 1981-85 to the concurrent "overvaluation" of the dollar relative to its (presumed) long-run equilibrium. Given the high and increasing exchange rate volatility over the last 15 years, however, it is far from obvious that currency risk factors are so unimportant. Indeed, it is at least conceivable that currency risk premia have increased enough to offset the tendency toward convergence in interest rate levels arising from the reductions in barriers to capital flows.

The main problem in resolving these questions is that neither exchange rate expectations nor currency risk premia are directly observable. Indeed, exchange rate expectations have been notoriously difficult to measure because of the high volatility of currency values. Any concrete analysis must be based upon proxies (preferably several) for expectations. One possibility is to use actual exchange rate changes over a given period as an approximation of the anticipated change during the same period in order to gauge the common currency yield differential. Conceptually, this indicator, which can be thought of as the ex post yield differential, is equal to the actual ex ante differential (reflecting currency risk as well as any remaining DOM and BAR) plus the market's forecast error in predicting the future exchange rate. *If* market forecasts are not systematically biased and forecast errors are roughly comparable among periods, this proxy will indicate the broad trends in actual common currency interest differentials.

Chart 3 shows the dispersion of the short-term interest rates expressed in dollars using the ex post measure. Divergences in ex post dollar yields have risen dramatically over time. The average divergence has ex-

ceeded 1000 basis points over the last decade, more than twice that recorded before 1973. Furthermore, the divergences have been somewhat greater during the 1980s than over 1973-79.

It is doubtful that these trends reflect increasing currency risk premia alone. In particular, the magnitude of the dispersion of ex post differentials seems implausibly large to represent risk premia. (Note that typical gaps between yields on very high risk junk bonds and AAA rated bonds are smaller than the differentials shown in Chart 3.) The fact that the dispersion of the ex post yields is nearly five times that of the unadjusted interest rates also suggests that forecast errors are largely responsible for the observed pattern in ex post yield dispersion. Thus, the increasing divergences shown in the chart are most likely the reflection of increasing currency volatility and unpredictability; they provide no conclusive evidence whether ex ante common currency interest differentials have converged.

Possibly more informative are various surveys of the exchange rate expectations of market observers and participants that have only become available during the 1980s.[14] Estimates of dollar depreciation based on a survey reported in the *Economist Financial Review* are presented in Table 2 along with the corresponding forward discount on the dollar quoted at the time of the survey. Recall that the forward discount on the dollar is equal conceptually to its expected depreciation plus the currency risk premium (CRISK). Thus the difference between the forward discount and the market survey expectations figure can be taken as a proxy for the currency risk.

As the table shows, survey estimates of dollar depreciation typically exceeded the forward discount for most of the 1980s, suggesting that investors viewed dollar assets as generally less risky than similar assets denominated in foreign currencies. The average size of these risk premia proxies is quite large, exceeding 500 basis points in many cases. Nonetheless, the survey measures and forward exchange premia do tend to vary together. As the table shows, both 3-month and 12-month forward discounts on the dollar are largest for those currencies against which the dollar is expected to depreciate most. Moreover, the expected depreciation and forward discount rates show a positive and statis-

---

Footnote 13 continued
currency swap quotes (essentially futures prices) for high-quality bonds issued in the Euromarkets.

[14]See the work of Jeffrey Frankel and Kenneth Froot: "Using Survey Data to Test Standard Propositions Regarding Exchange Rate Expectations," *American Economic Review*, vol. 77, no. 1, pp. 133-53; and "Interpreting Tests of Forward Discount Unbiasedness Using Survey Data on Exchange Rate Expectations," NBER Working Paper no. 1963, July 1986. See also Kathyrn Dominiquez, "Are Foreign Exchange Forecasts Rational?: New Evidence from Survey Data," Board of Governors of the Federal Reserve System, International Finance Discussion Papers, no. 241, May 1986. Here we use the *Economist Financial Review* survey data provided by Ken Froot.

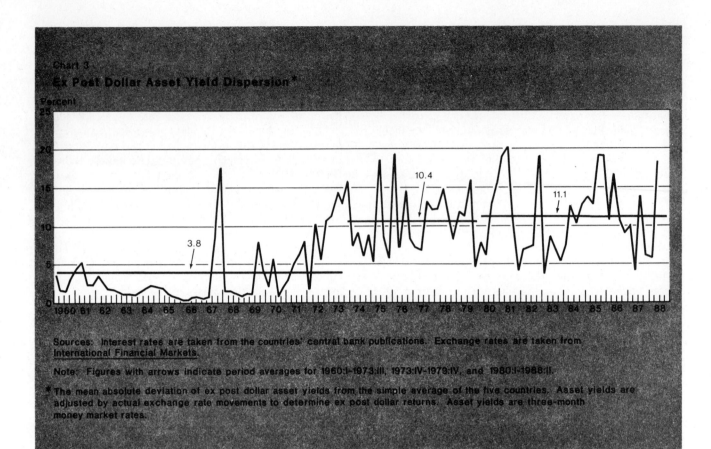

Chart 3

Ex Post Dollar Asset Yield Dispersion*

Percent

3.8

10.4

11.1

Sources: Interest rates are taken from the countries' central bank publications. Exchange rates are taken from International Financial Markets.

Note: Figures with arrows indicate period averages for 1960:I-1973:III, 1973:IV-1979:IV, and 1980:I-1988:II.

*The mean absolute deviation of ex post dollar asset yields from the simple average of the five countries. Asset yields are adjusted by actual exchange rate movements to determine ex post dollar returns. Asset yields are three-month money market rates.

Table 2

Survey Data and Foreign Exchange Rate Premia: June 1981-May 1987
(Period Average in Percent)

	German Mark		Japanese Yen		British Pound	
	3-Month Horizon	12-Month Horizon	3-Month Horizon	12-Month Horizon	3-Month Horizon	12-Month Horizon
Forward exchange premia on the dollar (+ = discount)	3.86	3.78	3.95	3.97	−0.94	−0.47
Survey-based estimates of dollar depreciation†	11.47	9.00	11.70	9.14	2.88	2.38
Estimated currency risk premia (+ = discount)	−7.61	−5.22	−7.75	−5.17	−3.82	−2.86
Memo: correlation of survey-based estimates of dollar depreciation and forward exchange premia	0.50	0.72	0.53	0.53	0.41	0.63

Source: Data provided by Ken Froot from data base used in Frankel and Froot, "Using Survey Data to Test Standard Propositions Regarding Exchange Rate Expectations," *American Economic Review*, March 1987.
†Survey-based data are from the *Economist Financial Report*.

tically significant association over time.[15]

As a whole, the survey evidence suggests that both expected exchange rate changes and currency risk premia are important components of forward premia and interest differentials across countries. This conclusion is consistent with the findings of most other recent studies of these questions.[16] But the data are too limited to draw more specific conclusions concerning the relative importance of currency expectations and risk premia or to assess the extent to which ex ante common currency yield differentials have changed over time.

Nature of expectations

Finally, to clarify the nature and importance of the exchange rate expectations, we ask whether they reflect differences in anticipated inflation rates, expected changes in real exchange rates, or both. Our earlier conceptual analysis implies that this question essentially concerns the behavior of real interest rates and their relation to the corresponding nominal rates. In particular, a comparison of relations (i) and (v) shows that real interest differentials reflect expectations of real exchange rate changes (as well as DOM, CRISK, and BAR) and, unlike their nominal counterparts, are not directly affected by anticipated currency movements arising from inflation differentials. Thus, comparing the dispersions of real and nominal interest rates should help to clarify the relative importance of expectations about inflation and about real exchange rate movements. Admittedly, real interest rates and the expected inflation rates underlying them are not directly observable; they can, however, be approximated using past inflation as a proxy for anticipated future rates.[17]

Chart 4 presents the dispersion of short-term and long-term real interest rates calculated in this manner. As a comparison of Charts 1 and 4 reveals, the dispersion

of real interest rates remained relatively close to that of nominal yields during the 1960s and early 1970s and rose above that of nominal rates by well over 100 basis points during 1973-75.[18] After 1975, however, the dispersion in real rates declined, dropping to roughly its pre-1973 average. In contrast, the dispersion of nominal yields continued to increase and during the 1980s has averaged nearly twice its pre-1973 level.

The clear implication that can be drawn from this evidence is that expectations concerning inflation (that is, differences in the rate anticipated for various countries) have been a significant source of interest differentials across countries during the era of floating exchange rates and indeed were the primary cause of the increased divergence in nominal rates observed after 1975. Consequently, it appears that currency expectations arising from inflation differences have been a significant contributor to international interest divergences, at least over the past 10 to 15 years. This result is not, of course, entirely surprising in view of the substantial increase in the variability and disparity of national inflation rates that occurred during the 1970s.

More striking, however, is that the average dispersion of real interest rates has been both substantial (generally above 100 basis points) and roughly constant over time. This relative stability in the average level of real interest rate dispersion is remarkable in light of the clear evidence that financial integration has virtually eliminated one of its most significant sources. The earlier analysis strongly suggests that barriers to capital mobility probably were the main contributor to real (as well as nominal) interest dispersion prior to 1973 and an important contributor during the latter 1970s. The role of capital controls, however, became minor during the 1980s. Thus, currency factors—currency risk premia and expectations about *real* exchange rates—have increased in size and now appear to be the main source of real interest divergences among the countries.

Furthermore, there is reason to believe that expectations about real exchange rate movements have been a significant contributor to real interest rate divergences, particularly in recent years. The evidence for this conclusion stems from the conceptual nature of real exchange rates and their actual behavior in the 1970s and 1980s. This same evidence also suggests, although only tentatively, that interest rate divergences adjusted for expected movements in real exchange rates were in fact smaller on average during the 1980s than in the

[15]In "Using Survey Data to Test Standard Propositions," Frankel and Froot also compare the forecast errors (prediction less actual change) implied by the survey data and corresponding forward premia. These errors are closely related, suggesting that expectations, at least as measured by the surveys, are an important element of the forward premia and corresponding interest differentials. The errors are also large, both absolutely and relative to the risk premia implied by the survey data. This result is consistent with our contention that forecast errors are largely responsible for the pattern of ex post nominal interest divergences.

[16]Most evidence suggests that currency risk premia exist, but considerable controversy remains over their empirical importance. The strongest evidence that currency risk premia play a major role in interest differentials across countries has been provided by Eugene Fama, "Forward and Spot Exchange Rates," *Journal of Monetary Economics*, November 1984, pp. 319-38; his results suggest that currency risk premia are more variable than exchange rate expectations and show a strong negative correlation with them.

[17]Here we use the past year's inflation (in the GNP deflator) to measure short-term real interest rates and the past two years' inflation for the long-term yields.

[18]In Japan and the United Kingdom during the mid-1970s, government controls sharply restricted the flexibility of nominal interest rates in adjusting to the severe fluctuations in inflation occurring at the time. This led to dramatic swings in real interest rates and largely explains the exceptionally large dispersion in these rates among the countries in the mid-1970s.

1970s.

As indicated earlier, the real exchange rate for a given country measures the average level of its product prices relative to those of its trading partners; hence real exchange rates are a key determinant of the nation's international competitiveness. It is therefore reasonable to suppose that at any time there is a long-run equilibrium real exchange rate level (consistent with a sustainable external payments position) toward which the actual exchange rate tends to move over time. This notion is the basis for the traditional and widely accepted notion of "purchasing power parity" (PPP), which in its strictest form implies that the equilibrium real exchange rate is constant in the long run. More realistic interpretations of PPP allow for some evolution in the long-run equilibrium arising from differences in productivity, demand, and other relevant trends across countries. Either interpretation implies, however, that short-term variations in real exchange rates represent, at least in part, departures from long-run values that tend to be reversed over time.[19]

Before the 1971 Smithsonian agreement to devalue the dollar, real exchange rates of the dollar and other major currencies were fairly stable, at least relative to their long-term trends. Fluctuations in the real value of the dollar became more considerable during the 1970s and, as Chart 5 reveals, became highly pronounced in the 1980s. The chart also shows that deviations of the real dollar from its past trend and period average, which can be viewed as very rough proxies for the long-run equilibrium, have also been quite large during the present decade, both in absolute terms and relative to

[19]Several recent studies of exchange rate behavior during the 1970s and 1980s imply that the long-run equilibrium real exchange rate changes fairly continuously. Some in fact suggest that actual real exchange rate changes largely reflect fluctuations in their long-run equilibrium and that there is virtually no tendency for current real exchange rate movements to be reversed in the future. See, for example, John Campbell and Richard Clarida, "The Dollar and Real Interest Rates," paper presented at the 1986 Carnegie-Rochester Conference on Public Policy, November 21-22, 1986.

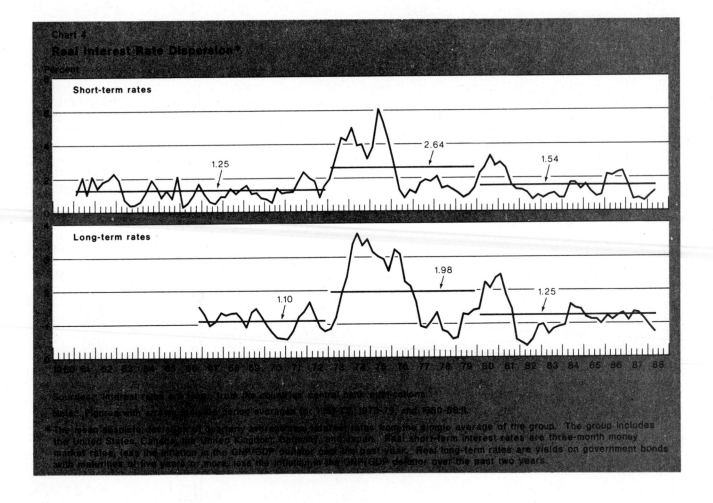

Chart 4
Real Interest Rate Dispersion*
Percent

the 1970s.

PPP theory strongly suggests that this behavior indicates a substantial "overvaluation" of the dollar relative to its long-term equilibrium during the first half of the 1980s. Similarly, the theory would attribute the sharp decline in the dollar after 1985 to a "correction" of this overvaluation. From this interpretation of the dollar's movements—which is supported by the unprecedented rise in the U.S. trade deficit after 1982—we can infer that anticipated changes in the real value of the dollar (at least over the medium term) have been sizeable and have contributed significantly to the divergences in real interest rates observed during the decade. The evidence from Chart 6 provides some support for this supposition:

the real long-term interest differential between the United States and the four major foreign countries rose with the appreciating real dollar over most of 1980-84; the real interest differential and the dollar also fell together after 1985.[20]

On balance these arguments suggest that expected movements in real exchange rates have been a significant source of real interest divergences during the

[20]There is, of course, no rigid linkage between real interest rates and exchange rates, either in theory or practice. As Chart 6 also shows, the dollar continued to rise over 1984-85 even when U.S. real interest rates fell relative to abroad. Nonetheless, the pattern evident before and after that period does support the hypothesis that expectations about future dollar movements were an important proximate source of real interest differentials observed at the time.

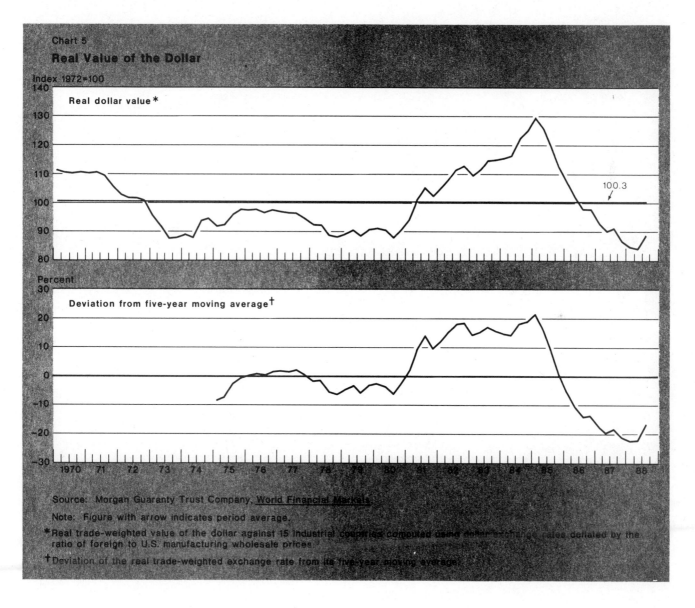

Chart 5
Real Value of the Dollar

Index 1972=100

Real dollar value*

100.3

Percent

Deviation from five-year moving average†

Source: Morgan Guaranty Trust Company, World Financial Markets.

Note: Figure with arrow indicates period average.

*Real trade-weighted value of the dollar against 15 industrial countries computed using dollar exchange rates deflated by the ratio of foreign to U.S. manufacturing wholesale prices.

†Deviation of the real trade-weighted exchange rate from its five-year moving average.

1980s; the role of real exchange rate expectations during the 1970s is less clear, but very likely less important than after 1980. More generally, this behavior provides further evidence of the major role that currency expectations, apparently reflecting perceptions about both the real and inflation components of exchange rates, have played in interest differentials across countries in recent years.

More speculatively, the apparent increase in importance of real exchange rate expectations may also mean that interest rates expressed, ex ante, in a common currency were more closely aligned in the 1980s, when international financial integration was greater than earlier. By definition, the real interest differential is equal to the expected change in the real exchange rate plus the common currency differential (see relations ii and v). Hence, the fact that the dispersion in real interest rates did not rise in the 1980s over the latter 1970s, while the magnitude of expected real exchange rate changes apparently did, suggests a possible decline in the dispersion of common currency differentials. Of course, the very rough and preliminary nature of our analysis makes

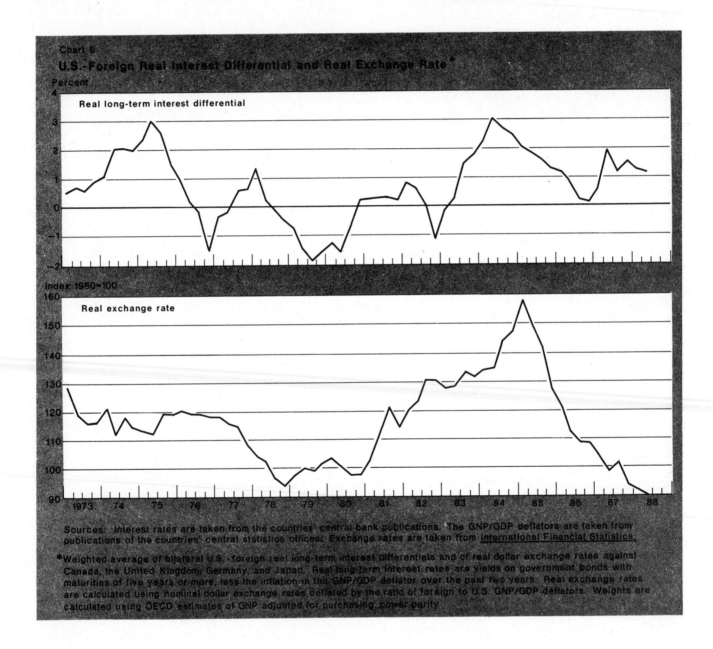

Chart 6
U.S.-Foreign Real Interest Differential and Real Exchange Rate*

Percent

Real long-term interest differential

Index 1980=100

Real exchange rate

Sources: Interest rates are taken from the countries' central bank publications. The GNP/GDP deflators are taken from publications of the countries' central statistics offices. Exchange rates are taken from International Financial Statistics.

*Weighted average of bilateral U.S.-foreign real long-term interest differentials and of real dollar exchange rates against Canada, the United Kingdom, Germany, and Japan. Real long-term interest rates are yields on government bonds with maturities of five years or more, less the inflation in the GNP/GDP deflator over the past two years. Real exchange rates are calculated using nominal dollar exchange rates deflated by the ratio of foreign to U.S. GNP/GDP deflators. Weights are calculated using OECD estimates of GNP adjusted for purchasing power parity.

this conclusion especially tentative.

Conclusion

It seems reasonably clear that international financial integration has increased considerably over the last decade. However, the effect of integration on the relationship of interest rates across countries has been somewhat different from that suggested by prior experience with the integration of domestic financial markets. Interest rates in the major U.S., European, and Japanese money markets now move very closely with their counterparts in the corresponding "offshore" Eurocurrency markets. Yet divergences among national interest rates, even for instruments with very similar characteristics, have often been very large in recent years.

As our analysis has shown, these patterns are not paradoxical; cross-country interest rate disparities are the natural consequences of differing currencies and jurisdictions that, while irrelevant or negligible within a single country, are potentially very important in an international context. In particular, in an environment of flexible exchange rates and divergent national economic conditions, interest differentials across countries can be expected to arise even when capital mobility and financial integration are "perfect." Of themselves, reductions in barriers to financial flows may be expected to reduce international interest rate divergences, but not if accompanied by increased exchange rate fluctuations and greater disparities in national economic policies.

These observations are reasonably consistent with the evidence cited in this article. There appears to be no systematic tendency for interest differentials to abate across countries over time; indeed nominal interest divergences during the 1980s have been greater on average than those observed during the previous two decades. Nonetheless, this analysis provides clear evidence that the sources of international interest differentials have changed. During the 1960s, interest rate divergences were sustainable under a fixed exchange rate regime in large part because of fairly stringent limitations on financial flows across national jurisdictions. With the substantial reduction in such barriers over the last 15 years, interest differentials across countries have become primarily associated with expected exchange rate changes—apparently reflecting both increased divergences in national inflation rates and greater real exchange rate fluctuations—and currency risk premia.

More fundamentally, this analysis has implications for the conduct of monetary policy in a financially integrated world economy. Our results suggest that the ability of monetary authorities to influence domestic interest rates independently of rates abroad has not declined significantly over time. In this narrow sense, the independence of national monetary policies may not have been appreciably reduced by international financial integration. Nonetheless, the reduction in barriers to international capital flows has strengthened the overall linkages among domestic interest rates, exchange rates, and foreign interest rates. As a result, domestic monetary policy actions influence and are influenced by foreign economic conditions more now than in the past. In a broader sense, therefore, increased international financial integration has led to greater *interdependence* among national monetary policies.

Bruce Kasman
Charles Pigott

Appendix: The Determinants of U.S.-Foreign Covered Interest Differentials

The closer alignment of covered interest rates across countries that has been documented in the text may reflect changes in several factors related to national jurisdiction. In addition to explicit restrictions on capital flows, perceived differences in U.S. and foreign assets arising from domestic tax systems, default risk, transaction costs, or political and sovereign risk are embedded in covered interest differentials. In this section we attempt to identify more clearly the role that factors specific to U.S. and foreign markets have played in the decline of covered interest differentials. To this end, we decompose each U.S.- foreign covered interest differential into the sum of the onshore-offshore differential for each country's assets and the offshore differential on U.S. and foreign assets:†

Covered differential = USDE + FORDE + USFORE

The first term, USDE, measures the interest differential between comparable dollar assets in domestic markets and Euromarkets. Since the United States has had vir-

†In more precise terms, any covered differential $[(1+i) - (1+i^*)f]$ can be seen to equal $(i-iE) + (iE^*-i^*)f + [(1+iE) - (1+iE^*f)]$, where i, i^*, iE and IE^* are U.S. onshore, foreign onshore, U.S. Euromarket, and foreign Euromarket rates, respectively, and f is the forward exchange rate premium.

Appendix: The Determinants of U.S.-Foreign Covered Interest Differentials *(continued)*

tually no capital controls from the early 1970s onward (with the exception of several months in 1980), this term captures the role of domestic U.S. regulations in generating covered interest differentials. The second term, FORDE, is a similar measure for foreign assets and again reflects the importance of foreign regulations, including the influence of any foreign capital controls.

The third term in this decomposition, USFORE, captures the covered differential in Euromarkets between dollar assets and assets denominated in foreign currencies. Since controls in these markets are insignificant and identical across the assets compared, this differential provides a measure of the impact of political risk considerations. Most studies have found these differentials to be rather small—indeed not significantly different from zero on average.‡

‡For a recent examination of covered interest differentials in Euromarkets, see Vincent Reinhart and Kenneth Weiller, "What Does Covered Interest Parity Reveal about Capital Mobility?" Federal Reserve Bank of New York, Research Paper no. 8713, in *International Integration of Financial Markets and U.S. Monetary Policy*, December 1987.

In the table, this decomposition of U.S.-foreign covered interest differentials is presented for a number of periods during the past 15 years. Focusing first on our bilateral covered differentials with Japan and the United Kingdom, we see that capital controls, reflected in the large size and variability of FORDE, were a major determinant of interest rate variations before 1980. After 1979, however, sharp declines emerge in the size and variability of the FORDE component for Japan and the United Kingdom, a finding consistent with other evidence indicating that these countries dismantled their controls at roughly that time. For Germany and Canada, two countries that loosened capital controls earlier, this component of the covered differential has been relatively small throughout our sample.§

The small size (generally below 20 basis points) and variability of these differentials for all the foreign countries since 1982 support the conclusion that foreign barriers

§There is substantial evidence, however, that at least until the mid-1970s capital controls in Germany were a significant component of covered interest differentials.

Decomposition of U.S.-Foreign Covered Interest Differentials
(In Percentage Points)

	Total Covered Differential†	USDE	FORDE	USFORE
Germany				
Jan. 74 - Aug. 77	−0.78 (0.50)	−0.61 (0.40)	−0.35 (0.30)	0.19 (0.20)
Sep. 77 - Nov. 79	−1.06 (0.43)	−0.60 (0.25)	−0.40 (0.27)	−0.06 (0.19)
Dec. 79 - Dec. 82	−1.65 (0.40)	−0.89 (0.29)	−0.48 (0.30)	−0.29 (0.20)
Jan. 83 - Sep. 88	−0.43 (0.40)	−0.25 (0.22)	−0.20 (0.17)	−0.01 (0.16)
Japan				
Jan. 74 - Aug. 77	−0.30 (5.17)	−0.61 (0.40)	NA NA	NA NA
Sep. 77 - Nov. 79	−2.20 (1.72)	−0.60 (0.25)	−1.83 (1.76)	0.22 (0.92)
Dec. 79 - Dec. 82	−0.82 (1.67)	−0.89 (0.29)	0.32 (0.72)	−0.26 (1.57)
Jan. 83 - Sep. 88	−0.50 (1.15)	−0.25 (0.22)	0.13 (0.25)	−0.41 (1.16)
Canada				
Jan. 74 - Aug. 77	−0.32 (0.72)	−0.61 (0.40)	NA NA	NA NA
Sep. 77 - Nov. 79	−0.69 (0.74)	−0.60 (0.25)	−0.09 (0.16)	0.00 (0.68)
Dec. 79 - Dec. 82	−0.87 (0.92)	−0.89 (0.29)	−0.18 (0.35)	0.19 (0.89)
Jan. 83 - Sep. 88	−0.15 (0.68)	−0.25 (0.22)	−0.13 (0.13)	0.20 (0.64)
United Kingdom				
Jan. 74 - Aug. 77	1.92 (1.77)	−0.61 (0.40)	1.62 (1.25)	0.92 (0.83)
Sep. 77 - Nov. 79	0.15 (0.92)	−0.60 (0.25)	0.56 (0.78)	0.19 (0.28)
Dec. 79 - Dec. 82	−1.05 (0.62)	−0.89 (0.29)	−0.08 (0.43)	−0.08 (0.53)
Jan. 83 - Sep. 88	−0.27 (0.33)	−0.25 (0.22)	−0.07 (0.11)	0.08 (0.23)

Note: Figures in parentheses are standard deviations.
†The total covered differential equals the sum of the other three differentials. Period averages may not sum exactly due to rounding errors.

Appendix: The Determinants of U.S.-Foreign Covered Interest Differentials *(continued)*

to capital mobility, while quite important in the past, have not been a significant proximate factor determining interest rate differentials during the 1980s.

A similar claim can be made regarding the importance of U.S. controls and political risk, factors embodied in the other components of the covered interest differentials, following 1982. Examining the interest differential between domestic U.S. and Eurodollar assets suggests that actions taken in U.S. markets might account, in part, for the large and volatile (uncovered) real interest differentials observed during 1980-82. Changes in Federal Reserve operating procedures in October 1979, combined with numerous reserve requirement shifts and the imposition of "voluntary" credit controls in 1980, led to increased interest rate divergence between these assets. Interest differentials on dollar assets here and in Euromarkets rose above 100 basis points during almost all of 1980, reaching a level that was double their average

for the 1974-79 period.‖ At the same time, Euromarket covered differentials between dollar assets and assets denominated in foreign currencies became more volatile during 1980-82, reflecting increased political uncertainty in the wake of the second oil price shock and the LDC debt crisis. However, with the possible exception of dollar-yen rates, Euromarket covered differentials have been insignificant since 1982. Interest differentials between domestic U.S. and Eurodollar assets have also fallen considerably since 1982, reflecting both the removal of controls (November 1980) and the closer integration of domestic and Eurodollar markets in recent years.

‖For a detailed discussion of the links between Eurodollar and U.S. domestic money markets during this period, see Lawrence L. Kreicher, "Eurodollar Arbitrage," this *Quarterly Review*, Summer 1982.

Part Four

Instruments of the Money and Capital Markets

The making of loans in modern financial systems results in the creation of financial instruments—bonds, notes, shares of stock, repurchase agreements, home mortgages, and government bills, to name only a few of the almost endless variety of financial instruments now being traded in markets around the globe. Indeed, with the advent of deregulation of financial institutions and markets in the U.S., Australia, Canada, Great Britain, Japan, and dozens of other nations, the menu of different financial instruments has expanded significantly, adding to an already impressive array of choices for investors with funds to lend. This section of the book examines the features of a select group of both old and new financial instruments.

The first two articles in this section look closely at two long-standing financial instruments—federal funds and repurchase agreements (RPs). *Federal funds* are simply short-term loans of reserves held by a financial institution (such as a bank or savings and loan association) or by a large depositor in a bank or savings association (such as a major corporation or security dealer). The reserves are held in such a way that they can be transferred immediately (usually by wire) to borrowers. Many federal funds loans, though certainly not all, involve reserve balances held at the Federal Reserve banks that can be moved by a simple bookkeeping entry from the lender's account to the borrower's account in seconds and then returned just as quickly when the loan matures. Most such "immediately available funds" are loaned overnight, with the borrower returning the funds plus interest the next day. Repurchase agreements, in contrast, are collateralized loans (unlike loans of federal funds, which are rarely backed by specific collateral) in which a borrowing bank, security dealer, or other institution can pledge high-grade securities it owns to back a loan.

As economists Marvin Goodfriend and William Whelpley in "Federal Funds: Instrument of Federal Reserve Policy," and Stephen A. Lumpkin in "Repurchase and Reverse Repurchase Agreements," point out, these credit instruments arose in earlier decades (reaching back into the 1920s and 1930s) when American banks and security dealers were looking for newer and more flexible ways to borrow short-term funds. While they started out as exclusively private financial instruments, these authors point out that both the federal funds and RP markets have attracted the attention and involvement of the federal government in recent years. The market for federal funds has become a conduit of monetary policy for the Federal Reserve System, supplying reserves to or absorbing reserves from this market in order to nudge interest rates and money growth toward the goals the Fed has in mind. Repurchase agreements have also attracted public attention in recent years as flexible ways to borrow money and relatively safe ways to lend money. However, the RP market has also been plagued by lawsuits and unresolved disputes over the competing rights and claims of borrowers and lenders. Recently Congress and federal

165

regulators have developed new procedures designed to reduce the risk of securities fraud in order to prevent troubled RP traders from misusing the collateral they have pledged behind loans. Despite these recent problems, however, the RP market appears to have a bright future.

While federal funds and repurchase agreements have a long history, *interest-rate swaps* are an invention of the 1980s. Economists Larry D. Wall and John J. Pringle in "Interest Rate Swaps: A Review of the Issues," note that interest-rate swaps have not attracted much notice from the general public, but in their own way are "quietly transforming" the markets for borrowing and lending. In a standard interest-rate swap, two borrowers of funds agree to *exchange* the interest payments each owes to third parties for a stipulated time period. Actually, each party to the swap does not pay all the interest owed by the other party; rather, the two parties exchange only the *difference* in interest owed by each of them. In this way each institution can more nearly match interest expenses to the interest revenues it receives. Launched in 1982, the swap market now is trading close to one trillion dollars in the principal amount of swaps outstanding.

Swaps were designed both to lower borrowing costs and to help *hedge* the parties to a swap against interest-rate risk. The same idea of interest-rate hedging has also recently spawned the development of *stripped securities*, which are created by separating the principal and interest payments promised by a debt security. The result is the creation of *two* financial claims to sell to interested investors: (1) a claim to an expected stream of interest payments only (an IO) and (2) a claim to the repayment of the principal value of the security only (a PO). Today most stripped securities arise from separating and selling IOs and POs on Treasury bonds and mortgage-backed securities. Economist Sean Becketti from the Federal Reserve Bank of Kansas City examines the characteristics, advantages, and problems posed by IOs and POs in "The Role of Stripped Securities In Portfolio Management." He points out that while these securities often help to reduce reinvestment risk, investors need to be cautious in the use of such instruments due to their price volatility and to the uncertainty over scheduled repayments that some of these financial instruments possess.

No exploration of financial instruments in the 1980s and 1990s would be complete without a close look at the market for low-grade (often called *junk*) bonds. Jan Loeys, senior economist at the Federal Reserve Bank of Philadelphia, provides us with a fascinating overview of how this market for speculative-grade corporate notes and bonds has blossomed and grown in the past decade. While much has been written in the press about the dangers of investing in junk bonds, most such securities are issued today by businesses that used to borrow from banks because their relatively small size and less-than-solid reputation shut them out of the bond market. However, with the help of investment banking houses and credit guarantors, the market for low-grade bonds has become one of the fastest growing financial innovations in recent years. Loeys explores both the risks and the advantages of this newly packaged financial instrument, finding in it not so much a threat to financial safety and stability as a "rechannelling of corporate borrowing" toward public securities and away from privately negotiated loans.

The final article in this section explores both the domestic commercial paper market in the United States—one of the oldest of all U.S. financial markets, dating back almost to the American Revolution—and the much newer Eurocommercial paper market. Robert N. McCauley and Lauren A. Hargraves ask: "Eurocommercial Paper and U.S. Commercial Paper: Converging Money Markets?" *Commercial paper* is a high-quality, short-term note that is sold by a large corporation or governmental agency with an impeccable credit rating or backed by a lending institution that has excellent credit credentials. McCauley and Hargraves find that these two paper markets—the American and the European—are becoming more and more alike, but also display important differences of which both borrowers and lenders should be aware.

Article 17

FEDERAL FUNDS: INSTRUMENT OF FEDERAL RESERVE POLICY

Marvin Goodfriend and William Whelpley

Federal funds are the heart of the money market in the sense that they are the core of the overnight market for credit in the United States. Moreover, current and expected future interest rates on Federal funds are the basic rates to which all other money market rates are anchored. Understanding the Federal funds market requires, above all, recognizing that its general character has been shaped by Federal Reserve policy. From the beginning, Federal Reserve regulatory rulings have encouraged the market's growth. Equally important, the Federal funds rate has been a key monetary policy instrument. This article explains Federal funds as a credit instrument, the funds rate as an instrument of monetary policy, and the funds market itself as an instrument of regulatory policy.

Characteristics of Federal Funds

Federal funds have three distinguishing features. First, they are short-term borrowings of immediately available money—funds which can be transferred between depository institutions within a single business day. The vast majority, roughly 80 percent, of Federal funds are overnight borrowings. The remainder are longer maturity borrowings known as term Federal funds. Second, Federal funds are liabilities of those depository institutions required to hold reserves with Federal Reserve Banks as defined by the Monetary Control Act of 1980. They are: commercial banks, savings banks, savings and loan associations, and credit unions. Third, historically Federal funds borrowed have been distinguished from other depository institution liabilities because they have been exempt from both reserve requirements

and interest rate ceilings.[1] Depository institutions are also the most important eligible lenders in the market. The Federal Reserve, however, also allows depository institutions to classify borrowings from Federal agencies and nonbank securities dealers as Federal funds.[2]

The supply and demand for Federal funds arises in large part as a means of efficiently distributing reserves throughout the banking system. On any given day, individual depository institutions may be either above or below their desired reserve position. Reserve accounts bear no interest, so banks have an incentive to lend reserves beyond those required plus any desired excess. Banks in need of reserves borrow them. The borrowing and lending of reserves takes place in the Federal funds market at a competitively determined interest rate known as the Federal funds rate.

The Federal funds market also functions as the core of a more extensive overnight market for credit free of reserve requirements and interest rate controls. Nonbank depositors supply funds to the overnight market through repurchase agreements (RPs) with their banks. The overnight repurchase agreement is a collateralized one-day loan, which requires actual transfer of title on the loan collateral. Under an overnight repurchase agreement, a depositor lends

This article was prepared for **Instruments of the Money Market**, 6th edition. The authors are Economist and Vice President, and Assistant Economist, Federal Reserve Bank of Richmond, respectively.

[1] This distinction has been blurred since passage of the Depository Institutions Deregulation and Monetary Control Act of 1980. Reserve requirements have been eliminated on some personal time deposits and interest rate controls have been removed on all liabilities except traditional demand deposits. However, interbank deposits are still reservable and explicit interest is still prohibited on interbank demand deposits.

In addition, our definition should be qualified because Repurchase Agreements (RPs) at banks have not had interest rate ceilings or reserve requirements. Strictly speaking, RPs are not Federal funds. Yet as we explain below, their growth and use have had much in common with the Federal funds market. And the point of view of this article is that they are close functional equivalents.

[2] A more complete list of eligible lenders is found in Board of Governors of the Federal Reserve System, **Federal Reserve Bulletin** 56 (January 1970), p. 38.

funds to a bank by purchasing a security, which the bank repurchases the next day at a price agreed to in advance. Overnight RPs account for about 25 percent of overnight borrowings by large commercial banks. Banks use RPs to acquire funds free of reserve requirements and interest controls from sources, such as corporations and state and local governments, not eligible to lend Federal funds directly. Total daily average gross RP and Federal funds borrowings by large commercial banks are roughly 200 billion dollars, of which approximately 130 billion dollars are Federal funds. Competition for funds among banks ties the RP rate closely to the Federal funds rate. Normally, the RP rate is around 25 basis points below the Federal funds rate; the lower rate being due to the reduced risk and additional transaction cost of arranging an RP.

Methods of Federal Funds Exchange

Federal funds transactions can be initiated by either the lender or borrower. An institution wishing to sell (loan) Federal funds locates a buyer (borrower) directly through an existing banking relationship or indirectly through a Federal funds broker. Federal funds brokers maintain frequent telephone contact with active funds market participants and match purchase and sale orders in return for a commission. Normally, competition among participants ensures that a single funds rate prevails throughout the market. However, the rate might be tiered, higher for a bank under financial stress. Moreover, banks believed to be particularly poor credit risks may be unable to borrow Federal funds at all.

Two methods of Federal funds transfer are commonly used. The first involves transfers conducted between two banks. To execute a transaction, the lending institution authorizes the district Reserve Bank to debit its reserve account and to credit the reserve account of the borrowing institution. Fedwire, the Federal Reserve System's wire transfer network, is employed to complete a transfer.

The second method simply involves reclassifying respondent bank demand deposits at correspondent banks as Federal funds borrowed. Here, the entire transaction takes place on the books of the correspondent. To initiate a Federal funds sale, the respondent bank simply notifies the correspondent of its intentions. The correspondent purchases funds from the respondent by reclassifying the respondent's demand deposits as "Federal funds purchased." The respondent does not have access to its deposited money as long as it is classified as Federal funds on the books of the correspondent. Upon maturity of the loan, the respondent's demand deposit account is credited for the total value of the loan, plus an interest payment for use of the funds. The interest rate paid to the respondent is usually based on the nationwide effective Federal funds rate for the day. In practice, the correspondent frequently resells the reclassified funds in the Federal funds market itself, earning the Federal funds rate in the process.

Types of Federal Funds Instruments

The most common type of Federal funds instrument is an overnight, unsecured loan between two financial institutions. Overnight loans are, for the most part, booked without a formal, written contract. Banks exchange verbal agreements based on any number of considerations, including how well the corresponding officers know each other and how long the banks have mutually done business. Brokers play an important role evaluating the quality of a loan when no previous arrangement exists. Formal contracting would slow the process and increase transaction costs. The verbal agreement as security is virtually unique to Federal funds.

In some cases Federal funds transactions are explicitly secured. In a secured transaction the purchaser places government securities in a custody account for the seller as collateral to support the loan. The purchaser, however, retains title to the securities. Upon termination of the contract, custody of the securities is returned to the owner. Secured Federal funds transactions are sometimes requested by the lending institution.

Continuing contract Federal funds are overnight Federal funds loans which are automatically renewed unless terminated by either the lender or borrower. This type of arrangement is typically employed by correspondents who purchase overnight Federal funds from a respondent bank. Unless notified by the respondent to the contrary, the correspondent will continually roll the interbank deposit into Federal funds, creating a longer term instrument of open maturity. The interest payments on continuing contract Federal funds loans are computed from a formula based on each day's effective Federal funds rate. When a continuing contract arrangement is made, the transactions costs (primarily brokers fees and funds transfer charges) of doing business are minimized because the entire transaction is completed on the books of the correspondent bank. In fact, additional costs are incurred only when the agreement is terminated by either party.

Determination of the Federal Funds Rate

To explain the determinants of the Federal funds rate, we present a simple model of the bank reserve market which incorporates the actions of both private banks and the Federal Reserve.[3] In this model, the funds rate is competitively determined as that value which equilibrates the aggregate supply and demand for banking system reserves.

The aggregate demand for bank reserves arises primarily from the public's demand for checkable deposits against which banks hold reserves. The aggregate quantity of checkable deposits demanded by the public falls as money market interest rates rise, raising the opportunity cost of holding checkable deposits. Hence, the derived demand for bank reserves is negatively related to market interest rates. The aggregate demand schedule for bank reserves is shown in Figure 1, where f is the funds rate and R is aggregate bank reserves.

The aggregate stock of reserves available to the banking system is determined by the Federal Reserve. In principle, the Federal Reserve could choose to provide the banking system with a fixed stock of reserves. If the Federal Reserve chose this strategy, a fixed stock of reserves, $\overline{R}$, would be provided through Federal Reserve purchases of government securities. The resulting funds rate would be f* in Figure 1, or the rate which equilibrates the aggregate supply and demand for bank reserves.

Such a Federal Reserve operating procedure, known as total reserve targeting, is the focus of hypothetical textbook discussions of monetary policy. The hallmark of total reserve targeting is that shifts in the market's demand for reserves are allowed to directly affect the funds rate. In practice, however, the Federal Reserve has never targeted total reserves. Instead, it has adopted operating procedures designed to smooth funds rate movements against unexpected reserve demand shifts.[4] The simplest smoothing procedure is Federal funds rate targeting, which involves selecting a narrow band, often fifty basis points or less, within which the funds rate is allowed to fluctuate. Explicit Federal funds rate targeting was employed by the Federal Reserve during the 1970s.

[3] Goodfriend [1982], pp. 3-16.

[4] Goodfriend [1986], contains a theoretical rational expectations model of interest rate smoothing and discusses its implications for money stock and price level trend-stationarity.

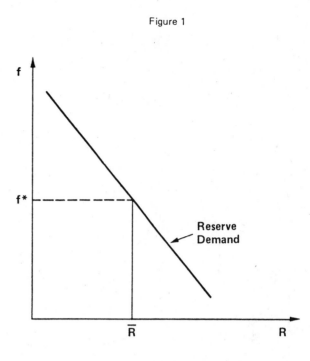

Figure 1

The funds rate can be targeted directly by supplying, through open market purchases of U. S. Treasury securities, whatever aggregate reserves are demanded at the targeted rate. For example, if the Federal Reserve chose to peg the funds rate at f* in Figure 1, it would have to accommodate a market demand for reserves of $\overline{R}$. In principle, either total reserve or funds rate targeting could yield the ex ante desired funds rate, f*, so long as the Federal Reserve had precise knowledge of the position of the reserve demand locus. There is, however, an important difference between these procedures. With a total reserve target, market forces directly influence the funds rate. They have no direct effect under a funds rate target. Instead, they affect the volume of total reserves.

Federal Reserve operating procedures become more complicated when reserves are provided by bank borrowing at the Federal Reserve discount window. Figure 2 shows the relationship between reserve provision and the Federal funds rate when there is discount window borrowing. The locus has a vertical and a nonvertical segment because reserves are provided to the banking system in two forms, as nonborrowed and as borrowed reserves. Nonborrowed reserves (NBR) are supplied by the Federal Reserve through open market purchases, while borrowed reserves (BR) are provided by discount window borrowing.

Figure 2

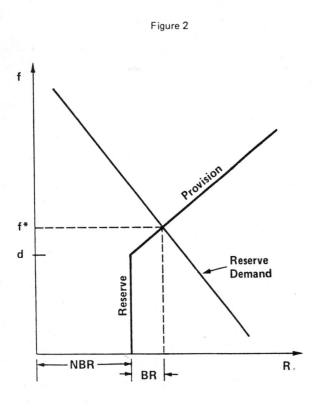

The distance between the vertical segment of the reserve provision locus and the vertical axis is determined by the volume of nonborrowed reserves. The reserve provision locus is vertical up to the point where the funds rate (f) equals the discount rate (d) because when the funds rate is below the discount rate, banks have no incentive to borrow at the discount window. Conversely, when the funds rate is above the discount rate borrowers obtain a net saving on the explicit interest cost of reserves. This net saving consists of the differential (f − d) between the funds rate and the discount rate. In administering the discount window the Federal Reserve imposes a noninterest cost of borrowing which rises with volume. In practice, higher borrowing increases the likelihood of triggering costly Federal Reserve consultations with bank officials. Banks tend to borrow up to the point where the marginal expected noninterest cost of borrowing just offsets the net interest saving. Consequently, borrowing tends to be greater the larger the spread between the funds rate and the discount rate. Hence, the reserve provision locus is positively sloped for funds rates above the discount rate.

Discount window borrowing plays a role in determining the funds rate whenever the Federal Reserve restricts the supply of nonborrowed reserves so that the funds rate exceeds the discount rate. In that case, the banking system's demand for reserves is partially satisfied by borrowing at the discount window. If the Federal Reserve chooses to keep nonborrowed reserves fixed in response to an unexpected shift in either reserve demand or the demand for discount window borrowing, then the procedure is called nonborrowed reserve targeting. Nonborrowed reserve targeting is a kind of cross between funds rate and total reserve targeting in the sense that the reserve provision locus is diagonal, rather than horizontal or vertical, thereby partially smoothing the funds rate against aggregate reserve demand shifts. The Federal Reserve employed nonborrowed reserve targeting between October 1979 and the fall of 1982.

By contrast, the Federal Reserve may choose to respond to a shift in reserve demand or the demand for discount window borrowing by adjusting the provision of nonborrowed reserves to keep aggregate discount window borrowing unchanged. The latter procedure, known as borrowed reserve targeting, is closely related to funds rate targeting. This is because, for a given level of the discount rate, targeting borrowed reserves determines the funds rate except for unpredictable instability due to shifts in the demand for discount window borrowing. Borrowed reserve targeting has been the predominant operating procedure since late 1982. An analytically similar procedure, known as free reserve targeting, was employed throughout the 1920s and in the 1950s and '60s.[5]

As can be seen in Figure 2, Federal Reserve discount rate policy plays an important role in determining the funds rate when f is greater than d under either nonborrowed or borrowed reserve targeting. As is easily verified diagrammatically, with a borrowed reserve target a discount rate adjustment changes the funds rate one-for-one. The effect is smaller with nonborrowed reserve targeting. Keep in mind, however, that the discount rate would be irrelevant for determination of the funds rate if the Federal Reserve were to supply a stock of nonborrowed reserves sufficiently large so that the funds rate fell below the discount rate, and banks had no incentive to borrow at the discount window. It is also irrelevant when the Federal Reserve targets the funds rate directly. Discount rate adjustments have played an important role since October 1979 in both the nonborrowed and borrowed reserve targeting periods, as they did in the 1920s, '50s and '60s under free

---

5 Free reserves are defined as excess reserves minus borrowed reserves, or equivalently nonborrowed reserves minus required reserves. Net borrowed reserves are negative free reserves.

reserve targeting. In contrast, discount rate adjustments had no direct impact on the funds rate when the funds rate itself was targeted during the 1970s. In that period, however, the announcement effect associated with discount rate changes sometimes signaled Federal Reserve intentions to change the funds rate target in the future.

The Federal Reserve, the Federal Funds Rate, and Money Market Rates

The Federal Reserve's operating procedures in the reserve market have varied greatly over the years. As we have seen, however, the Federal Reserve has always exercised a dominant influence on the determination of the Federal funds rate through setting the terms upon which it makes nonborrowed and borrowed reserves available to the banking system.

The funds rate is the base rate to which other money market rates are anchored. Market participants determine money market rates according to their view of current and expected future Federal

funds rates. In practice, because Federal Reserve monetary policy smooths funds rate movements, such views depend heavily on anticipated Federal Reserve policy intentions. As an example, consider bank certificates of deposit (CDs), which are generally arranged for a few months. CD rates, adjusted for reserve requirements, are roughly aligned with an average of expected future funds rates over the term of the CD. Banks can raise funds either through CDs or Federal funds and therefore choose whichever option is expected to be cheaper. Likewise, corporations considering a Treasury bill purchase have the option of lending their funds daily over the term of the bill at the overnight repurchase rate, which is closely tied to the Federal funds rate. As shown in Chart 1, arbitrage such as described above among alternative money market instruments generally keeps their yields in line, abstracting from differences due to interest rate spreads resulting from transaction costs and risk differentials.

Such considerations on the part of market participants make current and expected future Federal

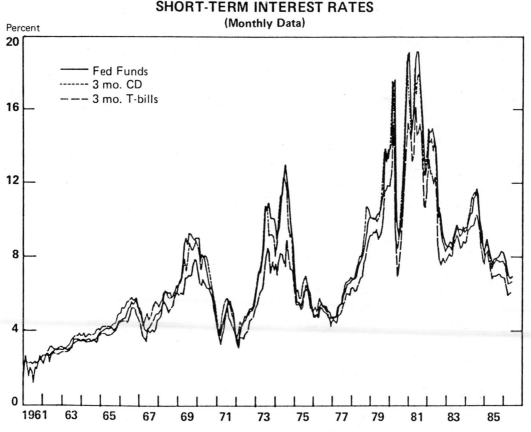

Chart 1
SHORT-TERM INTEREST RATES
(Monthly Data)

Source: *Federal Reserve Bulletin.*

Reserve policy toward the Federal funds rate the key determinant of money market rates in general. Having made this point, we must realize that it provides only a partial explanation of money market rates. A full explanation requires an understanding of Federal Reserve monetary policy. In particular, economy-wide variables such as unemployment and inflation do ultimately play an important role in the evolution of the funds rate through their effect on the Federal Reserve's monetary policy actions over time.

History of the Federal Funds Market

The birth of widespread trading in Federal funds is roughly pinpointed by a *New York Herald Tribune* article appearing in April 1928.[6] That article described the growing importance of Federal funds trading in the money market, reporting a typical daily volume of $100 million.[7] The primary purpose of the article was to announce the inclusion of the Federal funds rate in the *Tribune's* daily table of money market conditions.

As the *Tribune* described it, Federal funds transactions involved the exchange of a check drawn on the clearing house account of the borrowing bank for a check drawn on the reserve account of the lending bank. The reserve check cleared immediately upon presentation at the Reserve Bank, while the clearinghouse check took at least one day to clear. The practice thereby yielded a self-reversing, overnight loan of funds at a Reserve Bank; hence the name, Federal funds. By 1930, the means of trading Federal funds had expanded to include book-entry and wire transfer methods.[8]

The emergence of Federal funds trading constituted a financial innovation allowing banks to minimize transactions costs associated with overnight loans. By their very nature, Federal funds could be lent by member banks only, since only member banks held reserves at Reserve Banks. The beneficiaries on the borrowing side were also member banks, which could receive funds immediately through their Reserve Bank accounts. Federal funds offered member banks a means of avoiding reserve requirements on interbank deposits if they could be classified as "money borrowed" rather than deposits.

In September 1928 the Federal Reserve Board ruled that Federal funds should be classified as nonreservable money borrowed.[9] A further decision in 1930 found that Federal funds created by book-entry and wire transfer methods should also be nonreservable. These decisions provided the initial regulatory underpinnings for the Federal funds market of today. In both the 1928 and 1930 rulings, the Board indicated that it viewed Federal funds as a substitute for member bank borrowing at the Federal Reserve discount window. It argued that because discount window borrowing was not reservable, Federal funds borrowing should not be either. This view seemed appropriate because the mechanics of a Federal funds transaction restricted participation in the Federal funds market to member banks alone.

The Federal Reserve Board's decision to make Federal funds nonreservable is best understood as a means of encouraging the Federal funds market as an alternative to the two conventional means of reserve adjustment then in use: the discount window and the call loan market. Following World War I, aggregate Federal Reserve discount window borrowing generally exceeded member bank reserves. There was relatively little Federal Reserve discouragement of continuous borrowing at the window. Member banks could adjust their reserve positions directly with the Federal Reserve by running discount window borrowing up or down. In addition, banks had a highly effective means of reserve adjustment in the call loan market. Since the middle of the nineteenth century, banks had made a significant fraction of their loans to stockbrokers, secured by stock or bond collateral on a continuing contract, overnight basis.[10] A bank could obtain reserves on demand by calling in its broker loans, and it could readily lend excess reserves by increasing its supply of call loans. The call loan market was the functional equivalent of the Federal funds market for reserve adjustment purposes.

By 1928, however, the Federal Reserve had begun discouraging both the discount window and the call loan market as a means of reserve adjustment. Since 1922, substantial open market purchases had reduced borrowed reserves to less than one-third of total reserves.[11] Moreover, in an apparent effort to further

---

[6] **New York Herald Tribune** [1928].

[7] Willis [1970], p. 12, contains evidence of market activity as far back as 1922.

[8] Board of Governors of the Federal Reserve System, **Federal Reserve Bulletin** 16 (February 1930), p. 81.

[9] Board of Governors of the Federal Reserve System, **Federal Reserve Bulletin** 14 (September 1928), p. 656.

[10] See chapters 7 and 13 in Myers [1931].

[11] Board of Governors of the Federal Reserve System, **Banking and Monetary Statistics, 1914-1941**, pp. 368-96.

reduce the highly visible subsidy that member banks appeared to receive at the window, the Federal Reserve began actively discouraging continuous discount borrowing by individual banks.[12] Both policy actions tended to make discount window borrowing less effective for routine reserve adjustment purposes. This was particularly true for banks with undesired reserves, because with borrowing usually low or zero, they could not dispose of reserves by running down borrowings from the discount window. In addition, the Federal Reserve came to see the call loan market as an inappropriate means of financing security speculation during the stock market boom of the late 1920s. It went so far as to bring "direct pressure" on individual banks to restrict call loans.[13]

Apart from providing a substitute for the discount window and call loans, Federal funds helped to offset the increased cost of membership due to the more restrictive discount policy and the discouragement of call lending. Membership in the Federal Reserve System is voluntary, and throughout most of its history the Federal Reserve has been concerned about membership attrition. One of the significant costs of membership was the requirement that banks hold more non-interest-bearing reserves than nonmember banks had to hold. In making Federal funds nonreservable, the Federal Reserve reduced a cost of membership by providing member banks a means of more effectively competing for overnight interbank deposits.

Banking legislation in the 1930s further enhanced the attractiveness of Federal funds by enabling banks to continue to pay market interest on overnight interbank balances even after the Banking Act of 1933 prohibited explicit interest on demand deposits. This benefit was to prove particularly important in the high interest rate environment of the 1960s and '70s. In order to prevent excessive use of stock market credit, the Securities and Exchange Act of 1934 authorized the Federal Reserve Board to set margin requirements for both brokers and banks, and others if necessary, on loans collateralized by listed stocks and bonds. Relatively high margin requirements, coupled with other restrictions, brought about a permanent decline in the call loan market.[14]

Extremely low interest rates in the 1930s greatly reduced the interest opportunity cost of holding excess reserves. Consequently, banks held a large volume of excess reserves during this period and Federal funds trading virtually disappeared. Federal Reserve pegging of Treasury bill rates between 1942 and 1947 rendered the funds market superfluous for reserve adjustment purposes. Under this policy the Federal Reserve freely converted Treasury securities into reserves at a fixed price. Therefore, banks could use their inventory of Treasury bills for reserve adjustment purposes just as they had used their discount window borrowings in the early 1920s. The Federal Reserve abandoned its Treasury bill price peg in 1947 and Federal funds trading gradually reemerged as the most efficient means of reserve adjustment. Furthermore, higher market interest rates prevailing in the 1950s increased the opportunity cost of holding excess reserves, making more frequent reserve adjustment desirable. Consequently, the volume of trading in Federal funds grew sharply, with daily average gross purchases of large reserve city banks reaching about $800 million by the end of 1959.[15]

In the 1960s, the Federal funds market began to take on a broader role beyond that of reserve adjustment borrowing. Banks made more extensive use of Federal funds as a means of avoiding the reserve requirement tax and the interest prohibition on demand deposits, both of which became more burdensome as inflation and interest rates rose throughout the period. Although the Federal Reserve was responsible for enforcing both of these legislative restrictions, it had to be concerned throughout this period with offsetting the increased burden of membership in the System, and its actions during the period reflected this concern.[16]

The Board's first significant ruling with regard to the Federal funds market in this period was made in 1964 when it decided that a respondent bank, whether member or not, could request a correspondent member bank to simply reclassify a deposit as Federal funds, instead of having to transfer Federal funds through a Reserve Bank account.[17] This ruling probably had its major effect on smaller respondent

---

[12] Fifteenth Annual Report of the Federal Reserve Board **Covering Operations for the Year 1928** (Washington: Government Printing Office, 1929), pp. 7-10.

[13] See the discussion in Friedman and Schwartz [1963], pp. 254-66.

[14] The historical margin requirement series is reported in Board of Governors of the Federal Reserve System, **Banking and Monetary Statistics.**

[15] Board of Governors of the Federal Reserve System, **Federal Reserve Bulletin** 50 (August 1964), p. 954.

[16] Goodfriend and Hargraves [1983] document in detail how the membership problem dominated reserve requirement reform throughout this period.

[17] Board of Governors of the Federal Reserve System, **Federal Reserve Bulletin** 50 (August 1964), pp. 1000-1001.

banks, who had previously found use of Federal funds too costly for the size of their transactions. Allowing banks to simply reclassify their correspondent balances as Federal funds enabled smaller institutions to benefit from Federal funds, as large banks had already been doing. Moreover, it allowed Federal Reserve member correspondent banks to compete more effectively for interbank funds, thereby reducing a disincentive to membership. In 1986, for example, aggregate interbank reservable deposits at large commercial banks are only 25 to 30 percent of aggregate Federal funds borrowings.

Banks in the 1960s also had increasing incentive to give their nonbank depositors access to nonreservable, market interest-paying overnight loans. Nonbanks had always been prohibited from participating in the Federal funds market. But during the 1960s, widespread use of overnight repurchase agreements (RPs) by banks became popular as a means of allowing their nonbank depositors to earn an overnight rate only slightly below the Federal funds rate. As mentioned earlier, the lower rate is due to the reduced risk and additional transaction cost of arranging an RP. RPs do not allow nonbanks to lend Federal funds proper. Because RPs allow nonbanks to approximately earn the Federal funds rate, however, the RP market together with the Federal funds market constitutes a unified overnight loan market.

Obviously, nonbank depositors did not need access to a relatively unregulated overnight rate for reserve adjustment purposes. But the need to facilitate reserve adjustment had been the rationale for waiving reserve requirements and interest rate controls on Federal funds. Nevertheless, the Federal Reserve chose not to make RPs at banks subject to reserve requirements or interest rate controls, probably because doing so would have worsened the competitive position of member banks relative to nonmembers and increased membership attrition.

It was necessary, however, to face up to two consequences of allowing widespread use of RPs at banks. First, RPs were not covered by deposit insurance. Second, shifts from deposits to RPs reduced the reserve requirement tax base and consequently cost the U. S. Treasury tax revenue. A 1969 Federal Reserve rule restricting eligible bank RP collateral to direct obligations of the United States or its agencies, e.g., Treasury bills, responded to those concerns. In principal, requiring RPs to be collateralized with

liabilities of the United States made them free of default risk.[18] In addition, restricting bank RP paper exclusively to U. S. liabilities may have enhanced the demand for U. S. debt, offsetting somewhat the loss of reserve requirement tax revenue.

A 1970 Board ruling formally clarified eligibility for participation on the lending side of the Federal funds market. Eligibility was restricted to commercial banks whether member or nonmember, savings banks, savings and loan associations, and others.[19] In effect, the ruling explicitly segmented the overnight bank loan market into two classes of institutions, those that could lend Federal funds, and those that were required to pay somewhat more substantial transactions costs, through RPs, to earn a rate on overnight loans free of reserve requirements and interest rate controls. Because RPs were uneconomical in smaller volumes, smaller firms and households were unable to obtain nonreservable market yields on overnight money until the emergence of money market mutual funds in the late 1970s.

Conclusion

It is interesting to note how far the Federal funds market has come from its beginnings in the 1920s. Initially, the regulatory rationale for making Federal funds nonreservable was to provide member banks with a substitute for the discount window and call loans for reserve adjustment purposes. Participation in the Federal funds market was limited to member banks, i.e., banks holding required reserves at Reserve Banks. By the 1970s, however, that initial participation principle was effectively overturned. Nonbanks were not allowed to participate directly in the Federal funds market, but they were allowed to earn approximately the Federal funds rate through RPs at banks. Reserve adjustment obviously no longer provided a rationale for sanctioning access to an overnight loan rate free of reserve requirements and interest rate controls. Rather, the granting of such access is better explained as a means by which, in order to minimize membership attrition, the Fed-

---

[18] Even if collateralized by U. S. government secuirties, as a legal matter RPs might also be subject to custodial risk due to incompletely specified contracts. See Ringsmuth [1985].

[19] See footnote 2.

eral Reserve allowed member banks and their customers to avoid the reserve requirement tax and interest rate prohibition on overnight loans.

The Federal funds market today is in many ways a functional equivalent of the call loan market of the 1920s and earlier. The most notable differences are that the nonbank portion of the market is now a net lender rather than a net borrower, and the collateral used is exclusively debt of the United States government and its agencies rather than private stocks and bonds. Like the old call loan market, the Federal funds market of today facilitates the distribution of reserves among banks, and has much wider participation and a more general role as the core of an overnight credit market unencumbered by reserve requirements and legal restrictions on interest rates.

References

Board of Governors of the Federal Reserve System. *Annual Report of the Board of Governors*, various editions.

—————. *Banking and Monetary Statistics, 1914-1941*. Washington: Board of Governors, 1943.

—————. *Banking and Monetary Statistics, 1941-1970*. Washington: Board of Governors, 1976.

—————. *The Federal Funds Market—A Study by a Federal Reserve System Committee*. Washington: Board of Governors, 1959.

—————. *Federal Reserve Bulletin*, various issues.

"Federal Funds' Rate Index of Credit Status." *New York Herald Tribune*, April 5, 1928.

Friedman, Milton, and Anna J. Schwartz. *A Monetary History of the United States, 1867-1960*. Princeton, NJ: Princeton University Press, 1963.

Goodfriend, Marvin. "A Model of Money Stock Determination with Loan Demand and a Banking System Balance Sheet Constraint." Federal Reserve Bank of Richmond, *Economic Review* 68 (January/February 1982), pp. 3-16.

—————. "Interest Rate Smoothing and Price Level Trend-Stationarity." Federal Reserve Bank of Richmond, July 1986.

Goodfriend, Marvin, and Monica Hargarves. "A Historical Assessment of the Rationales and Functions of Reserve Requirements." Federal Reserve Bank of Richmond, *Economic Review* 69 (March/April 1983), pp. 3-21.

Myers, Margaret G. *The New York Money Market*, vol. 1. New York: Columbia University Press, 1931.

Ringsmuth, Don. "Custodial Arrangements and Other Contractual Considerations." Federal Reserve Bank of Atlanta, *Economic Review* 70 (September 1985), pp. 40-48.

Turner, Bernice C. *The Federal Fund Market*. New York: Prentice-Hall, Inc., 1931.

Willis, Parker B. *The Federal Funds Market: Its Origin and Development*. Boston: Federal Reserve Bank of Boston, 1970.

Article 18

REPURCHASE AND
REVERSE REPURCHASE AGREEMENTS

Stephen A. Lumpkin

Recent years have witnessed a considerable growth in the market for repurchase agreements (RPs), both in terms of daily activity and in the numbers and types of participants in the market. Many years ago RPs, or "repos" as they are frequently called, were used primarily by large commercial banks and government securities dealers as an alternative means of financing their inventories of government securities, but their use has expanded substantially in recent years. RPs are now used regularly by a variety of institutional investors in addition to banks and dealers, and the Federal Reserve Bank of New York (FRBNY) uses repo transactions to implement monetary policy directives and to make investments for foreign official and monetary authorities. This article describes RPs and their principal uses and discusses the factors influencing the growth and development of the RP market over the past few years.

What is a Repo?

A standard repurchase agreement involves the acquisition of immediately available funds through the sale of securities with a simultaneous commitment to repurchase the same securities on a date certain within one year at a specified price, which includes interest or its equivalent at an agreed upon rate.[1] Repo transactions have many characteristics of secured lending arrangements in which the underlying securities serve as collateral. Under this characterization, the sale of securities under an agreement to repurchase is a type of collateralized borrowing and represents a liability to the "seller," reflecting the contractual obligation to transfer funds to the "buyer" on the final maturity date of the agreement.

A reverse RP (technically a matched sale-purchase agreement) is the mirror image of an RP. In a reverse repo, securities are acquired with a simultaneous commitment to resell. Because each party to the transaction has the opposite perspective, the terms repo and reverse repo can be applied to the same transaction. A given transaction is a repo when viewed from the point of view of the supplier of the securities (the party acquiring funds) and a reverse repo when described from the point of view of the supplier of funds.[2] In general, whether an agreement is termed a repo or a reverse repo depends largely on which party initiated the transaction, but an RP transaction between a dealer and a retail customer usually is described from the dealer's point of view. Thus, a retail investor's purchase of securities and commitment to resell to a dealer is termed a repo, because the dealer has sold the securities under an agreement to repurchase.

There is no central physical marketplace in which RPs are negotiated. Rather, transactions are arranged over-the-counter by telephone, either by direct contact or through a group of market specialists (dealers or repo brokers). The securities most frequently involved in repo transactions are U.S. Treasury and federal agency securities, but repos are also arranged using mortgage-backed securities and various money market instruments, including negotiable bank certificates of deposit, prime bankers acceptances and commercial paper. If executed properly, an RP agreement is a low-risk, flexible, short-term investment vehicle adaptable to a wide range of uses. For instance, dealers use repo and reverse repo transactions not only to finance the securities held in their investment and trading accounts, but also to establish short positions, implement arbitrage activities, and acquire securities for their own purposes or to meet specific customer needs.[3] Investors in the repo market, such as nonfinancial corporations, thrift institutions, state and local government authorities, and pension funds, in turn, are provided with a low cost investment alternative which

---

The author is an economist at the Board of Governors of the Federal Reserve System. This article was prepared for *Instruments of the Money Market*, 6th ed., Federal Reserve Bank of Richmond.

[1] Immediately available funds include deposits in Federal Reserve Banks and certain collected liabilities of commercial banks that may be transferred or withdrawn on a same-day basis.

[2] For some participants, notably thrift institutions and the Federal Reserve, the terminology is reversed. That is, the Federal Reserve arranges RPs when it wants to inject reserves (supply funds) temporarily.

[3] A dealer establishes a short position by selling a security he does not have in his inventory. To make delivery of the securities the dealer either borrows them or acquires them by making reverse repurchase agreements.

offers combinations of yields, liquidity, and collateral flexibility not available through outright purchases of the underlying securities.

The key features of RP agreements are described in the following section. Subsequent sections explain the pricing of RP contracts and discuss the various procedures for transferring the different types of collateral between the repo counterparties.

Characteristics of RP Agreements

In most RP agreements, the purchaser of the repo securities acquires title to the securities for the term of the agreement and thus may use them to arrange another RP agreement, may sell them outright, or may deliver them to another party to fulfill a delivery commitment on a forward or futures contract, a short sale, or a maturing reverse RP. This feature makes RPs particularly useful for securities dealers, who use repos and reverses to implement a wide variety of trading and arbitrage strategies. As suggested previously, a wide range of other institutional participants also derive benefits from the RP market. The principal use of repos by these investors is the short-term investment of surplus cash either for their own accounts or on behalf of others in their fiduciary capacities or as agent. The various yields and maturities offered in RP transactions make them well-suited for this purpose.

Maturities RP agreements usually are arranged with short terms to maturity. Most RPs in Treasury securities, for example, are overnight transactions. In addition to overnight contracts, longer-term repos are arranged for standard maturities of one, two, and three weeks, and one, two, three, and six months. Other fixed-term multi-day contracts ("term repos") are negotiated occasionally and repos also may be arranged on an "open" or continuing basis. Continuing contracts in essence are a series of overnight repos in that they are renewed each day with the repo rate adjusted to reflect prevailing market conditions. These agreements usually may be terminated on demand by either party.

Yields In some RP agreements, the agreed upon repurchase price is set above the initial sale price with the difference reflecting the interest expense incurred by the borrower. It is more typical, however, for the repurchase price to be set equal to the initial sale price plus a negotiated rate of interest to be paid on the settlement date by the borrower. Repo interest rates are straight add-on rates calculated using a 360-day "basis" year. The dollar amount of interest earned on funds invested in RPs is determined as follows:

$$\text{Interest earned} = \text{Dollar amount invested} \times \text{Repo rate} \times \frac{\text{Number of days to maturity}}{360}$$

For example, a \$25 million overnight RP investment at a 6 3/4 percent rate would yield an interest return of \$4,687.50:

$$(\$25,000,000 \times .0675)/360 \times 1 = \$4,687.50$$

Suppose instead, that the funds were invested in a 10-day term agreement at the same rate of 6 3/4 percent. In this case, the investor's earnings would be \$46,875.00:

$$(\$25,000,000 \times .0675)/360 \times 10 = \$46,875.00$$

As a final example, suppose that the investor chose to enter into a continuing contract with the borrower at an initial rate of 6 3/4 percent, but withdrew from the arrangement after a period of five days. Suppose also that the daily RP rates over the five days were 6 3/4 percent, 7 percent, 6 1/2 percent, 6 3/8 percent, and 6 1/4 percent. Then the total interest earned on the continuing contract would be:

First day:
$$(\$25,000,000 \times .0675)/360 \quad \times 1 = \$\ 4,687.50$$
Second day:
$$(\$25,000,000 \times .07)/360 \quad \times 1 = \$\ 4,861.11$$
Third day:
$$(\$25,000,000 \times .065)/360 \quad \times 1 = \$\ 4,513.89$$
Fourth day:
$$(\$25,000,000 \times .06375)/360 \times 1 = \$\ 4,427.08$$
Fifth day:
$$(\$25,000,000 \times .0625)/360 \quad \times 1 = \underline{\$\ 4,340.28}$$

Total interest earned: \qquad \$22,829.86

If the investor had entered into a term agreement for the same period at the rate of 6 3/4 percent prevailing on the first day, he would have earned \$23,437.50 in interest. Thus, in this hypothetical example the movement in rates worked to the advantage of the borrower.

The purchaser of securities in a repo transaction earns only the agreed upon rate of return. If a coupon payment is made on the underlying securities during the term of the agreement, the purchaser in most cases must account to the seller for the amount of the payment. Securities in registered definitive form generally are left registered in the seller's name so that any coupon payments made during the repo term may be received directly.

Principal Amounts RP transactions are usually arranged in large dollar amounts. Overnight contracts and term repos with maturities of a week or less are often arranged in amounts of \$25 million or more, and blocks of \$10 million are common for longer maturity term agreements. Although a few repos are negotiated for amounts under \$100,000, the smallest customary amount is \$1 million.

Valuation of Collateral Typically, the securities used as collateral in repo transactions are valued at current market price plus accrued interest (on coupon-bearing securities) calculated to the maturity date of the agreement less a margin or "haircut" for term RPs.[4] Technically, the haircut may protect either the lender or the borrower depending upon how the transaction is priced. In the usual case, the initial RP purchase price is set lower than the current market value of the collateral (principal plus accrued interest), which reduces the lender's exposure to market risk. A dealer arranging a reverse RP with a nondealer customer frequently takes margin, which covers his exposure on the funds transferred.

To illustrate the computation of market risk haircuts, consider the case of a lender who in December 1984 was holding $10 million par value of 52-week Treasury bills as collateral for a 7-day term RP agreement. In 1984, the average week-to-week fluctuation in the yield of recently offered 52-week bills was 0.21 percent, measured as the standard deviation of the change in yield from Tuesday to Tuesday. The corresponding price volatility measure was 0.20 percent. To reflect a 95 percent confidence level the lender would compute a market risk haircut factor of 0.50 percent (2.5 times the standard deviation of week-to-week price changes). On December 27, for instance, year bills were trading at a discount rate of 8.38 percent or at a price of $91.504 per $100 par value. Thus, the current market value of the collateral was $9,150,361.11. The lender would calculate its per week risk of loss at $45,751.81 (the market risk haircut factor times the market value), and would value the collateral accordingly at $9,104,609.31 (the current market value less the haircut in dollars).

In principle, the dollar amount of the haircut should be sufficient to guard against the potential loss from an adverse price movement during the repo term. The sizes of haircuts taken in practice usually vary depending on the term of the RP contract, type of securities involved, and the coupon rate of the underlying securities. For example, discount bonds are more price volatile than premium bonds and thus are given larger haircuts. Similarly, haircuts taken on private money market instruments generally exceed those of comparable-maturity Treasury securities, due to an additional credit risk-induced component of price volatility. In general, haircuts are larger the longer the term to maturity of the repo securities, and larger haircuts are common for less liquid securities as well. Currently, market risk haircuts range

from about one to five percent, but may be as low as one-eighth of a point for very short-term securities.

Because both parties in a term repo arrangement are exposed to the risk of adverse fluctuations in the market value of the underlying securities due to changes in interest rates, it is common practice to have the collateral value of the underlying securities adjusted daily ("marked to market") to reflect changes in market prices and to maintain the agreed upon margin. Accordingly, if the market value of the repo securities declines appreciably, the borrower may be asked to provide additional collateral to cover the loan. However, if the market value of the collateral rises substantially, the lender may be required to return the excess collateral to the borrower.

Special Repo Arrangements The bulk of the activity in the RP market involves standard overnight transactions in Treasury and agency securities, usually negotiated between a dealer and its regular customers. Although standard overnight and term RP arrangements are most prevalent, dealers sometimes alter various provisions of these contracts in order to accommodate specific needs of their customers. Other arrangements are intended to give the dealer flexibility in the designation of collateral, particularly in longer-term agreements. For example, some contracts are negotiated to permit substitution of the securities subject to the repurchase commitment. In a "dollar repo," for instance, the initial seller's commitment is to repurchase securities that are similar to, but not necessarily the same as, the securities originally sold. There are a number of common variants. In a "fixed-coupon repo," the seller agrees to repurchase securities that have the same coupon rate as those sold in the first half of the repo transaction. A "yield maintenance agreement" is a slightly different variant in which the seller agrees to repurchase securities that provide roughly the same overall return as the securities originally sold. In each case, the maturity of the repurchased securities must be within an agreed upon range, but may be only approximately the same as that of the original securities. These agreements are frequently arranged so that the purchaser of the securities receives the final principal payment from the issuer of the securities.

In other repo arrangements, the repo counterparties negotiate flexible terms to maturity. A common example of this type of contract is the repo to maturity (or reverse to maturity for the lender of funds). In a repo to maturity, the initial seller's repurchase commitment in effect is eliminated altogether, because the purchaser agrees to hold the repo securities until they mature. The seller's repurchase commitment depends on the manner in which the final principal payment on the underlying

---

[4] The failure of Drysdale Government Securities in May 1982 and Lombard-Wall in August 1982 uncovered weaknesses in the pricing of RPs. RPs are now priced with accrued interest included in full in the purchase price, but prior to adoption of full accrual pricing in October 1982, it was common for RPs to be priced without accrued interest.

securities is handled. When the purchaser of the repo securities receives the final principal payment directly from the issuer of the securities, he usually retains it and nets it against the seller's repurchase obligation. However, if the seller of the repo securities receives the principal payment, he must pay the purchaser the full amount of the agreed upon repurchase price when the repo is unwound.

Reverses to maturity often involve coupon securities trading at a discount from the price at which the "seller" initially purchased them. Typically, reverses to maturity are initiated by an investor who is reluctant to sell the securities outright, because an outright sale would require taking a capital loss on the securities. A reverse to maturity enables the investor to acquire funds to invest in higher yielding securities without having to sell outright and realize a capital loss. The dealer participating in the transaction usually takes margin on the securities "purchased".

Participants in the RP Market

The favorable financing rates and variety of terms and collateral arrangements available have led government securities dealers to expand their use of repos in recent years. Many years ago, dealers relied primarily on collateralized loans from their clearing banks ("box loans") to meet their financing needs, but RPs and reverse RPs are now their principal sources of financing. Major dealers and large money center banks in particular finance the bulk of their holdings of Treasury and agency securities by RP transactions. Most of these transactions are arranged on a short-term basis (i.e., overnight or continuing contracts) via direct contact with major customers, typically banks, public entities, pension funds, money market mutual funds, and other institutional investors. The Federal Reserve Bank of New York also arranges repos and reverse repos with dealers to implement monetary policy directives and to make investments for foreign central banks and other official accounts.

Early each morning a dealer's financing desk arranges repo financing for expected changes in the firm's securities inventory ("long position") and for replacement of maturing RPs, and also arranges reverse RPs to cover known or planned short sales or to meet specific customer needs.[5] The bulk of these arrangements are finalized by 10:00 a.m. Eastern Time.

Dealers use reverse RPs to establish or cover short positions and to obtain specific issues for redelivery to customers. Major suppliers of securities to the market include large commercial banks, thrifts, and other financial institutions. Nonfinancial corporations and municipalities also supply collateral to this market. A dealer "reverses in" securities, in effect, by buying them from the holder under an agreement to resell; the term of the agreement usually ranges from a week to a month, but may also run for the remaining term to maturity of the securities (reverse to maturity). The use of reverse repos to cover short positions is similar to securities borrowing arrangements in which the dealer obtains securities in exchange for funds, other securities, or a letter of credit. However, reversing in securities typically is cheaper than borrowing the securities outright and also gives the dealer greater flexibility in his use of the securities. For instance, reverse RPs are arranged for fixed time commitments, but borrowing arrangements usually may be terminated on a day's notice at the option of the lender.

If a dealer has exhausted its regular customer sources but is still in need of funds or specific collateral, it may contact a repo broker. Dealers use repo brokers most often for term RP agreements and in arranging reverse RPs. The repo brokers market is particularly important for obtaining popular issues in short supply ("on special"). Although the use of bank loans as a source of financing has declined considerably, a dealer still may obtain financing from its clearing bank in the form of an overnight box loan if it has a negative balance in its cash account at the end of the day.[6] The rate the clearing bank charges is generally 1/8 to 1/4 of a point or more above the Federal funds rate, with slightly higher rates charged for loans arranged late in the day, so dealers acquire box loans only as a last resort. A dealer who is unable to obtain adequate financing using his own customer base, or has an unexpected receipt of securities late in the day, may choose to obtain a "position" loan from another bank rather than a box loan from his own clearing bank. Position loans are often available at more favorable rates than available on box loans. In these circumstances, the lender frequently wires the dealer's clearing bank the amount of the loan. The clearing bank, in turn, segregates the required amount of the dealer's securities as collateral for the loan and acts as custodian for the lender.

In addition to using repos and reverse repos to finance their long and short positions, dealers also use RP agreements in transactions in which they act as inter-

---

[5] A short sale is the sale of securities not currently owned, usually under the expectation that the market price of the securities will fall before the termination date of the transaction. The seller later purchases the securities at a lower price to cover his short position and earns an arbitrage profit.

[6] Securities received by a clearing bank on behalf of a dealer customer generally are delivered first into a central clearing account known as the "box." Any securities that have not been allocated to other uses by the dealer, and have not been financed through other means, may be used to collateralize an overnight loan (box loan) from the clearing bank.

mediaries between suppliers and demanders of funds in the repo market. A dealer acts as principal on each side of the arrangement, borrowing funds from one party (against the sale of securities) and relending the funds to another party (against the receipt of securities). The combination of repo and reverse repo transactions in this fashion is termed a "repo book." A repo book in which an RP and a reverse RP in the same security have equal terms to maturity is referred to as a "matched book." Larger, better capitalized dealers are able to borrow in the RP market at more favorable rates than smaller dealers and non-dealer customers, and thus can profit through arbitrage in matched transactions. Dealers also may profit from a differential in the margin taken on the underlying collateral in the two transactions.

At times, a dealer may choose not to match the maturities of the repo and reverse repo agreements in an effort to increase profits. For example, if interest rates are expected to rise during the term of the agreement, the dealer may arrange an RP with a longer term than the reverse RP in order to "lock in" the more favorable borrowing rates. Conversely, in a declining rate environment, a longer-term reverse RP may be financed through a number of shorter-term RPs arranged at successively lower rates.

Many types of institutional investors derive benefits from RP and reverse RP transactions with dealers, including nonfinancial corporations, state and local government authorities and other public bodies, banks, and thrift institutions. Repos are adaptable to many uses and RP maturities can be tailored precisely to meet the needs of lenders. This enables corporations and municipalities with temporary surplus cash balances to earn market rates of return on a timely basis but have their funds available when needed. Thus, in effect, RP agreements convert cash balances into interest-bearing liquid assets. In this fashion, RPs are more attractive investments than alternative money market instruments which do not offer the same combination of liquidity, flexibility, and ease of negotiation. Newly issued negotiable CDs, for example, must have a minimum maturity of at least 14 days and commercial paper is seldom written with maturities as short as a day.

Repos are also attractive investments for investors subject to restrictions on the types of assets in which they may invest. Many public bodies, for example, are required by law to invest their tax receipts and proceeds from note and bond sales in Treasury or federal agency issues until the funds are to be spent. As opposed to buying the securities outright, these entities often invest in repos collateralized by government securities and record the ownership of the securities rather than the repos on their books.

The Federal Reserve also is a major participant in the repo market. When the Manager of the System Open Market Account needs to inject reserves in the banking system overnight or for a few days, the Domestic Trading Desk of the FRBNY arranges RPs with primary dealers in government securities.[7] These agreements are arranged for specified periods of up to 15 days and are collateralized by Treasury and agency securities. Investments on behalf of foreign official and international accounts also involve RPs, either arranged in the market or internally with the System's Account. When the Manager wants to absorb reserves for a few days, the Desk arranges matched sale-purchase transactions with primary dealers, in which specific securities are sold from the System's portfolio for immediate delivery and simultaneously repurchased for settlement on the desired date.

Growth and Development of the RP Market

It is difficult to ascertain when the repurchase agreement originated. Some suggest that RPs date back to the 1920s, about the time that the Federal funds market evolved. Other sources state that the use of RPs was initiated by government securities dealers after World War II as a means of financing their positions. There is general agreement, however, that for many years RPs were used almost exclusively by government securities dealers and large money center banks. Since the late 1960s, however, the number and types of participants in the RP market has grown considerably.

A number of factors have influenced the growth and development of the RP market over this period, including changes in the regulatory environment, inflation, growth in federal debt outstanding, and increased interest rate volatility. The higher levels and greater volatility of interest rates since the 1960s have been particularly important. They have raised the opportunity cost of holding idle cash balances in demand deposit accounts, on which the explicit payment of interest is prohibited, and have led to an expanded use of active cash management techniques. Accompanying these developments have been key innovations in telecommunications and

---

[7] Primary dealers are a group of dealers who have met eligibility criteria established by the Federal Reserve Bank of New York (FRBNY). To be on the FRBNY's primary dealer list, a firm is expected to make markets in the full range of Treasury and agency issues under "good" and "bad" market conditions for a diverse group of nondealer customers, and to maintain certain minimum capital levels. The FRBNY selects appropriate counterparties from this list when it conducts open market operations.

computer technology, which have contributed to the development of sophisticated cash management systems for managing and transferring large volumes of funds. As a consequence, a variety of financial institutions, nonfinancial corporations, pension funds, mutual funds, public bodies, and other institutional investors have joined securities dealers and money center banks as active participants in the RP market.

As a result of this growth, the RP market is now considered to be one of the largest and most liquid markets in the world. Although total daily activity in the RP market is not known, as most agreements are negotiated directly between counterparties over the telephone, an indication of the growth in the market over recent years can be seen in the use of RPs and reverse RPs by primary dealers. As shown in Table I, on an annual average basis, repo financing by major dealers has nearly tripled since 1981. The same is true for the use of matched book transactions (Table II), which account for about half of all repo transactions. In fact, for some nonbank dealers matched book transactions account for as much as 90 percent of overall repo activity. Bank dealers are subject to capital requirements imposed by bank regulators, which raise the cost of using these transactions relative to alternative investments; thus, they have not participated as much in the use of matched RP agreements.

The rapid growth and development of the RP market over recent years has not occurred without incident. In particular, the failures of a few unregistered non-primary government securities dealers has had a significant effect on the operation of the market. These failures generally had some common characteristics, including the use of pricing techniques which ignored accrued interest in

Table I

ANNUAL AVERAGES OF OUTSTANDING REPURCHASE AND REVERSE REPURCHASE AGREEMENTS BY CATEGORY OF PRIMARY DEALER[1]

(Millions of Dollars)

Year	Bank Dealers	Nonbank Dealers	Total
1981	19,173	92,565	111,738
1982	22,337	147,890	170,227
1983	24,812	159,319	184,131
1984	26,706	218,282	244,988
1985	34,453	286,365	320,818

[1] Figures are obtained from reports submitted weekly to the Federal Reserve Bank of New York by the U. S. government securities dealers on its published list of primary dealers. Figures include matched agreements.

Table II

ANNUAL AVERAGES OF OUTSTANDING MATCHED REPURCHASE AND REVERSE REPURCHASE AGREEMENTS OF PRIMARY DEALERS[1]

(Millions of Dollars)

Year	Bank Dealers	Nonbank Dealers	Total
1981	6,167	51,177	57,344
1982	7,534	88,315	95,849
1983	6,839	84,523	91,362
1984	7,207	121,938	129,145
1985	9,118	152,914	162,032

[1] Figures are obtained from reports submitted weekly to the Federal Reserve Bank of New York by the U. S. government securities dealers on its published list of primary dealers. Figures include repurchase agreements, duebills, and collateralized loans used to finance reverse repurchase agreements, as well as the reverse side of these transactions.

computing the value of repoed securities, and the fraudulent use of customers' collateral. The failures resulted in considerable uncertainty regarding the legal status of repos and the contractual rights of the counterparties when one of them files for protection under federal bankruptcy laws.

Repurchase agreements have never been defined in a strict legal sense either as collateralized loans or as outright purchases and sales of securities. Under recent court rulings involving the bankruptcy proceedings of Bevill, Bresler, and Schulman, Inc., the court has determined that the appropriate characterization of a repo for legal purposes depends upon the manner in which the transaction was arranged. For instance, if the repo counterparties arranged the transaction as a consummated sale and contract to repurchase, then the court would adopt the same characterization in the event of a default and subsequent bankruptcy of one party.

Market participants have long operated under the assumption that the purchaser of repo securities is entitled to liquidate them if the seller is unable to fulfill the terms of the agreement at settlement, but the validity of this assumption relies importantly on the court's interpretation. For instance, in September 1982, in the bankruptcy proceedings involving Lombard-Wall, Inc., Federal Bankruptcy Judge Edward J. Ryan ruled that certain repos involved in that case were to be considered secured loan transactions for purposes of the proceedings.[8] As a consequence, under the existing law, RPs became

[8] Lombard-Wall failed in August 1982 when it was unable to return funds it had obtained in overvalued long-term RPs. The failure of Lombard-Wall occurred shortly after the collapse of Drysdale Government Securities, Inc. Drysdale failed in May 1982 when it was unable to make payments on accrued interest on securities it had acquired under RP agreements and could not return the securities it had obtained through over-collateralized reverse RPs.

subject to the "automatic stay" provisions of the Bankruptcy Code. The automatic stay provisions block any efforts of a creditor to make collections or to enforce a lien against the property of a bankrupt estate. Consequently, Lombard-Wall's repo counterparties could neither use the funds obtained nor sell the underlying repo securities without the court's permission, because to do so would constitute the enforcement of a lien and thus would violate the automatic stay provision.

As a result of the developments in the Lombard-Wall case, the perceived risks of lending in the RP market were raised, resulting in a contraction in the volume of repo transactions entered into by non-dealer entities, including mutual funds and state and local government authorities. With the reduction in a major source of repo funds, the financing costs for some non-primary dealers rose, as other participants regarded them as higher credit risks. At the same time RP rates paid by some well-capitalized firms declined somewhat. Similar movements in repo financing rates have occurred in the wake of failures of other government securities dealers, including the recent failures of E.S.M. Government Securities, Inc. and Bevill, Bresler, and Schulman Asset Management Corp. in 1985.

In response to the repurchase agreement issue, Congress, in June 1984, enacted the Bankruptcy Amendments Act of 1984, which amended Title 11 of the U. S. Code covering bankruptcy. The legislation exempts repurchase agreements in Treasury and agency securities, certain CDs, and bankers acceptances from the automatic stay provision of the Bankruptcy Code. Although the legislation does not resolve the question of whether an RP agreement is a secured lending arrangement or a purchase and sale transaction, it enables lenders to liquidate the underlying securities under either interpretation and resolves a major question about the status of RP collateral in bankruptcy proceedings.[9]

With the encouragement of the Federal Reserve Bank of New York (FRBNY), primary dealers began to include the value of accrued interest in the pricing of RPs and related transactions in October 1982. At that time, the FRBNY also recommended that dealers follow uniform procedures in establishing repo contract value for purposes of maintaining margin. These actions helped to correct certain inadequacies in standard repo pricing practices.

However, recent dealer failures have demonstrated that proper pricing of repo transactions alone is insufficient to ensure the safety of a repo investment. Investors must also concern themselves with the creditworthiness of their repo counterparties. For instance, many of the investors dealing with E.S.M. and Bevill, Bresler, and Schulman lost their money because they did not protect their ownership

interest in the repo securities pledged to them as collateral. Investors can best establish their ownership claim to repo securities by taking delivery of the securities, either directly or through a clearing bank-custodian.

Repo Collateral Arrangements

As mentioned previously, most RPs involve Treasury and federal agency securities, the bulk of which are maintained in book-entry form. Usually, when an RP is arranged, the underlying securities are transferred against payment over the Federal Reserve's securities wire ("Fedwire") to the lender/purchaser, resulting in a simultaneous transfer of funds to the borrower. At maturity, the RP collateral is returned over the wire against payment and the transfers are reversed. Direct access to the Federal Reserve's securities and payments transfer systems is restricted, so transfers of the repo securities usually are processed by means of Reserve Bank credits and debits to the securities and clearing accounts of depository institutions acting as clearing agents for their customers. Transfers of physical securities also frequently involve clearing agents.

The transaction costs associated with the payment and delivery of repo securities include some combination of securities clearance fees, wire transfer charges for securities in book-entry form, custodial fees, and account maintenance fees. The exact charges can vary considerably from case to case depending on the type of securities involved and the actual method of delivery. For example, Fedwire charges for securities transfers are higher for off-line originations than for transfers initiated on-line, and the fees for transfers of agency securities are slightly higher than those for Treasury securities. In any event, the total transaction costs to process transfers of securities from the seller/borrower to the buyer/lender are higher the greater the number of intermediate transactions. Although these costs are often inconsequential for longer-maturity transactions in large dollar amounts, they may add significantly to the overall costs of others. As a result, a number of repo collateral arrangements have been developed that do not involve the actual delivery of collateral to the lender. Not surprisingly, the rates available to investors in such nondelivery repos are higher than rates offered on standard two-party RPs with collateral delivery. Of course, the risks may be greater as well.

At one end of the spectrum of nondelivery repos is the "duebill" or letter repo. A duebill in essence is an unsecured loan similar in form to commercial paper; the borrower merely sends a transaction confirmation to the lender. Although specific securities might be named as collateral, the lender does not have control of the

[9] Note that the automatic stay provision is irrelevant if an RP is considered to be an outright purchase and sale of securities.

securities. Thus, the lender relies for the most part on the integrity and creditworthiness of the borrower. Duebills are used primarily in overnight arrangements that involve small par amounts of non-wireable securities.

A similar arrangement is the "hold-in-custody" repo in which the borrower retains possession of the repo securities but either transfers them internally to a customer account or delivers them to a bulk segregation account at its clearing bank; the securities are left in the dealer's name and not that of the individual customers. The extent to which the investor's ownership interest in the pledged securities is protected depends on the type of custody arrangement. If the borrower acts as both custodian and principal in the transaction, the investor relies on the borrower's integrity and creditworthiness.[10]

A lender can protect his ownership claim to repo securities by using "safekeeping" arrangements involving a clearing bank-custodian acting solely in its behalf or jointly as agent for both repo counterparties. The most popular of these arrangements is the "tri-party repo" in which a custodian, typically the borrower's clearing bank, becomes a direct participant in the repo transaction with the borrower and lender. The clearer-custodian ensures that exchanges of collateral and funds occur simultaneously and that appropriate operational controls are in place to safeguard the investor's ownership interest in the underlying collateral during the term of the agreement. When the repo is unwound at maturity, the clearer makes an entry in its internal records transferring the securities from the segregation account to the borrower's clearing account and wires the loan repayment to the lender.

The rates available to investors in tri-party repos are lower than those available on nonsegregated RPs without collateral delivery, but higher than the rates offered on standard two-party RPs with delivery. Thus, safekeeping arrangements of this type are attractive both to investors, who earn a higher risk-adjusted return than available on standard RPs, and to borrowers, whose total financing costs are lowered through the avoidance of clearance costs and wire transfer fees.

Determinants of RP Rates

The interest rate paid on RP funds, the repo rate of return, is negotiated by the repo counterparties and is set independently of the coupon rate or rates on the underlying securities. In addition to factors related to the terms and conditions of individual repo arrangements, repo interest rates are influenced by overall money market conditions, the competitive rates paid for comparable funds, and the availability of eligible collateral. As mentioned previously, changes in the perceived risks associated with RP investments also affect the level of RP rates and the spreads between RP rates and comparable money market rates.

Because repurchase agreements are close substitutes for Federal funds borrowings, overnight RP rates to a large extent are determined by conditions in the market for reserve balances and thus are closely tied to the Federal funds rate. For example, when the demand for reserves is high relative to the existing supply, depository institutions bid more aggressively for Federal funds, thereby putting upward pressure on the Federal funds rate. As the funds rate rises, some institutions will enter into repurchase agreements, which also puts upward pressure on the RP rate. Both rates will continue to rise until the demand and supply for reserves in the banking system is again in balance.[11] Federal Reserve policy actions have a major influence on overnight financing rates through their effect on the supply of reserves via open market operations and discount window policy.

Repo rates for overnight RPs in Treasury securities usually lie about 25 to 30 basis points below the Federal funds rate. Properly executed RP agreements are less risky than sales of Federal funds because they are fully backed by high-quality collateral. Thus, the rate spread generally reflects a risk premium paid to compensate investors for lending unsecured in the Federal funds market rather than investing in a collateralized RP agreement. The spread between the Federal funds rate and RP rate has narrowed when the perceived risks associated with RP investments have increased, e.g., when the legal status of the repo securities backing an RP agreement has come under question.

The spread between the funds rate and the RP rate can also depend on the supply of collateral held by government securities dealers. Dealers reduce their demand for RP financing when the dollar volume of securities they hold in their investment and trading accounts is low.[12] Other things the same, this also puts downward pressure on the RP rate relative to the Federal funds rate. Conversely, the RP rate rises, and the rate spread narrows, when the volume of securities to be financed is high relative to the availability of overnight financing. This

---

[10] Under the Uniform Commercial Code, an investor can establish an ownership interest in securities it has left with a dealer for a period of up to 21 days if it obtains a proper written agreement and "gives value" for the securities.

[11] See Kenneth D. Garbade [1982, Chapter 5].

[12] This sometimes occurs after major tax payments when incoming tax receipts exceed the capacity of Treasury Tax and Loan (TT&L) accounts at commercial banks and are transferred to the Treasury's account at Federal Reserve Banks. Because the transfer of funds from the public to the Federal Reserve (Fed) drains reserves from the banking system, the Fed often arranges RPs to inject reserves to offset the effect of the movement. These RPs must be collateralized, of course, and funds held in TT&L accounts also must be collateralized. Both actions tend to remove a large quantity of eligible collateral from the market.

sometimes occurs after Treasury mid-quarter refundings, particularly when the new issues are not well distributed to investors.

Conclusion

The use of RPs as a major financing vehicle is likely to continue to expand during the forseeable future, with a sizable increase in the volume of RPs outstanding and a broadening of the types of assets used as collateral. In coming years, the move toward a more complete globalization of securities markets and the associated growth in trading activity will further enhance the demand for flexible financing arrangements. This is likely to be associated with further efforts to clarify the rights of repo counterparties in written agreements and the expanded use of triparty agreements and other segregation arrangements.

References

Garbade, Kenneth D. *Securities Markets*. New York: McGraw-Hill, 1982.

Lucas, Charles, Marcos Jones, and Thomas Thurston. "Federal Funds and Repurchase Agreements." Federal Reserve Bank of New York, *Quarterly Review* (Summer 1977), pp. 33-48.

Simpson, Thomas D. "The Market for Federal Funds and Repurchase Agreements." Staff Studies 106. Washington, D.C.: Board of Governors of the Federal Reserve System, 1979.

Smith, Wayne J. "Repurchase Agreements and Federal Funds." *Federal Reserve Bulletin* (May 1978), pp. 353-60.

Stigum, Marcia. *The Money Market*. Rev. ed. Homewood, Illinois: Dow Jones-Irwin, 1983.

Article 19

Interest Rate Swaps: A Review of the Issues

Larry D. Wall and John J. Pringle

Interest rate swaps have gained considerable importance in capital markets in the six years since they were introduced. This article questions some of the conventional views regarding the use of interest rate swaps and presents information on swaps' pricing, risks, and regulation.

In the last two decades a myriad of new instruments and transactions have brought about significant changes in financial markets. Some of these innovations have attracted considerable publicity; stock index futures and options, for example, were an important element in the studies of the October 19, 1987, stock market crash.[1] However, not all of these new developments are well-known to the public. One recent innovation that is quietly transforming credit markets is interest rate swaps—an agreement between two parties to exchange interest payments for a predetermined period of time.

The interest rate swap market began in 1982. By 1988 the outstanding portfolios of 49 leading swap dealers totaled $889.5 billion in principal, of which $473.6 billion represented new business in 1987.[2] Reflecting their rapid growth, swaps have gained considerable importance in the capital markets. Thomas Jasper, the head of Salomon Brothers' swap department, has estimated that 30 to 40 percent of all capital market transactions involve an interest rate, foreign-exchange, or some other type of swap.[3]

Their rapid growth is one reason swaps have generated considerable interest among academics, regulators, accountants, and market participants alike. Paramount among the questions surrounding swaps are the reasons for their use and the basis of their pricing. Regulators are also keenly concerned with the risks swaps pose to financial firms, while accountants are debating appropriate reporting. This article reviews the current literature and presents some new research on interest rate swaps. Among the issues addressed are the workings of interest rate swaps, the reasons that firms use such swaps, the risks associated with interest rate swaps, the pricing of these swaps, the regulation of participants in the swap market, and the disclosure of swaps on firms' financial statements.

What Is an Interest Rate Swap?

Interest rate swaps serve to transform the effective maturity (or, more accurately, the repricing interval) of two firms' assets or liabilities. This type of swap enables firms to choose from a wider variety of asset and liability markets without having to incur additional interest rate risk, that is, risk that arises because of changes in market interest rates. For instance, a firm that traditionally invests in short-term assets, whose

The authors are, respectively, a senior economist in the financial section of the Atlanta Fed's Research Department and a professor of finance at the University of North Carolina at Chapel Hill. They wish to thank William Curt Hunter and Peter Abken for their comments.

returns naturally fluctuate as the yield on each new issue changes, may instead invest in a long-term, fixed-rate instrument and then use an interest rate swap to obtain floating-rate receipts. In this situation, one firm agrees to pay a fixed interest rate to another in return for receiving a floating rate.

Interest rate swaps have fixed termination dates and typically provide for semiannual payments. Either interest rate in a swap may be fixed or floating.[4] The amount of interest paid is based on some agreed-upon principal amount, which is called the "notional" principal because it never actually changes hands. Moreover, the two parties do not exchange the full amounts of the interest payments. Rather, at each payment a single amount is transferred to cover the net difference in the promised interest payments.

An example of an interest rate swap is provided in Chart 1. Atlanta HiTech agrees to pay Heartland Manufacturing a floating rate of interest equal to the London Interbank Offered Rate (LIBOR), which is commonly used in international loan agreements.[5] In return, Heartland Manufacturing promises to pay Atlanta HiTech a fixed 9.18 percent rate of interest. The swap transaction is ordinarily arranged at current market rates in order for the net present value of payments to equal zero. That is, the fixed rate on a typical interest rate swap is set so that the market value of the net floating-rate payments

exactly equals the market value of the net fixed-rate payments. If the swap is not arranged as a zero-net-present-value exchange, one party pays to the other an amount equal to the difference in the payments' net present value when the swap is arranged.

Chart 2 demonstrates three aspects of the swaps market: converting floating-rate debt to fixed-rate debt, converting a floating-rate asset to a fixed-rate asset, and using an intermediary in the swap transaction. In Chart 2, Widgets Unlimited can issue short-term debt but is averse to the risk that market interest rates will increase. To avoid this risk, Widgets enters into a swap in which it agrees to pay the counterparty a fixed rate of interest and receive a floating rate. This arrangement resembles long-term, fixed-rate debt in that Widgets' promised payments are independent of market interest rate changes. If market interest rates rise, Widgets will receive payments under the swap that will offset the higher cost of its short-term debt. Should market rates fall, though, under the terms of the swap Widgets will have to pay its counterparty money.

The combination of short-term debt and swaps is not identical to the use of long-term debt. One difference is that Widgets' interest payments are not truly fixed. The company is protected from an increase in market rates but not from changes in its own risk premium. The swap

Chart 1.
An Interest Rate Swap without a Dealer

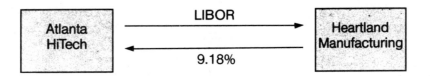

In this example, Atlanta HiTech agrees to pay Heartland Manufacturing a floating rate of interest equal to the London Interbank Offered Rate. In return, Heartland agrees to pay Atlanta HiTech a fixed 9.18% rate of interest. These two companies do not actually exchange the full amounts of the interest payments, but at each payment, a single amount is transferred to cover the net difference in the promised interest payments.

would not compensate Widgets if its own cost of short-term debt increased from LIBOR-plus-0.5 percent to LIBOR-plus-0.75 percent. If the cost of short-term debt to Widgets decreased to LIBOR-plus-0.30 percent, however, the cost of the debt issue would fall by 0.20 percent. In addition, the counterparty to the combination generally does not provide the corporation with the interest rate option implicit in many bonds issued in the United States, whereby they can be called in at a fixed price regardless of current market rates. Call options allow issuers to exploit large changes in market interest rates.[6] In contrast, standard interest rate swap contracts may be unwound or canceled only at prevailing market interest rates.

The other swap user in this example illustrates a swap's potential to convert a floating rate asset to one in which the rate is fixed. OneState Insurance, a small life insurance company, has long-term, fixed-rate obligations but would like to invest part of its portfolio in short-term debt securities. OneState Insurance can invest in short-term securities without incurring interest rate risk by agreeing to a swap in which the insurer pays a floating rate of interest and receives a fixed rate of interest. This combination provides the insurance company with a stream of income that does not fluctuate with changes in short-term market interest rates.

This example also demonstrates the usefulness of an intermediary in a swap. Although Widgets and OneState Insurance could have entered into a swap agreement with each other, in this example (see Chart 2), both Widgets Unlimited and OneState Insurance actually have

a swap agreement with DomBank. Numerous large commercial and investment banks as well as insurance companies have entered into the swap market as intermediaries. DomBank is compensated in an amount equal to the difference between what is received on one swap and what is paid under the other one. In this example, the fee is equal to 10 basis points.

Using DomBank is advantageous to Widgets and OneState Insurance for two reasons. First, the use of an intermediary reduces search time in establishing a swap agreement. DomBank is willing to enter into a swap at any time, whereas Widgets and OneState Insurance might take several days to discover each other, even with a broker's help. Second, an intermediary can reduce the costs of credit evaluation. Either of the participants in an interest rate swap may become bankrupt and unable to fulfill their side of the contract. Thus, each swap participant should understand the credit quality of the other party. In this example, Widgets and OneState are not familiar with each other, and each would need to undertake costly credit analysis on the other before agreeing to deal directly. However, total credit analysis costs are significantly reduced since both parties know the quality of DomBank and DomBank knows their respective credit standings.

Reasons for Interest Rate Swaps

Why do two firms agree to swap interest payments? They could either acquire assets or

Chart 2.
An Interest Rate Swap with a Dealer

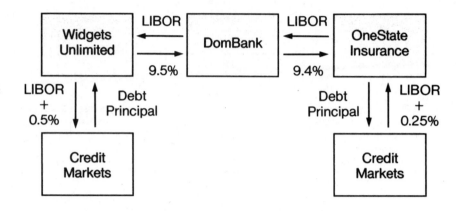

This chart demonstrates three aspects of the swaps market:

(1) *Converting floating-rate debt to fixed-rate debt (Widgets Unlimited)*
(2) *Converting floating-rate assets to fixed-rate assets (OneState Insurance)*
(3) *Using an intermediary (DomBank) to facilitate the swap*

issue liabilities with their desired repricing interval (or maturity) and eliminate the need to undertake a swap. An early explanation for swaps was that they reduce corporations' funding costs by allowing firms to exploit market inefficiencies.[7] Although this explanation remains popular with some market participants, academic analysis has questioned the ability of market inefficiencies to explain the existence and growth of the swap market. Several other explanations for the swap market's popularity that do not rely on market inefficiency have also been provided. The next section of this article presents both original research and a review of recent literature to determine alternative reasons for the surge in use of interest rate swaps.

Quality Spread Differential. The cost savings explanation of swaps claims that swaps allow corporations to arbitrage quality spread differentials. A *quality spread* is the difference between the interest rate paid for funds of a given maturity by a high-quality firm—that is, one with low credit risk—and that required of a lower-quality firm. The quality spread *differential* is the difference in quality spreads at two different maturities. Table 1 provides the calculation of the quality spread differential based on the example provided in Chart 1. Atlanta

HiTech, which has a AAA rating, can obtain short-term financing at six-month LIBOR-plus-0.20 percent or fixed-rate financing at 9.00 percent. Heartland Manufacturing can obtain floating-rate funding at six-month LIBOR-plus-0.70 or fixed-rate funds at 10.20 percent. For floating-rate funding, the quality spread, or difference in rates, between the two firms is 50 basis points, but it widens to 120 basis points for fixed-rate funding. The difference in quality spread, or the quality spread differential, in this example is 70 basis points.

The quality spread differential may be exploitable if Atlanta HiTech desires floating-rate funds and Heartland Manufacturing seeks a fixed rate. Table 2 shows how the quality spread differential is exploited through an interest rate swap. Atlanta HiTech issues fixed-rate debt, and Heartland issues floating-rate debt. Then the two firms enter into an interest rate swap. The net result is that Atlanta HiTech obtains funds at LIBOR minus 18 basis points and Heartland obtains fixed-rate funds at 9.88 percent. Compared with their cost of funds had they not used the interest rate swap strategy, this result represents a 38 basis point savings for Atlanta HiTech and a 32 basis point savings for Heartland. Note that the division of the gain in this

Table 1.
Numerical Example of a Quality Spread Differential

	Atlanta HiTech	Heartland Manufacturing	Quality Spread
Credit rating	AAA	BBB	
Cost of Raising Fixed-Rate Funding	9.00%	10.20%	1.20%
Cost of Raising Floating-Rate Funding	6-month LIBOR plus 0.20%	6-month LIBOR plus 0.70%	0.50%
Quality Spread Differential			0.70%

example is arbitrary and that the two parties could split the gains differently. However, the total gains to the swapping parties will always equal the quality spread differential—70 basis points in this example.

Table 2 clearly demonstrates the ability of swaps to help exploit apparent arbitrage opportunities. However, some observers question whether arbitrage opportunities actually exist. Stuart Turnbull (1987) argues that swaps are zero-sum games in the absence of market imperfections and swap externalities. He also suggests that quality spread differentials may arise for reasons that are not subject to arbitrage. Clifford W. Smith, Charles W. Smithson, and Lee Macdonald Wakeman (1986) note that, even if quality spread differential arbitrage were possible, such activity by itself would not explain swap market growth. In fact, the annual volume of new swaps should be declining as arbitrage becomes more effective.

If the quality spread differential is not entirely the result of market inefficiencies, why does it exist? In a 1987 research paper, the authors of this article point out that quality spread differentials could arise for a number of reasons, including differences in expected bankruptcy costs. Because the expected discounted value of bankruptcy-related losses increases at a faster pace for lower-rated corporations than for higher-rated ones, quality spreads increase with maturity. In this case, the lower initial cost of swap financing is offset by higher costs later.

Alternatively, Jan G. Loeys (1985) suggests that quality spread differentials could arise as

risk is shifted from creditors to shareholders. Creditors have the option of refusing to roll over their debt if the firm appears to be riskier than when the debt was incurred, and short-term creditors have more opportunities to exercise this option. Thus, the creditors of a firm that issues short-term debt bear less risk than the creditors of a firm that issues long-term debt. If the creditors of firms that issue short-term debt bear less risk, the equity holders and long-term creditors necessarily bear more risk.

A third possible explanation for the quality spread differential involves differences in short- and long-term debt contracts. Long-term contracts frequently include a variety of restrictive covenants and may incorporate a call option that is typically not present in short-term debt contracts. The differences in these contract provisions may be reflected in the interest rates charged on various debt contracts. For example, Smith, Smithson, and Wakeman point out that the long-term corporate debt contracts issued by U.S. firms in domestic markets typically have a call provision that is not adjusted for changes in market interest rates. However, long-term debt contracts issued in the Eurobond markets frequently have call provisions that adjust call prices for market rate changes. Thus, quality spread differentials will reflect differences in contract terms if they are calculated using domestic U.S. market rates for lower-quality firms and Eurobond rates for higher-quality firms.

In a forthcoming paper, one of the authors of this article suggests that the quality spread dif-

Table 2.
Numerical Example of a Swap's Ability to Reduce a Firm's Cost of Funding

	Atlanta HiTech	Heartland Manufacturing
Direct Funding Cost		
Fixed-rate funds raised directly by Atlanta HiTech	(9.00%)	
Floating-rate funds raised directly by Heartland		(6-month LIBOR + 0.70%)
Swap Payments		
Atlanta HiTech pays Heartland floating rate	(LIBOR)	LIBOR
Heartland pays Atlanta HiTech fixed rate	9.18%	(9.18%)
All-in cost of funding	LIBOR - 0.18%	9.88%
Comparable cost of equivalent direct funding	LIBOR + 0.20%	10.20%
Savings	38 basis points	32 basis points

ferential may reflect differences in the agency costs associated with short- and long-term debt. Agency costs arise because managers, owners, and creditors have different interests, and managers or owners may take actions that benefit themselves at the expense of the other parties and at the expense of total firm value. In particular, Larry D. Wall notes that the owners of firms that issue long-term, noncallable debt create an incentive to underinvest and to shift investments from low-risk to high-risk projects.[8] A firm may underinvest in new projects because most of the benefit of some projects is received by creditors in the form of a reduced probability that the firm will default. Owners will prefer a high-risk project to a low-risk project because they receive the gains on successful high-risk projects while creditors may suffer most of the losses if the projects fail. Creditors recognize the incentives created by long-term debt and demand a higher risk premium in compensation. The problems created by long-term debt may be reduced or eliminated by short-term debt, that is, debt which matures shortly after the investment decision.[9] An interest rate swap allows lower-quality firms to issue short-term debt while avoiding exposure to changes in market interest rates. Thus, the combination of short-term debt and swaps may be less costly than long-term debt.

In their 1987 paper, the authors also point to another agency cost—that of liquidating insolvent firms—which may be reduced by using short-term debt. Insolvent firms have an incentive to underinvest because, according to David Mayers and Clifford W. Smith (1987), creditors receive almost all of the benefit. Creditors of these firms can reduce the costs associated with underinvestment by taking control of the firm as soon as possible after the firm becomes insolvent. However, creditors may not gain control of a firm until it fails to make a promised debt payment. Short-term debt may hasten creditors' gaining control when a firm has adequate funds to pay interest but lacks the resources to pay interest on its debt and repay the principal.

According to Wall and John J. Pringle, the quality spread differential is not exploitable to the extent that it arises from differences in the expected costs of bankruptcy, shifts in risk from creditors to equityholders, or actual differences in contract terms. However, the quality spread differential can be exploited to the extent that it arises from agency costs. Moreover, arbitrage may eliminate differentials that arise from market inefficiencies, whereas one firm's swap does not reduce the potential agency cost savings to another firm. Thus, agency cost explanations could provide at least a partial explanation for the continuing growth of the swap market.

An important question facing the quality spread differential-based explanations is the extent to which the differential reflects exploitable factors. The authors note that the various explanations of the quality spread differential are not mutually exclusive. For example, if the differential is 70 basis points, then perhaps only 30 basis points may be exploitable.

One empirical study that has some bearing on the quality spread differential is by Robert E. Chatfield and R. Charles Moyer (1986). This study examines the risk premium on 90 long-term puttable bonds issued between July 24, 1974, and August 2, 1984, and a control sample of 174 nonputtable bonds. The put option on long-term, floating-rate debt gives creditors the option to force the firm to repay its debt if the firm becomes riskier.[10] The study finds that the put feature reduces the rate that the market requires on long-term debt by 89 basis points for the bonds in the sample. Chatfield and Moyer provide strong evidence that at least part of the quality spread differential does not arise due to inefficiencies in the markets for short- and long-term debt. However, the observed savings arising from the put feature may be attributable to some of the factors discussed earlier, including bankruptcy costs, risk shifting from creditors to equityholders, and agency costs. Thus, the Chatfield and Moyer results cannot be used to determine the magnitude of agency-cost savings available through interest rate swaps.

Other Explanations. Several explanations for the increased use of the interest rate swap market which do not depend on exploiting the quality spread differential are available. One is that swaps may be used to adjust the repricing interval (or maturity) of a firm's assets or liabilities in order to reduce interest rate risk. For example, a firm may start a period with an acceptable degree of exposure to changes in market interest rates. Subsequently, though, it desires a change in its exposure because of shifts in its product environment or in the volatility of interest rates. Swaps provide a low-cost method of making immediate changes in exposure to market interest rates. For example, suppose that a firm is initially fully hedged with respect to interest rate changes but that a subsequent change in its product markets increases its revenues' sensitivity to interest rates. This

company may be able to offset the increased sensitivity by entering into a swap whereby it agrees to pay a floating rate of interest, which better matches revenues, and receives a fixed rate of interest to cover payments on its outstanding debt.[11]

Smith, Smithson, and Wakeman (1987a) suggest that swaps may allow firms greater flexibility in choosing the amount of their outstanding debt obligations. In particular, reducing debt levels may be a problem if swaps are not used. To reduce its outstanding long-term debt, a firm may need to pay a premium (that is, the call price may exceed the current market value of the debt). On the other hand, if it issues short-term debt without a swap, it may be exposed to adverse changes in market interest rates. However, by issuing a combination of

---

"Swaps provide a low-cost method of making immediate changes in exposure to market interest rates."

---

short-term debt and swaps, the firm avoids the need to pay a premium to retire debt and simultaneously eliminates its exposure to changes in market interest rates.

Marcelle Arak and others (1988) present a general model in which firms will choose the combination of short-term debt and interest rate swaps over short-term debt; long-term, fixed-rate debt; and long-term, variable-rate debt. The model suggests that the combination will be preferred if the firm expects higher risk-free interest rates than does the market, the firm is more risk-averse than the market with respect to changes in risk-free rates, the firm expects its own credit spread to be lower than that expected by the market, and the borrower is less risk-averse to changes in its credit spread than is the market. The researchers also note that not all four conditions need to be met at the same time.

Arak and her colleagues' model is very broad and could include the agency cost models as subsets. An additional implication of their model is that firms may use swaps to exploit information asymmetries. Suppose that a company desires fixed-rate financing to fund a project. It could issue long-term debt, but, if management thought that the company would soon receive a better credit rating, issuing long-term debt would force the firm to pay an excessive risk premium. By issuing short-term debt, the firm could obtain a lower cost of long-term funds in the future when its credit rating improved. However, this strategy would expose the firm to interest rate risk. By instead issuing a combination of short-term debt and interest rate swaps the firm's managers can exploit their information about the true credit risk of the firm

---

"One limitation of the nonarbitrage explanation of swaps is that they provide only one reason for floating-rate payers to enter into swaps, namely, the ability to change the maturity structure of the firm's assets and liabilities."

---

without exposing the organization to changes in market interest rates.[12] When the good news comes, the firm's floating rate payments to outside creditors falls while its payments under the swap remain the same, thus reducing the firm's total financing costs. One important limitation of this explanation is that it applies only to firms that expect improved credit ratings in the near future.

In yet another alternative to the quality spread differential explanation, Loeys points out that swaps may allow firms to exploit differences in regulation. He notes that Securities and Exchange Commission (SEC) registration requirements raise the cost of issuing bonds in the United States by approximately 80 basis points above the cost of issuing bonds in the Eurobond markets. However, not all firms have access to the Eurobond market. Thus, the costs of obtaining fixed-rate funding may be reduced by having companies with access to the Eurobond market issue long-term debt and then enter into a swap with firms that lack access to but prefer fixed-rate funding. Smith, Smithson, and Wakeman, observing that a variety of regulations differ across countries in ways that can be exploited, refer to this explanation as tax and regulatory arbitrage.

A Review of the Explanations. The various explanations of interest rate swaps discussed above are not mutually exclusive, since different firms may use swaps for different reasons. One of the most popular explanations of interest rate swaps—that they allow arbitrage of the quality spread differential—is also the explanation with the weakest theoretical support. The other explanations are all theoretically plausible. Unfortunately, published empirical evidence on the reasons for using swaps is almost nonexistent. Linda T. Rudnick (1987) provides anecdotal evidence that reductions in financing costs are one of the primary reasons that firms enter into interest rate swaps. In research currently in progress, the authors of this article are examining the financial characteristics of firms that reported the use of swaps in the notes to their 1986 financial statements.

One limitation of the nonarbitrage explanations of swaps is that they provide only one reason for floating-rate payers to enter into swaps, namely, the ability to change the maturity structure of the firm's assets and liabilities. Moreover, this single explanation fails to provide a sound reason for a firm to issue long-term, fixed-rate debt and then enter into a swap agreement. If a company does issue long-term debt and then enters into a swap agreement as a floating-rate payer, either fixed-rate payers are sharing part of their gains with the floating-rate payer or floating-rate payers obtain some as yet undiscovered benefit from swaps.

Risks Associated with Swaps

Interest rate swap contracts are subject to several types of risk. Among the more important are interest rate, or position, risk and credit risk. Interest rate risk arises because changes in market interest rates cause a change in a swap's value. Credit risk occurs because either party may default on a swap contract. Both participants in a swap are subject to each type of risk.

Interest Rate Risk. As market interest rates change, interest rate swaps generate gains or losses that are equal to the change in the replacement cost of the swap. These gains and losses allow swaps to serve as a hedge which a company can use to reduce its risk or to serve as a speculative tool that increases the firm's total risk. A swap represents a hedge if gains or losses generated by the swap offset changes in the market values of a company's assets, liabilities, and off-balance sheet activities such as interest rate futures and options. However, a swap is speculative to the extent that the firm deliberately increases its risk position to profit from predicted changes in interest rates.

The determination of whether and how to use a swap is straightforward for a firm that is a user, one which enters into a swap agreement solely to adjust its own financial position.[13] First, the company evaluates its own exposure to future changes in interest rates, including any planned investments and new financings. Then, its views on the future levels and volatility of interest rates are ascertained. Firms wishing greater exposure to market rate changes enter into swaps as speculators. Alternatively, if less exposure is desired, the company enters into a swap as a hedge.

The problem facing a dealer—a firm that enters into a swap to earn fee income—is more complicated. A dealer may enter into a swap to hedge changes in market rates or to speculate in a manner similar to users. However, a dealer may also enter a swap to satisfy a customer's request even when the dealer wants no change in its interest rate exposure.[14] In this case, the dealer must find some way of hedging the swap transaction.

The simplest hedge for one swap transaction by a dealer is another swap transaction whose terms mirror the first swap. An example of this arrangement is given in Chart 2, in which the dealer's promised floating-rate payments of LIBOR to Widgets Unlimited is exactly offset by OneState's promise to pay LIBOR. Similarly, the fixed payments to OneState Insurance are covered by Widgets' promised fixed payments, and DomBank is left with a small spread. This combination of swaps is referred to as a *matched pair*. One problem with relying on matched

pairs to eliminate interest rate risk is that the dealer is exposed to interest rate changes during the time needed to find another party interested in a matching swap. Another problem is that the dealer may be relatively better at arranging swaps with fixed-rate payers and, thus, have problems finding floating-rate payers to execute the matching swap (or vice versa).

An alternative to hedging one swap with another swap is to rely on debt securities, or on futures or options on debt securities, to provide a hedge. Steven T. Felgran (1987) gives an example whereby a dealer agrees to pay a fixed rate and receive a floating rate from a customer. The dealer uses the floating-rate receipts to support a bank loan, which is then used to purchase a Treasury security of the same maturity and value as the swap. Any gains or losses on the swap are

---

"One problem with relying on matched pairs to eliminate interest rate risk is that the dealer is exposed to interest rate changes during the time needed to find another party interested in a matching swap."

---

subsequently offset by losses or gains on the Treasury security. Felgran does note one problem with using Treasury securities to hedge a swap: the spread between them and interest rate swaps may vary over time.[15] According to Felgran, dealers are unable to hedge floating-rate payments perfectly. Sources of risk include differences in payment dates and floating-rate reset days, disparities in maturity and principal, and "basis risk," that is, the risk associated with hedging floating payments based on one index with floating payments from another index.

Using the futures market to hedge swaps also entails certain drawbacks. Wakeman points to the "additional risk created by the cash/futures basis volatility." He also notes that matching the fixed-rate payments from a swap with the Treasury security of the closest maturity may not be optimal when the Treasury security is thinly traded. As an alternative he suggests that "on-the-run" (highly liquid) Treasury issues be used for hedging. The investment amount and type of issues to be used may be determined applying a duration matching strategy. Still, this approach is unlikely to eliminate interest rate risk for the swap dealer since duration matching provides a perfect hedge only under very restrictive assumptions.

Credit Risk. Aside from interest rate and basis risk, both interest rate swap participants are subject to the risk that the other party will default, causing credit losses. The maximum amount of the loss associated with this credit risk is measured by the swap's replacement cost, which is essentially the cost of entering into a new swap under current market conditions with rates equal to those on the swap being replaced.

"Aside from interest rate and basis risk, both interest rate swap participants are subject to the risk that the other party will default, causing credit losses."

A simple example can demonstrate the credit risk of swaps. Suppose that Widgets Unlimited agrees to pay a fixed rate of 9.5 percent to DomBank, and in return Widgets will receive LIBOR on a semiannual basis through January 1994. If the market rate on new swaps maturing in January 1994 falls to 8 percent, the swap has positive value to DomBank—that is, DomBank would have to pay an up-front fee to entice a third party to enter into a swap whereby DomBank receives a fixed rate of 9.5 percent. DomBank will suffer a credit loss if Widgets becomes bankrupt while the rate is 8 percent and pays only a fraction of its obligations to creditors. On the other hand, if the rate on swaps maturing in January 1994 rises to 10.5 percent and DomBank defaults, Widgets may suffer a credit loss.

This example demonstrates that both of the parties to an interest rate swap may be subject to credit risk at some time during the life of a swap contract. However, only one party at a time may be subject to credit risk. If rates in the above example fall to 8 percent, DomBank can suffer credit losses, but Widgets is not exposed to credit risk. That is, the swap has negative value to Widgets when the market rate is 8 percent; Widgets would be happy to drop the swap agreement if DomBank were to go bankrupt. In practice, though, Widgets is unlikely to receive a windfall from DomBank's failure. The swap contracts may provide for Widgets to continue making payments to DomBank or, if the contract is canceled, provide for Widgets to pay DomBank the replacement cost of the swap.[16]

One way of reducing the credit risk associated with swaps is for the party to whom the swap has negative value to post collateral equal to the swap's replacement cost. Some swaps provide for collateral but most do not. According to Felgran, swap collateralization is of uncertain value because such documentation has yet to be adequately tested in court. Moreover, some parties that would be happy to receive collateral are themselves reluctant to post it when swap rates move against them. Certain commercial banks in particular have a strong incentive to avoid collateralization. Such institutions take credit risks in the ordinary course of business and are comfortable with assuming credit risk on interest rate swaps. Investment bankers, on the other hand, are typically at risk for only short periods of time with their nonswap transactions and are not as experienced in evaluating credit risk. Thus, the continued presence of credit risk in the swap market strengthens the relative competitive position of commercial banks.

Several simulation studies have explored the magnitude of the credit risk associated with individual swaps or matched pairs of swaps. Arak, Laurie S. Goodman, and Arthur Rones (1986) examine the credit exposure—or maximum credit loss—of a single interest rate swap to determine the amount of a firm's credit line that is used by a swap.[17] They assume that short-term rates follow a random walk with no drift; in other words, the change in short-term rates does not depend on the current level of or on past changes in short-term rates. After the swap begins, the floating-rate component of the swap is assumed to move one standard deviation each year in the direction of maximum credit exposure. The standard deviation of interest rates is calculated using 1985 data on Treasury issues. Their results suggest that until the swap matures, maximum annual credit loss on swaps is likely to be between 1 and 2 percent of notional principal.

J. Gregg Whittaker (1987b) investigates the credit exposure of interest rate swaps in order to develop a formula for swap pricing. Using an options pricing formula to value swaps and assuming that interest rates follow a log-normal distribution and volatility amounts to one standard deviation, Whittaker finds that the maximum exposure for a 10-year matched pair of swaps does not exceed 8 percent of the notional principal.

The Federal Reserve Board and the Bank of England studied the potential increase in credit exposure of a matched pair of swaps.[18] The study's purpose is to develop a measure of the credit exposure associated with a matched pair of swaps that is comparable to the credit exposure of on-balance sheet loans. The results are used to determine regulatory capital requirements for interest rate swaps. The joint central bank research assumes that for regulatory purposes the swaps' credit exposure should be equal to its current exposure, that is, the replacement cost plus some surcharge to capture potential increases in credit exposure. The investigation uses a Monte Carlo simulation technique to evaluate the probabilities associated with different potential increases in credit exposure.[19] Interest rates are assumed to follow a log-normal, random-walk distribution with the volatility measure equal to the 90th percentile value of changes in interest rates over six-month intervals from 1981 to mid-1986. The credit exposure of each matched pair is calculated every six months and the resulting exposures are averaged over the life of the swap. The study concludes with 70 percent confidence that the average potential increase in credit exposure will be no greater than 0.5 percent of the notional principal of the swap per complete year; at the 95 percent confidence level it finds the average credit risk exposure to be no greater than 1 percent of the notional principal.

Terrence M. Belton (1987) follows this line of research in analyzing the potential increase in swap credit exposure, but he uses a different method of simulating interest rates. Belton estimates a vector autoregressive model over the period from January 1970 to November 1986 to estimate seven different Treasury rates. (Vector autoregressive models estimate current values of some dependent variables, in this case interest rates at various maturities, as a function of current and past values of selected variables. Belton uses current and past interest rates as explanatory variables.) Changes in the term structure are then simulated by drawing a set of random errors from the joint distribution of rates and solving for future values at each maturity. In effect, Belton's procedure allows the historical shape in the yield curve and historical changes in its level and shape to determine the value of various interest rates in his simulations. Belton's analysis differs from prior studies in that he uses stochastic, or random,

---

"[S]everal ways of estimating the increased credit exposure associated with matched pairs of swaps . . . might not be applicable to swap portfolios."

---

default rates rather than focusing exclusively on maximum credit exposure. His results imply that the potential increase in credit exposure of swaps caused by rate changes can be covered by adding a surcharge of 1 percent to 5 percent of the notional principal to the current exposure for swaps with a maturity of 2 to 12 years.

While the foregoing analyses suggest several ways of estimating the increased credit exposure associated with matched pairs of swaps, these approaches might not be applicable to swap portfolios. Starting with the assumption that dealers use matched pairs of swaps and that the swaps are entered into at market interest rates, Wall and Kwun-Wing C. Fung (1987) note that the fixed rate on the matched pairs will change over time as interest rates move up and down. Wall and Fung point out that if rates have fluctuated over a certain range, a bank may have credit exposure on some swaps in which it pays a fixed rate and on others in which it pays a floating rate. In this case, an increase in rates generates an increase in the credit exposure of swaps in which the dealer pays a fixed rate but also causes a decrease in the exposure of swaps in which the dealer pays a floating rate. Similarly, a decrease in rates will increase the exposure on the swaps in which the dealer pays a floating rate and decrease exposure on those in which the dealer pays a fixed rate.[20]

In a more empirical vein, Kathleen Neal and Katerina Simons (1988) simulate the total credit exposure of a portfolio of 20 matched pairs of interest rate swaps. The initial portfolio is generated by originating one pair of five-year swaps per quarter from the fourth quarter of 1981 through the fourth quarter of 1986 at the prevailing interest rate. For the period 1987

"[T]he maximum exposure on a matched pair of swaps is unlikely to exceed a small fraction of the swap's notional principal."

---

through 1991, the interest rates are generated randomly based on the volatility observed in historical rates.[21] The maturing matched pair is dropped each quarter from the sample and a new five-year swap is added to the portfolio at the simulated interest rates. After running "several thousand" simulations and assuming a portfolio of interest rate swaps with a notional principal of $10 million, Neal and Simons find the average maximum credit loss to be $185,000 and the 90th percentile exposure, $289,000.

No single correct approach is available to determine the expected credit exposure on an interest rate swap. The results may be influenced by the assumptions that are made about the distribution of future interest rates. However, several studies using different methodologies have reached the conclusion that the maximum exposure on a matched pair of swaps is unlikely to exceed a small fraction of the

swap's notional principal. Moreover, the analysis of a single matched pair may overstate the expected exposure of a swap portfolio. Therefore, additional simulations of portfolio analysis risk may be appropriate to determine the risk exposure of swap dealers. Dominique Jackson (1988) reports that a survey of 71 dealers showed that 11 firms had experienced losses with "total write-offs accounting for $33 million on portfolios which totaled a notional (principal) of $283 billion."

How Should Swaps Be Priced?

In addition to considering the reasons for engaging in swaps and the attendant risks, the literature on interest rate swaps addresses two important pricing questions: (1) how should the overall value of a swap be established, and (2) what spread between higher-rated and lower-rated firms is appropriate to cover swap credit risk? James Bicksler and Andrew H. Chen (1986) provide an analysis of a swap's overall value. They suggest that an interest rate swap be treated as an exchange of a fixed-rate bond for a floating-rate bond. According to this approach, the fixed-rate payer has in effect sold a fixed-rate bond and purchased a floating-rate bond. Bicksler and Chen suggest that pricing an interest rate swap is essentially the same as pricing a floating-rate bond.

Insight into the appropriate spreads between high- and lower-rated firms can be obtained by comparing the quality spreads on bonds versus those on swaps. Patrick de Saint-Aignan, the chairman of the International Swap Dealers Association and a managing director at Morgan Stanley, remarks that, "There's a credit spread of 150 basis points in the loan market but of only 5 to 10 basis points in swaps."[22] However, Smith, Smithson, and Wakeman (1987a) note that the risk exposure, as a proportion of notional principal for swaps, is far less than the exposure on loans. Lenders have credit exposure for all principal and interest payments promised on the loan, whereas a swap participant's credit exposure is limited to the difference between two interest rates. Thus, the credit risk borne by swap dealers is a far smaller proportion of the (notional) principal than that assumed by lenders.

Belton also addresses the question of appropriate spreads to compensate for swaps' credit risk by considering the default premium required to compensate one party for the expected value of the default losses from the other. For low-risk firms—companies with a 0.5 percent probability of default in one year and zero payment on default—the required premium is 0.70 basis points for a two-year swap and 3.02 basis points for a ten-year swap. For below-investment-grade firms—with a 2 percent probability of default per year and zero payment on default—the required premium ranges from 2.83 basis points for a two-year swap to 14.24 basis points for a ten-year swap. The differences in default premium of 2 to 14 basis points found by Belton for swaps is approximately in the 5 to 10 basis point range of the credit spread charged in swaps markets.

Whittaker (1987b) applies his options pricing method for calculating swaps' credit risk to the issue of swap pricing. He views a swap as a set of options to buy and sell a fixed-rate bond and a floating-rate bond. In his model default by the fixed-rate payer is analogous to a decision to exercise jointly a call option to purchase the fixed-rate bond and a put option to sell a floating-rate security. From this perspective, the decision to exercise one option is not independent of the decision to exercise another. Thus, one option may be exercised even though it is unprofitable to do so, provided that it is sufficiently profitable to exercise the other option. He then estimates the value of these options and suggests that "the market does not adequately take account of the exposure and pricing differentials across varying maturities." However, Whittaker claims that his results may not necessarily imply that the market is on average underpricing swap credit risk.

One limitation of the above studies is that they fail to combine into an integrated framework the distribution of interest rates and the credit risk associated with swaps. A conceptually superior approach to interest rate swap valuation begins by separating the payments. The result looks like a series of forward contracts in which the floating-rate payer agrees to buy a zero-coupon Treasury security from the fixed-rate payer. This forward contract may then be decomposed into two options, one in which the floating-rate payer buys a call from the fixed-

rate payer on the zero-coupon Treasury security and one in which the floating-rate payer sells a put on the security to the fixed-rate payer.

Unfortunately, the options derived from this analysis cannot be valued using standard options pricing formulas because both options are subject to credit risk. Herb Johnson and René Stulz (1987) analyze the problem of pricing a single option subject to default risk. However, swaps are a series of linked options whose payments in one period are contingent on the terms of the swap contract being fulfilled in prior periods. Thus, as Smith, Smithson, and Wakeman (1987b) suggest, to derive an optimal default strategy for swaps requires analysis of compound option issues similar to those discussed by Robert Geske (1977) for corporate coupon bonds.

"[T]he interest rate swap market is subject to remarkably little regulation and does not have a central exchange or even a central clearing mechanism."

The theoretical and pedagogical advantages of splitting a swap into a series of default-risky options are that the decomposition clearly illustrates the primary determinants of swap value: the distribution of the price of default-risk free bonds (interest rates), the possibility of default by either participant, and the linked nature of the options through time. The practical problem with the decomposition is that developing a pricing formula is not straightforward.

Requirements Imposed on Swaps

Regulation. In contrast to most other financial markets in the United States, the interest rate swap market is subject to remarkably little regulation and does not have a central exchange or even a central clearing mechanism. The terms of a swap agreement are determined by the parties to the contract and need not be disclosed. Nor does the existence of a swap need to be disclosed at the time the agreement is executed. (The financial statements' disclosure requirements for individual firms are discussed later in this article.) While certain regulators have a general responsibility for the financial soundness of some participants in the swap market, no public or private organization has overall responsibility for its regulation.

In general, this lack of regulation has not resulted in any major problems. Legislatures could make one potentially valuable contribution, though, by providing specific statutory language on the treatment of swap contracts when one party defaults. Market participants are currently waiting for the courts to determine

---

"Like regulatory requirements, accounting standards for swaps are minimal at best, owing largely to their rapid development."

---

if default procedures will follow the language of the swap contract or if the courts will impose some other settlement procedure. For example, many swaps are arranged under a master contract between two parties that provides for the netting of payments across swaps. This clause is desirable because it reduces the credit risk borne by both parties. However, the risk exists that a bankruptcy court will ignore this clause and treat each swap separately.

Even though the swap market is not subject to regulation, individual participants are. In particular, federal banking regulators in the United States are including interest rate swaps in the recently adopted risk-based capital standards. These standards are designed to preserve and enhance the safety and soundness of commercial banks by requiring them to maintain capital commensurate with the levels of credit risk they incur.[23]

Banks' capital standards first translate credit exposure on swaps into an amount comparable to on-balance sheet loans. The loan equivalent amount for swaps is equal to the replacement cost of the swap plus 0.5 percent of the notional principal. This loan equivalent amount is then multiplied by 50 percent to determine a risk-adjusted asset equivalent. Banks are required to maintain tier-one (or core) capital equal to 4 percent of risk-adjusted assets and total capital equal to 8 percent by 1992.[24]

The central banks of 12 major industrial powers have agreed to apply similar risk-based capital requirements to their countries' financial firms.[25] However, these standards do not apply to U.S. investment banks or insurance companies. Thus, capital requirements are not being applied to all swap dealers. Some market participants are concerned that the standards will place dealers that are subject to capital regulation at a competitive disadvantage.[26]

Accounting. Like regulatory requirements, accounting standards for swaps are minimal at best, owing largely to their rapid development. Existing accounting standards provide a general requirement that a firm disclose all material matters but do not require a company to disclose its participation in the interest rate swap market. Different firms appear to be following many of the same rules in accounting for the gains and losses under swap contracts, but some important discrepancies exist in practice.

Keith Wishon and Lorin S. Chevalier (1985) note that swap market participants generally do not recognize the existence of swaps on their balance sheets, a practice which is consistent with the treatment of futures agreements. However, they aver that the notes to the firm's financial statements should disclose the existence of material swap agreements and discuss the swap's impact on the repricing interval of the firm's debt obligations. Harold Bierman, Jr. (1987) recommends that firms also disclose the transaction's effects on their risk position.

Another issue at the inception of some swap contracts is accounting for up-front payments. Wishon and Chevalier believe that any up-front payments that reflect yield adjustments should be deferred and amortized over the life of the swap. While acknowledging that payers appear to be following this policy, the researchers note that some recipients have taken the position that all up-front fees are arrangement fees and may be immediately recognized in income. Bierman argues that yield-adjusting fees cannot be distinguished from others. Thus, all fees should be treated in the same manner. He further maintains that the most appropriate treatment is to defer recognition and amortize the payments over the life of the contract.

According to Wishon and Chevalier, regular payments and receipts under a swap agreement are frequently recorded as an adjustment to interest income when the swap is related to a particular debt issue. Though the receipts and payments are technically not interest, this approach is informative, especially if footnote disclosure is adequate. They report, nonetheless, that changes in the market value of the swap are generally not recognized in the income statement if gains and losses are not recognized on the security hedged by the swap. This treatment parallels that of futures, which meets the hedge criteria in the Financial Accounting Standards Board's Statement Number 80, "Accounting for Futures Contracts."

Another issue arising during the life of an interest rate swap is the presentation of the credit risk. For a nondealer, credit risk may not be material and, therefore, need not be reported. However, Wishon and Chevalier argue that the credit risk taken by a dealer is likely to be material and should be disclosed.

Some firms may enter into swaps as a speculative investment. Wishon and Chevalier contend that speculative swaps should be accounted for in the same manner as other speculative investments. Among the alternatives they discuss are using either the lower of cost or market method of valuation, with writedowns only for losses that are not "temporary," and the lower of cost or market in all cases. Both approaches are flawed. The treatment of some swap losses as "temporary" is inappropriate because objective and verifiable predictions of changes in interest rates are impossible.[27] Yet using the lower-of-cost-or-market method of valuation in all cases will always result in a swap's being valued at its historical low, an excessively conservative position. Probably the best approach is to report the swap's replacement cost and to recognize any gains or losses in the current period.

Bierman suggests that, when a speculative swap is terminated prior to maturity, the gain or loss should be recognized immediately. However, no consensus exists on the treatment if the swap is a hedge. Wishon and Chevalier report widespread disagreement on the appropriate treatment of a swap's termination. One common approach would defer and amortize any gains or losses on the swap over the life of the underlying financial instrument. The other calls for immediate recognition of any gains or losses. The treatment of gains or losses on futures hedges suggests that the deferral and amortization of early swaps termination is appropriate.

Eugene E. Comiskey, Charles W. Mulford, and Deborah H. Turner (1987-88), surveying the financial statements of the 100 largest domestic banks in 1986, discovered that some banks are deferring gains or losses in accordance with hedge accounting treatment even though hedge accounting would not be permitted in similar circumstances for futures.[28] They also found that five banks disclosed their maximum potential credit loss in the extremely unlikely event that every counterparty defaulted on all swaps that were favorable to the bank.

The Financial Accounting Standards Board issued an Exposure Draft of a proposed Statement of Financial Accounting Standards titled "Disclosures about Financial Instruments." The statement proposes disclosing a variety of new information about financial instruments, including the maximum credit risk; the reasonably possible credit loss; probable credit loss; the amount subject to repricing within one year, one to five years, and over five years; and the market value of each class of financial instrument. This statement specifically includes interest rate swaps in its definition of financial instruments. If, when, and in what form this proposal will be adopted is unclear.

Commercial banks in the United States are currently required to disclose the notional principal on their outstanding interest rate swap portfolio to the federal bank regulators.[29] It would seem that regulators should also consider requiring disclosure of the replacement cost of outstanding swaps given that replacement cost is an element of the risk-based capital standards.

Conclusion

This article surveys the literature and some research in progress on interest rate swaps. The extremely rapid growth of the market has left academics trying to explain the existence of the market and the pricing of these instruments, regulators attempting to determine what risks these instruments pose to financial firms, and accountants endeavoring to determine how institutions should report their use of swaps. Evidence is beginning to accumulate to dispel some of the early misconceptions about this market, but far more analysis remains before interest rate swaps can be fully understood.

Notes

[1] See Abken (1988) for a review of the studies of the stock market crash.

[2] The size of the interest rate swap market is typically stated in terms of the notional principal of the outstanding swaps. See the explanation of interest rate swap transactions for a discussion of the role of the notional principal. Refer to Jackson (1988) for a discussion of the size of the interest rate and currency swap markets.

[3] See Celarier (1987): 17. This estimating appears to encompass the effect of both interest rate swaps and a related instrument called a currency swap. A *currency swap* is an arrangement between two organizations to exchange principal and interest payments in two different currencies at prearranged exchange rates. For example, one corporation agrees to pay a fixed amount of dollars in return for receiving a fixed number of Japanese yen from another corporation. This article focuses on interest rate swaps, and hereafter the term *swaps* will be used as a synonym for interest rate swaps. Beckstrom (1986) offers a discussion of different types of swaps.

[4] Both fixed-rate interest payment to floating-rate payment swaps and floating-rate to floating-rate swaps whereby, for example, one party pays the London Interbank Offered Rate (LIBOR) while the other party pays the commercial paper rate, are observed in the market.

[5] LIBOR is the most common floating rate in interest rate swap agreements, according to Hammond (1987).

[6] However, the call option is not a free gift provided by the bond market to corporations. Corporations pay for this call option by paying a higher rate of interest on their bonds.

[7] See Bicksler and Chen (1986) as well as Whittaker (1987a) and Hammond (1987) for further discussion.

[8] See Myers (1977); Bodie and Taggart (1978); and Barnea, Haugen, and Senbet (1980).

[9] Long-term, callable debt may also reduce the agency problems of underinvestment and risk shifting problems. However, Barnea, Haugen, and Senbet point out that callable debt does not eliminate the underinvestment problem. Wall (forthcoming) suggests that callable bonds may not solve the risk shifting problem in all cases and also notes that short-term debt will solve both problems if it matures shortly after the firm makes its investment decision.

[10] Investors may also have an incentive to exercise the put option on fixed-rate bonds when interest rates increase. An easy way to control for this feature is to focus exclusively on floating-rate bonds. However, Chatfield and Moyers' study contained fixed-rate, puttable bonds. Their research controlled for the interest rate feature of the put option on these bonds by including a variable for the number of times per year the coupon rate on a bond adjusts and a measure of interest rate uncertainty.

[11] Bennett, Cohen, and McNulty (1984) discuss the use of swaps for controlling interest rate exposure by savings institutions.

[12] Robbins and Schatzberg (1986) suggest that callable bonds are superior to short-term debt in that they permit firms to signal their lower risk and to reduce the risk borne by equityholders. However, their results depend on a specific example. Wall (1988) demonstrates that the call-

able bonds may fail to provide a separating equilibrium if seemingly small changes are made to their example.

[13] This analysis does not consider the use of the futures, forward, and options markets. See Smithson (1987) for a discussion of the various financial instruments that may be used to control interest rate risk.

[14] The dealer may enter into a swap for a customer even though the dealer desires a change in exposure in a direction opposite to the swap.

[15] Indeed, some variation in the spread should be expected since the Treasury yield curve incorporates coupon interest payments and principal repayments at the maturity of the swap whereas the swap contract provides only for periodic interest payments.

[16] Widgets would probably prefer to cancel the contract and enter into a new swap contract with a different party. Otherwise, market rates could increase above 9.5 percent and then DomBank might be unable to make the promised payments. See Henderson and Cates (1986) for a discussion of terminating a swap under the insolvency laws of the United States and the United Kingdom.

[17] One way that banks typically limit their risk to individual borrowers is to establish a maximum amount that the organization is willing to lend to the borrower, called the borrower's credit line. The amount of a credit line used by a loan is the principal of the loan; however, the amount of the line used by a swap is less clear since a swap's maximum credit loss is a function of market interest rates.

[18] See also Muffet (1987).

[19] The Monte Carlo technique involves repeated simulations wherein a key value, in this case an interest rate, is drawn from a random sample.

[20] Consider two matched pairs of swaps. For the first matched pair the bank agrees to two swaps: 1) the bank pays a fixed rate of 11 percent and receives LIBOR on the first swap, and 2) the bank pays LIBOR and receives 11 percent. For the second matched pair the bank pays and receives a 9 percent fixed rate for LIBOR. Assume that the notional principal, maturity, and repricing interval of all swaps are equal. If the current market rate for swaps of the same maturity is 10 percent, the bank has credit exposure on the 9 percent fixed-rate swap in which it pays a fixed rate of interest and has credit exposure on the 11 percent fixed-rate swap in which it pays a floating rate of interest. If the market rate on comparable swaps increases to 10.5 percent, credit exposure increases on the 9 percent swap in which the dealer pays a fixed rate and decreases on the 11 percent swap in which the dealer pays a floating rate. Given the assumptions of this example, the change in exposure is almost zero when the market rate moves from 10 percent to 10.5 percent.

[21] The paper does not explain how swap replacement values and interest rate volatility were calculated.

[22] David Shirreff (1985): 253.

[23] The standards do not include any framework for evaluating the overall interest rate risk being taken by banking organizations.

[24] The standards effective in 1992 define core (tier-one) capital as common stockholders equity, minority interest in the common stockholders' equity accounts of con-

solidated subsidiaries, and perpetual, noncumulative preferred stock. (The Federal Reserve will also allow bank holding companies to count perpetual, cumulative preferred stock.) Total capital consists of core capital plus supplementary (tier-two) capital. Supplementary capital includes the allowance for loan and lease losses; perpetual, cumulative preferred stock; long-term preferred stock, hybrid capital instruments including perpetual debt, and mandatory convertible securities; and subordinated debt and intermediate-term preferred stock.

[25]The framework for risk-based capital standards has been approved by the Group of Ten countries (Belgium, Canada, France, the Federal Republic of Germany, Italy, Japan, the Netherlands, Sweden, the United Kingdom, and the United States) together with Switzerland and Luxembourg.

[26]Pitman (1988) discusses the capital standards' implications for various swap market participants.

[27]If the predicted changes in interest rates were subject to objective verification, that would suggest that arbitrage opportunities exist. That is, investors may be able to earn a profit with no net investment (financing the purchase of one debt security with the sale of another) and without assuming any risk (since objective verification proved that interest rates will move in the predicted direction). However, efficient markets theory implies that the market will immediately compete away any arbitrage opportunities.

[28]Deferral of gains or losses on futures is permitted only if the future is designated as a hedge for an "existing asset, liability, firm commitment or anticipated transactions," according to Comiskey, Mulford, and Turner, 4, 9.

[29]See Felgran (1987) for a listing of the top 25 U.S. banks by notional principal of swaps outstanding.

References

Abken, Peter A. "Stock Market Activity in October 1987: The Brady, CFTC, and SEC Reports." Federal Reserve Bank of Atlanta Economic Review 73 (May/June 1988): 36-43.

Arak, Marcelle, Arturo Estrella, Laurie Goodman, and Andrew Silver. "Interest Rate Swaps: An Alternative Explanation." Financial Management 17 (Summer 1988): 12-18.

Arak, Marcelle, Laurie S. Goodman, and Arthur Rones. "Credit Lines for New Instruments: Swaps, Over-the-Counter Options, Forwards and Floor-Ceiling Agreements." Federal Reserve Bank of Chicago, Conference on Bank Structure and Competition, 1986, 437-56.

Barnea, Amir, Robert A. Haugen, and Lemma W. Senbet. "A Rationale for Debt Maturity Structure and Call Provisions in the Agency Theoretic Framework." Journal of Finance 35 (December 1980): 1223-34.

Beckstrom, Rod. "The Development of the Swap Market." In Swap Finance, vol. 1, edited by Boris Antl, 31-51. London: Euromoney Publications Limited, 1986.

Belton, Terrence M. "Credit-Risk in Interest Rate Swaps." Board of Governors of the Federal Reserve System unpublished working paper, April 1987.

Bennett, Dennis E., Deborah L. Cohen, and James E. McNulty. "Interest Rate Swaps and the Management of Interest Rate Risk." Paper presented at the Financial Management Association meetings, Toronto, October 1984.

Bicksler, James, and Andrew H. Chen. "An Economic Analysis of Interest Rate Swaps." Journal of Finance 41 (July 1986): 645-55.

Bierman, Harold, Jr. "Accounting for Interest Rate Swaps." Journal of Accounting, Auditing, and Finance 2 (Fall 1987): 396-408.

Black, Fischer, and Myron Scholes. "The Pricing of Options and Corporate Liabilities." Journal of Political Economy 81 (1973): 637-59.

Bodie, Zvi, and Robert A. Taggart. "Future Investment Opportunities and the Value of the Call Provision on a Bond." Journal of Finance 33 (September 1978): 1187-1200.

Celarier, Michelle. "Swaps' Judgement Day." United States Banker (July 1987): 16-20.

Chatfield, Robert E., and R. Charles Moyer. "'Putting' Away Bond Risk: An Empirical Examination of the Value of the Put Option on Bonds." Financial Management 15 (Summer 1986): 26-33.

Comiskey, Eugene E., Charles W. Mulford, and Deborah H. Turner. "Bank Accounting and Reporting Practices for Interest Rate Swaps." Bank Accounting and Finance 1 (Winter 1987-88): 3-14.

Federal Reserve Board and Bank of England. "Potential Exposure on Interest Rate and Exchange Rate Related Instruments." Unpublished staff paper, 1987.

Felgran, Steven D. "Interest Rate Swaps: Use, Risk and Prices." New England Economic Review (November/December 1987): 22-32.

Geske, Robert. "The Valuation of Corporate Liabilities as Compound Options." Journal of Financial and Quantitative Analysis 12 (1977): 541-52.

Hammond, G.M.S. "Recent Developments in the Swap Market." Bank of England Quarterly Review 27 (February 1987): 66-79.

Henderson, Schuyler K., and Armel C. Cates. "Termination Provisions of Swap Agreements under U.S. and English Insolvency Laws." In Swap Finance, vol. 2, edited by Boris Antl, 91-102. London: Euromoney Publications Limited, 1986.

Jackson, Dominique. "Swaps Keep in Step with the Regulators." Financial Times, August 10, 1988, 22.

Johnson, Herb, and René Stulz. "The Pricing of Options with Default Risk." Journal of Finance 42 (June 1987): 267-80.

Loeys, Jan G. "Interest Rate Swaps: A New Tool For Managing Risk." Federal Reserve Bank of Philadelphia Business Review (May/June 1985): 17-25.

Mayers, David, and Clifford W. Smith. "Corporate Insurance

and the Underinvestment Problem." *Journal of Risk and Insurance* 54 (March 1987): 45-54.

Muffet, Mark. "Modeling Credit Exposure on Swaps." Federal Reserve Bank of Chicago, *Conference on Bank Structure and Competition,* 1987, 473-96.

Myers, Stewart C. "Determinants of Corporate Borrowing." *Journal of Financial Economics* 5 (November 1977): 147-76.

Neal, Kathleen, and Katerina Simons. "Interest Rate Swaps, Currency Swaps, and Credit Risk." *Issues in Bank Regulation* (Spring 1988): 26-29.

Pitman, Joanna. "Swooping on Swaps." *Euromoney* (January 1988): 68-80.

Robbins, Edward Henry, and John D. Schatzberg. "Callable Bonds: A Risk Reducing, Signalling Mechanism." *Journal of Finance* 41 (September 1986): 935-49.

Rudnick, Linda T. "Discussion of Practical Aspects of Interest Rate Swaps." Federal Reserve Bank of Chicago, *Conference on Bank Structure and Competition,* 1987, 206-13.

Shirreff, David. "The Fearsome Growth of Swaps." *Euromoney* (October 1985): 247-61.

Smith, Clifford W., Charles W. Smithson, and Lee Macdonald Wakeman. "The Evolving Market for Swaps." *Midland Corporate Finance Journal* 3 (1986): 20-32.

_____ , _____ , and _____ . "The Market for Interest Rate Swaps." University of Rochester Working Paper Series No. MERC 87-02 (May 1987a).

_____ , _____ , and _____ . "Credit Risk and the Scope of Regulation of Swaps." Federal Reserve Bank of Chicago, *Conference on Bank Structure and Competition,* 1987b, 166-85.

Smithson, Charles W. "A LEGO® Approach to Financial Engineering: An Introduction to Forwards, Futures, Swaps, and Options." *Midland Corporate Finance Review* 4 (Winter 1987): 16-28.

Stulz, René M., and Herb Johnson. "An Analysis of Secured Debt." *Journal of Financial Economics* 14 (December 1985): 501-21.

Turnbull, Stuart M. "Swaps: A Zero Sum Game?" *Financial Management* 16 (Spring 1987): 15-21.

Wakeman, Lee Macdonald. "The Portfolio Approach To Swaps Management." Chemical Bank Capital Markets Group unpublished working paper, May 1986.

Wall, Larry D. "Interest Rate Swaps in an Agency Theoretic Model with Uncertain Interest Rates." *Journal of Banking and Finance* (forthcoming).

_____ . "Alternative Financing Strategies: Notes Versus Callable Bonds." *Journal of Finance* 43 (September 1988): 1057-65.

_____ , and Kwun-Wing C. Fung. "Evaluating the Credit Exposure of Interest Rate Swap Portfolios." Federal Reserve Bank of Atlanta Working Paper 87-8 (December 1987).

_____ , and John J. Pringle. "Alternative Explanations of Interest Rate Swaps." Federal Reserve Bank of Chicago, *Conference on Bank Structure and Competition,* 1987, 186-205.

Weiner, Lisabeth. "Dollar Dominates Swaps, Survey Shows: Deals in U.S. Currency Outstrip Yen, Deutsche Mark by Far." *American Banker,* February 26, 1988, 2.

Whittaker, J. Gregg. "Interest Rate Swaps: Risk and Regulation." Federal Reserve Bank of Kansas City *Economic Review* (March 1987a): 3-13.

_____ . "Pricing Interest Rate Swaps in an Options Pricing Framework." Federal Reserve Bank of Kansas City unpublished working paper RWP 87-02. Presented to the Financial Management Association Meetings, Las Vegas, October 1987b.

Wishon, Keith, and Lorin S. Chevalier. "Interest Rate Swaps—Your Rate or Mine?" *Journal of Accountancy* (September 1985): 63-84.

Article 20

The Role of Stripped Securities In Portfolio Management

By Sean Becketti

A wave of new financial products has been generated in recent years by the combined pressures of increased financial market volatility, technological innovation and regulatory change. Many of these new products are valuable additions to the tools investors and financial intermediaries use in managing their portfolios. Such new products as financial futures, options and swaps provide better means of hedging interest rate risk while other products increase investment opportunities. But the novelty and complexity of some of these products raise regulatory concerns about their possible misuse, particularly by federally insured financial institutions.

One of the most interesting examples of financial product innovation is the development of stripped securities. These securities are created by separating (stripping) the principal and interest payments from an underlying debt security and selling the claims to the payment streams as new and separate securities. In recent years, stripped securities have been created from Treasury bonds and from mortgage-backed securities.

The main reason for stripping is to create new securities with properties different from those of the underlying security. For example, the sensitivity of a stripped security's price to interest rate changes can be very different from the price sensitivity of the underlying security. This property can make the stripped security a useful hedging device. However, an investor who does not fully understand the behavior of stripped securities in different interest rate environments can be exposed to sizable losses. In fact, federal bank regulators recently issued guidelines noting the extreme price volatility of some of these stripped securities and warning banks to avoid adding stripped securities to their portfolios.

This article provides an introduction to stripped securities and their uses in investment and portfolio management strategies. Despite apparent similarities in the process of stripping Treasury and mortgage-backed securities, the resulting stripped securities have very different properties and usually appeal to different investors. The article first examines the conceptually simpler

Sean Becketti is an economist at the Federal Reserve Bank of Kansas City. Deana VanNahmen, a research associate at the bank, assisted in the preparation of this article.

Treasury-backed stripped securities and then examines mortgage-backed stripped securities. Both discussions are organized into three parts: a description of the underlying Treasury or mortgage-backed securities used to create the stripped securities, a discussion of how stripped securities are created and their key properties, and a look at the evolution of the markets for stripped securities.

Treasury-backed stripped securities

Properties of Treasury securities

To understand the mechanics of Treasury strips and their appeal to investors, it is useful to look first at the main features of the underlying Treasury securities that are stripped. An investor purchasing a Treasury bond pays the Treasury the face value (principal) of the bond and receives in return semiannual payments of interest at a fixed coupon rate plus the return of the principal at maturity. For example, an investor buying a $10,000 10-year Treasury bond at an 8 percent coupon rate pays the Treasury $10,000 and receives 20 semiannual interest payments of $400 each plus the $10,000 principal at maturity.

From an investor's standpoint, Treasury securities have both advantages and disadvantages. One key advantage is the absence of credit (default) risk. A second advantage is the absence of interest rate risk if the security is held to maturity.

In contrast to these positive attributes, there are two potential drawbacks to an investment in Treasury securities. First, if the investor sells the security before its maturity, the price received for the security may be less than the par value, reducing the effective yield on the investment. This risk of capital loss would be eliminated if the investor could match the maturity of the Treasury security to the timing of his payment needs. A second potential disadvantage is that, if the interest earnings from the Treasury security are reinvested at the current market rate, the rate of return on the reinvestment may be lower than the coupon rate of the Treasury security.

Creating stripped securities

Treasury-backed stripped securities are created by separating or stripping the principal and interest payments from a Treasury security and selling the claims to these payment streams as new and separate securities. A claim to the principal portion of the underlying Treasury security is called a PO (principal-only) security. A claim to an interest payment is called an IO (interest-only) security. Thus the 10-year Treasury security discussed above can be subdivided into 20 interest-only strips, each representing a $400 interest payment and one principal-only strip representing payment of $10,000 principal.

The properties of stripped securities can be very different from the properties of the underlying Treasury security. These properties can make stripped securities a valuable addition to an investment portfolio. In particular, Treasury strips allow an investor to avoid the reinvestment risk of regular Treasury securities and give the investor greater flexibility in matching the maturity of his investment to the timing of his payment needs.

Treasury strips avoid the reinvestment risk of regular Treasury securities because each IO strip and PO strip is, in effect, a zero-coupon bond. Such a bond is a discount security with no periodic interest payments and one lump sum repayment of the principal at maturity. Investors earn a return on a zero-coupon bond by purchasing the bond at discount, that is, by paying less than the face value of the bond. Since there are no periodic interest payments to reinvest, there is no reinvestment risk. The yield of a zero-coupon bond held to maturity is the yield quoted when the bond is sold.

Like a zero-coupon bond, each IO strip and PO

strip obtained from a Treasury security represents a promise to pay a fixed amount of money at a specific date in the future. An investor purchases a strip at a discount from its face value, the amount of the discount determining the effective yield of the strip. By buying one of the IO or PO strips, the investor can lock in a fixed yield for maturities starting at six months and extending to the maturity of the bond.

An investor also can better match the maturity of his investment to his need to make other payments by buying a combination of IO and PO strips. Treasury securities are issued in a limited number of different maturities. By buying an appropriate assortment of strips, the investor can pick investment maturities that more closely coincide with his need to make payments.

Another important property of stripped securities is the sensitivity of their price to interest rate changes. The interest sensitivity of stripped securities can be very different from the interest sensitivity of the underlying Treasury securities. This property can be advantageous to investors who want to change the overall interest sensitivity of their investment portfolios. This same property can potentially be dangerous to unwary investors who add stripped securities to their portfolios without examining their potential price behavior in different interest rate environments.

The relationship between the interest rate and the value of Treasury strips is straightforward. As with the underlying Treasury security, the prices of the strips and interest rates move inversely. As the interest rate rises, the prices both of the strips and of the underlying Treasury security fall. Similarly, as the interest rate falls, the prices of these securities rise.

While the prices of all these securities move in the same direction when the interest rate changes, the magnitude of the price change increases with the maturity of the Treasury strip. In other words, the prices of the strips with the longest maturities are most sensitive to interest rate changes.[1] The PO strip of a Treasury security represents the payment with the longest maturity. Thus, the price of the PO strip is most sensitive to changes in market interest rates. In contrast, the individual IO strips or combinations of the IO strips have shorter effective average maturities so that the values of these strips are less sensitive to interest rate changes. The interest sensitivity of the underlying Treasury security is a weighted average of the sensitivities of all the strips.[2]

To see the practical importance of this relationship between the maturity of a strip and its interest sensitivity, consider an investor with a 10-year horizon who has the choice of buying a regular 10-year Treasury security or a PO strip with the same maturity. The investor might prefer the PO strip in order to avoid the reinvestment risk of the Treasury security. However, if the investor has to sell the security before maturity, he must recognize that changes in market rates will have a greater impact on the value of the PO than on the value of the underlying security.

Evolution of the market for Treasury strips

Like most financial innovations, stripped

---

[1] To see how a longer maturity increases interest rate sensitivity, consider a zero-coupon bond that pays F dollars K years from today. If the market interest rate is r, then the present value, P, of this bond is:

$$P = \frac{F}{(1+r)^K}.$$

If the interest rate falls by one percentage point, the value of the zero-coupon bond will increase $K/(1+r)$ percent, a change that grows larger as the maturity, K, increases.

[2] Some of the IO strips that mature later will be more interest rate sensitive than the underlying Treasury security. However the PO strip and the latest IO strip will be more interest rate sensitive than either the underlying Treasury security or any of the other IO strips. (The latest IO strip represents the final coupon payment, which is made at the same time the principal is repaid.)

securities arose as a solution to specific financial problems. The organized market for Treasury strips originated in the early 1980s, partly in response to high interest rates and partly in response to loopholes in tax laws that made investments in stripped securities attractive.

Investors purchasing 20-year Treasury bonds in 1981 could earn record high coupon rates, close to 16 percent. However, as market rates fell from these elevated levels, the interest from the semiannual coupon payments would have to be reinvested at lower rates. With the creation of Treasury-backed stripped securities, investors could avoid reinvestment risk by locking in the high rates for the maturity of the investment.

Tax laws also stimulated the development of Treasury strips. Prior to 1982, investors did not have to report the implied interest accrual on a zero-coupon bond as current income. In addition, tax accounting rules tied the taxable value of a bond to its principal. Since the price of a PO strip is less than the price of an underlying Treasury security, institutions could buy Treasury securities, create PO strips, and sell the PO strips at a loss for tax purposes. These loopholes were eliminated in the Tax Equity and Fiscal Responsibility Act of 1982.

Treasury strips were originally developed by investment banks to meet the demand for zero-coupon Treasury securities. In 1982, Merrill Lynch created TIGRs (Treasury Investment Growth Receipts), the first zero-coupon derivative security based on Treasury securities.[3] Merrill Lynch bought Treasury securities, deposited them as an irrevocable trust handled by a custodian bank, and sold zero-coupon TIGRs with maturities that matched the maturities of the interest and principal payments of the pool of Treasury securities. Other investment banks followed Merrill Lynch's approach and created their own proprietary, zero-coupon securities collateralized by pools of Treasury securities.

The market for Treasury strips changed dramatically in 1985 when the Treasury announced its own STRIPS (Separate Trading of Registered Interest and Principal of Securities). Prior to 1982, the Treasury had been opposed to Treasury strips because of their tax loopholes. Once the tax loopholes were closed, stripping became attractive to the Treasury because the demand for STRIPS increased the total demand for Treasury securities and, thus, lowered the cost of issuing government debt.

Under the STRIPS program, Treasury securities with maturities of ten years or more can be submitted to the Treasury for stripping. The Treasury provides PO and IO strips in book-entry form to the investors and stands ready to reconstitute the STRIPS by exchanging the underlying Treasury securities for the pieces of the STRIPS.[4]

The market for stripped securities has grown steadily. Privately issued zero-coupon securities dominated the Treasury-backed stripped securities market from August 1982 until the beginning of the Treasury's STRIPS program in February 1985. In these 31 months, investment bankers stripped $33.7 billion (par value) of Treasury securities. Of this amount 91 percent was accounted for by three products—Salomon Brothers' CATS, the generic TR's (a product supported by a group of investment banks), and

---

[3] Prior to the development of TIGRs, a few dealers stripped Treasury securities for their customers. The customer received the stripped components of the Treasury security itself, that is, the actual pieces of paper that constitute the Treasury security. TIGRs were a *derivative* security that represented claims to portions of the receipts from a pool of Treasury securities.

[4] Although the STRIPS program began in February 1985, the reconstitution program did not start until May 1987. Reconstitution is a desirable feature because it increases the liquidity of STRIPS.

CHART 1
Treasury STRIPS outstanding
February 1985 to February 1988

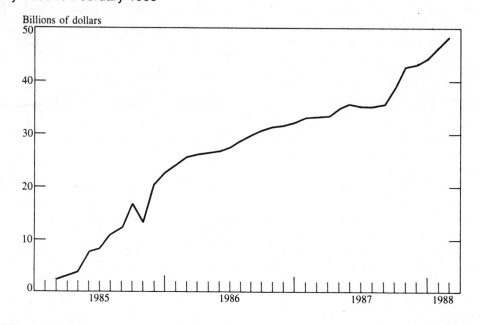

Billions of dollars

Merrill Lynch's TIGRs.[5]

The growth of the Treasury's STRIPS program is displayed in Chart 1. The amount of STRIPS outstanding increased from $2.4 billion in February 1985 to $48.2 billion in February 1988. This latter amount represents 4 percent of all outstanding Treasury notes and bonds and 19 percent of all outstanding Treasury securities eligible for stripping. The increase from February 1985 to February 1988 represents an annual growth rate of 172 percent in the amount outstanding. The reconstitution feature of the STRIPS program is also actively used. Reconstitution increased from $2.6 billion in August 1987 (7 per-

cent of outstanding STRIPS) to $8.1 billion in February 1988 (17 percent of outstanding STRIPS).

Mortgage-backed stripped securities

The creation of new securities by stripping interest and principal payments from existing securities has been extended recently to the market for mortgage-backed securities. But just as mortgage-backed securities differ fundamentally from Treasury securities, so do the properties of mortgage-backed strips differ from those of Treasury strips. As a result, mortgage-backed stripped securities play a different role in the portfolios of investors and financial institutions.

Properties of mortgage-backed securities

Mortgage-backed securities (MBSs) are pass-

---

[5] These figures are taken from Thomas J. Kluber and Thomas Stauffacher, "Zero Coupon Treasury Securities," in *The Handbook of Treasury Securities: Trading and Portfolio Strategies*, edited by Frank J. Fabozzi, Probus Publishing Co., 1987.

through securities, that is, securities representing an undivided interest in the principal and interest payments from an underlying pool of mortgages.[6] MBSs are more attractive to some investors than whole mortgage loans because the securities are more liquid and are backed by federal or private insurance guarantees. Correspondingly, yields on MBSs are generally lower than on whole mortgage loans.

Mortgage securities and Treasury securities are similar in that they both have low default risk. There are, however, two important differences between MBSs and Treasury securities. First, mortgage principal is amortized over the life of the mortgage so that some principal is included in each mortgage payment. Moreover, the proportion of each payment that represents principal increases steadily while the proportion that represents interest declines. In contrast, a Treasury security has one principal payment at maturity and all other payments represent a constant amount of interest.

Second, and more important, mortgage borrowers have the option of prepaying their mortgages at any time. Prepayments affect the pattern of mortgage payments in two ways. First, prepayment accelerates the mortgage holder's receipt of principal. Second, because mortgage interest payments are calculated as a percentage of the remaining unpaid principal, interest payments cease when principal is repaid early. Thus, the cash flow from an MBS can be altered significantly by a change in prepayments.

Creating mortgage-backed stripped securities

Mortgage-backed stripped securities are created

in much the same way as Treasury strips, by separating the principal and interest payments streams and selling them as separate securities. However, unlike Treasury securities, which are stripped into separate securities for each interest payment and the principal payment, mortgage securities are generally stripped into only two parts: a PO strip representing all principal payments and an IO strip representing all interest payments.[7] Thus, mortgage strips do not have the zero-coupon feature of Treasury strips.[8]

Because of this difference in construction, mortgage-backed strips play a different role in portfolio management than Treasury strips. Indeed, the two primary functions of Treasury strips—reduction of reinvestment risk and maturity matching—cannot be performed by mortgage strips. Mortgage strips do not have the zero-coupon feature of Treasury strips and thus do not reduce reinvestment risk. Moreover, because of prepayments, the effective maturity of mortgage strips is uncertain so they cannot be used for maturity matching.

The feature that makes mortgage strips most useful in portfolio management is their interest rate sensitivity. In principle, mortgage strips can be very useful hedging devices for a variety of investors and portfolio managers. However determining the degree of interest sensitivity of mort-

---

[6] The term "MBS" is used in this article as a generic term for a pass-through security backed by a pool of mortgages. For the purposes of this article, mortgage-backed bonds are not included in MBSs.

[7] This arrangement, that is, the separation of mortgage cash flows into a single PO security and a single IO security, describes the Federal National Mortgage Association's (Fannie Mae) current method of stripping MBSs. The Fannie Mae program represents the majority of stripped MBSs.

Other methods of separating mortgage cash flows were used early in the development of this market and continue to be used to create so-called strip classes of collateralized mortgage obligations (CMOs), which are multiclass mortgage-backed bonds. Other than noting these techniques here, this article restricts its attention to the simpler Fannie Mae method of stripping MBSs.

[8] Because mortgage principal is amortized over the life of the mortgage, even the PO portion of an MBS represents a sequence of payments rather than a single zero-coupon type of payout.

gage strips in different interest rate environments is extremely complicated. Thus, they are potentially dangerous in the hands of unsophisticated or unwary investors.

The key factor determining the interest sensitivity of PO and IO mortgage strips is the rate of prepayment on the underlying mortgages. Prepayment rates depend primarily on interest rates. A fall in interest rates tends to increase home sales, causing existing mortgages to be retired. A drop in rates can also cause an increase in mortgage refinancing. Refinancing requires the payment of discount points and other fees. When interest rates fall far enough, though, as they did in the spring of 1986, refinancings and the rate of prepayments can skyrocket. In contrast, when interest rates rise, slower home sales and fewer refinancings cause prepayments to slow.

Prepayments make the price of PO mortgage strips extremely sensitive to interest rate changes —much more sensitive than the price of the underlying MBSs. To see this, it is helpful to divide the change in value of a PO strip into two parts: a discounting effect and a prepayment effect.[9] Even with prepayment rates held constant, a fall in interest rates induces a rise in the value of a PO strip because the stream of principal payments is discounted at a lower interest rate. Since prepayments rise when interest rates fall, there is a further rise in the value of the PO strip because principal payments are received earlier than expected and thus have higher present value. Taken together, these two effects make the value of PO mortgage strips highly sensitive to interest rate changes.

Prepayments are also crucial in determining the interest sensitivity of IO mortgage strips. Indeed, prepayments can cause the value of an IO strip to move in the opposite direction from the value of fixed-income securities, making the IO strip potentially useful as a hedging instrument. To see this, consider the effect of a fall in market interest rates with prepayments held constant. As rates drop, the discounting effect causes the value of the stream of interest payments to rise. Thus, the discounting effect causes the price of IO strips to rise, just like the prices of other fixed-income securities, when market rates fall. But if prepayments also increase as rates drop, the expected stream of future interest payments is cut short, reducing the value of the IO strip. If the prepayment effect is large enough, it can outweigh the discounting effect, causing the value of the IO strip to fall. That is, with a strong enough prepayment effect, the value of IO mortgage strips can move in the opposite direction of the prices of other fixed-income securities.

An example may be helpful in illustrating both the importance of the prepayment effect and the heightened interest rate sensitivity of the stripped securities. Consider the effect of a one-percentage-point decrease in the interest rate, from 9 percent to 8 percent, on the value of a $100,000 share in a pool of newly issued, 30-year mortgages.[10] The drop in interest rates increases the value of the share to $104,511, a 4.5 percent gain. This increase reflects the combined effect of the discounting and prepayment effects. The discounting effect alone—that is, the effect of holding

---

[9] This division of the effect of interest rate changes into two parts is only a conceptual separation. When interest rates change, the discounting and prepayment effects simultaneously influence MBS values. Only the ultimate changes in values can be observed. Nonetheless it is helpful to analyze these influences separately.

[10] The methods used to calculate the effects described in this example are explained in Edward A. Hjerpe III, "Stripped Mortgage-Backed Securities: An Economic Analysis and Valuation Simulation," Research Working Paper 130, Federal Home Loan Bank Board, June 1987. The prepayment assumptions used in the example are taken from the estimates in Frank J. Navratil, "The Estimation of Mortgage Prepayment Rates," Research Working Paper 112, Federal Home Loan Bank Board, April 1984.

prepayments constant and discounting future cash flows at 8 percent rather than 9 percent—raises the value of the share $6,819, or 6.8 percent.[11] However, the drop in interest rates also increases prepayments. These prepayments raise the present value of the principal payments, but, by retiring principal early, they reduce the amount of the interest payments. The net result of this prepayment effect is to reduce the value of the share $2,308, or 2.3 percent. The combined effect of the discounting and prepayment effects is the total increase of $4,511 (=$6,819-$2,308).[12] In this example the discounting effect is larger than the prepayment effect.

The values of both the PO and the IO components of this share in a pool of mortgages are more sensitive to interest rate changes than is the underlying share. In addition, the prepayment effect is more important than the discounting effect in determining the value of the PO and IO components. When rates drop from 9 to 8 percent, the value of the principal payments increases a whopping 51.4 percent, from $42,210 to $63,911. But only 15 percent of that increase ($3,239) is due to the discounting effect. Fully 85 percent of the increase ($18,462) reflects the early repayment of the principal.

The value of the IO component is also extremely sensitive to interest rate changes. When rates drop from 9 to 8 percent, the value of the interest payments decreases by 30.0 percent, from $57,790 to $40,600. For the IO component, the discounting and prepayment effects work in opposite directions. The fall in interest rates gives future interest payments a higher present value. This discounting effect raises the value of the IO component 6.2 percent ($3,580). However the early retirement of principal associated with the fall in rates reduces the amount of interest received. This prepayment effect lowers the value of the IO component 35.9 percent ($20,770). The combination of these effects accounts for a $17,190 (=$3,580-$20,770) loss in the value of the IO component.

The precise sensitivity of MBSs and their associated stripped securities to interest rate changes depends on many factors. However this example does illustrate the three most important. First, the prepayment effect makes the interest rate sensitivity of MBSs different from the interest sensitivity of Treasury securities. Second, the prepayment effect makes the PO and IO mortgage-backed strips much more sensitive on average to interest rates than the underlying MBS. Third, the prepayment effect is sometimes so strong that an IO mortgage-backed strip will rise in value when interest rates rise and fall in value when rates fall—precisely the opposite relationship from other fixed income securities. This last feature of stripped mortgage-backed securities, the positive relationship between the value of some IO strips and interest rates, is particularly useful to investors who need to hedge a portfolio of other fixed-income securities.

To see how IO strips can act as a hedge, consider the effect of interest rate changes on the value of a portfolio containing both IO strips and ordinary fixed-income securities. When interest rates rise, the increase in the value of the IOs tends to balance the decrease in the value of the other securities. When interest rates fall, the decrease in the value of the IOs tends to balance the increase in the value of the other securities. The right proportions of IO strips and other securities can insulate the value of the combined portfolio

---

[11] Since Treasury securities do not prepay, this is the same increase in value that would be enjoyed by a "comparable" Treasury security. The difference in the timing of principal and interest payments between mortgage and Treasury securities makes it difficult to decide what a comparable Treasury security might be. Nonetheless it is still true that the interest rate sensitivity of Treasury securities reflects only the discounting effect.

[12] Note that the share increases in value less than a Treasury security when interest rates fall. The share also decreases in value more than a Treasury security when interest rates rise.

CHART 2

The interest rate sensitivities of two mortgage-backed IOs

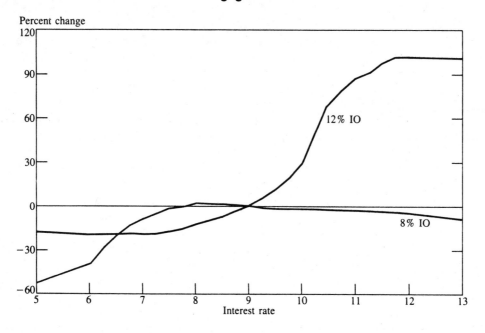

from interest rate changes.

The precise relationship between the value of stripped mortgage-backed securities and interest rates is complicated. The relationship can vary greatly, depending on the difference between the current interest rate and the coupon rate on the underlying MBS.

Chart 2 presents an example of how different these interest rate sensitivities can be. The chart displays the hypothetical change in the market values of two IO strips at different interest rates.[13] One of the IO strips is based on an MBS with a coupon rate of 8 percent. The other IO strip is based on an MBS with a coupon rate of 12 per-

cent. The chart is drawn under the assumption that the market interest rate is initially 9 percent.

While both IO securities tend to increase in value as interest rates rise, their interest sensitivities are different in many respects. The value of the 12-percent IO, for example, benefits greatly from increases in interest rates above the initial 9 percent because these rate increases reduce the incentive to refinance the underlying 12-percent mortgages. As a result, interest rate increases reduce prepayments and increase interest receipts. The value of the 8-percent IO, in contrast, responds very little to interest rate increases, even large increases. At an initial interest rate of 9 percent, 8-percent mortgages are already prepaying slowly, and further interest rate increases have little additional effect. Interest rate declines initially lower the value of the 12-percent IO, but these losses level out after rates fall to 7 percent. However the 8-percent IO is very vulnerable to

---

[13] The data for this chart are taken from Edward A. Hjerpe III, "Stripped Mortgage-Backed Securities: An Economic Analysis and Valuation Simulation," Research Working Paper 130, Federal Home Loan Bank Board, June 1987.

decreases in rates. Again, the differences derive from prepayment behavior. The 12-percent mortgages are already prepaying rapidly when the interest rate is 9 percent, and further interest declines have little additional effect. The 8-percent mortgages just begin to prepay as rates fall below 7 percent or so.

Chart 2 highlights the complexity of stripped MBSs. Investors who buy these stripped MBSs as hedging assets without fully understanding the properties of these securities may not achieve their investment goals. In addition, the potential for enormous swings in the value of the stripped MBSs magnifies the cost of small errors in portfolio management. Stripped mortgage-backed securities are for only the most sophisticated investors, and even these investors must constantly monitor the performance of these assets.

None of these cautions, however, erases the usefulness of stripped MBSs to certain classes of investors. As was noted above, the value of the IO strips may rise with interest rates, hence, they can be used to hedge other fixed-income assets. Such investors as thrifts and other institutional investors that hold portfolios of MBSs and other fixed-income securities may find IOs useful as a hedging asset.

PO strips may appeal to investors who wish to hedge fixed-income liabilities. Such investors include insurance companies and corporations that have issued long-term bonds. Since the values of fixed-income securities move inversely with interest rates, the debt burdens of investors that issue fixed income liabilities also move inversely with interest rates. If these investors hold PO strips as assets, then changes in the burden of their debt induced by changes in interest rates are balanced to some extent by changes in the value of their PO strip holdings.

Another group of investors that may wish to purchase PO strips are mortgage servicing corporations and issuers of collateralized mortgage obligations (CMOs). Mortgage servicing fees and the residual payments that accrue to CMO issuers are similar to interest-only securities.[14] As a result, these investors can purchase PO strips to balance their IO-like assets.

Evolution of the market for mortgage-backed strips

Like Treasury-backed strips, stripped MBSs arose as a solution to specific financial problems. The record-high interest rates of the early 1980s seriously hurt many depository institutions. Savings and loan associations (S&Ls), in particular, found themselves saddled with long-term mortgage loans with low, fixed interest rates while, at the same time, they were forced to pay higher market rates to obtain the deposits to fund these loans. When rates dropped from their peaks, S&Ls faced a new problem: mortgages made at peak interest rates began prepaying rapidly.

These experiences alerted depository institutions to the need to insulate their portfolios from unexpected swings in interest rates. Financial markets experimented with ways of restructuring traditional mortgage-backed securities to obtain new securities with properties that are helpful in portfolio management. One example of this experimentation was the appearance in 1983 of CMOs.

The market acceptance of CMOs led to the development of the market for stripped mortgage-backed securities. As noted earlier, the CMO residuals—the excess of mortgage receipts over

---

[14] Mortgage servicing fees are paid as a thin slice of the mortgage interest payments. These fees account for much of the difference between the contract rate on the mortgages in a pool and the lower rate paid to holders of the mortgage-backed securities. CMOs are multiclass, mortgage-backed bonds. CMO residuals are the funds left after the bond obligations are met. These residuals reflect the overcollateralization of the bonds. The complicated structure of CMOs makes the CMO residuals, in effect, interest-only securities. Many market observers count CMO residuals as IO strips when they measure the amount of mortgage-backed stripped securities.

CHART 3
Stripped mortgage-backed securities outstanding
August 1986 to March 1988

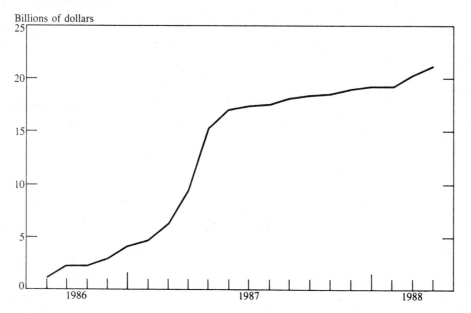

Billions of dollars

bond obligations—are similar to IO mortgage strips. In addition, some CMO bond classes are like PO mortgage strips. From these "near-stripped" CMO securities, it was a short step to an explicitly stripped mortgage-backed security.

The organized market for mortgage-backed stripped securities began in July 1986 when the Federal National Mortgage Association (Fannie Mae) issued its first stripped MBSs backed by $200 million of FHA/VA mortgages. For technical reasons, Fannie Mae issued "almost principal-only" and "almost interest-only" securities.[15] The "almost PO" security received 99 percent of the principal payments and 45 percent of the interest payments. The "almost IO" security

received 1 percent of the principal payments and 55 percent of the interest payments.

Fannie Mae issued 12 of these pairs of partially stripped mortgage-backed securities before it created its current SMBS (stripped MBS) Trust program. The SMBS Trusts issue "pure" PO and IO securities collateralized by pools of MBSs.[16] Fannie Mae has formed 32 SMBS Trusts so far. Private investment banks have also issued some stripped mortgage-backed securities.

The growth of the market for mortgage-backed strips is shown in Chart 3.[17] The amount of strips outstanding increased from $1.02 billion in August 1986 to $21.03 billion in March 1988. New issues of mortgage strips were halted briefly

[15] For several reasons, it was not possible at that time to enter IO mortgage securities in the Federal Reserve Bank of New York's book entry system or to transfer such securities by Fedwire, the Federal Reserve's electronic system for transferring funds and securities. These problems have since been overcome.

[16] SMBS Trust No. 25 is an exception to this rule.

[17] The data in Chart 3 include the Fannie Mae issues and the stripped classes of CMOs. No attempt has been made to account for the partial retirement of these securities. Because most of these securities were issued very recently, this procedure should

after Merrill Lynch lost $250 million on its portfolio of mortgage strips in April 1987. The market has recovered slowly from the shock of this loss. But investment bankers report recent increases in the trading of existing stripped securities. Some investment bankers estimate that as much as $200 million of stripped mortgage-backed securities changes hands daily.

Summary and conclusion

Specific financial market problems led to the creation of both Treasury-backed and mortgage-backed stripped securities. Investors' desire to lock in record-high interest rates accounts for the initial interest in Treasury strips. Thrift institutions' need to insulate portfolios of mortgages and mortgage-backed securities from unpredictable shifts in interest rates stimulated experimentation that ultimately produced stripped MBSs.

Treasury and mortgage strips are very different securities, even though the mechanics of their creation are similar. The most important feature of Treasury strips is that they are zero-coupon bonds with the safety of Treasury securities. Treasury strips are useful to investors who wish to avoid reinvestment risk and who need to time their investment receipts to match their obligations to make payments. The most important feature of mortgage-backed strips is their heightened and varied sensitivities to interest rate changes. Mortgage strips are useful to investors who wish to hedge their portfolios against unexpected changes in rates.

Because their interest rate sensitivity is similar to that of the underlying Treasury securities, Treasury strips are easily understood. Although

introduce relatively small errors. The data in Chart 3 do not include CMO residuals, which total approximately $5.1 billion in February 1988. The author would like to thank R. Blaine Roberts, managing director of government bond research, Bear, Stearns & Co., Inc. for information on CMO issues and CMO strip classes.

Treasury POs are more sensitive to interest rate changes than the underlying Treasury securities, the general shape of their relationship to interest rates mimics that of the Treasury securities. Furthermore, investors, such as municipal bond issuers, who use Treasury strips simply to match future payments obligations need not worry about the interest rate sensitivity of Treasury strips. The zero-coupon character of Treasury strips eliminates the reinvestment risk such investors would otherwise face. However, as guidelines recently issued by federal bank regulators point out, few depository institutions require zero-coupon bonds in their portfolios, hence few depository institutions are likely to purchase these assets.

Because mortgage-backed stripped securities are so volatile and because their interest rate sensitivity is so complicated, only the most sophisticated investors should consider using them. Mortgage strips are unlike any other fixed-income securities in their interest rate sensitivity, including the underlying MBSs. Investors' experience with other securities will not prepare them to manage a portfolio containing stripped MBSs. However the extreme volatility of these stripped securities may make them a very effective hedging asset. Some of their properties may not be obtainable from other assets or combinations of assets.

Guidelines recently issued by federal bank regulators warn banks against incorporating mortgage-backed stripped securities in their portfolios. The riskiness of mortgage strips and the relatively short term of most bank assets suggests that mortgage strips are not suitable for bank portfolios. Savings and loan associations, in contrast, hold high proportions of their assets in long-term, interest-sensitive mortgages and mortgage-backed securities. For some sophisticated S&Ls, mortgage strips can be a useful hedging tool. However the extreme price volatility of mortgage strips may make other hedging assets a better choice for the majority of thrifts.

Article 21

Low-Grade Bonds:
A Growing Source of Corporate Funding

Jan Loeys*

In recent years, a growing part of corporate borrowing has taken the form of "low-grade bonds." Called "junk bonds" by some, and "high-yield bonds" by others, these bonds are rated as speculative by the major rating agencies, and they are therefore considered more risky than high- or investment-grade bonds. Lately, low-grade bonds have received a lot of public attention because of their use in corporate takeovers. But in fact, most low-grade bond issues are not used for this purpose.

Corporations that now issue low-grade bonds

*Jan Loeys is a Senior Economist in the Macroeconomics Section of the Research Department at the Federal Reserve Bank of Philadelphia.

are firms that, because of their lack of size, track record, and name recognition, used to borrow mostly via bank loans or privately placed bonds. Recently, investors have become more willing to lend directly to smaller and less creditworthy corporations by buying these low-grade bonds. There are several reasons for the new popularity of these bonds. But before discussing those reasons, it is useful to examine in more depth exactly what low-grade bonds are and how their market first developed.

WHAT ARE LOW-GRADE BONDS?

Low-grade bonds represent corporate bonds that are rated below investment grade by the major rating agencies, Standard & Poor's and

Moody's. These ratings, which firms usually request before issuing bonds to the public, reflect each agency's estimate of the firm's capacity to honor its debt (that is, to pay interest and repay principal when due). The highest rating is AAA (for firms with an "extremely strong" capacity to pay interest and repay principal), and then AA ("very strong"), A ("strong"), and BBB ("adequate"). Bonds rated BB, B, CCC, or CC are regarded as "speculative" with respect to the issuer's capacity to meet the terms of the obligation.[1] Firms generally strive to maintain at least a BBB rating because many institutions or investment funds cannot, because of regulation, or will not, because of firm policy, invest in lower-grade bonds. This explains why bonds rated below BBB are also known as "below-investment" grade bonds.

There is no set formula for determining a bond rating—the rating agencies say they look at the entire spectrum of financial and product market conditions. But a certain issue may be considered too risky to be rated investment grade for several reasons. For one, certain financial ratios—such as a high debt-equity ratio or a high ratio of interest expenses to total income—may indicate that even moderate fluctuations in cash flow could endanger the issuer's capacity to pay the bondholders. Or the firm's assets may not be well diversified (too dependent upon a single product), which also makes the firm's revenues highly variable. Alternatively, if the firm is relatively new and thus lacks a proven track record, the firm's cash flow might be hard to predict. Finally, the firm or its industry may be considered in decline, which increases the likelihood of a default.

THE MARKET FOR LOW-GRADE BONDS

Low-grade bonds have received widespread attention from the press in recent years, largely because of their association with certain corporate takeover techniques.[2] But low-grade bonds have been around for a long time. In fact, during the 1920s and 1930s, about 17 percent of domestic corporate bond offerings (that is, new issues) were low grade.[3] Furthermore, as the Depression of the 1930s wore on, many bonds that were originally issued with a high-grade rating were downgraded to below-investment grade. These so-called "fallen angels" were bonds of companies that had fallen on hard times. By 1940, as a result of both these downgradings and the earlier heavy volume of new low-grade offerings, low-grade bonds made up more than 40 percent of all bonds outstanding.

After 1940, the market for new public offerings of low-grade bonds shrank significantly. Many investors avoided low-grade bonds due to their high default rate during the 1930s—an average of almost 10 percent of outstanding low-grade bonds (valued at par) defaulted each year.[4] Most additional low-grade bonds represented only new fallen angels. By the mid-1970s, only about 4 percent of all public corporate bonds outstanding in the U.S. consisted of low-grade bonds.[5]

---

[1]These are the ratings for Standard & Poor's. The corresponding ratings for Moody's are Aaa, Aa, A, Baa, Ba, B, Caa, and Ca, with ratings below Baa considered below investment grade. For both agencies, the rating C is reserved for bonds on which no interest is being paid, while bonds rated D are in default.

[2]For a discussion of these issues, see Kevin F. Winch and Carol Kay Brancato, "The Role of High-Yield Bonds (Junk Bonds) in Capital Markets and Corporate Takeovers: Public Policy Implications," in *The Financing of Mergers and Acquisitions*, Hearing before the Subcommittee on Domestic Monetary Policy of the Committee on Banking, Finance and Urban Affairs, House of Representatives, 99th Congress, 1st session (May 3, 1985) pp. 246-297.

[3]See W. Braddock Hickman, *Corporate Bond Quality and Investor Experience*, (Princeton University Press, 1958) p. 153.

[4]See W. Braddock Hickman, *Corporate Bond Quality and Investor Experience*, p. 189.

[5]Edward I. Altman and Scott A. Nammacher, "The Anatomy of the High Yield Debt Market," Morgan Stanley (September 1985), Table 2. These and the following data refer only to publicly issued, nonconvertible debt that is rated below BBB (or Baa). Including unrated debt, which would probably be low grade if it were rated, and debt that is convertible into stock, would raise the outstanding amount of low-grade bonds by up to 30 percent.

In 1977, Drexel Burnham Lambert, an investment bank that was already making a secondary market in fallen angels, started an effort to revitalize the market for original-issue low-grade bonds by underwriting new issues and subsequently making a secondary market in them. By 1982, low-grade bond issuance had grown gradually to about $2.8 billion per year (or 6 percent of total corporate bonds issued publicly that year). In 1983, the market started growing much faster, reaching an annual issue volume of about $15 billion in 1985 (or 15 percent of total corporate issues that year; see Figure 1). Most low-grade bonds were issued by industrial companies and utilities, accounting for more than a third of the bonds raised by these firms in 1985. By the end of 1985, the total stock of low-grade bonds outstanding reached about $75 billion (or 14 percent of the total), less than a third of which consisted of fallen angels.

Historically, default rates on low-grade bonds have been much higher than those on high-grade bonds, lending credibility to the speculative rating of low-grade bonds. A recent study finds that between 1970 and 1984, this average annual default rate for low-grade bonds was only 2.1 percent, while the default rate for investment-grade debt was close to zero percent.[6]

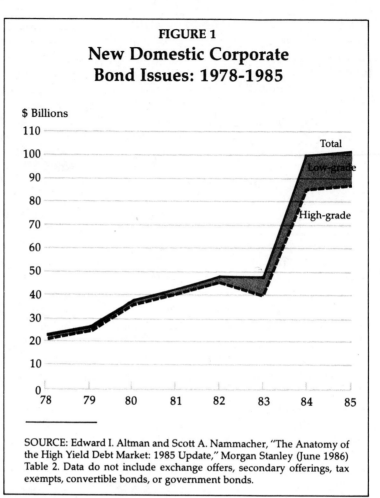

FIGURE 1

New Domestic Corporate Bond Issues: 1978-1985

SOURCE: Edward I. Altman and Scott A. Nammacher, "The Anatomy of the High Yield Debt Market: 1985 Update," Morgan Stanley (June 1986) Table 2. Data do not include exchange offers, secondary offerings, tax exempts, convertible bonds, or government bonds.

This average for low-grade bonds, however, hides a lot of year-to-year variability: it varied from a high of 11.4 percent in 1970, when Penn Central went under, to a mere 0.15 percent in 1981, when only two firms defaulted on their bonds (see Figure 2, p. 6).

To compensate investors for the risk they bear by holding low-grade debt—or indeed any debt of private firms—rather than (presumably) default-free Treasury securities, firms promise to pay higher yields on their debt than the

---

[6]Edward I. Altman and Scott A. Nammacher, "The Anatomy of the High Yield Debt Market: 1985 Update," Morgan Stanley (June 1986) Table 10. One must be careful in interpreting these data. A default does not necessarily mean that bondholders lose all of their investment. If the firm in default has some assets left, bondholders may still retrieve part of their investment, although it may be some time before these funds are returned.

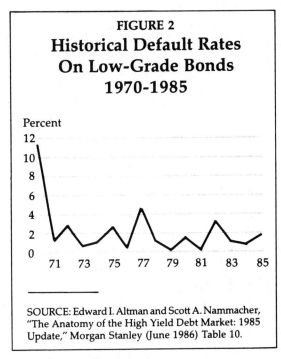

FIGURE 2
Historical Default Rates On Low-Grade Bonds 1970-1985

Percent

SOURCE: Edward I. Altman and Scott A. Nammacher, "The Anatomy of the High Yield Debt Market: 1985 Update," Morgan Stanley (June 1986) Table 10.

Treasury does.[7] This difference between yields is called a "risk premium." In general, the lower a firm's rating, the higher the risk premium will be. As Figure 3 shows, high-grade (AAA) bonds usually yield only 50 to 100 basis points more than Treasury bonds, while medium-rated (BBB) bonds may yield from 150 to 300 basis points above Treasury yields. The risk premium of lower-grade bonds over Treasuries, however, has run from 300 to 600 basis points over the last five years. But default risk is probably not the only reason for these yield differentials. Low-grade bonds may require a higher return to compensate investors for the fact that the secondary market for low-grade securities is much less liquid than that for Treasury securities.[8]

Actual realized returns frequently differ from promised returns, however. Aside from the promised return, the actual return includes capital gains and losses due to defaults, upgradings and downgradings, and changes in market interest rates. For example, from 1978 to 1985, low-grade bonds realized an average annual return of 12.9 percent, compared with 10.8 percent on Treasury bonds.[9]

This average return hides a lot of variability, however. In 1983, low-grade bonds outperformed Treasury securities by almost 20 percentage points (see Figure 4, p. 8). But in 1982, and again in 1985, as yields on new Treasury issues dropped much more than the yield on new low-grade issues, the larger capital gains on Treasury securities allowed them to beat low-grade bond returns by almost 10 percentage points. Therefore, although low-grade bonds have yielded a higher return than Treasury or investment-grade bonds on average, there is no guarantee that they will do so in any given year.

The recent revival of the low-grade bond market raises the question of why this product has become successful again. One popular misconception is that these bonds are used solely to finance corporate takeovers. But while the sudden rise in corporate mergers and acquisitions in the last few years did contribute to the growth in low-grade bond offerings, the market had taken off well before the first major use of low-grade bonds in corporate takeover attempts in 1983. And even in 1985—a year of unprecedented merger activity—low-grade bonds issued for takeover purposes made up only about 38 percent of total low-grade bond issuance (see LOW-GRADE BONDS AND TAKEOVERS, p.

[7]Sometimes this compensation takes the form of a "warrant," which gives the bondholder the right to buy equity in the firm at an attractive price, or an option to convert the bond to the common stock of the firm. These so-called "equity kickers" allow bondholders to benefit from any improvements in the value of the firm.

[8]In addition, unlike most Treasury securities, most corporate bonds are callable; that is, the issuer has the option to

pay off part (or all) of the issue at a predetermined price during a predetermined period prior to maturity. The issuer pays for this option in the form of a higher yield.

[9]Edward I. Altman and Scott A. Nammacher, "The Anatomy of the High Yield Debt Market: 1985 Update," Table 1. See also Marshall E. Blume and Donald B. Keim, "Risk and Return Characteristics of Lower-Grade Bonds," Rodney L. White Center for Financial Research, University of Pennsylvania (August 1986).

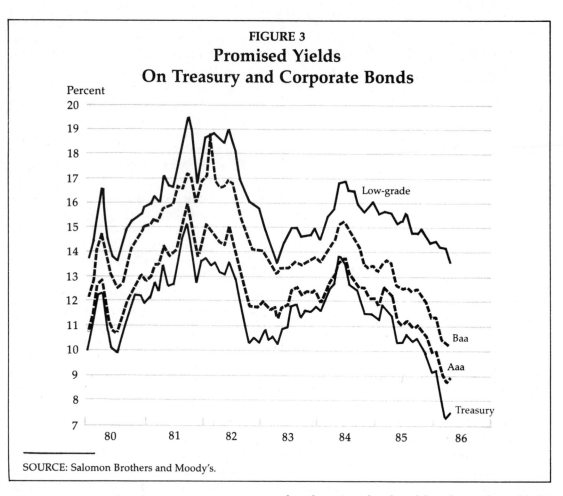

FIGURE 3
Promised Yields
On Treasury and Corporate Bonds

Percent

SOURCE: Salomon Brothers and Moody's.

9). Rather than reflecting a rise in one particular use for low-grade bonds, the reemergence of the market paralleled more fundamental changes in financial markets that made low-grade bonds relatively more attractive compared with other forms of financing.

WHY DID THE MARKET GROW?

The main alternative to issuing public debt securities directly in the open market is to obtain a loan from a specialized financial intermediary that issues securities (or deposits) of its own in the market. These alternative instruments usually are commercial bank loans—for short- and medium-term credit—or privately placed bonds —for longer-term credit. Unlike publicly issued bonds, privately placed bonds can be sold directly to only a limited number of sophisticated investors, usually life insurance companies and pension funds.[10] Moreover, privately placed bonds are held for investment purposes rather than for resale, and they have complex, custo-

---

[10]The Securities Act of 1933 exempts privately placed bonds from the normal registration process that the Securities and Exchange Commission enforces on public securities offerings. For more details on this market, see John D. Rea and Peggy Brockschmidt "The Relationship Between Publicly Offered and Privately Placed Corporate Bonds," Federal Reserve Bank of Kansas City *Economic Review,* (November 1973) pp. 11-20, and Patrick J. Davey, "Private Placements: Practices and Prospects," *The Conference Board Information Bulletin* (January 1979).

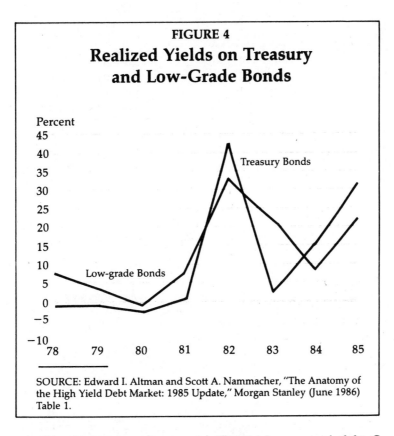

FIGURE 4

Realized Yields on Treasury and Low-Grade Bonds

Percent

Treasury Bonds

Low-grade Bonds

78 79 80 81 82 83 84 85

SOURCE: Edward I. Altman and Scott A. Nammacher, "The Anatomy of the High Yield Debt Market: 1985 Update," Morgan Stanley (June 1986) Table 1.

mized loan agreements (covenants). The restrictions in the covenants range from limits on dividend payments to prohibitions on asset sales and new debt issues. They provide a series of checkpoints that permit the lender to review actions by the borrower that have the potential to impair the lender's position.[11] Thus, these agreements have to be regularly renegotiated prior to maturity. As a result, these privately placed bonds in effect are much more like loans than public securities.

Before the reemergence of original-issue low-grade bonds, only large, well-known firms with established track records found it economical to raise money by issuing their own debt securities in the public capital markets. For smaller, relatively new or unknown firms, the expense was usually prohibitive. Because of the risk of underwriting low-grade bonds, investment bankers would demand hefty underwriting fees. Also, less creditworthy issuers would have had to pay a very high premium on their debt because investors perceived them as particularly risky investments.

Such borrowers thus found it more economical simply to obtain a loan from a bank or to place a private bond issue with a life insurance company. These alternatives proved cheaper because banks and life insurance companies specialize in credit analysis and assume a large amount (if not all) of a borrower's debt. Consequently, they could realize important cost savings in several functions, such as gathering information about the condition of debtor firms, monitoring their actions, and renegotiating loan agreements.

The reemergence of a market for public original-issue low-grade bonds suggests that this situation is changing. Certain lower-rated corporations now apparently find it economical to issue their own bonds directly in the public capital markets (see THE GROWTH OF SECURITIES MARKETS, p. 10). As with many financial innovations, it is impossible to identify all the factors responsible for this development. But it is possible to suggest several important ones that may have made a contribution to the reemergence of original-issue low-grade bonds, and three seem particularly noteworthy—a greater demand by investors for marketable assets; lower information costs; and changes in

---

[11]See Edward Zinbarg, "The Private Placement Loan Agreement," *Financial Analyst Journal* (July/August 1975) pp. 33-35 and 52.

Low-Grade Bonds and Takeovers

Low-grade bonds became the center of public attention because of their association with corporate takeover attempts. In a takeover, one firm or a set of investors acquires the stock (and thus ownership) of another firm. When the stock purchase is not financed with cash or newly issued stock of the acquiring firm, the acquisition is financed by borrowing funds. As a result, equity in the combined firm is replaced with debt and its debt-equity ratio rises. Many of these cases involve so-called "leveraged buyouts" (LBOs), in which a group of investors, usually including the management of the firm being acquired, buy out stockholders in order to take the firm private.[a]

In the past, there was little LBO borrowing and what there was took the form of bank loans. However, because an increased debt-equity ratio raises the default risk of a firm's debt, bank loans usually come with a lot of restrictions and collateral requirements. In response to an increased demand for LBO financing, Drexel Burnham Lambert, in late 1983, started using its extensive network of private and institutional buyers of low-grade debt to float LBO bonds. These bonds are frequently rated below investment grade, especially when they are junior to already existing debt, and when cash flow projections barely exceed the higher required interest payments. The flexibility of this new source of LBO financing allows some investors to attempt acquisitions of firms several times their own size.[b]

In contrast to the amount of public discussion about this topic, low-grade bond issues actually involved in takeovers make up only a small part of the market. During 1984, LBOs amounted to only $10.8 billion, compared with $122.2 billion in total merger and acquisition activity.[c] Drexel estimates that of about $14 billion in publicly issued low-grade bonds in 1984, only "approximately 12 % was issued in acquisition or leveraged buyout transactions, of which a de minimis amount was connected with the financing of unsolicited acquisitions."[d] By 1985, however, other analysts had estimated that the proportion of new low-grade issues used to finance acquisitions and LBO transactions had risen to 38 percent.[e]

---

[a]For details, see Carolyn K. Brancato and Kevin F. Winch, "Merger Activity and Leveraged Buyouts: Sound Corporate Restructuring or Wall Street Alchemy?" U.S. Congress, House, Committee on Energy and Commerce, Subcommittee on Telecommunications, Consumer Protection, and Finance, 98th Congress, 2nd Session (November 1984).

[b]Early in 1986, the Board of Governors of the Federal Reserve System ruled that bonds that are issued by a corporation with no business operations and no assets other than the stock of the target company, are functionally equivalent to borrowing to buy stock (that is, buying stock on margin). Therefore, these bonds are subject to a 50 percent margin as required by Regulation G. That is, only 50 percent of the stock purchase can be financed with borrowed funds. However, the Board specifically excluded bonds that are issued simultaneously with the consummation of the merger or LBO—a standard practice in LBOs—because the assets of the firm, and not its stock, would be the source of repayment of the bond issue. For details, see Federal Reserve System 12 C.F.R. Part 207 (Regulation G; Docket No. R-0562).

[c]W. T. Grimm & Co. "1984 Merger/Acquisitions Set Ten-Year Record: Total Dollar Value Rose to 67% to a Record-Breaking $122.2 Billion," (Chicago: W. T. Grimm & Co., 1985). Press release, undated, duplicated.

[d]Drexel Burnham Lambert, Inc., "Acquisitions and High Yield Bond Financing," submitted to the Subcommittee on Telecommunications, Consumer Protection, and Finance (March 20, 1985) p. 14.

[e]Martin Fridson and Fritz Wahl, "Plain Talk About Takeovers," *High Performance* (February 1986) p. 2. Fridson and Wahl use a more restrictive definition of the size of the low-grade market than Drexel does.

---

investors' risk perceptions.

Marketability vs. Covenant Restrictions. One reason for the growth in the public issuance of low-grade bonds is that buyers of privately placed bonds have become more willing to trade some of the safety they found in the contractual restric-tions they placed on borrowers in return for the marketability and higher yields of publicly issued low-grade bonds. Private placements are bilateral, customized loan agreements with complex contractual restrictions on borrowers' actions. However, the lack of standardization of these

The Growth of Securities Markets

The growth of low-grade bond offerings is not an isolated phenomenon. In several other financial markets there is also a growing tendency for corporate borrowing to take the form of negotiable securities issued in the public capital markets rather than in the form of nonmarketable loans negotiated with financial intermediaries. For example, in the short-term credit market, commercial paper has become increasingly competitive with bank loans. By the end of 1985, bank loans constituted only 24 percent of short-term debt at large manufacturing firms, compared with 59 percent in early 1974.[a] And even in the Eurodollar market, large corporations are more frequently bypassing syndicated loans in favor of financing arrangements that allow them to issue debt under their own names. In fact, by 1985, financing in the form of securities made up 80 percent of total funds raised in international financial markets, compared to only 33 percent in 1980.[b]

This move towards borrowing in the form of securities reduces the role of the traditional intermediary that just makes loans and issues deposits. These financial intermediaries will still help link ultimate savers and borrowers, although the way in which they do business may change substantially. The traditional intermediary provides all forms of financial intermediation under one roof: it pools the funds of many small savers, issues insured deposits, provides a payments mechanism, and lends out the funds in a different form to a diverse set of borrowers. The new growth of securities markets implies an "unbundling" of this process with many of these services being provided by different intermediaries: a commercial bank or thrift may originate the loan; an investment bank may package it into a security and distribute it; an insurance company may insure it; and a mutual or pension fund may end up financing it by attracting funds from a large number of small savers.

[a]Large manufacturing firms are firms with more than $1 billion in assets. Source: *Quarterly Financial Report*, U.S. Department of Commerce (1st Quarter 1975) p. 69, and (4th Quarter 1985) p. 134.

[b]*Financial Market Trends*, OECD (March 1986) p. 7, and earlier issues. See also *Recent Innovations in International Banking*, Bank for International Settlements (April 1986) Chapter 5.

covenants and the frequent need for renegotiation when borrowers want to transgress the covenant restrictions make it very costly to have a lot of lenders per issue, or to change the identity of the lenders. As a result, there is not much of a secondary market for private placements. That is, they are not marketable.

Low-grade bonds, in contrast, are public securities and are issued with relatively simple, standardized contracts without cumbersome restrictions on borrowers' actions, in order to facilitate their trading in a secondary market. And in exchange for the added freedom from covenant restrictions, borrowers pay a higher yield on low-grade bonds than on private placements. The marketability and liquidity of low-grade bonds still are not comparable to those of Treasury or high-grade bonds. But the recent development of a secondary market for low-grade bonds and the increasing number of dealers in this market do make these securities much more liquid and marketable than privately placed bonds.

Historically, life insurance companies, to which most private placements were sold, had no great need for marketability or liquidity. They held long-term liabilities and received highly predictable cash flows. They had no particular preference for marketable securities because they expected to hold their investments to maturity.

But recent economic developments have forced life insurance companies to abandon their traditional buy-and-hold-to-maturity policy and to become more active in money management.[12]

[12]See James J. O'Leary, "How Life Insurance Companies Have Shifted Investment Focus," *Bankers Monthly Magazine*

On the asset side, life insurance companies, as well as other financial intermediaries, have been faced with increased interest rate volatility and higher credit risk.[13] On the liability side, increases in loan requests by holders of whole life insurance policies and the growth of "separate accounts"—accounts managed temporarily for pension funds or other types of mutual funds— convinced life insurance companies that their liabilities have become much more volatile. In order to gain more flexibility in responding to unexpected cash outflows or to changing perceptions about firms, industries, or interest rates, life insurance companies shifted their investment focus away from nonmarketable, illiquid assets, such as private placements, toward publicly traded securities, including low-grade bonds.[14]

Information Costs. A second factor contributing to the growth of the low-grade bond market is that, in recent years, it has become much easier for individual and institutional investors to obtain and maintain information about the condition of corporate borrowers. Thus lenders are now more likely to find it cost-effective to lend directly to smaller and less well-known corporations, rather than indirectly through financial intermediaries such as commercial banks.

(June 15, 1982) pp. 2-28, and Timothy Curry and Mark Warshawsky, "Life Insurance Companies in a Changing Environment," *Federal Reserve Bulletin* (June 1986) pp. 449-459.

[13]The early 1980s saw severe sectoral problems—for example in the farm and the energy sectors—and a third-world debt crisis. From 1980 to 1983, the business failure rate—that is, the annual number of failures per 10,000 listed enterprises—averaged 76, more than twice its level during the 1970s. See *The Economic Report of the President* (Washington, DC: GPO, February 1986) Table B-92. For evidence on interest volatility, see Harvey Rosenblum and Steven Strongin, "Interest Rate Volatility in Historical Perspective," Federal Reserve Bank of Chicago *Economic Perspectives* (January/February 1983) pp. 10-19.

[14]Timothy Curry and Mark Warshawsky, "Life Insurance Companies in a Changing Environment," p. 456, report that: "In recent years, however, life insurance companies have been committing to private placements smaller percentages of their investable cash flow: 25 to 30 percent in 1984, down from a historical level of 40 to 50 percent."

Indeed, recent technological improvements in such areas as data manipulation and telecommunications have reduced greatly the costs of obtaining and processing information about the conditions—whether international or domestic, industry-wide or firm-specific—that affect the value of a borrowing firm. Any analyst now has computerized access to a wealth of economic and financial information at a relatively low cost. New information reaches investors across the world in a matter of minutes. Given the reduction in information costs, the cheapest method of lending to certain smaller and less creditworthy borrowers may no longer require a specialized intermediary as the sole lender to these borrowers, especially after recognizing the other expenses of using the intermediary.[15] For many institutional investors—such as mutual funds, pension funds, and insurance companies—the costs of being informed about certain borrowers have dropped enough that it has become profitable to acquire relatively small amounts of debt directly from those firms. As a result, firms that now issue their own low-grade bonds in the open market face a growing acceptance of their securities.

Risk Perceptions. A third explanation of the growth in low-grade bond offerings is more on the psychological side. Investors are not only better informed about the risks they take on, but they may have also become more willing to invest in risky securities. After the 1930s, the market for newly issued low-grade bonds shrank as most investors—with the losses incurred during the Depression still vividly in mind—turned to high-grade securities and left it to financial intermediaries to manage the risk of lending to less creditworthy borrowers. But as time passed and the memory of the 1930s faded, portfolio managers probably started to discount the proba-

---

[15]These added costs of using a financial intermediary instead of lending directly to a firm by buying its debt securities involve, for example, taxes, administration costs, and the costs of monitoring the condition and behavior of the intermediary.

bility that the economy would again become subject to a major system-wide shock.[16] It is thus possible that, as new generations of portfolio managers with no direct experience of the Depression took over, financial markets as a whole became more receptive to riskier securities, such as low-grade bonds.

SUMMARY

Low-grade bonds are bonds that are rated "speculative" by the major rating agencies and that are therefore considered very risky investments. These bonds are either corporate bonds that have been downgraded, or, more recently, bonds that are issued originally with a rating below investment grade. Original-issue low-grade bonds are issued mostly by corporations that previously borrowed in the form of commer-

cial loans or privately placed bonds.

Several factors seem to have contributed to the growth in low-grade bond offerings. For one, increased volatility in their sources of funds and a worsening of interest rate and credit risk have forced life insurance companies, which are the major buyers of private placements, to shift their investment focus towards assets that are somewhat more marketable and liquid, such as low-grade bonds. Also, improvements in computer technology have lowered the information and monitoring costs of investing in securities and have thus allowed smaller and less known corporations to borrow directly from private and institutional investors. Third, it may be that the favorable post-World War II default experience on low-grade bonds has made investors more receptive towards investing directly in riskier securities, including low-grade bonds.

The growth in low-grade bond offerings thus represents mostly a rechanneling of corporate borrowing, away from individually negotiated loans, towards public securities. As such, it exemplifies a continuing effort by financial market participants to search out the most cost-effective way to channel funds from lenders to borrowers.

---

[16]For a discussion of this type of behavior, see Jack Guttentag and Richard Herring, "Credit Rationing and Financial Disorder," *The Journal of Finance* (December 1984) pp. 1359-1382. As an example, the authors describe the behavior of a driver who has just witnessed a car accident. His immediate reaction is to drive much more cautiously. But gradually, as time passes and the image of the accident recedes from memory, the driver reverts to less cautious behavior.

Eurocommercial Paper and U.S. Commercial Paper: Converging Money Markets?

The showing of U.S. banks in securities markets abroad has influenced the debate over new powers for banks in the United States. Observers have for some time looked to the Euromarket as an appropriate laboratory for testing the performance of U.S. banks as underwriters. To some, the test results from Eurobond underwriting are positive: in 20 years of existence, with the important participation by U.S. banks, the Eurobond market has proven "orderly and efficient" and underwriters have not taken on excessive risks.[1] To others, the recent record of "huge losses" suggests the possibility of a "disaster" that might prove costly to the federal deposit insurance system.[2]

Attention is now shifting to the Eurocommercial paper (ECP) market because the power of the test provided by the Eurobond market has waned recently. In particular, U.S. banks have fallen in the ranks of Eurobond underwriters in the face of stiff competition from affiliates of Japanese securities firms and Continental banks. At the same time, after years of rapid growth, Eurobond issuance in 1987 is running well behind the 1986 pace. Some investors are avoiding the Eurobond market because of concern over market liquidity.

But even as they have ceded market share in Euro-bond underwriting, some U.S. banks have sought to establish themselves as dealers in the rapidly-growing market for short-term Euronotes or Eurocommercial paper. And the performance of U.S. banks in the ECP market, just as in the Eurobond market, can inform the current debate on bank powers.

There is a danger, however, that the debate will take the domestic and offshore paper markets to be basically identical. This article underscores the differences between the Eurocommercial paper market and the U.S. commercial paper (CP) market. We point to significant differences in credit assessment and quality, buyers, liquidity, clearing, and settlement, and we argue that these differences are unlikely to disappear.

Now is an opportune time to contrast and to compare the two markets. While the amount of commercial paper outstanding in London promises to double again in 1987 to over $60 billion,[3] structure and practice in the ECP market are becoming well established. If London is coming through a formative period, New York may be on the eve of a shake-up: banking powers may be expanded to allow bank underwriting of commercial paper.

Some differences between the two markets are likely to persist while others disappear. Ongoing differences include the following:

- Buyers of ECP, coming from a broad range of countries, draw credit distinctions but do not divide issuers consistently by nationality; U.S. investors

[1]Richard M. Levich, "The Experience with Unregulated Underwriting Activities in the Eurobond Market and Recent International Financial Market Innovations," testimony before the Senate Banking Committee, October 13, 1987; see also the same author's "A View from the International Capital Markets," in Ingo Walter, ed., *Deregulating Wall Street* (New York: Wiley, 1985), pp. 255-92.

[2]Testimony of Robert Gerard, Managing Director of Morgan Stanley and Company, before the Subcommittee on Telecommunications, Consumer Protection, and Finance of the House Committee on Energy and Commerce, October 14, 1987.

[3]For data on the growth of Europaper issuance, see "Statistics on Euronotes and Eurocommercial Paper," Bank of England *Quarterly Bulletin*, vol. 27 (November 1987), pp. 533-35.

in CP systematically require foreign issuers to offer higher yields than like-rated U.S. issuers.

- The distribution of U.S. issuers in the ECP market is of significantly lower quality than the distribution of U.S. issuers in the U.S. CP market; foreign issuers in the United States show a distribution of quality significantly better than that of U.S. issuers here.
- Central banks, corporations, and banks are important parts of the investor base for particular segments of the ECP market; the most important holders of U.S. CP, money market funds, are not very important abroad.
- The average maturity of ECP remains about twice as long as the average maturity of U.S. CP.
- ECP continues to be actively traded in the secondary market; most U.S. CP is held to maturity by the original investors.
- Issuing, clearance, and payment of ECP are more dispersed geographically and more time-consuming than those same processes for U.S. CP.

The following differences are likely to prove transitory:

- Dealing is very competitive in the Europaper market; just two firms deal half of dealer-placed U.S. CP.
- To date, all ECP has been placed by third parties; many U.S. CP issuers place paper directly with investors.
- Credit ratings are necessary in the domestic market; in the Euromarket they are common but not required.
- ECP has been and mostly continues to be priced in relation to bank deposit interest rates; pricing in the U.S. is based on absolute rates that vary in relation to rates on Treasury bills and bank certificates of deposit (CDs).

Permanent differences

The foreign premium

A cosmopolitan market, the ECP market brings together issuers and investors from a wide range of nations. Buyers and sellers in the U.S. market, by contrast, are overwhelmingly U.S.-based. Foreign banks, companies and sovereigns and their U.S. affiliates have issued only about one-tenth of outstanding U.S. CP (Chart 1).

Buyers in the U.S. CP market have exacted a yield premium from foreign issuers over like-rated U.S. issuers. The premium started at almost one-half of a percentage point in the mid-1970s and declined to around one-quarter by the early 1980s.[4] In the past year

[4]Marcia Stigum, The Money Market (Homewood, Illinois: Dow Jones-Irwin, 1983), p. 64.

it has reached eight to ten basis points.

The foreign premium in the U.S. CP market may be traced to restrictions on buying foreign paper, to the greater difficulty of analyzing foreign firms, and to differences in name recognition. Some investors are prohibited by articles of incorporation or by boards of directors from buying foreign-issued paper. Most foreign issuers of commercial paper have attempted to circumvent such restrictions by establishing financing corporations, frequently in Delaware.[5] But some investors abide by the spirit of such restrictions and even refrain from buying paper issued by U.S. subsidiaries of foreign entities. Other investors, including insurance companies, have internal limits on foreign assets that, defined broadly rather than legally, constrain their purchase of such paper.

A second source of the foreign premium is the difficulty faced by investors who must perform their own analysis of foreign issuers of paper. Accounting standards differ, disclosure requirements vary, and available information remains less accessible. While the rating

[5]See Peter V. Darrow and Michael Gruson, "Establishing a U.S. Commercial Paper Programme," International Financial Law Review, April 1985, pp. 8-12.

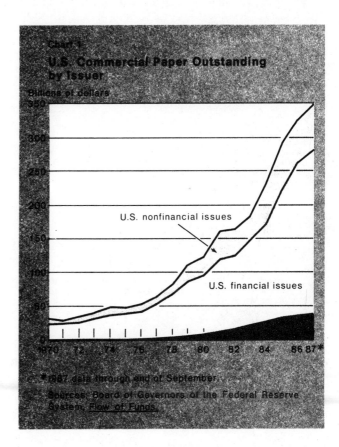

Chart 1
U.S. Commercial Paper Outstanding by Issuer

Billions of dollars

U.S. nonfinancial issues

U.S. financial issues

*1987 data through end of September.

Sources: Board of Governors of the Federal Reserve System, Flow of Funds.

agencies may be given access to information not publicly available, a buyer of foreign CP cannot easily form an independent judgment.

A final source of the foreign premium is lack of name recognition. Some investors in commercial paper emphasize liquidity and safety; if they are not effortlessly assured of both, they will not buy paper, even from a well-rated issuer.

Some of the same factors that created the foreign premium in the first instance help to account for its decline in recent years. As more information on foreign companies becomes available, paper buyers should require less of an inducement to buy foreign paper. Several forces have worked to increase information over the past twelve years. U.S. banks have widened their relationships with foreign corporations and have thereby given bank trust departments greater access to information on foreign borrowers. In addition, U.S. securities firms have stepped up research on foreign corporations in line with the growing investment by pension funds, mutual funds, and insurance companies in foreign equities. To serve these investors, some foreign firms issue English language annual reports. As for name recognition, the mere presence of Electricité de France in the U.S. CP market for over a dozen years should

have an effect.

Another development that has promoted acceptance of foreign names in the U.S. CP market and has helped to reduce the foreign premium is the rise of money market mutual funds (MMMFs) to their current status as the largest single type of CP buyer. The growth of MMMFs has in fact closely paralleled the decline of the foreign premium. MMMFs came out of nowhere in the mid-1970s to comprise a $292 billion portfolio at end-1986; the reduction in the foreign premium took place over the same period.

Although this coincidence suggests a link between the growth of MMMFs and the declining foreign premium, the demonstrated readiness of the funds to buy foreign CP provides more convincing evidence. An analysis of the top ten MMMF portfolios shows that, while they vary considerably in the weight given to foreign CP holdings, in aggregate, they do overweight foreign CP. That is, the top MMMFs have allocated 16 percent of their CP holdings to foreign CP (Table 1). This portfolio share stands quite a bit higher than the 10 percent share of foreign CP in the market as a whole. If the top ten funds, which have about half of all MMMF holdings of CP, are representative, MMMFs hold almost half the foreign CP outstanding, as against less than a third of

Table 1

The Holding of Foreign Commercial Paper by Top Ten Money Market Mutual Funds Investing in Commercial Paper*

	Total Assets	Total CP	Foreign CP	Foreign CP	
		(In Millions of Dollars)		As Percent of Assets	As Percent of Total CP
Merrill Lynch CMA Money Fund†	17,959	5,117	307	1.7	6.0
Merrill Lynch Ready Assets Trust‡	10,578	7,190	284	2.7	3.9
Dreyfus Liquid Assets§	7,235	1,497	1029	14.2	68.7
Dean Witter/Sears Liquid Asset Fund‖	6,869	3,646	25	0.4	0.7
Fidelity Cash Reserves¶	6,604	2,528	1309	19.8	51.8
Temporary Investment Fund**	5,782	5,541	129	2.2	2.3
Cash Equivalent Fund—Money Market Portfolio††	5,556	4,153	1540	27.7	37.1
Institutional Liquid Assets—Prime Portfolio‡‡	5,191	4,008	0	0.0	0.0
Prudential-Bache Moneymart Assets‡‡	4,308	2,653	520	12.1	19.6
Kemper Money Market Fund§§	4,174	3,862	1418	34.0	36.7
Total of top ten	74,256	40,195	6,561	8.8	16.3

* Two funds in the top ten, the Trust for Short-Term Government Securities and the Trust of U.S. Treasury Obligations, are specialized funds that invest only in specific government-backed paper.
† As of March 31, 1986.
‡ As of June 30, 1986.
§ As of March 12, 1986.
‖ As of February 28, 1986.
¶ As of November 30, 1986.
** As of September 30, 1986.
†† As of July 15, 1987.
‡‡ As of December 31, 1986.
§§ As of July 31, 1986.
Sources: Fund Annual and Semiannual Reports.

all CP outstanding. So it seems fair to conclude that the foreign premium fell as more money was channelled to money managers quite prepared to accept a foreign name.

It is understandable that managers of MMMFs have been more willing than the average CP buyer to buy the paper of foreign borrowers. Money fund managers are viewed as more aggressive in seeking yield than many CP buyers. A reason may be that MMMFs are compared and judged exclusively on the basis of their success in managing strictly short-term liquid funds. Managers of insurance companies, bank trust accounts or pension funds, by contrast, pay less attention to the allocation among money-market instruments than to the more consequential weighting of equities and bonds as against money in managed portfolios.

That some sensitivity to foreign paper remains among even MMMF managers is evident from the individual fund portfolio weights. Despite the premium, no MMMF held more than 69 percent of its total commercial paper as foreign CP. And only two funds had as much as one-half of their CP in foreign names. At the same time, the sixth-ranked fund, Goldman Sachs' Institutional Liquid Assets-Prime Portfolio, has virtually no foreign CP. In managing the top two funds, Merrill Lynch significantly underweights foreign CP. Thus, the two major dealers in U.S. CP both avoid foreign CP in managing their institutional and individual money funds.

Credit quality

Starting with Electricité de France in 1974, relatively high quality foreign corporations first entered the New York CP market in search of a wider investment base and better pricing. To this day, foreign issuers in the U.S. market still have a significantly better distribution of ratings than U.S. issuers in the U.S. market.

Consequently, it would be natural to assume that high quality U.S. names predominate in the ECP market. After all, the Eurobond market has for years skimmed the cream of U.S. borrowers.[6] In fact, in contrast to the Eurobond market, the ECP market takes only the milk. U.S. issuers in the Euromarket have a significantly worse distribution of ratings than all U.S. issuers in the U.S. CP market.

The contrasting behavior of New York and London provides clues to the development of the ECP market. Since top-rated European corporations always paid more in the U.S. CP market than top-rated U.S. borrowers, they were quick to seize the opportunity offered by the emerging ECP market. This step allowed them to sell paper at or below the London interbank rates in 1985

as those rates fell toward U.S. CP rates.[7] As a consequence, non-U.S. names in the ECP market tended to be among the best. But the first U.S. issuers in London included electric utilities with unfinished or unlicensed nuclear power plants that had found it hard to obtain credit in the United States but found willing lenders in banks across the Atlantic.

Looked at superficially, the ratings of issuers of ECP appear better than those of CP issuers. A statistical comparison[8] of the distribution of ratings of all rated issuers in the CP market to the distribution of ratings in Europe appears to confirm that a better cut of borrowers sells ECP (Table 2).[9] But there is an adverse selection problem: high quality European borrowers may disproportionately pay the cost of recasting their accounts, meeting with the raters and paying for the ratings. Thus, that unrated issuers in Europe are generally worse credits than the rated invalidates the comparison to the U.S. CP market, where all issuers are rated.

More revealing is the comparison of non-U.S. borrowers in the U.S. CP market to U.S. names in the same market (Table 3). Non-U.S. CP issuers exhibit a significantly better distribution of ratings than native issuers. In particular, over 70 percent of the foreign firms have the highest paper rating while less than half the U.S. issuers do.

This skewed distribution is caused by the foreign premium. This has kept most good-quality, as distinct from top-quality, non-U.S. credits out of the U.S. market. The distribution of the foreign names in the U.S. CP market is truncated: since merely good-quality foreign names are treated like medium-quality U.S. names, the former do not go through the expense to enter the market. By contrast, no set of borrowers is consistently foreign to the purchasers of ECP.

Also revealing is the comparison of U.S. names in the Euronote/ECP market and the distribution of U.S. CP

---

[7]For a discussion of cross-market arbitrage opportunities for U.S. issuers, see Rodney H. Mills, "Euro-Commercial Paper Begins to Compete," *Euromoney*, February 1987, pp. 23-24. The foreign premium renders the ECP market more competitive than Mills reckons.

[8]The statistical test used here and throughout this article is the chi-square test. It determines whether factors—credit quality and nationality of issuer or market of issue—covary. It tests whether the distribution of observations is what one would expect knowing only the marginal totals or whether knowing one factor helps predict the other. In this case, a chi-square statistic comparing ECP issuers to U.S. CP issuers was computed. It allowed us to reject the null hypothesis that the rating of the firm and the market in which it is issuing are independent. The probability of error of the test is less than 0.01.

[9]Note the existence of "junk" CP, rated B and C. Issuers in these rating categories are regarded as having only adequate or doubtful capability for payment on maturity of the paper.

[6]See Hendrick J. Kranenburg, "Reaching for 'Quality' Debt," Standard and Poor's *Credit Week International*, Fourth Quarter 1984, pp. 11, 16.

Table 2

Ratings of U.S. and Eurocommercial Paper Issuers*
December 1986

	A-1 +	A-1	A-2	A-3	B	C	Total	Percent
U.S. CP issuers	529	301	184	12	2	7	1035	93.2
Eurocommercial paper issuers†	47	16	12	1	0	0	76	6.8
Total	576	317	196	13	2	7	1111	—
Percent	51.8	28.5	17.6	1.2	0.2	0.6	—	—

*The commerical paper ratings used here consist of three categories, ranging from 'A' for the highest quality obligations to 'C' for the lowest. The 'A' category is refined into four subcategories, ranging from 'A1 +' for the highest to 'A-3' for the lowest. The universe of U.S. CP issuers excludes those whose credit is supported by bank letters of credit and similar guarantees.

†The ECP sample contains only active programs. Where no ECP rating was available, the U.S. CP rating was substituted.

Computed chi-square statistic: 194.2 (5 degrees of freedom). A statistic in excess of 15.086 allows the rejection of the null hypothesis that the rating of the issuer and the market in which it is issuing are independent factors with a probability of error less than 0.01.

Sources: U.S.: Standard & Poor's *Commercial Paper Ratings Guide.*
Euro: List of active programs was obtained from major market makers.

issuers from which they were selected. U.S. issuers abroad are not representative of the run of U.S. credits in the U.S. CP market (Table 4). U.S. issuers of ECP show a significantly lower distribution of ratings than U.S. CP issuers.

An explanation of this finding may lie in the importance of banks as buyers of less than prime paper in the Euromarket. Some banks take the time to perform their own credit assessment; less careful ones take comfort in the size of a U.S. corporation or familiarity with its name. In addition, unlike many buyers of U.S. CP, few buyers of ECP are required to expose their portfolios to public scrutiny.

A comparison of ECP issuance by the finance companies of General Motors, Ford, and Chrysler supports the conclusion drawn from the distribution of ratings at a point in time. A2/P2-rated Chrysler Financial Corporation started selling ECP as early as 1984, and is one of the largest ECP issuers. A1+/P1-rated General

Table 3

Ratings of U.S. Commercial Paper Issuers
December 1986

	A-1 +	A-1	A-2	A-3	Total	Percent
U.S. issuers	391	249	182	12	834	81.3
Non-U.S. issuers	138	52	2	0	192	18.7
Total	529	301	184	12	1026	—
Percent	51.6	29.3	17.9	1.2	—	—

Computed chi-quare statistic: 5194.2 (3 degrees of freedom). A statistic in excess of 11.341 allows the rejection of the null hypothesis that the rating of the issuer and its nationality are independent factors with a probability of error less than 0.01.

Source: U.S.: Standard & Poor's *Commercial Paper Ratings Guide.*

Table 4

Ratings of U.S. Issuers of Eurocommercial and U.S. Commercial Paper
December 1986

	A-1 +	A-1	A-2	A-3	Total	Percent
U.S. market	391	249	182	12	834	96.9
Euro-market*	8	6	12	1	27	3.1
Total	399	255	194	13	861	—
Percent	46.3	29.6	22.5	1.5	—	—

*The ECP sample contains only active programs. Where no ECP rating was available, the U.S. CP rating was substituted.

Computed chi-square statistic: 119.4 (3 degrees of freedom). A statistic in excess of 11.341 allows the rejection of the null hypothesis that the rating of the issuer and the market in which it issues are independent factors with a probability of error less than 0.01.

Sources: U.S.: Standard & Poor's *Commercial Paper Ratings Guide.*
Euro: List of active programs was obtained from major market makers.

Motors Acceptance Corporation (GMAC) and Ford Motor Credit only started selling ECP in 1986, and outstanding ECP by each has not generally matched that of Chrysler.

That some issuers sell paper without credit enhancement in London but with a guarantee in New York gives further evidence of the quality difference between the markets. For example, buyers of the obligations of the Australian natural resource companies Comalco and CRA in London accept their credit risk, but buyers of the same firms' U.S. commercial paper look to the banks that have written letters of credit as the ultimate obligors.

Investor base

The role of central banks and commercial banks as investors in ECP distinguishes the market from the U.S. CP market. Central banks investing their dollar reserves in a substitute for U.S. Treasury bills or bank CDs have come to dominate one whole segment of the ECP market. It is difficult to know precisely how much ECP commercial banks buy for their own account, since they also buy for their trust accounts and for distribution to their institutional and individual clients. But it is clear that banks take a considerable share of ECP onto their books, although it is also clear that this share has fallen in 1987. By contrast, banks in the United States buy little CP for their own accounts. Also distinguishing the European markets is the very small representation of money funds in Europe; their U.S. counterparts are the largest investors in U.S. CP.

The buyers of ECP differ among the four distinct ECP issuer classes: sovereigns, top-quality corporates, prime corporates and the rest. In the market for high-quality sovereign paper, central banks account for most of the demand, perhaps 80 percent. The rest is split between fund managers and market makers.

Top quality corporate paper, rated A1+/P1, is bought by fund managers and other corporations. Fund managers include managers of pension funds, bank trusts, and insurance companies. Prime quality paper, rated A1/P1, is bought not only by fund managers and corporations but also by financial institutions, mostly banks. The rest of investment grade paper, rated A2/P2, and unrated paper are bought largely by banks.

The quality spectrum corresponds to the pricing spectrum. Sovereign ECP yields the London Interbank Bid Rate (LIBID) less 10 to 25 basis points; A1+/P1 corporate and bank paper yields a bit below LIBID, in general, and rarely above it; A1/P1 paper yields range from LIBID to midway between the interbank bid and offer range rates (usually LIBID plus 6.25 basis points); and A2/P2 paper and unrated paper yield from just below the offered rate, LIBOR, to well above LIBOR.

Banks' own funding costs incline them to buy the less-than-prime ECP. Since most banks can fund themselves only at LIBID or perhaps a bit less, they cannot make money holding A1+/P1 paper. Of course, with overnight or weekly rates lower than three- or six-month rates, banks can add a funding spread to the slim intermediation spread by funding their purchases of longer-maturity ECP with shorter-maturity money, but thereby they expose themselves to interest rate risk.

Maturity

Most ECP matures in 60 to 180 days; most U.S. CP matures in less than 60 days. From the perspective of the Euromarket, this difference may partly reflect the emergence of ECP from the note issuance facility market and, more generally, from syndicated loans. Instead of borrowing from banks that in turn sell CDs to fund loans, ECP issuers offer paper of like maturity directly to investors. From the U.S. perspective, the maturity difference reflects the fact that the U.S. market caters to entities such as automobile finance companies and credit card affiliates of banks that must manage shorter, more predictable cash flow schedules. The well-developed secondary market in ECP makes it difficult to explain the difference from the buyer's side. Secondary market activity suggests that the average holding period of ECP is roughly half of its maturity.

Secondary market

Partly as a result of the maturity difference, the ECP market has an active secondary market, with weekly turnover in a range of 40 to 60 percent of total ECP turnover (Chart 2). As the market has matured, secondary trading has tended to fall in relation to primary market turnover. Formerly, banks with little placing power bid aggressively for paper to impress borrowers, only to dump it into the secondary market. But such behavior neither earned money nor, ultimately, won over issuers. Many borrowers do not like the loss of control over pricing that secondary market trading can bring. And so great is competition in the market that dealers will sometimes report to an issuer another dealer's disposal of recently issued paper in the secondary market.

There is some evidence that the secondary market turnover increases in relative terms when interest rates are falling (Chart 3). Most recently, as interest rates have risen, the secondary market turnover has dropped. Consistent with this pattern is the tendency of market makers and bank treasuries that actively manage their ECP portfolios to buy more paper when interest rates decline and profits can be earned by funding three-month paper with money borrowed overnight.

Motors Acceptance Corporation (GMAC) and Ford Motor Credit only started selling ECP in 1986, and outstanding ECP by each has not generally matched that of Chrysler.

That some issuers sell paper without credit enhancement in London but with a guarantee in New York gives further evidence of the quality difference between the markets. For example, buyers of the obligations of the Australian natural resource companies Comalco and CRA in London accept their credit risk, but buyers of the same firms' U.S. commercial paper look to the banks that have written letters of credit as the ultimate obligors.

Investor base

The role of central banks and commercial banks as investors in ECP distinguishes the market from the U.S. CP market. Central banks investing their dollar reserves in a substitute for U.S. Treasury bills or bank CDs have come to dominate one whole segment of the ECP market. It is difficult to know precisely how much ECP commercial banks buy for their own account, since they also buy for their trust accounts and for distribution to their institutional and individual clients. But it is clear that banks take a considerable share of ECP onto their books, although it is also clear that this share has fallen in 1987. By contrast, banks in the United States buy little CP for their own accounts. Also distinguishing the European markets is the very small representation of money funds in Europe; their U.S. counterparts are the largest investors in U.S. CP.

The buyers of ECP differ among the four distinct ECP issuer classes: sovereigns, top-quality corporates, prime corporates and the rest. In the market for high-quality sovereign paper, central banks account for most of the demand, perhaps 80 percent. The rest is split between fund managers and market makers.

Top quality corporate paper, rated A1+/P1, is bought by fund managers and other corporations. Fund managers include managers of pension funds, bank trusts, and insurance companies. Prime quality paper, rated A1/P1, is bought not only by fund managers and corporations but also by financial institutions, mostly banks. The rest of investment grade paper, rated A2/P2, and unrated paper are bought largely by banks.

The quality spectrum corresponds to the pricing spectrum. Sovereign ECP yields the London Interbank Bid Rate (LIBID) less 10 to 25 basis points; A1+/P1 corporate and bank paper yields a bit below LIBID, in general, and rarely above it; A1/P1 paper yields range from LIBID to midway between the interbank bid and offer range rates (usually LIBID plus 6.25 basis points); and A2/P2 paper and unrated paper yield from just below the offered rate, LIBOR, to well above LIBOR.

Banks' own funding costs incline them to buy the less-than-prime ECP. Since most banks can fund themselves only at LIBID or perhaps a bit less, they cannot make money holding A1+/P1 paper. Of course, with overnight or weekly rates lower than three- or six-month rates, banks can add a funding spread to the slim intermediation spread by funding their purchases of longer-maturity ECP with shorter-maturity money, but thereby they expose themselves to interest rate risk.

Maturity

Most ECP matures in 60 to 180 days; most U.S. CP matures in less than 60 days. From the perspective of the Euromarket, this difference may partly reflect the emergence of ECP from the note issuance facility market and, more generally, from syndicated loans. Instead of borrowing from banks that in turn sell CDs to fund loans, ECP issuers offer paper of like maturity directly to investors. From the U.S. perspective, the maturity difference reflects the fact that the U.S. market caters to entities such as automobile finance companies and credit card affiliates of banks that must manage shorter, more predictable cash flow schedules. The well-developed secondary market in ECP makes it difficult to explain the difference from the buyer's side. Secondary market activity suggests that the average holding period of ECP is roughly half of its maturity.

Secondary market

Partly as a result of the maturity difference, the ECP market has an active secondary market, with weekly turnover in a range of 40 to 60 percent of total ECP turnover (Chart 2). As the market has matured, secondary trading has tended to fall in relation to primary market turnover. Formerly, banks with little placing power bid aggressively for paper to impress borrowers, only to dump it into the secondary market. But such behavior neither earned money nor, ultimately, won over issuers. Many borrowers do not like the loss of control over pricing that secondary market trading can bring. And so great is competition in the market that dealers will sometimes report to an issuer another dealer's disposal of recently issued paper in the secondary market.

There is some evidence that the secondary market turnover increases in relative terms when interest rates are falling (Chart 3). Most recently, as interest rates have risen, the secondary market turnover has dropped. Consistent with this pattern is the tendency of market makers and bank treasuries that actively manage their ECP portfolios to buy more paper when interest rates decline and profits can be earned by funding three-month paper with money borrowed overnight.

Goldman Sachs.[11] Merrill Lynch officials lay claim to leadership among U.S. dealers, with a market share just short of 30 percent.[12] Merrill's acquisition of A. G. Becker from Paribas in 1984 put it into position to overtake Goldman.

The degree of concentration is much lower in the Euromarket. Estimates vary widely on market shares in the amount of paper issued, but the consensus is that the top six dealers place somewhere around 70 to 75 percent of ECP by value. No dealer can credibly claim a market share much in excess of 20 percent. In terms of number of dealerships for both ECP and Eurodollar certificates of deposit, the top six dealers share less than 50 percent of the market.[13] By either measure, ECP dealing is less concentrated than CP dealing.

The entry of U.S. banks into the U.S. CP market is sharpening competition. Thus far they have acted only as placing agents, finding buyers for CP without buying the paper themselves. But despite their restricted role as agents, banks are seeking to prove themselves reliable placers, at times offering paper to investors at a favorable, slightly higher yield to ensure its sale. At the same time, by charging a very modest placing fee, the banks raise funds for the issuer at a favorable, slightly lower net cost of funds. By early 1987, U.S. banks served as exclusive placers of CP for 65 issuers with over $7 billion in paper outstanding. They shared placing in 70 other programs with over $19 billion outstanding.[14] While these figures indicate a market share for all U.S. banks of about 5 percent or more, they do suggest some measure of success in entry despite ongoing legal restrictions on underwriting. Citicorp's purchase in November 1987 of Paine Webber's CP operation, with paper outstanding in the amount of about $3 billion under about 40 programs, adds clout to an already sizable placer.

In addition, foreign securities firms are entering the U.S. CP market as dealers for foreign issuers. In late 1986, U.S. affiliates of foreign securities firms, mostly Canadian and Japanese, shared placing in 25 programs with approximately $5 billion outstanding. The foreign-based securities firms uniformly deal in paper of borrowers from their home country, probably because long-standing relations incline the borrowers to give their dealers an opening. It should be noted, however, that none of the foreign securities dealers serves as a sole placer of U.S. CP.

The competitive challenge in U.S. CP has led a market leader to change a long-held business policy in favor of practice typical of the ECP market. Heretofore Goldman Sachs insisted on a company's sole use of Goldman to place the company's CP. Now, Goldman is prepared to play co-dealer, particularly on large paper programs where the firm has not played a role to date.[15] Although the previous policy might have spurred the dealer to win wide acceptance of an issuer's paper in order to capture all the business so generated, issuers now seem keen to encourage more direct competition.

While U.S. banks have entered the business of placing CP in New York, a U.S. bank ranks among the top ECP dealers in London. It is generally acknowledged that Citicorp Investment Bank, Limited leads its competitors in the amount of paper placed, although the market share it claims is much disputed. Other leaders are the affiliates of U.S. securities firms—Merrill Lynch, Morgan Stanley, and Shearson Lehman—Swiss Banking Corporation International, and the U.S.-Swiss hybrid Credit Suisse First Boston. Each of these six probably enjoys a market share between 10 and 20 percent. All are trying to secure their positions before Japanese institutions enter the market.

The superior performance of Citicorp Investment Bank, Limited in the ECP market is attributable in part to its strength in a traditional banking activity. Most observers credit its leadership to its mixing dollar paper with forward sales of dollars against a variety of currencies to create "cocktail" paper. In effect, buyers of such mixtures get CP in their currency of choice, although they also expose themselves to Citicorp on the forward transaction.

Other U.S. banks are making serious, if less successful, efforts to compete in ECP dealing. U.S. banks represent no less than 8 of the 20 top dealers of ECP and Euro-CDs. Taken together, U.S. banks probably have carved out a market share of a quarter or more. The resources devoted by U.S. banks to the ECP market must be understood in light of their overall investment banking strategies and, in particular, their

[11]Moody's *Short-Term Market Record;* Standard and Poor's *Commercial Paper Rating Guide.* The Federal Reserve Board, noting the concentration of dealerships in the U.S. CP market, adduced the public benefit of fostering competition in explaining its decisions to permit banks to place and to deal in U.S. CP. See "Bankers Trust New York Corporation," and "Citicorp, J.P. Morgan & Co, Incorporated, Bankers Trust New York Corporation," *Federal Reserve Bulletin,* vol. 73 (February 1987 and June 1987), pp. 148 and 490. For a review of the Federal Reserve rulings, see Terrance W. Schwab and Bernard J. Karol, "Underwriting by Bank Affiliates," *Review of Financial Services Regulation,* vol. 3 (May 20, 1987), pp. 93–100.

[12]In computing Merrill's market share, the official excluded paper issued by dealers on behalf of their own affiliates to eliminate the effect of Merrill's sizable fund-raising. See Tom Herman, "Goldman Sachs Abandons Policy It Says Hurt Growth in Commercial Paper Field," *Wall Street Journal,* October 2, 1987, p. 29.

[13]*International Financing Review,* July 4, 1987, p. 2202.

[14]Moody's *Short-Term Market Record;* Standard and Poor's *Commercial Paper Rating Guide.*

[15]Tom Herman, "Goldman Sachs Abandons Policy."

interest in demonstrating the inappropriateness of Glass-Steagall restrictions.

Greater competition among dealers in the ECP market brings lower prices for their services. U.S. CP dealers used to collect a fee of one-eighth of a percent for buying paper from the issuer and reselling it or, failing that, taking any unsold paper into position. This fee works out to $3.47 per million dollars per day until maturity at issue.[16] More recently, fees have fallen to around ten basis points or even lower. In the Euromarket, the spread between what dealers pay for ECP and sell it for averages three basis points. This spread works out to only $75 for placing $1 million of 90-day paper. When working as agents for some high-quality issuers who do not want anyone but end-investors to own their paper, ECP placers also make a commission of less than five basis points. Little money is being made at these rates. And some dealers have accepted paper at rates lower than they can place it, to gain market share.

Such intense competition for market share may suggest that a great deal of money is at stake. It appears, however, that dealing dollar CP in New York and London produces only modest revenues. If dealing in the U.S. fetches ten basis points per year on placements of $180 billion, only $180 million is earned. If dealing generates three basis points on the roughly $50 billion outstanding in London, only $15 million is at stake, matched, perhaps, by another $10 million in the secondary market. These are estimates of gross revenue out of which overhead and expense must be paid. Only very rapid growth of these markets can justify the resources that financial firms are devoting to them.

The entry of foreign securities firms and U.S. banks as dealers will make the U.S. CP market increasingly competitive. It was this prospect that prompted the exit in October 1987 of Salomon Brothers from the U.S. CP market, where it had achieved a market share in excess of 10 percent. The outlook for the rapidly growing ECP market is less certain: the current competitiveness of the market may continue if heavier future volume is spread out over the current dealing capacity, or it may end in a shake-out that would remove some capacity. Already in 1987, J.H. Shroder Wagg and Salomon Brothers have withdrawn from the ECP market. The more heterogeneous investor base in the ECP market may leave room for more players. In any case, it is likely that the U.S. CP and ECP markets will converge somewhat in the competitive structure of dealing.

Direct issuance
Changes in the degree of concentration of dealers in

the two markets may reduce another market difference: the fact that no Europaper issuer issues directly. In the United States, finance companies, representing a substantial share of the market, place their own paper directly with investors (Chart 4); in the smaller, less developed Euromarket, no issuer has yet found it worthwhile to bypass the dealers.

Note that foreign issuers in the U.S. CP market, even those with large and long-standing programs, do not directly place paper. It appears that U.S. buyers demand that dealers sell them the paper. The reason usually given is the desire for the monitoring of the more remote borrower's credit standing by the dealer. For direct issuance to take hold in the Euromarket, the buyer of the paper must not make a similar demand for dealers to monitor the credit of foreign borrowers.

A direct issuer of CP in the U.S. essentially replaces the dealer on commission with in-house dealers. Dealer fees of about one-eighth of a percent can exceed the cost of hiring a full-time staff to manage a program, provided that outstandings are sufficiently large, normally in the $200-250 million range. Thus the concentration of dealers in U.S. CP does not necessarily mean that they have a hold on the business and can exact

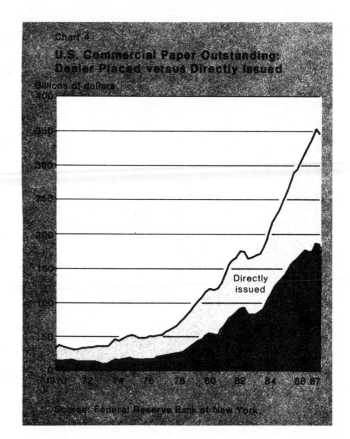

Chart 4
U.S. Commercial Paper Outstanding:
Dealer Placed versus Directly Issued
Billions of dollars

Directly issued

Source: Federal Reserve Bank of New York.

---

[16]Stigum, p. 639.

oligopolistic returns. CP dealers face a potential competitor in each customer.

The U.S. CP market looks much less concentrated if the relevant market is taken to be the CP market as a whole rather than dealer-placed CP. Merrill Lynch and Goldman Sachs together place little more than a quarter of *all* U.S. CP. The fourth-ranked placer is the first-ranked direct issuer, GMAC, with about a 10 percent market share. As a group the top four placers share well less than half the market. On this showing, the U.S. CP market looks much more competitive.

It is reasonable to take the whole CP market as the relevant market for the assessment of concentration even though direct issuance cannot substitute perfectly for hiring a dealer. A direct issuer performs most of the functions that a dealer performs: making arrangements with buyers, assessing the market, posting rates, and closing sales. The direct issuer must set up dealers in a dealing room and buy telephones and screens. The direct issuer cannot, however, free himself of the risk that paper may not be sold in the desired quantity at the posted rates. Still, the direct issuer may fund the shortfall in much the same way that the dealer would fund an overnight CP position, with repos or same-day bank credit. On balance, direct issuance substitutes closely for hiring a dealer; therefore, it makes sense to measure concentration in terms of the CP market as a whole.

Sharpened competition that drives down dealers' fees may over time shift the composition of U.S. CP to more dealer-placed paper. With lower fees, the threshold amount that an issuer must sell regularly before it can break even issuing directly should rise. Over time, one would expect the share of paper directly placed to fall.

Since dealer fees in Europe are currently less than half those in the United States, outstandings of perhaps $1 billion would be required before savings on dealer fees would outweigh direct issuance costs. At this point, even Chrysler generally has less than that amount of ECP outstanding. Again, the more heterogeneous nature of the investor base for ECP may raise the threshold for an issuer to internalize the dealing function. But as the market grows, it seems safe to anticipate the appearance of direct placement in the Euromarket, especially if the exit of current dealers or other factors should cause dealer fees to rise.

Importance of credit ratings

Euromarket practice should converge to U.S. market practice in requiring paper to be rated. Only about 45 percent of active ECP issuers at end-1986 were rated, while credit ratings are ubiquitous in the United States. There are two plausible explanations for this difference. First, Euromarket investors generally have not relied on

credit agencies and their ratings. This year, an agency called EuroRatings was set up by Fitch Investors Service and Compagnie Belge d'Assurance Credit to serve the Euromarket exclusively. As of September, 1987, EuroRatings advertises 67 short-term ratios, of which 9 are for U.S. firms. By contrast, buyers of U.S. corporate debt have consulted credit ratings for generations. In the United States, regulation has reinforced tradition: prime quality paper, distinguished by a high rating, need not be registered with the Securities and Exchange Commission.[17] Second, borrowers in the Euromarket have not encountered severe liquidity problems or defaulted on their paper. It was only in the wake of the largest shock to the U.S. CP market, Penn Central's default on $82 million of outstanding paper, that multiple ratings became as widespread in the United States as they are today.[18] But even though Europe has not witnessed such an episode, ratings are becoming more important there as well, as investors become accustomed to the concept.

Tough competition among paper dealers is paralleled by competition among raters. While the third-ranked U.S. CP rater, Fitch, has teamed up with a European partner, the two major raters in the United States have both adopted strategies to establish their position in the Euromarket. Standard and Poor charges an entity with a U.S. rating only $5000 for an ECP rating on top of the $25,000 annual U.S. fee. Moody's has gone a step further by making its CP ratings global paper ratings, applicable in any market or currency.

Increasing reliance by Euromarket investors on ratings will undermine the distinction between ECP and Euronotes. Euronotes are said to be underwritten, meaning that the contract governing their issuance also contains an undertaking by a group of banks to buy the paper in the event that it cannot be sold at a yield less than LIBOR plus an agreed spread. For years, however, the U.S. rating firms have required that an issuer of commercial paper have sufficient access to bank credit to repay maturing paper in the event that new paper could not be sold. So rated issuers of ECP must have access to bank credit, even if that access is not contractually bundled with the paper issuance. A rating thus substitutes for an announced, "underwritten" program of paper issuance, and ratings have gained in Europe even as the announcement of Euronote programs has fallen off.

[17]Low-rated paper is issued under the private placement exemption that restricts sales to a limited number of sophisticated investors, at the cost of market width and higher yields. See Darrow and Grusen, "Establishing a U.S. Commercial Paper Programme," pp. 10-11.

[18]See Thomas M. Timlen, "Commercial Paper—Penn Central and Others," in Edward I. Altman and Arnold W. Sametz, eds., *Financial Crises: Institutions and Markets in a Fragile Environment* (New York: John Wiley, 1977), pp. 220-25.

Pricing base

Pricing differences between the two markets persist but are showing signs of erosion. CP dealers in the U.S. market post absolute rates, while the Euromarket has traditionally based pricing on LIBID or LIBOR, plus or minus a spread. Specifically, a rise in the yield spread between U.S. Treasury bills and Eurodollars would lead ECP rates to rise with the Eurodollar rates one-for-one. U.S. CP rates, by contrast, vary with respect to both Treasury bill rates and Eurodollar rates and generally split the difference when the latter two diverge.[19]

But yields on some ECP, that issued by sovereigns, have developed in 1987 a noticeable independence from bank deposit rates. At the beginning of the year, dollar paper for Sweden and Spain gave a return to investors generally 0-10 basis points below the bid rate for Eurodollar deposits with banks (Chart 5). In the spring the Treasury cut back on its issuance of Treasury bills in response to unanticipated tax revenue and recurring approaches to the legislated debt limit. Reduced supply met an increased demand, as central banks sought to invest reserves acquired in support of the dollar, and, consequently, Treasury bill rates hardly rose as three-month Eurodollar rates rose through 7 percent in April. Sovereign ECP rates, however, did not quite rise in step with bank deposit rates. In late April and early May, sovereign ECP offered investors 10-20 basis points less than Eurodollar deposits in banks. When Treasury bill rates rose in late July and Eurodollar rates remained steady, the difference between the yields of sovereign ECP and bank deposits narrowed again.

Sovereign ECP yields thus stray from Eurodollar deposit rates to stay closer to Treasury bill rates when the Treasury and Eurodollar rates diverge; ECP yields approach Eurodollar deposit rates when Treasury and Eurodollar rates converge. When the Treasury-Eurodollar spread has been less than 100 basis points this year through September, the Kingdom of Sweden's ECP has yielded an average of about 5 basis points less than LIBID; when the Treasury-Eurodollar spread has reached over 100 basis points, Sweden's ECP has yielded an average of 14 basis points less.

The investment behavior of central banks lies behind these changing rate relations. Formerly, U.S. CP sold by either French state corporations or banks with a government guarantee competed with U.S. Treasury bills in offering sovereign risk on dollar paper. Now central banks can spread their dollars across paper issued by or guaranteed by most of the governments of Western Europe. By investing in sovereign ECP, central banks can pick up more than 100 basis points while sacrificing

[19]See Nancy J. Kimmelman and Gioia M. Parente, "The TED Spread—Outlook and Implications," Salomon Brothers Bond Market Research Memorandum, July 15, 1987.

liquidity only modestly: for this reason, such investments are becoming increasingly common.

The pricing of other ECP has not similarly diverged from interbank rates. The ECP yield index that the Bank of England has published just since late August 1987 shows little independence of ECP rates. In particular, the rates published for three-month ECP prime corporate and bank holding company borrowers range narrowly from 0-3 basis points above the London Interbank Bid Rate.

Convergence of rates in the two markets would require ECP rates to fall relative to Eurodollar bank deposit rates. Alternatively, U.S. CP rates could rise relative to domestic bank CD rates. Indeed, with heavy

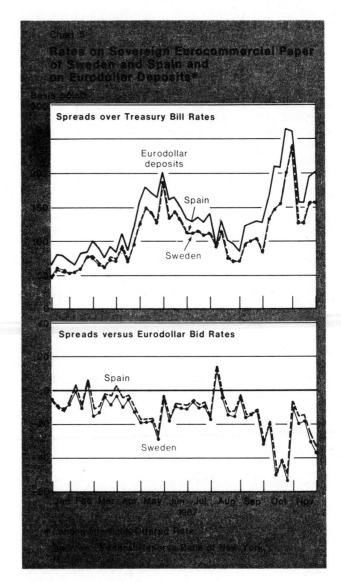

Chart 5
Rates on Sovereign Eurocommercial Paper of Sweden and Spain and on Eurodollar Deposits*

issuance of CP, CP rates have approached and sometimes have exceeded domestic CD rates. But since a domestic reserve requirement and a Federal Deposit Insurance Corporation insurance premium drive a wedge of 30 basis points or so between domestic bank rates and Eurodollar deposit rates, considerable distance still generally separates pricing in the two markets, especially for direct issuers in the U.S. market.[20] The experience of GMAC, which has not been able to maintain $1 billion of ECP outstanding at prices no higher than at home, underscores this point. Along the way to convergence, foreign issuers could be expected to exit from the U.S. market, given the foreign premium. Thus, convergence of rates might well be associated with greater specialization by nationality of issuance in the two markets.

Conclusion

This article argues that the Eurocommercial paper market and the U.S. commercial paper market are likely to continue to differ in some important respects. In particular, the U.S. market will probably remain less cosmopolitan than the ECP market, requiring foreign issuers to pay a higher interest rate than U.S. issuers of like quality. As a consequence of the diminished but persistent foreign premium in the U.S. market, the U.S. market funds a prime selection of foreign credits. Conversely, the less quality-conscious ECP market offers funds to a distribution of U.S. borrowers of lower quality than the general run of U.S. issuers of CP. In addition, the ECP market is likely to remain a market for longer-maturity paper with much greater reliance on secondary market trading to provide liquidity. Issuance, clearance

and settlement of ECP span half the globe and take two days while these same processes in the U.S. CP market are carried out in one city in the course of a day.

Other differences are likely to prove transitory. Although dealing in ECP appears much more competitive than dealing in U.S. CP, the entry of U.S. banks serving as placing agents and of foreign securities firms is increasing competition among U.S. dealers in New York. And if direct issuers are recognized as competitors of U.S. securities firms, the market appears even more competitive. In addition, ratings are likely to become as necessary in Europe as they are in the United States. Finally, both pricing methods and levels are likely to converge in the two markets, although this convergence may coincide with greater segmentation by nationality of issuers in the two markets.

Out of these differences come three useful points for the ongoing debate over banks' underwriting in the U.S. CP market. First, dealing in the U.S. CP market is less competitive than dealing in ECP, but the difference is both easy to overstate and already narrowing. Second, foreign issuers of U.S. CP and smaller U.S. firms that do not have programs large enough to warrant direct issuance would be the principal beneficiaries of further competition and lower dealing rates in the United States. Third, since the total revenues at stake, particularly in the competitive circumstances characteristic of the ECP market, do not seem large, only explosive growth of CP issuance would make the policy question at hand decisive for commercial bank revenues or profitability.

---

[20]See Lawrence L. Kreicher, "Eurodollar Arbitrage," this *Quarterly Review*, Summer 1982, pp.10-21.

Robert N. McCauley
Lauren A. Hargraves

Part Five

_____

International Finance

The operations of financial institutions and markets have increasingly become international. Large commercial banks operate multinationally and frequently have larger amounts of deposits and loans in foreign countries than in their home countries. Often large financial service organizations, especially securities-related and insurance firms, operate globally. Moreover, money and capital market instruments trade throughout the world. Twenty-four hour continuous trading of financial instruments in Tokyo, London, New York, and other major markets is fast becoming the norm.

Each of the five articles in this section deals with some important aspect of the international dimensions of financial markets and institutions. While this section is exclusively devoted to the international aspect of financial markets and institutions, there are a number of other articles in this book that also relate to international finance. For example, in Part One, "The Risk-Based Capital Agreement: A Further Step towards Policy Convergence," discusses the actions by the major central banks to develop a uniform set of capital requirements for the principal multinational banks. Similarly, in Part Three, "Interest Rate Divergences among the Major Industrial Nations," has an international perspective. This illustrates the fact that the separation and compartmentalization of international finance within a treatment of financial institutions and markets is now possible only from an organizational perspective.

The first article in this section, "Europe 1992: Implications for U.S. Firms" by Thomas Bennett and Craig Hakkio, discusses the potential significance of the proposed integration of major European markets in 1992. Perhaps one of the most significant economic events of recent history, the establishment of a single market encompassing 12 separate nations with a total population exceeding 300 billion people should produce significant benefits for consumers in those nations. However, while some firms will benefit, others will be harmed. The effects on U.S. commercial banks operating in Europe are particularly important and are discussed.

The second article, "International Policy Cooperation: Building a Sound Foundation," by Brian Cody is closely related to the first. The integration of markets for goods among nations and the growing integration of financial markets makes it more important for policymakers to coordinate their macroeconomic policies. Cody discusses the significance of such coordination and the steps that various nations have taken toward that goal.

International integration of markets requires the dismantling of barriers to trade. The reduction and ultimate elimination of tariffs is the most common focus of the discussion about free trade. Yet, as Coughlin and Wood point out in "An Introduction to Non-Tariff Barriers to Trade," while tariffs have been reduced in the 1980s, nontariff barriers have multiplied. These nontariff barriers can of course have the same adverse effect on trade as tariffs. Moreover, the chances for reversing the trend appear to be limited.

The last two articles in this section deal with the same general topic—the credit risk exposure of U.S. banks through their international loan portfolio. In "U.S. Banks' Exposure to Developing Countries: An Examination of Recent Trends," Barbara Bennett and Gary Zimmerman provide historical evidence of the growth of LDC lending by U.S. banks, and seek to determine whether that expansion was due to involuntary lending or other factors. In contrast to this historical perspective, Chien Nan Wang, in "The Costs of Default and International Lending," explores the potential costs and benefits of defaults by LDC countries from the perspectives of both lenders and borrowers.

Article 23

Europe 1992: Implications for U.S. Firms

By Thomas Bennett and Craig S. Hakkio

In 1946 Winston Churchill stood before the people of an economically ravaged Europe and said, ''We must build a United States of Europe.'' Churchill's dream was to tear down barriers to trade and commerce within Europe so that European nations could enjoy economic freedom and prosperity. Today the 12 members of the European Community (EC) are closer than ever to making Churchill's dream a reality. But some observers fear that the EC's current initiative, Europe 1992, might become ''Fortress Europe,'' a community of nations bent on tearing down internal walls only to build them externally against foreign competitors.

The implications of Europe 1992 for U.S. firms doing business with Europe are not clear—and the stakes are high. Two types of U.S. firms do business with Europe: U.S.

exporters and subsidiaries of U.S. firms.[1] In 1987 U.S. sales in the EC were 56 percent more than U.S. sales in Canada and Japan combined. If members of the EC encourage a world trade system unencumbered by barriers to trade, a single economic market in Europe could prove beneficial to U.S. firms. However, if EC members strive to close their markets to outsiders, Europe 1992 could prove costly to U.S. firms.

This article examines the implications of Europe 1992 for U.S. firms doing business with Europe, focusing on nonfinancial firms and banks. The article concludes that U.S. firms will benefit from Europe 1992 unless the EC members raise external trade barriers or adopt discriminatory financial regulations. The first

Thomas Bennett is a research associate at the Federal Reserve Bank of Kansas City. Craig S. Hakkio is an assistant vice president and economist at the bank.

[1] In this article the term ''Europe'' designates the 12 EC member countries: Belgium, Britain, Denmark, France, Greece, Ireland, Italy, Luxembourg, the Netherlands, Portugal, Spain, and West Germany.

The European Community

Economic integration has been a European goal for 30 years, with Europe 1992 the most recent and most ambitious initiative. The information contained here briefly reviews the history of European integration leading up to Europe 1992. Key dates in the history of the EC are listed in the table.

In 1951 the European Coal and Steel Community established the framework for European integration. The original six members of the Community—Belgium, the Federal Republic of Germany, France, Italy, Luxembourg, and the Netherlands—subsequently signed the Treaty of Rome in 1957, which formally established the European Community (EC). The principal aims of the treaty were to preserve and strengthen peace; to create a region with the free movement of goods, people, services, and capital; and ultimately to form a political union.

Following the signing of the Treaty of Rome, barriers to trade began to fall. Tariffs between EC member countries were eliminated by 1968, 18 months ahead of the schedule in the Treaty of Rome. And, while not the sole reason, eliminating tariff barriers probably contributed to Europe's strong economic performance over the next 15 years. From 1958 to 1972 the EC's economy expanded nearly 5 percent per year, while intra-European trade grew about 13 percent per year (measured in constant dollars).[1]

The period from 1973 to the early 1980s, in contrast, was a difficult one for European integration. The oil price shocks in 1973-74 and

1979 led to numerous problems, most importantly, a slowdown in economic growth. Real gross domestic product growth averaged 2.4 percent from 1972 to 1979 and 1.4 percent from 1979 to 1985. Partly in response to slower economic growth, integration slowed, or even reversed, as member states levied new border taxes, reintroduced trade quotas, increased subsidies, and established implicit barriers against both outside countries and other EC countries.

The movement toward integration resumed in the 1980s. Europeans became convinced that raising trade barriers did not improve economic growth and that low growth resulted from inefficient and inflexible economies. Moreover, the stubbornly high unemployment rates of the 1980s—relative to the 1960s and relative to the United States—provided additional incentive to integrate. Finally, increased international competition from the United States and Japan convinced Europeans of the need for economic integration.

In the mid-1980s, the EC launched a systematic program to eliminate trade barriers and create a single European marketplace. The 1985 White Paper, officially known as "Completing the Internal Market," established the program to create a single European marketplace for goods and financial services. The White Paper included approximately 300 directives designed to eliminate barriers to the free movement of goods, people, services, and capital among the 12 EC member states. The Single European Act—ratified in 1986—adopted the White Paper, amended the Treaty of Rome, and set 1992 as the completion date of the Internal Market.

---

[1] The Commission of the European Communities, *The European Community* (Brussels: 1987), p. 7.

section of the article describes the goals of Europe 1992 and discusses the extent to which the initiative might become a reality. The second section shows that, in the absence of external walls against international trade, Europe 1992 would help U.S. firms operate more efficiently in Europe. The third section examines why some U.S. firms are apprehensive about Europe 1992.

The dimensions of Europe 1992

The road to a fully integrated Europe has not been smooth. An important milestone was achieved in 1957 when the six members of the European Coal and Steel Community—Bel-gium, West Germany, France, Italy, Luxembourg, and the Netherlands—signed the Treaty of Rome. The Treaty of Rome established the EC and set forth goals of economic integration. By 1968, EC members had eliminated all tariffs within the EC. Due in part to the removal of tariffs, economic growth in the EC was strong from 1958 to 1972. Slow growth returned to the EC following the oil price shocks of the 1970s, however, prompting member countries once again to protect themselves against foreign competitors, including other EC countries. Border taxes, trade quotas, and subsidies were reintroduced. It was not until the mid-1980s, amid stubbornly high unemployment and rising international competition, that Europeans gave economic integration another big push: the Europe 1992 initiative (see box).[2]

What is Europe 1992?

In 1985 the EC issued a White Paper titled "Completing the Internal Market." The White Paper set forth about 300 directives designed to create a single European market for goods and financial services. Full implementation of the White Paper's directives was set for 1992. Currently, about 40 percent of the directives have been approved and are being implemented. When Europe 1992 is completed, goods, services, and capital will no longer be restricted from moving freely across European borders. But before this can happen, remaining trade barriers and financial restrictions need to be torn down.

Goods market integration. The EC hopes to create a single European market for goods; however, three major types of barriers stand in the way of integrating the 12 separate markets of the EC. All three types of barriers—technical, fiscal, and physical—need to be eliminated before goods can move freely within the EC.

One set of technical barriers comprises health, safety, and environmental standards. Such standards can impede the flow of goods from one country to another. In some cases, these standards reflect varying national preferences for safety and consumer protection.

However, many believe that some of the standards were established simply to keep foreign goods out of domestic markets.

Under the Europe 1992 program, health, safety, and environmental standards will be standardized among EC members.[3] The guiding principle in setting standards will be if a product is good enough to be offered in one EC country—and meets minimal EC requirements—it is good enough to be offered in all EC countries. This principle is called mutual recognition.

Another set of technical barriers relates to the selection process for public contracts. Public contracts represent about 15 percent of the EC's gross domestic product. However, most successful bids for government projects come from firms in the home country; only 2 percent of public supply and public construction contracts are awarded to firms from other member nations.[4] In an attempt to open up bidding on public contracts, the EC has adopted common standards in the procurement process. The EC also plans to extend competitive bidding to telecommunications, water distribution, energy, and transportation industries.

The second type of barriers to be removed

---

[2] For further information on Europe 1992, see Kristina Jacobson, "A United European Community by 1992," *Financial Letter*, Federal Reserve Bank of Kansas City, September 1988.

---

[3] Prior to the adoption of the White Paper, European integration was slow because it was thought that national standards had to conform to European standards. In addition, decisions previously required unanimous approval. Consequently, integration was difficult to achieve. *The Economist* ("Europe's Internal Market," July 9, 1988, p. 7) put it as follows: "It was a hopeless prospect wherever countries were asked to take unanimous decisions over national quirks that were dear to them."

[4] "The Economics of 1992," *The European Economy* (Brussels: Commission of the European Communities, March 1988), p. 55.

TABLE 1
VAT rates in the European Community (April 1987, percent)

	Low rate*	Basic rate	High rate*
Belgium	1 and 6	19	25 and 33
Denmark	—	22	—
France	2.1 to 7	18.6	33⅓
Germany	7	14	—
Greece	6	18	36
Ireland	2.4 and 10	25	—
Italy	2 and 9	18	38
Luxembourg	3 and 6	12	—
Netherlands	6	20	—
Portugal	8	16	30
Spain	6	12	33
United Kingdom	—	15	—
Europe 1992 proposal	4 to 9	14 to 20	abolished

*Imposed on necessities such as food and children's items.
**Imposed on luxury items.

Source: "The Economics of 1992," *European Economy* (Brussels: Commission of the European Communities, March 1988), p. 61.

is fiscal barriers, such as differences in tax rates. The value-added tax (VAT), a form of sales tax, provides an example.[5] Broad differences in VAT rates throughout the EC require that individual countries control the movement of goods to prevent consumers and firms from buying goods where VAT rates are low and bringing them into countries where VAT rates are high.

VAT rates vary in several ways from one EC country to another. Member countries have both different levels of rates and different goods that are covered. Table 1 shows the range of VAT rates for EC countries. The basic VAT rate ranges from 12 percent in Spain and Luxembourg to 25 percent in Ireland. In addition, many countries impose a lower VAT rate on necessities. The United Kingdom, for example, imposes no value-added tax on food or children's clothes. Some countries also impose a higher VAT rate on luxuries. Italy, for exam-

[5] A value-added tax is an indirect broad-based consumption tax. It is essentially equivalent to a retail sales tax except in the method of administration. For a detailed discussion of the VAT, including a comparison with a retail sales tax, see Glenn H. Miller, Jr., "The Value-Added Tax: Cash Cow or Pig in a Poke?" *Economic Review*, Federal Reserve Bank of Kansas City (September/October 1986), pp. 3-15.

ple, imposes a tax of 38 percent on automobiles.

Under the Europe 1992 program, the EC proposes to standardize VAT rates by establishing two ranges of tax rates. The low VAT rate will range from 4 percent to 9 percent, and the basic VAT rate will range from 14 percent to 20 percent (see the bottom line in Table 1). In addition, the high VAT rate currently used by some EC countries will be abolished.[6]

The third type of barriers confronting European nations is physical barriers, namely, border controls. Border controls are perhaps the most visible obstacles to the free movement of goods across borders in the EC. Member countries use border controls to collect VAT taxes, to ensure conformity with varying health and safety regulations, and to regulate products subject to import quotas.

Some progress has been made toward eliminating border controls. For example, in January of last year the EC adopted a policy of permitting truck drivers to pass through customs by showing a single document. In the past, drivers had to show border officials copies of invoices, forms for import statistics, and reports for tax authorities—sometimes up to 100 separate documents—before entering the country. Consequently, a 750-mile trip from London to Milan, for example, routinely took about 58 hours (excluding crossing the channel), while today a similar trip might take only about 36 hours.[7]

Financial market integration. Just as the EC hopes to create a single European market for goods, it also hopes to create a single market for financial services. Market forces, such as the globalization of capital markets and financial innovations, are moving the world toward a single capital market. To complement these market forces, the EC under Europe 1992 will work to streamline financial operations within member countries. Capital controls will be eliminated, and banks that are licensed in one country will automatically be allowed to establish branches in any other EC country.

Many kinds of capital market controls will be eliminated in an integrated Europe. Firms in one EC member country will be permitted to issue bonds denominated in the currency of another EC country without obtaining approval from that country's central bank. EC citizens will be allowed to hold bank accounts and tap into credit markets throughout the EC. All restrictions on short-term capital flows will be removed, and capital flows between EC countries and non-EC countries will be liberalized.[8] Three countries—the United Kingdom, Germany, and the Netherlands—have already liberalized capital movements, and an EC directive

---

[6] Recent discussion in the EC has led to possible new approaches to harmonizing tax rates. One idea is to keep the lower band at 4 to 9 percent, but to give the high band a floor of 17 percent and no ceiling. Other discussion focuses on changing the lower band to accommodate the United Kingdom's and Ireland's desires for having no taxes on some items.

[7] Kate Bertrand, "Scrambling for 1992," *Business Marketing,* February 1989, p. 54.

[8] As long as some EC country does not restrict capital movements from non-EC countries, restricting capital movements between an EC country and a non-EC country would be pointless. The reason is simple: If, for example, U.S. funds can flow freely into the United Kingdom, and if U.K. funds can flow freely into Italy, then there is no reason to prohibit U.S. funds from flowing freely into Italy.

TABLE 2
Permissible banking activities under Europe 1992

(1) Deposit-taking and other forms of borrowing;
(2) lending (including consumer credit, mortgage lending, factoring and invoice discounting, and trade finance);
(3) financial leasing;
(4) money transmission services;
(5) issuing and administering means of payment (credit cards, travelers' checks, and bankers' drafts);
(6) guarantees and commitments;
(7) trading for the institution's own account or for the account of its customers in (a) money market instruments (such as checks, bills, and CDs), (b) foreign exchange, (c) financial futures and options, (d) exchange and interest rate instruments, and (e) securities;
(8) participation in share issues and the provision of services related to such issues;
(9) money brokering;
(10) portfolio management and advice;
(11) safekeeping of securities;
(12) credit reference services; and
(13) safe custody services.

Source: Annex to the Second Banking Coordination Directive.

adopted in June 1988 requires the other member countries to remove all remaining capital controls by 1990.[9]

Moreover, banks will be allowed to operate throughout the EC under a single banking license. The same principle that is applied to technical standards for goods—mutual recognition—will govern EC banking. In other words, a bank established in one EC country will be allowed to branch into any other member country without obtaining permission from authorities in that country.

The EC has proposed a list of activities permissible to European banking. The list adopts the universal banking principle; that is, EC banks will be allowed to provide securities-related and advisory services in addition to commercial banking services (Table 2). As long as the country in which a bank is domiciled (the home country) permits its banks to engage in one of the essential activities, then those banks may engage in that activity in another country (the host country), even if the activity is prohibited to domestic banks in the host country.

Bank supervision under Europe 1992 will generally be the responsibility of the home country. Bank regulators in the home country can impose restrictions to ensure the safety and soundness of banks domiciled in their country. In three areas, however, banks will be subject

---

[9] Four countries that are heavily reliant on capital controls have an extended deadline: Spain and Ireland, 1992; Greece and Portugal, mid-1990s.

to host-country supervision. First, branches will be subject to host-country rules imposed for monetary policy purposes. For example, reserve requirements on various assets will be set by the host country. Second, the host country will supervise the securities activities of banks. And third, the host country will retain primary responsibility for supervision of liquidity.

Eventually, a common set of banking regulations will likely emerge within the EC. Because banks domiciled in different countries will initially face different regulations, banks located in countries with stringent regulations will be at a competitive disadvantage. Over time, one would expect political pressures to remove regulatory disparities. To keep these political pressures from leading to regulatory anarchy, however, the EC plans to adopt some essential requirements for safety and soundness. For example, minimum standards will be set for capital adequacy, and minimum levels for deposit insurance will be established.[10] Moreover, procedures will be established for handling bank failures.

Thus, like goods market integration, financial market integration is moving ahead. Europe

1992, if fully integrated, would reduce burdensome financial regulations.

How likely is full implementation of Europe 1992?

A common desire for the benefits of integration has given Europe 1992 an irreversible momentum. EC officials estimate that if Europe 1992 becomes a full reality, by 1997 the EC's real gross domestic product will be increased 7 percent, 5 million new jobs will be created, and consumer prices will be lowered 4.5 percent.[11] Such benefit estimates have bolstered the EC's commitment to Europe 1992. Yet many roadblocks remain. Two major obstacles are a reduction of national sovereignty and a temporary increase in unemployment.

Any movement toward uniform EC standards reduces national sovereignty. Standardizing VAT rates, for example, requires countries to change their tax systems. In many cases, the philosophy behind a tax system is deeply rooted in a nation's psyche. For example, taxes on necessities, such as children's clothes, are much lower in some countries than in others. Europe 1992 will take this power to tax according to national beliefs out of the hands of the governments in individual countries.

Viewed another way, full integration represents a shift in the center of power from national governments to the governing bodies of the EC in Brussels—a shift that politicians and civil ser-

---

10 Capital adequacy standards will be based on the work of the Basel Committee on Banking Regulations and Supervisory Practices. The Basel Committee is made up of representatives from the G-10 countries (Belgium, Canada, France, West Germany, Italy, Japan, the Netherlands, Sweden, the United Kingdom, and the United States), plus Switzerland and Luxembourg. For additional information on the Committee's proposal, see "Fed Staff Summary and Recommendations on Risk-Based Capital Plan," *BNA's Banking Report,* vol. 51 (Washington, D.C.: The Bureau of National Affairs, Inc., 1988).

---

11 Glennon J. Harrison, "The European Community's 1992 Plan: An Overview of the Proposed Single Market," a report prepared for Congress by the Congressional Research Service, September 21, 1988, p. 9.

vants may regard as a personal threat. Each sovereign country's reluctance to transfer power to Brussels may slow the momentum of Europe 1992.

The second roadblock to Europe 1992 is a potential short-run increase in unemployment. Unemployment will rise temporarily as less efficient or highly protected firms are forced to adjust to heightened competition. The EC estimates that job losses during the first years of the program will amount to more than 250,000 per year.[12] As a result, despite projections of large unemployment decreases in the long run, some governments may be reluctant to permit short-run increases, causing a strain on the movement toward free markets.

Although the EC has made substantial progress in adopting the Europe 1992 directives, many difficult issues still need to be resolved. As of late January 1989, about 85 percent of the White Paper's directives had been submitted to the EC's decision-making body, the Council. Half of the directives submitted to the Council have been adopted. However, some of the most controversial proposals, such as standardizing tax rates, have not been acted upon.[13]

---

[12] Harrison, ''The European Community's 1992 Plan . . . ,'' p. 12.

[13] The EC's decision-making process on many issues has changed from unanimous consent to qualified majority. Qualified majority voting refers to weighing each member state's votes according to its population. Thus, France, the Federal Republic of Germany, Italy, and the United Kingdom have ten votes each. Spain has eight. Belgium, Greece, the Netherlands, and Portugal have five votes each. Denmark and Ireland have three each, and Luxembourg has two. To pass a proposal requires at least 54 out of the total 76 votes. This prevents the four largest countries from dominating community decisions and removes the possibility of one country imposing a veto. Unanimous voting is still required for the harmonization of tax rates.

Potential benefits of Europe 1992 for U.S. firms

Europe 1992 will replace 12 separate national markets with a single EC market. The EC comprises 320 million people, a third more than live in the United States. The EC's gross domestic product is $4.6 trillion, nearly equal to that in the United States. As long as the EC market remains open to outsiders, increased uniformity brought about by the Europe 1992 initiative will prove advantageous to U.S. firms. As restrictions are removed, nonfinancial U.S. firms will be able to operate more freely throughout the EC, thereby reducing their production and distribution costs. And U.S. banks will be able to branch throughout the EC while providing a greater range of financial services.

Potential benefits for nonfinancial U.S. firms

Removing physical and technical barriers will reduce the cost of U.S. firms doing business with Europe. Without physical barriers, such as border controls, U.S. firms will obviously be able to reduce transportation costs. Without technical barriers U.S. firms will benefit in several ways. First, U.S. firms will be able to realize economies of scale in production and distribution. Second, U.S. firms will be able to sell their products in a market not inhibited by overlapping or conflicting regulations and standards. And third, U.S. firms will be able to use a base in one country to develop a network for selling their products throughout the EC, resulting in lower transportation and capital costs.

Moreover, U.S. firms stand to benefit from their experience in highly competitive markets. As existing trade barriers fall, inefficient domestic firms will no longer be protected from outside competition. As competiton increases, more efficient U.S. firms will be rewarded.

To take advantage of the benefits of an integrated market, some U.S. firms may change the way they operate in Europe. Once technical standards become uniform, subsidiaries of U.S. firms may choose to expand the scale of their European operations. U.S. exporters to Europe may choose to move production from the United States to Europe, perhaps by forming European subsidiaries. And because Europe 1992 is leading firms to become ''European'' rather than simply national, some U.S. firms may try to gain sales by shedding their foreign image—that is, they may try to merge or form joint ventures with European firms.

Potential benefits for U.S. banks

If the Europe 1992 proposals are adopted by the EC, banks will be able to operate in all 12 member countries under a single banking license and under a universal banking concept. The single license will enable all banks in Europe, including banks from the United States, to realize a number of cost benefits. The universal banking concept will expand the powers of U.S. banks providing services in Europe.

A single banking license will directly lower bank costs by enabling banks to operate throughout the EC using common distribution networks, managers, and support staffs. Additional cost savings could be realized by centralizing funding of loans. Moreover, operating under a single banking license will enable banks to reduce risk by diversifying the geographic distribution of their loans. For example, if a bank's portfolio includes loans to farmers in one country, the risk to the bank may be very high

due to the possibility of drought. However, a portfolio with loans to farmers in all EC countries may be much less risky, since crop damage is less likely across all EC countries than within a single country.

A single banking license and home-country supervision of banks will also indirectly lower bank costs in Europe. Currently, to operate in all 12 EC countries, a bank must meet the standards set by each country's regulators. However, with a single banking license and home-country supervision, a bank need meet only one set of regulations—those set by the home country. If overlapping or conflicting standards and regulatory procedures are eliminated, the cost of banking in Europe will decline. Furthermore, whereas in the past a bank might have chosen to locate and operate in only the larger European markets, it will now be able to establish itself in one market and then branch into all the other markets of the EC.

U.S. banks, like others, will have an incentive to expand into new countries because the prices of banking services vary greatly from one country to another. Chart 1 shows that the prices of two banking services, commercial loans and credit cards, differ considerably among EC countries.[14] To the extent these differences persist, at least temporarily, countries with high prices will attract new entrants. Some U.S. banks may also attempt to gain presence in the EC market by merging with existing European banks.

As noted earlier, under the Europe 1992 pro-

---

[14] For more detail on the calculations shown in Chart 1, see ''The Economics of 1992,'' *European Economy,* (Brussels: Commission of the European Communities, March 1988), pp. 86-94.

CHART 1
Prices of banking services in selected European countries

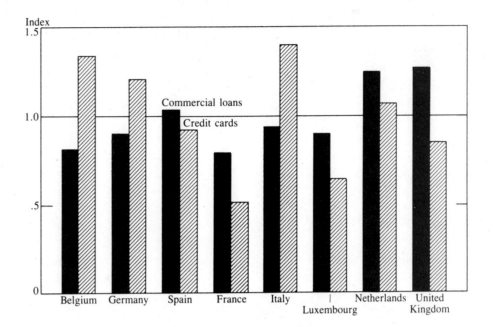

Note: Prices for each country are expressed as a fraction of the average price in the eight countries. The price for a commercial loan is the annual cost (including commissions and charges) to a midsized firm of a 250,000 ECU commercial loan; the price for credit cards is the difference between the interest rate on a 500 ECU debit and money market rates.

Source: "The Economics of 1992," *European Economy* (Brussels: Commission of the European Communities, March 1988), p. 91.

gram universal banking will become the norm for European banking. Subsidiaries of U.S. banks operating in the EC will be able to engage in capital market activities, such as underwriting securities—unlike their parent banks operating in the United States, which are prohibited from underwriting securities by the Glass-Steagall Act. These expanded powers will give U.S. banks the opportunity to use their expertise to earn additional income in European capital markets. Furthermore, with U.S. banks underwriting securities in Europe, the U.S.

Congress may be more inclined to repeal the Glass-Steagall Act and thus increase the international competitiveness of U.S. banks.

Thus, if adopted, Europe 1992 will enable both nonfinancial U.S. firms and U.S. banks to operate more efficiently in Europe. Nonfinancial U.S. firms, unhampered by costly overlapping standards and regulations, will be able to reduce both production and distribution costs. And U.S. banks will benefit from both expanded powers and the ability to operate in all 12 EC countries.

U.S. apprehensions of Europe 1992

Europe 1992 presents U.S. firms not only with opportunities but also with potential dangers. Access to a barrier-free market with a population that is one-third larger than the United States opens up lucrative possibilities. However, these possibilities will be realized only if the EC's markets remain open. If the EC becomes a Fortress Europe by raising trade barriers against foreign competition or by adopting financial regulations that discriminate against foreign banks, U.S. firms will be harmed.

Implications of a Fortress Europe

Many apprehensions of a Fortress Europe arise because the international implications of Europe 1992 for non-EC members are still not clear. The EC's 1985 White Paper focused on the internal aspects of integration rather than on its external implications. In the fall of 1988 the EC approved a 300-page document outlining member-country views on the external aspects of the Europe 1992 program. Currently, however, only a six-page summary of the document is available. The summary suggests that the EC does not intend to become a Fortress Europe; however, few specifics are given. Consequently, the possibility that the EC will close its doors to foreign competition has many U.S. firms worried.

Protectionist measures by the EC, if adopted, would threaten U.S. firms in two fundamental ways. First, U.S. firms doing business with Europe could be discriminated against. For example, if the EC limits imports, U.S. exporters will lose sales. Such a loss could be significant since U.S. exports to the EC in 1987 amounted to $120 billion, 28 percent of total U.S. exports. Additionally, if the EC adopts laws favoring European firms over foreign firms operating in Europe, subsidiaries of U.S. firms could lose sales. Such sales totaled about $350 billion in 1987.[15]

The second fundamental way that U.S. firms would be threatened, and perhaps the most important danger of a Fortress Europe, is that protectionist measures by the EC would inevitably force the United States and other nations to respond in kind. One round of protectionist policies is bad; ensuing rounds—a trade war—would be disastrous to all parties involved.[16]

Will trade barriers be erected?

Some observers are apprehensive that the EC may erect trade barriers against nonfinancial

---

[15] U.S. Secretary of Commerce C. William Verity, "U.S. Business Needs to Prepare Now for Europe's Single Internal Market," *Business America,* August 1, 1988, p. 2.

Some subsidiaries of U.S. firms operating in Europe could actually be helped if the EC adopts discriminatory regulations against foreign firms. Some EC countries have local content requirements that determine whether a firm is considered "European." For example, a U.S. firm may need to purchase 60 percent of its inputs from an EC country in order to be considered European. Therefore, although discriminatory regulations would harm subsidiaries of U.S. firms that were not sufficiently European, subsidiaries of U.S. firms that were sufficiently European could gain business.

[16] Recent tensions between the United States and the EC exemplify the potential problems from protectionist policies. For instance, on New Year's Day the EC imposed health regulations barring imports of the United States' and other countries' beef from cattle implanted with growth-inducing hormones. In retaliation, the United States placed a 100 percent tariff on certain European products.

U.S. firms. One reason is that EC countries and industries will be subject to short-run unemployment increases resulting from integration; consequently, they may try to offset unemployment costs by stifling competition from abroad. And perhaps more important, EC countries may erect trade barriers simply to keep all the benefits of Europe 1992 to themselves.

Seemingly conflicting statements by European officials underscore the uncertainty regarding the EC's policies toward foreign competitors. Some Europeans argue that the EC, as the world's largest trading bloc, has a vital interest in maintaining and expanding the trading system. For example, West German Chancellor Kohl has asserted, "We are aware of our responsibility in maintaining a world trade system that is free of protectionism and impediments to trade. I assure you that it isn't our goal to tear down barriers internally, only to resurrect them outwardly again."[17] In contrast, other Europeans feel the benefits from integration should accrue primarily to members of the EC. According to Jacques Delors, president of the European Commission, "We are not building a single market in order to turn it over to hungry foreigners."[18]

Potential trade barriers can take many forms. Currently, some countries have quotas on as many as 1,000 individual items. The EC will have to decide whether to completely eliminate these quotas or to establish EC-wide quotas.[19] Alternatively, EC standards for certain products, the so-called essential requirements, could be written in such a way that they discriminate against the products of non-EC countries. Furthermore, EC legislation might establish local content laws requiring products to contain a certain percentage of local labor, materials, and capital to be considered domestic.

Thus, whether the EC will ultimately decide to erect external trade barriers is still an open question. Some EC member countries may be tempted to limit access by foreign firms to European markets. Others will likely be committed to keeping markets open to all firms.

Will discriminatory financial regulations be adopted?

Apprehensions that U.S. banks might be discriminated against arise because the EC has not made it clear how it will treat foreign banks. The EC has indicated that access to a single European financial market will be limited to banks from those countries outside the EC that provide reciprocal treatment to banks from all EC countries.[20] Unfortunately, the EC's definition of reciprocity is unclear—both in its meaning and its implications. Reciprocity may mean

[17] Remarks by West German Chancellor Helmut Kohl to a gathering of diplomats in Bonn, Telerate Systems, November 18, 1988, p. 155.

[18] Scott Sullivan, "Who's Afraid of 1992?" *Newsweek,* October 31, 1988, p. 34.

[19] A related concern is how Europe will treat "Japanese" autos produced in the United States. For example, if Hondas are exported from the United States, will they be treated as Japanese autos or U.S. autos?

[20] While reciprocity provisions could be applied to any product or firm, they have been incorporated only into directives on banking, investment services, and public procurement.

either "national" treatment or "mirror-image" treatment. National treatment would strengthen U.S. banks; but mirror-image treatment would severely limit the powers of U.S. banks operating in the EC.

As a matter of policy, the United States accords national treatment to foreign banks. Under national treatment, all powers granted to U.S. banks are also granted to foreign banks operating in the United States. By allowing domestic and foreign firms to compete on an equal footing, national treatment is nondiscriminatory.

U.S. policymakers have urged the EC to provide national treatment to U.S. banks operating in the EC. An official of the U.S. Treasury Department has argued, for example, that national treatment is consistent with our treaties with European nations, with the codes and instruments of the Organization for Economic Cooperation and Development, and with U.S. federal law.[21] U.S. officials further argue that since the United States provides national treatment to foreign banks, the EC should provide national treatment to U.S. banks.

If the EC adopts national treatment as its definition of reciprocity, U.S. banking in the EC will not be unduly restricted. Since EC banks can branch throughout Europe and underwrite securities, national treatment will allow U.S. banks operating in Europe to do likewise.

On the other hand, if the EC adopts a mirror-image definition of reciprocity, U.S. banking activity in the EC will be severely restricted. Under mirror-image reciprocity, treatment of U.S. banks in the EC will mirror the treatment of EC banks in the United States. Since the United States prevents EC banks (and U.S. banks) from branching throughout the United States and from underwriting securities, mirroring that treatment in the EC will prevent U.S. banks from branching throughout Europe and underwriting securities. Thus, U.S. banks would be unable to compete effectively against European banks, which would have much wider powers.

The October 1988 document on the external aspects of Europe 1992 has allayed some of the apprehensions about the reciprocity provisions. Lord Cockfield, Internal Market Commissioner of the EC, assured foreign bankers that the reciprocity provisions will not be applied retroactively.[22] As a result, U.S. banks already established in the EC will be treated the same as European banks, regardless of the definition of reciprocity.

Lord Cockfield also asserted, however, that reciprocity provisions will be applied to "newcomers." In the event that reciprocity is defined as mirror-image, Lord Cockfield's assertion raises several questions. Suppose, for instance, a nonfinancial company already established in the EC establishes a new financial services subsidiary. Is the firm a newcomer? Alternatively, suppose a U.S. bank becomes established in the EC between 1990 and 1992. Is it a newcomer?

---

[21] U.S. Deputy Secretary of the Treasury M. Peter McPherson, "The European Community's Internal Market Program: An American Perspective," remarks before the Institute for International Economics, Washington, D.C., August 4, 1988, p. 6.

[22] "EC Allays Freeze-Out Fears," *American Banker*, October 24, 1988, p. 6.

Or suppose a U.S. bank, already established in the EC, reorganizes or adds another subsidiary. Is the reorganized bank a newcomer? Is the new subsidiary a newcomer?

As debate has continued within the EC over the treatment of foreign banks, U.S. policymakers have emphasized the importance of adopting the national treatment definition of reciprocity. For example, Governor Heller of the Federal Reserve System stressed that anything other than national treatment "would be detrimental not only in that it would harm the ability of U.S. banks to compete in the European market for financial services, but it could lead to further protectionist pressures that would be harmful to all."[23] And Mr. McPherson, then Deputy Secretary of the Treasury, argued that mirror-image reciprocity "could be applied in a manner that would discriminate against firms in the United States seeking entry to the EC," concluding that the U.S. government finds this reciprocity concept "particularly troubling."[24]

---

[23] *Daily Report for Executives,* November 3, 1988, p. A-12.

[24] M. Peter McPherson, "The European Community's Internal Market Program . . . ," pp. 4-6.

Summary

With Europe 1992, members of the European Community are creating a single market for goods and financial services. Tearing down trade barriers and removing financial restrictions will strengthen the EC's economic power, create millions of new jobs for its citizens, and lower consumer prices.

The implications of Europe 1992 for U.S. firms doing business with Europe are not clear, however. If the EC keeps open its doors to world trade, U.S. firms could share in the benefits of a single European market. On the other hand, if the Europeans close their doors to foreign competitors, some U.S. firms could pay a high price. This article argues that U.S. firms will benefit unless the EC raises external trade barriers or adopts discriminatory financial regulations.

Complete integration of Europe 1992, as envisioned by the White Paper, may not become full reality by 1992. Disagreement on such central issues as tax rates, banking control, and national sovereignty may take years to unravel. Yet there is little doubt that Europe 1992 is moving strongly toward implementation —and that it will have significant ramifications for U.S. firms.

International Policy Cooperation: Building a Sound Foundation

Brian J. Cody*

Policymakers have long recognized that the welfare of their economies is tied to the welfare of the world economy. Because goods, services, capital, and even labor are mobile internationally, economic policies in one country invariably have spillover effects on others. Having decided they can no longer ignore these global effects, and hoping to build a more stable world

economy, governments have made some heroic attempts to coordinate their economic policies. Unfortunately, their efforts have been largely unsuccessful. Now policymakers are attempting more modest steps toward cooperation.

The seven leading industrial nations—Canada, France, West Germany, Italy, Japan, the United Kingdom, and the United States—are now developing a new system for sharing economic information. A good deal of economic data (inflation statistics, for example) is currently available, but different countries use different

* Brian J. Cody is an Economist in the Macroeconomics Section of the Philadelphia Fed's Research Department.

methods to calculate, analyze, and forecast economic indicators. To overcome the difficulties created by these differences, the major countries are working out a set of "objective indicators"—indicators with well-articulated definitions across countries. The hope is that these indicators will lead to a single analytical framework and a coherent set of economic forecasts. Ultimately, these efforts should enhance policymakers' understanding of how their actions affect not only their own economy but others as well, enabling them to design harmonious national policies.

An exchange of economic indicators may seem like a small step, perhaps even a retreat from past efforts. In large part, however, it is lack of information that has hampered previous attempts at policy coordination. A seemingly modest program of information-sharing can help overcome problems undermining more ambitious plans and provide the foundation for broader agreements down the road.

COOPERATION: WHAT'S IN IT FOR A COUNTRY?

Cooperative policymaking can take many forms, but in general it occurs whenever officials from different countries meet to evaluate world economic conditions.[1] During these meetings, policymakers may present briefings on their individual economies and discuss current policies. Such meetings would represent a simple form of cooperation. A more involved interchange might include economists' reports on a specific problem, coupled with an in-depth discussion of possible solutions. True *policy coordination*, however, goes much further than either of these two cooperative forms:

---

[1] For a formal definition of policy cooperation, see Jocelyn Horne and Paul R. Masson, "Scope and Limits of International Economic Cooperation and Policy Coordination," International Monetary Fund Staff Papers (June 1988).

policy coordination is a formal agreement among nations to enact specific policies. Recent attempts by the leading industrial nations to design and jointly implement specific economic policies fall into this last category.

In a sense, it is surprising that previous efforts have not been more successful. Theoretically, any group of nations whose economies interact and influence one another can benefit from policy coordination. Regardless of national economic objectives, policy coordination can, in principle, make each participating nation better off than if it chose to operate in isolation.

If policy coordination offers so many benefits, then why have previous attempts at it failed? In large measure, the problem has been lack of information. Achieving true policy coordination, with agreement to jointly implement specific policies, requires a greater capacity to collect and analyze data jointly than countries now have. A simple example helps demonstrate the potential benefits of economic policy coordination—and highlights the potential problems.

Two Countries Whose Situations Are Less Than Ideal. Suppose there are just two countries in the world, the Highlands and the Lowlands. They freely trade goods and services with each other, but want to pursue national economic interests. Highlanders expect their government to keep the economy close to full employment and to avoid trade deficits with the Lowlands. Meanwhile, Lowlanders expect their government to keep the economy close to full employment and to avoid trade deficits with the Highlands.

The current economic situation in the two countries is less than ideal: trade between them is balanced, but both economies are operating below full employment. Each government has considered increasing its spending in order to bolster domestic demand, raise output, and increase employment. Each has also rejected the idea, recognizing the adverse impact it would have on the trade balance. The Highlands' government knows that more employment and higher incomes for Highlanders would mean a greater tendency for them to buy imports from the Lowlands and thereby drive their trade account with the Lowlands into deficit. Similarly, the Lowlands government sees that spending to boost national employment and incomes would raise Lowlanders' tendency to import goods from the Highlands and thereby drive their trade account with the Highlands into deficit. Consequently, neither government acts and unemployment persists in both countries.

How Policy Coordination Can Benefit Both. Given their choices, both the Highlands and the Lowlands can clearly benefit from policy coordination.[2] If both governments agreed to increase their spending at the same time, then output, employment, and incomes would expand in both countries simultaneously. While higher incomes for Highlanders would tend to increase their demand for goods from the Lowlands, Lowlanders' incomes would also be rising, which would tend to increase their demand for goods from the Highlands. Let's say that government spending in both countries were increased by an appropriate amount. In that case, each country's increased demand for imports would be matched by an increased demand for its exports, maintaining balanced trade between the Highlands and the Lowlands. In this example, policy coordination—that is, mutual adoption of expansionary policies—would allow each country to attain its goal of full employment while avoiding a trade deficit.

Things Are More Complicated in the Real World. This hypothetical example paints a

rosy picture of policy coordination. The coordinated effort seemed easy because the economic problem was so simple—two economies, two goals. In the real world, coordination typically involves many countries and many diverse goals. Recent coordination attempts have involved the seven leading industrial countries and have focused on a broad range of goals—balanced trade, inflation reduction, and output and employment growth.

Even with fewer countries and simpler goals, there is no guarantee that governments can design and carry out coordinated economic policies. In our example, we tacitly assumed that each country possessed perfect information—an assumption that eliminates many potential problems. First, perfect information implies that the Highlands and the Lowlands know the structure of their economies.[3] Consequently, they can calculate precisely their policies' effects on output, employment, incomes, and trade. The assumption of perfect information also implies that when policies do not produce the desired effects, policymakers can quickly pinpoint the cause and renegotiate the agreement. Thus, our example has not considered the effects of an

---

[2] In "Macroeconomic Strategy and Coordination Under Alternative Exchange Rates" (in *International Economic Policy*, edited by R. Dornbusch and J. A. Frenkel, London: Johns Hopkins Press, 1979), Koichi Hamada presents the classic arguments in favor of international policy coordination.

[3] Using the simulations generated by large macroeconomic forecasting models, two recent papers have demonstrated that unless officials coordinate their policies based upon the "correct" model of the world, policy coordination can reduce general economic welfare rather than increase it. See J. A. Frankel and K. Rockett, "International Macroeconomic Policy When Policymakers Do Not Agree on the True Model," *American Economic Review* (June 1988) pp. 318-340, and M. Canzoneri and H. Edison, "A New Interpretation of the Coordination Problem and Its Empirical Significance," a paper prepared for the Federal Reserve Board Conference "Monetary Aggregates and Financial Sector Behavior in Interdependent Economies," Washington, D.C., May 26-27, 1988. See also J. Frankel, "Obstacles to International Macroeconomic Policy Coordination," International Monetary Fund Working Paper, WP/87/29 (April 21, 1987), and A. Ghosh and P. Masson, "International Policy Coordination in a World with Model Uncertainty," International Monetary Fund Staff Papers (June 1988) pp. 230-258.

unexpected change in economic conditions—an investment boom in the Highlands, for example.

The assumption of perfect information also solves another, different kind of problem. Any situation offering gains from cooperating also offers the potential for even bigger gains from cheating—that is, signing an agreement to do something (in this case, increase government spending) and then reneging. In our example, both the Highlands and the Lowlands would like the other to increase spending unilaterally, mainly because the country that holds the line on spending (while the other spends more) stands to benefit from higher foreign demand for its goods. The increased foreign demand stimulates output and employment, while generating a trade surplus. Perfect information, however, can cramp a country's ability to cheat because it suggests that each country can precisely monitor the policies of the other. Thus, any attempt by one country to cheat on a cooperative agreement would be uncovered immediately by the other country.

Unfortunately, policymakers in the real world have imperfect information. They cannot assume away the difficulties involved in *designing*, *renegotiating*, and *monitoring* an agreement. In fact, it is imperfect information that has stymied past attempts at coordination.

HOW CAN INDICATORS HELP?

Beginning a couple of decades ago and continuing today, the United States and its major trading partners have strengthened international policy *cooperation* through such efforts as the Economic Policy Committee and its Working Party 3 at the Organization for Economic Cooperation and Development, the series of annual economic summits, and the International Monetary Fund's world economic outlook process. Since the early 1970s, however, these countries have engaged in three major attempts at *coordinated* policymaking. (See *Three Examples of Policy Coordination*, p.8.)

Each of these real-world agreements has faced difficulties. In two cases, the Smithsonian Agreement and the Bonn Summit, the coordinated policies broke down completely. The third coordinated policy—initiated with the Plaza and Louvre accords and developed at subsequent meetings—has survived, though it has produced somewhat disappointing results. The current coordination attempt can benefit from (and perhaps previous agreements could have been saved by) a better system for sharing economic information.

Perceiving the benefits of shared information, policymakers from the G-7 countries, under the auspices of the IMF, have begun to develop a set of objective indicators of economic performance.[4] The sharing of objective indicators—so named because their definitions and measures are accepted across countries—will increase the quality and range of information available to governments.[5] In general, an appropriate indicator is any economic variable that can be used to measure policymakers' actions, the performance of an individual econ-

---

[4] There have been widespread calls for the use of "objective indicators" in the policy cooperation process. Recent publications by the International Monetary Fund have presented thorough summaries of the recent developments concerning the use of economic indicators. See A. Crockett and M. Goldstein, "Strengthening the International Monetary System: Exchange Rates, Surveillance, and Objective Indicators," International Monetary Fund Occasional Paper, No. 50 (February 1988); J. Horne and P. R. Masson "Scope and Limits of International Economic Cooperation and Policy Coordination," International Monetary Fund Working Paper, WP/87/24 (April 7, 1987).

[5] At the close of the Toronto summit in June 1988, the G-7 countries summarized the ongoing advances made in the use of objective indicators, stating, "We welcome the progress made in refining the analytical use of indicators, as well as the addition to the existing indicators of a commodity-price indicator. The progress in coordination is contributing to the process of further improving the functioning of the international monetary system" ("Economic Declaration," Final Toronto Economic Summit Communique, issued June 21, 1988).

omy, or the spillover effects of one nation's policies on another. Not open to confusion over definitions, objective indicators provide policymakers with the basic data they need to overcome three information problems that have frustrated past attempts at policy coordination.

Policymakers Disagree over Appropriate Policies... In our example, we assumed that policymakers had sufficient information to understand how their policies would affect both economies. For instance, we assumed that the Highlands' officials knew how much they would have to raise government spending in order to reach full employment. We assumed also that the Highlands' economists had sufficient information to predict what effect this policy would have on their trade account with the Lowlands. Of course, the Lowlands' economists had analyzed the same questions and had reached the same conclusions.

In the real world, neither economists nor policymakers have complete information. Moreover, the study of economics has not yet reached a stage that would end honest disagreements over interpretations of a single set of data. The seeming inability of economists to agree on anything has even led some skeptics to contend that if all of the economists in the world were laid end to end, they would still not reach a conclusion. If policymakers and economists can reasonably disagree using the same data, then the potential for disagreement is simply magnified if they lack a common framework.

Our experience since the recent Plaza and Louvre accords illustrates the difficulty of designing appropriate policies when governments disagree about economic fundamentals. To effect the accords' goals—a sustainable, balanced pattern of international trade and continued economic growth—the United States agreed to follow a less stimulative fiscal policy; meanwhile, other governments, in particular

West Germany and Japan, were to implement more stimulative policies. Although economic growth has continued since these accords, improvements in the U.S. current account and fiscal deficits and reductions in other countries' trade surpluses have been slower than was hoped.

The accords' limited success in trade adjustment can be traced, at least in part, to the countries' lack of agreement over appropriate policies to follow. In the summer and autumn of 1987, West German officials approached cautiously the implementation of a coordinated fiscal policy expansion, fearing that such a policy could ignite domestic inflation. The U.S. government, on the other hand, argued that West Germany's inflation rate, at 2 percent, was low enough—and the coordinated expansion moderate enough—to preclude any exacerbated price pressures from an expansionary fiscal policy.

Moreover, the slow progress on deficit reduction in the United States, particularly in the autumn of 1987, has raised questions about the U.S. government's implementation of the agreements. With its concerns about accelerating inflation, the West German government has been reluctant to enact stimulative policies without evidence of fiscal restraint in the United States.[6]

These disagreements would be reduced if policymakers can 1) develop a common framework in which to measure fiscal policy changes and analyze the potential for noninflationary growth in the United States, Western Europe, and Japan and 2) agree on which variables best

---

[6] For some background on these disagreements, see *The New York Times*, "Long Road For Tokyo and Bonn," October 1, 1987, and "3 European Allies Reduce Key Rates to Spur Economies," November 25, 1987; and "Restoring International Balance: The Federal Republic of Germany and World Economic Growth," Joint Economic Committee, June 2, 1988.

Smithsonian Agreement (December 1971)

Background: Under the Bretton Woods system of fixed exchange rates, set up after World War II, the U.S. was committed to maintaining the dollar as the anchor of the world exchange rate system by stabilizing the dollar price of gold at $35 an ounce. All other participating countries then pegged the value of their currency to the dollar. In the face of large and growing current account deficits, which were threatening the stability of the dollar, President Nixon suspended the convertibility of the dollar into gold in August 1971, effectively ending the system of fixed exchange rates.

Agreement: In December 1971, officials from the 10 largest economies in the Organization for Economic Cooperation and Development met at the Smithsonian Institute in Washington D.C. to draw up a new exchange agreement. The dollar was devalued by raising the official price of gold to $38 an ounce, from $35. The German mark and the Japanese yen were revalued against the dollar by 17 and 14 percent, respectively. Since gold convertibility was not restored, the world was not on a gold standard but a dollar standard. President Nixon promised that the U.S. current account deficit would be adjusted so that the dollar would not experience any further weakness.

Result: Continued weakness in the U.S. current account in 1972 led to speculation that the agreement was not working and that the dollar would have to be devalued again. The U.S. currency was devalued by 10 percent in February 1973, and the agreement was finally abandoned one month later, when the major industrialized countries decided to allow their currencies to float against the dollar.

Bonn Summit (July 1978)

Background: The strong U.S. recovery from the 1974-75 recession contributed to a U.S. current account deficit and a weakening dollar. This condition produced calls for other countries, in particular West Germany and Japan, to enact expansionary fiscal and monetary policies. Such policies, it was hoped, would increase demand for U.S. goods, thereby helping to reduce the U.S. trade deficit and strengthen the dollar. There was also widespread sentiment abroad that artificially low oil prices in the United States

measure that potential.[7]

...But Indicators Can Help Answer Basic Questions. Policymakers recognize that they can never be sure of the outcome of their actions. By gradually introducing objective indicators into the Plaza and Louvre accords, however, policymakers hope to obtain a clearer picture of the prospects for noninflationary growth in Western Europe, Japan, and the United States. Following their May 1986 summit in Tokyo, the seven leading industrial nations announced their intention to adopt a group of useful indicators, including GNP growth rates, inflation rates, interest rates, unemployment rates, fiscal deficit ratios, current account and trade balances, money growth rates, foreign exchange reserves, and exchange rates.[8] As this program develops, policymakers should be better equipped to design workable

---

[7] In describing the Plaza and Louvre accords, we have focused on the uncertainties surrounding a fiscal policy solution to trade imbalances. Policymakers could also use monetary policy to address this problem. Unfortunately, no matter which course is followed, policymakers cannot be sure of the impact on the current account. A contractionary monetary policy in the deficit country, for instance, would tend to discourage imports, as higher interest rates resulting from the policy induce consumers to spend less and save more. However, the boost to interest rates would also cause the domestic currency to appreciate, thereby reducing the cost of foreign goods and stimulating imports. These offsetting effects make it difficult to assess the linkages between even monetary policy and the trade balance.

---

[8] See "Tokyo Economic Declaration," Final Tokyo Economic Summit Communique, issued May 6, 1986.

Policy Coordination

were exacerbating the U.S. trade imbalance.

Agreement: West Germany would expand government spending by 1 percent of GNP. The U.S. would introduce a program to reduce oil imports and undertake anti-inflationary measures.

Result: As West German policy was having its effect, the OPEC countries engineered a sharp increase in crude oil prices, fueling inflationary fears in West Germany. Despite efforts to reduce the U.S. trade imbalance, the dollar continued to weaken into 1979. The United States tried to persuade West Germany to intervene in the foreign exchange markets, while the West Germans called for further adjustments in U.S. policy. The onset of unexpected inflation and conflicts over continued adjustment of policies led to abandonment of the agreement.

Plaza Agreement/Louvre Accord (September 1985/February 1987)

Background: By early 1985, there was widespread agreement that the dollar was "overvalued" and that the U.S.'s twin deficits (trade and federal budget) were too large.

Agreement: In order to stimulate demand, West German and Japanese officials agreed to more stimulative fiscal policies, accelerating planned tax cuts and expanding spending programs, respectively. For its part, the U.S. agreed to attempt to bring down its budget deficit. Moreover, all participants agreed to intervene in the currency markets, when necessary, to further the dollar's orderly decline.

Result: The accord has been viewed as a success, though not an unqualified one. In 1987, citing increased inflationary pressures, West German officials approached cautiously the implementation of a coordinated fiscal policy expansion. This development has not set well with the United States, which disagrees over the extent to which accelerating inflation is a problem in West Germany. The slow progress on reducing the federal budget deficit in the United States, particularly during the second half of 1987, has also strained the agreement. Other countries have been understandably reluctant to enact stimulative policies without evidence of fiscal restraint in the United States. The accord has, however, survived numerous attacks, with the participating countries repeatedly expressing their support for it.

policies that facilitate international adjustment and continued economic growth.

Responding to Unexpected Events Is Costly... Working from a set of objective indicators has other benefits, as well. Sometimes policymakers observe an event and know that it will affect their agreement. Changing economic conditions pose a problem for policy coordination, precisely because a new set of circumstances calls for changes in policy. Unfortunately, simply observing the event is no guarantee that policymakers will agree on how the event has changed the world economy or that they can successfully renegotiate their agreement. Rather, the countries also need enough information to form a consensus about the nature of the problem and the appropriate response.

A classic example of problems that can follow an unexpected event is the breakdown of the program designed at the 1978 Bonn Summit. At that summit, the largest industrialized democracies agreed to policies that would spur growth in Europe and Japan and fight inflation in the U.S. West Germany, Japan, and the United States faithfully enacted the programs, but just as the policies began to take hold, the OPEC countries engineered a dramatic run-up in crude oil prices and inflation accelerated. As inflationary pressures mounted, policymakers debated whether the run-up in prices was due to the oil price shock, the coordinated fiscal policies, or both. Not surprisingly, West Germany and Japan became increasingly reluctant to carry out the expansionary policies for fear of exacerbating domestic inflation.

Clearly, the coordinated expansion was no longer appropriate and the agreement needed to be renegotiated. Without a common economic framework and consistent information on wages, input prices, and government expenditures, however, they could not agree on a common interpretation of the crisis, nor could they formulate a coordinated response. The lack of a common framework made renegotiation so costly in terms of time and effort that each country withdrew from the agreement and formulated its own course of action.

...But Indicators Would Reduce Renegotiation Costs. This breakdown might not have happened, however, had policymakers agreed to use objective indicators of wages and other input prices in addition to indicators of inflation and output. If such a system had been in place, U.S., West German, and Japanese officials could have quickly, and with less disagreement, analyzed the economic impacts of the oil price shock. This analysis would have speeded a negotiated, coordinated response to rising world inflation.

In developing and exchanging objective indicators, policymakers can review, each month or quarter, the consistency between the indicators and the coordinated policy. They can compare the desired path for inflation, say, with the value of each country's objective inflation indicator and determine if policy changes are warranted. The uninhibited flow of data and multilateral surveillance of general indicators can help policymakers recognize and respond to unexpected events much more rapidly than they could in isolation. Moreover, if everyone shares the same data and analyzes them using the same criteria, disagreements over the appropriate multilateral response can be reduced.

It's Hard to Enforce Agreements... As we've seen, coordinated policies do not always produce the desired results. Unfortunately, policymakers are not always able to trace the problem back to a particular event. When something goes wrong, policymakers often are not sure why.

If the agreement suddenly starts to produce unexpected results, policymakers can become suspicious. Recognizing that an incentive to cheat exists, they may wonder if everyone is honoring the agreement. A change in the world economy would only compound the problem, since it would make cheating even harder to detect. A country could simply hold the unexpected event responsible for the policy's poor performance, deflecting blame from itself.

The breakdown of the 1971 Smithsonian Agreement exemplifies the problems that can arise when an agreement is clearly not working and there is insufficient information to tell whether the world has changed or if someone is cheating. In the early 1970s, the United States was running a sizable trade deficit, which produced a burgeoning supply of dollars on foreign exchange markets. This excess supply was depressing the dollar's value, thereby jeopardizing its role as the reserve currency.[9] Attempting to restore stability to the dollar, the Smithsonian Agreement called for devaluing the dollar, both by raising the official price of gold to $38 per ounce, from $35, and by raising the dollar values of the West German mark and Japanese yen by 17 percent and 14 percent, respectively. The agreement also sought U.S. policies to correct the U.S. trade deficit.

After the agreement was signed, however, the trade balance did not improve and dollars continued to flood the foreign exchange markets. Other countries viewed their growing dollar balances as prima facie evidence that the United States had abandoned the maintenance

[9] Under the international monetary system outlined in the Bretton Woods agreement, the dollar served as the chief international asset, or reserve currency, held by governments. They held dollars in anticipation of possible future payments deficits that would have to be settled. Thus, we refer to the dollar during this period as the international reserve asset or reserve currency.

of its external position as a domestic policy goal. In essence, they accused the United States of cheating.

The United States responded that it had implemented the policies, but that the world economy had changed and that the coordinated policies would no longer produce the desired results. Confusion ensued and policymakers, despite the need for further action, could not resolve their differences. The failure to renegotiate a coordinated plan fueled speculation that the dollar's value could not be sustained, and eventually the agreement broke down.

...But Indicators Can Help Monitor Compliance. The conflict surrounding the Smithsonian Agreement was spawned by inadequate measures of U.S. commitment to the policy. U.S. officials viewed their implementation of the mandated policies as sufficient evidence of their fidelity to the agreement. Other countries, however, doubted the U.S. commitment because the U.S. current account had failed to improve. While data both on the U.S. current account and on policy actions, such as the dollar's devaluation, were already available, the policymakers had not agreed on a uniform framework in which to evaluate U.S. performance. If the agreement had explicitly stated which objective indicators would be used to monitor policy compliance—the dollar, the U.S. current account, or some other measure—it would have been much easier to determine whether the U.S. trade balance had worsened because the agreement had been violated or because the policy was no longer appropriate.

In general, if participants agree to exchange data on their policy actions, the chore of monitoring everyone's behavior will be eased.[10] For

instance, if a coordinated policy required each country to enact anti-inflationary monetary policies, then officials could first select, as an objective indicator, a particular interest rate or monetary aggregate to follow. They would also choose an indicator of inflation. If after some time inflation had not abated, the indicators would reveal whether each country had faithfully implemented the coordinated policy—or whether their economies had changed and the policy needed to be redesigned.

CONCLUSION

Recognizing that their policies can have significant impacts on trading partners—and that their economies are not immune to the effects of changing economic conditions abroad—countries have often attempted to cooperate in setting economic policies. They have acted on the theory that a system of coordinated policies produces the greatest improvement in economic welfare.

Attempts by the United States and its major trading partners to coordinate policies have met with only limited success. Rather than calling into question the theoretical conclusion that coordination is best, experience suggests that when coordinated policies began producing unexpected results, policymakers lacked the information needed either to decipher the cause or to redesign the policy.

In response to this problem, policymakers have begun to develop a system for sharing objective indicators of economic performance. The hope is that these indicators will sharpen policymakers' understanding of the world

---

[10] Charles Schultze, in "International Macroeconomic Coordination—Marrying the Economic Models with Political Reality," *International Economic Cooperation*, Martin Feldstein (ed.), National Bureau of Economic Research

(1988), suggests that much of the conflict surrounding policymakers' goals arises from officials considering policies, such as tax reform, as ends in themselves rather than as tools to achieve more general economic and social goals. Forcing policymakers to express their goals in terms of quantifiable economic aggregates may help eliminate some of this confusion.

economy, thereby facilitating the policymaking process. When problems do arise, the indicators will help policymakers determine whether a participant is reneging on the agreement or if the world has somehow changed. While we are still a long way from a successful coordinated policy, the use of objective indicators should help resolve some of the problems that have complicated efforts in the past.

Cletus C. Coughlin
and Geoffrey E. Wood

Cletus C. Coughlin is a senior economist at the Federal Reserve Bank of St. Louis and Geoffrey E. Wood is a professor of economics at City University, London. Thomas A. Pollmann provided research assistance.

An Introduction to Non-Tariff Barriers to Trade

RESTRICTIONS on international trade, primarily in the form of non-tariff barriers, have multiplied rapidly in the 1980s.[1] The Japanese, for example, began restricting automobile exports to the United States in 1981. One year later, the U.S. government, as part of its ongoing intervention in the sugar market, imposed quotas on sugar imports.

The increasing use of protectionist trade policies raises national as well as international issues. As many observers have noted, international trade restrictions generally have costly national consequences.[2] The net benefits received by protected domestic producers (that is, benefits reduced by lobbying costs) tend to be outweighed by the losses associated with excessive production and restricted consumption of the protected goods. Protectionist trade policies also cause foreign adjustments in production and consumption that risks retaliation by the affected country.

As a type of protectionist policy, non-tariff barriers produce the general consequences identified above; however, there are numerous reasons, besides their proliferation, to focus attention solely on non-tariff barriers.[3] Non-tariff barriers encompass a wide range of specific measures, many of whose effects are not easily measured. For example, the effects of a government procurement process that is biased toward domestic producers are difficult to quantify. In addition, many non-tariff barriers discriminate among a country's trading partners.

This discrimination violates the most-favored-nation principle, a cornerstone of the General Agreement on Tariffs and Trade (GATT), the multinational agreement governing international trade. Not only does the most-favored-nation

---

[1] See Page (1987) for a general discussion indicating that the proliferation of trade restrictions in recent years has taken the form of non-tariff, as opposed to tariff, barriers. A recent Congressional Budget Office study (1987) notes that the average tariff rate for most developed countries is less than 5 percent. There is no evidence of rising tariff rates or coverage. For example, U.S. tariff revenue as a percentage of total imports has changed very little between 1975 (3.9%) and 1986 (3.6%). See the *Statistical Abstract of the United States* (various editions) for the figures for other years.

[2] For example, see Coughlin et al. (1988).

[3] See chapter 1 in Laird and Yeats (forthcoming) for a discussion of the policy issues raised by non-tariff barriers.

principle require that a country treat its trading partners identically, but it also requires that trade barrier reductions negotiated on a bilateral basis be extended to all GATT members. By substituting bilateral, discriminatory agreements for multilateral approaches to trade negotiations and dispute settlement, countries raise doubts about the long-run viability of GATT.

This paper provides an introduction to non-tariff barriers. We begin by identifying numerous non-tariff barriers and document their proliferation. We then use supply and demand analysis to identify the general effects of two frequently used non-tariff barriers: quotas and voluntary export restraints. Next, we consider why non-tariff barriers are used instead of tariffs. A brief history of GATT's attempts to counteract the expansion of non-tariff barriers completes the body of the paper.

NON-TARIFF BARRIERS: TYPES AND USE

A tariff is a tax imposed on foreign goods as they enter a country; non-tariff barriers, on the other hand, are non-tax measures imposed by governments to favor domestic over foreign suppliers. Non-tariff barriers encompass a wide range of measures. Some have relatively unimportant trade effects. For example, packaging and labeling requirements can impede trade, but usually only marginally. Other non-tariff measures such as quotas, voluntary export restraints, trade restraints under the Multifiber Arrangement, non-automatic import authorizations and variable import levies have much more significant effects.[4] These "hard-core" non-tariff measures are designed to reduce imports and, thereby, benefit domestic producers. The discussion below focuses on these hard-core barriers.

Quotas

A quota is simply a maximum limitation, specified in either value or physical units, on imports of a product for a given period. It is enforced through licenses issued to either importers or exporters and may be applied to imports from specific countries or from all foreign

countries generally. Two examples illustrate these different characteristics. The United States imposes a general quota on dried milk imports; licenses are granted to certain U.S. trading companies, who are allowed to import a maximum quantity of dried milk based on their previous imports. In a different situation U.S. sugar imports are limited by a quota that specifies the shares of individual countries; the right to sell sugar to the United States is given directly to the governments of these countries.

Voluntary Export Restraints and the Multifiber Arrangement

Voluntary export restraints, which are nearly identical to quotas, are agreements between an exporting and an importing country limiting the maximum amount of exports in either value or quantity terms to be sold within a given period. Characterizing these restraints as "voluntary" is somewhat misleading because they are frequently designed to prevent official protective measures by the importing country. In the 1980s, for example, exports by the Japanese automobile industry to the United States and the United Kingdom have been limited "voluntarily" to prevent the governments of these countries from directly limiting imports of Japanese autos.

An example of a voluntary export restraint on a much broader scale is the Multifiber Arrangement. Originally signed in 1974 as a temporary exception to GATT and renewed three times since, the Multifiber Arrangement allows for special rules to govern trade in textiles and apparel. Under this agreement, quotas are set on most imports of textiles and apparel by developed countries from developing countries, while imports of textiles and apparel from other developed countries except Japan are not subject to any restrictions. Multilateral voluntary export restraint agreements are frequently called "orderly marketing agreements."

Non-Automatic Import Authorizations

Non-automatic import authorizations are non-tariff barriers in which the approval to import is not granted freely or automatically. There

---

[4]This subset of non-tariff barriers is taken from Laird and Yeats (forthcoming). This subset excludes a number of non-tariff barriers that can also have sizeable effects. Among these are government procurement policies, delays

at customs, health and sanitary regulations, technical standards, minimum import price regulations, tariff quotas and monitoring measures. See appendix 4 in Laird and Yeats for a glossary of terms associated with non-tariff barriers.

are two general categories of non-automatic licensing.

Discretionary licensing, often called liberal licensing, occurs when an importer's government must approve a specific import; however, precise conditions to ensure approval are not specified. Frequently, this form of licensing is used to administer quantitative limits. Under the current restraints on U.S. imports of steel, a domestic user can request authorization to exceed the maximum import limitation if the specific product is unavailable domestically at a reasonable cost. Exactly how availability and cost considerations affect the probability of an approval are left to the discretion of the authorities.

The second category of non-automatic import licensing requires the importer to meet specific conditions, such as minimum export performance, the use of the imported good for a specific purpose or required purchases of domestic products. In an export-import linkage scheme, a firm's value of imported components is limited to a maximum percentage of the value of its exports. This measure is intended to improve a country's trade balance and protect domestic producers of components.[5] Export-import linkage requirements are numerous. For example, in Yugoslavia during the early 1980s, authorized importers of automobiles were required to export goods totaling at least 30 percent of the value of each imported automobile.[6]

Variable Import Levies

Variable import levies are special charges set to equalize the import price of a product with a domestic target price. The levies are variable so that as the world price of a product falls (rises), the levy rises (falls).[7] The result is that price changes in the world market will not affect directly the domestic price. These measures are an integral aspect of the European Community's Common Agricultural Policy. For example, in March 1987, the European Community's price for wheat was $8.53 per bushel, while the world price was $1.95 per bushel. Prospective importers were faced with a levy of $6.58 per bushel.[8]

The Use and Expansion of Non-Tariff Barriers

In a current study, Laird and Yeats (forthcoming) measure the share of a country's imports subject to hard-core non-tariff barriers. Because countries frequently impose non-tariff barriers on the imports of a specific good from a specific country, but not on imports of the same good from another country, they disaggregated each country's imports by both product and country of origin to permit calculation of the total value of a country's imports subject to non-tariff barriers. Each country's "coverage ratio" is simply the value of imports subject to non-tariff barriers divided by the total value of imports.[9]

Table 1 shows the trade coverage ratio for 10 European Community and six other industrial countries for 1981 and 1986. In computing this ratio, the 1981 and 1986 non-tariff measures are applied to a constant 1981 trade base. Thus, the figures identify changes in the use, but not the intensity, of specific non-tariff measures, while holding constant the effects of trade changes.

---

[5]See Herander and Thomas (1986) for a theoretical demonstration that an export-import linkage scheme might not improve a country's trade balance.

[6]For details on the policies of Yugoslavia as well as numerous other countries, see ''Survey of Automotive Trade Restrictions Maintained by Selected Nations'' (1982).

[7]Variable import levies, which are actually variable tariffs, are considered non-tariff barriers in this study for two reasons. First, the international trade literature generally characterizes variable import levies as non-tariff barriers. See Nogués et al. (1986) for another list of non-tariff barriers that includes variable import levies. Second, Laird and Yeats (forthcoming) provide the most up-to-date data on non-tariff barriers and we have no way to remove variable import levies from their data.

[8]The numerical example is from Coughlin and Carraro (1988).

[9]One weakness of the coverage ratio as a measure of protectionism is that more-restrictive non-tariff barriers tend to receive a lower weight in the construction of the coverage ratio than less-restrictive ones. For example, a non-tariff barrier that eliminated all imports of a good from a country would have a smaller impact on the coverage ratio than a less-restrictive measure. Assume that one country's imports are valued at $100, $15 of which comes from country A, and there are no non-tariff barriers. In this case, the coverage ratio is zero. Suppose that a non-tariff barrier is now imposed on imports of goods from country A. In the first case, assume that imports from country A decline from $15 to $10; alternatively, suppose that imports decline from $15 to zero. The non-tariff barrier in the second case is more restrictive; however, the change in the coverage ratio does not reflect this fact. The coverage ratio becomes 10.5 percent ($10/$95) in the first case and zero percent ($0/$85) in the second. Thus, the "intensity" of the protection provided by non-tariff barriers is not measured accurately by this coverage ratio. An alternative measure focusing on the share of trade "affected" by non-tariff barriers, which also highlights the proliferation of non-tariff barriers, can be found in Laird and Yeats (1989).

Table 1

Non-tariff Trade Coverage Ratios for OECD Countries

Importer[1]	Trade Coverage Ratio[2]		
	1981	1986	Difference
Belgium-Luxembourg	12.6%	14.3%	1.7%
Denmark	6.7	7.9	1.2
Germany, Fed. Rep.	11.8	15.4	3.6
France	15.7	18.6	2.9
Greece	16.2	20.1	3.9
Great Britain	11.2	12.8	1.6
Ireland	8.2	9.7	1.5
Italy	17.2	18.2	1.0
Netherlands	19.9	21.4	1.5
EC (10)[3]	13.4	15.8	2.4
Switzerland	19.5	19.6	0.1
Finland	7.9	8.0	0.1
Japan	24.4	24.3	−0.1
Norway	15.2	14.2	−1.0
New Zealand	46.4	32.4	−14.0
United States	11.4	17.3	5.9
All above	15.1	17.7	2.6

NOTE: Non-tariff measures include variable import levies, quotas, non-automatic import authorizations including restrictive import licensing requirements, quantitative "voluntary" export restraints and trade restraints under the Multifiber Arrangement.

[1] The following Organization for Economic Cooperation and Development (OECD) countries — Australia, Canada and Sweden — were excluded from the computations because of problems in compiling their non-tariff measures.

[2] The share of total imports (by value) subject to hardcore non-tariff measures. In computing this index, 1981 and 1986 non-tariff measures are applied to a constant 1981 trade base. Petroleum products have been excluded from the calculations.

[3] European Community intra-trade is excluded.

SOURCE: Laird and Yeats (forthcoming).

A number of facts emerge. First, the coverage ratio varies substantially across countries. In 1981, the coverage ratio ranged from 6.7 percent in Denmark to 46.4 percent in New Zealand and, in 1986, from 7.9 percent in Denmark to 32.4 percent in New Zealand. Second, for most countries, the coverage ratio has increased. This caused the coverage ratio using the world trade figures of all 16 countries to increase from 15.1 percent in 1981 to 17.7 percent in 1986. Third, the United States had the largest percentage-point increase, as its coverage ratio increased from 11.4 percent in 1981 to 17.3 percent in 1986. The 5.9 percentage-point increase was more than double the increase for all countries.

Laird and Yeats provide evidence that exports from developing countries to industrial countries are affected to a larger extent than trade among industrial countries. For example, the 1981 trade coverage ratio was 18.8 percent for developing country exports to industrial countries and 14.3 percent for intra-industrial country trade. A similar pattern prevailed in 1986 with a coverage ratio of 20.6 percent for developing country exports to industrial countries and 17.5 percent for intra-industrial country trade.[10]

Table 2 contains coverage ratio data on a product basis. As a result of the Multifiber Arrangement, trade in textiles and clothing is subject to non-tariff barriers. For example, slightly more than one-third of European Community and U.S. imports of textiles are affected, while approximately two-thirds of European Community and three-quarters of U.S. imports of clothing are affected. Since these goods are among the most important manufactured exports from developing countries, coverage ratios for imports from developing countries relative to industrial countries tend to be higher.

Table 2 also identifies some other manufactured goods affected substantially by non-tariff barriers, especially iron and steel and transport equipment. More than three-quarters of U.S. imports of iron and steel and more than 40 percent of transport equipment are affected. The corresponding figures for the European Community are 46.2 percent and 23.6 percent.

While trade in manufactured goods is affected substantially by non-tariff barriers, trade in agricultural goods is affected to an even greater extent. The coverage ratios for agricultural goods shown in table 3 are substantially above those for manufactured goods shown in table 2. The agricultural coverage ratios frequently exceed 70 percent; see, for example, the U.S. ratios for sugar and honey (91.9 percent), dairy products (87.8 percent) and oil seeds and nuts (74 percent). Even higher agricultural coverage

---

[10] While this differential may reflect discrimination directed at developing countries, another interpretation is that the differential is product-based. Chow and Kellman (1988), for example, show that the relatively higher tariff rates faced by developing countries can be explained by product characteristics.

Table 2

Coverage Ratios of Selected Non-tariff Measures on Selected Manufactured Goods: 1986

SITC	Description	EC (10)[1]	Switzerland	Finland	Japan	Norway	New Zealand	United States
61	Leather products	7.7%	30.8 %	0.0%	47.0 %	0.0%	59.9%	0.0%
62	Rubber products	9.1	0.0	0.0	13.6	0.7	53.9	0.0
63	Wood and cork	1.0	1.9	0.0	0.0	0.0	53.0	0.0
64	Paper and articles	5.9	0.0	0.0	0.0	0.0	48.6	0.0
65	Textiles	34.7	0.0	1.6	55.5	6.1	27.4	34.5
66	Cement, clay and glass	2.9	0.0	0.0	24.1	0.0	54.5	0.1
67	Iron and steel	46.2	1.0	0.0	0.0	0.0	64.1	76.3
68	Non-ferrous metals	0.8	1.9	3.5	0.4	0.0	8.7	0.0
69	Metal manufactures, n.e.s.	2.1	5.6	0.0	1.0	0.0	35.3	11.0
71	Non-electric machinery	3.1	4.7	0.0	4.4	0.0	35.9	0.0
72	Electric machinery	11.1	0.0	0.0	0.3	0.0	64.0	1.4
73	Transport equipment	23.6	84.7	0.0	17.3	0.0	22.1	41.1
81	Plumbing & lighting fixtures	0.0	0.0	0.0	0.0	0.0	68.2	0.0
82	Furniture	0.3	0.0	0.0	0.0	0.1	0.0	1.1
83	Travel goods	0.9	53.0	0.0	0.0	0.0	100.0	18.9
84	Clothing	65.7	18.6	12.1	11.3	86.5	52.2	76.4
85	Footwear	11.3	74.6	0.0	6.9	0.3	82.9	0.1
86	Instruments	3.8	0.0	0.0	14.1	0.0	5.3	0.0

NOTE: See table 1 for the list of hard-core non-tariff measures. The coverage ratio is, for each given product and country, the imports subject to a hard-core non-tariff measure divided by total imports.

[1]European Community intra-trade is excluded.

SOURCE: Laird and Yeats (forthcoming).

Table 3

Coverage Ratios of Non-tariff Measures on Selected Agricultural Goods: 1986

SITC	Description	EC (10)[1]	Switzerland	Finland	Japan	Norway	New Zealand	United States
00	Live animals	60.2%	100.0%	95.3%	1.2%	98.0%	0.0%	0.0%
01	Meat	77.8	97.8	89.3	65.7	99.7	14.4	0.0
02	Dairy products	99.7	45.5	100.0	73.2	82.1	12.7	87.8
03	Fish and seafood	4.6	58.3	9.7	100.0	80.4	3.6	0.0
04	Cereals and preparations	96.9	87.8	83.4	32.5	100.0	5.1	0.0
05	Fruits and vegetables	36.0	44.8	51.6	18.3	100.0	39.2	0.9
06	Sugar and honey	85.8	0.0	89.1	84.6	100.0	0.9	91.9
07	Coffee and cocoa	17.5	0.0	0.0	0.0	100.0	0.9	2.3
08	Animal feeds	11.9	30.9	5.3	13.7	92.7	16.9	0.3
09	Food preparations	10.2	13.4	0.0	17.3	100.0	73.7	0.4
11	Beverages	24.9	76.4	88.0	70.7	100.0	5.6	0.0
12	Tobacco	0.0	0.0	0.0	84.3	0.0	5.1	0.0
21	Hides and skins	0.0	99.1	0.0	18.1	0.0	0.0	3.2
22	Oil seeds and nuts	24.8	56.0	100.0	4.3	100.0	0.0	74.0
23	Rubber	0.0	0.0	0.0	0.0	0.0	0.0	0.0
24	Wood and cork	0.6	39.6	0.0	0.0	0.0	2.4	0.0
25	Pulp and paper	0.0	0.0	0.0	0.0	0.0	0.0	0.0
26	Silk, wool, cotton, etc.	9.0	24.8	0.0	1.2	4.6	16.4	2.1
29	Crude animal & vegetable matter	19.0	78.0	5.3	51.8	69.1	11.2	11.0

NOTE: See table 1 for the list of hard-core non-tariff measures. The coverage ratio is, for each given product and country, the imports subject to a hard-core non-tariff measure divided by total imports.

[1]European Community intra-trade is excluded.

SOURCE: Laird and Yeats (forthcoming).

Table 4

The Use of Selected Non-tariff Measures

Importer	Share of Imports Facing NTMs, 1981[1]					Change in the Share of Imports Facing NTMs, 1981-86[2]				
	QUOT	VER	MFA	NAIA	VIL	QUOT	VER	MFA	NAIA	VIL
Belgium-Luxembourg	0.3%	5.1%	1.2%	5.7%	5.2%	1.1%	2.2%	0.0%	0.0%	0.0%
Denmark	0.3	2.6	2.3	1.1	1.4	0.1	1.2	−0.1	0.0	0.0
Germany, Fed. Rep.	0.5	3.0	4.9	3.0	2.0	0.4	2.0	−0.6	0.0	0.0
France	5.8	1.2	1.8	7.1	2.2	1.6	1.8	0.0	0.0	0.0
Greece	8.2	4.8	1.2	3.9	3.8	0.4	4.4	0.0	0.0	0.0
Great Britain	2.2	2.0	2.9	5.1	4.4	−0.9	2.3	0.0	0.0	0.0
Ireland	0.1	4.6	1.3	2.2	2.2	0.1	1.5	0.0	0.0	0.0
Italy	7.5	0.8	1.8	7.0	6.6	0.6	1.2	−0.1	0.0	0.0
Netherlands	0.4	2.0	3.0	14.0	6.3	2.5	3.6	−0.2	0.0	0.0
EC (10)[3]	2.6	2.3	3.0	5.6	3.7	0.5	2.1	−0.2	0.0	0.0
Switzerland	2.5	0.0	0.4	2.8	0.5	0.0	0.0	0.0	0.0	0.0
Finland	0.9	0.0	0.2	6.7	1.8	0.0	0.0	0.1	0.0	0.0
Japan	14.2	0.0	0.0	7.7	1.8	0.1	0.0	0.0	0.0	0.0
Norway	5.2	0.0	0.0	2.2	0.0	−0.5	0.0	0.0	1.1	0.0
New Zealand	25.3	0.0	0.0	25.6	0.0	1.6	0.0	0.0	−8.8	0.0
United States	0.5	6.9	3.2	0.0	0.0	1.5	4.4	0.0	0.0	1.4
All above	4.0	3.1	2.3	4.2	2.0	0.7	2.2	−0.1	−0.1	0.4

[1]Petroleum products have been excluded from the calculations. The abbreviations for the non-tariff measures are as follows: QUOT—quotas; VER—voluntary export restraints; MFA—restrictions under the Multifiber Arrangement; NAIA—non-automatic import authorizations; and VIL—variable import levies.

[2]The change is the 1986 share less the 1981 share.

[3]European Community intra-trade is excluded.

SOURCE: Laird and Yeats (forthcoming).

ratios are found for the European Community and Japan.

Another dimension of the use of non-tariff barriers concerns differences in the use of specific barriers across countries. Table 4 shows the share of imports (by country) that faced different non-tariff measures in 1981 and how this share changed by 1986. A number of facts emerge. In 1981, non-automatic import authorizations and quotas affected the largest share of imports when all 16 countries are considered; by 1986, this was no longer the case. Voluntary export restraints, whose use in the United States, Greece, the Netherlands and Great Britain rose substantially, affected the largest share of imports (5.3 percent) by 1986. Meanwhile, the share of imports affected by quotas rose from 4 percent in 1981 to 4.7 percent by 1986.

Comparisons of the specific measures across countries indicate that voluntary export restraints were used more extensively by the United States than by other countries. By 1986, 11.3 percent of U.S. imports were affected by voluntary export restraints; Greece, with 9.2 percent, had the next-highest share of its imports affected by these restraints.

SUPPLY AND DEMAND ANALYSIS USING QUOTAS AND VOLUNTARY EXPORT RESTRAINTS

Although the quantitative effects of non-tariff barriers are not always easily identified and measured, a theoretical identification of their major effects can be derived using supply and demand analysis. We begin by examining the effects of a quota, then discuss how a voluntary export restraint can be analyzed similarly.

In figure 1, DD represents the U.S. import demand curve for some good produced by U.S. and foreign producers. The foreign supply curve (that is, the supply curve for imports into the United States) for the good is SS. With free trade, the United States will import Q_F units of the good and pay a price per unit of P_F.

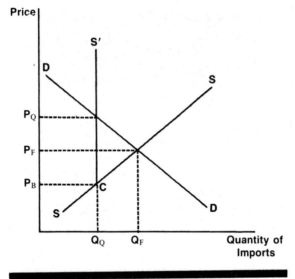

Figure 1
The Price and Quantity Effects of a Quota and a Voluntary Export Restraint

Now, suppose that an import quota of Q_Q is imposed by the United States. This restriction causes the import supply curve to become vertical at the restricted quantity. Thus, the import supply curve is the kinked curve SCS'. The restriction reduces the quantity of imports from Q_F to Q_Q, the domestic price to rise from P_F to P_Q, and the foreign price to decline from P_F to P_B.[11] The higher domestic price reduces total U.S. consumption of the good, but increases U.S. production; thus, U.S. producers of the good benefit at the expense of U.S. consumers in general. The difference between what domestic and foreign consumers pay, $P_B P_Q$, is a premium per unit of imports that can be appropriated by exporters, importers or government. The method used to allocate import licenses determines the distribution of these premiums among the potential claimants.

A voluntary export restraint has the same general effects as an equivalent quota. A volun-

tary export restraint reduces the quantity of imports, which, in turn, causes the domestic price to rise and the foreign price to fall as shown in figure 1. Again, the higher domestic price benefits U.S. producers of this good at the expense of U.S. consumers. Finally, the difference between what domestic and foreign consumers pay, $P_B P_Q$, is a premium per unit of imports that can be captured by exporters, importers or government.

While the supply and demand analysis isolates the major effects of two frequently used non-tariff barriers, it conveys virtually no information about either the magnitude of the costs and benefits of non-tariff barriers or their dynamic consequences.[12] Various case studies, however, have provided estimates of these costs and benefits. A review of this literature can be found in Laird and Yeats. Two case studies are provided in the shaded inserts on pages   and   as examples of such analyses. The first example examines the impact of the U.S. quota on sugar imports; the second examines the effect of the U.S.-Japanese agreement to limit Japanese automobile exports to the United States.

As a protectionist policy, non-tariff barriers are a method for redistributing wealth from consumers in general to selected firms and workers. This redistribution is abetted by consumer ignorance and the costs of mobilizing an effective force to counteract protectionist demands. As Coughlin et al. (1988) have demonstrated recently, the benefits received by selected groups of firms and workers are far outweighed by the costs borne by the rest of the population.

WHY USE NON-TARIFF BARRIERS INSTEAD OF TARIFFS?

Since non-tariff barriers have been used increasingly in recent years, an obvious question is why non-tariff barriers rather than tariff bar-

---

[11]Figure 1 can also be used to illustrate a variable import levy. While a quota limits the quantity of imports, a variable import levy is used to fix the price. Assuming a target (domestic) price of P_Q, when world prices fall below this price, the levy will be altered automatically to maintain the price of P_Q. Thus, no matter how far world prices decline, the quantity of imports will not rise above Q_Q. Consequently, a variable import levy and a quota have the same effect, even though they are implemented differently.

[12]Theoretical research on the impact of non-tariff barriers has explored various issues that we do not mention in the

text, two of which are mentioned below. Since many markets for internationally traded goods are imperfectly competitive, a standard topic in introductory international trade texts is to identify the effect of an import quota in the presence of monopoly. See Krugman and Obstfeld (1988) for an elementary discussion. Since voluntary export restraints discriminate among trading partners, the effects of this differential treatment have been explored. See Jones (1984) for such an analysis.

A Voluntary Export Restraint in Practice: The U.S.-Japanese Automobile Agreement

One well-known example of a voluntary export restraint is the Japanese restraint on automobile exports to the United States. In early 1981, the Japanese imposed restraints to preempt more restrictive measures advocated by many, especially labor groups, within the United States.[1] These protectionist pressures increased during the late 1970s and early 1980s as automobile sales by U.S. producers declined and foreign producers captured larger shares of the U.S. market.

Collyns and Dunaway (1987), as well as many others, estimated the effects of the restraints. These authors examined the restraints from 1981 to 1984. The examination revealed that the expected results did materialize.

With the restraints, the prices paid by U.S. consumers for Japanese automobiles rose. This reduced the competitive pressures on U.S. producers and non-Japanese exporters to the United States with the effect of increasing prices for these automobiles, but not as much as the rise in Japanese prices. The higher automobile prices reduced U.S. purchases, but the effects on U.S. and non-Japanese producers were mitigated by the relatively larger rise in the prices of Japanese automobiles and the resulting shift away from Japanese automobiles.

The restraints also induced quality changes as Japanese producers shifted their mix of exports toward larger and more luxurious models that generated more profits per unit. In addition, more "optional" equipment was installed in each unit. Consequently, the average transaction price of Japanese automobiles increased because of the pure price effect as well as the quality effects associated with the restraints.

In fact, the factors underlying the price change affect the prices of all automobiles sold in the United States and complicate the estimation. For all new cars sold in 1984, Collyns and Dunaway (1987) estimated an average increase of $1,649 (17 percent), which consisted of a pure price effect of $617 per car and a quality effect of $1,032 per car. The higher price led to a reduction in 1984 purchases of approximately 1.5 million.

As suggested above, the export restraints had differential effects. For example, the price increase for domestically produced automobiles of $1,185 (12 percent) was less than the increase for imports from Japan of $1,700 (22.5 percent). This relative price change allowed the U.S. producers to increase their market share by 6.75 percentage points, enough to leave domestically produced unit sales unchanged despite a decline of unit sales in the United States. Thus, the U.S. reduction in 1984 purchases of 1.5 million was borne by foreign producers. These production changes were estimated to generate increased U.S. automotive employment in a range from 40,000 to 75,000 jobs.

The higher automobile prices represent one facet of the losses for consumers. The pure price effect caused U.S. consumers to suffer a loss of consumers' surplus of $6.6 billion in 1984. In addition, U.S. consumers were worse off to the extent that quotas limited their range of automotive choices. Purchases of increased quality resulting from the quota totaled $10.75 billion in 1984. The welfare loss associated with these quality expenditures was not estimated, but it is clear that this loss is possibly greater than the loss associated with the pure price effect.

The losses of U.S. consumers are primarily transfers from consumers to domestic and foreign producers. Estimates of the benefits for domestic and foreign producers hinge on

---

[1]Feenstra (1985) provides numerous details concerning legislation designed to restrict imports. In early 1981, Sens. Danforth and Bentsen introduced a bill to restrict automobile imports from Japan to 1.6 million units annually during 1981-83, which is very close to the voluntary export restraint of 1.68 million. Other proposed legislation was more restrictive in providing for smaller import quotas and in specifying the minimum content of American parts and labor for automobiles sold in the United States.

the assumption about the distribution of the pure price effects. If the export restraints led to equivalent pure price effects on domestic and imported cars, then U.S. producers gained $5 billion in 1984 and foreign producers gained $1.5 billion. Of the foreign producers' gain, Japanese producers received $1 billion. On the other hand, if the export restraints led to equivalent quality effects, then U.S.

producers gained $1.25 billion in 1984 and foreign producers gained $5.5 billion. Of the foreign producers' gain, Japanese producers received $5.25 billion. If accurate, this figure provides an obvious reason why the Japanese government continued the restraints beyond early 1985 when the Reagan administration decided not to request an extension of the agreement.[2]

---

[2]In early 1985, the Reagan administration decided that the domestic automobile industry had adjusted to foreign competition and announced they would not ask for an extension. Nevertheless, in early 1985, the Japanese government extended the restraints through early 1987 at a level 24 percent above the previous

level and in 1987 extended the restraints for another year without a further increase in the ceiling. The unilateral decision to extend the restraints is a clear indication that the Japanese, especially automobile producers, were benefiting from the restraints.

---

riers have become so popular.[13] A review by Deardorff (1987) concludes that there currently is no definitive answer to this question; however, numerous reasons have been suggested.

The Impact of GATT: An Institutional Constraint on the Use of Tariffs

GATT is an institution whose original mission was to restrict the use of tariffs. Given this constraint, policymakers willing to respond to protectionist demands were forced to use non-tariff devices. Thus, in this case, non-tariff barriers are simply a substitute for tariffs. In fact, research by Ray (1981) indicates that non-tariff barriers have been used to reverse the effects of multilateral tariff reductions negotiated under GATT.[14]

Certainty of Domestic Benefits

Deardorff (1987) suggests that non-tariff barriers are preferred to tariffs because policymakers and demanders of protection believe that the effects of tariffs are less certain. This perception could be due to various reasons, some real and some illusory. For example, it may be much easier to see that a quota of 1 million limits automobile imports to 1 million than to demonstrate conclusively that a tariff of, say, $300 per car would result in imports of only 1 million automobiles.

In part, doubts that tariffs will have the desired effect is based on the possibility of actions that could be taken to offset the effects of higher tariffs. For example, the imposition of a tariff may induce the exporting country to subsidize the exporting firms in an attempt to reduce the tariff's effectiveness. The effects of quotas, on the other hand, are not altered by such subsidies.[15]

---

[13]Dating from Bhagwati's seminal discussion in 1965, comparisons of the theoretical effects of tariffs and non-tariff barriers have been a frequent topic in the international trade literature. Under various circumstances, a tariff and a specific non-tariff barrier, say, a quota, can cause different final prices and production despite reducing trade by equal amounts. These circumstances produce what is termed nonequivalence. Tariffs and quotas are equivalent when markets are perfectly competitive. In this case, there is no reason to prefer one to the other.

Bhagwati (1965, 1968) has demonstrated that the equivalence of tariffs and quotas breaks down in imperfectly competitive markets. Numerous situations can be characterized as imperfectly competitive. To date, however, the literature has provided no compelling reasons for preferring non-tariff over tariff barriers. For a recent example from this literature, see Krishna (1985).

[14]A question remains, however, as to why the framers of GATT chose to focus primarily on tariffs rather than non-tariff barriers.

[15]Deardorff's (1987) review provides another perspective on the role of uncertainty. The optimality of trade policy tools has been explored extensively using trade models with uncertainty. These models, which rely on risk aversion (that is, an individual requires a higher expected return as compensation for an increase in risk) and uncertainty originating outside a country, conclude that quotas are preferred to tariffs. The country is insulated from the uncertainty stemming from randomness in world prices or import supply curves by a quota that stabilizes the price and quantity of imports. One problem with this explanation, however, is that the quota is instituted before the uncertain state of the world is known, while in the real world protection is generally provided after a change in the world market.

A Non-Tariff Barrier in Practice: The U.S. Sugar Import Quota

Since 1982, the United States has imposed quotas on sugar imports to support a domestic price guarantee by the federal government that exceeds world market levels.[1] The high price has stimulated U.S. sugar production and shifts in demand toward other sweeteners, which has necessitated large reductions in sugar import quotas in recent years.

Tarr and Morkre (1984) estimated the costs of the sugar import quota for fiscal year 1983 (October 1982-September 1983). Actually, the quota is combined with a tariff, so tariff revenues as well as quota revenues arise. The quota revenues are captured by 24 foreign countries who have the right to sell sugar in the United States.

Figure 2 illustrates some of the effects of the U.S. trade restrictions in 1983. The lines SS and DD are the U.S. supply and demand curves for sugar. The world price was 15 cents per pound, and U.S. purchases were assumed to have no effect on this price. With free trade, U.S. production, consumption and imports would have been 6.14 billion pounds, 19.18 billion pounds and 13.04 billion pounds. To raise the internal (U.S.) price to 21.8 cents per pound, a tariff of 2.8 cents per pound and a quota of 5.96 billion pounds were used. The value of the quota is 4.0 cents per pound, because 2.8 cents per pound of the 6.8 cents per pound differential between the U.S. price and the world price is due to the tariff.

The welfare effects of the trade restrictions are indicated by the areas f, g, h, i and j. The price-increasing effects of the trade restrictions cause consumers to suffer a loss of consumer surplus equal to $1.266 billion, the sum of areas f, g, h, i and j.[2] Producers gain, in the form of producer surplus, area f whose value is $616 million. The U.S. government also gains $167 million in tariff reve-

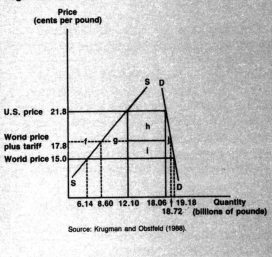

Figure 2
The Effects of Trade Restrictions on the U.S. Sugar Market

Source: Krugman and Obstfeld (1988).

nue, which is represented by area i. Consequently, the net effect for the United States is a loss of $483 million, which is the sum of areas g, j and h. Area g is the loss due to inefficient production and area j is the loss due to inefficient consumption. Area h, which is equal to $238 million, is the value of the import licenses received by foreign suppliers. In other words, the quota entails a transfer from U.S. consumers to foreign producers of $238 million.

The preceding analysis, while effectively highlighting the winners and losers from the U.S. sugar program, is not the entire story. These estimates pertain to one year only. Since the U.S. sugar policy is ongoing, the losses are ongoing as well. In addition, important dynamic interrelationships between policy changes and production and trade changes exist.

[1]Maskus (1987) concluded that U.S. sugar production and trade have been directed by government policies almost continuously for 200 years.

[2]Tarr and Morkre's (1984) estimate of the consumer cost of the U.S. sugar program is consistent with other studies. Maskus (1987) surveyed studies of the costs borne by U.S. consumers and found estimates ranging from $1 billion to $2.7 billion.

Maskus (1987) has identified a number of the dynamic consequences of the U.S. sugar program, many stemming from the fact that sugar has several close substitutes. Corn sweeteners, non-caloric sweeteners, honey and specialty sugars are all close substitutes. Higher sugar prices have induced the production of alternative sweeteners that compete with and, consequently, threaten U.S. sugar producers.

The fact that sugar is used in different goods has set in motion a number of adjustments. Examples abound of the distortions induced by the artificially high U.S. sugar price. For example, the large price differential between U.S. and foreign sugar provides a cost advantage to foreign, especially Canadian, food-processing firms. The sugar policy can be viewed as a tax on U.S. refiners and processors that was not levied on foreign firms.

Trade flows responded to these price changes as a rapid expansion in imports of sugar-containing goods ensued. In fact, the differential between U.S. and world sugar prices became so large at one time that sugar-containing goods were imported solely for their sugar content. For example, during 1985, world sugar prices declined so sharply that, in June 1985, the U.S. sugar price was 776 percent of the world price. This difference induced some firms in the United States to import Canadian pancake mix, which was not subject to the quota, and process it to extract the sugar.

The induced changes in production and trade have forced a number of additional U.S. actions to maintain the sugar prices. For fiscal year 1985, the U.S. sugar import quota was reduced 17 percent. This was followed by reductions of 27.6 percent in 1986 and 45.7 percent in 1987. Trade restrictions on sugar substitutes also have resulted. Two of these are: 1) an emergency ban on imports of certain syrups and blended sugars in bulk in June 1983; and 2) emergency quotas on a broad range of sugar-containing articles in both bulk and retail forms in January 1985.

The increasingly restrictive import barriers have produced tensions with numerous exporters of sugar, most of whom are developing countries. To conform with the General Agreement on Tariffs and Trade, the import quotas must be applied in a non-discriminatory fashion. The United States applied this provision by basing its quota allocation on imports during the relatively free-market period of 1975-81. Attempts to maintain constant shares for most countries, however, ran into practical problems. Countries experiencing rapid growth in sugar exports to the United States between 1975 and 1981 were subjected to substantial cuts between the end of the free-market period and the beginning of the quotas. For example, sugar exports from Honduras were reduced from 93,500 tons in 1981 to 28,000 tons in 1983.

The effect of this cut was mitigated somewhat in 1983 when the United States transferred 52 percent of Nicaragua's quota to Honduras, an action that simultaneously punished the Sandinista regime and rewarded a neighboring state thought to be in danger from the Nicaraguan-supported rebellion. This action violated GATT rules and generated much criticism of the United States. Such a quota system increases the likelihood that trade policy is used for noneconomic reasons.

The lessons from the U.S. sugar program are straightforward. First, significant costs have been imposed on U.S. consumers. Second, the resulting distortions in economic incentives have harmed U.S. producers dependent on sugar. Third, economic responses to the legislation have revealed a number of loopholes that have necessitated additional restrictions and distortions so that U.S. sugar producers could continue to benefit. Fourth, U.S. attempts to ensure fairness have necessitated substantial resources to ascertain production and trade behavior. Finally, the program has been used for political purposes to reward and punish foreign countries.

Benefits to Other Parties

The supply and demand analysis of quotas and voluntary export restraints highlights the difference per unit of import between what domestic and foreign consumers pay. This price differential reflects the extent of the gains that are available for some group to appropriate. With tariffs, the price differential is captured by the domestic government in the form of tariff revenue. With non-tariff barriers, the domestic government is not a direct beneficiary unless it sells the rights to import to the highest bidders. Otherwise, domestic importers, foreign exporters and foreign governments capture these gains. The potential distribution of these benefits can influence the domestic government's choice between tariff and non-tariff barriers.

With voluntary export restraints, the price differential identified above is typically captured by the exporting firms from the foreign country. This result may reduce the likelihood that the foreign country will retaliate against such restrictions. Given certain demand conditions in both the U.S. and foreign markets, voluntary export restraints can entail a substantial redistribution from consumers in the importing country to selected producers in the exporting country. For example, Collyns and Dunaway (1987) estimate that the U.S.-Japanese voluntary export restraint on automobiles yielded increased benefits to selected Japanese auto producers ranging from $1 billion to $5.25 billion in 1984.

Hillman and Ursprung (1988) extend the preceding idea using a simple model of trade policy formulation in which a democratic government is choosing between a tariff and a voluntary export restraint.[16] A simplification in this model, whose importance is discussed below, is that rival political candidates place no value on tariff revenue. Assume a voluntary export restraint and a tariff generate identical domestic producer benefits. Politicians will support the voluntary export restraint over the tariff because the voluntary export restraint generates benefits for foreign producers that, in turn, can be appropriated partially by the politicians in the form of campaign contributions. On the other hand, the tariff revenue is assumed to have no value for politicians. Candidates for elective office are viewed as announcing trade policy positions to maximize campaign contributions from domestic and foreign producer interests.

In addition to increasing the probability that protectionism will take the form of voluntary export restraints rather than tariffs, the argument reveals a way that political candidates can personally capture revenues that, with tariffs, would have accrued to the domestic government. Nonetheless, the assumption about the perceived value of tariff revenue to politicians and the fact that consumer interests are ignored in the analysis suggests one should be cautious in generalizing this result.

The possible benefits to domestic politicians of using non-tariff rather than tariff barriers are not restricted to campaign contributions. For example, a tariff is an explicit tax on consumers while a quota is an implicit tax on them. Policymakers might find it easier to support quotas and other non-tariff barriers because they will not be directly associated with a tax increase that consumers, as voters, might resist.[17]

---

[16]Husted (1986) also connects foreign lobbying to the domestic economy. He finds that the dollar value of foreign lobbying in the United States is small relative to other traded service flows and that the returns to foreign lobbying generate large returns. For example, Husted calculated that the expenditure in the United States of $1.4 million on foreign lobbying by the world automobile industry came primarily from Japan. Given the estimates by Collyns and Dunaway (1987) and others indicating Japanese automobile rents exceeded $1 billion in 1984, U.S. politicians do not appear to be capturing much of these rents.

[17]A neglected issue in the preceding comparison of non-tariff barriers with tariffs is the distribution of these restrictions across industries. While Ray (1981) found that non-tariff barriers and tariffs are biased toward industries in which the United States has a comparative disadvantage, he also found some major differences. Tariffs are biased toward low-skill rather than capital-intensive industries and are unrelated to product heterogeneity and the geographical dispersion of domestic production facilities. On the other hand, non-tariff barriers are biased toward capital-intensive industries producing fairly homogeneous products. Production in these industries tends to be distributed across regions consistent with the distribution of population.

GATT AND NON-TARIFF BARRIERS

The history of multilateral trade negotiations dealing with non-tariff barriers is brief.[18] Multilateral trade negotiations are conducted under the auspices of the General Agreement on Tariffs and Trade, which was created shortly after World War II. GATT, a term that encompasses the multilateral agreement governing international trade, the bodies administering the agreement, and all associated trade-related activities, has focused on the reduction of tariff rather than non-tariff barriers. To date, seven rounds of GATT negotiations have been completed, with the first six concerned almost exclusively with tariffs.[19]

The Tokyo Round

The Tokyo Round, the most recently completed round lasting from 1973 to 1979, was a comprehensive effort to reduce trade obstacles stemming from tariffs and non-tariff measures. New or reinforced agreements, called "codes," were reached on the following non-tariff measures: 1) subsidies and countervailing duties; 2) government procurement; 3) technical standards; 4) import licensing procedures; 5) customs valuation; and 6) anti-dumping.[20]

The code on subsidies and countervailing duties prohibits direct export subsidies, except under certain situations in agriculture. This code is noteworthy in extending GATT's prohibition of export subsidies to trade in raw materials. Because nearly all governments subsidize domestic producers to some extent, the code established criteria to distinguish between a domestic and an export subsidy. Domestic subsidies that treat domestic and export activities identically are generally allowed. Countervailing duties, which are tariffs to offset a subsidy received by a foreign exporter, are prohibited unless the subsidized goods are shown to be causing (or threatening) "material" injury to a domestic producer. This code also allows a country to seek redress for cases in which another country's subsidized exports displace its exports in third-country markets.

The code on government procurement states that, for qualifying nonmilitary purchases, governments (including government-controlled entities) must treat foreign and domestic producers alike. In addition to resolving disputes, the code establishes procedures for opening and awarding bids.

The code on technical standards attempts to ensure that technical regulations and product standards such as labeling, safety, pollution and quality requirements do not create unnecessary obstacles to trade. The code does not specify standards; however, it establishes rules for setting standards and resolving disputes.

The code on import licensing procedures, similar to the code on technical standards, is not spelled out in detail. Generally speaking, governments stated their commitment to simplify the procedures that importers must follow to obtain licenses. Reducing delays in licensing and paperwork are two areas of special interest.

The code on customs valuation established a uniform system of rules to determine the customs value for imported goods. This code uses transaction prices to determine value and is designed to preclude the use of arbitrary values that increase the protective effect of a tariff rate.

Finally, the anti-dumping code prescribes rules for anti-dumping investigations, the imposition of anti-dumping duties and settling disputes. The standards for determining injury are clarified. This code obligates developed countries to treat developing countries preferentially.

---

[18]For a brief history of multilateral trade negotiations, as well as details on the current negotiations, see *The GATT Negotiations and U.S. Trade Policy*, a 1987 study by the Congressional Budget Office. For additional details on the current multilateral negotiations, see Anjaria (1986) and the 1987 report by the United States International Trade Commission, *Operation of the Trade Agreements Program*.

[19]The sixth round, known as the Kennedy Round, marked the first time for a GATT agreement on non-tariff barriers. Agreements were reached on an anti-dumping code and the elimination the U.S. system of American Selling Prices, which applied a tariff rate for certain imports to an artificially high dutiable value. The dutiable value was set equal to the price of a competing good produced domestically instead of to the import's actual invoice price. This system was applied to a small portion of total imports, primarily benzenoid chemicals and rubber footwear. Both agreements were blocked by Congress, but were accepted in the next round of negotiations.

[20]Non-tariff barriers were also reduced in civil aircraft and selected agricultural goods, primarily meat and cheese.

The Uruguay Round

The Tokyo Round codes have relied on good-faith compliance, which has tended to undermine their effectiveness. Streamlining and resolving disputes is a priority during the current round of multilateral negotiations, the Uruguay Round. The Tokyo Round codes will be reviewed and possibly modified during the Uruguay Round. In particular, broadening the government procurement code to include service contracts will be discussed. Concerning the technical standards code, agreements dealing with the mutual acceptance of test data generated by other parties and the openness of the activities of standards bodies will be sought. A major issue in the anti-dumping code is how to handle input dumping (that is, export sales of products that contain inputs purchased at dumped prices).

The Uruguay Round, begun in September 1986, has and will discuss a number of non-tariff barrier issues, many of which extend beyond the codes of the Tokyo Round. Trade issues involving agriculture and services (banking, construction, insurance and transportation) are of paramount importance. The United States has proposed the elimination of all trade- and production-distorting agricultural policies. While the major agricultural nations have agreed to the principle of liberalizing agriculture, the sweeping nature of the U.S. proposal has been resisted by some nations, especially the European Community. With respect to services, the primary goal is to establish principles for extending GATT coverage to this trade.

A recent study by the Congressional Budget Office (1987) predicts that the performance of the Uruguay Round will be judged largely on its handling of non-tariff barrier issues. GATT has not effectively combatted rising non-tariff barriers for many reasons. Two reasons are that the effects of non-tariff barriers are less transparent than the effects of tariffs and, in many cases, non-tariff barriers are designed to satisfy a domestic rather than an international objective. A major obstacle is determining at what point a national economic policy, whose international effects are somewhat uncertain, becomes an internationally unacceptable non-tariff barrier. These national economic policies have frequently resulted from the lobbying efforts of strong domestic constituencies such as agricultural interests. Thus, major trade policy

reform will be met with much resistance from these groups.

CONCLUSION

Non-tariff barriers have effects similar to those of tariffs: they increase domestic prices and impede trade to protect selected producers at the expense of domestic consumers. As shown in the case studies of sugar and automobiles, they also have other effects, generally adverse.

Despite the adverse national consequences, the use of non-tariff barriers has increased sharply in recent years. The chances for a reversal of this trend appear to be small. The variety of non-tariff measures, the difficulties of identifying and measuring their effects and the benefits received by specific groups combine to make a significant reduction of non-tariff barriers in the ongoing Uruguay Round negotiations unlikely.

The original mission of GATT, which has been largely achieved, was to reduce tariffs. The question, however, of why policymakers have preferred to use non-tariff barriers rather than tariffs in recent years remains. The more certain protective effects of non-tariff barriers is one plausible explanation. A second explanation, which focuses on the distribution of the benefits, is that the benefits of non-tariff barriers can be captured by foreign producers and domestic politicians. Such an allocation of benefits increases the probability that the political process generates larger amounts of non-tariff barriers relative to tariffs. A final explanation is that their adverse effects are generally less obvious to consumers than the effects of tariffs.

REFERENCES

Anjaria, S.J. "A New Round of Global Trade Negotiations," *Finance and Development* (June 1986), pp. 2-6.

Bhagwati, Jagdish N. "On the Equivalence of Tariffs and Quotas," in R.E. Caves et al., eds. *Trade, Growth, and the Balance of Payments: Essays in Honor of Gottfried Haberler* (Rand McNally, 1965), pp. 53-67.

————. "More on the Equivalence of Tariffs and Quotas," *American Economic Review* (March 1968), pp. 142-46.

Chow, Peter C. Y., and Mitchell Kellman. "Anti-LDC Bias in the U.S. Tariff Structure: A Test of Source Versus Product Characteristics," *Review of Economics and Statistics* (November 1988), pp. 648-53.

Collyns, Charles, and Steven Dunaway. "The Cost of Trade Restraints: The Case of Japanese Automobile Exports to the United States," *International Monetary Fund Staff Papers* (March 1987), pp. 150-75.

Coughlin, Cletus C., and Kenneth C. Carraro. "The Dubious Success of Export Subsidies for Wheat," this *Review* (November/December 1988), pp. 38-47.

Coughlin, Cletus C., K. Alec Chrystal, and Geoffrey E. Wood. "Protectionist Trade Policies: A Survey of Theory, Evidence and Rationale," this *Review* (January/February 1988), pp. 12-29.

Deardorff, Alan V. "Why do Governments Prefer Nontariff Barriers?" in Karl Brunner and Allan H. Meltzer, eds. *Bubbles and Other Essays,* Carnegie-Rochester Conference Series on Public Policy (North-Holland, 1987), pp. 191-216.

Feenstra, Robert C. "Automobile Prices and Protection: The U.S.-Japan Trade Restraint," *Journal of Policy Modeling* (Spring 1985), pp. 49-68.

Herander, Mark G., and Christopher R. Thomas. "Export Performance and Export-Import Linkage Requirements," *Quarterly Journal of Economics* (August 1986), 591-607.

Hillman, Arye L., and Heinrich W. Ursprung. "Domestic Politics, Foreign Interests, and International Trade Policy," *American Economic Review* (September 1988), pp. 729-45.

Husted, Steven. "Foreign Lobbying and the Formation of Domestic Trade Policy," paper presented at Western Economic Association Meeting, San Francisco, July 1986.

Jones, Kent. "The Political Economy of Voluntary Export Restraint Agreements," *Kyklos* (1984), pp. 82-101.

Krishna, K. "Trade Restrictions as Facilitating Practices," National Bureau of Economic Research, Working Paper #1546 (1985).

Krugman, Paul R., and Maurice Obstfeld. *International Economics* (Scott, Foresman, 1988).

Laird, Sam, and Alexander Yeats. "Nontariff Barriers of Developed Countries, 1966-86," *Finance & Development* (March 1989), pp. 12-13.

Laird, Sam, and Alexander Yeats. *Quantitative Methods for Trade Barrier Analysis* (Macmillan, forthcoming).

Maskus, Keith E. "The International Political Economy of U.S. Sugar Policy in the 1980's," United States Department of State, Bureau of Economic and Business Affairs, Planning and Economic Analysis Staff, Working Paper #1 (September 1987).

Nogués, Julio J., Andrzej Olechowski, and L. Alan Winters. "The Extent of Nontariff Barriers to Industrial Countries' Imports," *The World Bank Economic Review* (1986), pp. 181-99.

Page, Sheila. "The Rise in Protection Since 1974," *Oxford Review of Economic Policy* (Spring 1987), pp. 37-51.

Ray, Edward John. "The Determinants of Tariff and Nontariff Trade Restrictions in the United States," *Journal of Political Economy* (February 1981), pp. 105-21.

"Survey of Automotive Trade Restrictions Maintained by Selected Nations." Office of International Sectoral Policy, U.S. Department of Commerce, in hearings on *Fair Practices in Automotive Products Act* before the Subcommittee on Commerce, Transportation and Tourism, March 2, 1982, pp. 113-23.

Tarr, David G., and Morris E. Morkre. *Aggregate Costs to the United States of Tariffs and Quotas on Imports: General Tariff Cuts and Removal of Quotas on Automobiles, Steel, Sugar, and Textiles,* Bureau of Economics Staff Report to the Federal Trade Commission (December 1984).

U.S. Congress, Congressional Budget Office. The *GATT Negotiations and U.S. Trade Policy* (GPO, June 1987).

U.S. Department of Commerce, Bureau of the Census. Statistical Abstract of the United States: 1988 (GPO, 1987).

U.S. International Trade Commission. Operation of the Trade Agreements Program—39th Report, 1987 (USITC, July 1988).

Article 26

U.S. Banks' Exposure to Developing Countries: An Examination of Recent Trends

Barbara A. Bennett and
Gary C. Zimmerman

Economists, Federal Reserve Bank of San Francisco. Outstanding research assistance provided by Alice Jacobson, John Nielsen, and Steven Dean. Special thanks to Emily Kwok and Irene Tong for assistance with the database. Editorial committee members were Hang-Sheng Cheng, Chris James and Vivek Moorthy.

U.S. banks' total LDC loan exposure and exposure relative to assets and capital have declined since the LDC debt crisis began in 1982. The authors find, however, that exposure to troubled LDCs has not fallen as much as exposure to more creditworthy borrowers, and that exposure has become increasingly concentrated at the largest U.S. banks. They posit three possible explanations: involuntary lending, banks' relative advantages in working with troubled borrowers, and the existence of deposit insurance, which distorts lending decisions.

In February 1987, the government of Brazil announced that it was suspending interest payments on its debts to commercial banks. This debt-service moratorium came as no surprise to the international financial community since Brazil's ability to meet the regularly scheduled payments of principal and interest on its obligations had been deteriorating for some time. Nonetheless, Brazil's action underscored the lingering concerns about a number of lesser developed country (LDC) debtors following the 1982 debt crisis.

In view of renewed worries about the economic health of LDC debtors and the continued high level of exposure to those borrowers within the U.S. banking industry, a number of U.S. banks took action to increase their loan loss reserves in June 1987. All told, these additions to loan loss reserves amounted to over $15 billion. Bank stock values responded favorably, but questions remain concerning the adequacy of these actions.

Moreover, bank regulators remain concerned about U.S. banks' exposure to developing countries. For example, as part of its risk-based capital proposal announced in July 1987, the Federal Reserve Board suggested that all banks with large exposures to high-risk countries be required to maintain capital positions above the minimum ratios.

This paper examines U.S. banks' exposure to international borrowers, with a particular emphasis on the subset of troubled LDCs. It attempts to explain the pattern of exposure that apparently concentrates international lending risk in the banking system. The paper is organized in the following way. In the first and second sections, we describe the events leading up to the debt crisis that erupted in August 1982, when Mexico announced a moratorium on debt service, and how the debt crisis affected bank lending to developing countries.

Readers who are familiar with this background material may wish to turn directly to the third section where we take a closer look at U.S. banks' exposure to developing countries since the debt crisis. We find a number of surprising and possibly disturbing developments, including an increase in U.S. banks' exposure to troubled LDCs relative to their exposures to other international borrowers and an increasing concentration of that total exposure at the largest U.S. banks. In the fourth section, we attempt to explain these developments. The paper concludes with a discussion of policy implications.

I. LDC Lending in Historical Perspective

Prior to the 1970s, longer term lending to developing countries occurred primarily through official sources. The bulk of private capital flows, to the extent they occurred, took the form of foreign direct investment. Private lenders such as commercial banks tended to provide funds primarily to finance trade.

Even before the first oil crisis in 1973-74, however, the role of private lenders began to change dramatically. Some have suggested that the rapid rise in the U.S. money supply in the early 1970s and the adoption of floating exchange rates increased liquidity, particularly in the form of Eurodollars, and led to a rise in international lending by commercial banks. The first oil shock then generated current account deficits for oil-importing countries and equally large surpluses in the current accounts of the Persian Gulf countries. Private lenders, most notably commercial banks, facilitated the flow of funds between lending and borrowing countries.

Chart 1 shows the growth in the external indebtedness of Latin American countries to all countries from 1970 through 1984. It is clear that private lenders' (primarily banks) share of the total funds advanced to those countries increased significantly. Moreover, data on bank lending suggests that U.S. banks took an active role in supplying credit to LDCs generally, with exposure reaching a peak of $166.2 billion in 1983.

Although several developing countries experienced debt service problems during this period, in general, the high inflation of the middle and late 1970s guaranteed that the real, or inflation-adjusted, debt service burden was quite low because loans were repaid in devalued dollars. Moreover, rapid growth of the economies of the industrial countries generated strong demand for the exports of developing countries. Consequently, very few LDCs experienced payment difficulties despite the rapid growth in the nominal value of their indebtedness.

Beginning in the early 1980s, a number of factors combined to increase LDC debtors' real debt burdens. First, real interest rates rose dramatically as central banks moved to reduce inflation by tightening credit. The rise in real interest rates was translated immediately to LDCs' borrowing costs since most of LDCs' debt was short- or medium-term at floating rates tied to a market rate, such as LIBOR (London Inter-Bank Offer Rate). Second, in 1982, worldwide inflation unexpectedly abated. Long-term debt obligations that were contracted on the assumption that export prices would continue rising suddenly became more costly in real terms. Worse yet, the decline in inflation was not translated into lower nominal interest rates.

Moreover, the value of the dollar, the currency in which most loans to LDCs were denominated, rose relative to

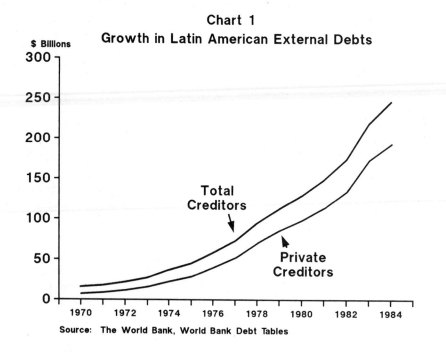

Chart 1
Growth in Latin American External Debts

Source: The World Bank, World Bank Debt Tables

LDC currencies, making it more expensive for developing countries to earn dollars with which to service their debts. Ordinarily, the rise in the value of the dollar would have stimulated demand for developing countries' exports, enabling them to generate additional foreign exchange. Instead, a worldwide recession reduced the demand for developing countries' exports and made it extraordinarily expensive for LDCs to obtain foreign exchange to service their debt obligations.

These developments culminated in Mexico's announcement in August 1982 that it was imposing a moratorium on the payment of interest on its debt obligations. A payments "crisis" ensued. Mexico's creditors were able to negotiate a "restructuring" of Mexico's debt to alleviate near-term debt service problems, but by then a number of other LDCs were experiencing similar difficulties.

At this point, default on LDC loans and the potential for collapse of the international financial system became a real concern. Official policymakers and private lenders adopted similar approaches to managing the crisis for all debtors experiencing difficulties. First, to obtain short-term financing from the IMF (International Monetary Fund), the debtor country had to reach an agreement with the IMF concerning an economic reform program designed to improve the longer term outlook for its debt service capacity. Second, once an IMF agreement was reached, banks had to reach an agreement with the debtor to reschedule their loans. Initially, these reschedulings established higher fees and spreads over the cost of funds to compensate banks for lengthening loan maturities. In subsequent reschedulings, spreads and fees were reduced even as loan maturities were extended. (Actually, funds provided by the IMF also were conditioned upon the country reaching an agreement with its bank creditors.) Finally, in a number of cases, banks also provided additional new funds at reduced interest rates primarily to enable countries to cover their contractual interest payments. Typically, banks participated in these new loans in proportion to their outstanding exposures to the borrower.[1]

II. Bank Lending and Changing Risk Perceptions

As the crisis unfolded, investors abruptly changed their assessment of the probability of default on LDC debt obligations. This sort of change in perceived default probabilities can be inferred from the sharp decrease in the value of outstanding claims on LDCs. The behavior of prices in the bond, bank loan, and, indirectly, the bank equities market is consistent with this view.

Articles by Edwards (1986), Folkerts-Landau (1985) and Dornbusch (1986) examine the international bond and bank loan markets' reactions to Mexico's announcement. These articles compare yields on international and foreign bonds issued by individual developing countries with those issued by industrial countries. They find that the yield spread increased dramatically in the third quarter of 1982, suggesting that investors required substantially higher default risk premia for LDC debt than previously. It is interesting to note, moreover, that default risk premia increased for all the major non-OPEC LDC debtors, suggesting an across-the-board reassessment of default probabilities with respect to LDC debt. Edwards also finds that the international bond market only anticipated the debt crisis by a few weeks, and then only partially.

In addition to the evidence from the international bond market, these articles find that risk premia on bank loans to LDCs rose during the early 1980s, as well. Terrell (1984), for example, notes that spreads over LIBOR for selected major LDCs increased from an average of 125 basis points through the first seven months of 1982 to 217 basis points during 1983.

Additional evidence for the change in perceived default risk is available from the secondary market for bank loans to LDCs. This market has existed for some time but became more prominent after the onset of the debt crisis. For example, the financial press noted the emergence of secondary market discounts of 10 to 25 percent relative to the face value of LDC loans in 1983.[2] (Secondary market discounts of 50 percent or more are not uncommon for loans to certain LDCs today.) Since the trading volume in this market was (and still is) quite thin, prices may not give an accurate indication of the *level* of default risk, but the *change* in those prices provides at least some indication that investors' assessment of default risk changed for the worse.[3]

Other studies have focused on the stock market's reaction to the debt crisis. In general, these studies conclude that investors tended to discount the market values of banks that had large exposures to developing country debt. Beebe (1985), for example, found that between 1982 and the end of 1984, the sharp downward valuation of the equities of the largest bank holding companies (those with assets over $10 billion) can be explained in part by their individual exposures to Latin American debtors, specifically Argentina, Brazil, Mexico, and Venezuela. Kyle and Sachs (1984) likewise find evidence that the market tended to discount the share prices of banks with significant exposures to Argentina, Brazil, Chile, Mexico, and Venezuela between September 1982 and June 1983.[4]

Given the strong evidence for an increase in perceived default risk following Mexico's actions, one would expect to see a sharp decrease in the supply of loans to LDCs. While it may be difficult to attribute patterns in LDC lending to supply versus demand factors, the observed decline in new lending is at least consistent with the view that lenders became less willing to extend credit after the debt crisis. According to data published by the Organization for Economic Cooperation and Development (OECD), new medium- and long-term bank lending to LDCs dropped from an average of $39.2 billion a year in the period between 1978 and 1982 to $24.1 billion after 1982.[5]

Moreover, only a relatively small proportion of the "new" lending to LDCs after the crisis actually represents a net increase in the amount of borrowed funds available to those countries. Instead, most of the new lending reported by the OECD involves rollovers of maturing obligations and/or reschedulings. Net new funds typically have been provided only to enable the borrower to meet interest payments coming due on outstanding obligations. In addition, most of the lending (whether on a net or a gross basis) has been considered "involuntary" in the sense that it takes place at below-market clearing rates and commercial bank lending syndicates have had to invoke "fair-share" rules with varying degrees of success as a means of inducing members to continue to provide funds.

In fact, because commercial bank lending to LDCs dropped off so dramatically, in October 1985, Treasury Secretary Baker announced the so-called Baker Plan. The Plan established modest goals for concerted net new lending by commercial banks in conjunction with increased official lending to the fifteen principal LDC debtors. (For a list of the "Baker Fifteen," see Appendix A.) Nonetheless, net new lending to these countries has been meager at best. In 1986, loans outstanding actually declined by nearly $3 billion.[6]

III. Effect on U.S. Bank Portfolios

The increase in the perceived probability of default on LDC loans lowered the value of the loans outstanding to LDCs. As a result, U.S. banks suffered market value capital losses even though they generally did not re-value LDC loans on their books, or increase their loan loss reserves significantly until the spring of 1987. Based on data compiled from a variety of sources, U.S. banks apparently wrote down only $2.2 billion, or approximately 1.7 percent, of their loans to non-OPEC LDCs between 1982 and 1985.[7] Moreover, total provisions to increase loan loss reserves likewise were modest, averaging approximately 0.51 percent of assets per year during this period.[8]

However, U.S. banks did take other steps to counter the effects of the decline in the market values of their portfolios. For example, banks raised additional capital through increased retained earnings, asset sales, and sales of new equity and subordinated debt. They also curtailed asset growth overall, and LDC loan growth particularly. Terrell (1984) notes, for example, that banks raised front-end fees on LDC loans as a means of curtailing lending. Outstanding loans to LDCs fell from a total of $152.6 billion in 1981 to $133.6 billion at the end of 1986. As a result of these actions, exposure to LDC debtors steadily fell between 1982 and 1986.

Charts 2 and 3 show the marked change in U.S. banks' LDC debt exposure, in relation both to total assets and book value capital for those banks with significant international lending exposure.[9] In the years preceding the debt crisis, both total assets and book capital grew at roughly the same annual rate (11.9 and 11.6 percent, respectively), while loans to LDCs grew at a faster rate (14.9 percent, on an annual basis). As a result, both measures of LDC loan exposure rose between 1977 and 1982, the former reaching more than 13 percent of assets and the latter more than 243 percent of capital. Then, beginning in 1982, exposure relative to capital, in particular, declined. By 1986, it was about half the level of 1981.

Most of this decline is the result of banks' efforts to raise book capital. Between 1982 and 1986, banks increased capital at a 13.2 percent annual rate, while LDC loans outstanding declined at only a 5.0 percent annual rate. Most of these loans originally were short-term, and banks, in theory, could have chosen not to refinance them upon maturity. In practice, once the credit had been extended, banks apparently were unable to force repayment of principal.

Moreover, closer examination of the patterns of exposure — among LDCs and other international borrowers, as well as exposure by size of bank — yields some interesting and possibly disturbing observations. First, exposure to all nations excluding LDCs, declined more rapidly than total LDC exposure. For example, U.S. banks' exposure to the major industrial nations, that is, the

G-10 countries plus Switzerland, declined 57.3 percent from 210 percent of capital in 1981 to 90 percent in 1986. Total international loan exposure relative to capital declined by 55.2 percent. In contrast, LDC loan exposure declined by 52.7 percent. Thus, the decline in LDC loan exposure is not nearly as dramatic when one considers the decline in lending to other, more creditworthy international borrowers.

Second, within the category of LDC borrowers, the decline in U.S. bank exposure has varied, with more dramatic declines reported for the LDCs that are not experiencing debt problems. To analyze this development, we grouped LDCs into two categories — "troubled" and "not troubled". The troubled borrowers were selected according to the following criteria: they received a rating of worse than average by *Institutional Investor*, and/or their outstanding bank loans were trading at a discount of more than ten percent of face value in the secondary market. Furthermore, in most cases, troubled countries have a recent history of balance of payments difficulties, economic instability, and actual defaults on their obligations. (Appendix A contains a list of the countries that fall into the troubled category, as well as a list of the "Baker Fifteen" countries.)

One way of measuring the change in banks' exposure to these two groups that attempts to control for the common factors that may have caused a general decline in international lending is to examine the change in these borrowers' shares of U.S. banks' international loan portfolios. Thus, Table 1 shows that exposure to what we have termed troubled LDCs has risen from 26.1 percent of banks' international loan portfolios in 1982 to 29.4 percent in 1986. Moreover, exposure to the Baker Fifteen has risen from 25.9 to 31.3 percent of banks' international loan portfolios. At the same time, loans to industrialized countries have fallen from 39.7 percent to 37.7 percent, and loans to nontroubled LDCs have fallen from 12.0 percent to 11.5 percent.

Thus, although borrowing by troubled LDCs has declined in absolute terms, borrowing by more creditworthy borrowers has declined by more. As a result, banks' relative exposure to troubled LDCs has risen. By implication, banks have tended to keep the worst risks in their portfolios. Consequently, the decline in total LDC exposure observed in Charts 2 and 3 overstates the decline in U.S. banks' exposure to default risk associated with lending to LDCs.

A third observation is that exposure by size of bank also has varied, with the nine largest banks holding a larger percentage of troubled LDC loans now than in 1981. As a percentage of total loans outstanding to troubled borrowers, the nine money center banks reporting on the

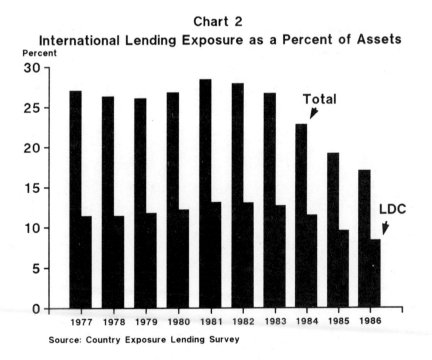

Chart 2
International Lending Exposure as a Percent of Assets

Source: Country Exposure Lending Survey

Table 1
Shares of U.S. Banks' International Loans Outstanding by Country Group
(Millions of Dollars; Percent of Total)

Year	Total		G-10 and Switzerland		Non G-10 Developed		OPEC LDCs		Non-OPEC LDCs Non-Troubled		Non-OPEC LDCs Troubled		Baker 15		Other	
1977	$194571	100%	$83610	43.0%	$16114	8.3%	$15945	8.2%	$14479	7.4%	$50699	26.1%	$40992	21.1%	$13723	7.1%
1978	217337	100	92044	42.4	17172	7.9	21342	9.8	17337	8.0	54117	24.9	47485	21.8	15324	7.1
1979	246161	100	99065	40.2	18330	7.4	22347	9.1	22958	9.3	63716	25.9	54826	22.3	19745	8.0
1980	286527	100	118503	41.4	20997	7.3	23319	8.1	29935	10.4	74739	26.1	66846	23.3	19034	6.6
1981	332057	100	131422	39.6	26084	7.9	25441	7.7	37626	11.3	87708	26.4	81520	24.6	23776	7.2
1982	352293	100	139824	39.7	29742	8.4	27760	7.9	42424	12.0	92033	26.1	91084	25.9	21509	6.1
1983	357343	100	136766	38.3	32417	9.1	28613	8.0	43717	12.2	93897	26.3	94229	26.4	21933	6.1
1984	323324	100	113400	35.1	30529	9.4	26164	8.1	39019	12.1	93819	29.0	95375	29.5	20393	6.3
1985	294542	100	105528	35.8	26986	9.2	22242	7.6	33761	11.5	87257	29.6	90525	30.7	18769	6.4
1986	275639	100	104017	37.7	22728	8.2	19550	7.1	31676	11.5	81112	29.4	86172	31.3	16556	6.0
Mean				39.3		8.3		8.2		10.6		27.0		25.7		6.7
Standard deviation				2.5		0.7		0.7		1.7		1.6		3.6		0.6

Figures may not add due to rounding
Source: Country Exposure Lending Survey, Federal Reserve Board

Table 2
Shares of U.S. Banks' Exposure to Troubled LDCs by Size of Bank
(Millions of Dollars; Percent of Total)

Year	Total		Nine Money Center Banks		Next 14 Largest Banks		All Other Banks	
1977	$50699.4	100	$30757.0	60.7	$ 9389.5	18.5	$10552.9	20.8
1978	54116.7	100	32585.3	60.2	10155.8	18.8	11375.6	21.0
1979	63715.7	100	39482.7	62.0	11320.3	17.8	12912.7	20.3
1980	74738.8	100	44388.0	59.4	13273.2	17.8	17077.6	22.8
1981	87707.8	100	50099.5	57.1	16565.1	18.9	21043.2	24.0
1982	92033.3	100	51925.2	56.4	18249.9	19.8	21858.2	23.8
1983	93896.8	100	53571.3	57.1	18594.1	19.8	21731.4	23.1
1984	93819.2	100	56004.5	59.7	18492.3	19.7	19322.4	20.6
1985	87257.0	100	54084.3	62.0	15496.7	17.8	17676.0	20.3
1986	81112.0	100	50884.0	62.7	14521.0	17.9	15707.0	19.4
Mean				59.7		18.7		21.6
Standard deviation				2.1		0.8		1.6

Figures may not add due to rounding
Source: Country Exposure Lending Survey, Federal Reserve Board

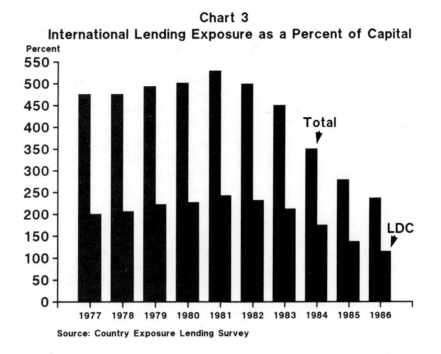

Chart 3
International Lending Exposure as a Percent of Capital

Percent

Source: Country Exposure Lending Survey

CELS now hold 63 percent compared to a low of 56 percent in 1982. Table 2 shows that, in contrast, the other two groups of banks — the next 14 largest and all other international lenders — systematically reduced their proportional shares of the total U.S. bank exposure to troubled LDCs. To a certain extent, this reduction represented a shift toward more creditworthy borrowers and a general tendency to reduce international lending altogether.

In terms of absolute changes in exposure, the nine money center banks reduced their troubled LDC loans outstanding by only $1 billion, while the next 14 largest banks and all other banks reduced theirs by $4 billion and

$6 billion, respectively, from 1982-1986. The latter two groups tended to be more active sellers of loans in the secondary markets. Also, the non-money center banks' participation in involuntary new lending arrangements associated with debt reschedulings has been relatively limited. For example, *Fortune Magazine* reported in July 1983 that many of the nine largest banks provided more than their proportional shares of the rescheduled loans to Brazil because the other lenders, including many in the next-largest category, provided substantially less than their original shares.[10]

IV. Explanations

Many observers now suggest that involuntary lending provides an explanation for these patterns in U.S. banks' exposure to LDCs. As noted earlier, LDC borrowers were able to meet debt service obligations through additional borrowing prior to the crisis. However, with the decline in the market's perception of these borrowers' creditworthiness, new funds became scarce.

To induce existing lenders to provide some relief, a number of debtors threatened to default. Lenders with outstanding claims against these borrowers, then, were faced with the choice of forbearing and/or rescheduling those claims, selling the claims at a discount to other

creditors, or declaring the borrowers in default and attempting to recover value through whatever remedies might be available. The sale of such claims at a discount would have involved the recognition of accounting losses, and declaration of default probably would have entailed even greater losses since the value of collateral generally was less than the discounted value of the claim. Lenders therefore may have been reluctant to pursue either of these two options, particularly when the exposure to a given borrower was large relative to the lender's capital. Consequently, lenders — particularly the largest ones with the largest exposures and thus the most to lose in the event of default — may have "chosen" to reschedule existing loans and even to extend new loans to cover interest payments on existing obligations to avoid losses associated with default.

However, because *all* existing lenders, whether they participated or not, would have benefitted from the extension of new credit, LDC lending syndicates had to invoke fair-share rules to ensure that adequate additional funds were provided to prevent default. Nonetheless, lenders with relatively small outstanding exposures had little incentive to participate in such lending. This may explain the difference in the patterns of exposure among the three size categories of U.S. banks.[11]

While the involuntary lending explanation is consistent with the patterns we have observed for banks, it is not entirely satisfactory. A number of troubled LDCs also had bonds outstanding prior to the crisis. In the absence of distortions, one would expect, on the basis of the involuntary lending explanation, the two groups of lenders — the bondholders and the banks — to respond similarly to the debt crisis. Yet the two appear to have responded quite differently.

Nearly all accounts of the management of the debt crisis suggest that it was the bank lenders and *not* the bondholders that were involved in debt reschedulings and extensions of new credit. Moreover, data on funds raised in international capital markets also suggest that unlike bank loans, bond financing, at least for certain countries, became nonexistent after the crisis.

This implies, in other words, that reliance on bank loans increased relative to bonds as the credit rating of the borrower declined. Moreover, nonbank creditors apparently became even more reluctant to supply funds to a borrower with a given low credit rating after the crisis than before.

To show the difference in the way bank lenders and bondholders behaved, we regressed the ratio of bank loans to total external funds raised (including bonded debt) in international capital markets by a given country in a given year on the credit rating of that country for that year. Clearly, because of the way this ratio is defined, an increase implies that reliance on bonded debt has decreased. Bank loans were defined as the sum of international bank loans and foreign bank loans, but not floating

Table 3

Percent of Bank Loans to Total Funds Raised (OECD)

Year	G-10	Non-LDC	LDC	Non-Troubled	Troubled	Baker 15
1977	34.2	37.1	80.9	74.5	78.1	78.3
1978	65.1	61.4	86.6	86.5	88.0	87.5
1979	42.7	51.1	93.9	95.2	92.9	93.7
1980	55.6	59.3	95.4	97.0	93.9	95.1
1981	27.1	34.3	79.1	89.5	72.8	73.8
1982	38.5	43.3	82.1	75.7	84.6	86.1
1983	20.4	26.2	85.7	72.3	98.0	98.2
1984	44.1	46.2	89.4	75.6	100.0	100.0
1985	35.7	38.0	74.7	61.8	98.8	99.3
1986	20.5	25.7	76.0	73.9	38.0*	42.3*

* The relatively low ratio of bank loans to total funds raised by these countries reflects the problems Mexico and Brazil encountered in rescheduling their bank loans in 1986. If Mexico's rescheduled debt, which appears in the second quarter of 1987 figures were included in the 1986 total, these ratios would be close to 100 percent.

rate notes held by banks. For the credit rating, we used the country ratings published annually by *Institutional Investor* as a proxy for creditworthiness. Ideally, some sort of market measure like the actual market prices of loans would be appropriate. However, the secondary market for bank loans is thin and quotes prices for only a handful of countries. A test of the extent to which the *Institutional Investor* ratings are a good instrument for the secondary market discounts revealed that at least for the few countries for which discounts are quoted, the ratings are indeed a good proxy.[12]

To test for a change in LDCs' access to nonbank sources of funds after the crisis (and controlling for changes in creditworthiness), we included a dummy variable that takes the value of zero prior to 1982 and the value of each country's credit rating afterwards.

We used data compiled by the OECD for a sample of approximately 62 countries between 1980 and 1986.[13] These countries represent the major international borrowers during this period and include 23 industrial countries, as well as 10 OPEC, 24 non-OPEC LDCs, and 5 Eastern Bloc countries. Table 3 presents the OECD data grouped by type of borrower.

The results of our pooled cross-section time-series regression are summarized in Table 4. The negative and statistically significant coefficient on the credit rating

Table 4

Reliance on Bank Lending vs. Bond Financing

Dependent Variable:	Ratio of International and Foreign Bank Loans to Total External Funds raised on International Markets by Country.

Independent Variable	Parameter Estimate
Intercept	1.185**
	(36.99)
Rating	−0.007**
	(−11.12)
Rating Dummy*	−0.003**
	(−6.10)

Number of Observations	492
Adjusted R-squared	.36
t-statistics are in parentheses	

* *Rating Dummy: Rating * Dummy post-1982 (= 1 after 1982).*
** *Significant at the 1 percent level.*

suggests that as LDCs' creditworthiness deteriorated, bond financing "dried up" and they were forced to rely increasingly on bank loans as a source of funds. Moreover, the negative and significant coefficient on the credit rating dummy variable suggests that for a given level of creditworthiness, access to alternative sources of funds diminished after the crisis.

These findings are consistent with the view that after the debt crisis, a number of LDC borrowers were unable to obtain funds from other sources and that it was the *banks* that were "forced" to renew and reschedule existing loans to avoid defaults and to protect their investments. This would explain the small decline in banks' exposure to troubled borrowers relative to the decline in exposure to more creditworthy borrowers.

Given that the banks appear to have responded differently to the debt crisis than did the bondholders, the question remains as to why. The involuntary lending explanation does not adequately address this issue. Assuming that neither the bankers nor the bondholders were willing to "throw good money after bad," bankers must have had some inducements to continue lending that bondholders did not have. Two explanations come to mind. First, bankers may have had superior information on the ability of LDC debtors to repay, and/or superior ability to obtain repayment. Second, bank lenders may have had regulatory incentives to lend that were not available to bondholders.

In the analysis that follows, these two alternatives are examined as two different (but not necessarily mutually exclusive) factors that may have played a significant role in determining banks' willingness to lend to LDCs both before and after the crisis.[14] The first one, the "efficiency factor," has to do with advantages banks may have relative to bondholders in assessing and monitoring riskier credits and in handling problem loan workout situations. The second factor, the "subsidy factor," relates to the effects government subsidies (implicit or explicit) may have had on banks' and investors' portfolio decisions.

Efficiency Factor

One factor that may account for the increase in banks' exposure to LDCs throughout the 1970s, and, therefore, may have had a bearing on banks' response to the debt crisis is what we have termed the efficiency factor. This explanation focuses on banks' relative advantages as agents for investors in assessing the creditworthiness of borrowers, monitoring borrowers, and working through repayment problems. It draws on insights from models of principal/agent problems in lending.[15]

Broadly speaking, borrowers and investors (that is, the ultimate lenders) may use two types of financial instruments to transfer savings. These can be characterized as bonds (direct finance) on the one hand, and bank loans (intermediated finance) on the other. The choice between the two will depend on the one that provides borrowers with the cheapest source of funds and investors with the highest return net of the costs associated with administering their investment. Among the usual costs associated with administering an investment are the costs of collecting and maintaining records of scheduled principal and interest payments, but they also include the cost of more or less continuously monitoring the borrower's financial condition. This sort of monitoring is necessary to prevent borrowers from engaging in activities that reduce the value of the lenders' claims.

For some borrowers, the costs of such monitoring are relatively modest since publicly available information conveys an accurate picture of their true net worth and, therefore, the likelihood of default. Since investors can readily determine when action is needed to protect the value of their claims, these borrowers generally will prefer bond finance because the standard covenants contained in bond indentures will provide adequate protection for investors at the lowest cost.[16, 17]

For other borrowers, however, monitoring may be costly because their assets are not traded and are therefore difficult to evaluate. In these cases, the standard financial ratios on which bond covenants rely will not convey accurate information about the borrower's true condition. In fact, if these borrowers were to use bond finance, it is possible that they might violate standard bond covenants and therefore be forced to seek new sources of credit or even be forced into liquidation, even though better information would have indicated that such actions were unnecessary and costly to both borrower and investor.

These borrowers therefore will prefer bank loans because banks typically have access to information about their condition that is not readily available to investors directly. For example, banks may have information about a borrower's payments activity and transactions balances that investors do not. Consequently, banks will be able to monitor the condition of these borrowers more cheaply than could the individual investors, making bank loans the cheaper source of funds. In a sense, then, the obligations of these borrowers could be worth more to investors when held in bank portfolios.

This analysis is applicable to international lending, although solvency may not always be the proper measure of default risk. Instead, a more general approach would be to treat default risk as a function of the cost of default. In cases where actual insolvency is not at issue, default risk would be defined as the value of unrestricted future access to external borrowed funds plus the value of seizable assets, to the extent such assets exist.[18] Thus, a sovereign borrower will not default as long as the cost of doing so exceeds the value of its external obligations.

Assuming investors can readily determine the value of a given borrower's external obligations relative to the cost of defaulting on those obligations, bonds will be the preferred financing vehicle. Presumably, most industrial countries as well as those LDCs with relatively small amounts of debt outstanding, significant wealth, and high returns to capital investment will be the countries that can tap the bond markets.

In contrast, LDCs that have high amounts of debt outstanding relative to GNP or other measures of capacity, or have unstable political regimes such that default through repudiation is a possibility, have found their ability to raise external funds through bond finance severely limited, and thus have had to rely chiefly on bank loans. To the extent that investors are willing to hold these obligations at all, they appear to prefer to hold them indirectly because banks can monitor and work with problem borrowers more cheaply, and because banks have better access to assets that may be seized than do individual investors.

Banks' apparent advantage in providing credit to higher risk borrowers suggests that, given the increase in demand for external funds on the part of LDCs in the 1970s, banks would have been the logical ones to supply most of the needed funds. Moreover, this analysis suggests that once the debt crisis erupted and investors became less certain of the chances of being repaid, the value of banks' ability to gauge solvency risk and to handle workout situations would have increased. Therefore, one would expect to see banks holding proportionately more of troubled LDCs' debt than before the crisis. One might also expect the banks' share of the outstanding obligations of nontroubled borrowers to fall as the debt crisis changed the relative values of these obligations as well.

This theory is consistent with the results of our regression findings that banks and *not* bondholders were involved in continued lending to troubled LDCs. Moreover, it helps to explain why banks continued to lend to the smaller borrowers even though, according to the involuntary lending explanation, there may have been less incentive to do so because exposure to these borrowers was small. A recent study by Gluck (1987) supports this view. He found that as the creditworthiness of selected LDCs improved in the years after the debt crisis, they were able to obtain bond financing and forego bank loans as a source of funds.

Folkerts-Landau (1985) and Edwards (1986) also provide some interesting evidence that is consistent with the relative advantage argument. They suggest that because banks are in a better position to reschedule and renegotiate a borrower's obligations than are bondholders, whose primary recourse is declaring default on the obligation, risk premia on the two types of instruments should reflect these differences. Consistent with this hypothesis, they observe that default risk premia rose by substantially more on bonds than on bank loans after the onset of the debt crisis.

The relative advantage argument, then, suggests that once the debt crisis erupted and investors became more concerned about the probability of default on the part of at least some of the LDC debtors, one would expect to see an even greater preference for bank loans as opposed to bonds in those countries. As default risk increased, banks' superior ability to work with troubled debtors and ultimately, to seize assets, would have become more valuable to investors. This would explain why U.S. banks' exposure to troubled LDCs rose relative to their exposure to more creditworthy international borrowers. It also would explain why exposure became more concentrated at the nine largest banks. Since those banks are the ones most actively involved in the international payments network and in trade finance, they are also the banks best able to monitor and seize assets if necessary.

Moreover, in workout situations, lenders need to act cohesively and the fewer lenders there are, the easier it would be to achieve consensus. This view suggests first that bond finance is particularly unsuited to workout situations since it is unlikely that the myriad bondholders could be forced to work cohesively. It also suggests that the banks with the largest exposures to begin with (that is, the nine money center banks) would have had the greatest incentive to work cohesively and to continue lending to the troubled debtors.

Subsidy Factor

A second and possibly more important factor that may have induced banks to continue lending to troubled LDCs is the existence of regulatory incentives or subsidies. In general, government subsidies, either of the lender's assets or its liabilities, will distort decisions regarding risk. If the government were to underwrite at least a portion of the increased risk, lenders would have an incentive to make and hold riskier loans than they otherwise would.

These subsidies can arise in two ways. First, the government (or a multilateral official institution such as the IMF) may subsidize exposure to LDCs *directly* by providing a guarantee of the loans to LDCs. With a guarantee of this sort, the guarantor would repay the lender up to the face value of the guarantee in the event of default by the LDC debtor. Clearly, such guarantees will encourage banks to make and hold LDC debt because some or all of the

increased risk is borne by the guarantor (that is, the government) and not the lender.

Of course, there have been no public pronouncements that provide unequivocal evidence of the existence of such guarantees. Sachs (1987), however, maintains that loan guarantees were an explicit part of the negotiations involving rescheduled debt.[19] Moreover, a number of other studies have argued that bank managers and investors behaved as if *implicit* guarantees existed, in part because there are clear public policy goals served by lending to LDCs. For example, Folkerts-Landau (1985) argues that the governments of the major industrial countries informally encouraged banks to lend to developing countries on the implicit understanding that the central banks would fulfill a lender-of-last-resort function if necessary.[20] Likewise, Guttentag and Herring (1985) suggest that one reason that banks allowed exposure to LDCs to become so high may be the existence of official international support for developing countries through such programs as the IMF's adjustment assistance programs.[21]

In contrast, there is little evidence that direct guarantees, whether explicit or implicit, were available for bonded debt. If guarantees were to apply only to bank loans, this would explain the willingness of bank lenders to continue lending while bondholders became more reluctant after the crisis.

A second way that the government could have subsidized lending to LDCs is indirectly — through (underpriced) guarantees of banks' liabilities. Of course, such subsidies are not available to bondholders. This sort of deposit insurance subsidy increases banks' willingness to hold risky assets generally. Since lending to LDCs was considered riskier than lending to industrial countries even prior to the debt crisis, banks would have had incentives to increase their exposure to LDC borrowers, particularly as the demand for external funds apparently increased throughout the 1970s. This could explain why a very large share of the private lending to LDCs even prior to the crisis took the form of bank loans as opposed to bonds.

Once the debt crisis erupted, the response of bank share prices and of new bank lending to troubled LDCs would have depended on the nature of the subsidy. Direct subsidies in the form of loan guarantees likely would have had less impact on stock prices and lending behavior than indirect subsidies. Specifically, with direct subsidies, one would not expect bank share values nor secondary market values of outstanding LDC loans to decline since the guarantor would have been the one to bear the losses.

The actual decline in share values and secondary market prices after the crisis suggests either that direct subsidies were not a significant factor in banks' international lending decisions, or that investors and bank managers were unsure of the strength of such implicit subsidies. The fact that banks tended to view IMF assistance and involvement in the rescheduling of a troubled country's debt as a prerequisite for providing new funds to that country may be a reflection of this uncertainty. Alternatively, Sachs has argued that banks have been willing to continue lending as a *quid pro quo* for IMF protection with respect to outstanding obligations.[22]

Regardless of the significance of direct subsidies in banks' lending decisions, indirect subsidies (that is, subsidies associated with deposit insurance protection) almost certainly played an important role. There is a large and growing body of evidence on the so-called deposit insurance problem which suggests that indirect subsidies exert a strong influence on banks' domestic lending. Foreign lending should be no different in this regard. Moreover, the declines in bank share prices and secondary market prices for LDC loans are both consistent with this type of subsidy. Unlike direct subsidies, in the event of default, bank shareholders do bear the risk of loss with indirect subsidies even though insured depositors do not.

Also, banks' willingness to continue lending to troubled LDCs after the crisis is consistent with the view that indirect subsidies were a significant factor in lending decisions. For example, one could argue, as Furlong and Keeley (1987) have, that a lender's incentive to hold risky assets increases the closer the lender is to insolvency. Thus, the decline in the market value of banks' net worth following the debt crisis probably provided banks with an *additional* incentive to maintain their exposure to the riskier LDCs.

Finally, the regulatory accounting treatment of rescheduled and nonaccruing LDC debt also is consistent with the existence of indirect subsidies. Regulators have allowed banks to record most LDC loans at book value as long as there is some "reasonable" prospect that the bank will be repaid at least its principal investment. As a result, banks have not had to record capital losses for LDC loans even though the market value of LDC loans declined precipitously following the 1982 crisis. By allowing this sort of indirect subsidy through "capital forbearance," bank regulators may have provided some additional inducements to continue lending. (Of course, regulators have required banks to improve their book value capital-to-assets ratios since then, so the forbearance may not have been as great as it might have first appeared.)

In sum, subsidies of various sorts probably help to explain why U.S. banks' exposure to developing countries reached such a high level in the 1970s. Once the debt crisis erupted, uncertainty over how the regulators would respond to the increased possibility of default probably also helps to explain why bank share values subsequently declined and why banks reduced their new lending to troubled LDCs. Moreover, the apparent tendency for banks to keep the riskiest debt may be consistent with this view, particularly if the regulators' actions over time could be interpreted as providing assurances of willingness to forbear.

However, the existence of subsidies does not necessarily explain why seemingly only the nine largest banks could take advantage of them, unless the subsidies were directed at a group of banks considered, by both the regulators and the market, as too large to be allowed to fail. Otherwise, subsidies would have been perceived to extend to other large banks as well, if not also to the smaller banks.

Assessment

The available evidence on lending to LDCs cannot clearly distinguish among the three explanations: the involuntary lending argument, the efficiency factor, and the subsidy factor. More sophisticated tests might shed some light and, in fact, work in progress by James suggests that indirect deposit subsidies have had a lot to do with LDC lending.

However, it is likely that all three influences have been operating since they are not mutually exclusive and may even be complementary. For example, part of the reason that the governments of industrial countries may have chosen to provide protection for bank loans to LDCs may have been that, in the event of a crisis, bank lenders have a relative advantage in monitoring the borrower and in handling a problem loan workout. Moreover, multilateral organizations like the IMF may have encouraged continued lending and helped to enforce fair-share rules because the amount of funds provided otherwise would have been inadequate. Thus, the three influences could have been and probably were mutually reinforcing.

V. Summary and Policy Implications

Mexico's announcement in August 1982 had a profound impact on the market's assessment of the default probabilities associated with lending to developing countries. Specifically, default risk premia increased and the holders of existing debt suffered large market value capital losses. As a result, lenders have become less willing to extend new loans to the countries perceived as most risky. Moreover, the outstanding exposure of U.S. banks has declined through actual write-offs, repayments, and, primarily, through growth in capital accounts.

The decline in exposure to troubled LDCs, however, is not very dramatic when compared to the declines in exposure to more creditworthy international borrowers. Likewise, the largest U.S. banks now have a larger share of troubled LDC exposure than when the debt crisis erupted. This paper has posited a number of possible explanations, all of which imply that after 1982 investors developed a decided preference for holding the obligations of troubled LDCs in the form of bank loans as opposed to bonds.

Previously cited work by James suggests that indirect subsidies have played a significant role in keeping U.S. banks' exposure to the riskiest developing countries high. Consequently, bank regulators must continue to monitor these exposures carefully and encourage banks to continue to raise capital to prevent further distortions in international lending decisions.

At the same time, however, bank lending to troubled LDCs also may be a reflection of the superior monitoring capabilities banks have in working with problem debtors. As a result, the true value of these loans on banks' books may lie somewhere between their book values and their values to nonbank investors on the secondary market. Such considerations are important to proposals that would require banks either to mark their LDC loan portfolios to market and/or to hold substantially more book capital.

APPENDIX A

International Banking
List of Country Groups

G-10 Plus Switzerland

Switzerland	Germany	Canada	Sweden
Italy	United States	France	United Kingdom
Belgium-Luxembourg	Japan	Netherlands	

Non-G-10 Developed Countries

Australia	Ireland	New Zealand	Norway
Austria	Spain	Denmark	Portugal
Finland	Greece	Iceland	Turkey

OPEC LDCs

Bahrain	Kuwait	Brunei	Iraq
Oman	Nigeria	Trinidad & Tobago	Libya
Algeria	Saudi Arabia	Ecuador	Qatar
Gabon	Venezuela	Indonesia	United Arab Emirates
Iran			

Non-OPEC Developing Countries, Troubled Debtors

Argentina	Liberia	Bahamas	Jamaica
Barbados	Malawi	Bermuda	Madagascar
Bolivia	Morocco	Brazil	Mexico
Chile	Panama	Columbia	Nicaragua
Costa Rica	Peru	Cuba	Paraguay
Dominican Republic	Senegal	El Salvador	Philippines
Guatemala	Uruguay	Guyana	Sudan
Haiti	Zambia	Honduras	Zaire
Ivory Coast			

Non-OPEC Developing Countries, Nontroubled Debtors

Angola	Mauritius	Antigua	Mozambique
Botswana	Nauru	Burma	Nepal
Burundi	North Korea	Cameroon	Netherlands-Antilles
China PR	Pakistan	Congo	Papua New Guinea
Cyprus	Puerto Rico	Egypt	Singapore
Ethiopia	Solomon Islands	Fiji	South Korea
Ghana	Sri Lanka	Guinea	Swaziland
Hong Kong	Syria	India	Taiwan
Israel	Tanzania	Jordan	Upper Volta
Kenya	Vietnam	Lebanon	Yemen
Lesotho	Yugoslavia	Macao	Zimbabwe
Malaysia		Mauritania	

Baker's List of 15 Largest LDCs with Debt Servicing Problems

Brazil	Philippines	Morocco	Ivory Coast
Mexico	Chile	Colombia	Uruguay
Argentina	Yugoslavia	Peru	Bolivia
Venezuela	Nigeria	Ecuador	

FOOTNOTES

1. See Sachs (1987) for a more complete description of the rescheduling arrangements.

2. Cited in Kyle and Sachs (1984).

3. In addition, the average (for all rated countries) country risk rating published by *Institutional Investor* fell from 52.3 to 41.0 between 1980 and 1983.

4. There are a number of other studies on the impact of LDC exposure on bank share prices. See, for example, Smirlock and Kaufold (1987) and Cornell and Shapiro (1986).

5. The data on external funds raised in international markets come from the OECD's *Financial Statistics Monthly*. All data are reported in U.S. dollars and are converted on the basis of the average spot rate for the month the bonds or loans were reported. For this paper, we use year-end figures that reflect the sum of all new lending, including bond financing over the year. It should be noted, however, that these figures represent total funds raised, including reschedulings and refinancings, as opposed to net new funds raised.

6. Morgan Guaranty Trust Company, *World Financial Markets*, June/July 1987.

7. Rodney Mills, "Foreign Lending by Banks: A Guide to International and U.S. Statistics," *Federal Reserve Bulletin*, October 1986.

8. It should be noted, however, that this increase in loan loss reserves also is the result of anticipated loan losses arising from banks' domestic loan portfolios at this time.

9. Data on U.S. banks' international loan exposure come from the Federal Reserve Board's *Country Exposure Lending Survey* (CELS). This survey was first conducted in 1977 in response to a perceived need for better data on the cross-border claims of consolidated banking organizations domiciled in the U.S. with foreign branches and majority-owned foreign subsidiaries. The data are now collected on a quarterly basis. U.S. bank exposure to over one hundred countries and a number of international organizations are reported by type of borrower and time remaining to maturity, with adjustments for loan guarantees that shift exposure across countries.

CELS data are reported for three subsets of banks: the nine money center banks, the next 14 largest banks, and the remaining banks with at least $30 million in consolidated claims on non-U.S. residents and that have at least one foreign branch or foreign subsidiary (about 160 in number).

The major drawbacks of these data are that they do not cover the claims held by all U.S. banks and the country-by-country breakdown only covers exposures that exceed three-fourths of one percent of a reporting bank's capital. Also, CELS data do not cover local-currency-denominated claims.

10. Reported in Sachs (1987), cited above.

11. Krugman (1985) and Sachs (1984) have developed models that show once a sovereign borrower has run into debt problems, it may be in the interests of all the lenders involved to reschedule the outstanding obligation and extend additional funds to reduce the borrower's near-term debt burden and enhance long-term repayment prospects. However, because there is a public good aspect to new lending in that the value of any given lender's outstanding exposure will be enhanced whether or not that lender participates in providing new funds, the lenders with the smallest exposures will have an incentive to "free ride" on the new lending of the others.

12. The Spearman Rank Test showed that correlation between the *Institutional Investor* rating and the loan discount for a given country was 0.843, at a significance level of 0.0001.

13. OECD, *Financial Statistics Monthly*.

14. There may be other factors, as well. For example, Guttentag and Herring (1985) argue that bank lending to developing countries can be explained by a concept drawn from current research in cognitive psychology called "disaster myopia." However, because this view has not gained wide acceptance in the literature, it is not addressed in this article.

15. Berlin and Loeys (1986), James (forthcoming) and implicit in Folkerts-Landau (1985).

16. These covenants typically require the borrower to meet certain readily observed conditions which, presumably, are good indicators of the borrower's true net worth. These conditions include among other things, restrictions on the types of assets the borrower may invest in, the maintenance of certain financial ratios, and the maintenance of a minimum level of capital adequacy. Violations of these covenants imply that the borrower is close to insolvency, giving bondholders the right to accelerate the maturity of their claim even to the point of forcing liquidation of the borrower's assets in bankruptcy.

17. For example, the growth in the commercial paper market largely is due to the ability of larger, well-established borrowers to raise funds directly at a lower cost than through bank loans.

18. See Niehans (1985) and Glick (1986).

19. Sachs (1987), p. 21.

20. Folkerts-Landau (1985), p. 324.

21. Guttentag and Herring (1985), p. 136.

22. Sachs (1987), p. 21.

The Costs of Default and International Lending

by Chien Nan Wang

In August 1982, Mexico announced that it was unable to service its nearly $80 billion foreign debt. Brazil, Argentina, Venezuela and other debtor countries soon announced their own debt-servicing difficulties.

Initially, it was feared that these borrowers might flatly refuse to repay their debts, thus repudiating their loan obligations. Because debt repudiation could severely hurt both creditors and debtors, the threat became the focus of what became known as the 1982 less-developed-country (LDC) debt crisis.

Between 1983 and 1986, creditors, debtors, and the International Monetary Fund (IMF) generally were able to work together to manage the debt problems, keeping interest payments on schedule by restructuring old loans and by making new loans in what can be described as a process of "cooperative interruptions."[1]

However, in 1986, Peru limited debt-service payments to not more than 10 percent of its export revenues. More strikingly, in February 1987, despite an ongoing effort to reschedule and refinance its debt, Brazil unilaterally delayed interest payments. In addition to Brazil, seven other Latin American countries, together with several smaller African countries, delayed interest payments in 1987. However, as will be discussed later, most of these interrupted payments were renegotiated, with interest payments resuming within a year, through a set of arrangements that has been described as a "conciliatory default."[2] Earlier this year, Brazil again announced several measures designed to delay the repayment of its debts.

Conciliatory default, cooperative interruptions, and outright debt repudiation can each be regarded as a type of debt servicing failure—that is, of a borrower's failure to service and repay its debt as originally specified in the loan agreement. There are important distinctions among the types of debt-service failure. Outright repudiation is the most extreme form of noncooperative default, and occurs rarely. In contrast, both conciliatory default and cooperative interruption are characterized by important elements of mutual agreement, or at least acceptance of the need to modify the original loan agreement. Of these two, the latter procedure is the most amicable. However one describes the process, the international debt-service difficulties of recent years raise questions that are worth exploring.

First, any type of debt servicing failure can hurt creditors and debtors alike. Creditors see their capital eroded, threatening their solvency; debtors damage their own creditworthiness, perhaps impairing their ability to borrow again. Given such significant costs, how do borrowers choose the appropriate response to their debt servicing problems?

During the past few years, a number of less developed countries (LDCs) have had difficulty repaying their foreign debt. Sometimes payments have been suspended or delayed—making it necessary for debtors and creditors to renegotiate or reschedule loan payments. These problems have raised questions about the costs and benefits of different types of debt repayment negotiations and their implications for the future of international lending. This article investigates these questions.

Second, international lending to LDCs currently is declining. Declining capital inflows make it even more difficult for LDCs to service their debts and to finance their growth. Considering the huge amount of old debt and the uncertain prospects for future repayment, it is difficult to restore lenders' incentives to make new loans. Even if overall indebtedness were reduced to a more manageable level, for example, how could lenders really be confident that debtors would not default again in the future? Finally, do widespread problems with international debt service reveal a fundamental weakness in the structure of international private lending that does not exist in purely domestic lending?

The key to answering these questions centers on the benefits and costs of default in its various forms. This *Economic Commentary* investigates these aspects of default, using the current LDC debt problem to illustrate several issues that seem especially important for future international lending.

■ The Benefits and Costs of Default

International credit agreements involving the direct or indirect obligations of governments present the most difficult problems for creditors. The ultimate defenses for creditors against nonpayment —such as seizure of collateral and recourse to legal proceedings—are not fully available in international lending, so that repayment from sovereign debtors is not strictly enforceable.

A country may choose not to repay, even if it can. When unwillingness to repay motivates a sovereign debtor's debt-service decision, this decision is usually made after comparing the costs and benefits involved in a continuum of options ranging from timely debt service to extreme forms of default. One such option may be to alter the terms of repayment.

The primary benefit of altering the terms of repayment is the ability in the short run to save foreign exchange for domestic consumption and promotion of economic growth. The amount of foreign exchange saved is larger in repudiation cases than in conciliatory defaults because the former reduces the debt-servicing load for a longer period of time than the latter. While conciliatory default relieves or delays full debt-service payments for a period of time, cooperative interruption still assumes a certain amount of debt servicing for that period, thus reaping fewer benefits.

Debtors may also think that altering debt-service obligations will enhance domestic political tranquility. It is reasonable for debtors to believe that reducing debt service will permit increased domestic consumption and improve the resident population's immediate living standard. Altering the terms

of debt-service agreements may help consolidate the political regime, particularly for countries with pressing demands for a higher living standard. The longer-run effect is less certain. The costs of default may make it impossible to maintain a higher growth profile that will improve the future living standard, although this will depend on the severity and the effectiveness of the creditors' sanctions.

Altering debt-service agreements, while perhaps economically and politically attractive, is not cost-free, however. The costs and benefits for the debtor depend importantly on a wide range of factors, including the ability to negotiate new terms with lenders. In extreme cases of unilateral default, the borrower often faces trade and financial sanctions that impede the ability of the debtor country to maintain its overall consumption level when its income is low and then to repay when its income is high. Profitable investment opportunities may also be lost, and trade credit may be reduced or eliminated. Trade embargoes imposed by the lender's government may cause severe damage to countries dependent on trade, which includes most major debtors.

Default may also result in seizure of a defaulter's foreign assets or exports. Sovereign immunity from foreign interference with commercial transactions once was a basic principle in international law. However, the 1976 Foreign Sovereign Immunity Act (FSIA) in the U.S. and the 1978 State Immunity Act (SIA) in the United Kingdom established the legal liability of foreign governments for their acts of a purely commercial nature.

FSIA and SIA are crucial statutes because most international loan contracts are signed under U.S. or British law. As a result, borrowing countries typically waive sovereign immunity in commercial loan contracts.

There have been several instances in which a sovereign defaulter's foreign assets were seized by creditors. In

1979, for example, Morgan Guaranty Trust Company successfully attached the Iranian government's stake in Fr. Krupp AG through the German courts. Also, in 1981, the Cuban ship I Congresso del Partido was seized by Chilean plaintiffs for a default by Cubazucar, the state sugar monopoly. In general, however, the relatively limited resort to seizure by creditors suggests that it is a useful option only in the most extreme circumstances of debt-resolution failure.

■ The Uncertain Costs of Default

Economic issues, such as debt repayments, are only one dimension of a country's overall relationship with debtors, so that it may be difficult to define the national interest of the creditor's country narrowly enough to impose sanctions. Disagreements may exist either between various interest groups within a creditor country or between creditor nations about whether or not to sanction a defaulter. For example, exporters, nonexporters, regional banks, and multinational banks within the creditor country may take different positions on proposed sanctions. Finally, economic sanctions, if imposed, may be of limited effectiveness, because trade and financial flows are multilateral. Factors such as these and others may operate to reduce the threat of default penalties from the debtor's perspective. If debtors regard efforts to alter debt-service terms as unlikely to provoke a strong response, they are likely to press forward with some initiatives.

It may also be a misconception to believe that all foreign economic interests would unite to cut off future loans to a defaulting country. A permanent interruption of debt service on medium-term bank debts, for example, would cut a country off from new medium-term bank loans for a substantial period. However, if the debt service interruption is either temporary or occurs within a framework of ongoing negotiation and of acceptance by the borrower of the need to resume debt service, then eventual renegotiation of the loan contract is likely to restore access to credit. In such a setting, the reactions of nonbank foreign traders, multinational direct investors, and providers of short-term, direct-trade finance to a defaulting country might not be as serious. Foreign equity investors could very well retain their equity intact, and trade credits might still be serviced.

Trade retaliation against a defaulting nation is another option available to creditors, although such restrictions are most effective when applied by the creditors' governments. Moreover, the impact of trade embargoes is often diluted by trade with other countries and triangular-trade arrangements through third-country firms.[3]

The effectiveness of legal sanctions against sovereign defaulters is also limited. Although the legal position of creditors against the sovereign immunity defense has been improved substantially since 1976, the practical remedies for creditors still are limited.

For example, the Act of State principle, an established tenet of U.S. law, prevents U.S. courts from passing judgment on foreign countries' actions in cases involving our national interest. Execution of judgment under the legal process also usually does not apply to foreign diplomatic, military, and central bank properties in the U.S. Private property of individual foreign nationals located in the creditor country also is usually protected. Finally, legal actions may be avoided simply because they diminish the debtor's incentive to renegotiate the debt.

The argument that sovereign nations can avoid or reduce the cost of altering the terms of debt service implies that the benefits of such efforts may often be greater than the costs. While outright permanent and unilateral abrogations of lending agreements are uncommon, cooperative interruptions and conciliatory default, as part of an ongoing effort to reduce debt-service obligations, have occurred often since 1982. However, the infrequency of outright debt repudiation suggests that both debtors and creditors saw benefits in renegotiation and new repayment terms.

There are two other factors that seem to be important explanations of the willingness of debtor countries to renegotiate new repayment terms. National pride and a sense of fairness often require making the necessary payments. However, a borrowing country may simply be unable to generate enough foreign exchange through export expansion, import reduction, or acquisition of new capital to repay its debts, thus becoming unable to make the capital transfer.

Both the reputation factor and the transfer problem have been important underlying factors in the default and repayment experiences following the onset of the LDC debt crisis. During this period, most LDC debtors tightened their belts in order to generate sufficient trade surpluses to service their debts, both for preventing sanctions and for maintaining their reputations.

After the 1982 debt crisis, extensive debt restructuring was negotiated, usually requiring debtors to adopt International Monetary Fund (IMF) adjustment programs. These restructuring packages included lowering interest terms and stretching out interest or principal payment schedules, which increased the benefits of interrupting the debt servicing in a cooperative way. The restructuring packages also included refinancing arrangements that lowered the costs of cooperative interruptions. Therefore, debtors, after examining the costs and benefits, did not choose repudiation.

■ **Changing Situation**
Recently, lending to LDCs has been shrinking. In 1983, new bank lending to developing countries was $34.3 billion; in the first half of 1987, new lending fell to $3.4 billion. Reduced lending reduces the benefits to debtors of debt service because not much new financing is likely to be forthcoming whether they repaid or not. Also, the longer that debt stalemates continue, the longer would the benefits of withholding debt service accrue to debtor countries for enhanced economic growth, living standards, and political

stability. A probable result of these changes in the cost-benefit effect was the 1987 Brazilian interest moratorium. More than 10 other LDCs also delayed interest payments in the same year.

Brazil's interest moratorium did not last, however; Brazil and its creditors were able to negotiate lower fees and interest on restructured loans, and assemble new-money financing packages. The possibility that creditors would seek more extreme measures in order to maintain their reputation for debt-repayment enforcement also may have contributed to the reluctance of Brazil to remain in arrears.

For some countries in arrears, private medium-term financing virtually ceased, and short-term trade credits also declined. Peru, for example, has received few new agreements on short-term trade credits since its default. As for Brazil, it reportedly experienced difficulties in obtaining trade financing. (According to Brazil's Finance Minister, Mailson Ferreira da Nobrega, Brazil's 1987 interest moratorium was a mistake because it created new economic uncertainty and affected credit flows from abroad.)[4]

The bank trade credit loss for Brazil was estimated to be a moderate 20 percent. Once Brazil publicly expressed its intention to renew debt servicing, a record-high $82 billion restructuring package was assembled by Brazil's bank creditors. This event illustrates that, overall, the costs of debt service interruptions can be low as long as debtors show evidence of a cooperative attitude.

■ **Conclusion**
After the 1982 debt crisis, difficulties in securing debt repayment in the terms as originally agreed upon has emphasized the risks in international lending, and has contributed to a decline in lending. In 1983, involuntary bank lending to Latin America was $13.3 billion; it dropped to $2.0 billion in the first three quarters of 1987. In 1981, voluntary bank lending to Latin America was

$24.3 billion; in 1987, it fell to only $0.1 billion in the first three quarters.[5]

Various financial plans have been advanced to resolve the ongoing LDC debt repayment and economic growth problems. The proposals are divided between plans favoring an increase in lending to buy time and to finance structural reforms, and plans favoring a reduction in debt that is compatible with the debtor's ordinary servicing capacity. No matter how the current LDC debt and economic growth problems are managed, in the long run the difficulties encountered in enforcing international loan agreements seem likely to limit lenders' confidence in the likelihood of complete repayment.

The debt servicing difficulties of the past several years have increased lender's perceptions of risks to such a degree that a resumption of international lending may require basic and complicated structural changes in the framework of lending itself. Making these changes will prove to be very difficult, but if the volume of lending could be increased as a result, then both borrowers and lenders would benefit accordingly.[6]

Creditor and debtor nations will continue to struggle with their debt resolution efforts for many years. Parties on both sides will undoubtedly search for new ways to prevent overborrowing and overlending from repeating. They will also continue to calculate the costs and benefits of defaults on current obligations, and act accordingly.

■ **Footnotes**

1. See IMF Staff, *Recent Developments in External Debt Restructuring* (Washington D.C.: IMF, 1983, 1985), Occasional Paper, No. 25, 40.

2. Anatole Kaletsky is probably the first person to use the term "conciliatory default." Refer to the discussion of the costs of default in his book, *The Costs of Default* (New York: Priority Press Publications, 1985).

3. See Gary C. Hufbauer and Jeffrey J. Schott, *Economic Sanctions in Support of Foreign Policy Goals* (Washington D.C.: Institute for International Economics, 1983).

4. See "Brazil's Reversal of Debt Strategy," New York Times, February 22, 1988.

5. See IMF Staff, International Capital Markets (Washington D.C.:IMF, 1988), World Economic and Financial Surveys Series.

6. Various sanctions can deter defaults and enable lenders to extend credit to developing countries. See Jonathan Eaton and Mark Gersovitz, "Poor Country Borrowing in Private Financial Markets and the Repudiation Issue," Princeton Studies in International Finance, No. 47, June 1981.

Chien Nan Wang is an economist at the Federal Reserve Bank of Cleveland. The author would like to thank John Davis, William Gavin, Owen Humpage, Mark Sniderman, E.J. Stevens, and Walker Todd for helpful comments.

The views stated herein are those of the author and not necessarily those of the Federal Reserve Bank of Cleveland or of the Board of Governors of the Federal Reserve System.

Part Six

Macroeconomics and Financial Policy

Financial institutions and markets are created to serve the public—to efficiently produce and sell financial services that meet the needs of businesses and households. Yet, it is not just the public to whom these markets and institutions must respond and not just the public that influences and evaluates their performance. *Government*, too, plays a profoundly important role in determining the kinds of financial institutions that will be allowed to operate, the services these institutions can offer, and the prices attached to those services. Governments are customers of the financial system, especially in borrowing money and making payments, and, in this customer role, demand an adequate supply of financial services at low cost. Even more important, however, governments represent the public interest in promoting a sound financial system in which the public's savings are managed prudently, scarce resources are utilized efficiently, and financial conditions are established that contribute to broad national goals.

While governments at all levels affect the workings of the financial system, two governmental institutions stand out in influencing the performance of financial institutions and in shaping financial market conditions. These governmental units are: (1) the central bank—in the United States, the Federal Reserve System (the Fed); and (2) the government's fund raiser and borrower—in the United States, the Treasury Department. This section of the book is devoted to these two dominant governmental institutions in the financial system. Our purpose is to see more clearly how these institutions interact with private financial institutions and the public to influence the availability and cost of financial services and the stability of the financial system.

The younger of the two is the Federal Reserve System, chartered by act of Congress in 1913. The Fed possesses great financial power and it has been vested by Congress with numerous supervisory and service responsibilities over the banking system. The Federal Reserve's most important task, however, is carrying out *monetary policy*—managing the supply of money and credit in order to achieve full employment, low inflation, sustainable economic growth, and a stronger balance-of-payments position vis-à-vis the rest of the world. Several articles in this portion of the book describe in detail how the Fed conducts monetary policy and some of the key problems it faces in pursuit of these national economic goals.

For example, in the first article in this section, John R. Walter, economist at the Federal Reserve Bank of Richmond, provides an excellent overview of the various measures of the *money supply* and reserves held by banks. These highly publicized money measures include M1, M2, M3, and the monetary base. All are widely followed by investors and financial analysts as barometers of monetary policy. Walter carefully explains how these measures are calculated and how they have changed over time.

Understanding monetary measures is a necessary prelude to understanding the important linkages between changes in the money supply and the performance of the economy. One of these linkages—the connection between money and inflation—is explored by two economists from the Federal Reserve Bank of Dallas, W. Michael Cox and Harvey Rosenblum. Their article, "Money and Inflation in a Deregulated Financial Environment: An Overview," looks at three key issues occasioned by recent state and federal deregulation of banks and other depository institutions. Specifically, they ask if deregulation has changed the public's demand for money. Has deregulation impacted the relationship between the money supply and the high-powered reserves held by banks and the currency and coin held by the public? And, which money measure should the Federal Reserve use as a target in the conduct of monetary policy? They conclude, tentatively, that people's money-using habits *have* changed, redistributing funds between money and other assets. Moreover, the money supply now seems more responsive to changes in money demand, and the linkages between some forms of money (specifically, M2) appear to be relatively stable, suggesting that inflation can be significantly reduced by a well-designed monetary policy.

Economists Joseph H. Haslag and Scott E. Hein, also writing for the Dallas Federal Reserve Bank, take up roughly where Cox and Rosenblum leave off, looking in detail at the *monetary base* as a possible guiding star and target for monetary policy. Their article "Reserve Requirements, the Monetary Base, and Economic Activity" is a careful analytical study of which measure of the monetary base the Federal Reserve should target in order to stabilize the economy's growth and contribute to the nation's broad economic goals. They conclude that one measure of the monetary base—called the *adjusted base*, which accounts for changes in deposit reserve requirements—would be a useful future target for the central bank in regulating the economy. The adjusted monetary base displays a high positive correlation with changes in the nation's income and spending.

As we noted at the outset of this section, the Treasury Department also has an important effect on economic and financial conditions. The Treasury exerts its most potent effects through two primary channels: (1) *fiscal policy*—taxing and spending activities; and (2) *debt management policy*—issuing new debt and refunding outstanding debt. Both of these forms of government economic policy share with monetary policy the same broad national economic goals for full employment and low inflation. Certainly fiscal policy and debt management policy have attracted much public and political attention in recent years due to record-high federal budget deficits and a federal debt that has soared to unprecedented heights.

The highly controversial issues surrounding the impact of deficit spending by the federal government are examined in some depth by economists K. Alec Chrystal of the City University of London and Daniel L. Thornton of the Federal Reserve Bank of St. Louis in "The Macroeconomic Effects of Deficit Spending: A Review." Their analysis of federal deficits begins by carefully defining the different types of budget deficits that exist and by carefully evaluating each of the arguments for and against running budget deficits. Chrystal and Thornton conclude that much of the literature surrounding the impact of government deficits is ambiguous, but that research evidence is growing that indicates deficits have *no* long-run effects on either national output or employment. However, they observe, government deficits may tend to redistribute income in the economy.

Finally, economist Owen Humpage of the Federal Reserve Bank of Cleveland looks at the process and the impact of government intervention in international currency markets. In "Should We Intervene in Exchange Markets?" Humpage takes us through three different channels by which government treasuries and central banks can influence currency prices, the money supply, and the public's expectations. He argues that exchange-rate intervention can be useful in reinforcing monetary and fiscal policies when market uncertainty over the government's policies appears to be on the rise.

Article 28

MONETARY AGGREGATES: A USER'S GUIDE

John R. Walter

The monetary aggregates are measures of the nation's money stock. The most narrowly defined monetary aggregate, M1, is the sum of the dollar amounts of currency and nonbank travelers checks in circulation, plus checkable deposits. M2 includes M1 plus overnight repurchase agreements, overnight Eurodollar deposits, general purpose and broker/dealer money market fund balances, money market deposit accounts, and savings and small time deposits. M3 is the sum of M2 and large time deposits, term repurchase agreements, term Eurodollar deposits, and balances in money market funds employed solely by institutional investors. Analysts study the relationships among these monetary measures and other macroeconomic variables, such as national income, employment, interest rates, and the price level. These relationships are then used to forecast changes in economic activity, interest rates, and inflation. The Board of Governors of the Federal Reserve System defines the aggregates and calculates and reports their values.

This article explains the origin and evolution of the monetary aggregates and discusses how they are prepared and released, how they are used, and when and why they are revised. Information on the monetary base is also included.

How the Monetary Aggregates Evolved

Over the years economists have proposed many different groupings of financial assets into something called "money." No single definition of money has been universally acceptable. Two approaches have been used to define money. The first is to identify what financial assets are commonly used for certain purposes. Analysts using this approach generally include as money financial assets serving (1) as a medium of exchange, i.e., assets widely acceptable in payment for goods, services, and debts, and (2) as a store of value. A second approach to defining money is to find the groupings of financial assets the movements of which are most closely correlated with the movements of certain macroeconomic variables such as national income, employment, and prices. Both approaches have contributed to the development of the monetary aggregates constructed by the Federal Reserve. A brief chronology of the evolution of these measures is given below.

In 1944 the Board of Governors of the Federal Reserve System began reporting monthly data on two types of exchange media, (1) currency outside of banks, and (2) demand deposits at banks, i.e., non-interest-bearing deposits transferable by check or convertible into cash "on demand." It also reported the sum of these two. The Board's expressed intent in reporting the data was "to increase the information available to the public on current changes . . . in the nation's money supply." In time the sum of currency outside banks and demand deposits came to be called M1, the narrowest of the Fed's monetary aggregates.

Until 1971 M1 was the only monetary aggregate for which estimates were published by the Board of Governors. In that year, however, the Board began reporting data for two additional aggregates, M2 and M3. Interest in these latter variables reflected the growing importance of the monetary aggregates in formulating monetary policy. It also reflected the view among some economists that the appropriate definition of money should include assets capable of providing a temporary store of value. Accordingly, M2 was defined to include M1 plus savings deposits at commercial banks and time deposits at commercial banks except large negotiable certificates of deposit. Similarly M3 was defined as the sum of M2 and deposits at mutual savings banks and savings and loan associations.

In 1975, the Board began publishing data for even broader collections of financial assets, namely M4 and M5. M4 included M2 plus large negotiable certificates of deposit. M5 was the sum of M3 and large negotiable certificates of deposit.

The decade of the 1970s witnessed the development of many financial instruments. Some of the new assets were close substitutes for demand deposits, namely negotiable order of withdrawal (NOW) accounts which are interest-bearing checkable accounts, savings accounts featuring automatic transfer to checking accounts (ATS accounts), credit union share draft accounts, and money market mutual funds with checking privileges. These new accounts began to be used as exchange media but were not counted in M1 until 1980.

The introduction of these new assets also coincided with what some economists interpreted as changes in the relationships between the monetary aggregates and economic variables such as income, employment, and prices. These apparent changes provided some of the Fed's motivation for modifying its definitions of the aggregates in 1980.[1] At that time the Fed replaced its M1 definition of money with M1A and M1B. M1A was equivalent to the old M1, including only currency and demand deposits; M1B included all of M1A plus NOW and ATS balances at banks and thrifts, credit union share draft balances, and demand deposits at mutual savings banks.[2] At the same time old M2 through M5 were replaced with new measures of M2 and M3. New M2 included all of M1B and a number of other assets that are easily convertible to transaction account deposits or that can be used in transactions to a limited degree. These were overnight repurchase agreements (RPs) issued by commercial banks and certain overnight Euro-dollars held by nonbank U.S. residents, money market mutual fund shares, and savings and small-denomination time deposits at all depository institutions.[3] New M3 added to M2 large-denomination time deposits at all depository institutions and term RPs at commercial banks and savings and loan associations.

In January 1982 the Board of Governors stopped reporting M1A and redesignated M1B as M1. Since then the definitions have been modified only slightly. Table I shows the current magnitudes of M1, M2, and M3.

Monetary Base

The monetary base is composed of currency held by the public and in vaults of depository institutions, plus reserves of depository institutions. In 1968 the Federal Reserve Bank of St. Louis began publishing figures on the monetary base. In 1979 the Board of Governors of the Federal Reserve System also began publishing data on a somewhat different version of the monetary base.

The base can be viewed as the foundation upon which the superstructure of deposits is erected. An increase in the reserves component of the base allows the system of depository institutions to expand deposits. Initially, an increase in reserves—resulting from open market operations or loans by the Fed—

leads to an increase in "excess" reserves, that is, reserves beyond the amount needed to meet reserve requirements at depository institutions. These institutions use the excess reserves to make loans and investments which soon become deposits. When these deposits are spent and redeposited, they create additional excess reserves and lead to the extension of more loans. Through a multiplicative process the money supply is increased by a multiple of the Fed's original addition to the monetary base. The extent to which the money stock increases upon an increase in the monetary base depends on the percentages of required and excess reserves held by depository institutions and on the public's holdings of cash relative to deposits.[4]

As noted above, the Board of Governors' and the St. Louis Federal Reserve Bank's estimates of the monetary base differ, and do so in three respects. First, the Board and St. Louis adjust the base differently to cleanse it of changes that are simply the result of changes in reserve requirements.[5] Second, the Board and St. Louis account for vault cash differently. Third, they seasonally adjust their estimates differently.[6]

Preparation and Release of Monetary Data

The Board of Governors constructs its estimates of the monetary aggregates from information supplied by depository institutions, the U.S. Treasury, money market mutual funds, New York State investment companies, nonbank issuers of travelers checks, and foreign central banks. Some of these institutions report every week, others report less frequently. Some report in an abbreviated form not available to larger institutions. To produce weekly and monthly estimates of the aggregates, the Board estimates missing data where detail or frequency of reporting

[1] See Board of Governors (June 1976) and Board of Governors (January 1979), p. 24.

[2] M1A excluded demand deposits held by foreign commercial banks and foreign official institutions while old M1 did not.

[3] For a thorough discussion of RPs see Stephen A. Lumpkin's article "Repurchase and Reverse Repurchase Agreements" in Cook and Rowe (1986), pp. 65-80.

[4] Humphrey (1987) describes the theory of deposit expansion and its history. Most introductory level college money and banking texts provide a basic discussion of how monetary actions of the Fed affect the base and the money stock. Burger (1971) goes into great detail.

[5] For example, when the reserve requirement against business time deposits with maturities of 2-1/2 to 3-1/2 years was dropped in April 1983, the amount of reserves banks were required to hold declined by $80 million. In order to prevent a corresponding increase in excess reserves the Fed concurrently withdrew this $80 million through open market operations, leading to an identical decline in the monetary base. The Board of Governors and the Federal Reserve Bank of St. Louis then eliminated this $80 million decline in their adjusted monetary base data.

[6] Burger (1979) discusses the causes of the differences between the Board of Governors' and St. Louis' monetary base estimates.

Table I

COMPONENTS OF THE MONETARY AGGREGATES AND MONETARY BASE AND THEIR LEVELS
August 1988
Billions of dollars

M1	**782.5**
Currency	207.2
Travelers checks	7.2
Demand deposits	290.0
Other checkable deposits	278.1
M2	**3032.0**
M1	782.5
Overnight RPs	64.9
Overnight Eurodollars	15.8
MMF balances (general purpose and broker/dealer)	231.2
MMDAs	517.1
Savings deposits	433.8
Small time deposits	985.2
M3	**3847.3**
M2	3032.0
Large time deposits	514.7
Term RPs	121.0
Term Eurodollars	102.4
MMF balances (institution only)	84.0
Monetary Base	**271.2**
Currency	207.2
Reserves	61.1

Sources: Data for M1, M2, M3 and their components are from Board of Governors of the Federal Reserve System H.6 release, "Money Stock, Liquid Assets, and Debt Measures," dated October 6, 1988. Data for Monetary Base are from Board of Governors of the Federal Reserve System H.3 release, "Aggregate Reserves of Depository Institutions and the Monetary Base," dated October 6, 1988. The Currency figure shown below Monetary Base is from H.6 while the Reserves figure is from H.3.

Explanation: M2 and M3 both differ from the sums of their components because these aggregates are seasonally adjusted by adjusting the non-M1 components of M2 and the non-M2 components of M3 as blocks. Several of these components are not reported in seasonally adjusted form while those that are have been adjusted individually. Monetary Base differs from its components because the currency component the Board uses in its Monetary Base computation includes some adjustments excluded from the H.6 currency figure. The Board does not publish the currency portion of Monetary Base separately.

Other checkable deposits are negotiable order of withdrawal (NOW) accounts, automatic transfer service (ATS) accounts, credit union share draft accounts, and demand deposits at thrift institutions.

RPs, repurchase agreements, are loan arrangements in which the borrower sells the lender securities with an agreement to repurchase them at a future date.

Eurodollars are dollar-denominated deposits issued to U.S. residents by foreign branches of U.S. banks worldwide.

MMF, money market mutual funds, are funds investing in money market instruments, offered by investment companies.

MMDA, money market deposit accounts, are savings deposits on which only a limited number of checks can be drawn each month.

Savings deposits are liabilities of depository institutions that do not specify a date of withdrawal or a time period after which deposited funds may be withdrawn, although depository institutions must reserve the right to require at least seven days written notice before withdrawal of savings deposits.

Time deposits are liabilities of depository institutions payable on a specified date, or after a specified period of time or notice period, which in all cases may not be less than seven days following the date of deposit.

Term, as in Term RPs and Term Eurodollars, means maturities of greater than one day.

The *Reserves* component of Monetary Base is total reserves of depository institutions with Federal Reserve Banks plus vault cash used to satisfy reserve requirements and is adjusted for reserve requirement changes.

For a detailed description of each of the components of M1, M2, and M3 see any recent H.6 release or footnotes to the table entitled "Money Stock, Liquid Assets, and Debt Measures," in the statistical section of a recent *Federal Reserve Bulletin.* For a detailed description of the Reserves component of Monetary Base see the footnotes to the H.3 release, or footnotes to the table entitled "Reserves and Borrowings, Depository Institutions" in the statistical section of a recent *Federal Reserve Bulletin.* The Federal Reserve Bank of Richmond's *Instruments of the Money Market* includes a chapter for each of the major money market instruments, including Eurodollars, RPs, and MMF, listed above.

The Federal Reserve, in its H.6 release and in the tables of its *Federal Reserve Bulletin,* publishes estimates of liquid assets and total debt of nonfinancial sectors with the monetary aggregates even though these are not considered monetary aggregates. The liquid assets measure is called L and is made up of M3 plus U.S. savings bonds, short-term Treasury securities, commercial paper, and bankers acceptances. The aggregate labeled "Debt" includes the debt of the U.S. government, state and local governments, and private nonfinancial sectors. L first appeared in the *Federal Reserve Bulletin* in 1980, with Debt following in 1984. Items in L and Debt fall outside of the category of assets that most economists would call money.

---

are lacking. Table II lists, by component, sources of data used by the Board to calculate the monetary aggregates.

The Board of Governors reports figures for M1, M2, and M3 each week (usually on Thursday afternoon at 4:30 eastern time). Reported values are weekly averages of daily figures for the week ending ten days earlier. The Board publishes both seasonally adjusted and not seasonally adjusted data. Revisions of the seasonally adjusted aggregates can be large due to changing seasonal patterns over time.[7]

---

[7] For a discussion of the difficulties of seasonal adjustment see Hein and Ott (1983).

The Board of Governors releases its most recent estimates of the monetary base every two weeks. These figures are two-week averages of daily figures for the two weeks ending eight days earlier. The Board publishes a seasonally adjusted monetary base figure adjusted for changes in reserve requirements, a not seasonally adjusted base figure adjusted for changes in reserve requirements, and a not seasonally adjusted figure not adjusted for reserve requirement changes. The St. Louis Federal Reserve Bank also releases a new estimate of the average monetary base every two weeks. It provides only a base figure adjusted for reserve requirement changes and for seasonal change.

Table II

SOURCES OF DATA USED BY THE BOARD OF GOVERNORS IN THE
ESTIMATION OF THE MONETARY AGGREGATES AND THE MONETARY BASE

Component	Description of Component	Source of Data on Component and Frequency
M1		
Currency	Currency and coin in the hands of the nonbank public.	Consolidated Statement of Condition of All Federal Reserve Banks (H.4.1)—weekly; vault cash data from Report of Transaction Accounts, Other Deposits and Vault Cash (FR 2900)—weekly, and Quarterly Report of Selected Deposits, Vault Cash, and Reservable Liabilities (FR 2910Q).
Nonbank travelers checks	Travelers checks issued by institutions other than banks. Included in M1 because they can be used directly for purchases.	Report of Travelers Checks Outstanding (FR 2054)—monthly.
Demand deposits and Other checkable deposits	Checkable deposits including regular non-interest-bearing checking accounts, NOW balances, ATS balances, and credit union share draft balances.	FR 2900; FR 2910Q; Reports of Condition and Income (Call Reports)—quarterly; internal Federal Reserve float data; Weekly Report of Assets and Liabilities for Large Banks (FR 2416).
M2		
M1		
Overnight repurchase agreements	Overnight and continuing contract repurchase agreements (RPs) issued by commercial banks. Included in M2 because they are generally considered short-term investments used in managing demand deposit balances.	Report of Selected Borrowings (FR 2415)—weekly; Annual Report of Repurchase Agreements (FR 2090A); Weekly Report of Assets of Money Market Mutual Funds (FR 2051A); Weekly Report of Assets for Selected Money Market Mutual Funds (FR 2051C).
Overnight Eurodollars	Overnight Eurodollars issued to U.S. residents by foreign branches of U.S. banks worldwide. Short-term investments like RPs.	Report of Selected Deposits in Foreign Branches Held by U.S. Residents (FR 2050)—weekly; FR 2051A; FR2051C.
Money market mutual fund (MMF) balances (general purpose and broker/dealer)	Often checkable, but included in M2 rather than M1 because turnover rates are more like savings instruments than transactions instruments.	Investment Company Institute (ICI) gathers FR 2051A and FR 2051C for Fed covering all MMFs.
Money market deposit accounts (MMDAs)	Limited check writing features and turnover rates like savings rather than transactions accounts cause Fed to include this asset in M2 rather than M1.	FR 2900; FR 2910Q; Call Reports.
Savings deposits	Passbook and telephone transfer accounts.	FR 2900; FR 2910Q; Call Reports; FR 2416.
Small time deposits	Time deposits at depository institutions with denominations less than $100,000. Includes RPs with denominations less than $100,000.	FR 2900; FR 2910Q; Call Reports; Monthly Survey of Selected Deposits and Other Accounts (FR 2042); Report of Repurchase Agreements on U.S. Government and Federal Agency Securities (FR 2090Q)—quarterly; FR 2090A.
M3		
M2		
Large time deposits	Time deposits at depository institutions with denominations of $100,000 or more. Held largely by institutions.	FR 2900; FR 2910Q; Call Reports; FR 2416; FR 2051A; FR 2051C.
Term RPs	Denominations $100,000 or greater with more than one day maturity. Held largely by institutions rather than individuals.	FR 2415; FR 2090A; Call Reports; FR 2051A; FR 2051C.
Term Eurodollars	More than one day maturity, held largely by institutions rather than individuals.	Weekly Report of Foreign Branch Liabilities to, and Custody Holdings for, U.S. Residents (FR 2077); information from Bank of Canada and Bank of England; FR 2051A; FR 2051C.
MMF balances (institution only)	Balances held by institutions rather than individuals.	FR 2051A; FR 2051C.
Monetary Base		
Currency	Currency and coin in the hands of the nonbank public plus currency and coin in bank vaults not used to satisfy reserve requirements.	H.4.1; FR 2900; FR 2910Q; Call Reports.
Reserves	Reserves of depository institutions held with Federal Reserve Banks plus vault cash used to satisfy reserve requirements.	FR 2900; H.4.1.

The Board of Governors publishes historical series of the monetary aggregates and many of the components making up the aggregates. These series are periodically updated to reflect revisions or redefinitions of the aggregates. Both the Board and the St. Louis Fed produce historical series for the base. Table III lists the monetary aggregates and their component series as well as the monetary base and its component series available from the Board and St. Louis.

How The Monetary Aggregates Data Are Used

The Fed's legislative mandate is to set a monetary policy consistent with high employment, stable prices, and moderate long-term interest rates. In semiannual testimony to Congress, the Chairman of the Board of Governors of the Federal Reserve System reports the targets set by the Federal Open Market Committee (the Fed's monetary policy-making body)[8] for growth of the monetary aggregates. The Chairman also relates these targeted growth rates to forecasted rates of unemployment, output growth, and inflation. Because of concern with the instability of the behavior of M1, the Federal Open Market Committee has not specified an M1 target range since 1986, although it has continued to set target ranges for M2 and M3.

The Federal Reserve cannot directly control the quantity of money. It can, however, control

---

[8] The President of the Federal Reserve Bank of New York is a permanent voting member of the Federal Open Market Committee while the other eleven Federal Reserve Bank presidents share four voting memberships on a rotating basis. All seven members of the Board of Governors are also permanent voting members.

Table III

AVAILABILITY OF TIME-SERIES ON MONETARY AGGREGATES AND COMPONENTS MAKING UP MONETARY AGGREGATES

Series	Weekly Averages Available Beginning: sa	nsa	Monthly Averages Available Beginning: sa	nsa
Aggregates				
M1	1/75	1/75	1/59	1/47*
M2	1/81	1/81	1/59	1/59
M3	1/81	1/81	1/59	1/59
Monetary Base—Board				
Adjusted	1/59**	1/59**	1/59	1/59
Unadjusted		1/59**		1/59
Monetary Base—St. Louis				
Adjusted	1/72**	1/72**	1/50	1/29
Unadjusted		1/72**		1/19
Components of Ms				
Currency	1/75	1/75	1/59	1/47*
Demand deposits	1/75	1/75	1/59	1/47*
Other checkable deposits	1/75	1/75	1/63	1/63
Overnight RPs		1/75		11/69
Overnight Eurodollars		12/79		2/77
MMMF (general purpose and broker/dealer)		2/80		11/73
MMMF (institution only)		2/80		4/74
Nonbank travelers checks	1/75	1/75	1/59	1/59
Savings deposits	1/81	1/81	1/59	1/59
Small time deposits	1/81	1/81	1/59	1/59
Large time deposits	1/81	1/81	1/59	1/59
MMDA		12/82		12/82
Term RPs		1/75		10/69
Term Eurodollars		12/79		1/59
Components of Base				
Reserves—Board				
Adjusted	1/59**	1/59**	1/59	1/59
Unadjusted		1/59**		1/59
Reserves—St. Louis				
Adjusted			1/50	1/47
Currency—St. Louis		1/72**		1/50

Sources: Board of Governors of the Federal Reserve System, H.6, "Historical Money Stock Data," March 1988; Board of Governors of the Federal Reserve System, H.3, "Reserves of Depository Institutions, Historical Data," June 1988; *Banking and Monetary Statistics, 1941-1970*, Board of Governors of the Federal Reserve System, 1976; The Federal Reserve Bank of St. Louis.

* Data from 1/47 until 12/70 can be found in *Banking and Monetary Statistics, 1941-1970*, Board of Governors of the Federal Reserve System, 1976, while data for 1/59 to current are available from Board of Governors of the Federal Reserve System, H.6, "Historical Money Stock Data," March 1988. Definitions used in these two sources differ.

** Weekly data are available until 2/84, after which only biweekly data are available.

sa = Seasonally adjusted

nsa = Not seasonally adjusted

variables that influence short-term interest rates, namely the quantity of reserves held by depository institutions and the monetary base, and thereby influence the growth rate of the aggregates. Greater provision of reserves through Federal Reserve open market purchases of securities tends to push down the federal funds rate and other short-term interest rates. Lower interest rates, in turn, help determine the quantities of the monetary aggregates demanded by the private sector. Downward pressure on federal funds and other rates makes holding money balances, which pay no or low rates of interest, less costly. The lower cost of holding money increases the quantity of money demanded. Assuming money supply equals money demand, the result is an increase in the level of monetary aggregates. Changes in the aggregates normally are followed by temporary changes in aggregate output and employment and by permanent changes in prices.[9] Chart 1 illustrates the relationship between M2 and the price level. As is conventional in such comparisons, M2 is shown per unit of real output, i.e., is divided by real GNP, to adjust for growth in the economy.[10]

The monetary aggregates have been watched closely by those attempting to predict Fed policy moves.[11] In periods when the Fed sought tight control of the growth rate of the aggregates, unusually fast or slow money growth has generated expectations of subsequent policy actions by the Fed to arrest or reverse these movements. In such periods, the financial markets react to the announcement of the weekly M1 figure. The announcement of a higher than expected M1 figure, for example, leads market participants to increase their estimate of the probability that the Fed will put upward pressure on the funds rate, and other short-term rates rise in reaction to these changed expectations.[12]

Many economists study the aggregates to improve their understanding of the links between monetary growth and changes in other macroeconomic variables. Prior to the 1980s empirical studies generally found stable relationships between M1 growth and inflation and GNP growth. These findings were important to the Fed's decision to place more emphasis on the monetary aggregates in monetary policymaking during the 70s and early 80s. With the financial deregulation and disinflation of the early 1980s

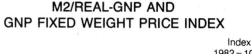

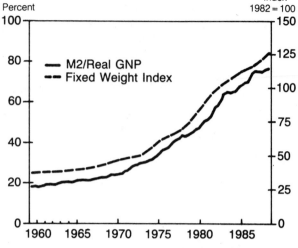

however, studies began to find that the once stable relationships between M1 growth and inflation and GNP growth were breaking down. These findings led the Federal Reserve in 1982 to de-emphasize M1 in its monetary policymaking process.[13] Recent studies, however, suggest that changes due to disinflation and deregulation have had a smaller effect on M2 than on M1 growth, and that the relationship between M2 growth and inflation has remained fairly stable.[14] In his February 1989 testimony before Congress the Chairman of the Board of Governors stated that "over the long haul there is a close relationship between money [M2] and prices." The Fed, consistent with the view that further reductions in the growth rate of M2 are necessary to achieve long-run price stability, reduced its target range for M2 in both 1988 and 1989.[15]

Revisions to the Monetary Aggregates

Major revisions to the published data on the monetary aggregates occur for four reasons. First, the data are revised as reporting or processing errors are discovered. Second, the aggregates are revised annually to incorporate "benchmark" changes. Third, the seasonally adjusted data are revised annually to incorporate new seasonal adjustment factors. Finally, the historical series are revised whenever there is a redefinition of the aggregates.

---

[9] See Board of Governors (July 1988), pp. 419-20, and Broaddus (1988), pp. 45-49.

[10] Friedman (1969), p.177.

[11] Loeys (1984).

[12] Walter (1988), pp. 222-25.

[13] Friedman (1988) and Bernanke and Blinder (1988).

[14] Hetzel and Mehra (1988), Mehra (1988), and Reichenstein and Elliott (1987).

[15] Greenspan (April 1989) and Board of Governors (March 1989).

With thousands of institutions reporting to the Federal Reserve System on a weekly basis, it is impossible for the Fed to find and correct all errors before the first release of monetary aggregate data. As errors are discovered the Board revises the data. Most revisions occur within the first month following initial release of a figure, although some can take place months later.

As noted above, to produce estimates of the monetary aggregates the Board of Governors must estimate the deposits held in financial institutions not reporting on a weekly basis. Most of these institutions do report data on a quarterly or annual basis, however. When these quarterly or annual figures become available, they provide points of reference, or "benchmarks," which the Board uses to make more accurate estimates for intervening dates. The Board makes these benchmark revisions to the aggregates each February.

The monetary aggregates are seasonally adjusted to remove those movements that tend to recur at the same time each year, such as the temporary increases in transactions balances before Christmas and before the due date for tax payments. To determine the proper seasonal adjustment factors to apply to a given month's or week's aggregates the Board normally uses data on the aggregates for three years before and three years after the month or week in question. No later data are available for the most recently released aggregates so the Board forecasts fifteen months of the data and appends it to the actual aggregate data. As time passes, the estimates of the seasonal factors can be made more accurately as forecasted data are replaced by actual data and as data errors are corrected and new benchmarks become available. Each February, the Board re-estimates the seasonal factors for the data series used in the monetary aggregates and revises the seasonally adjusted data accordingly.[16]

As discussed earlier, the Federal Reserve changes the definitions of its aggregates from time-to-time following financial market innovations and regulatory changes that affect the way money is held. Some definitional changes are minor and produce only small revisions in the aggregates; others, such as those occurring during the early 1980s, lead to major revisions. When the Fed changes the definitions of the monetary aggregates, it revises the historical data to be consistent over the whole period of the series. (For a list of the beginning dates of various series see Table III.) Previously published data, however, may not bear the same definitions. Thus when comparing data at different dates, users should take care to determine that the data definitions are consistent.

Sources of Data

Monetary aggregate data are available from many sources. On each Friday *The Wall Street Journal* publishes a table giving the money stock data released on Thursday afternoon. Historical data can be found in the *Federal Reserve Bulletin*, in the Board of Governor's H.6 release, in the Board's annual historical supplement to the H.6, "Historical Money Stock Data," in the Federal Reserve's *Banking and Monetary Statistics, 1914-1941, Banking and Monetary Statistics, 1941-1970*, and *Annual Statistical Digest* for years since 1970.

Historical data on the monetary base are available directly from the St. Louis Federal Reserve Bank and from the Board of Governors, or in the Board's H.3 release as well as the Board's historical supplement to the H.3, "Reserves of Depository Institutions, Historical Data." Normally, on Friday, *The Wall Street Journal* publishes a table including the most recent figures on the monetary base from the H.3 release.

Suggestions for Further Reading

Most college level money and banking texts discuss the monetary aggregates and the monetary base and their relationship to economic variables. James N. Duprey's "How the Fed Defines and Measures Money" in the Spring-Summer 1982 issue of the *Quarterly Review* of the Federal Reserve Bank of Minneapolis, examines the aggregates and discusses their construction. "Data Sources Used In Constructing the U.S. Monetary Aggregates," a 1984 monograph by Cynthia Glassman of the Board of Governors of the Federal Reserve System, details the sources used in the estimation of the monetary aggregates. The debate among economists over the best definition of money is discussed in Alfred Broaddus's "Aggregating the Monetary Aggregates: Concepts and Issues" in the *Economic Review* of the Federal Reserve Bank of Richmond, November/December 1975.

The footnotes found in the Board of Governor's weekly H.6 release provide detailed definitions of the aggregates. The H.6 release also describes components included in each of the aggregates and reports their estimated levels over time.

The February 1980 *Federal Reserve Bulletin* article "The Redefined Monetary Aggregates" by Thomas Simpson, describes the events and intellectual forces that led the Fed to redefine its aggregates in 1980

---

[16] Lawler (1977), Hein and Ott (1983), pp. 16-20, and Cook (1984), pp. 22-25.

and specifies how the redefinition was accomplished. This article includes time series charts showing the growth of the pre-1980 aggregates and the post-1980 aggregates.

A Monetary History of the United States, 1867-1960, by Milton Friedman and Anna Schwartz provides a seminal discussion of how changes in growth of the money stock have affected the American economy. The authors discuss and make use of the Fed's monetary aggregates throughout much of the book. *Monetary Statistics of the United States*, also by Friedman and Schwartz, provides estimates of the quantity of money for the period 1867-1968 and discusses sources and methods of construction of historical money stock estimates. This volume also devotes more than 100 pages to alternative approaches to the definition of money.

The *Federal Reserve Bulletin* and the Board of Governors' *Annual Report* generally document and explain definitional changes in the monetary aggregates. *Banking and Monetary Statistics, 1941-1970*, published by the Board of Governors, includes a detailed discussion of the Fed's money stock measures.

"The Monetary Base—Explanation and Analytical Use," by Leonall C. Anderson and Jerry L. Jordan, in the August 1968 Federal Reserve Bank of St. Louis *Review*, explains the construction of the St. Louis version of the monetary base and points out why that concept is of importance to monetary economists. The Board of Governors' H.3 release gives a complete definition of the Board's monetary base in its footnotes. Carl M. Gamb's "Federal Reserve Intermediate Targets: Money or the Monetary Base?" in the January 1980 Federal Reserve Bank of Kansas City *Economic Review*, discusses the pros and cons of use of the monetary base in monetary control and provides a good review of the Board's and St. Louis' construction of the base.

References

Anderson, Leonall C., and Jerry L. Jordan. "The Monetary Base—Explanation and Analytical Use." Federal Reserve Bank of St. Louis *Review* 50 (August 1968): 7-11.

Bernanke, Ben S., and Alan S. Blinder. "Credit, Money, and Aggregate Demand." *American Economic Review* 78 (May 1988): 435-39.

Board of Governors of the Federal Reserve System. "A Proposal for Redefining the Monetary Aggregates." *Federal Reserve Bulletin* 65 (January 1979): 13-42.

——————. *Banking and Monetary Statistics, 1914-1941*. Washington, 1976.

——————. *Banking and Monetary Statistics, 1941-1970*. Washington, 1976.

——————. "Implementing Monetary Policy." *Federal Reserve Bulletin* 74 (July 1988): 419-29.

——————. "Improving the Monetary Aggregates." Report of the Advisory Committee on Monetary Statistics. June 1976.

——————. "Monetary Aggregates and Money Market Conditions in Open Market Policy." *Federal Reserve Bulletin* 57 (February 1971): 79-95.

——————. "Monetary Policy Report to the Congress." *Federal Reserve Bulletin* 74 (August 1988): 517-33.

——————. "Monetary Policy Report to the Congress." *Federal Reserve Bulletin* 75 (March 1989), forthcoming.

——————. "Money Stock Revisions." (Annual historical supplement to the Board of Governors of the Federal Reserve System release H.6, "Money Stock, Liquid Assets, and Debt Measures"). March 1988.

——————. "New Monetary and Banking Statistics." *Federal Reserve Bulletin* 30 (February 1944): 134.

——————. "Notes to Table 1.21." *Federal Reserve Bulletin* 72 (November 1986): A14.

——————. "Reserves of Depository Institutions." (Annual historical supplement to the Board of Governors of the Federal Reserve System release H.3, "Aggregate Reserves of Depository Institutions and the Monetary Base"). June 1988.

——————. *69th Annual Report*, 1982. Washington: Board of Governors, 1983.

——————. *The Federal Reserve System: Purposes & Functions*. 7th ed. Washington: Board of Governors, 1984.

Broaddus, Alfred. "Aggregating the Monetary Aggregates: Concepts and Issues." Federal Reserve Bank of Richmond *Economic Review* 61 (November/December 1975): 3-12.

——————. *A Primer on the Fed*. Richmond: Federal Reserve Bank of Richmond, 1988.

Broaddus, Alfred, and Marvin Goodfriend. "Base Drift and the Longer Run Growth of M1: Experience from a Decade of Monetary Targeting." Federal Reserve Bank of Richmond *Economic Review* 70 (November/December 1984): 3-14.

Burger, Albert E. "Alternative Measures of the Monetary Base." Federal Reserve Bank of St. Louis *Review* 61 (June 1979): 3-8.

——————. *The Money Supply Process*. Belmont, California: Wadsworth Publishing Co., Inc., 1971.

Cook, Timothy Q. "The 1983 M1 Seasonal Factor Revisions: An Illustration of Problems That May Arise in Using Seasonally Adjusted Data for Policy Purposes." Federal Reserve Bank of Richmond *Economic Review* 70 (March/April 1984): 22-33.

Cook, Timothy Q., and Timothy D. Rowe, eds. *Instruments of the Money Market*, 6th ed. Richmond: Federal Reserve Bank of Richmond, 1986.

Duprey, James N. "How the Fed Defines and Measures Money." Federal Reserve Bank of Minneapolis *Quarterly Review* (Spring-Summer 1982), pp. 10-19.

Federal Reserve Bank of St. Louis. "Monetary Trends." Various dates.

——————. "U.S. Financial Data." Various dates.

Friedman, Benjamin M. "Monetary Policy Without Quantity Variables." *American Economic Review* 78 (May 1988): 440-45.

Friedman, Milton. *The Optimum Quantity of Money and Other Essays*. Chicago: Aldine Publishing Company, 1969.

Friedman, Milton, and Anna Jacobson Schwartz. *A Monetary History of the United States, 1867-1960*. Princeton, N.J.: Princeton University Press, 1963.

——————. *Monetary Statistics of the United States, Estimates, Sources, Methods*. New York: National Bureau of Economic Research, 1970.

Gambs, Carl M. "Federal Reserve Intermediate Targets: Money or the Monetary Base?" Federal Reserve Bank of Kansas City *Economic Review* 65 (January 1980): 3-15.

Glassman, Cynthia A. "Data Sources Used in Constructing the U.S. Monetary Aggregates." Paper presented at 21st Meeting of Technicians of Central Banks of the American Continent. Washington: Board of Governors of the Federal Reserve System, Division of Research and Statistics, Financial Reports Section, 1984.

Greenspan, Alan. "Statement before the Committee on Banking, Finance and Urban Affairs, U.S. House of Representatives, February 21, 1989." *Federal Reserve Bulletin* 75 (April 1989), forthcoming.

Hein, Scott E., and Mack Ott. "Seasonally Adjusting Money: Procedures, Problems, Proposals." Federal Reserve Bank of St. Louis *Review* 65 (November 1983): 16-24.

Hetzel, Robert L., and Yash P. Mehra. "The Behavior of Money Demand in the 1980s." Federal Reserve Bank of Richmond, June 1988. Photocopy.

Humphrey, Thomas M. "The Theory of Multiple Expansion of Deposits: What It Is and Whence It Came." Federal Reserve Bank of Richmond *Economic Review* 73 (March/April 1987): 3-11.

Lawler, Thomas A. "Seasonal Adjustment of the Money Stock: Problems and Policy Implications." Federal Reserve Bank of Richmond *Economic Review* 63 (November/December 1977): 19-27.

Lindsey, David E., and Henry C. Wallich. "Monetary Policy." In *The New Palgrave, A Dictionary of Economics*, edited by John Eatwell, Murray Milgate, and Peter Newman, vol. 3. London: The MacMillan Press Limited, 1987, pp. 508-15.

Loeys, Jan G. "Market Views of Monetary Policy and Reactions to M1 Announcements." Federal Reserve Bank of Philadelphia *Business Review* (March/April 1984), pp. 9-17.

Mehra, Yash P. "The Forecast Performance of Alternative Models of Inflation." Federal Reserve Bank of Richmond *Economic Review* 74 (September/October 1988): 10-18.

McCarthy, F. Ward, Jr. "Basics of Fed Watching." In *The Handbook of Treasury Securities*, edited by Frank J. Fabozzi. Chicago: Probus, 1987.

Reichenstein, William, and J. Walter Elliott. "A Comparison of Models of Long-Term Inflationary Expectations." *Journal of Monetary Economics* 19 (May 1987): 405-25.

Simpson, Thomas D. "The Redefined Monetary Aggregates." *Federal Reserve Bulletin* (February 1980): 97-114.

Stone, Courtenay C., and Jeffrey B. C. Olson. "Are the Preliminary Week-to-Week Fluctuations in M1 Biased?" Federal Reserve Bank of St. Louis *Review* 63 (December 1978): 13-20.

Taylor, Herb. "What Has Happened to M1?" Federal Reserve Bank of Philadelphia *Business Review* (September/October 1986), pp. 3-14.

Walter, John R. "How to Interpret the Weekly Federal Reserve Data." In *The Financial Analyst's Handbook*, 2nd. ed., edited by Sumner N. Levine. Homewood, Illinois: Dow Jones-Irwin, 1988.

Article 29

W. Michael Cox

Vice President and Economic Advisor
Federal Reserve Bank of Dallas

Harvey Rosenblum

Senior Vice President and
Director of Research
Federal Reserve Bank of Dallas

Money and Inflation in a Deregulated Financial Environment: An Overview

Much attention has centered on the recent monetary and inflationary experience of the United States and on the role played by financial deregulation in the economic history of the 1980s.[1] While little doubt exists that there are many major differences in the financial landscape today as compared with only a few years ago, there is also little doubt that an understanding of these differences is essential to the proper management of the economy.[2]

Understanding the likely macroeconomic effects of financial deregulation is clearly important to the Federal Reserve in view of the direct linkage to monetary policy. The selection of a monetary aggregate, of an operating procedure, and of policy indicators or guidelines must all be reexamined in light of the new and deregulated financial environment. This is admittedly an ambitious challenge and one that will require substantial resources and extended research—effort certainly beyond the scope of any single study.

The work here provides an overview of the macroeconomic effects of financial deregulation and outlines extended research in this area that we plan over the coming months.[3] In this article, we specifically address three questions. First, what effect has financial deregulation had on the demand for money? Second, has financial deregulation significantly altered the money supply process—specifically, the relationship between base money and the monetary aggregates?[4] And third, which measure of money should the Federal Reserve target in the deregulated financial environment?

As we review these key questions, provisional answers are suggested whenever possible.[5]

Our findings at this stage should be viewed as tentative. Nevertheless, we find substantial support for several basic conclusions from the mone-

[1] We use the term "financial deregulation" to refer not only to legislated changes in the regulatory environment that have taken place over the past few years (such as the Depository Institutions Deregulation and Monetary Control Act) but also to private-sector financial innovations, which clearly have equally altered the financial landscape. We recognize also that financial deregulation has been somewhat a gradual process rather than an immediate one. See Gilbert (1986, 31) for details of the steps in the phaseout of Regulation Q.

[2] While we explicitly only consider the effects of financial deregulation, many other changes have taken place in the macroeconomic environment over the past few years—such as disinflation, the deposit insurance crisis, the transition to interstate banking, shocks in oil prices, and changes in tax laws. These changes have altered the underlying economics of the banking industry and contributed, at least temporarily, to the hostile banking environment.

[3] The work reported here draws in part from Cox and Haslag (1989).

[4] By definition, base money (sometimes called the monetary base, or high-powered money) is currency held by the nonbank public plus reserves of banks. See Table 1 for a complete listing and description of the components of the M1 and M2 monetary aggregates as well as the monetary base.

[5] For earlier acknowledgment of some of the potential effects of financial innovations, see Santomero and Siegel (1981), Tatom (1983), and Thornton (1983). More recently, see Roley (1985); Bradley and Jansen (1986); Christiano (1986); Keeley and Zimmerman (1986); Darby, Poole, Lindsey, Friedman, and Bazdarich (1987); Roth (1987); Stone and Thornton (1987); B. Friedman (1988); Motley (1988); and Wenninger (1988).

tary and financial data of the 1980s. First and most important, because of financial deregulation, there appears to have been a permanent shift in the way in which people distribute their holdings of wealth among moneys and other assets. But this shift has been almost entirely among the components of the M2 monetary aggregate; to a much lesser extent, there have been shifts between M2 and other assets. As a result, there appears to be a stable long-term relationship between M2 and the price level, which reaffirms the notion that inflation is primarily a monetary phenomenon—at least, once you understand the evolving and proper definition of money.

Financial deregulation also appears to have altered the behavior of the multiple relationship between the monetary aggregates and base money. In particular, the two primary effects of financial deregulation here appear to have been a slowing in the rate of growth of the M2-to-base money ratio but an increased responsiveness of money supply to temporary disturbances in money demand. Thus, for purposes of pursuing long-term goals for nominal GNP growth (that is, for inflation), M2 appears to dominate both the more narrow M1 and the monetary base as a tar-

get for Federal Reserve policy. But, for purposes of pursuing short-term objectives for nominal GNP growth, base money now deserves more attention as a potential monetary target.

Overview of the policy problem faced by the Federal Reserve

Before specific questions are considered, we will first set out the monetary problem faced by the Federal Reserve. By carefully defining our view of the Federal Reserve's objective and by outlining the various factors affecting achievement of that objective, we intend to put in perspective the specific questions addressed in this article. In addition, we hope to limit the ambiguities that naturally arise when pursuing a relationship between two variables, such as money and economic activity. While our decision to narrow the scope of possible linkages between these two variables is necessary for tractability, we recognize that there is no unanimously accepted view of the exact way in which monetary policy affects the economy.

Chart 1 provides a diagrammatical overview of the monetary policy problem faced by the Fed-

Chart 1
Overview of the Policy Problem of the Federal Reserve

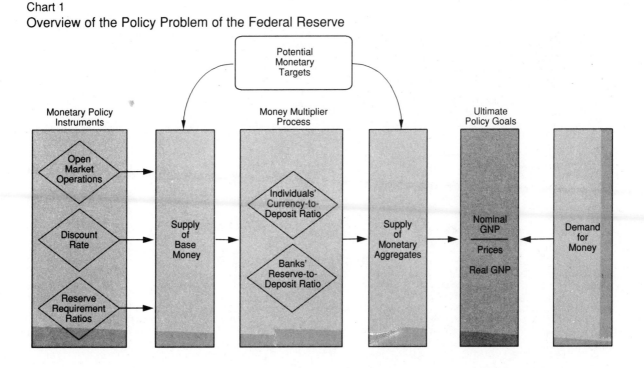

eral Reserve. Economic activity is viewed as being affected primarily by the two sides of the money market—money supply and money demand.[6] On the one side, the private sector demands various types of moneys—currency, bank reserves, demand deposits, other checkable deposits, money market deposit accounts, money market mutual funds, and so on.[7] On the other side, the Federal Reserve, together with private banks and households, determines (through a mechanism described later and known commonly as the money multiplier process) the supplies of the various moneys. These supplies include three simple-sum monetary measures—base money and the M1 and M2 monetary aggregates. (See Table 1 for a listing and description of the various types of money, including the monetary base and the M1 and M2 monetary aggregates.)

The Federal Reserve's objective, broadly speaking, is to achieve some ultimate policy *goal*—defined here as a particular level of nominal GNP—by manipulating its policy instruments. These are open market operations, reserve requirement ratios, and the discount rate.[8] In choosing particular values for these policy instruments, the Federal Reserve determines a specific magnitude for base money in the economy, which, through the money multiplier process, implies a level for each monetary aggregate.

Because variations in the private sector's demand for money (or moneys) render the existing stock of money (or moneys) inadequate or in excess, thereby affecting the economy's level of nominal GNP, the Federal Reserve may for practical reasons choose to adopt an intermediate policy goal, or monetary *target*. But also, because of variability in the money multiplier process, the Federal Reserve must decide whether that monetary target should be a more immediately controllable one, such as base money, or one further separated, such as M1 or M2.

These considerations frame the subject of the sections that follow. To proceed in a useful way, however, we need to clarify further and

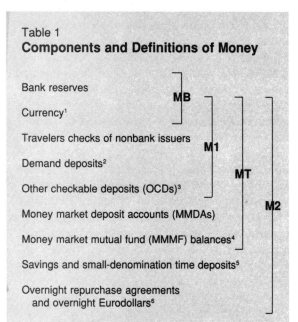

Table 1
Components and Definitions of Money

Bank reserves

Currency[1]

Travelers checks of nonbank issuers

Demand deposits[2]

Other checkable deposits (OCDs)[3]

Money market deposit accounts (MMDAs)

Money market mutual fund (MMMF) balances[4]

Savings and small-denomination time deposits[5]

Overnight repurchase agreements and overnight Eurodollars[6]

MB

M1

MT

M2

[1] Currency outside the Treasury, Federal Reserve Banks, and the vaults of depository institutions.

[2] Demand deposits at all commercial banks other than those due to depository institutions, the U.S. government, and foreign banks and official institutions less cash items in the process of collection and Federal Reserve float.

[3] Consist of negotiable order of withdrawal (NOW) and automatic transfer service (ATS) accounts at depository institutions, credit union share draft accounts, and demand deposits at thrift institutions.

[4] Balances in both taxable and tax-exempt general purpose and broker-dealer MMMFs.

[5] Time deposits, including retail repurchase agreements (RPs), in amounts of less than $100,000.

[6] Overnight (and continuing contract) repurchase agreements issued by all commercial banks and overnight Eurodollars issued to U.S. residents by foreign branches of U.S. banks worldwide.

NOTE: M2 excludes individual retirement accounts (IRAs) and Keogh balances held at depository institutions and money market funds and all balances held by money market funds (except institution-only funds), U.S. and foreign commercial banks, and the U.S. and foreign governments.

[6] To center attention on the role played by monetary factors, all other influences on economic activity are ignored in Chart 1 and in the accompanying discussion.

[7] The term "bank" is used as a generic shorthand here, and throughout this study, to refer equally to all depository institutions.

[8] We are assuming here, of course, that the chain of the causality runs primarily from base money to the monetary aggregates and then to nominal income, rather than other possible scenarios.

narrow somewhat the policy problem that we consider. Two caveats are thus made.

The first caveat concerns our interpretation of the use of nominal income as a policy objective of the Federal Reserve. By definition, nominal income is the level of *real* GNP evaluated at current prices. While it is reasonable that the Federal Reserve may have the ability, in the short run, to affect *both* real GNP and prices through expansion or contraction of the money supply, it is generally accepted that significant permanent effects of monetary policy on real GNP are not achievable. On the contrary, monetary policy in the long run is seen as affecting only prices. We thus find it convenient to retain nominal income as an overall goal of monetary policy, with the understanding that this variable is used to reflect movements in both real GNP and prices in the short run but as a guide to controlling inflation in the long run. With this clarification, we hope that the reader will not be distracted as we move sometimes synonymously between nominal GNP and prices in the discussion and charts that follow.

The second caveat concerns our definition and selection of variables to consider as money. What is money?[9] Does money include currency, bank reserves, demand deposits, other checkable deposits, money market mutual funds, money market deposit accounts, savings accounts, or what? Can money be measured accurately and usefully as a simple-sum variable—such as M1, M2, or base money? Or must money be aggregated in some other way to be valid? We admit at the outset that there is an extensive debate on this subject. And, frankly, no conclusive answer has yet emerged. Thus, for purposes of tractability, for ease of direct comparison, and because we

wish later to consider monetary targets of the type historically employed, we choose to narrow the set of possible money measures to those of the purely simple-sum variety. These are M1, M2, and the monetary base.[10]

In view of the central role played separately by both the demand for and the supply of money in the Federal Reserve's policy problem, we turn now to focus on each of these in more detail. This is followed by an analysis and discussion of the issue of choosing a suitable monetary target. We begin our overview by looking at the effects that financial deregulation has had on the demand for the monetary aggregates.

Effect of financial deregulation on demand for the monetary aggregates

In this section, we examine the behavior of the demand for M1 and M2 over the period 1960–88. We postpone analysis of the demand for base money until the money multiplier process is considered. Although it would be possible, by separately studying banks' demand for reserves and households' demand for currency, to examine directly the demand for base money also, we choose the alternative strategy of treating base money usage as a *derived* demand—derived, that is, from the demand for the monetary aggregates and linked by means of the money multiplier process. We follow this strategy because, as shown later, we feel that there is valuable information to be learned from a separate study of the behavior of the money multiplier process over the period 1960–88.

As Table 1 shows, the task of defining money demand is complicated because there is no single measure of money. A question of central importance, then, is whether there has been a permanent change in the way in which people distribute their holdings of wealth among moneys and other assets because, at least in part, of financial deregulation. As Chart 2 shows, over the past decade there has been tremendous growth in the demand for three new financial instruments— other checkable deposits (which include NOW and Super NOW accounts), money market mutual funds, and money market deposit accounts—all of which are now fully and competitively interest-bearing and enjoy checking privileges to some

---

[9] One could argue that the measures of money considered here reflect more the liquidity concept of money, rather than a transactions concept or net wealth concept of money. For a discussion of the various concepts of money and of the issue of money in a deregulated financial system, see, for example, O'Driscoll (1985, 1986) and Osborne (1985).

[10] We consider, as potential targets, neither individual monetary components (currency, demand deposits, etc.) nor monetary variables other than those of the simple-sum variety. In addition, we do not consider nonmonetary variables, such as nominal income or the interest rate.

Chart 2
Transactions Balances

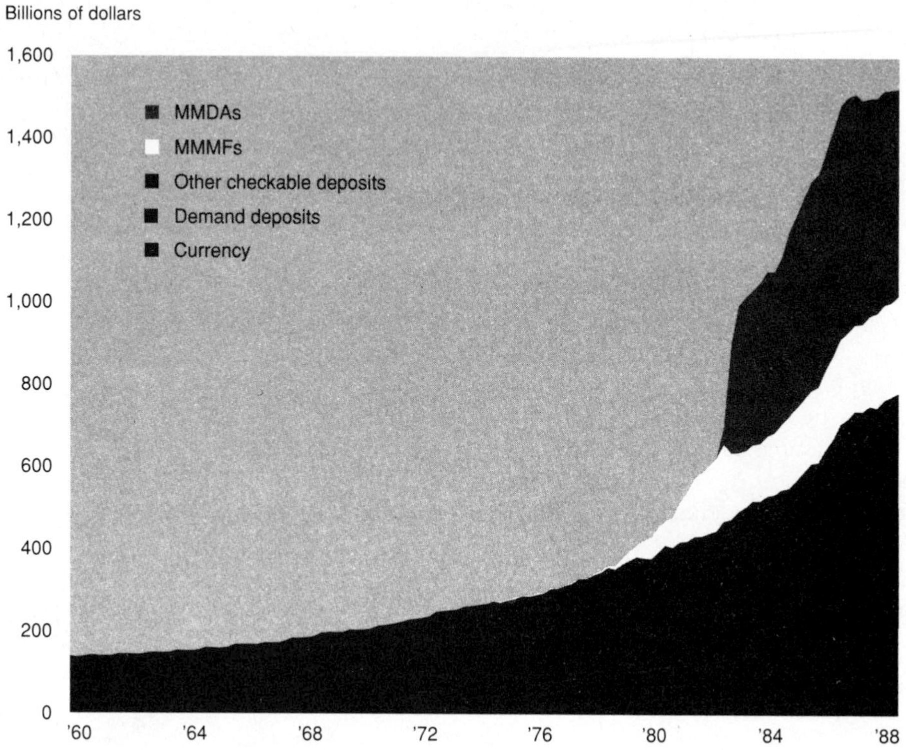

Billions of dollars

Legend:
- MMDAs
- MMMFs
- Other checkable deposits
- Demand deposits
- Currency

SOURCE: Board of Governors, Federal Reserve System.

degree.[11] Such tremendous growth in demand has no doubt been due largely to the interest-bearing nature of these accounts and to the rates they offer compared with those on alternative investments.

Now that a large part of money is explicitly interest-bearing, will the demand for some, or perhaps all, moneys grow more rapidly than in the past? Will money demand shrink? Or will it return to previous patterns of growth? To investigate these questions, we will ignore briefly the fact that there are various moneys as well as various alternative assets (securities, stocks, real property, etc.) and think generically in terms of "money" and "securities." This allows attention to be focused on the "opportunity cost" concept of holding money.

At any point in time, individuals choose to hold particular amounts of money and securities relative to their income, such ratios depending on

interest rates paid on money compared with those offered on alternative assets.[12] The spread between interest rates paid on securities and those paid on money measures the opportunity cost of holding money compared with alternative assets.

[11] NOW accounts were authorized for all depository institutions as of January 1, 1980, and Super NOWs as of January 5, 1983. A Super NOW is defined as a NOW account involving an agreement between the depositor and depository institution that requires a $2,500 minimum balance ($1,000 effective January 1, 1985) and provides that funds deposited are eligible to earn more than 5.25 percent interest. Beginning in 1986, the distinction between NOW accounts and Super NOWs was removed, and all accounts thereafter were classified as NOWs.

[12] This choice depends also, of course, on individuals' tastes and on transactions technology.

Chart 3 shows one measure of this opportunity cost—the spread between the interest rate paid on one-year U.S. Treasury securities and the rates paid on checkable deposits (calculated on a weighted-average basis)—over the period 1960–88.[13] Clearly, the spread between interest rates paid on checkable deposits and those on alternative assets has narrowed substantially as a result of financial deregulation.[14]

Because interest-bearing checking accounts have made money more like bonds, financial deregulation could have resulted in a sharp increase in the demand for money relative to income, leading even to unruly behavior of the demand for money. The latter would be the case, for example, if changes in the interest rate differential between money and securities encouraged individuals to shift more sharply back and forth between these forms of wealth than previously was

[13] The interest rate on checkable deposits referred to here is calculated as a weighted average of the interest rates paid on demand deposits (that rate being treated as zero), other checkable deposits (in particular, the average interest rate paid on NOW and Super NOW accounts), money market deposit accounts, and money market mutual funds. Specifically, $R_{CD} = (OCD/CD)R_{OCD} + (MMDA/CD)R_{MMDA} + (MMMF/CD)R_{MMMF}$, where R_{CD} is the average interest rate on checkable deposits (CD), R_{OCD} is the interest rate on other checkable deposits (OCD), R_{MMDA} is the interest rate on money market deposit accounts (MMDA), and R_{MMMF} is the interest rate on money market mutual funds (MMMF). (Before 1982, interest rate data on NOW and Super NOW accounts are unavailable and are estimated.) We explicitly exclude from this calculation the interest rate paid on savings accounts because those interest rate data are generally available only in terms of legal maximums (see footnote 36) and not as market rates. The spread is calculated as the one-year Treasury security rate less the calculated rate on checkable deposits.

[14] The spread may be measured with a variety of interest rates on moneys and alternative assets. We have chosen to measure the spread in a way that approximates both the opportunity cost to households of demanding interest-bearing checkable deposits and the profit to banks of supplying those deposits. It should be pointed out, though, that the spread behaves very similarly across a variety of interest rate comparisons, so the choice here is not critical. See footnote 13 for a description of how the interest rate on checkable deposits is constructed. Also, we recognize that banks implicitly offered positive rates of return on checkable deposits before financial deregulation. To circumvent legal prohibition of interest, for example, banks often offered "gifts."

Chart 3
Interest Rates

Percent per year

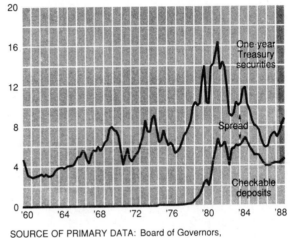

SOURCE OF PRIMARY DATA: Board of Governors, Federal Reserve System.

Chart 4
The Demand for Money Per Dollar of Income

(Ratios)

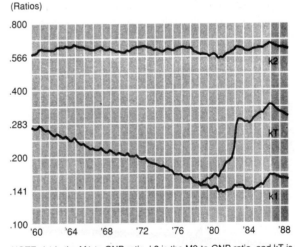

NOTE: k1 is the M1-to-GNP ratio, k2 is the M2-to-GNP ratio, and kT is the MT-to-GNP ratio. See Table 1 for a description of the M1, M2, and MT monetary aggregates.
SOURCES OF PRIMARY DATA: Board of Governors, Federal Reserve System. U.S. Department of Commerce.

the case.[15] The effects on the demand for money of the emergence of interest-bearing checking accounts can be seen by examining the historical behavior of the money-income ratio. Chart 4 shows three monetary aggregates—M1, M2, and a transactions aggregate, MT—relative to GNP over the period 1960–88.[16] These ratios are denoted as k1, k2, and kT, respectively.

Has financial deregulation led to a permanent and radical change in the way people distribute their holdings of wealth among moneys and other assets? Is the demand for money now very different from that in the past and perhaps much more erratic? As Chart 4 shows, the demand for M1 does appear to have changed dramatically over the past decade. The k1 ratio—which fell at an average annual rate of roughly 3 percent from 1960 to 1981—began to grow in the early 1980s.[17] While not obvious from Chart 4, M1 has also become much less *predictable*, with the variability in the growth rate of the M1-to-GNP ratio increasing by nearly 2½ times since 1981. In short, there is reason to suspect a deterioration in the stability of the demand for M1. This deterioration is even more notable in a broader transactions aggregate, MT—defined as the sum of currency, demand deposits, other checkable deposits, money market mutual funds, and money market deposit accounts.[18]

In the case of M2, however, apparently no significant deterioration has been caused by the movement from a regulated financial environment to a deregulated one.[19] The demand for M2 relative to income has remained remarkably stable over this entire period, as seen in Chart 4 by the relatively flat line for the k2 ratio (the M2-to-GNP ratio) compared with the lines for k1 and kT. The finding suggests that the increased demand for transactions balances has come largely at the expense of other M2 components—in particular, savings and small time deposits—and only slightly at the expense of other assets. Chart 5 further supports this finding.[20]

A closer look at the k2 ratio gives us a better idea of just how much difference the emergence of interest-bearing checkable deposits has made to the demand for M2. Chart 6 compares recent movements in the k2 ratio with those of the interest rate spread between one-year Treasury securities and checkable deposits. The chart points out

two important relationships. First, the demand for M2 relative to income is closely related to the spread in interest rates. Specifically, as the spread falls, the demand for M2 rises. Second and more

[15] Preliminary statistical tests indicate a heightened sensitivity of money demand to changes in the interest-rate-spread variable over the period 1983–88 compared with 1960–81. This result suggests a potentially increased substitutability between money and alternative assets (due presumably to the interest-bearing nature of money accounts). For evidence on the substitutability among various monetary assets, see Gauger and Schroeter (1989).

[16] See Table 1 for definitions of the monetary aggregates.

[17] While financial deregulation has been more of a gradual process than an immediate one, for purposes of comparisons between the regulated environment and the deregulated one, we need to separate the data into clearly defined periods. The procedure we opted for was to divide the data into three periods—a period generally characterizing a regulated financial environment, one characterizing a deregulated environment, and a transition period (treated as one year) between these two. Tests were then conducted examining the behavior of several monetary and financial variables reported here, such as the money-to-GNP ratios and the M2 money multiplier, to determine the period of maximum likelihood of a break in the data. The suggested subperiods from those tests were found to be 1960–81 and 1983–88.

[18] This monetary aggregate is sometimes referred to as M1+ or M2–.

[19] In response to the proliferation of new financial instruments offered by both bank and nonbank financial institutions in the second half of the 1970s, the Federal Reserve was compelled to redefine the monetary aggregates in 1980 (see Simpson 1980). At that time, it was not known whether (or how) prior, existing, and anticipated deregulation of banking would affect the relationships between the various monetary aggregates and nominal income, inflation, and other real-sector and financial variables. Given nearly a decade for these relationships to evolve and to be measured and understood, we now find M2 emerging as the most useful monetary aggregate. When the monetary aggregates were in the process of redefinition, few economists would have forecast this result. And as deregulation or reregulation takes new directions, these relationships may change. Such changes may necessitate the preeminence of another monetary aggregate and/or further redefinition of the monetary aggregates as new financial instruments are created with medium-of-exchange or store-of-value properties.

[20] Chart 5 excludes one component of M2—overnight repurchase agreements and overnight Eurodollars—which make up approximately only 2½ percent of M2.

Chart 5
M2 Components

Billions of dollars

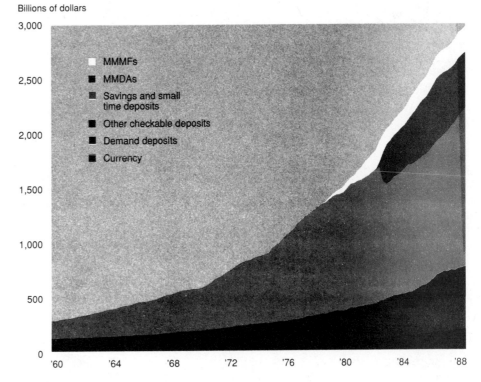

- MMMFs
- MMDAs
- Savings and small time deposits
- Other checkable deposits
- Demand deposits
- Currency

SOURCE: Board of Governors, Federal Reserve System.

Chart 6
Interest Rate Spread and Demand for M2

k2
(Ratio)

Spread
Percent per year

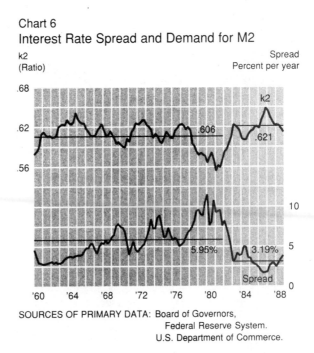

k2

.606

.621

5.95%

3.19%

Spread

SOURCES OF PRIMARY DATA: Board of Governors,
Federal Reserve System.
U.S. Department of Commerce.

important, the reduction in the spread caused by financial deregulation has not had a significant effect on the demand for M2. We estimate that deregulation of the financial environment has reduced the spread in interest rates to an average of 3.2 percent from 5.9 percent. In response, however, the demand for M2 per dollar of income has increased to only 62.0 cents from 60.6 cents. That is, the demand for M2 per dollar of income has increased by roughly only 2 percent during the period of financial deregulation.[21]

Effect of financial deregulation on the money supply process

In addition to affecting households' demand for the various types of money, financial deregulation may have significantly altered the process of money supply creation.[22] In this section, we examine the effect that financial deregulation has had on the relationship between the aggregates and base money over the period 1960–88. Particular attention is paid to the M2 money multiplier—that is, to the relationship between base money and the M2 monetary aggregate.

In the previous section, we examined the historical linkage between the monetary aggregates and nominal GNP. As Chart 1 points out, however, one other linkage is equally important in the overall connection between Federal Reserve policy instruments and policy goals. It is the linkage between base money (referred to alternatively as the monetary base, or high-powered money) and the monetary aggregates—known commonly as the money multiplier process.

By definition, base money is the total volume of currency held by the nonbank public plus reserves of banks (adjusted for changes in reserve requirements).[23] The monetary base is one important and useful measure of money because it is the measure over which the Federal Reserve has most immediate control. Base money rises, for example, as the Federal Reserve either purchases some asset, reduces its nonmonetary liabilities (through either the open market or the discount window), or lowers reserve requirements of banks. As a practical matter, open market purchases and sales of government securities are the medium most often associated with changes in the base. Indeed, open market operations are the central tool with which the Federal Reserve guides monetary policy over the long run.

Because of the fractional reserve nature of banking, an increase in base money causes a multiple increase in each of the monetary aggregates. Consider, for example, the M2 monetary aggregate and its relationship to the monetary base. Recall that M2 consists of currency plus deposits (demand deposits plus other checkable deposits plus money market deposit accounts plus money market mutual funds plus savings and small time deposits), and base money is currency plus bank reserves.[24] Using c to denote the ratio at which

[21] In contrast to M1 money demand, M2 money demand also appears to be more stable. In particular, in statistical tests relating the (log of the) level of $k1$ and $k2$, individually, to the interest rate spread (and to a constant and time), significantly more of the variation in $k2$ is shown as explained in the period 1983–88 (compared with the period 1960–81) but significantly less for $k1$.

[22] For an overview of the behavior of the M1 and M2 money multipliers over the period 1960–87 (and a brief discussion of the role played by the emergence of interest-bearing checking accounts), see Burger (1988).

[23] In practice, there are two measures of the monetary base—the source base and the adjusted monetary base. These measures differ primarily on the basis of whether they adjust for changes in reserve requirements. The source base is a simple accounting construct equal to net assets of the Federal Reserve System. The source base rises, for example, when the Federal Reserve purchases some asset or reduces its nonmonetary liabilities. As a practical matter, the source base is manipulated either through an open market purchase or sale of government securities by the Federal Reserve System or by System lending through the discount window. The adjusted monetary base, on the other hand, additionally adjusts the source base to account for the magnitude of reserves freed by a change in reserve requirements. A reduction in reserve requirements, for example, frees bank reserves in an amount that could have been achieved directly through an open market purchase of government securities by the System. Thus, to capture the effects of changes in all three of the System's policy instruments—open market operations, the discount rate, and reserve requirement ratios—we use the adjusted monetary base. In particular, we use the St. Louis adjusted monetary base. See Haslag and Hein (1989) for a more thorough description of the monetary base and its relationship to GNP.

[24] Again, for exposition, we are ignoring overnight repurchase agreements and overnight Eurodollars.

individuals wish to hold currency relative to M2 deposits, e as the ratio at which banks hold reserves (in excess of those required) relative to M2 deposits, and B as the monetary base (adjusted for reserve requirements), it is easy to show that M2 is a multiple of base money.[25] Specifically, the relationship is $M2 = a2 \cdot B$, where $a2 = (c + 1)/(c + e)$ is the M2 "money multiplier." This equation says simply that open market purchases or sales of government securities by the Federal Reserve (as well as other operations on base money) have an eventual multiple impact on the M2 supply of money, where the *size* of that multiple depends on the preferences of individuals regarding their holdings of currency relative to deposits (c) and depends on banks' preferences (e) regarding the amount of reserves to hold relative to deposits.

To illustrate the money multiplier process further, consider the case where the Federal Reserve wishes to increase the monetary aggregates. The Federal Reserve, say, purchases government securities held by banks, which increases bank reserves and, thus, base money. Banks, in turn, loan out a portion of the additional reserves (depending on their choice of e), of which individuals redeposit a portion (depending on their choice of c), thus providing additional deposits, of which banks loan out a portion, and so on. This progression of redepositing and relending is termed the money multiplier process, because it is through this mechanism that an increase in the monetary base has an eventual multiplier impact on any given monetary aggregate.

In essence, the money multiplier is the transmission in the linkage between the engine of base money growth and the speed, or growth rate, of the monetary aggregates. This transmission depends on the preferences of both individuals and banks, which, in turn, depend on underlying economic variables (such as transactions technology, tastes) and, also, on the spread between interest rates paid on money and those on alternative assets.

For purposes of seeing the effect that financial deregulation has had on the money supply process, we must understand next the role that the interest rate spread plays in banks' choice of the excess reserve-to-deposit ratio. On the one hand, deposits held as reserves serve a direct economic function to banks in that they allow banks to meet unanticipated cash drains, manage the efficient allocation of bank liabilities and assets over time, and satisfy reserve requirements without borrowing at the discount window. On the other hand, though, the spread reflects the potential net unit profit to banks from borrowing funds in the deposit market and investing those funds elsewhere (drawing down reserves).[26] A decrease in the spread, then, is apt to increase banks' chosen excess reserve-to-deposit ratio as it lowers the economic benefit to banks of lending

Chart 7
Currency Relative to M2 Deposits,
Excess Reserves Relative to M2 Deposits,
and the M2 Money Multiplier

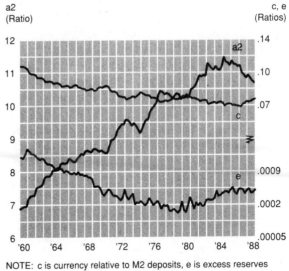

NOTE: c is currency relative to M2 deposits, e is excess reserves
relative to M2 deposits, and a2 is the M2 money multiplier.
SOURCE: Board of Governors, Federal Reserve System.

[25] We recognize that not all M2-type deposits are at institutions defined as "depository institutions" and under the direct supervision of the Federal Reserve. Examples of these are cash management accounts at money market brokerage firms.

[26] For the sake of exposition, this discussion ignores other types of institutional borrowing and lending costs (loan origination costs, advertising costs, etc.) that might affect banking profitability. In addition, banks are treated as lending in the same investment market generally available to individuals, so the spread shown earlier for individuals (the opportunity cost concept) may be used to approximate that pertinent to the borrowing and lending decisions faced by banks.

deposits instead of retaining those deposits as reserves.

Chart 7 shows the behavior of the excess reserve-to-deposit ratio and the M2 money multiplier over the period 1960–88. As that chart reveals, the excess reserve-to-deposit ratio, which fell steadily through the period 1960–80, began to level off in the early 1980s and has in recent years shown signs even of growth. Apparently, the emergence of interest-bearing checkable deposits and the implied narrowing of the spread between borrowing and lending rates of banks have had a significant impact on banks' chosen reserve-to-deposit ratio.[27]

Note also, though, in view of the relatively small magnitude of the excess reserve-to-deposit ratio, that this effect on the M2 money multiplier has not been the predominant one. Even more significantly impacting the M2 money multiplier has been the emergence of a new pattern of behavior for the currency-to-deposit ratio. As Chart 7 shows, the currency-to-M2 deposit ratio, which fell at an average annual rate of 1.4 percent over the period 1960–81, has altered its long-term course and in recent years has *grown* at an average annual rate of 0.3 percent. Such an increase

in relative currency holdings might have been expected, in part, given the general decline in interest rates on alternative investments over the decade (encouraging households to substitute out of these interest-bearing instruments and into cash). Still, the increase would *not* have been predicted from the emergence of interest-bearing deposit accounts. Indeed, one might have expected that financial deregulation would *reduce* the currency-to-deposit ratio as households reduced their cash balances and sought the attractiveness of interest-bearing checking accounts.[28]

The basic lesson to be learned from studying the new and puzzling behavior of the currency-to-deposit ratio, then, is that there remains a good deal of uncertainty about the way in which financial deregulation has affected the money multiplier process.[29] Nonetheless, the M2 money multiplier has departed from its established pattern of 2.1-percent average annual growth over the period 1960–81 and has slowed to virtually no growth (with some signs, in fact, of declining over the past three to four years). Furthermore, the variability in the growth rate of the M2 money multiplier has increased sharply over the past few years.[30] And as a result, the transmission mechanism from the Federal Reserve's operating variable—base money—to the ultimate monetary target(s)—the monetary aggregate(s)—has been made potentially less certain because of financial deregulation.

Chart 8 shows the implications of these results for the demand for base money. Reflecting a

Chart 8
The Demand for Base Money Per Dollar of Income

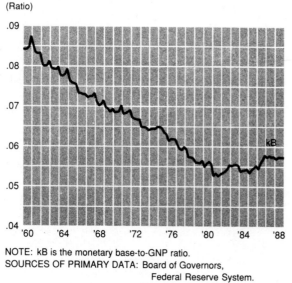

(Ratio)

NOTE: kB is the monetary base-to-GNP ratio.
SOURCES OF PRIMARY DATA: Board of Governors,
Federal Reserve System.
U.S. Department of Commerce.

[27] This result is strongly supported by statistical analysis, indicating a highly statistically significant relation between the interest-rate-spread variable introduced here and both the excess reserve-to-deposit ratio and the M2 money multiplier.

[28] Of course, there is also the potential effect that deregulation has had, through heightened financial fragility, on the currency-to-deposit ratio.

[29] See Burger (1988) for a discussion of the recent behavior of the currency-to-deposit ratio.

[30] Specifically, the variance in the annualized quarterly growth rate of the M2 money multiplier has increased from an average of 0.18 percentage point over the period 1960–80 to 0.26 percentage point over the period 1982–88.

Table 2
Trend Growth and Deviations from Trend Growth in a2 and the k Ratios

(Annual averages, in percentage points)

	Trend growth				Deviation from trend growth			
	k1	k2	a2	kB	k1	k2	a2	kB
1960–81	–3.18	–0.18	2.12	–2.30	1.75	2.55	2.32	1.87
1983–88	1.13	0.25	–0.29	0.55	5.15	2.99	1.79	2.28

NOTE: a2 is the M2 money multiplier calculated as the ratio of M2 to base money. k1 is the M1-to-GNP ratio, k2 is the M2-to-GNP ratio, and kB is the base money-to-GNP ratio. See footnote 17 for an explanation of the choice of periods over which these variables are compared.
SOURCES OF PRIMARY DATA: Board of Governors, Federal Reserve System.
U.S. Department of Commerce.

disturbance to nominal GNP growth—short and long run—and to evaluate the relative merits of pursuing different monetary targets in terms of their abilities to achieve *both* short-run and long-run desired rates of GNP growth.

In sum, then, the problem we are considering is one where the Federal Reserve wishes to control nominal GNP growth as much as possible, both in the long run and in the short run, by adopting a constant growth rate rule for either M1, M2, or the monetary base. What are the relative merits of targeting each of these money variables to achieve this goal? As Table 2 shows, the answer to this question is not immediately straightforward because there are generally two types of shocks that may occur (and have historically occurred) to money demand and to money supply growth, each of which affects nominal GNP growth differently. Broadly speaking, these two types of shocks are temporary shocks and permanent shocks.

Consider first the case of permanent shocks to the growth rate in money demand or money supply. Examples of these shocks are shown in Charts 4, 6, and 7 and Table 2, where arguably permanent shifts have occurred in the growth rates of the k1 ratio, the k2 ratio, and a2 (the M2 money multiplier) over the past decade. As shown in Table 2, over the past few years the average annual rate of growth in k1 has risen to

1.1 percent from –3.2 percent previously—a shift of 4.3 percentage points. Thus (by our calculations), continuing to target M1 over this period—that is, continuing to allow M1 to grow at its 1960–81 average annual value—would have tightened nominal GNP growth to under 2.4 percent from its actual average of nearly 6.3 percent. Targeting the monetary base, in turn, would have tightened nominal GNP growth to 3.1 percent, because of the sharp downward shift (a shift of 2.4 percentage points) in the trend rate of growth of the M2 money multiplier. Targeting M2, on the other hand, would have produced almost no discernible effect on the growth rate of nominal GNP, as the k2 ratio remained stable throughout this period (a trend shift of only 0.4 percentage point). On the basis of these results and for purposes of achieving long-term objectives for nominal GNP growth (inflation), a policy of targeting M2 would then be implied.

Charts 9, 10, and 11 further underscore this point.[32] While M1 has been led astray by the

---

[32] In Charts 9, 10, and 11, the lines depicting the level of prices have been adjusted by adding respective constant rates of growth quarterly. These constants are calculated, in each case, as the average quarterly growth rate of real GNP plus the average quarterly growth rate of the individual money-to-GNP ratio over the period 1960–88.

higher demand for both bank reserves and currency relative to M2 deposits and currency, the base-to-GNP (kB) ratio has departed in recent years from its historically declining pattern. Specifically, while the kB ratio fell at an average annual rate of 2.3 percent over the period 1960–81, this ratio has grown over the past six years at an average annual rate of nearly 0.6 percent.

The Federal Reserve's money target in the new financial environment

We turn now to the issue of establishing targets to guide monetary policy. In the past, repeated arguments have been made for targeting M1 and M2 and, more recently, for targeting the monetary base.[31] Arguments have also been made that the Federal Reserve should target both interest rates and nominal income. Practically speaking, these are too many targets to consider within the scope of this article. For simplification and for ease of direct comparison, then, we consider only three potential Federal Reserve targets. These are base money, M1, and M2—all, notably, monetary targets.

In this section, we set out a simple rule for monetary targeting and then evaluate the implications of applying three alternative targets to follow that rule. We admit at the outset that our choice of a targeting procedure is potentially overly simple. Nonetheless, it serves as a useful device for comparing the merits of alternative targets, while also providing a valuable benchmark against which to judge more sophisticated targeting procedures. We should also indicate that, whereas our discussion to this point has been cast in terms of *levels* of variables, for purposes of considering alternative targets by which to achieve both short-term *and* long-term goals, it is much

more meaningful to conduct the analysis henceforth in terms of rates of growth.

Is there some monetary variable that the Federal Reserve can target in an effort to control nominal GNP growth and, if so, what is that variable? To investigate this question, we must first define our use of the term "monetary targeting procedure." Should the procedure be one of allowing the monetary variable to grow within certain prespecified ranges; should there be some "feedback" rule for money growth from observing nominal GNP, interest rates, or some other policy indicator; should the Federal Reserve adopt, say, a constant growth rate rule for the monetary variable in question, as has been frequently suggested; or should some other targeting procedure be followed?

Given the complexities of this problem and in view of our desire to focus on the merits of pursuing alternative monetary targets (rather than alternative targeting *procedures*), we adopt the simplest monetary targeting procedure—a constant growth rate rule. That is, whichever of the three monetary variables the Federal Reserve targets, a constant growth rate is presumed to be adopted for that variable. This is accomplished for base money by direct control of the Federal Reserve balance sheet. Achievement of a constant growth rate for each of the monetary aggregates would admittedly be more difficult (if not impossible in the very short run) because of the influence of private forces on the money multiplier process. Nevertheless, this rule is achievable in principle (certainly, at least approximately) by raising or lowering the growth rate of the monetary base to offset movements in either of the money multipliers.

We must also specify whether the Federal Reserve's objective is to achieve a desired nominal GNP goal in the short run (a goal for real GNP and the price level combined), in the long run (a goal for prices), or both. There is no necessary reason why a goal of minimizing temporary disturbances in nominal GNP would call for the same monetary target as would a goal of preventing deviations from a desired permanent path for nominal GNP (inflation). This is an important distinction and one that we feel should not be ignored. Our approach, thus, is to assume that the Federal Reserve is concerned about each type of

---

[31] For early historical support for the choice of M2 as the appropriate monetary aggregate to target, see Friedman and Schwartz (1963). More recently, see McMillin and Fackler (1984), Judd and Trehan (1987), M. Friedman (1988), Mehra (1988), and Wenninger (1988). Support for targeting the monetary base may be found, for example, in Fama (1983), Andersen (1975), Andersen and Karnosky (1977), McCallum (1987, 1988), Hall (1988), Neal (1988), and Shadow Open Market Committee (1985–).

newfound attractiveness of interest-bearing deposits (Chart 9) and while the relationship between the monetary base and prices has been impaired by the effects of financial deregulation on the money multiplier process (Chart 10), the relationship between M2 and prices (Chart 11) has remained remarkably stable.[33] There *has* been a permanent change in the way in which people distribute their holdings of wealth between moneys and other assets because of financial deregulation, *but* this shift has been almost entirely among the components of M2 and not between M2 and other assets. It is for this reason that the long-term relationship between M2 and prices has not been significantly damaged by financial deregulation.

Consider now the implications of temporary shocks to money demand and money supply growth, shown in Table 2 as deviations from the trend rates of growth for each of the periods 1960–81 and 1983–88. What are the effects of these types of monetary shocks on nominal GNP growth? To answer this question, recognize first that money supply adjusts partially and automatically to meet disturbances in money demand. Consider, for example, the case of an increase in money demand. An increase in the demand for money relative to other assets causes a widening of the spread between interest rates on deposits and those on alternative investments, thereby inducing banks to make more loans, which, through the money multiplier process described above, increases the money supply. Part of this automatic adjustment process was in place before financial deregulation because interest rates on alternative assets could respond to changes in the demand for money; but now, *deposit* interest rates also can respond, which aids in the automatic adjustment of money supply to accommodate shifts in money demand.

In short, there are fundamental economic reasons why households' demand for M2 per

dollar of income (k2) and the M2 money multiplier (a2) would historically be significantly correlated—indeed, even more correlated in a deregulated financial environment. While potentially tentative, our estimates confirm that the statistical correlation between the quarterly growth

Chart 9
M1 and Prices

(Indexes, 1981:Q4 = 100)

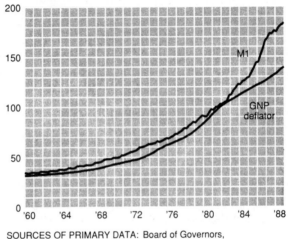

SOURCES OF PRIMARY DATA: Board of Governors,
Federal Reserve System.
U.S. Department of Commerce.

Chart 10
Base Money and Prices

(Indexes, 1981:Q4 = 100)

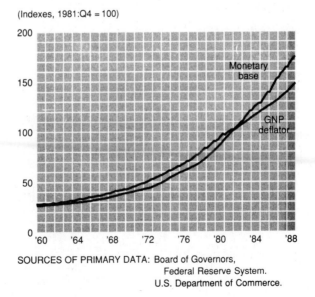

SOURCES OF PRIMARY DATA: Board of Governors,
Federal Reserve System.
U.S. Department of Commerce.

---

[33] *Our choice to represent the relationship between money and prices in terms of levels in Charts 9, 10, and 11, and in the accompanying discussion, is statistically supported by evidence that the level of prices is co-integrated (at the 10-percent level or greater) with each of the variables M1, M2, and the monetary base.*

rates of k2 and a2 has increased to 0.72 over the period 1983–88 from 0.49 during the period 1960–81.

What implications does this hold for the choice of an appropriate monetary aggregate with which to achieve short-term stability in nominal GNP growth? Because a policy of targeting the monetary base allows the money multiplier to remain freely flexible and available to help equilibrate the money market—that is, to absorb disturbances in money demand or money supply—such a policy potentially lessens the transmission of those disturbances to nominal GNP growth in the economy.[34] A policy of targeting M2, on the other hand, ignores the benefits of the automatic equilibrating mechanism offered by the money multiplier process, thereby allowing those disturbances to be transmitted more fully to nominal GNP in the economy.

In sum, then, there are merits to targeting M2 and the monetary base and relatively little merit to targeting M1. The merits of targeting M2 lie primarily with the fact that the M2-to-GNP ratio has proven quite stable historically; thus, targeting M2 growth is a relatively simple way of achieving long-term goals for inflation. The merits of targeting base money, on the other hand, lie primarily with the stabilizing nature of the money multiplier

process; monetary aggregates can adjust to accommodate partially any temporary shocks to money demand.

The bottom line, then, is that, if the Federal Reserve is concerned primarily with controlling inflation, a constant growth rate rule for M2 may be the more reasonable policy to pursue. If the goal is more one of temporary stability in nominal GNP growth, then such a targeting rule for the monetary base is likely preferred, especially in a deregulated financial environment. In either case, there is good reason to argue that M1 has lost much of its reliability as a monetary target.

Conclusions and projections

Over the past decade, the banking and monetary system of the United States has fundamentally and perhaps irrevocably changed. There are clearly many major differences in the financial environment today as compared with only a few years ago. Perhaps the greatest of these differences is the way in which people hold money and wealth.[35] As recently as 10 years ago, individuals used chiefly currency and demand deposits for transactions balances, while they preferred savings accounts, interest-bearing securities, and other assets as stores of value. In this old, regulated financial environment, checkable bank deposits were prohibited from paying interest, and rates on savings deposits were limited to a maximum of 5½ percent.[36]

Chart 11
M2 and Prices

(Indexes, 1981:Q4 = 100)

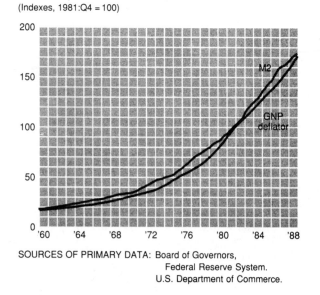

SOURCES OF PRIMARY DATA: Board of Governors,
Federal Reserve System.
U.S. Department of Commerce.

[34] See Santomero and Siegel (1981) for theoretical examination of the effects of financial deregulation on the stability of the macroeconomy.

[35] See Santoni (1987) for an exposition of the relationship between national wealth and M1 money demand over the period 1960–86.

[36] The 5.5-percent legal maximum became effective January 1, 1984. Before that time (and over the period with which this study is concerned), the legal maximums were as follows: January 1, 1957–December 31, 1961, 3 percent; January 1, 1962–January 20, 1970, 4 percent; January 21, 1970–June 30, 1973, 4.5 percent; July 1, 1973–June 30, 1979, 5 percent; July 1, 1979–December 31, 1983, 5.25 percent; and beginning January 1, 1984, 5.5 percent. Note also that transferability between savings and checking deposits was severely restricted by regulation.

Induced by inflation and high interest rates in the late 1970s, however, financial innovations, such as money market mutual funds, began to change the way in which people hold money and wealth. And with the subsequent enactment of the Depository Institutions Deregulation and Monetary Control Act of 1980, a new era of money and banking was officially ushered in. The act guaranteed full rite of passage to a new and *de*regulated financial world and codified changes in the nature of money that had evolved over the prior decade. In short, a large part of what is called "money" became explicitly interest-bearing and, thus, much more like bonds and other earning assets than previously.

The emergence of a new market-determined "price" for checkable deposits has had, and will continue to have, important effects on the economy. For one, the narrowing of the interest rate spread between "funds borrowed and funds lent" by depository institutions implies potentially fundamental changes in banking profitability, bank failure rates, the composition of bank loan portfolios, and so on. These microeconomic, or structural, ramifications of financial deregulation are important to the economy, and they are important to the Federal Reserve because they bear directly on the function of supervision and regulation. But financial deregulation also has important *macro*economic effects on the level and stability of prices, interest rates, and GNP in the economy.

This article provides an overview of some key questions regarding the impact of financial deregulation on the macroeconomy. We have four basic conclusions.

1. Financial deregulation does appear to have caused a permanent shift in the way in which people distribute their holdings of wealth among moneys and other assets. But this shift has been almost entirely among the components of the M2 monetary aggregate and not between M2 and other assets.

2. There appears to be a stable relationship between M2 and the price level. This stability reaffirms the notion that inflation is primarily a monetary phenomenon once one understands the evolving and proper definition of money.

3. Financial deregulation appears to have altered the relationship between the monetary aggregates and the Federal Reserve's primary instrument of monetary control—base money. In particular, financial deregulation has apparently slowed the rate of growth of the M2-to-base money ratio but has yielded an increased responsiveness of money supply to temporary disturbances in money demand.

4. Thus, for purposes of pursuing long-term goals for nominal GNP growth (goals for inflation), M2 appears to dominate both the more narrow M1 and the monetary base as a target for Federal Reserve policy. But for purposes of pursuing short-term goals for nominal GNP growth, base money is likely the preferred target, especially in the deregulated financial environment.

Based on these findings, what can we point to as reducing inflation in the United States during the early 1980s, and what projections can be made about the nation's future course of inflation? The work here indicates that the inflationary era of the late 1970s can be linked largely to excessive growth in the M2 monetary aggregate during that period.[37] Furthermore, the deceleration in inflation during the early 1980s appears to be due largely to deceleration in the rate of M2 money growth and can be credited only a little to financial deregulation or innovations in the payments mechanism. Because financial deregulation has not significantly altered the long-term relationship between M2 money and prices, the future course for inflation will continue to depend largely on the course of M2 money growth, which the Federal Reserve is obliged to restrain for price stability.

---

[37] M2 grew at an annual rate of 10 to 13 percent for a 10-quarter period ending in the fourth quarter of 1978. This was followed by a buildup in inflation averaging 8 to 10 percent at an annual rate over an 11-quarter period ending in the fourth quarter of 1981.

References

Andersen, Leonall C. (1975), "Selection of a Monetary Aggregate for Economic Stabilization," *Federal Reserve Bank of St. Louis Review,* October, 9–15.

Andersen, Leonall C., and Denis S. Karnosky (1977), "Some Considerations in the Use of Monetary Aggregates for the Implementation of Monetary Policy," Federal Reserve Bank of St. Louis *Review*, September, 2–7.

Board of Governors of the Federal Reserve System (1977), "The Impact of the Payment of Interest on Demand Deposits," Staff Study (Washington, D.C.: Board of Governors, 31 January).

Bradley, Michael D., and Dennis W. Jansen (1986), "Deposit Market Deregulation and Interest Rates," *Southern Economic Journal* 53 (October): 478–89.

Brainard, William C. (1964), "Financial Intermediaries and a Theory of Monetary Control," *Yale Economic Essays* 4 (Fall): 431–82.

Burger, Albert E. (1988), "The Puzzling Growth of the Monetary Aggregates in the 1980s," Federal Reserve Bank of St. Louis *Review*, September/October, 46–60.

Christiano, Lawrence J. (1986), "Money and the U.S. Economy in the 1980s: A Break from the Past?" *Federal Reserve Bank of Minneapolis Quarterly Review*, Summer, 2–13.

Cox, W. Michael, and Joseph H. Haslag (1989), "The Effects of Financial Deregulation on Inflation, Velocity Growth, and Monetary Targeting," Federal Reserve Bank of Dallas Research Paper no. 8907 (Dallas, May).

Darby, Michael R., William Poole, David E. Lindsey, Milton Friedman, and Michael J. Bazdarich (1987), "Recent Behavior of the Velocity of Money," *Contemporary Policy Issues* 5 (January): 1–33.

Dwyer, Gerald P., Jr., and R. W. Hafer (1988), "Is Money Irrelevant?" Federal Reserve Bank of St. Louis *Review,* May/June, 3–17.

Fama, Eugene F. (1983), "Financial Intermediation and Price Level Control," *Journal of Monetary Economics* 12 (July): 7–28.

Friedman, Benjamin M. (1988), "Lessons on Monetary Policy from the 1980s," *Journal of Economic Perspectives* 2 (Summer): 51–72.

Friedman, Milton (1988), "Money and the Stock Market," *Journal of Political Economy* 96 (April): 221–45.

Friedman, Milton, and Anna Jacobson Schwartz (1963), *A Monetary History of the United States, 1867–1960* (Princeton: Princeton University Press for National Bureau of Economic Research).

Gauger, Jean A., and John R. Schroeter (1989), "Measuring the Nearness of Modern Nearmonies: Evidence from the 1980s" (March, Photocopy).

Gilbert, R. Alton (1977), "Effects of Interest on Demand Deposits: Implications of Compensating Balances," Federal Reserve Bank of St. Louis *Review*, November, 8–15.

———— (1986), "Requiem for Regulation Q: What It Did and Why It Passed Away," Federal Reserve Bank of St. Louis *Review*, February, 22–37.

Hall, Thomas E. (1988), "McCallum's Base Growth Rule: Results for the United States, West Germany, Japan, and Canada," PAS Working Paper Series, no. 11, U.S. Department of State (Washington, D.C.: U.S. Department of State, Bureau of Economic and Business Affairs, Planning and Economic Analysis Staff, December).

Hallman, Jeffrey J., Richard D. Porter, and David H. Small (1989), *M2 per Unit of Potential GNP as an Anchor for the Price Level*, Staff Studies, no. 157 (Washington, D.C.: Board of Governors of the Federal Reserve System, April).

Haslag, Joseph H., and Scott E. Hein (1989), "Reserve Requirements, the Monetary Base, and Economic Activity," Federal Reserve Bank of Dallas *Economic Review*, March, 1–15.

Judd, John P., and Bharat Trehan (1987), "Portfolio Substitution and the Reliability of M1, M2 and M3 as Monetary Policy Indicators," Federal Reserve Bank of San Francisco *Economic Review*, Summer, 5–29.

Keeley, Michael C., and Gary C. Zimmerman (1986), "Deposit Rate Deregulation and the Demand for Transactions Media," Federal Reserve Bank of San Francisco *Economic Review*, Summer, 47–62.

McCallum, Bennett T. (1987), "The Case for Rules in the Conduct of Monetary Policy: A Concrete Example," Federal Reserve Bank of Richmond *Economic Review*, September/October, 10–18.

———— (1988), "Robustness Properties of a Rule for Monetary Policy," *Carnegie-Rochester Conference Series on Public Policy* 29:173–203.

McMillin, W. Douglas, and James S. Fackler (1984), "Monetary vs. Credit Aggregates: An Evaluation of Monetary Policy Targets," *Southern Economic Journal* 50 (January): 711–23.

Mehra, Yash P. (1988), "The Forecast Performance of Alternative Models of Inflation," Federal Reserve Bank of Richmond *Economic Review*, September/October, 10–18.

Motley, Brian (1988), "Should M2 Be Redefined?" Federal Reserve Bank of San Francisco *Economic Review*, Winter, 33–51.

Neal, Stephen L. (1988), *Report on the Conduct of Monetary Policy*, prepared by the Subcommittee on Domestic Monetary Policy for the use of the House Committee on Banking, Finance and Urban Affairs, 100th Cong., 2d sess., Committee Print 100-5.

O'Driscoll, Gerald P., Jr. (1985), "Money in a Deregulated Financial System," Federal Reserve Bank of Dallas *Economic Review*, May, 1–12.

———— (1986), "Deregulation and Monetary Reform," Federal Reserve Bank of Dallas *Economic Review*, July, 19–31.

Osborne, Dale K. (1985), "What Is Money Today?" Federal Reserve Bank of Dallas *Economic Review*, January, 1–15.

Rasche, Robert H. (1989), "Some Evidence on the Elusive 1982 Shift in Velocity Drift," in Shadow Open Market Committee, "Policy Statement and Position Papers," Public Policy Working Paper Series, no. PPS 89-01, University of Rochester (Rochester, N.Y.: University of Rochester, Bradley Policy Research Center, 19–20 March), 41–49.

Roley, V. Vance (1985), "Money Demand Predictability," *Journal of Money, Credit, and Banking* 17 (November, pt. 2): 611–41.

Roth, Howard L. (1987), "Has Deregulation Ruined M1 as a Policy Guide?" Federal Reserve Bank of Kansas City *Economic Review*, June, 24–37.

Santomero, Anthony M., and Jeremy J. Siegel (1981), "Bank Regulation and Macro-Economic Stability," *American Economic Review* 71 (March): 39–53.

Santoni, G. J. (1987), "Changes in Wealth and the Velocity of Money," Federal Reserve Bank of St. Louis *Review*, March, 16–26.

Shadow Open Market Committee (1985–), "Policy Statement and Position Papers," Public Policy Working Paper Series, University of Rochester (Rochester, N.Y.: University of Rochester, Bradley Policy Research Center).

Siegel, Diane F. (1986), "The Relationship of Money and Income: The Breakdowns in the 70s and 80s," Federal Reserve Bank of Chicago *Economic Perspectives*, July/August, 3–15.

Simpson, Thomas D. (1980), "The Redefined Monetary Aggregates," *Federal Reserve Bulletin* 66 (February): 97–114.

Stockton, David J., and James E. Glassman (1987), "An Evaluation of the Forecast Performance of Alternative Models of Inflation," *Review of Economics and Statistics* 69 (February): 108–17.

Stone, Courtenay C., and Daniel L. Thornton (1987), "Solving the 1980s' Velocity Puzzle: A Progress Report," Federal Reserve Bank of St. Louis *Review*, August/September, 5–23.

Tatom, John A. (1983), "Was the 1982 Velocity Decline Unusual?" Federal Reserve Bank of St. Louis *Review*, August/September, 5–15.

Thornton, Daniel L. (1983), "Why Does Velocity Matter?" Federal Reserve Bank of St. Louis *Review*, December, 5–13.

Tobin, James (1969), "A General Equilibrium Approach to Monetary Theory," *Journal of Money, Credit, and Banking* 1 (February): 15–29.

Tobin, James, and William C. Brainard (1963), "Financial Intermediaries and the Effectiveness of Monetary Controls," *American Economic Review* 53 (May, Papers and Proceedings, 1962): 383–400.

Wenninger, John (1988), "Money Demand—Some Long-Run Properties," Federal Reserve Bank of New York *Quarterly Review*, Spring, 23–40.

Article 30

Joseph H. Haslag
Economist
Federal Reserve Bank of Dallas

Scott E. Hein
Professor of Finance
Texas Tech University
Consultant
Federal Reserve Bank of Dallas

Reserve Requirements, the Monetary Base, and Economic Activity

The search for the right target for U.S. monetary policy remains a focal point of debate among monetary economists and policymakers. Although unanimity has proven elusive, sentiment favoring the monetary base has grown. For many years, the Shadow Open Market Committee has recommended targeting the growth rate of the monetary base.[1] Recently, McCallum (1988) has provided empirical evidence that suggests a monetary base rule would have resulted in more stable growth of nominal GNP (gross national product) over the period 1954–85.[2] Even Congress has recently gotten into the act. The House Subcommittee on Domestic Monetary Policy, for example, has suggested that the Federal Reserve "give serious consideration to reporting target ranges for the monetary base."[3]

Apart from the question of conviction to targeting the monetary base, there remains the issue of **which** base measure to use. Although not a generally recognized fact, two different measures of base money exist—source base and adjusted monetary base.[4] The fundamental difference between these two measures is the treatment of changes in reserve requirement ratios. The source base measure comes directly from the Federal Reserve's balance sheet and ignores the role of reserve requirement ratios. The adjusted monetary base combines the source base with a term that accounts for changes in reserve requirement ratios.

Choosing between the source base and the adjusted monetary base as prospective policy targets amounts to making suppositions about the importance of changes in reserve requirement ratios. If changes in reserve requirement ratios are important for economic stabilization purposes, then the adjusted monetary base would be the better target for monetary policy. If, on the other hand, reserve requirement ratio changes are negligible and unimportant, then the source base would serve equally well as a target.

The purpose of the present article is twofold. First, the aim is to make clear the difference between the source base and the adjusted monetary base. A complete description of the two measures is provided, including a discussion of the methodology adopted to account for changes in reserve requirement ratios.

The authors wish to thank W. Michael Cox, R. Alton Gilbert, Evan F. Koenig, and Kenneth J. Robinson for helpful comments. Of course, any remaining errors are solely our responsibility.

[1] In addition, Andersen (1975) and Andersen and Karnosky (1977) find evidence that supports the monetary base as the appropriate monetary aggregate to control nominal GNP.

[2] See McCallum for a complete discussion of the merits of the proposed "base" rule.

[3] In Report on the Conduct of Monetary Policy, prepared for the use of the House Committee on Banking, Finance and Urban Affairs, 100th Cong., 2d sess., 1988, Committee Print 100-5, 32.

[4] Actually, there are four base measures. In addition to the source base and adjusted monetary base calculated by the Federal Reserve Bank of St. Louis, two are calculated by the Federal Reserve Board of Governors—a monetary base that is adjusted for reserve requirement ratio changes and one that is not.

The second aim is to examine the question, Which base measure bears the strongest relationship to economic activity? Such a question highlights the role that reserve requirement ratios have played in economic stabilization over the past 30 years. The evidence in this article supports the notion that changes in reserve requirement ratios have been large and important enough that ignoring them gives a distorted impression of monetary policy. Based on the evidence presented here, the adjusted monetary base is judged a better gauge of monetary policy than the source base, which is a simple balance sheet relationship.

Conducting monetary policy: an overview

Chart 1 broadly characterizes the monetary policy process originating at the policymaker's decision stage and leading ultimately to economic activity. The chain of events begins with a decision to alter monetary policy, which is implemented through the three tools of the Federal Reserve—open market operations, the discount rate, and reserve requirement ratios. These tools directly affect the operating targets—the source base, the reserve adjustment magnitude, and the adjusted monetary base—which, in turn, influence

the monetary aggregates and, finally, the ultimate goals of policy.

As Chart 1 shows, the monetary policy decision can be implemented through one or more of three tools; moreover, these tools can be coordinated to achieve a desired policy outcome. From the standpoint of the operating targets, transactions in the open market and changes in the discount rate both lead to changes in the source base. Changes in reserve requirements, on the other hand, do *not* lead to changes in the source base but show up as changes in the reserve adjustment magnitude, referred to as RAM. Because the source base and RAM sum to the adjusted monetary base, changes in any of the three tools will be captured in this broader base measure.

The sequence laid out in Chart 1 indicates some of the problems associated with selecting the appropriate gauge of monetary policy. The source base is considered important by monetary policy experts but omits the effects of changes in reserve requirement ratios. Though generally less well understood, the adjusted monetary base reflects all policy actions undertaken. It is important, therefore, to describe and understand both the source base and the adjusted monetary base. By doing so, analysts will be better able to judge

Chart 1
Monetary Policy Overview

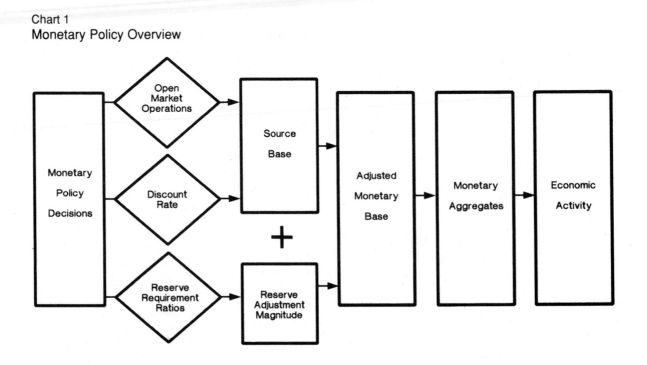

the merits of each as an indicator of monetary policy.

Describing the source base

Calculation of the source base follows directly from the Federal Reserve System's consolidated balance sheet. Assets are identified as "sources" of the base because the Federal Reserve System generally creates base money in acquiring Federal Reserve assets. Liabilities other than Federal Reserve notes outstanding and accounts held at the Federal Reserve by depository institutions are labeled "uses" of the base because these other liabilities absorb base money. The major monetary liabilities of the Federal Reserve System are Federal Reserve notes outstanding and accounts held at the Federal Reserve by depository institutions. In sum, these two liabilities represent the public's claims against the Federal Reserve, otherwise known as Federal Reserve credit, and make up the source base.

Table 1 breaks the Federal Reserve balance sheet into its two components—sources and uses—as of February 1, 1989. Operationally, the sum of Federal Reserve assets less the value of the nonmonetary liabilities of the Federal Reserve System is sources less uses and is equal to the source base. As of February 1, 1989, the source base totaled $272.82 billion.

Implementing monetary policy through the source base

What actions can the Federal Reserve undertake to change the source base? Traditionally, the most important asset alterations have occurred through open market operations—the buying and selling of U.S. government securities. As the Federal Reserve buys, for example, U.S. government securities, it generally pays for these assets by creating liabilities against itself, called financial institution deposits at the Fed. In short, the open market purchase results in an increase in Federal Reserve assets (sources of the base) without an offsetting decrease in other Federal Reserve liabilities (uses of the base). Thus, this action increases the source base. (Of course, selling government securities corresponds to the Federal Reserve buying deposits back from financial institutions. Such

Table 1
Sources and Uses of Source Base, February 1, 1989

(Billions of dollars)

Sources	
Holdings of securities	$240.97
Loans	.96
Float	.33
Gold stock	11.06
Special drawing rights	5.02
Treasury currency outstanding	18.86
Other Federal Reserve assets	19.91
Total sources	$297.11

Uses	
Treasury deposits at Federal Reserve Banks	$ 13.30
Treasury cash holdings	.41
Foreign deposits with Federal Reserve Banks	.22
Other liabilities and capital accounts	7.84
Other Federal Reserve deposits	.51
Service-related balances and adjustments	1.99
Total uses	$ 24.27
Source base = total sources − total uses	$272.82

NOTE: Totals may not add because of rounding.
SOURCE: Federal Reserve Bank of St. Louis.

action results in a contraction of the source base.)

The Federal Reserve maintains a fairly large stock of U.S. government securities (roughly $233 billion as of November 1988), and it is primarily through open market operations that the source base is managed. In addition to open market operations, though, the source base may be altered through raising or lowering the discount rate. A reduction in the discount rate means lower borrowing costs for financial institutions, which, in turn, induce greater borrowings at the discount window. The increase in discount loans ("loans" in Table 1) will result in an increase in depository institutions' account balances at the Federal Reserve. Provided such loans do not directly generate offsetting reductions in other Federal Reserve assets or expansions in nonmonetary liabilities, the increase in loans results in an increase in the source base.

While open market operations and discount rate changes are two of the Federal Reserve's most visible means of altering the source base, in essence, *any* increase in asset holdings of the Federal Reserve (or any reduction in nonmonetary liabilities) matched by a change in Federal Reserve credit will necessarily alter the source base. If, for example, the Federal Reserve were to make a $500 million purchase of new computer equipment, this action alone would have the same effect on the source base as a $500 million purchase of U.S. government securities, provided these assets were purchased with monetary liabilities.

In short, the source base is a summary of all the monetary policy actions that the Federal Reserve may take concerning its own balance sheet.

An important use of the source base, therefore, is to enumerate in one comprehensive measure all policy actions as they pertain to the balance sheet of the Federal Reserve.

Implementing monetary policy through reserve requirements

In addition to having the authority to undertake open market operations and change the discount rate, the Federal Reserve System may also vary, for specified deposit classifications, the proportion of funds that depository institutions must hold as required reserves. These proportions are commonly referred to as reserve requirement ratios. Required reserves must be held either as vault cash or as deposits at a Federal Reserve Bank, and they earn no interest for depository institutions.

Suppose, for example, that the Federal Reserve were to lower reserve requirement ratios for all depository institutions. For a given amount of deposits, lower reserve requirement ratios would call for smaller holdings of reserve balances by depository institutions. Because this action is not itself a Federal Reserve balance sheet transaction, it would not result in a change in the source base.[5] The reduction in reserve requirement ratios, however, would allow depository institutions to increase their deposit liabilities. And the money stock would grow, even though the source base did not change. The increase in the money stock, in turn, would presumably allow an increase in total spending in the economy. This action is not captured by the source base; therefore, the source base is not a perfect indicator of all the methods by which monetary policy may be implemented in order to affect economic activity.

Hence, while the source base reflects two of the Federal Reserve's three monetary policy tools—open market operations and the discount rate—it does not reflect the third policy tool—reserve requirements. There is, thus, one potential shortcoming of the source base as a measure of monetary policy. Namely, the source base does not capture the effects on the money supply and on economic activity that occur when the Federal Reserve changes reserve requirement ratios.

---

[5] Changes in reserve requirements are likely to affect the lending behavior of depository institutions and, therefore, cause further changes in the money supply. Such portfolio actions of depository institutions, however, do not affect the source base (because the Federal Reserve's balance sheet is not affected), but, instead, allow a given level of the source base to support a higher level of the money supply. Source base movements will occur only when coordinated with open market operations, discount rate changes, or some other Federal Reserve portfolio adjustment.

Describing the adjusted monetary base

The potential shortcoming of ignoring reserve requirement ratios in calculating the source base has long been recognized by monetary policy analysts. For many years, both the Federal Reserve Board of Governors ("Board") and the Federal Reserve Bank of St. Louis ("St. Louis") have estimated base measures that correct for this shortcoming. The essence of each correction procedure is to adjust the source base to account for changes in reserve requirement ratios. Both the Board's "monetary base adjusted for changes in reserve requirements" and St. Louis' "adjusted monetary base" are measures that summarize all three tools of monetary policy. The aim of the following discussion is to provide a basic understanding of the adjustment procedure adopted by St. Louis. Readers who want more detail or wish to understand the Board's measure are referred to Gilbert (1983).[6]

Adjusting for changes in reserve requirements

How is the source base adjusted to account for changes in reserve requirement ratios? Formally, the St. Louis adjusted monetary base (AMB) is calculated as

$$(1) \qquad AMB = SB + RAM,$$

where SB is the source base and RAM is the reserve adjustment magnitude. For comparison with the source base calculation presented in Table 1, Table 2 presents the AMB calculation for February 1, 1989. As this table shows, AMB as of that date was roughly $8.5 billion larger than the source base. Two questions must now be answered: How is this $8.5 billion adjustment determined, and what factors affect RAM? In order to answer these questions, it is helpful to understand the reserve adjustment procedure.

Consider a simple example where there is only one deposit classification against which depository institutions must hold reserves.[7] Suppose that the reserve requirement ratio is reduced from some original-period value, r_0, to a new lower level, r_1, so that $r_0 - r_1 > 0$. Given this reduction in the reserve requirement ratio, the St. Louis RAM is

Table 2
Components of Adjusted Monetary Base, February 1, 1989

(Billions of dollars)

Source base	$272.82
Reserve adjustment magnitude (RAM)	8.54
Adjusted monetary base (AMB)	$281.36

SOURCE: Federal Reserve Bank of St. Louis.

defined as

$$(2) \qquad RAM_1 = (r_0 - r_1)\, D_1,$$

where D_1 is the level of reservable deposits in the later period.[8]

Note that with r_1 less than r_0, RAM_1 is positive. The interpretation of this calculation is that a decrease in the reserve requirement ratio "frees" reserves. In other words, the reduction is viewed as having the same effect on the liquidity of depository institutions as would an injection of reserves through open market operations.

---

[6] See Gilbert (1983) and Haslag and Hein (1988) for a comparison of these two measures.

[7] In the discussion in the text, only one reservable deposit classification is considered. In reality, there is more than one reservable classification. The appropriate procedure requires separate adjustment, as in equation 2, for each deposit classification. As a result, RAM will be affected by deposit shifts when these moves are between deposits with different reserve requirement ratios. Thus, RAM can change even though all reserve requirement ratios remain unchanged. In this circumstance, RAM changes reflect the amount of reserves absorbed or freed by such deposit shifts. The RAM still attempts to summarize monetary policy concerns—not spending relationships, as the monetary aggregates attempt to capture.

[8] Gilbert (1980) and Tatom (1980) discuss some of the issues involved in selecting a base period. Specifically, both authors point to problems introduced by the sweeping reforms of the Monetary Control Act of 1980.

As equation 2 indicates, the reduction in the reserve requirement ratio results in an increase in RAM and, hence, an increase in AMB relative to the source base. With an increase in the reserve requirement ratio, however, RAM would decrease, thus indicating an "absorption" of reserves. The decrease in RAM would cause AMB to be less than the source base.

In short, the RAM component of AMB quantifies the amount of reserves that are freed or absorbed when reserve requirement ratios are lowered or raised, respectively. In this sense, RAM "dollarizes" changes in reserve requirement ratios.

One important assumption implicit in the RAM adjustment should also be noted here. As equation 1 indicates, RAM is simply *added* to the source base to obtain AMB. That is, the adjustment treats $1 freed through reductions in reserve requirement ratios as having the same effect on the banking system and economy as a $1 increase in the source base. Constructing AMB in this manner presumes that a single number is sufficient to summarize all monetary policy actions; therefore, separating the effects is not helpful.

Are changes in reserve requirements empirically important?

As the previous section indicates, monetary policy analysts have two summary measures of actions taken by the Federal Reserve—the source base and AMB. The only difference between the two measures is that the source base ignores changes in reserve requirement ratios, while AMB quantifies such changes and adjusts for them through the RAM component. But is this adjustment to the source base really important? Or could analysts get by with looking at the source base only?

---

[9] In calculating this ratio, we use data from February 1, 1989.

[10] The RAM component of AMB is calculated as

$$RAM_t - RAM_{t-1} / [(AMB_t + AMB_{t-1})/2].$$

Thus, it is the year-over-year growth rate of RAM relative to the total AMB that is presented in the bottom panel.

It is noteworthy that, when viewed in terms of levels, RAM is estimated to be only about 3 percent of AMB, so RAM is dwarfed by the source base.[9] One might be led to conclude from this comparison that reserve requirements are relatively unimportant and could be ignored. Whether such a conclusion is, in fact, proper can be seen by examining and comparing the behavior of RAM and AMB both in terms of absolute levels and in terms of growth rates. This additional comparison, based on percentage rates of change, is justified because the Federal Reserve announces its targets for the monetary aggregates (annually) in terms of growth rates.

Chart 2 sheds some light on the differences between comparing the *levels* and the *growth rates* of RAM. The upper portion of the chart portrays the level of the RAM over the period 1960:Q1–1988:Q2. Two points can be made from this chart. First, the level of RAM has generally been comparatively small. Second, however, the level of RAM is far from constant. Indeed, RAM is highly variable, indicating that despite its relatively small absolute magnitude, RAM may play a potentially critical role in gauging the true posture of monetary policy.

The bottom portion of Chart 2 details the quarterly weighted-average growth rate of the RAM component.[10] The quarterly growth rates are highly variable, ranging from a low of –2 percent to a high of +5 percent. Thus, while the absolute level of RAM is generally small relative to that of the total adjusted monetary base, there have been substantial changes in the RAM variable over time.

A sizable portion of AMB growth, therefore, has historically come about through the RAM component, so it is far from obvious that RAM can be neglected. Judging the importance of reserve requirement ratios on the basis of the level of RAM relative to AMB is not sound.

What if reserve requirement changes are ignored?

Reserve requirements have obviously changed substantially through time, but whether the implied changes in RAM have been empirically important in judging monetary policy is yet to be determined. One way of examining this issue is to investigate the relationship between

Chart 2
Level and Growth Rate of Reserve Adjustment Magnitude

Billions of dollars

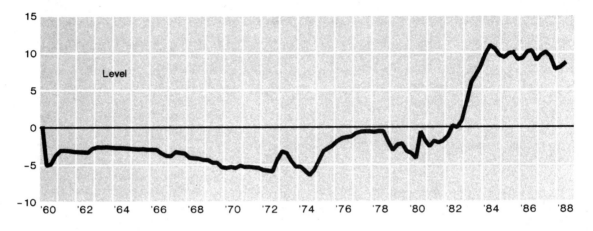

Percent

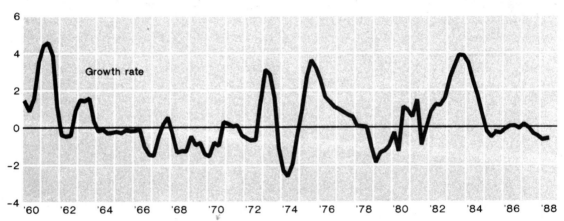

monetary policy and nominal GNP, using only the source base as the gauge. Interestingly enough, analysts who totally ignored RAM over the period 1960–88 would have concluded that monetary policy actions have *no* systematic relationship to nominal GNP. Statistical tests show, for example, that there is no correlation between nominal GNP growth and source base growth over this 29-year period.[11] Therefore, analysts using the source base to gauge the thrust of monetary policy would conclude that policy is powerless to affect nominal GNP.

Why is the source base a poor policy indicator?

To see why source base growth may bear no statistical relationship to nominal GNP growth, consider three separate scenarios. First, consider a simple case in which the Federal Reserve has determined that the economy is growing too rapidly and decides to use open market operations to restrict the growth rate of nominal GNP. Policymakers reduce the rate of purchases of government securities, decreasing the growth rate of the source base. Presumably, this decrease in base growth is associated with a slower rate of growth of the monetary aggregates and, subsequently, a slower rate of growth of nominal GNP.

In Chart 3, Scenario 1 illustrates this chain of events, which follows closely the linkage laid out in Chart 1. Note that the reduction in source base growth is associated with a reduction in nominal GNP growth. That is, this scenario involves a positive association between source base growth and growth of nominal GNP. Monetary policy has been successful in slowing the pace of economic activity.

Consider next a second scenario, in which the Federal Reserve believes that the economy is growing too slowly and determines that the needed pickup in economic activity could be set in place by reducing reserve requirements. Although reserve requirements could, in theory, be lowered by an amount that would exactly achieve the desired goals for GNP growth, (for reasons that will be discussed later) the Federal Reserve reduces reserve requirements by an amount that would overstimulate economic activity.[12] Thus, the Federal Reserve decides to offset partially the reduction in required reserves by slowing the rate of growth of the source base. What is the observed association between source base growth and nominal GNP growth in Scenario 2? As the second panel of Chart 3 indicates, the association is now negative. Slower source base growth is accompanied by faster nominal GNP growth.

Consider finally a scenario in which the Federal Reserve believes that the present rate of economic growth is acceptable and that no change in monetary policy is called for. By other criteria, however, the Federal Reserve judges reserve requirements to be "too high."[13] A decrease in reserve requirements alone would be associated with higher growth rates of the monetary aggregates and, ultimately, faster nominal GNP growth. Consequently, the Federal Reserve must offset the expansionary effects of the reduction in reserve requirements. This offset can be accomplished by simultaneously decreasing the rate of growth of the source base. By design, the net effect of both actions is no change in the growth rate of the adjusted monetary base and no change in the growth rate of nominal GNP.

Note that, in this case, there is an apparent absence of association between the rate of growth

---

[11] *The estimated regression for the source base was*

$$Y_t = .011 + .849\, Y_{t-1} + .025\, SB_{t-1},$$
$$(.004)\quad (.055)\qquad (.055)$$

Durbin's h = 2.93.

where Y is the rate of growth of nominal GNP. (Figures in parentheses are standard errors.) The results indicate that the coefficient on source base growth is not significantly different from zero. In another test, the hypothesis that the long-run effect is equal to zero was not rejected. Thus, the results suggest that there is no statistical association between changes in source base growth and nominal GNP growth.

[12] *Mishkin (1986) points out that extremely small reserve requirement ratio changes are costly to administer. He proceeds to point out that "using reserve requirements to engineer 'fine-tuning' adjustments to the money supply is like trying to use a jackhammer to cut a diamond" (p. 371).*

[13] *For example, the Federal Reserve observes banks taking more of their operations overseas, where reserve requirement ratios are nonexistent. To offset this outflow of banking activity, the Federal Reserve lowers reserve requirement ratios, at the same time not wanting to affect economic activity directly.*

Chart 3
Three Scenarious Relating the Growth Rate of the
Source Base to the Growth Rate of Nominal GNP

Scenario 1: Open Market Sale, No Change in Reserve Requirements, Net Contractionary Effect

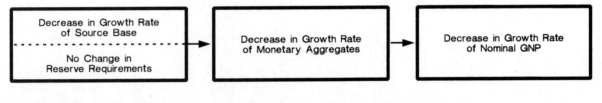

Scenario 2: Open Market Sale, Lower Reserve Requirements, Net Expansionary Effect

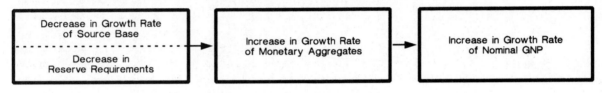

Scenario 3: Open Market Sale, Lower Reserve Requirements, No Net Effect

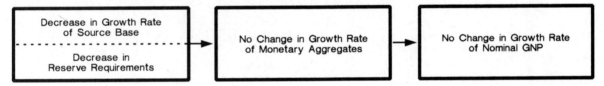

Chart 4
Contributions of Growth of the Source Base and the Reserve
Adjustment Magnitude to Growth of the Adjusted Monetary Base

Percent

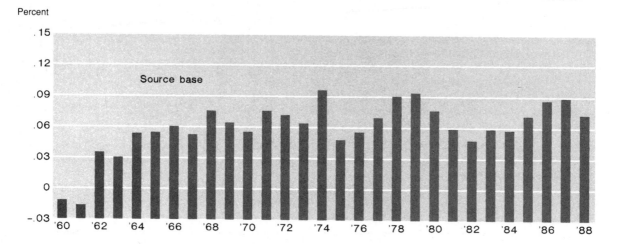

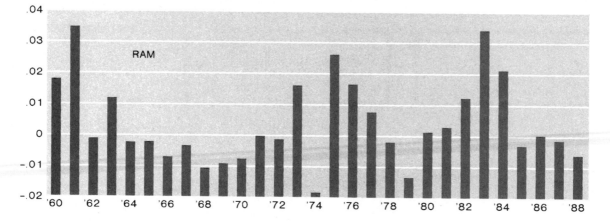

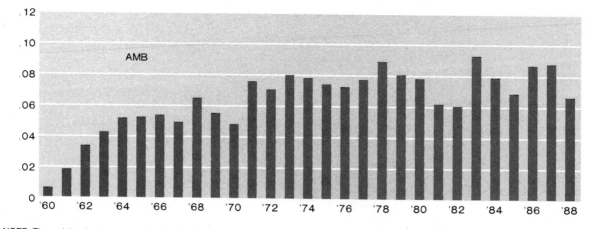

NOTE: The weighted-average growth rates for the source base and for RAM are calculated as described in footnote 14.

of the source base and that of nominal GNP. In short, as shown by Chart 3, the source base and nominal GNP appear independent.

What primary inference can be drawn from reviewing these three scenarios? In each case, the rate of growth of the source base has declined. Yet in each case, the final implication for nominal GNP growth is quite different. For this reason, the source base is potentially a poor indicator of monetary policy.

Are monetary policy tools coordinated?

Has the source base historically been used to offset changes in reserve requirement ratios? To answer this question, Chart 4 presents information on the annual growth rates of the source base, RAM, and AMB over the 1960–88 period. Consider first the top and middle portions of Chart 4, which plot the weighted-average growth rate of the source base and that of RAM.[14] In general, the higher the RAM contribution to AMB growth, the lower is the source base contribution to AMB growth. This tendency suggests that movements in source base growth *are* coordinated with reserve requirement changes.

The bottom portion of Chart 4 presents the annual average growth rate of the adjusted monetary base. As such, it reveals the bottom-line movement in AMB growth as a composite of growth of the source base and that of RAM. Growth of the adjusted monetary base shows far less volatility than growth of either component (source base or RAM) individually. Thus, this chart further suggests a coordination of the tools of monetary policy and underscores the potential fallacy in using the source base alone as a gauge of monetary policy.

The coordination of source base and RAM is further indicated by simple correlation of the growth rates of the two AMB components.[15] Over the 1960–88 period, the estimated correlation coefficient for the growth rate of the source base component and that of the RAM component is −0.61 and is statistically significant.[16] This is strong evidence of a negative association between the growth rates of the source base and RAM. The implication is that when the Federal Reserve lowers reserve requirement ratios, a simultaneous contraction in the growth rate of the source base is typically undertaken.

Why is the source base used to offset changes in reserve requirements?

As discussed previously, the Federal Reserve has historically used the source base to offset movements in reserve requirements. At first, this practice may seem counterproductive, but there are basically two reasons why policymakers might choose to pursue this strategy.

The first reason concerns the costs to depository institutions of changes in reserve requirements. Reserve requirement ratios play a direct and important role in portfolio management by depository institutions. Even when small in magnitude, increases in reserve requirement ratios oblige depository institutions to liquidate a portion of their interest-bearing assets, alter the maturity structure of existing loans, and pursue other investment strategies. Decreases in reserve requirements similarly involve "fixed" loan-production and other costs that depository institutions must bear. The portfolio management problem historically has been further complicated by variation in the structure of deposit classifications against which reserve requirements apply. As Table 3 shows, a variety of reserve requirement structures and deposit categories have been administered over the past 10 years.

Given these considerations, periodic and repeated changes in reserve requirements unduly complicate the task of portfolio management.

---

[14] The source base and RAM components are defined as

$$SB_t - SB_{t-1} / [(AMB_t + AMB_{t-1})/2]$$

and

$$RAM_t - RAM_{t-1} / [(AMB_t + AMB_{t-1})/2],$$

respectively. Thus, the growth rates of both components are measured relative to the total adjusted monetary base.

[15] This coefficient ranges in value from −1.0 to +1.0. A negative coefficient indicates that the two variables move in opposite directions, and a positive coefficient indicates that the two variables move in the same direction.

[16] The correlation between growth rates of the source base and RAM components over the 1960:Q1–1979:Q4 subperiod is estimated to be −0.71. This correlation is also significantly different from zero at the 5-percent level.

Consequently, the Federal Reserve has altered reserve requirements sparingly. And when changes in reserve requirements have been administered, the Federal Reserve has often done so without regard to the objective of fine-tuning the economy.

The second reason why the Federal Reserve has historically used the source base to offset movements in reserve requirements pertains, broadly speaking, to the "other" factors behind reserve requirement decisions. An example of these considerations is pointed out by McNeill (1980). Referring to the intentions of the Monetary Control Act of 1980, McNeill stated, "the Board has emphasized the need for universal reserve requirements in order to meet the problem of attrition in membership and weakening of the Board's monetary reserve base" (p. 444).[17] This argument reflects a concern during the late 1970s that the exodus of banks from membership in the Federal Reserve System (and to the jurisdiction of state banking authorities) due to lower reserve requirements elsewhere might continue.[18] The Federal Reserve reacted by altering reserve requirement ratios to retain deposits and to bring the depository institutions back to the System. Thus, for reasons other than ultimately affecting economic activity, the Federal Reserve may choose to raise or lower reserve requirements.

Are economic activity and the adjusted monetary base empirically related?

In a previous section, it was established that nominal GNP bears no significant relationship to the source base. Having uncovered the negative correlation between the source base and the reserve adjustment magnitude, the evidence suggests that this lack of significance is due chiefly to the coordination of monetary policy tools. This

---

Table 3

Reserve Requirements of Depository Institutions as of Selected Dates

(Dollar amounts in millions)

January 31, 1989
All Depository Institutions

Type of deposit, deposit interval	Percent of deposits[1]
Net transaction accounts	
$0–$41.5	3
More than $41.5	12
Nonpersonal time deposits	
By original maturity	
Less than 1 1/2 years	3
1 1/2 years or more	0
Eurocurrency liabilities	
All types	3

January 31, 1979
All Member Banks

Type of deposit, deposit interval	Percent of deposits
Net demand deposits	
$0–$2	7
$2–$10	9 1/2
$10–$100	11 3/4
$100–$400	12 3/4
Over $400	16 1/4
Time deposits	
Savings deposits	3
Other time deposits	
$0–$5, maturing in—	
30 to 179 days	3
180 days to 4 years	2 1/2
4 years or more	1
Over $5, maturing in—	
30 to 179 days	6
180 days to 4 years	2 1/2
4 years or more	1

[1] A zero-percent reserve requirement applies to total reservable liabilities not in excess of $3.4 million.
SOURCE: Board of Governors, Federal Reserve System.

---

[17] See McNeill (1980) for a complete description of the principal elements of the Monetary Control Act.

[18] The reserve requirement ratio is also considered a "tax" on depository institutions. Because reserves are non-interest-bearing, reserve requirements impose a portfolio restriction. See Santoni (1985) for a complete discussion of how reserve requirements act as a tax on depository institutions.

Chart 5
Estimated Initial and Cumulative
Effects on Nominal GNP Growth
of a 1-Percentage-Point Change in
Source Base and Adjusted Monetary Base

Percent

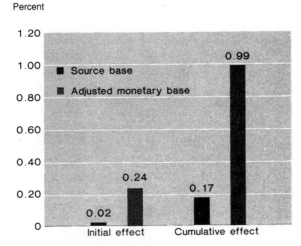

lyst using the adjusted monetary base, instead of the source base, to gauge monetary policy intent would conclude that monetary policy does affect economic activity.

Summary

This article outlines the distinction between two measures of the monetary base—the source base and the adjusted monetary base—and focuses on which is more helpful in explaining movements in aggregate economic activity. As shown, the adjusted monetary base is essentially the source base plus a second component—the reserve adjustment magnitude. That magnitude (RAM) is designed to account for changes in reserve requirement ratios.

Evidence is provided that over the past 30 years, changes in reserve requirements have been large and important enough to have significant effects on economic activity. By ignoring the role of reserve requirements, then, the source base ap-

section focuses on the question, Is the *adjusted* monetary base helpful in explaining movements in nominal GNP?

Chart 5 illustrates the initial (one-quarter-ahead) expansion in nominal GNP growth estimated from a 1-percentage-point increase in the source base and, separately, from a 1-percentage-point increase in the adjusted monetary base.[19] With a 1-percentage-point increase in the source base, nominal GNP growth is estimated to remain essentially unchanged. With a 1-percentage-point increase in the adjusted monetary base, however, GNP growth is higher.

Chart 5 also illustrates the cumulative, or long-run, effect on nominal GNP growth of a 1-percentage-point increase in both the source base and AMB.[20] Again, the long-run effect of a 1-percentage-point increase in the source base is not statistically different from zero. On the other hand, a 1-percentage-point increase in AMB growth yields a significantly positive increase in nominal GNP growth. In fact, the estimated cumulative effect is not different from unity; a permanent 1-percentage-point increase in the growth rate of the adjusted monetary base generally results in a permanent 1-percentage-point increase in the nominal GNP growth rate.[21] Thus, an ana-

[19] The estimated regression for the adjusted monetary base was

$$Y_t = .004 + .759\ Y_{t-1} + .238\ AMB_{t-1} .$$
$$(.004)\ (.054)\ \phantom{Y_{t-1} + }(.067)$$

Durbin's $h = 3.35$.

(Figures in parentheses are standard errors.) The results suggest that changes in the growth rate of the adjusted monetary base are related to changes in nominal GNP growth. The coefficient on the adjusted monetary base variable is statistically significant. Moreover, the hypothesis that the long-run multiplier is equal to 1 is not rejected. (See the Appendix for a detailed discussion of the GNP specifications.)

[20] The estimated long-run elasticity of a 1-percentage-point increase in the source base is calculated as 0.025/(1−0.849), which equals 0.166. For AMB, the estimated cumulative effect is calculated as 0.238/(1−0.759), which equals 0.988.

[21] The result that the long-run multiplier for the adjusted monetary base is equal to unity is essentially the notion conveyed by Dwyer and Hafer (1988) in their Proposition Ia. These results are also in line with our findings reported in Haslag and Hein (1988), where a more general model was used in the investigation.

pears to give a distorted picture of monetary policy over this period. The primary reason is that Federal Reserve changes in the reserve requirement ratio over the past 30 years have typically been coordinated with offsetting balance sheet operations affecting the source base. Looking at source base alone, therefore, is misleading because the source base does not capture the full intent of monetary policy. By combining both the source base and RAM, on the other hand, the adjusted monetary base *does* appear quite adequate in gauging the full thrust of monetary policy. Our conclusion is supported by a variety of tests showing essentially no relationship between the source base and nominal GNP but a strong positive relationship—indeed, a proportionate one—between the adjusted monetary base and aggregate nominal GNP.

Appendix

Alternative Nominal GNP Specifications

The time paths of the effects of source base growth and adjusted monetary base growth on nominal GNP growth are derived from the results reported in footnotes 11 and 19, respectively. The sample period was 1960:Q1–1988:Q2. Furthermore, to allow for seasonal variation in all the variables, we calculated year-over-year changes using quarterly observations, as follows:

$$\dot{x}_t = \frac{x_t - x_{t-4}}{(x_t + x_{t-4})/2}.$$

Taking four-quarter differences with quarterly observations appears to allow for much of the common quarterly seasonal pattern, as indicated by the sample autocorrelation functions provided in Haslag and Hein (1988).

Presenting the results from only one specification (correctly) piques a researcher's interest. How robust are these findings to alternative model specifications? The primary justification for adopting this regression form is the simple dynamic structure. McCallum (1988) also used a model with only one lag of monetary base growth to explain nominal GNP behavior.

Two criticisms of the simple model were considered and addressed. First, the Durbin's *h* statistics reported for both regressions suggest that the residuals are autocorrelated. This evidence, of course, violates the classical regression assumption that errors are independent. Using ordinary least squares to estimate a regression when the residuals are not white noise renders the statistical inferences questionable.

Second, the lag structure warrants further consideration. For example, do the results change if additional lags, or perhaps even contemporaneous values, are included in the regression? Misspecification bias may also stem from having too few lags. The final prediction error is used to determine the "optimal" lag length. Similarly, omitting a fiscal policy measure may also affect the outcomes of the regression analysis.

To address both issues—autocorrelated errors and potential misspecification bias—simultaneously, a more general model was estimated. Testing the hypothesis that the long-run effect of a change in adjusted monetary base growth on nominal GNP growth equals unity fails to be rejected using the results from the general model. But the hypothesis that the total multiplier for the effect of a change in source base growth on nominal GNP growth is unity is rejected. Thus, the evidence suggesting that reserve requirement ratio changes affect nominal GNP behavior is left intact when a more general model specification is considered.

References

Andersen, Leonall C. (1975), "Selection of a Monetary Aggregate for Economic Stabilization," Federal Reserve Bank of St. Louis *Review*, October, 9–15.

Andersen, Leonall C., and Denis S. Karnosky (1977), "Some Considerations in the Use of Monetary Aggregates for the Implementation of Monetary Policy," Federal Reserve Bank of St. Louis *Review*, September, 2–7.

Dwyer, Gerald P., Jr., and R. W. Hafer (1988), "Is Money Irrelevant?" Federal Reserve Bank of St. Louis *Review*, May/June, 3–17.

Gilbert, R. Alton (1980), "Revision of the St. Louis Federal Reserve's Adjusted Monetary Base," Federal Reserve Bank of St. Louis *Review*, December, 3–10.

————— (1983), "Two Measures of Reserves: Why Are They Different?" Federal Reserve Bank of St. Louis *Review*, June/July, 16–25.

Haslag, Joseph H., and Scott E. Hein (1988), "Evidence on the Two Monetary Base Measures and Economic Activity," Federal Reserve Bank of Dallas Research Paper no. 8810 (Dallas, December).

McCallum, Bennett T. (1988), "Robustness Properties of a Rule for Monetary Policy," *Carnegie-Rochester Conference Series on Public Policy* 29:173–203.

McNeill, Charles R., with Denise M. Rechter (1980), "The Depository Institutions Deregulation and Monetary Control Act of 1980," *Federal Reserve Bulletin* 66 (June): 444–53.

Mishkin, Frederic S. (1986), *The Economics of Money, Banking, and Financial Markets* (Boston: Little, Brown).

Santoni, G. J. (1985), "The Monetary Control Act, Reserve Taxes and the Stock Prices of Commercial Banks," Federal Reserve Bank of St. Louis *Review*, June/July, 12–20.

Tatom, John A. (1980), "Issues in Measuring an Adjusted Monetary Base," Federal Reserve Bank of St. Louis *Review*, December, 11–29.

K. Alec Chrystal and Daniel L. Thornton

K. Alec Chrystal is the National Westminster Bank Professor of Personal Finance at City University, London, and Daniel L. Thornton is a research officer at the Federal Reserve Bank of St. Louis. Dawn M. Peterson provided research assistance.

The Macroeconomic Effects of Deficit Spending: A Review

FOLLOWING the Keynesian Revolution in macroeconomics, a large number of economists argued that deficit spending was required to achieve two of the stated national economic objectives: full employment and a high rate of economic growth.[1] Society was thought to benefit from deficit spending because of the reduction in lost output and because the economy would achieve a higher rate of growth.

This view of deficit spending has been challenged increasingly over the years. A sizable number of economists now believe that deficit spending has little effect on employment and output, especially in the long run, and that it primarily results in a redistribution of output, either within the private sector or as a transfer of resources from the private to the public sector.[2] Support for this viewpoint has produced a growing concern about the potentially harmful effects of deficit spending and the size of the public debt.[3]

The existence and magnitude of the benefits from deficit spending have important implications for the public policy debate. Presumably, the decision to incur deficits is affected by the public's belief about whether deficits provide benefits to some individuals at little or no cost to others, or whether they merely redistribute income. Hence, a central issue in the debate over deficit spending is whether, and to what degree, it can be used to produce net benefits for society as a whole. The purpose of this paper is to examine some of the arguments and evidence on whether deficit spending yields net benefits to society.

DEFICIT SPENDING: SOME KEY TERMS

The phrases "deficit spending" and "fiscal policy" are not necessarily synonymous. While deficit spending is a particular fiscal policy action, not all

---

[1] One of Keynes' initial arguments was that saving would exceed investment at a level of output consistent with the full employment of labor. That is, the U.S. savings rate was too high. The view that the budget should be in persistent deficit was termed the "new fiscal policy." To see how opinions about deficit spending have changed in two decades, compare the deficit discussions in Levy (1963) with those in Levy, et. al. (1984).

[2] The once-common view that the market economy cannot sustain full-employment equilibrium has given way to the concept of the natural rate of unemployment. For a discussion of these issues, see Modigliani (1986b), Blinder (1986) and Laidler (1988).

[3] For a discussion of the potential harmful effects of the public debt, see Bruce and Purvis (1986), Barro (1987) and Levy, et. al. (1984).

fiscal policy actions produce or involve deficits.[4] For example, the government could devise a policy whereby expenditures and taxes are changed by the same amount. This well-known "balanced budget" operation affects aggregate demand, because the change in government expenditures affects aggregate demand more than the change in taxes, but does not affect the deficit.[5]

Despite the balanced-budget multiplier, the stance of fiscal policy today is often associated with, and frequently measured by, the size of the federal budget deficit.[6] Thus, in this article, deficit spending and the stance of fiscal policy will be treated as synonymous. Furthermore, since they both produce the same qualitative shift in aggregate demand, no distinction will be made between deficits that arise from increases in government spending and those that result from tax reductions.

Cyclical and Structural Deficits and Discretionary Fiscal Policy

It is important to differentiate between "cyclical" and "structural" deficits when examining the effects of policy changes on the economy. Tax revenues rise during the expansion phase of the business cycle and fall during the contraction phase; in contrast, certain government expenditures (e.g., unemployment compensation) fall during expansions and rise during contractions. These counter-cyclical components of the

deficit—the so-called automatic stabilizers—are intended to smooth cyclical swings in income.

The structural deficit, on the other hand, reflects discretionary fiscal policy actions.[7] It is the part of the deficit that is invariant to the phase of the business cycle. Chart 1 presents measures of the actual and cyclically adjusted budget deficit. Although these measures depart substantially at times, generally they move together. While the analysis in this paper applies equally well to cyclical and structural deficits, from now on the discussion will focus solely on structural deficits.

THE NET BENEFITS FROM DEFICIT SPENDING

The effectiveness of deficit spending depends on two factors: the slope of the aggregate supply curve and the extent to which deficit spending shifts the aggregate demand curve. These factors are discussed in detail in latter sections of the paper. In this section, we present some general notions underlying the view that society can be a net beneficiary from deficit spending.

The initial popularity of using deficit spending to increase output was based on the belief that the market economy is unable to sustain aggregate demand at a level consistent with full-employment output. This idea of persistent unemployment is illustrated in chart 2 which shows a gap between actual and "potential" real output.[8] The

---

[4]There is a well-known caveat to this statement. Government tax rate changes are not neutral. The government may change certain marginal tax rates and simultaneously alter government expenditures to produce no net effect on aggregate demand, all other things constant. The ultimate effect on aggregate output, however, need not be neutral; the non-neutrality of the tax rate change could produce changes in aggregate supply.

Such analysis underlies much of the recent work by Auerbach and Kotlikoff (1987) and Kotlikoff (1988). Consequently, they have challenged the usual convention of associating deficit spending with fiscal policy. For example, Kotlikoff (1988), pp. 489–90, states that ". . . fiscal policies can matter a lot, but deficits may nonetheless tell us nothing useful about the true stance of fiscal policy." They argue that, within their life-cycle model, the labels "taxes" and "spending" are arbitrary. For them, a tight fiscal policy occurs when a larger burden of "government consumption" is borne by current rather than future generations.

[5]Aggregate demand increases because the marginal propensity to spend of the public sector (1) is greater than the marginal propensity to spend of the private sector (<1). If the private sector's marginal propensity to spend is large, the difference between the marginal propensities will be small and so, too, will be the effect of tax-financed expenditures on aggregate demand.

[6]It is common to measure fiscal action by the full-employment budget surplus or deficit. For a discussion of this, see Carlson (1987) and Seater (1985).

[7]See de Leeuw and Holloway (1983) for a detailed discussion of these concepts and Fellner (1982) for a critique of these measures. For a discussion of these concepts and a breakdown of the deficit, see Erceg and Bernard (1988).

[8]There is an issue, not taken up here, about the extent to which such unemployment is "involuntary." According to the usual textbook definition, involuntary unemployment occurs when individuals are willing to work at the market wage but are unable to find employment; that is, when there is an excess supply of labor at the market wage rate. If the market is competitive, the wage rate should fall to eliminate the involuntary unemployment. Hence, nearly all theories of involuntary unemployment require some form of nominal or real wage rigidity.

In early Keynesian models, involuntary unemployment was due to nominal rigidities in wages. This explanation requires real wages to fall when output rises. Empirical evidence, however, suggests that real wages are pro-cyclical. Recently, research by "New Keynesian Economists" suggests that persistent under-employment equilibria and involuntary unemployment can result from nominal price rigidities in the output market because of monopolistically competitive firms, and because of rigidities in real wages due to "efficiency wages." See Blinder (1988), Mankiw (1988), Rotemburg (1987), Prescott (1987), The New Keynesian Microfoundations (1987) and the cited references.

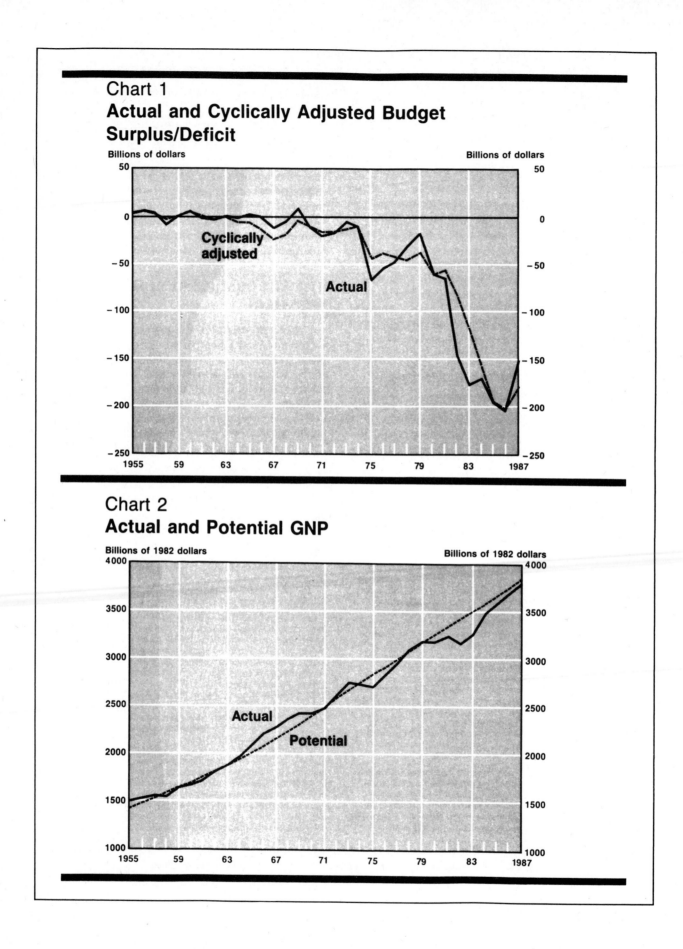

Chart 1
Actual and Cyclically Adjusted Budget Surplus/Deficit

Billions of dollars

Billions of dollars

Cyclically adjusted

Actual

Chart 2
Actual and Potential GNP

Billions of 1982 dollars

Billions of 1982 dollars

Actual

Potential

potential path of real output usually is associated with some full-employment rate of unemployment. Periods in which real output falls below its potential represent episodes of persistent excessive unemployment. If the economy is prone to periods of prolonged unemployment due to deficient aggregate demand for goods and services, the government could run a sustained deficit to make up for the deficiency. If successful, this deficit would keep output closer to its full-employment potential. Moreover, on average, real output growth would exceed the rate that would otherwise occur.

Deficit Spending and Capital Accumulation

Deficit spending could have a secondary effect on the rate of economic growth. Production of real output (y) is related to factor inputs, labor (N) and capital (K), via a production function, that is, $y = f(N,K)$. The marginal products of both labor and capital are positive: for any quantity of capital (labor), output increases as more labor (capital) is used. The growth of the labor force is often considered synonymous with population growth, which is determined in part by factors that are independent of economic considerations. The size of the capital stock, on the other hand, is usually assumed to be related to economic factors. The higher the rate of capital formation (investment), the higher the rate of economic growth.

Firms determine the most profitable level of output and, simultaneously, the optimal capital/labor ratio. Because of the nature of capital goods, the decision to acquire capital is based (among other things) on expectations of output growth. If the market economy is subject to prolonged periods of unemployment and slow growth because of insufficient demand, expectations for output growth and investment will be lower than if these periods did not occur. If deficit spending raises the path of real output over what it would achieve otherwise, investment and, thereby, potential real output growth should rise even higher. Thus, deficit spending could produce a higher rate of actual and potential growth because of increased capital formation.[9]

Deficits and Symmetric Business Cycles

The gains in output discussed so far are predicated on the assumption that cyclical swings in output around its potential path are asymmetric: cyclical downturns are longer and more pronounced than cyclical upturns. Since we are assuming that cyclical swings are due to variation in the demand for goods and services, this means that increases in the demand for goods and services are less frequent and smaller than decreases. If, on the other hand, fluctuations in aggregate demand around potential output are symmetric, periods during which output is above or below the potential path also will be symmetric.[10] This is illustrated by path 1 in figure 1 and by the aggregate demand and supply curves in figure 2. Given the slope of the aggregate supply curve, symmetric variation in aggregate demand produces symmetric movements in output about the potential level, y^*. On average, there are no "net output" gains to be achieved from deficit spending over the cycle. Periods of deficit spending when the economy is below the full-employment path would be matched by periods of budget surplus when output is above the path, so the budget would be balanced over the cycle and the average output level would be the same as with no fiscal action.

Society still may benefit, however, if the government runs deficits during the contraction phase of the cycle and surpluses during expansions. A cyclically balanced budget could stabilize aggregate demand and reduce the variability in output; this is illustrated by path 2 in figure 1.[11]

The Benefits From Stable Output

More stable output could reduce the risk associated with capital investment and, as a result, increase investment.[12] Consequently, the capital

---

[9]Achieving a higher rate of economic growth was part of the fiscal policy agenda during the 1960s. See Levy (1963).

[10]Recently, Sickel (1988) has investigated the asymmetry of the business cycles. He tests for both the "steepness" and "deepness" of post-World War II cycles and finds evidence that cyclical troughs are deeper than cyclical peaks.

[11]This discussion implicity assumes that deficit spending does not alter the path of y^*, i.e., that deficit spending merely dampens the cycle.

[12]Many authors merely assert that there are benefits from more stable output growth without identifying these gains, e.g.,

Modigliani (1986a), (1986b) and Bossons (1986). At other times explanations of these gains sound hollow. For example, Bruce and Purvis (1986), pp. 60–61, argue for the benefits of avoiding a cyclical downturn by stating that "a government deficit will provide some stimulus to the economy and hence help reduce *the dead-weight costs of unemployment that would have occurred in the absence of the deficit.*" In the case where the government runs a surplus in order to prevent an economic boom, they argue that the surplus helps "avoid the *dead-weight costs that again arise because the economy is away from its long-run equilibrium.*" (Italics added.)

Figure 1
Symmetric Swings in Output

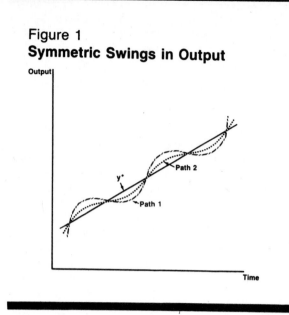

Figure 2
Symmetric Swings in Output and Aggregate Demand and Supply

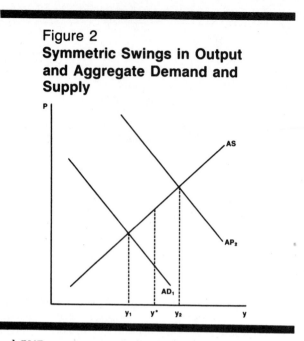

stock would increase, as would the level of potential output.[13] The economy would then achieve a higher rate of growth than otherwise.

Additional benefits could arise if more stable output growth results in more stable consumption. Economists usually argue that people maximize the utility of their consumption over some planning horizon and that the utility gains from increased consumption are smaller than the losses from equally probable decreases in consumption.[14] Even if the distribution of shocks to income and, therefore, consumption are symmetric, the distribution of utility gains and losses will be asymmetric. Consequently, the expected utility of consumption rises as income is stabilized.

The Benefits from Stabilizing Nominal GNP

There are additional benefits from stabilizing aggregate demand if cyclical movements in nominal GNP are symmetric, but cyclical movements in real output are asymmetric. That is, the aggregate supply curve is more steeply sloped above potential output as in figure 3. In this case, random variation in aggregate demand would produce larger changes in real output below the potential output level than above it. Of course, the change in nominal spending above and below potential output must be the same if variations in aggregate demand are symmetric about the natural rate. Stabilizing discretionary fiscal policy reduces both inflation and unemployment over the cycle and, thus, the cost of lost output associated with unemployment *and* the cost of inflation.[15]

Finally, deficit spending could yield net benefits if it merely offsets downward shifts in aggregate demand. For example, assume that cyclical swings in real output are symmetric so that there are no output gains on average over the cycle from stabilizing aggregate demand. Deficit spending still could result in net output gains for society, if de-

---

[13]The issue is whether the growth rate of real output is made *permanently* higher. Certainly, if economic stabilization policy merely causes the level of real output to be higher but does not affect the rate of real output growth permanently, there would still be a period immediately following the enactment of stabilization policy in which the observed rate of real output growth would exceed the full-employment growth rate.

[14]That is, the utility function is concave. Such gains from economic stabilization have been suggested by New Keynesian economics. See Rotemburg (1987), p. 83. To illustrate this point, assume that consumption is a random variable that is uniformly distributed on the closed interval 1 to 2, and let the utility of consumption be the simple concaved function, $u = C^{.5}$. In this case, the expected value of utility is 1.22. Now assume that income and, hence, consumption are more variable, but

with the same expected value. Specifically, assume that consumption is now uniformly distributed on the closed interval 0 to 3. In this case, the expected value of utility of consumption is reduced to 1.15. Hence, reducing the variability of consumption increases the expected (average) utility of consumption. Of course, consumption may fluctuate much less than output over the business cycle if the life-cycle or permanent income theories of consumption are correct.

[15]The costs of expected inflation are in terms of its effects on long-term bond markets, the misallocation of productive resources and its effects on regulations. The casts of unexpected inflation are primarily in terms of its redistribution of wealth. For a discussion of these costs, see Leijonhufvud (1987) and the references cited there.

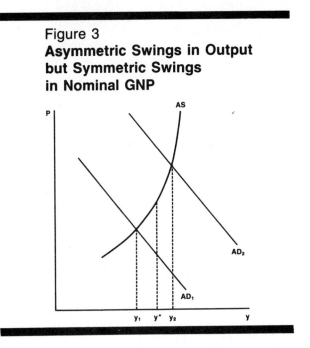

Figure 3
Asymmetric Swings in Output but Symmetric Swings in Nominal GNP

ficits were incurred when aggregate demand was weak, but surpluses were not incurred when aggregate demand was strong. Of course, in this case, the level of government debt would rise, both over the cycle and over time.

CRITICISMS OF THE ALLEGED BENEFITS OF DEFICIT SPENDING

As we have seen, the gains from deficit spending consist of reducing "lost" output due to reduced employment, increasing the growth rate of real output or stabilizing output and consumption. To achieve these gains, deficit spending must shift the aggregate demand schedule and the aggregate supply curve must be upward-sloping, at least in the short run. If the aggregate supply curve were vertical, shifts in the aggregate demand schedule would not affect output. Consequently, there could be no output gains from offsetting shifts in aggregate demand. Of course, if the aggregate supply curve were positively sloped, deficit spending would be effective only if it succeeds in shifting the aggregate demand curve. Attacks on the efficacy of fiscal policy have focused, therefore, on

the slope of the aggregate supply curve and the ability of deficit spending to shift aggregate demand.[16]

Asymmetric Cyclical Variation in Output

Both the Great Depression of the 1930s and the rise of Keynesian economics, with its emphasis on underemployment equilibrium, led to the acceptance of the notion that the market economy is neither able to sustain a full-employment level of output nor able to move back to it quickly when aggregate demand failures occur.[17] Prior to Keynes, it was commonly believed that output would naturally move to the level consistent with no involuntary unemployment. While shocks to either aggregate demand or supply might cause temporary periods of unemployment, resources were thought to be sufficiently mobile and wages and prices sufficiently flexible that the economy would return to its full-employment equilibrium fairly quickly.

Keynes argued that the economy might remain permanently below its full-employment level because of insufficient aggregate demand and market imperfections.[18] This below-full-employment equilibrium requires an upward-sloping aggregate supply curve. Typically, it was also argued that the aggregate supply curve would become steeper around the full-employment level of output, like the aggregate supply curve in figure 3.

The Phillips Curve

The Keynesian view was strengthened by the discovery of what appeared to be a stable long-run empirical relationship between the rate of inflation and the unemployment rate; this relationship was called the Phillips Curve.[19] If unemployment was too high (relative to the full-employment rate), policymakers could achieve a permanent increase in output by increasing aggregate demand through deficit spending. The cost would be a permanent increase in inflation. The extent of the cost is determined by the slope of the Phillips Curve. The closer income was to its full-

[16]This applies to monetary policy as well.

[17]For an interesting discussion of Keynesian and classical economics, see Blinder (1986), Laidler (1988), Eisner (1986) and Niehans (1987).

[18]There is a problem in defining "persistent" unemployment and establishing if and when it differs from cyclical unemployment. Many economists argue that there is no such thing as persistent unemployment because the market economy eventually

will adjust to the point at which the labor market clears. Keynes himself almost certainly believed this to be true in the long run; however, he regarded the long run to be too long for the adjustment to be left to market forces alone. His much-quoted defense of his view was that ". . . in the long run we are all dead."

[19]This apparent empirical regularity was first discovered by Phillips (1958) who used wages and unemployment.

employment level, the steeper the slope and, consequently, the higher the inflation rate. Presumably, without deficit spending, the economy would be stuck permanently below the full-employment level of output.

The Natural Rate Hypothesis and Rational Expectations: A Counter View to the Phillips Curve

The view that the economy could remain permanently at underemployment equilibrium was challenged by the Natural Rate Hypothesis.[20] It reintroduced the once-prevalent argument that the economy eventually will return to its full-employment equilibrium. That is, the Natural Rate Hypothesis implied that the long-run Phillips Curve is vertical at the natural rate of unemployment.

The implications of the Natural Rate Hypothesis were enhanced by the rational expectations revolution, which argued for the same conclusions, albeit along different theoretical lines. Rational expectations models of the business cycle showed that systematic stabilization policies could not affect real output permanently in markets populated by "rational" individuals.[21]

Both theories argue that the employment rate will tend toward its natural rate; consequently, demand management policies will be unable to keep the unemployment rate below the natural rate in the long run. The natural rate of output, y_n, is determined solely by the level of employment N_n, consistent with the natural rate of unemployment, given the stock of capital K. That is,

$$y_n = f(N_n, K).$$

Since demand management policies have no lasting effect on employment or the capital stock, they have no effect on the natural rate of output. In effect, these theories make it less likely that there will be asymmetries in the business cycle, thus, eliminating the possibility of permanent gains in net output from deficit spending. Unless shocks to demand or supply are asymmetric, on average, cyclical downturns need be no more pronounced nor of longer duration than cyclical upturns.[22]

The Natural Rate Hypothesis asserts that the long-run aggregate supply curve is vertical at an output level consistent with the natural rate of unemployment. It does not assert, however, that the short-run aggregate supply curve will be vertical at this level of output.[23] Hence, accepting the Natural Rate Hypothesis does not imply that society cannot benefit from appropriately timed and implemented deficit spending; however, it limits significantly the benefits that society can receive from deficit spending. As discussed previously, society benefits only if deficit spending reduces cyclical swings in output or nominal GNP.[24]

CAN DEFICIT SPENDING SHIFT THE AGGREGATE DEMAND SCHEDULE?

Even when the aggregate supply curve (short- or long-run) is upward-sloping, deficit spending will have little effect on output or prices if the increase in aggregate demand that it produces is largely offset by a deficit-induced decrease in private spending, that is, if deficit spending fails to change aggregate demand.

Competition for Credit—Indirect Crowding Out Through Interest Rates

When the government runs a deficit, it issues government debt.[25] Thus, the demand for credit increases relative to the supply. All other things

---

[20]See Friedman (1968) and Phelps (1967).

[21]Neither the Natural Rate Hypothesis nor many rational expectations models give rise to involuntary unemployment as defined in footnote 8. Many rational expectations models, however, give rise to cyclical movements in the natural rate of unemployment. See Fischer (1977), Taylor (1988) and McCallum (1986). For a list of other factors that could cause the unemployment rate to change without involuntary unemployment, see Blinder (1988).

[22]In chart 2, "potential" output is defined arbitrarily. Consequently, persistent unemployment can exist by definition. This applies to estimates of "potential" GNP as well as cyclically-adjusted deficits, etc. See Fellner (1982) and de Leeuw and Holloway (1982) for a discussion of this point.

[23]Also, it does not say explicitly what the level of the natural rate is. See Carlson (1988) for a discussion of the level of the natural rate.

[24]Actually, in such models, deficits can provide benefits in the absence of stabilizing output. These benefits come from smoothing taxes over the cycle. Public finance theory asserts that variation in tax rates across goods or activities results in welfare losses under most conditions. Consequently, it would be more efficient to run deficits and surpluses over the business cycle rather than balance the budget annually by altering tax rates. See Bossons (1986) and the references cited there.

[25]In models with a government budget constraint deficits are often financed directly through money creation. Given the current institutional structure, however, the government must initially issue debt even if it is subsequently monetized. See Thornton (1984a). See Thornton (1984b) for a discussion of and evidence on debt monetization.

unchanged, this causes interest rates to rise, reducing private expenditures in interest-sensitive sectors of the economy. Hence, the increase in aggregate demand associated with the deficit could crowd-out private expenditures indirectly by affecting interest rates.[26] Since investment spending is one of the most interest-sensitive components of spending, analysts often argue that deficit spending might retard the rate of capital formation and, hence, economic growth.[27]

Deficit Spending and the Trade Deficit

Assuming that deficit spending increases the demand for credit, its effect on interest rates depends on whether the economy is "open" or "closed." In the preceding example, we implicitly assumed that the economy was closed so that the government ran a deficit by borrowing from the private sector. In an open economy with a floating exchange rate and perfect capital flows, the results would be somewhat different.[28]

An increase in the budget deficit puts upward pressure on domestic interest rates. This leads to inflows of financial capital and an appreciation of the exchange rate. This appreciation, together with the higher domestic demand, is associated with a current account deficit in the balance of payments. In effect, the government deficit is

financed by a larger trade deficit.[29] The economy may gain in terms of higher short-term consumption, but at a cost of an increase in external debt.

The decline in private expenditures is affected through higher interest rates, a larger trade deficit or both. In any event, the result is the same: the group that gains directly from deficit expenditures does so at the expense of those who lose, with little or no net increase in aggregate demand. The only difference is that those who gain directly are more readily identified than those who suffer indirect losses through higher interest rates or increased foreign claims on U.S. assets.[30]

Ricardian Equivalence

Another argument, referred to as the "Ricardian Equivalence Hypothesis," holds that deficit spending cannot shift the aggregate demand curve.[31] The closed-economy conclusion that deficit spending does not crowd-out private spending directly implies that government debt is net wealth to society. In other words, when the government issues debt to purchase goods and services, the holder of the debt views it as an asset; but the taxpayer does not view it as a liability (or, at least, views it as a smaller liability). That is, individuals believe that they will not have to pay current or future taxes to service or retire the debt.

[26]This problem cannot be solved by monetizing the debt. The increased rate of money growth will result merely in a higher rate of inflation and, hence, higher nominal interest rates. Many advocates of countercyclical fiscal policy view this as one of the most serious drawbacks to deficit spending. See Modigliani (1986b).

[27]This argument ignores how the deficits are spent. Recently, Heilbroner (1988) has argued that deficit spending is necessary to finance the purchase of public capital, that is, infrastructure. Other economist (for example, see Sturrock and Idan (1988)) argue that the real burden of deficits comes only when they are used to finance current consumption. This does not establish the desirability of deficit spending; it merely asserts that spending for infrastructure capital may increase the rate of economic growth, depending primarily on the relative productivity of the factor resources in the two sectors and on the productivity of public versus private capital.
The idea that such expenditures should be financed by deficits rests largely on the long-lived nature of capital goods. Since these capital goods provide services over a number of years, it is argued that public sector capital goods should be financed by borrowing just as businesses or households finance their acquisition of durable goods. In the case of businesses, however, debt service is financed out of the increased earnings that the capital goods are expected to provide. In the case of households, deficit financing is used to better match the desired consumption with expected future income. Hence, households, too, expect to service the debt through higher incomes. No similar increased earnings necessarily accrues from the acquisition of public capital. Income will increase only if the marginal product of public capital is larger than that of private capital. This is a difficult point to establish. Proponents of this view point to the productivity gains that could accrue

from public expenditures on education and the like; however, these services could be provided by the private sector. Hence, this argument is about the appropriate role for government and public goods. See Aschauer and Greenwood and Aschauer (1988a, b and c) for a discussion of the benefits from social infrastructure expenditures. Hence, the only real argument for deficit financing of such expenditures is that it would equalize their costs and benefits across generations. This implies, however, that the increased indebtedness that such expenditures necessitate will eventually be retired through increased taxes unless the infrastructure acquired is infinitely lived.

[28]The assumption of perfect capital flows means that domestic real interest rates could not rise above world levels without inducing an inflow of financial capital from overseas. For a situation in which there is no expectation of exchange rate changes, this means that domestic and foreign nominal interest rates must be equal.

[29]See Mundell (1963). This result assumes no change in monetary policy to accommodate the deficit.

[30]In this model, the real market value of government debt is part of society's net wealth. In the closed economy model, at the natural rate of unemployment, the increase in wealth resulting from the increase in nominal debt due to deficit spending is just offset by a decline in wealth due to higher prices, interest rates or both. In the open economy model, it is offset by a reduced stock of national wealth due to increased claims by foreigners on U.S. assets.

[31]Technically, Ricardian Equivalence argues that, for a given level of government expenditures, aggregate demand will not change as the government switches from tax to bond financing. As O'Driscoll (1977) points out, Ricardo was merely offering this as a theoretical possibility and did not himself believe it.

Ricardian Equivalence, on the other hand, asserts that public and private debt are perfect substitutes. Individuals believe that they or their heirs will have to pay taxes equal to the deficit-financed expenditures, so an increase in present value of the expected future taxes just equals the current deficit.

At the macroeconomic level, Ricardian Equivalence implies that deficit spending will not be associated with increases in real interest rates, output, prices or the trade deficit.[32] Consequently, the Ricardian view yields a radically different notion of the national debt. For those who believe in the benefits of deficit spending, the national debt, which is the accumulated deficits, should be viewed as a blessing, not a curse. For those who believe in Ricardian Equivalence, deficit spending merely results in a redistribution of income and the national debt represents the cumulative amount of this net transfer.

Can Discretionary Fiscal Policy Be Successfully Implemented?

There is also an argument against the usefulness of deficit spending that is independent of its ability to shift aggregate demand. It is critically dependent, however, on the Natural Rate Hypothesis and on whether shifts in aggregate demand caused by other factors are temporary or permanent. It has been suggested that policymakers do not have the information needed to offset shifts in aggregate demand to stabilize output.[33] This argument is usually couched in a discussion of the lags in economic policymaking. For fiscal policy, the most important of these are the "recognition" and "implementation" lags. The recognition lag is the time between when a need for corrective action arises (an exogenous shift in aggregate demand) and when policymakers recognize the need. The issue is simply whether policymakers know where the economy is in the business cycle at any particular point in time.

The implementation lag is the time between when the need for corrective action is recognized and when policymakers take action. Thus, even if policymakers are quick to recognize that the demand has shifted, by the time they react to the situation, it may have changed and the need for corrective action may have vanished.

This argument is presented graphically in figure 4a. Assume that the Natural Rate Hypothesis holds and that the short-run aggregate supply curve is symmetric around the level of output consistent with the natural rate of unemployment. Assume further an exogenous decrease in aggregate demand, shifting it from AD to AD′. Now if policymakers did not react to the shift in demand immediately, the process of adjustment toward the natural rate would begin; the price level would decline and the quantity of output demanded would increase. Once policymakers reacted to the problem by increasing deficit spending, they would shift the aggregate demand curve upward, bringing output back to its natural-rate level.

If the shift in aggregate demand were temporary, a delay in policy might actually exacerbate the situation if deficit spending coincided closely with the return of aggregate demand to its former level. This is illustrated in figure 4b, where the simultaneous increase in deficit spending and the return of aggregate demand to its former level shift aggregate demand to AD″.

Of course, if the decline in aggregate demand were permanent, the timing of policy would be less important. Deficit spending eventually would move the economy back to the natural rate; the timing of the policy action would determine only how quickly deficit spending moved the economy back to its full-employment potential. Of course, the economy would move back eventually to full employment even without deficit spending.

Demand or Supply Disturbances

Another problem is that policymakers must be able to differentiate between demand- and supply-side disturbances. Recently, some have suggested that business cycles can be explained solely by supply-side disturbances. Indeed, some "real business cycle" models have successfully produced cyclical swings in output that mimic real world data. Whether all cyclical swings in economic activity can be explained by such models is the subject of intense debate. Nevertheless, to the extent that some cyclical swings are the result of supply-side shocks, fiscal policy can succeed in stabilizing output only by exacerbating movements in prices (or it can help stabilize the price level only by exacerbating movements in output).

---

[32]Analysts frequently argue that Ricardian Equivalence must be invalid because the necessary microeconomic conditions for its validity are so stringent that they cannot possibly be satisfied. For example, see Buiter (1985). Also, see McCallum (1984).

[33]It is argued that inappropriately timed policy might destabilize the economy. See Friedman (1968).

Figure 4
The Timing of Changes in Fiscal Policy

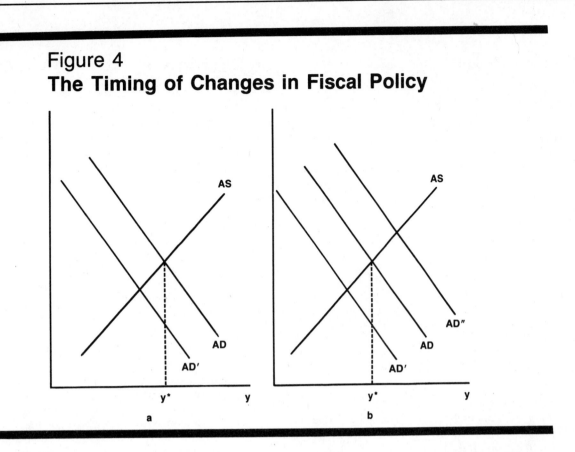

a

b

Consequently, policymakers must know not only where in the business cycle the economy is at any point in time, but whether its position was caused by a shift in aggregate demand, aggregate supply or, perhaps, simply the cyclical dynamics of the economy, unrelated to exogenous disturbances in either aggregate demand or supply. In short, some would argue that the information required to use discretionary fiscal policy effectively is simply too great.

WHAT IS THE EVIDENCE?

Assessing the evidence on discretionary fiscal policy is difficult. Effective discretionary fiscal policy implies that output should be more stable and suggests that perhaps the rate of real output growth should be higher on average when fiscal policy was used aggressively. It also suggests that deficit spending should be positively correlated with interest rates, prices (or inflation) or trade deficits.

A number of large-scale econometric models suggest that fiscal policy has significant short-run and, in some cases, long-run effects. Estimates of reduced-form models, however, typically show no long-run effects of deficit spending and, often, only weak short-run effects.[34] Hence, such models essentially substantiate the Natural Rate Hypothesis. These studies are subject to considerable controversy because of the difficulty in finding commonly accepted variables that reflect discretionary changes in fiscal policy and the continued controversy over reduced-form estimation.

The greatest challenge to the orthodox view of deficit spending comes from the Ricardian Equivalence Hypothesis.[35] Macroeconomic evidence from three recent surveys is largely consistent with the Ricardian view.[36] In general, there is no statistically significant relationship between structural deficits and interest rates or inflation, or between the budget and trade deficits.[37] These results are bolstered by work that shows a high negative correla-

---

[34]One of the earliest of these was the Andersen-Jordan equation. See Andersen and Jordan (1968).

[35]See Barro (1987), Bernheim (1987) and Aschauer (1988a). For more recent studies which report results consistent with Ricardian Equivalence, see Evans (1988), Koray and Hill (1988) and Leiderman and Razin (1988).

[36]The microeconomic evidence yields mixed results.

[37]Barro (1987) reports that he finds a statistically significant correlation between government deficits and the trade deficit only if 1983 is included.

tion between public and private savings.[38]

The Evidence on Stabilization

One commonly cited piece of evidence that demand management can stabilize the economy is a comparison of the volatility of U.S. output, unemployment and industrial production, before and after World War II. The fact that the pre-war series are more volatile than the post-war series has been cited as evidence of both the inherent instability of unmanaged capitalism and the success of demand management policies in stabilizing the economy.

There are several criticisms of this evidence. First, pre- and post-war data vary in terms of a quality and uniformity. Indeed, some argue that the excessive pre-war volatility of the commonly used series on unemployment, GNP and industrial production is due to various quirks in their construction.[39]

Second, even if the post-war economy is more stable, this may be due to other changes in economic fundamentals, not to discretionary fiscal policy per se.[40] Furthermore, even if fiscal policy is responsible for the apparently more stable post-war economy, this may be the result of increased relevance on the automatic stabilizers, not to discretionary fiscal policy.

Also, post-war real output growth in the United States is below its pre-war growth. The discrepancy is even larger if the Depression years are omitted.[41] Moreover, there has been a secular rise in the unemployment rate. These adverse movements roughly coincide with a secular rise in the U.S. structural deficit.[42] Hence, if the more stable post-war economy is used as evidence on the success of fiscal policy, the associated slower output growth and higher unemployment must be considered the costs of stability.

CONCLUSION

This paper has examined the theoretical arguments about the wisdom of deficit spending. The once-prevalent Keynesian approach, which concludes that such gains clearly exist, has come under attack. Increasingly, both theoretical innovations and empirical evidence suggest that modern economies are not well characterized by the Keynesian view. Support for the Natural Rate Hypothesis, which argues that deficit spending has no effect on the equilibrium level of output and employment in the long run has grown. If this hypothesis is valid, the gains from deficit spending result from stabilizing output around the level consistent with the natural rate of unemployment. Such an effective use of deficit spending, however, imposes information requirements on policymakers that are unlikely to be attained.

In general, empirical evidence on the effects of deficit spending is sparse and, for the most part, ambiguous. Most persuasive is the growing macroeconomic evidence, consistent with Ricardian Equivalence, that deficit spending has no long-run effect. The challenge for those who argue that deficit spending merely redistributes income and that stabilization policy will likely hurt is to explain phenomena like the Great Depression. Through adherents to both extreme Keynesian and extreme rational expectations views (and everything between) usually are able to rationalize historical events on their own terms, the Great Depression is as likely to be seen as an example of what bad policy can create as it is of what good policy can eradicate.

REFERENCES

Andersen, Leonall C., and Jerry L. Jordan. "Monetary and Fiscal Actions: A Test of Their Relative Importance in Economic Stabilization," this *Review* (November 1968), pp. 11–24.

---

[38]Of course, in a closed economy with output unchanged, the public sector deficit must equal the private sector surplus. Other studies of consumption have tried to determine whether government debt is net wealth, e.g., Tanner (1979) and Kochin (1974). Again, the results are consistent with the Ricardian Equivalence Hypothesis.

[39]See Romer (1986a, 1986b, 1986c and 1988). Romer's evidence has been challenged by Weir (1986) and Lebergott (1986).

[40]Pre- and post-war real output series for the United Kingdom, Germany and Italy show significant decreases in the variability of real output of a similar order of magnitude as that of the United States. The pre-war standard deviations of annual output growth for the United States, United Kingdom, Germany and Italy were 6.61, 3.98, 6.10 and 4.79, respectively. The post-war standard deviations were 2.83, 2.00, 2.45 and 3.49. In all cases, the decline in variability was statistically significant at the 5 percent level. The data were obtained from Liesner (1985).

[41]The growth rate of real output from 1869 to 1938 was 3.1 percent, from 1945 to 1983, 2.7 percent, and from 1965 to 1983, 3.7 percent. These growth rates were calculated from data in Gordon (1986).

[42]The unemployment rate averaged 4.5 percent in the 1950s, 4.8 percent in the 1960s, 6.2 percent in the 1970s and 7.7 percent in the 1980s, respectively.

Aschauer, David. "The Equilibrium Approach to Fiscal Policy," *Journal of Money, Credit and Banking* (February 1988a), pp. 41–62.

_____. "Is Government Spending Stimulative?" Federal Reserve Bank of Chicago Staff Memoranda SM 88-3 (1988b).

_____. "Public Spending and the Return to Capital," Federal Reserve Bank of Chicago Staff Memoranda SM 88-2, (1988c).

Aschauer, David A., and Jeremy Greenwood. "Macroeconomic Effects of Fiscal Policy," *Carnegie-Rochester Series on Public Policy* (Autumn 1985), pp. 91–138.

Auerbach, Alan J., and Laurence J. Kotlikoff. "Evaluating Fiscal Policy with a Dynamic Simulation Model," *The American Economic Review* (May 1987), pp. 49–55.

Barro, Robert J. "The Ricardian Approach to Budget Deficits," Henry Thornton Lecture, City University Business School, London, November 1987.

Bernheim, B. Douglas. "Ricardian Equivalence: An Evaluation of the Theory and Evidence," NBER Working Paper No. 2330 (July 1987).

Blinder, Alan S. "The Challenge of High Unemployment," *The American Economic Review* (May 1988), pp. 1–15.

_____. "Keynes After Lucas," *Eastern Economic Journal* (July-September 1986), pp. 209–16.

Bossons, John. "Issues in the Analysis of Government Deficits," in John Sargent, ed., *Fiscal and Monetary Policy* (University Toronto Press, 1986), pp. 85–112.

Bruce, Neil and Douglas D. Purvis. "Consequences of Government Budget Deficits," in John Sargent, ed., *Fiscal and Monetary Policy* (University of Toronto Press, 1986), pp. 43–84.

Buiter, William H. "A Guide to Public Sector Debt and Deficits," *Economic Policy: A European Forum* (November 1985), pp. 14–79.

Carlson, Keith M. "How Much Lower Can the Unemployment Rate Go?," this *Review* (July/August 1988), pp. 44–57.

_____. "Federal Fiscal Policy Since the Employment Act of 1946," this *Review* (December 1987), pp. 14–30.

de Leeuw, Frank, and Thomas M. Holloway. "The High-Employment Budget and Potential Output: A Response," *Survey of Current Business* (November 1982), pp. 33–35.

Eisner, Robert. "The Revolution Restored: Keynesian Unemployment, Inflation and Budget Deficits," *Eastern Economic Journal* (July-September 1986), pp. 217–21.

Erceg, John J., and Theodore G. Bernard. "Federal Budget Deficits: Sources and Forecasts," Federal Reserve Bank of Cleveland, *Economic Commentary* (March 15, 1988).

Evans, Paul. "Are Consumers Ricardian? Evidence for the United States," *Journal of Political Economy* (October 1988), pp. 983–1004.

Fellner, William. "The High-Employment Budget and Potential Output: A Critique," *Survey of Current Business* (November 1982), pp. 26–33.

Fischer, Stanley. "Long Term Contracts, Rational Expectations, and the Optimal Money Supply Rule," *Journal of Political Economy* (February 1977), pp. 191–205.

Friedman, Milton. "The Role of Monetary Policy," *The American Economic Review* (March 1968), pp. 1–17.

Gordon, Robert J., ed. *The American Business Cycle: Continuity and Change*, NBER (University of Chicago Press, 1986).

Heilbroner, Robert L. "The Importance of Red Ink: How I Learned to Love the Deficit," *The New York Times,* September 4, 1988.

Kochin, Levis A. "Are Future Taxes Anticipated by Consumers?" *Journal of Money, Credit and Banking* (August 1974), pp. 385–94.

Koray, Faik, and R. Carter Hill. "Money, Debt, and Economic Activity," *Journal of Macroeconomics* (Summer 1988), pp. 351–70.

Kotlikoff, Laurence J. "What Macroeconomics Teaches Us about the Dynamic Macro Effects of Fiscal Policy," *Journal of Money, Credit and Banking* (August 1988, Part 2), pp. 479–95.

Laidler, David. "Taking Money Seriously," *Canadian Economic Journal* (forthcoming).

Lebergott, Stanley. "Discussion," *The Journal of Economic History* (June 1986), pp. 367–71.

Leiderman, Leonardo, and Assaf Razin. "Testing Ricardian Neutrality with an Intertemporal Stochastic Model," *Journal of Money, Credit and Banking* (February 1988), pp. 1–21.

Leijonhufvud, Axel. "Constitutional Constraints on the Monetary Powers of Governments," in James A. Dorn and Anna J. Schwartz, ed., *The Search for Stable Money: Essays on Monetary Reform* (University of Chicago Press, 1987).

Levy, Michael E. *Fiscal Policy, Cycles and Growth* (The Conference Board, 1963).

Levy, Michael E., et. al. *Federal Budget Deficits and The U.S. Economy* (The Conference Board, 1984).

Liesner, Thelma. *Economic Statistics: 1900–1983* (The Economist Publications Ltd., 1985).

Mankiw, N. Gregory. "Recent Developments in Macroeconomics: A Very Quick Refresher Course," *Journal of Money, Credit and Banking* (August 1988, Part 2), pp. 436–49.

McCallum, Bennett T. "Are Bond-financed Deficits Inflationary?: A Ricardian Analysis," *Journal of Political Economy* (February 1984), pp. 123–35.

_____. "On 'Real' and 'Sticky-Price' Theories of the Business Cycle," *Journal of Money, Credit and Banking* (November 1986), pp. 397–414.

Modigliani, Franco. "Comment on R. J. Barro, 'U.S. Deficits Since World War I,' " *The Scandinavian Journal of Economics,* Vol. 88, No. 1 (1986a), pp. 223–34.

_____. *The Debate over Stabilization Policy* (Cambridge University Press, 1986b).

Mundell, R. A. "Capital Mobility and Stabilization Policy under Fixed and Flexible Exchange Rates," *The Canadian Journal of Economics and Political Science* (November 1963), pp. 475–85.

The New Keynesian Microfoundations: "Discussion," in *NBER Macroeconomics Annual 1987* (1987), pp. 114–16.

Niehans, Jurg. "Classical Monetary Theory, New and Old," *Journal of Money, Credit and Banking* (November 1987), pp. 409–24.

O'Driscoll, Gerald P., Jr. "The Ricardian Nonequivalance Theorem," *Journal of Political Economy* (February 1977), pp. 207–10.

Phelps, Edmund S. "Phillips Curves, Expectations of Inflation, and Optimal Unemployment Over Time," *Economica* (August 1967), pp. 254–81.

Phillips, A. W. "The Relation Between Unemployment and the Rate of Change of Money Wage Rates in the United Kingdom, 1861–1957," *Economica* (November 1958), pp. 283–99.

Prescott, Edward C. "Comment," *NBER Macroeconomics Annual 1987*, pp. 110–14.

Romer, Christina D. "Is the Stabilization of the Postwar Economy a Figment of the Data?" *The American Economic Review* (June 1986a), pp. 314–34.

————. "Spurious Volatility in Historical Unemployment Data," *Journal of Political Economy* (February 1986b), pp. 1–37.

————. "New Estimates of Prewar Gross National Product and Unemployment," *The Journal of Economic History* (June 1986c), pp. 341–52.

————. "World War I and the Post War Depression: A Reinterpretation Based on Alternative Estimates of GNP," *Journal of Monetary Economics* (July 1988), pp. 91–115.

Rotemberg, Julio J. "The New Keynesian Microfoundations," *NBER Macroeconomics Annual 1987*, pp. 69–104.

Seater, John J. "Does Government Debt Matter?: A Review," *Journal of Monetary Economics* (July 1985), pp. 121–32.

Sickel, Daniel E. "Business Cycle Asymmetry: A Deeper Look," unpublished manuscript, Board of Governors of the Federal Reserve System (1988).

Sturrock, John, and George Iden. "Deficits and Interest Rates: Theoretical Issues and Empirical Evidence," Congressional Budget Office Staff Working Paper (1988).

Taylor, John B. "Aggregate Dynamics and Staggered Contracts," *Journal of Political Economy* (February 1980), pp. 1–23.

Tanner, J. Ernest. "An Empirical Investigation of Tax Discounting," *Journal of Money, Credit and Banking* (May 1979), pp. 214–18.

Thornton, Daniel L. "The Government Budget Constraint with Endogenous Money," *Journal of Macroeconomics* (Winter 1984), pp. 57–67.

————. "Monetizing the Debt," this *Review* (December 1984b), pp. 30–43.

Weir, David R. "The Reliability of Historical Macroeconomic Data for Comparing Cyclical Stability," *The Journal of Economic History* (June 1986), pp. 353–65.

Article 32

ECONOMIC COMMENTARY

Should We Intervene in Exchange Markets?

by Owen F. Humpage

The Group of Five countries (France, Germany, Japan, the United Kingdom and the United States), plus Canada, met in Paris on February 21 and 22, seeking ways to eliminate huge trade imbalances in the United States, Japan and Germany, to encourage greater exchange-market stability, and to thwart growing protectionism.[1]

The recent rapid depreciation of the dollar, which poses major problems both for the United States and for our major trading partners, prompted the Paris meeting. As the dollar depreciates relative to other currencies, foreign exporters find it difficult to compete against U.S. goods in world markets. The dollar depreciation already has contributed to a sharp slowdown in Japan's economic growth. For the United States, fear of continued rapid dollar depreciation increases the risk that international investors will shift funds out of dollar-denominated assets and, thereby, force up U.S. interest rates. Federal Reserve Chairman Paul A. Volcker repeatedly has cautioned about this possible effect. The depreciation also will contribute to higher prices in the United States.

Although vague on the issue, the Paris meeting increased speculation that the participating countries would intervene more forcefully in an attempt to limit movements in key exchange rates. As newspapers recently have reported, Japan, and to a lesser extent, Germany have committed large sums to exchange-market intervention. In contrast, however, the United States has been reluctant to intervene in the exchange market, believing that when nations conduct intervention independent of their monetary policies it has, at best, a limited influence on exchange rates.

This *Economic Commentary* discusses the U.S. reluctance to intervene in exchange markets. We present three theoretical channels through which exchange-market intervention could influence exchange rates: the monetary channel, the portfolio-adjustment channel, and the expectations channel.[2]

A Definition

Exchange-market intervention refers to official purchases and sales of foreign exchange, which nations undertake through their central banks to influence the exchange value of their currencies. Although nations have many ways to influence their exchange rate—such as using monetary and fiscal policy, capital controls and trade barriers— exchange-market intervention seems the most direct and most flexible method. Many nations, therefore, frequently resort to intervention. Members of the European Monetary System, for example, routinely intervene to keep their exchange rates within narrow margins.[3]

Much of the recent interest in intervention stems from the belief that intervention enables nations to influence their exchange rates without altering monetary and fiscal policies. To understand this, we first must distinguish between *sterilized* and *nonsterilized* intervention. When a country undertakes sterilized intervention, it engages in other transactions to prevent either the purchase or sale of foreign currency from influencing its money-supply growth. In contrast, nonsterilized intervention can alter a country's money supply.

An example can help clarify the important distinction between sterilized and nonsterilized intervention. Suppose the United States wants to slow a depreciation of the dollar relative to the German mark. At the direction of the Treasury Department, the Federal Reserve System would buy dollars with German marks through its foreign-exchange desk in New York. Because this transaction reduces the supply of dollars in the foreign-exchange market, the dollar should then appreciate relative to the German mark. The foreign-exchange desk's purchase of dollars, however, also contracts the money supply in the United States. At this point, the intervention transaction is nonsterilized.

The reduction in the money supply resulting from intervention might be inconsistent with the domestic objectives of monetary policy. Consequently, the Federal Reserve then might wish to offset the impact of the intervention purchases of dollars by purchasing Treasury bills through the System's open-market desk at the Federal Reserve Bank of New York. The purchase of Treasury bills supplies reserves to the banking system and increases the money supply. Thus, by coordinating the activities of the foreign-exchange and open-market desks, the Federal Reserve can offset, or sterilize, the monetary impact of its exchange-market activities.

Owen F. Humpage is an economist at the Federal Reserve Bank of Cleveland.

The views stated herein are those of the author and not necessarily those of the Federal Reserve Bank of Cleveland or of the Board of Governors of the Federal Reserve System.

1. This article was revised and published after the February Group of Five meeting and has been backdated in order to maintain the continuity of the *Economic Commentary* series - editor.

2. The author presents a more detailed analysis of intervention and a survey of the literature in: "Exchange-Market Intervention: The Channels of Influence," *Economic Review,* Federal Reserve Bank of Cleveland, Quarter 3, 1986, pp.2-14.

3. The United States intervened quite frequently during much of the 1970s, but has intervened relatively infrequently in the 1980s.

While sterilized intervention has no effect on the money stock, it does change the public's relative holdings of U.S. Treasury securities and foreign securities. In our example, sterilized intervention reduces the supply of dollar-denominated Treasury securities in the market.[4]

The Impact of Nonsterilized Exchange-Market Intervention

Nonsterilized intervention alters nations' money supplies, whereas sterilized intervention alters relative supplies of government securities.[5] Consequently, we initially discuss the influence of a change in monetary policy on the exchange rate and then describe the unique influence of sterilized intervention. Both types of intervention can influence expectations, which we also will discuss.

Economists have long recognized a relationship between changes in countries' monetary growth rates and changes in exchange rates (or in the balance of payments under fixed exchange rates). Although economists might disagree about the timing, about the precise chain of causation, and about the relative importance of money for determining exchange rates, few would object on theoretical grounds to the inclusion of money among the key determinants of exchange rates.

A common description of the chain of events connecting a reduction in money growth to a currency appreciation would be as follows: If the United States were to slow its money growth, say from 10 percent per year to 8 percent, with other factors unchanged, it would experience an increase in its interest rates, at least initially. If foreign countries maintain their interest rates, international investors will transfer funds from assets denominated in foreign currencies, say German marks, to assets denominated in dollars. To obtain dollars, these investors will trade German marks for dollars in the exchange market. The increased supply of German marks and increased demand for dollars will tend to cause the dollar to appreciate relative to the mark.

The reduced rate of U.S. money growth also might slow the pace of economic activity and reduce the rate of inflation in the United States. But, prices typically adjust more slowly than the exchange rate, so the initial slowing in the money growth rate will cause the dollar to appreciate both on a nominal basis and on an inflation-adjusted, or *real*, basis.[6] The real appreciation of the dollar will make U.S. goods less competitive in world markets, until the U.S. inflation rate adjusts to the slower pace of money growth in the United States.

In summary, nonsterilized intervention is identical to central bank open-market operations, except that the bank would slow the money supply growth through sales of foreign exchange instead of securities. A slower rate of money growth resulting from nonsterilized intervention can result in a persistent nominal appreciation of the dollar and a temporary real appreciation of the dollar. Nonsterilized intervention thus will not have a long-term impact on a nation's competitive position.[7]

Sterilized Intervention and Portfolio Adjustments

While little disagreement exists about the ability of nonsterilized intervention to alter exchange rates through changes in money growth, disagreement about the potency of sterilized intervention abounds. Economists have suggested two theoretical channels through which sterilized intervention might influence exchange rates. These are the portfolio-adjustment channel and the expectations channel.

According to the portfolio-adjustment channel, sterilized intervention, which alters the amounts of U.S. Treasury securities relative to foreign government securities in private hands, can cause investors to reorganize their portfolios. This re-diversification can affect exchange rates.

To understand how the portfolio-adjustment effect operates, consider a world in which risk-averse investors, facing uncertain rates of return on an array of assets, diversify their portfolios instead of holding only the single asset currently yielding the highest rate of return. When we acknowledge that assets denominated in different currencies can carry varying degrees of exchange risk and political risk, a strong incentive then exists for investors worldwide to diversify their portfolios across currencies.[8] In the case of major developing countries, most analysts attach the greatest importance to exchange risk. Economists believe that the exchange risk associated with bonds denominated in a particular currency increases with the proportion of similarly denominated bonds held by investors.

Since sterilized intervention alters the relative amounts of bonds in the hands of the public, it has the potential to affect risk-based premiums. Consider our original example. If the Federal Reserve undertakes open-market operations to sterilize the impact of the dollar purchases on the U.S. money supply, it will reduce the amount of dollar-denominated securities in the hands of the public. The change in the relative supply of dollar- and mark-denominated assets then could lower the relative risk premium associated with dollar assets. Moreover, if the German Bundesbank also sterilized the impact of our sales of German marks through its own open-market operation, it would further affect the relative supplies of securities and the risk premium. The lower risk premium could entice international investors to diversify into dollar assets, thereby causing the dollar to appreciate relative to the mark.

For the portfolio balance approach to operate, investors must view dollar-and foreign-currency denominated bonds as imperfect substitutes because of differences in the risk premium associated with each. If, in our example, investors viewed U.S. and German bonds as perfect substitutes with equal risks, they would willingly substitute German securities for dollar securities in their portfolios. They would see no need to diversify their portfolios and, consequently, no exchange-rate movements would result.

Empirical research does not strongly support the portfolio-adjustment channel. Although the issue remains unresolved, the evidence on the existence of

---

4. The purchase of dollars with marks also will increase the German money supply. We assume throughout our example that the Germans sterilize the influence on their money supply by selling government securities to the market.

5. See: "The Channels of Influence," op. cit., pp. 4-5.

6. The *nominal* exchange rate is the rate that traders and newspapers typically quote. The *real* exchange rate is equal to the nominal exchange rate adjusted for inflation-rate differentials between the countries in question.

7. This description ignores the important contribution of expectations. Expectation, however,

will not alter the outcome of a decrease in the rate of money growth, but can alter the speed and contours with which events take place.

8. *Exchange risk* is the uncertainty associated with unanticipated exchange-rate movements; *political risk* refers to the probability that governments will impose capital controls.

a risk premium between similar assets denominated in currencies of different major developed countries is mixed. But, even if the relevant bonds are imperfect substitutes, it appears that the response to small changes in the risk premium is quite low.

Michael Hutchison, for example, noted that the change in the total outstanding publicly held government debt was the relevant variable for portfolio decisions.[9] Total government debt responds to intervention, to changes in the budget deficit, and to monetary policy. The volume of exchange-market intervention is usually too small, compared to the total volume of outstanding debt, to have a significant impact on portfolio choices. With the publicly held federal debt in excess of $1.7 trillion, the Federal Reserve and foreign central banks probably would need to undertake a massive volume of intervention before it had a significant impact on investors' portfolio decisions.

Expectations

Even in the absence of a significant portfolio-adjustment effect, sterilized intervention could affect exchange rates by altering market expectations. Exchange markets are highly efficient processors of information. Traders make full use of all currently available information, including information about predictable future events and policy decisions. Exchange rates on any given day embody all of this information. Changes in exchange rates reflect new information that has altered traders' expectations. Intervention thus could alter exchange rates if it provided new information to the market.

The scope for altering expectations through official purchases or sales of foreign exchange seems rather narrow. First, the Federal Reserve and the U.S. Treasury probably do not have better information than the market concerning day-to-day developments. Nevertheless, officials do, from time to time, possess better information in the

important sense that market participants might be confused or unsure of the future course of monetary or fiscal policy. If intervention can clarify policy intentions, it thus could alter expectations and exchange rates.

The decision of the Group of Five countries to intervene in late September 1985 (the Plaza decision) seems to represent a recent example of successful intervention that altered expectations in the foreign-exchange market. Prior to the meeting, the dollar was depreciating, but the market seemed uncertain about the future course of U.S. monetary and fiscal policies. The narrowly defined money stock was growing in excess of its target range, suggesting to many observers that the Federal Reserve might reduce money growth.

On the other hand, economic activity seemed weak at the time; many complained that the dollar was overvalued, and banks continued to experience difficulties with agricultural and international loans. These events suggested to many observers that the Federal Reserve might take no action to slow money growth. The United States intervened forcefully immediately following the G-5 meeting, but did not continue to intervene beyond the fourth quarter. Foreign-exchange market participants seemed to view the decision to intervene as a signal that U.S. monetary policy would not move in a direction that might strengthen the dollar. Money continued to grow above the target range and the dollar continued to depreciate.

Designing and implementing exchange-market intervention to influence expectations presents many difficulties. As already noted, the authorities must provide new information to market participants, but the possibilities of doing so seem limited. Experienced market participants will anticipate and adjust for policy decisions. Consequently, intervention will alter expectations only when it is not routine, and when a credible change in monetary policy accompanies it.

If the market believes domestic economic or political consideration prohibit a tightening of monetary policy, it will not respond favorably to intervention

that is designed to slow a dollar depreciation. Such was the case in the late 1970s. Heavy U.S. intervention in 1978 and 1979 to stem the dollar's decline appeared to have little effect, because the market believed that the United States lacked the resolve to end inflation. Only after the Federal Reserve re-established credibility with a new chairman and with a new operating procedure did the dollar begin to appreciate.

If we accept the argument that the authorities have the ability to influence foreign-exchange-market expectations by providing new information about policy, is intervention then the most effective vehicle for introducing this information? Could the central bank not provide the same information more effectively through the announcement of monetary-policy intentions or by altering an instrument of monetary policy?

One reason for thinking that actual currency purchases or sales might be more effective in convincing the market about central-bank intentions is that they represent a bet by the central bank on its own information. Profitable central-bank intervention—buying foreign currency when it is cheap relative to the dollar and selling it when it is expensive relative to the dollar—tends to smooth fluctuations in the exchange rate. As Dale Henderson has noted, when the prospects are such that the central bank will incur a loss on its intervention activity if it does not follow through with the correct change in monetary policy, the market has greater reason to trust that the central bank, in fact, will initiate the appropriate monetary adjustment.[10]

One also might wonder about the extent to which intervention, which alters expectations about future monetary policy, is truly sterilized. Many observers believe that such intervention, when accompanied by a future change in monetary policy, has a significantly larger impact on the market than an unaccompanied change in monetary policy.[11] Nevertheless, ability to alter expectations clearly depends on fulfillment of the expectations.

9. See Hutchison, Michael M. "Intervention, Deficit Finance and Real Exchange Rates: The Case of Japan." *Economic Review*, Federal Reserve Bank of San Francisco, Winter 1984, pp. 27-44.

10. See Henderson, Dale W. "Exchange Market Intervention Operations: Their Role in Financial Policy and Their Effects," in John F. O. Bilson and Richard C. Marston, eds. *Exchange Rate Theory and Practice*, Chicago: University of Chicago Press, 1984.

11. See Jurgensen, Phillippe (Chairman). *Report of the Working Group on Exchange Market Intervention*, processed, March 1983.

Conclusion

Most analysts believe that growing U.S. trade deficits cannot continue. As our international indebtedness grows, foreigners will become increasingly reluctant to acquire additional dollar-denominated assets. This will initiate adjustments in many economic variables, including exchange rates and interest rates, to bring the international economy back into balance. How and how quickly these adjustments take place depends in large part on how rapidly the market decides to adjust its holdings of dollar-denominated assets.[12]

Depreciation of the dollar can contribute to the adjustment process by increasing the competitiveness of U.S. goods and services in world markets. Nevertheless, economists have long realized that the ability of an economy to meet increased demands for its goods and services limits the contribution of a currency depreciation to improving its trade balance. If the economy is operating at full capacity, the depreciation will not generate much improvement in the trade balance. Ultimately a reduction in the trade deficit requires that the United States reduce its budget deficit, that it promotes savings, and that it encourages production of tradable goods and services.

Exchange-market participants understand these relationships and look for compatible developments in U.S. economic policies. If they believe that the United States is attempting to force a dollar depreciation through an inflationary increase in money growth or that the United States is not taking credible steps to reduce its budget deficit, international investors, who have played an important role in helping finance U.S. credit demands, could shift rapidly out of dollars into assets denominated in other currencies. Under such circumstances, no amount of exchange-market intervention could supplant appropriate monetary or fiscal policies.

If, on the other hand, monetary and fiscal policy are consistent with a reduction in the trade deficit and an orderly depreciation of the dollar, then intervention can play a useful role in reinforcing the intention of policy should market uncertainty arise. Policymakers should clearly state the objectives of such policies. Under these circumstances, monetary and fiscal policies will help minimize market uncertainty and, hence, the need for intervention.

12. See Humpage, Owen F. "Should We Be Concerned About the Speed of the Depreciation?" *Economic Commentary,* Federal Reserve Bank of Cleveland, March 15, 1986.

Part Seven

Financial Innovation

Without question the financial markets have been more exciting and more stressful places in which to work in recent years. New financial services and new variations on such traditional financial services as deposits and loans have opened up a broad menu of products offered to business and household customers. The list of these new services is already long, and growing daily. Examples include home-equity loans, securitized assets, stock-index futures, standby credit letters, and the net-working of credit and debit cards to serve customers regardless of where they may travel.

The *consequences* of this trend toward service innovation are both positive and negative. The *positive* aspects seem to lie where economists argue they should be found—with the financial-services customer. The customer is offered a wider array of financial services, which increases the probability that he or she will find service offerings that fit exactly a particular need. Moreover, deregulation and increased competition have encouraged financial firms to listen more carefully to their customers in designing new services.

The *negative* consequences of today's drive toward financial and technological innovation seem to lie mainly with those who work in the financial-services industry or who invest in financial firms. The development and introduction of new services and new service delivery systems sharply increases operating and financial risk. Some new services and service delivery systems will turn out to be little more than "trial balloons," drifting about looking for a favorable public reception and collapsing when they find none. And, the financial institutions marketing those services may fail as well due to unrecovered costs. Indeed, failure rates of financial institutions have climbed dramatically in recent years to the highest levels since the Great Depression of the 1930s.

The articles in this section deal with some of the most important financial-service innovations of recent years. For example, the first article, by John J. Merrick, Jr., of the Federal Reserve Bank of Philadelphia, examines the use of stock-index futures contracts traded on major securities exchanges. He points out in "Fact and Fantasy about Stock Index Future Program Trading" that, contrary to popular opinion, these contracts calling for the future delivery of cash depending on changes in the value of a stock index were designed to help investors *reduce* the risk of loss from changing stock prices. Nevertheless, trading in stock-index futures was widely blamed for the stock market crash in October 1987. Merrick argues, however, that arbitrage ("program trading") between stocks and stock-index futures tends to increase market liquidity and results in fairer pricing of securities.

A related innovation that first appeared in 1987 is the *market-index deposit*—a CD or time deposit sold by a bank, savings and loan, or other institution, whose return is linked in some way to stock price movements. Index CDs were developed in the 1980s to attract investors away from a soaring stock market. Economists Stephen King and Eli M. Remolona examine the methods and pitfalls involved in pricing this new breed of deposit instruments. Of special concern is the possibility of a sharp increase in risk exposure for depository institutions issuing such deposits. This innovation may have to wait awhile before winning a strong customer following, however. Many of the stock-index deposit programs were shut down after the stock market crash of October 1987.

Governments can have a profound impact on the speed and type of financial innovation. No better example exists today than the *home-equity loan*—a loan line of credit that is supported by pledging the borrower's home as collateral. Home-equity loans increased dramatically in importance after the U.S. Congress, in the 1986 Tax Reform Act, called for phasing out the tax deductibility of interest owed on consumer credit unless such loans were secured by residential property. Many banks and other lending institutions rushed in to offer home-secured loans and take advantage of their tax-deductibility feature. And many household customers liked the idea of using the accumulated equity value in their homes to fund nonhousing-related expenditures, such as a college education. Unfortunately, as Randall Pozdena, assistant vice president at the Federal Reserve Bank of San Francisco, observes in "Home Equity Lending: Boon or Bane?" there are some pitfalls with these loans that both lenders and their borrowing customers must understand and deal with.

Increasingly intense competition for loanable funds among banks, savings associations, and thousands of other credit-granting institutions in recent years has set in motion a search for new ways to raise funds. One relatively new source of loanable funds is *securitization*—the pooling of assets held by a financial institution and the selling of shares of participation in the income generated by that asset pool. An investor buying such a share receives both the interest payments earned by the asset pool and any repayments of principal that occur. Christine Cumming, writing for the Federal Reserve Bank of New York, looks at the causes behind the rapid growth of securitization in recent years. In "The Economics of Securitization" she finds that sluggish growth of traditional funds sources (such as deposits), greater demands for liquidity, and better risk-management techniques all have played major roles in the trend toward securitization.

As popular as securitization is today, investors in securitized assets must be aware of the risks associated with these new financial instruments. Writing for the Federal Reserve Bank of Kansas City, senior economist Sean Becketti explains that the use of pools of home mortgages as collateral for securitizations exposes investors to a new kind of risk—*prepayment risk*, the danger that some home mortgage loans may be paid off earlier than expected, while others may take much longer than average to pay out. Either way, the investor may lose some of his or her expected return, particularly if interest rates have fallen and the funds returned to the investor from early payouts of loans must then be reinvested at lower interest rates. Becketti's article, "The Prepayment Risk of Mortgage-backed Securities," explores both the causes and the possible consequences of this form of investment risk.

Finally, Barbara Bennett of the Federal Reserve Bank of San Francisco examines the pressing issue of risk-exposure to banks and other depository institutions from the growth of *contingent* obligations. Her particular focus is on *standby letters of credit* (SLCs), agreements by a bank to provide funds if a customer cannot pay off a loan previously taken out. In "Off Balance Sheet Risk in Banking: The Case of Standby Letters of Credit," economist Bennett points out that contingent obligations can come home to hurt the originating financial institution if business bankruptcies begin to rise or if interest rates move in an unexpected direction. She suggests that bank regulatory authorities must devise ways to insure that banks hold enough capital to fully support the risks inherent in standby credit letters.

Article 33

Fact and Fantasy About Stock Index Futures Program Trading

*John J. Merrick, Jr.**

INTRODUCTION

Exchange-traded stock index futures contracts** have been among the most important financial innovations of the 1980s. With these products, investors can adjust the exposure of their portfolio to fluctuations in the average level of stock prices quickly and cheaply. This capability is extremely attractive to pension fund managers and other institutional investors. In

fact, in less time than the typical reader will take to read this article, he or she could buy an index futures contract, change opinion on the market and sell it off, and, upon further reflection, revise opinion once again and buy it back.

Trading in these futures contracts has grown enormously since their introduction in the early 1980s. During fiscal 1986, the dollar value of the Standard and Poor's (S&P) 500 stock index** futures contracts that traded hands was about 60 percent greater than the value of actual stock trading on the floor of the New York Stock Exchange. The four major stock index futures contracts are the Chicago Mercantile Exchange's S&P500 index contract (by far the most active), the New York Futures Exchange's New York

* John Merrick, Associate Professor of Finance, New York University Graduate School of Business Administration, prepared this article while he was a Visiting Scholar in the Macroeconomics Section of the Philadelphia Fed's Research Department.
**See the Glossary (pp. 24-25) for a definition of this and other terms with ** throughout the text.

Stock Exchange Composite** index contract, the Kansas City Board of Trade's Value Line** index contract, and the Chicago Board of Trade's Major Market** index contract.[1]

Perhaps because of the astounding growth in these index futures markets, traders, investors, and the financial press have made much ado about their possible adverse effects. In particular, the impact of program trading** between index futures and cash market** stocks by arbitragers** has become a hot contract design and market regulation issue. The concern centers on whether program trading has increased price volatility** in the cash stock markets. Excess price volatility is undesirable because investors may have to buy stocks at artificially high prices or sell them at artificially depressed prices, thus creating windfall gains and losses in a market where the gains and losses from the "fundamentals" are variable enough.[2]

As it turns out, the adverse impacts of arbitrage program trading probably have been overblown. It is true that, during the so-called "Triple Witching Days" that occur four times a year when the major stock index futures contracts expire, program trading magnifies stock market price volatility. However, in more normal circumstances, available evidence indicates that such trading has had no significant impact on volatility.

Moreover, the arbitrage process underlying program trading provides important benefits to investors, through both enhancing the liquidity** of futures trading and ensuring fairer relative pricing between stock and stock index futures markets. In conjunction with attempts to lessen the pricing distortions that occur when index futures expire, the exchanges and their regulators should avoid inhibiting overall activity in the arbitrage sector.

---

[1]*Options* on stock indexes and options on stock index futures also have attracted large trading interest. In fact, today, the most actively traded options are the Chicago Board Options Exchange's S&P100 stock index option contracts.

[2]Excess stock price volatility is also undesirable since it decreases the informational content of prices.

INDEX FUTURES CONTRACTS AND THEIR MARKETS

A futures contract is a standardized agreement to buy or sell a particular asset or commodity at some deferred date.[3] The underlying "asset" for a stock index futures contract is a specific price index of cash market stocks. For example, the S&P500 stock index futures contract is based upon the S&P500 index of stock prices, a weighted average of the prices of all 500 stocks comprising Standard and Poor's list.[4] (Each S&P500 index futures contract represented about $145,000 of stock market value as of May 1987.) Stock index futures contracts cover only four expiration months a year—March, June, September and December. Thus, in May 1987, the June 1987 expiration contract was the "near" contract. The nearest expiration contract tends to be the most actively traded of all contracts up to a short time prior to its expiration day.

Traditional futures contracts, such as those for gold or Treasury bills, allow final settlement by delivery of the underlying assets. In stock index futures, actual physical securities (the individual stocks themselves) are not involved. Instead, stock index futures make their final settlement through a cash payment. For example, on each third Friday of the months of March, June, September and December, the nearest S&P500 index contract expires. At the expiration moment, the contract is assigned a value based upon the current value of the underlying cash market index. The net gain or loss on an index futures position depends upon the change in the futures price between the time when the contract is entered initially and the date it expires

---

[3]For a short introductory guide to financial futures markets, see John J. Merrick, Jr. and Stephen Figlewski, "An Introduction to Financial Futures Markets," *Occasional Papers in Business and Finance*, Salomon Brothers Center for the Study of Financial Institutions, No. 6 (August 1984).

[4]The weight for each individual stock price in the index is the ratio of the total dollar value of all outstanding shares of the stock to the total dollar value of all 500 stocks in the index (that is, each stock price in the index is "capitalization-weighted").

or the position is offset**. (Most users of futures will close their futures contract position out prior to expiration through a reversing trade—for example, selling another contract to offset one previously bought.)

The terms of the S&P500 index futures contract are that each one point move in the futures price is worth $500. For example, a rise in an S&P500 index futures contract's price from 290 to 291 would entail a gain of $500 to investors who were long** the contract (that is, those who had bought) and an equivalent loss to those who were short** (that is, those who had sold). The final cash settlement feature of the stock index futures contract is designed to avoid the costs and inconvenience of final settlement through physical delivery which, in the case of the S&P500 contract, would involve the purchase, delivery and (probably) resale of the properly weighted basket of 500 individual stocks.

Stock Index Futures Lower Portfolio Management Costs. Investors find stock index futures useful because they are a convenient and relatively low-cost way to speculate on future movements in the stock market or to hedge the market risk of a stock portfolio. Speculators who are confident in their ability to predict swings in stock prices find long or short index futures positions convenient ways to take on desired market risk exposure. Other, perhaps less confident, investors enter index futures positions designed to hedge their current cash market positions. For example, if the hedger is holding a cash market portfolio of stocks (that is, if he is long cash stocks), he will sell a properly weighted number of stock index futures contracts to reduce his net market risk exposure.[5] The hedge works to reduce total return risk since a loss (gain) from a fall (rise) in cash market stock prices will be at least partially offset by a gain (loss) from

the short futures position as long as futures prices move in the same direction taken by cash prices.

Of course, investors could speculate or hedge their risks without resorting to futures market transactions. The would-be bullish speculator could simply buy a broad portfolio of stocks (or shares in a mutual fund). The would-be hedger could simply sell out the stock portfolio and invest the proceeds in Treasury bills until a less uncertain environment prevailed. However, executing these strategies in the cash market can be cumbersome. The speculator would be hampered because only 50 percent of a stock position can be financed by margin loans. Similarly, the hedger who sold off the stock portfolio would bear not only the direct costs of selling these stocks, but also the costs of reconstructing the perhaps painstakingly acquired initial position at the onset of more favorable market conditions.

While transactions in standardized index-based futures contracts also entail margin requirements and direct trading costs, these are substantially lower than those for the cash market. For example, the direct commission cost of a "round-trip" purchase and sale of 100 S&P500 index futures contracts is about $2,500. Assuming commission costs in the cash market of $.07 per share and an average share price of $45, the cost of buying and then selling an equivalent amount of stocks (roughly $14.5 million in May 1987) would be about $45,100. Thus, stock index futures contract purchases and sales provide large investors with cost-efficient means of making desired portfolio adjustments and are properly viewed as institutional solutions to trading problems.

INDEX FUTURES ARBITRAGE: LINKING CASH AND FUTURES MARKETS

Index Futures Prices Versus the Cash Index. Since an index futures contract is a close substitute for the basket of stocks underlying the cash market index for many users, one might expect the index futures price to be closely related to the cash index. Certainly the tie between the

---

[5]A thorough practical treatment of hedging using financial futures markets is contained in *Hedging with Financial Futures for Institutional Investors*, by Stephen Figlewski with Kose John and John J. Merrick, Jr. (Cambridge, MA: Ballinger Publishing Company, 1985).

futures price and the cash index value is tight on the contract's expiration day when, by the contract's design, the two are equal. However, prior to expiration day, the potential user of the futures should "comparison shop" to see whether the contract is overpriced or underpriced relative to the prices of the stocks in the cash market. For example, is it cheaper to buy a one-year-to-maturity S&P500 futures contract at 300 or the underlying portfolio of stocks if the cash S&P500 index stands at 286? Clearly, the futures should usually sell for more than the cash index since, while both futures and cash indexes converge within a year, there is a net cost to carrying** the stock portfolio (financing costs less dividends earned).[6] However, is 300 too high or too low?

As it happens, answering the question of fair relative pricing between futures and cash markets also explains how arbitragers make money by trading between the two markets following what are called "program trading" rules. While comparison shopping by hedgers and speculators puts some limits on potentially abnormal deviations of index futures prices from their cost-of-carry values, most of the responsibility for maintaining fair pricing between the futures and cash markets falls on "program traders"—members of the arbitrage community who have come to specialize in intermarket trading. Program traders attempt to extract profits from any discrepancy that arises between the futures contract's price and its cost-of-carry value, following the old adage "buy cheap, sell dear." That is, they buy (or sell) index contracts in the futures market and sell (or buy) the equivalent value of the actual stocks in the cash market.

Cost-of-Carry Pricing and Arbitrage. The theoretical difference between the initial futures price and the initial index value is solely determined by the difference between the stock portfolio's financing cost and its dividend yield.** For example, suppose that the S&P500 stock index currently is 286; that the dividend yield on the underlying cash market S&P500 stock portfolio is 3.2 percent; that the one-year interest rate is 7.1 percent; and that transactions costs can be ignored. In this case, the net cost of carry equals 3.9 percent—the 7.1 percent financing rate less a 3.2 percent dividend yield. The cost-of-carry pricing argument would maintain that a one-year-to-expiration S&P500 index futures contract should sell for 297.15 index points, or 3.9 percent above the current cash index value.

To see why this pricing structure makes sense, consider what happens when an arbitrager purchases the stocks and sells the futures. He is assured of making the current futures-cash index spread** (297.15-286 = 11.15 index points) via convergence *regardless* of whether the year-end level of the index is higher, equal to, or lower than its current level. For example, if the expiration day closing index value is 300, the cash position gains 14 points (300-286) and the short futures position loses 2.85 (297.15-300) for a net gain of 11.15. If, instead, the index closes out at 275, the cash position loses 11 points (275-286), but the futures position gains 22.15 (297.15-275) to again net a gain of 11.15. "Convergence" ensures that the initial 11.15 point spread between the futures and the cash index (297.15-286) is earned. This position also will earn 9.15 points in dividends (.032x286 = 9.15). Thus, total gross earnings for this riskless investment will be 20.3 index points. However, this gross profit is exactly what the initial capital would return if it were invested at the current interest rate of 7.1 percent (.071x286 = 20.3).

The futures price of 297.15 is fair relative to the current cash index value precisely because the "program" of buying cash stocks and selling index futures is a perfectly hedged position. If the futures were selling at 298 instead, this riskless buy/sell program would gross 21.15 points (yielding 100x21.15/286 = 7.40 percent). Such a program would dominate the simple 7.1 percent riskless investment. Thus, this particular program trade by arbitragers, or other investors seeking to swap the riskless cash/futures program

---

[6]The futures position entails no meaningful initial investment but accrues no dividends.

for a "plain vanilla" riskless investment (say, a Treasury bill) whenever rate of return discrepancies arise, would drive the futures price down (and/or the cash price up) if the futures rose above 297.15. Likewise, if the futures price fell below 297.15, arbitragers would profit from the *reverse* trade of selling the stock basket and buying the underpriced futures. Again, the result would be pressure on both cash and futures prices to return to their fair relative values.

These calculations ignore transactions costs. Typically, the largest players in index futures program trading are the major stock brokerage houses. These firms already have invested in developing economical systems for trading stocks. For a S&P500 index futures program trade by a major brokerage house arbitrager, total transactions costs might be reasonably approximated as 0.5 percent of the S&P500 cash index (or, 1.43 index points in the example above).[7] Thus, the futures price actually could wander anywhere within a band between 298.58 and 295.72 without violating fair pricing boundaries.[8] Certainly, the proposed price of 300 that began this discussion is too high in this sense. However, some hedgers and speculators would still find the futures an attractive buy at 300 if their cash market trading costs were relatively high (greater than 2.85 index points), or if it were important to avoid delay in executing the trade.

In sum, deviations from cost-of-carry pricing that cannot be attributed to transactions costs present signals for arbitragers to buy cheap and sell dear. These program traders enter both a position in index futures contracts and an offsetting position in an appropriately selected basket of stocks. The basket is constructed in such a way that movements in its value mirror movements in the stock index upon which the futures contract is based. The position is designed to deliver a "riskless" hedged return that yields more than alternative riskless securities.[9] The arbitrage process should continue until the futures and cash stock markets have returned to a fair relative pricing relation.

The Economic Role of Arbitragers. As explained above, arbitragers seek to profit from misaligned relative prices. This last statement might be construed as an academic way of stating that "these people make easy money at the expense of true investors." However, such an interpretation would be misleading. First, the arbitrage process itself is costly. Arbitrage firms must invest heavily in communication, trade evaluation, and trade execution systems. Second, the trades themselves are not completely riskless. Risk enters because of the marked-to-market** daily settlement feature of futures, because of restrictions on short sales of stocks, and because the stock baskets assembled by the arbitrager do not always track the stock index perfectly.[10]

But most importantly, it can be argued that arbitragers actually help true investors. By working to bring about cost-of-carry pricing, arbitragers allow speculators and hedgers to

---

[7]See Hans Stoll and Robert Whaley, "Expiration-Day Effects of Index Options and Futures," *Monograph Series in Finance and Economics,* Salomon Brothers Center for the Study of Financial Institutions, New York University (1986).

[8]This 0.5 percent or 1.43 index point transactions cost estimate overstates the average transactions costs incurred by active arbitragers who constantly look either to unwind their positions early at a reversed mispricing or to roll their hedges into the next contract expiration at a more favorable price spread. These arbitragers receive additional arbitrage profits without incurring the full set of additional transactions costs. Thus, some aggressive players might choose to be active even at futures prices that lie within the transactions costs bounds described. One active arbitrager estimates his average transactions cost at about one S&P500 index point.

[9]The hedge underlying intermarket arbitrage trading can also be constructed by combining the cash market stocks with index option positions. Thus, arbitragers will use both options and futures programs depending upon which hedge yields the highest riskless return.

[10]Gains and losses from futures price changes are settled in cash at the end of each day by means of marked-to-market settlement. Therefore, losses on futures contracts are not "paper losses," but entail real cash outlays even when the position has not yet been closed. Likewise, gains on futures positions entail immediate cash inflows. Short sales of stock refer to sales of stock temporarily borrowed from other investors.

open and close futures positions at prices that are fairer relative to the underlying cash market than those they would have obtained without arbitrage trade price pressures.[11] Thus, arbitragers help reduce some of the uncertainty that users of futures markets bear. Furthermore, arbitrage trading adds to market liquidity. Additional liquidity in a market benefits all market users. In particular, it lowers total transactions costs by shrinking the bid-ask spread** and allows larger orders to be placed with shorter time delay.

One useful way to view the contribution of arbitragers concerns the sequence of events surrounding the decision of a previously bullish portfolio manager to turn bearish on the stock market. However, assume that the portfolio manager still believes that his individual stock "picks" will outperform the market over time.[12] Consequently, he keeps his portfolio intact, but sells S&P500 futures contracts of equivalent value to hedge his position against market risk. Since no sell order on the cash side is entered, only the futures market is initially affected by the portfolio manager's change of heart: In order to find buyers to absorb this new futures contract sell order, the index futures price is nudged down a bit.

If prices were initially in their fair cost-of-carry relation, now they are slightly misaligned (futures are cheap relative to cash). This is the signal for the arbitrager to act. He buys the underpriced futures contract and sells a basket of stocks carefully selected to mimic the value change of the S&P500 index.[13] The arbitrager's orders put some upward pressure on the index futures price and (at last) downward pressure on the prices of the stocks comprising his basket.

The net effect of the portfolio manager's shift to bearish sentiments is to lower both futures *and* cash stock prices. In effect, the portfolio manager made the sell decision, but delegated responsibility for the actual stock market sales to the arbitrager. The "fee" collected by the arbitrager consists of the spread implicit in the initially underpriced futures. The portfolio manager was willing to pay this fee (that is, sell the futures at less than full cost-of-carry) because the implied transactions costs of accepting this "low" futures price were lower than his direct transactions costs of selling out and then subsequently rebuilding his cash stock portfolio. Also, the futures sale is accomplished almost immediately, whereas the liquidation of a large portfolio might take some time.

Through implicitly delegating his cash market sales to the arbitrager, the portfolio manager shifts the burden of selling a large complex stock portfolio to an agent who has come to specialize in such sales (or purchases). Thus, one can interpret the advent of stock index futures arbitragers as a response to the institutional investor's desire to develop low-cost ways to acquire or liquidate large portfolio holdings. In fact, the term "program trading" as applied to futures/cash arbitragers makes perfect sense in this regard, since investment houses servicing large-scale portfolio restructurings for institutional investors traditionally referred to their services as "doing a program" long before the advent of index futures trading. For the case of arbitrage in futures, however, the stock portfolio involved is always the index-based basket or a reasonable facsimile.

ARBITRAGE EFFECTS ON THE CASH STOCK MARKET

The Historical Evidence. Data on the volume of futures contracts give us a clear picture of how active these instruments are and how actively

---

[11]See John J. Merrick, Jr., "Hedging With Mispriced Futures," Federal Reserve Bank of Philadelphia Working Paper No. 87-11, June 1987 for an analysis of the interrelationships between arbitrage sector performance and hedging cost and effectiveness.

[12]That is, he thinks that the portfolio will lose less than the S&P500 in bear markets and gain more than this index in bull markets.

[13]The arbitrager may accomplish the stock sale half of the position either by selling out of his firm's preexisting inventory (a swap) or by short sales.

arbitragers have been involved with them. Between 1983 and 1986, while the dollar volume of stocks traded on the cash markets of the New York Stock Exchange broke records, the dollar volume of S&P500 futures contracts rose even higher (see Figure 1a, FUTURES CONTRACTS SOAR . . .). Arbitrage activity can be inferred from looking at the growth in the number of contracts settled in cash on expiration day. Market participants other than arbitragers, who use futures contracts to hedge their portfolios or to speculate, are less inclined to hold expiration-month contracts to their final settlement day. Instead, these traders typically would roll their contract positions over to maintain their hedge or open speculative position. Between 1983 and 1986, the volume of contracts settled in cash (presumably by arbitragers) more than quin-tupled, from about 6,000 to almost 33,000. In addition, the relative importance of arbitragers has increased. The increased presence of arbi-tragers can be inferred by comparing the growth in the number of contracts settled in cash relative to the growth of the average month-end open interest** (see Figure 1b, . . . AND ARBITRAGE ACTIVITY GROWS, TOO). Over this time per-iod, the proportion of cash-settled contracts rose from about 28 percent to 38 percent of average month-end open interest.

Deviations From Cost-of-Carry Pricing. Fig-ure 2 (p. 20) presents a plot of the percentage deviation of the actual daily closing prices for near expiration S&P500 index futures contracts from their theoretical cost-of-carry levels for the May 17, 1982 to May 30, 1986 period. It is clear that while most of the deviations are within the 0.5 percent transaction cost bounds (shown as a shaded band), there have been instances in which such deviations were large and persistent. For example, the futures was grossly overpriced throughout the month of October 1984. In the 1985-86 period, however, instances of mis-pricings in excess of transactions costs are less frequent than·in the earlier 1982-84 period,

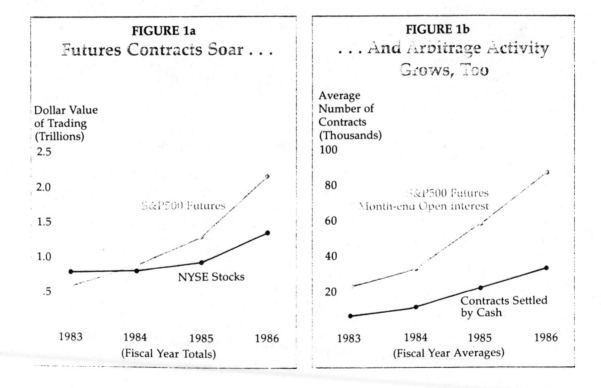

FIGURE 1a
Futures Contracts Soar . . .

Dollar Value of Trading (Trillions)

S&P500 Futures

NYSE Stocks

1983   1984   1985   1986
(Fiscal Year Totals)

FIGURE 1b
. . . And Arbitrage Activity Grows, Too

Average Number of Contracts (Thousands)

S&P500 Futures Month-end Open Interest

Contracts Settled by Cash

1983   1984   1985   1986
(Fiscal Year Averages)

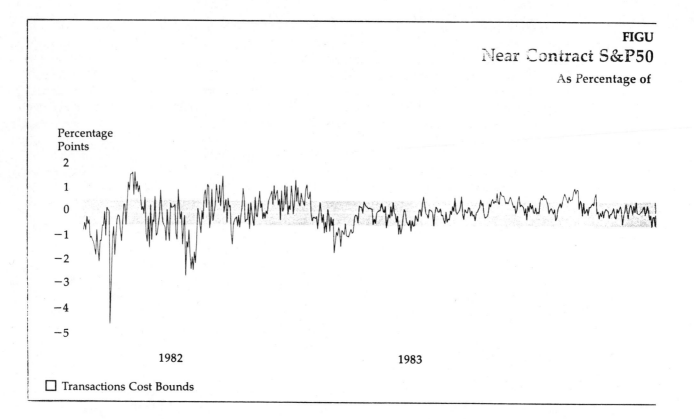

Percentage
Points

☐ Transactions Cost Bounds

probably because of the marked expansion of the arbitrage sector during the later years.

Volume, Volatility, and the Arbitrage Deviation. It's natural to ask why mispricing might ever arise in the face of expanded arbitrage trading activity. While it is certainly true that index futures arbitrage programs pour millions of dollars into these trades, arbitragers apparently are not always able to bring prices back into their cost-of-carry relation quickly. Thus, one might be suspicious of at least some of the charges linking volume and price volatility effects to arbitrage activity.

In fact, looking at daily data for non-expiration months over the 1982-1986 period, recent research has uncovered virtually no evidence that arbitrage mispricings predict any significant percentage of the variation in daily return volatility (for both S&P500 and NYSE cash indexes). There *is* evidence linking futures/cash arbitrage mispricings to increased NYSE cash market trading volume. Such effects have become more pronounced in the recent 1985-1986 period. However, fluctuations in trading volume are more highly correlated with return volatility than with arbitrage mispricings.[14] In addition, there is stronger evidence that fluctuations in trading volume and return volatility portend larger arbitrage mispricings than vice versa.

The evidence that the volume effects of arbitrage trading have become more important recently does not necessarily make arbitragers the ultimate source of cash stock price movements. Certainly arbitragers cause pressures on

[14]See John J. Merrick, Jr., "Volume Determination in Stock and Stock Index Futures Markets: An Analysis of Volume and Volatility Effects," Federal Reserve Bank of Philadelphia Working Paper No. 87-2, January 1987 (forthcoming in *The Journal of Futures Markets*, October 1987).

RE 2

0 Futures Mispricing

Theoretical Value

1984   1985   1986

Daily Data: 5/17/82 — 5/30/86

cash market prices. However, such price pressures generated by arbitrage trading only bring the cash market in line with the valuation reflected by the previous movement in the futures. For instance, suppose that, as in the earlier "bearish portfolio manager" example, the futures shifts down suddenly from an initial full cost-of-carry equilibrium and becomes underpriced relative to the cash index. Suppose further that, as the prices become realigned through arbitrage activity, cash prices fall more than futures prices rise. Indeed, while cash market selling by program traders directly leads to the cash index decline, in this instance the cash market fell because of the previous weakness in the futures price. The futures market "discovered" the new bearish sentiments of the investing public.[15] Arbitragers

ensured that this "bad news" was transmitted to the cash markets in individual stocks. While investors holding positions in these stocks need not be pleased, there is no reason to adopt a "kill the messenger" attitude.

"Triple Witching Hour" Congestion Effects. One adverse effect of index futures arbitrage on cash stock markets that *does* receive strong empirical support is the so-called "Triple Witching Hour" congestion. Prior to the June 1987 expirations, the Triple Witching Hour occurred at the 4:00 p.m. close of trading on the New York

---

[15]The available evidence suggests that the S&P500 index futures market has played the dominant price discovery role

(relative to the cash market) since 1985. Prior to 1985, the cash stock market dominated the price discovery process. This reversal in price discovery dominance roles occurred not long after the volume of trading in the futures market eclipsed that in the cash market. For details, see John J. Merrick, Jr., "Price Discovery in the Stock Market," Federal Reserve Bank of Philadelphia Working Paper No. 87-4, March 1987.

Stock Exchange on the quarterly expiration Fridays of the stock index futures contracts. Stock index options and options on individual stocks also have expirations that occur at this time.

Taken at face value, contract expirations would not appear to be such dramatic events. After all, trade in the various commodity and other financial futures contracts has occurred for years, and individual contract expirations have come and gone with very little public attention. However, the cash settlement design of the stock index futures (and index options) contracts presents special problems on expiration days when arbitragers "unwind" their positions.

Recall that arbitragers hold offsetting positions in stocks and index futures. Their return is hedged perfectly if they liquidate their stock basket at the moment the futures contract expires, since the futures price is marked to the value of the cash stock index at that time. Thus, the planned expiration day strategy of the arbitrager was to submit market-on-close** orders to the specialist** on the floor of the exchange trading each stock held in the stock basket.[16] On expiration days that the net (long or short) aggregate stock position of arbitragers was large, order imbalances appeared in each specialist's book at the market's close, which produced unusual temporary price swings in one direction or the other. The imbalance occurs because the index futures are settled in cash, not through *delivery* of the securities. In brief, at market close on expiration day, arbitragers supplied or demanded an abnormal quantity of stocks, but nothing in the futures settlement process provided an automatic mechanism to generate offsetting stock orders to absorb the disturbance.

Congestion effects in the cash markets during the last hour of trading on index futures expiration days have been documented. Specifically, three effects have been found for index component stocks: cash market volume in the last hour of trading is approximately double that of non-expiration Fridays; last-hour cash market return volatility for index component stocks is significantly higher than for non-expiration days; and abnormal price reversals occur on the morning following these quarterly expirations.[17] The symptoms accompanying expiration days have been likened to the temporary cash market distortions of "block" trades in individual stocks.

Since these expiration day effects are so localized, two reactions are defensible. The first would be to live with the problem in its present form, though endeavoring to educate investors concerning the increased uncertainties of trading during these four days of the year. There is some reason to believe that, with proper market education, the expiration day problem would correct itself. Small investors would be wary of trading on expiration days. In contrast, large investors might choose to act strategically, altering their normal behavior to pick up "bargains" through either selling at the temporarily high or buying at the temporarily low cash market prices induced by expiration day price "spikes".[18] Both sets of market responses would tend to ameliorate expiration day pricing distortions.

The second response would be to attempt some fine-tuning of either the design of the

----

[16]Actually, the trigger for the unwinding is related more closely to the return of the futures price to its cost-of-carry relationship. Of course, this return is assured at expiration by the contract's convergence feature. But if a return to cost-of-carry pricing (or an appearance of a reverse mispricing) occurs before the expiration, arbitragers who close out early will earn higher returns than they initially expected. For example, early close-outs were optimal for short futures/long cash positions during the weeks leading up to the September 1986 contract expiration since the previously overpriced September futures became substantially underpriced (in fact, futures were trading at a discount to the cash market stock index).

----

[17]These results are found in Stoll and Whaley, "Expiration-Day Effects of Index Options and Futures." Stoll and Whaley find smaller price and volume effects on days on which index options expire but index futures do not.

[18]Such strategic positioning is not without risks, in that the direction of expiration day congestion price effects is not perfectly predictable.

stock index futures contracts or trading procedures. However, many of the solutions proposed to date have adverse effects on the smooth functioning of the market—especially in diminishing market liquidity—which may outweigh their calculable benefits.[19] One major change effective with the June 1987 contracts for the S&P500 and NYSE index futures is to shift the expiration of these contracts to the cash market's *open* rather than its close. This change should help reduce excess expiration day volatility since it effectively expands the amount of time that NYSE specialists have to assemble large orders to offset any imbalances created by arbitragers. First, arbitragers must submit their market-on-open unwinding orders prior to 9:00 a.m. on expiration day. Second at 9:00 a.m., the New York Stock Exchange will announce any buy or sell order imbalances of 50,000 shares or more in 50 selected "blue chip" stocks. Furthermore, as on any other day, the specialists will be able to advertise unusual excess demand or supply situations by indicating the expected opening price prior to the actual opening of trading. Finally, as on any other day, each specialist will retain the prerogative to delay the opening of trading for stocks faced with unusual pricing patterns. In turn, potential buyers or sellers of the stock, given extra time and more complete information about the nature of net arbitrager activity, should find it easier to

respond to perceived imbalances with offsetting orders.

CONCLUSIONS

"Program trading" based upon stock index futures arbitrage is growing in practical importance. The positive effects of arbitrage trading include increased market liquidity and fairer pricing. Both factors benefit "true investors" (hedgers and speculators). One adverse effect of arbitrage is the temporary distortion in the cash stock markets caused by the unwinding of positions by arbitragers on the days of the quarterly futures contract expirations. However, these distortions are not particularly serious, especially since their effects are so localized.

The evidence that arbitragers distort cash markets on non-expiration days is scant. There is very little evidence that daily cash index return volatility is affected by observed index futures mispricing. In fact, the evidence suggests that the degree of mispricing itself is influenced by fluctuations in volatility.

The periods of persistent mispricing of index futures contracts observed since the beginning of trading in 1982 appear to indicate that the arbitrage sector has historically been under-capitalized or otherwise impeded. Because of these implied imperfections in this sector, futures-cash mispricing inefficiencies tended to persist, and hedgers were forced to bear undesired excess risk on positions closed out prior to contract expiration. Pricing performance by an expanded arbitrage sector has improved in recent years. For this reason, as they grapple with the expiration-day congestion issue, futures exchanges and their regulators should ensure that any possible contract redesign or other trading change does not hamper the arbitrage sector in a manner that will eliminate the recent gains in contract pricing efficiency.

---

[19]These anti-congestion proposals include (1) altering the cash settlement procedure on the index futures contract, (2) telescoping of position limits on the futures, (3) restricting expiration day market orders, and (4) requiring early disclosures of expiration day futures and options positions by large traders (the Securities and Exchange Commission sponsored a 3:30 p.m. expiration day stock position disclosure policy which came into effect as of the September 1986 expiration). See Franklin R. Edwards, "Stock Index Futures and Stock Market Volatility: Evidence and Implications," *Commodities Law Letter*, 6 (November/December 1986) pp. 3-6, and Stoll and Whaley for discussion.

Arbitrage   A strategy designed to create riskless profits through taking matched opposite positions in two investments that have identical payoffs but are trading at different prices.

Bid-ask spread   The difference between the price currently bid on the exchange floor for the purchase of a stock (or futures contract) and the price currently asked for the sale of that same stock. "Market" orders to buy a stock will be transacted at the asked price. "Market" orders to sell a stock will be transacted at the bid price.

Cash market   The market for (immediate) exchange of title of a security or other asset for cash.

Dividend yield   The dividend income accruing to, say, a portfolio of stocks expressed as a fraction of the stock or portfolio value.

Futures contract   A standardized agreement to buy or sell a particular asset or commodity at some deferred date.

Liquidity   The continuity of the order flow and therefore the orderliness of price changes in an asset market. Other things held constant, a market's liquidity rises with its size.

Long position   The position created through the purchase of a contract.

Marked-to-market settlement   The procedure by which all open accounts are debited or credited the cash amount of the change in contract value due to the daily change in the futures price.

Major Market index   An equally-weighted index of 20 "blue-chip" stocks which tends to track the popular Dow Jones Industrial Average.

Market-on-close order   Order placed with the specialist to buy or sell the stock at the market asked or bid price at the 4:00 p.m. close of trading. This type of order was particularly attractive to program traders who want to unwind their cash stock positions at the futures expiration.

Net cost-of-carry   The difference between the financing cost and the productive yield of a cash market position over the period ending with the future's expiration date.

New York Stock Exchange Composite index   A capitalization-weighted index of the prices of all stocks traded on the New York Stock Exchange.

Open interest   The number of contracts entered but as yet neither offset nor otherwise satisfied by a final settlement such as delivery.

Option contract   A contract that gives the right but not the obligation to buy an asset (a "call" option) or sell an asset (a "put" option) at a fixed price on or before a specified expiration date.

Position offset   An equal and opposite ("reversing") transaction to counteract a previously established position. For example, a sale of a June futures contract on May 15 to close out a position established previously by an April 25 purchase of a June futures contract.

Program trading   The popular name given to arbitrage trading between the stock index futures market and the cash market in stocks.

S&P500 index   An index number that relates the current value of a weighted average of the prices of the stocks that comprise Standard and Poor's list of 500 stocks to that of a historical base period.

Short position   The position created through the sale of a futures contract or the sale of borrowed stock.

Specialist   The marketmaker—price setter and order flow matcher—for a stock in the New York Stock Exchange system for stock trading.

Spread   The difference between the prices of two assets.

Transactions costs   Costs of executing a trading strategy. For the program trader, these costs consist of commissions and the bid-ask spread on the cash stock side and the commission and one-half of the bid-ask spread on the futures side.

Value Line composite index   A geometric average of 1,700 stock prices. It is the broadest of the four indexes on which actively traded futures contracts are based. This stock index places relatively more weight on smaller stocks than the other major indexes.

Volatility   A measure of the dispersion of possible percentage price changes about their mean value.

Article 34

The Pricing and Hedging of Market Index Deposits

Commercial banks and other financial institutions are currently devising new ways of tailoring their debt instruments to the portfolio needs of their customers. A recent innovation has been deposits with returns linked not to market interest rates but to the performance of indexes or prices in markets other than those for fixed-income instruments. These market index deposits (MIDs) offer a specified portion of any gain in a market index and guarantee a minimum return. Two U.S. banks have recently begun to issue MIDs: Chase Manhattan has deposits linked to the S&P 500 Index and Wells Fargo has deposits linked to the price of gold. This article explains the pricing of such deposits and the means by which risks to the issuing banks can be controlled by hedging.

The new deposits are similar to index and gold warrants issued in the international bond market. These warrants, however, have been available only to large investors. A few mutual funds also provide returns linked to gains in the S&P 500 and offer a floor on the value of shares. In addition, a major investment bank offers a menu of short-term instruments, called PIPs,[1] allowing investors to choose from various combinations of minimum returns and links to foreign currencies and interest rates, equity indexes, and commodities prices. MIDs differ from these other instruments in that they are both available in retail denominations and carry FDIC insurance.[2] While the focus of this paper is on banks issuing MIDs, the analysis also applies to other institutions offering instruments with characteristics of options.

Our analysis suggests that, barring a severe market downturn, banks can offer MIDs without exposing themselves to excessive risk. In principle, they can price and hedge these deposits so that they cost no more than conventional deposits regardless of market performance. To hedge, banks need only purchase the appropriate options, which provide a payoff matching that of an MID. When the right options are unavailable, as is frequently the case in practice, banks may construct synthetic ones. The strategy of hedging with synthetic options, however, has yet to be tested by an extreme market move.

We first outline the hedging of a prototypical MID and the pattern of returns that can be generated by such a deposit. A central choice that the bank must make is to determine the proportion of increases in the index that it will pass on to depositors. We show that the issuing bank faces a trade-off between the maturity, guaranteed minimum return, and proportion of index gain that it can offer at any given cost. We illustrate this trade-off for the case of a deposit linked to the S&P 500. This trade-off will not remain constant over time, and we next demonstrate the extent to which market fluctuations would have affected the terms of a hypothetical MID between July 1983 and June 1987.

We also show the return that a depositor would have

---

[1]These are described in *Performance-Indexed Paper: An Indexed Money Market Instrument*, by Rajiv Nanda and James Callahan, Salomon Brothers, July 1987.

[2]The minimum for the Chase index deposit is $1,000 and for the Wells Fargo gold deposit, $2,500. Even the "retail" currency

Footnote 2 continued
warrants that Citicorp has recently issued can be exercised only in lots of about $7,000 each, compared to the $55 to $80 value of the option embedded in a one-year $1,000 MID that guarantees only principal.

received over that period from an efficiently priced MID linked to the S&P 500. We contrast this return with the yield that would have been obtained from an investment in an index fund (i.e. one whose performance equals that of the S&P 500) and with an investment in a conventional bank certificate of deposit (CD). Our analysis demonstrates that investors in an MID would have realized returns that were generally between those obtained on a conventional CD and those obtained in the stock market, and with risk characteristics that also fell between these two alternative investments.

We then discuss in greater detail appropriate hedging strategies for the issuing bank. Because the strategies proposed do not perfectly hedge the bank's exposure, we assess the risks to the hedging strategy that might result from unanticipated jumps in the market index. We suggest that the risks to any bank that offers such a deposit can be attenuated *provided the bank is able to execute its hedging strategy.*

Pricing the deposit

An MID will pay at maturity either (1) a guaranteed minimum return, or (2) a fixed proportion of any gain in the market index over the life of the deposit, whichever is greater. The guaranteed return may be positive, zero, or even negative.[3] We call the fixed proportion of market gain the "upside capture."[4] If the MID is efficiently priced and hedged, it will offer terms that will cost the bank neither more nor less than alternative sources of funds of the same maturity.[5]

If a bank were to offer such a deposit without hedging it, then the cost of the deposit would be unknown at the time the bank issued it. Only when the deposit matured, and the value of the market index became known, would the bank know its cost. If the market were to remain constant or fall, the cost of the deposit would be simply the guaranteed minimum return. If the index were to rise, however, the cost could exceed the guaranteed return and, in principle, rise without limit. A bank could reduce the uncertainty about its cost of funds by hedging its exposure to such risk.

The bank could protect itself against a large increase in the index over the life of the deposit by purchasing call options on the index that expire at the same time as the deposit.[6] The calls would have a strike price corresponding to the guaranteed return on the MID. In the case of an MID that guarantees only principal, for example, the strike price would be equal to the initial index value.[7] The payoff on an index option depends only on the value of the index when the option is exercised and is independent of the previous movements of the index. Since the return on an MID similarly depends only on the value of the index at maturity, an option is the ideal hedge instrument. When the appropriate options are difficult to obtain, it may be cheaper for the bank to construct synthetic options by using other financial instruments, such as futures, sometimes in combination with purchased options. We discuss this technique, known as "dynamic hedging," below and in Appendix 1.[8] The price of an option or the cost of a synthetic one will be determined primarily by market volatility, short-term interest rates, and the option's expiration date.

For the deposit to be efficiently priced, the cost of calls purchased must be equal in present value to the potential interest payments saved—specifically, the differential between the conventional CD rate and the guaranteed minimum return on the MID. The size of this differential therefore determines the amount that the bank can profitably invest in options to hedge its deposit. The number of options the bank can purchase in turn determines the amount of upside capture it can profitably offer depositors. The upside capture will therefore depend negatively on both the guaranteed return and the price of a call option.[9]

Suppose a bank wishes to raise $1000 in one-year funds by issuing either a 6 percent one-year CD or a one-year MID with a guarantee of principal only, that is, with zero guaranteed interest. The present value of the interest payment on the conventional CD would be $56.60 ($60/(1.06)). For the same cost, the bank could offer an MID and hedge by purchasing $56.60 worth of calls with a strike price equal to the current index value. If the price of one such "at-the-money" call were $113.20 per $1,000 of the underlying asset, the

[3]By guaranteeing a floor on the return that the depositor will receive, the bank is effectively offering its depositors "portfolio insurance." Portfolio insurance is discussed in Mark Rubinstein, "Alternative Paths to Portfolio Insurance," *Financial Analysts Journal*, July/August 1985, pp. 42-55.

[4]Upside capture is sometimes called the "participation rate."

[5]More precisely, the bank should equate marginal costs across all funding sources of any given maturity. For example, the marginal cost of 6-month funds from an MID should be the same as that of 6 month funds from any other source.

[6]A call option confers on its purchaser the right, but not the obligation, to purchase at the strike price the underlying index. Settlement of an index option consists of a cash payment representing the difference between the current index value and the strike price. Options, including index options, are discussed in Laurie S. Goodman, "New Option Markets," this *Quarterly Review*, Autumn 1983, pp. 35-47.

[7]The precise relationship between the guaranteed return and the strike price is given in Appendix 2.

[8]However, the realized cost and payoff of a synthetic option no longer has the desirable property of being independent of the path that the index follows before expiration.

[9]The exact formula for the upside capture is provided in Appendix 2.

bank could purchase half a call. Because it could thus hedge only half the deposit, the bank would offer an upside capture of only one-half. If the index then rose over the year, the bank would exercise its half of a call to receive a payoff just sufficient to pay the MID depositor. If the index fell, the call would expire worthless while the depositor would be owed no interest. In either case, the MID would cost the bank the same as the conventional CD.

In principle, given MIDs that are efficiently priced, the relationship among upside capture, guaranteed return, and maturity is precise. Chart 1 shows the various amounts of upside capture that could be offered on an MID that would cost the bank the same as a conventional CD paying a 6 percent annual return. The three curves show the combinations of guaranteed annual return and upside capture for maturities of 6, 12, and 36 months.[10] On any point on any of the curves, the bank's cost for the MID is the same 6 percent annual

[10]The example assumes that the CD rate and dividend yield are 6 percent and 3.5 percent, respectively, and that market volatility on the S&P 500 is 17 percent. These assumptions are consistent with actual market conditions in the first half of 1987.

rate. The lower the guaranteed return or the longer the maturity, the higher the upside capture.

For each curve, upside capture falls to zero as the guaranteed return approaches 6 percent. If the bank guarantees a return of 6 percent—its assumed marginal cost of funds—it cannot offer any additional return linked to the index. For any given maturity, a lower guaranteed return implies a larger interest differential relative to a conventional CD and a larger sum to allocate to the purchase of options, and thereby greater upside capture. Given the guaranteed return, a longer maturity also allows greater upside capture, since the savings from the interest differential rise faster with time to expiration than do call prices.[11]

The top curve shows that if maturity is long enough, an MID can offer more than 100 percent of the gain in the stock index and still guarantee no capital loss. Such an MID, however, is not a way to beat the market. Since stock index gains represent only capital appreciation, the MID holder does not receive the dividends from the stocks underlying the index. Hence, the expected return to the depositor will be lower than that on an index fund. Chase Manhattan, for example, introduced an MID for large investors that initially offered 115 percent of the S&P 500 over three years with a guaranteed minimum return of zero.[12] Given a dividend yield of 3.5 percent on the S&P 500, the index would have to rise more than 30 percent a year for the Chase account to outperform an index fund. Since the index is unlikely to do so well for three years, investors in the account are sacrificing some expected return to protect the value of their principal.

Deposit behavior over time

To get a sense of the effect of actual market conditions on MIDs, we can observe how these deposits would have behaved over time had they been issued in the past. Such a demonstration serves to illustrate the risk and return characteristics of an MID in comparison with those of alternative instruments. In this section, we track the behavior of hypothetical 90-day MIDs with zero guaranteed return, assuming they had been issued each month from July 1983 through June 1987. First we illustrate the upside capture a bank could have offered. We then compare the performance of the MID with that of an index fund and a conventional CD.

Upside capture—Chart 2 plots the monthly upside capture that a bank could have offered on the 90-day

[11]This property can be shown from the formula in Appendix 2. See also Chapter 5, "An Exact Pricing Formula," in John C. Cox and Mark Rubinstein, *Options Markets* (Prentice-Hall, 1985).

[12]Salomon Brothers has issued SPINs offering the greater of a guaranteed return of 2 percent and 100 percent of the percentage increase in the S&P 500 over four years.

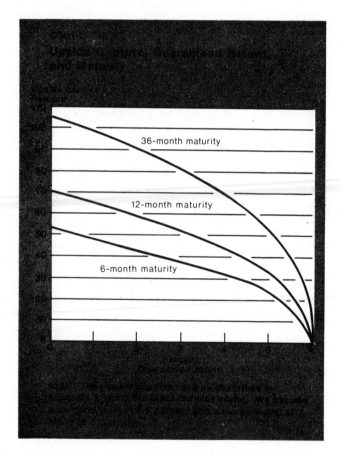

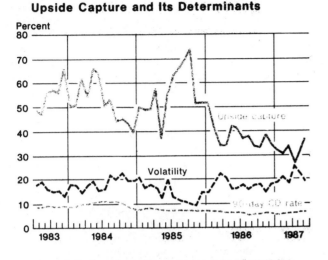

Chart 2

Upside Capture and Its Determinants

Note: The chart shows the upside capture of a 90 day MID with guaranteed return of principal, and its two key determinants: the annual volatility implied by traded call option prices and the interest rate on conventional CDs

MID with zero guaranteed return. The feasible upside capture is chosen so as to cost the bank the same amount as a conventional 90-day CD issued in the same month.[13] The chart shows two principal determinants of upside capture: the volatility of stock returns and the interest rate on the conventional CD. The CD rate and upside capture are both generally high at the beginning of the sample period and low towards the end. This pattern reflects the fact that when CD rates are high, the bank's interest savings allow the purchase of more call options. Month-to-month variation in the upside capture, however, is dominated by movements in volatility,[14] which has a major influence on the price of the relevant call option. The chart also shows that a bank offering efficiently priced MIDs would be expected to change the terms of the deposit—at least one term among the guaranteed return, upside capture, and maturity—quite sharply over time.

Risk and return—Although an efficiently priced MID will cost the bank the same as a conventional CD, the yield that a depositor actually receives will not, in general, be expected to equal the CD rate. Indeed the MID would be expected to yield a return that is higher on

[13]The feasible upside capture is computed iteratively using the principle described in the previous section (and specified precisely in Appendix 2), together with the Black-Scholes formula.

[14]The volatility measure is an average for the month of the volatility implied by current call option prices and the Black-Scholes formula.

average than that on a CD, but one that is more variable. Chart 3 plots the annualized returns on: (1) the S&P 500 with dividends reinvested,[15] (2) the 90-day MID (with the same upside capture as in Chart 2), and (3) a 90-day CD. The returns are computed ex-post, that is, they represent the yield that an investor would have realized over 90 days, rather than the yield the investor had expected at the time of the investment.

The chart illustrates vividly the differences between returns on the alternative investments. The role of the MID in putting a floor on the returns is apparent from the fact that the MID line never dips beneath zero. The cost of this floor protection is shown clearly by the fact that the MID investor would receive only around one-half of the positive yields that a stock market investor would obtain. It should be stressed, however, that had the market fallen over the period, rather than risen, the MID investor would have benefited more frequently from the floor protection provided by the MID. Between July 1983 and March 1987, the mean ex-post annualized yield on the efficiently priced MID was 9.3 percent, compared to 19.1 percent on the S&P 500, and 8.5 percent on the 90-day CD. The standard deviation for

[15]Equivalently, the chart plots the yield that would be obtained by investing in an S&P 500 index fund.

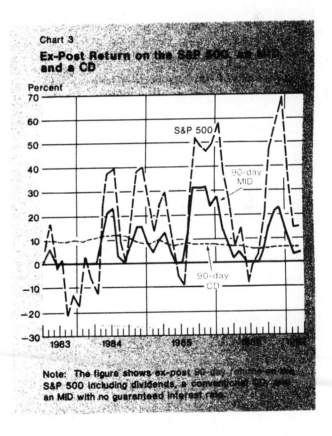

Chart 3

Ex-Post Return on the S&P 500, an MID and a CD

Note: The figure shows ex-post 90 day returns on the S&P 500 including dividends, a conventional CD, and an MID with no guaranteed interest rate

the MID return was 10.1 percent, less than half that for the S&P 500, which was 23.0 percent.[16]

Choice of hedging instrument

A bank issuing a market index deposit could hedge its risk exposure with a number of alternative instruments, used separately or in combination with each other. To hedge a deposit linked to a stock index, the bank could use the stocks comprising the index, index options, index futures, or options on index futures. To hedge a deposit linked to a commodity price, the bank could use the actual commodity, commodity futures, or options on commodity futures. We discuss below the advantages and disadvantages of these alternative hedging instruments.

Listed options—The hedging instruments that are the simplest conceptually would be exchange-traded European options[17] with maturities and strike prices matching exactly the terms of the deposit. If such options were available, the bank using them would be exposed to no hedging risk other than the credit risk of the exchange. The Chase and Wells Fargo deposits, for example, are issued weekly and should be hedged with European calls expiring each Tuesday, the day on which the deposits mature. While some listed index options are European, they expire at most once a month and are not available for maturities longer than five months, with most of the trading concentrated in the nearest months.[18] Listed options on index futures are American, expire only quarterly and are not available for longer than three quarters. Strike prices for either type of option on the S&P 500 are available only in increments of five index points. The mismatch in maturities or strike prices would make the use of listed options more expensive than is necessary for the hedging bank's purposes. Hedging with an option expiring after the deposit matures, for example, would mean paying for some of the remaining time value of the option.

Over-the-counter options—The bank could hedge with over-the-counter European options, which might be tailored to have exactly the right maturities and strike prices. This approach, however, is likely to be infeasible because of the lack of liquidity in this market. The bank would have to find suitable option writers each time it issued a deposit.

Stocks or commodities—In the absence of appropriate options, the bank could create synthetic options by holding a portfolio of stocks or commodities and adjusting its position in response to price movements. Using a method known as "dynamic hedging," the bank could, in principle, replicate the risk-return profile of any option by taking varying positions in the underlying asset and cash. In the case of an index option, the underlying asset would be the portfolio of stocks making up the index. In the case of a commodity option, the asset would be the physical commodity. We illustrate the operation of dynamic hedging in Appendix 1.

A shortcoming of dynamic hedging is that the method works imperfectly in practice. As we explain in the next section, the method is subject to tracking error and execution risk, which allow only an approximate replication of options. How close the approximation is depends on the skill of the hedger and the state of the market. Moreover, positions are revised so frequently in dynamic hedging that transactions costs are significant. One practitioner has estimated that the transactions costs involved in replicating a one-year option on the S&P 500 with stocks would amount to 56 basis points.[19] In commodity markets, transactions costs are likely to be even higher.

Futures—Synthetic options could be created out of futures instead of the underlying asset. Futures usually have the advantage of liquidity; the markets in the S&P 500 index futures and in gold futures are both highly liquid. As a result, it is relatively cheap to transact trades. In the case of the S&P 500, for example, dynamic hedging implemented with futures is estimated to entail transactions costs only one-third those of hedging with stocks.[20] Futures, however, are one market removed from the market on which the relevant index or commodity price is based. Since arbitrage between markets is imperfect, some mispricing of futures relative to the underlying asset is to be expected. Moreover, this mispricing—or "cash-futures basis"—works against the dynamic hedger. Despite this limitation, however, futures tend to be the preferred instrument for dynamic hedging because of advantages in liquidity and transactions costs.

---

[16]These numbers can also be compared to an ex-post mean annual yield of 9.1 percent on a 90-day MID with a guaranteed minimum return of 1 percent. In this case, the standard deviation was 9.3 percent.

[17]A European option permits exercise only at the expiration date. By contrast, an American option may be exercised on or before expiration.

[18]Since American options allow early exercise, they may be more expensive than European options with otherwise identical terms. For purposes of hedging an MID, however, early exercise would be necessary only if options with the same maturity as the MID were unavailable. Hence, if both types of options had the right maturity, the bank would prefer the European. Of course, if maturities cannot be matched precisely, American options would be preferable to European options, since the former can be exercised as deposits mature. European options include those on the Institutional Index (on the American Stock Exchange) and the S&P 500 (on the Chicago Board Options Exchange).

[19]See Rubinstein, "Alternative Paths."

[20]See Rubinstein, "Alternative Paths."

Risks of dynamic hedging

Dynamic hedging has become a familiar technique in portfolio insurance, and there is now some experience with its performance under moderate market conditions. The technique entails buying more of futures or the underlying asset as prices rise, and selling off as prices fall. Buying high and selling low in this way necessarily implies capital losses. In the absence of transactions costs, these losses should equal in present value the price of the option being replicated. However, two specific types of problems arise with option-replicating strategies: (1) tracking error and (2) execution risk.[21] We discuss these two problems in terms of hedging with futures for MIDs.

Tracking error—Tracking error occurs when the hedger fails to hold the right positions in futures that will replicate the call option. The exact positions are calculated from an options-pricing model. We consider below three conceptually distinct reasons why the hedger might fail to hold the correct positions: (1) inadequacies of the model used, (2) variations in the cash-futures basis, and (3) incorrect forecasts of index volatility or short-term interest rates. One practitioner estimates the cost of tracking error from the three sources together for hedging with index futures to be typically about 20 basis points.[22] This cost is in addition to transactions costs, which, as we have pointed out, are also significant in dynamic hedging.

First, the assumptions underlying the options pricing model may be violated, in which case the model may fail to simulate the actual market precisely. Second, the cash-futures basis is such that futures generally trade at a premium when prices are rising and at a discount when prices are falling. Since the dynamic hedger buys as prices rise and sells as prices fall, this systematic mispricing adds to the cost of the strategy.

The third source of error is incorrect estimation of volatility or interest rates. If volatility is underestimated at the time the MID is priced, the deposit will end up costing more than anticipated. The hedger will be buying at high prices and selling at low prices more frequently than anticipated, thereby incurring greater capital losses than expected. On the other hand, if volatility is overestimated, the hedger will make larger trades than are warranted by price movements, and the MID will still end up costing more than necessary. In Chart 4, we show the losses the bank would incur if it incorrectly estimated volatility in hedging a 90-day deposit linked to the S&P 500 with zero guaranteed minimum return. The relationship is not quite linear even for an at-the-money option. However, over a wide range of volatilities, the bank would lose 20 basis points for each 1 percent error in the volatility estimate.[23]

Similarly, if short-term interest rates are initially underestimated, the deposit will end up costing more than anticipated. Unlike volatility changes, however, interest rate changes are easily observed, so the hedging program can in principle be revised to replicate the appropriate option at the lowest cost possible.

Execution risk—Execution fails when the hedging bank is unable to adjust its portfolio sufficiently rapidly in response to price movements. This risk is illustrated in the final section of Appendix 1. Clearly the problem is most severe when the hedger is obliged to make large transactions at the same time that the market price is changing rapidly. When the option is deep-in- or deep-out-of-the-money, or when the expiration date of the option is distant, the hedge adjustments required by the synthetic option are generally small. However, when the asset is close to maturity and near-the-money, the logic of dynamic hedging will imply large portfolio changes.

[23]The costs portrayed in Charts 4 and 5 were computed using the Black-Scholes option-pricing formula.

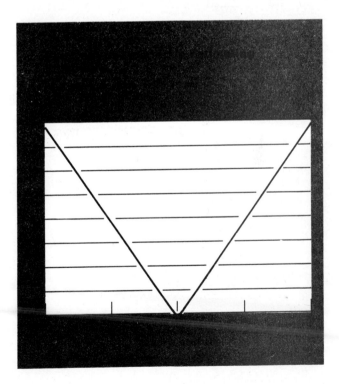

[21]Appendix 1 provides an illustration. For an introductory exposition, see Mark Rubinstein and Hayne Leland, "Replicating Options with Positions in Stock and Cash," *Financial Analysts Journal*, July/August 1981, pp. 63-72. Since option-replicating strategies involve considerable amounts of trading, the hedger may also be exposed to problems that might arise in existing settlement and payments systems.

[22]This estimate assumes the hedging program is executed well. See Richard Bookstaber, "Does Execution Matter?" Morgan Stanley Fixed Income Research Special Report, 1987.

Intuitively, these large portfolio changes result from the requirement of the technique that, just before the expiration of the option, the investor be either fully in cash or fully in the index future. The investor should be fully in cash if the option is out-of-the-money, and fully in the index future if the option is in-the-money. If the option is at-the-money immediately before expiration, the portfolio will be 50 percent invested in cash. The bank will then be faced with trading half of its portfolio in a very short period of time.

We can calculate the potential costs of execution risk in a "worst case" scenario. We assume that the hedger is completely unable to execute any portfolio transactions at a time when there is an adverse 4 percent shock to the S&P 500 index.[24] Chart 5 shows how the

[24]This was the magnitude of the decline in the S&P 500 on September 11, 1986, the third largest single-day decline in history. William Brodsky, Chairman of the Chicago Mercantile Exchange, stated that few portfolio insurers were practicing intraday adjustment at that time. He further noted that few portfolio insurers were able to execute on January 23, 1987, during the 70 minutes when the S&P 500 dropped 6 percent, producing a record trading range for a day.

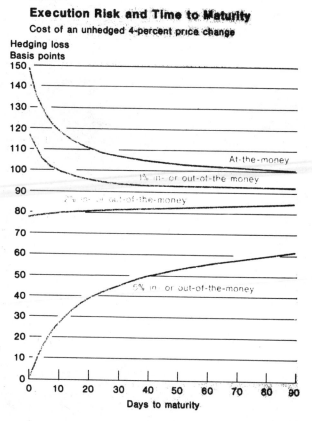

Chart 5

Execution Risk and Time to Maturity

Cost of an unhedged 4-percent price change

cost varies with time to maturity and "closeness-to-the-money" for a 90-day deposit under current market volatility and interest rates.[25] As we explained above, the largest costs are incurred on an at-the-money option that is close to maturity, and these can be as high as 150 basis points.[26] Options that are "away-from-the-money" suffer lower costs at all maturities. The chart demonstrates that an option that is 5 percent away-from-the-money suffers very little from an unexpected price change that occurs near maturity, because the change makes little difference to the probability that the option will expire in-the-money. The chart suggests that a bank dynamically hedging $100 million of 90-day MIDs outstanding would expect to lose between $400,000 and $1 million in this scenario. Having said this, we should emphasize that the performance of synthetic options has not been tested in market conditions more adverse than those assumed above. It is possible that actual trading losses could exceed the above amounts.

Conclusion

Commercial banks have recently begun to attract funds by offering accounts that return to depositors the greater of a guaranteed minimum return and a proportion of any increase in a market index. Such a market index deposit potentially exposes the issuing bank to considerable risk. We have shown, however, the ways in which the issuing bank can minimize its risk when liquid instruments are available for hedging.

Clearly, investors with access to options or futures markets could to some degree replicate the investment characteristics of MIDs. Such replication, however, would be impractical for small investors. Existing MIDs may appeal to the latter group because they offer straightforward access to options with low transactions costs and FDIC insurance, and because they require minimal effort on the part of the investor.

For MIDs to appeal to larger investors, banks will have to offer more than simple convenience; they will have to provide value added. MIDs could be attractive to some investors, particularly institutions that are not large enough to replicate at reasonable cost the risk-return profile that the deposit offers. Deposits linked to an index on which there are no publicly traded options with

Footnote 24 continued
(See *International Financing Review*, March 21, 1987, pp. 1001-1005.)

[25]The costs are calculated as the difference between the theoretical price of a call option immediately before and immediately after the 4 percent index shock.

[26]Execution risk in dynamic hedging can be reduced by combining futures with purchased options in a technique called "delta-gamma hedging." See *Recent Innovations in International Banking*, Bank for International Settlements, Basel, April 1986, pp. 101-120.

the maturity that the bank offers would therefore represent potentially viable products. In such a case, the bank would be providing portfolio insurance by using dynamic hedging techniques that would be uneconomic to the individual investor. It remains to be seen if this type of wholesale deposit will prove to be more successful than competing financial instruments.

Stephen R. King
Eli M. Remolona

Appendix 1

Hedging the Market Index Deposit: A Simple Numerical Example

With this numerical example, we first show various ways to hedge a market index deposit (an MID) using options, stocks, and index futures. Then we illustrate the execution risk of a hedge that relies on a synthetic option of either stocks or futures.

Pricing the MID

An MID that is properly priced and hedged must cost the issuing bank neither more nor less than alternative sources of funds regardless of index performance.

Consider an MID linked to the S&P 500 Index. Suppose the current value of the index is 300. Divide the time until the deposit matures into two periods. Over the first period, the index can move with equal probability either up to 336 or down to 267. If it moves up to 336, then over the second period it can move to either 376 or 300. If it moves down to 267, then it can move to either 300 or 238. These index movements result in three possible outcomes, as shown in the top panel of Figure A-1. Outcome I represents a gain of slightly more than 25 percent over two periods; in outcome II there is no gain or loss, and in outcome III there is a loss of about 21 percent.

Suppose the marginal cost of bank funds, say the interest rate on a conventional CD, is 8 percent over two periods. Suppose also the MID pays a minimum return of zero (that is, only the principal is guaranteed). Then under outcomes II and III, the MID pays zero while the conventional CD pays 8 percent. For the MID to cost the same as the alternative source of funds under these outcomes, the spread between zero and 8 percent must be the cost of the hedge. Specifically, on a deposit size of D, the hedge must cost $0.08 \times D$ at maturity or $0.08 \times D/1.08$ at the start of the first period.*

One way to hedge would be to purchase call options on the index with the same maturity as the MID and a strike price equal to the initial value of the index.† Under outcome I, the call would be worth 76 index points at maturity (an index value of 376 minus a strike price of 300) and zero under outcomes II and III. The call would end "in-the-money" under outcome I, "at-the-money" under outcome II, and "out-of-the-money" under outcome III. The bottom panel of Figure A-1 shows how the price of this call would move with the index. At the start of the first period, the price of the call would be about 30 index points. If the index rose to 336 at the end of the first period, the price of the call would be about 48 index points, and if the index fell to 267, the price would be zero.‡

Suppose the deposit principal is $3,000 and an index point is worth $10. If the bank held one call against the MID, the proceeds from the call at maturity would allow the bank to pass on to depositors the entire gain in the index should it rise, and to guarantee the principal should the index fall. Under outcome I, the bank would exercise the call at maturity to receive $760 (76 index points times $10 per point), an amount that would be just sufficient to pay on the MID a return equal to the percentage change in the index. Under outcomes II and III, the bank would not exercise, thus losing no money on the index and thereby retaining its ability to guarantee the deposit principal. However, to purchase a call in the beginning would have cost the bank $300 (30 index points times $10 per point), while the spread between the cost of funds and the minimum return specifies a hedge costing only $222 ($0.08 \times \$3000/1.08 \approx \$222$). If the bank held one call against the MID and the call ended out-of-the-money, the MID would turn out to be a more costly source of funds than a conventional CD.

The cost of the hedge requires the bank to purchase

Footnote † continued
$1 + r^G/\phi$ times the initial value of the index. Hence, in the case where $r^G > 0$, the option price and proportion of index gain have to be solved for simultaneously.

---

*If r^G is the guaranteed minimum return and r is the cost of funds, the cost of the hedge must be $(r - r^G) \times D$ at maturity or $(r - r^G) \times D/(1 + r)$ at the start.

†If the guaranteed minimum return is r^G and the offered proportion of index gain is ϕ, the strike price should be

‡Option prices here assume that writers of the index call face the same 8 percent cost of funds and that the stocks underlying the index pay no dividends. The prices are derived using the binomial approach in Cox, Ross, and Rubinstein, "Option Pricing: A Simplified Approach," *Journal of Financial Economics*, Vol. 7 (1979), pp. 229-263.

Hedging the Market Index Deposit *(continued)*

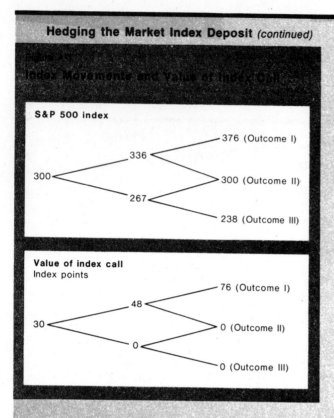

Index Movements and Value of Index Call

S&P 500 index

- 300
  - 336
    - 376 (Outcome I)
    - 300 (Outcome II)
  - 267
    - 300 (Outcome II)
    - 238 (Outcome III)

Value of index call
Index points

- 30
  - 48
    - 76 (Outcome I)
    - 0 (Outcome II)
  - 0
    - 0 (Outcome II)
    - 0 (Outcome III)

---

just three-quarters of a call ($222/$300 ≈ 3/4) and thus to offer to compensate the MID depositor for only 75 percent of the gain in the index. Hence the relationship between minimum return and upside capture (or proportion of index gain) can be expressed in terms of (1) the price of an appropriately specified option, and (2) the spread between the bank's marginal cost of funds and the minimum return it guarantees. In Appendix 2, we present the general formula for this relationship.

Hedging with a purchased call

The table shows how the hedge would work on the $3,000 MID offering 75 percent of the gain in the index. Under outcome I, the bank would pay the depositor a return of 19 percent (0.75 times the index gain) or $570. This payment would be fully covered by the exercise of the three-quarters of a call the bank would be holding (3/4 times $760 option value at maturity is $570). Under outcomes II and III, the bank would pay no interest on the MID, and the call would expire with zero value. Given the 8 percent cost of funds, the $222 starting price of three-quarters of a call would cost the bank $240 at maturity (1.08 × $222), an amount equal to the interest that the bank would pay if it took the $3,000 as a conventional CD. Hence, the MID would cost the bank nei-

---

ther more nor less than a conventional CD under any outcome.

Hedging with a stock portfolio

With dynamic hedging, the bank may also hedge by actively trading a portfolio of stocks replicating the S&P 500 Index.§ The idea is to hold a portfolio with the same risk profile as the index call—in effect, to construct a synthetic option. At each point in time, the size of the stock position we need for the synthetic index call is given by the option's "hedge ratio" or "delta," usually computed from an options-pricing model such as Black-Scholes. In our example, the delta at the start of each period is calculated as the ratio of (1) the difference between the high and low values of the index call on the next move, and (2) the difference between the high and low values of the underlying index on the next move.‖ Hence, at the start of the first period, (1) is 48 − 0 = 48, and (2) is 336 − 267 = 69, so the delta is about 0.7 (≈48/69). At the start of the second period, there are two possible deltas. If the index rose to 336, the delta would be (76 − 0)/(376 − 300) = 1. If the index fell to 267, the delta would be (0 − 0)/(300 − 238) = 0.

---

§One way to do this would be to trade shares in an index fund based on the S&P 500.

‖Again see Cox, Ross, and Rubinstein, "Option Pricing." In general, the delta depends on the interest rate, the current price of the underlying asset, the volatility of the asset's return, the strike price, and the time to maturity.

Cash Flows for a Hedged MID and a Conventional CD

		Maturity Date	
	Starting Date	Outcome I	Outcomes II and III
S&P 500 MID			
Take MID	3,000	−3,570	−3,000
Borrow at 8%	222	−240	−240
Buy 3/4 call	−222	570	0
Total	3,000	−3,240	−3,240
Conventional CD			
Take deposit	3,000	−3,240	−3,240

Assumptions: The MID pays 0.75 of the gain in the S&P 500 Index and guarantees the principal. The outcomes refer to Figure A-1 with each index point assumed to be worth $10.

Hedging the Market Index Deposit (continued)

Figure A-2 shows how the bank would construct the synthetic option needed to hedge the $3,000 MID offering 75 percent of the market gain. At the start of the first period, a delta of 0.70 applied to three-quarters of a call tells the bank to buy an S&P 500 stock portfolio worth $1,575 (0.70 × (3/4) × $3,000), financing its purchase with funds costing 8 percent.

If the index then rose to 336, the value of the portfolio underlying one index call would be $3,360 (336 index points times $10 a point). A delta of one for three-quarters of a call would then tell the bank to hold a stock portfolio worth $2,520. Since the stock portfolio carried over from the first period would now be worth about

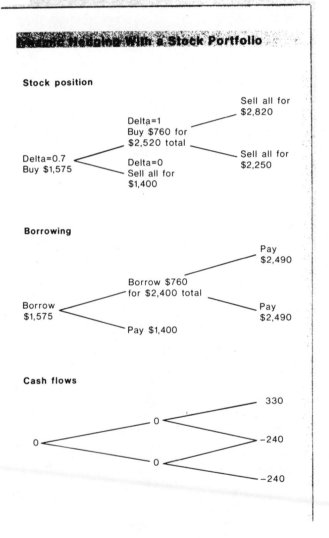

Dynamic Hedging With a Stock Portfolio

Stock position

Delta=0.7
Buy $1,575

Delta=1
Buy $760 for
$2,520 total — Sell all for $2,820

Delta=0
Sell all for
$1,400 — Sell all for $2,250

Borrowing

Borrow
$1,575

Borrow $760
for $2,400 total — Pay $2,490 / Pay $2,490

Pay $1,400

Cash flows

0
0 — 330 / −240
0 — −240

$1,760,¶ the bank would buy $760 more of the portfolio, again borrowing the amount for the purchase.

Under outcome I, the bank would end up with a stock position worth about $2,820. At the same time the bank would owe about $1,700 (1.08 × $1,575) from the first loan and about $790 from the second. After the bank liquidates the stocks and pays off the loans, it would have $330 left. Since the interest payment on the MID would be $570, the hedge and the MID would cost the bank $240 net, exactly the cost of a conventional CD. Discounted to the start of the first period, this is also the price of a purchased option, as we saw in the last section.

Under outcome II, the stock portfolio would be worth $2,250. Paying off $2,490 in loans would again leave the bank $240 short. Since the MID would require no interest, the cost of the hedge would exactly match the cost of a conventional CD.

If the index fell to 267 at the end of the first period, the bank would be holding $1,400 in stocks. A delta of zero would then tell it to liquidate its stock position. After using the proceeds to pay its loan, the bank would still owe about $235 at the start of second period or $240 at maturity. Since only outcomes II and III would be possible, the MID would require no interest, and again the cost of the hedge would be the cost of a conventional CD.

Hedging with index futures

The bank may also choose to form its synthetic option out of index futures. Index futures are priced to require no exchange of cash in the beginning, except for the initial margin.** This amounts to setting the price at a premium to the underlying index to reflect borrowing costs (less dividend yield if any). During the course of the contract, each price change is settled in cash.†† The side favored by the price change receives a payment while the other side pays. As shown in Figure A-3, when the index is 300 and the "cost-of-carry" is 8 percent over two periods, a futures contract expiring at the end of two periods would be priced at 324 points (1.08 × 300). If the index went to 336 at the end of the first period, the futures price would be 349 points (1.04 × 336), and the holder would receive the cash equivalent of 25 points (349 − 324). If the index fell to 267, the futures price would be 278 points, and the holder would pay 46 points

¶Recall that we assume no dividend payments.

**The initial margin on an S&P 500 futures contract is $10,000 and each index point is worth $500.

††In practice, this is done daily. The cash settlement is called a "variation margin."

Hedging the Market Index Deposit *(continued)*

(324 − 278). At maturity, the futures price necessarily reverts to the value of the index. A final cash payment is made to reflect the last price change, and the contract expires.

Dynamic hedging with futures uses the same delta that is used for dynamic hedging with stocks. To create a synthetic index call, the bank would start with a delta of 0.70. At this point, a whole futures contract would be priced at $3,240 (at an assumed $10 per index point). However, replicating three-quarters of a call with index futures does not mean buying $1,700 worth of the contract (a delta of 0.70 times three-quarters times $3,240). Because of the cash settlement following each price

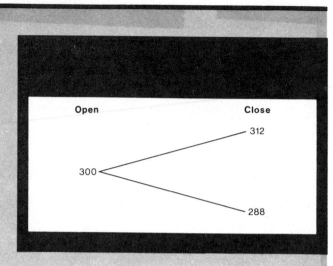

change, we need to discount for the fact that the futures price reflects a two-period premium. As Figure A-3 shows, the correct amount to buy would be about $1,635 ($1,700/1.04), so that the bank, in effect, would pay only for one period of carrying costs.

If the futures price then rose to 349 points at the end of the first period, the bank would be holding futures worth about $1,760 ($1,635 × 349/324), and it would receive $125 in cash ($1,760 − $1,635) from the price change. The new delta of one would tell the bank to buy about $855 more futures for a total of about $2,615 (three-quarters of a call times $3,490). Under outcome I, the bank's futures position would be about $2,815 at maturity. The bank would receive $200 in cash ($2,815 − $2615) as final settlement. At the same time, the earlier cash settlement would have grown to about $130 (1.04 × $125), so the bank would come out $330 ahead. It would then pay $570 on the MID for a net cost of $240, exactly what a conventional CD would cost. Under outcome II, the futures position would be about $2,250. The bank would pay a final cash settlement of roughly $370. This time the MID would require no interest payment. With the earlier cash settlement, the net cost of the MID would again be $240.

If the futures price fell to 278 points at the end of the first period, the bank's futures position would decline to about $1,405, requiring a cash payment of $230 ($1,635 − $1,405). The new delta of zero would tell the bank to sell all its futures. The sale would be carried out without any further exchange of cash. At the end of the second period, the cash payment made earlier would cost the bank about $240 (1.04 × $230). There would be no interest payment on the MID and no other gains or losses from the hedge. Again the net cost of the MID would be the same as that of a conventional CD.

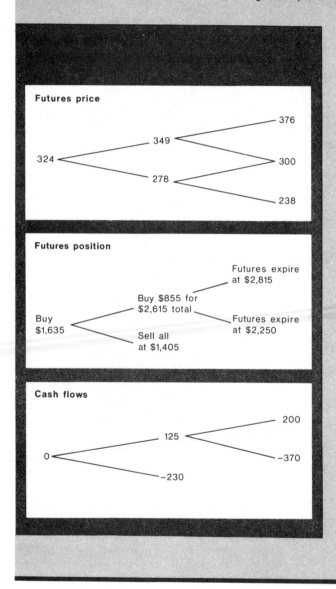

Hedging the Market Index Deposit (continued)

Execution risk

In existing markets, large changes in either stock or futures positions are hard to execute when prices are moving swiftly. Thus a dynamic hedger faces execution risk when the delta happens to be very sensitive to prices during a period of unusually wide price swings. In this situation, the delta would require a large hedge adjustment at the very time that prices are moving too fast to allow the hedger to execute a large trade. The delta is most sensitive to prices when the option to be replicated is both near maturity and at-the-money.

In order to illustrate execution risk when the delta is most sensitive to prices, let us suppose that we have the same $3,000 MID as before. But this time, suppose that on the maturity date, as shown in Figure A-4, the index opens at 300 and can close at either 312 or 288 (with the MID linked to the closing value).§§ Hence, the trading day opens with the synthetic option being at-the-money. At this point the delta is one-half and the bank should hold $(0.5) \times (0.75) \times \$3,000 = \$1,125$ in stocks or futures for its dynamic hedge. Suppose that the bank is able to implement this investment position at the start of the day, but that during the day, prices move too quickly for the bank to execute any further adjustment.

If the index rose to 312, the bank would be holding a position worth $1,170 ($1,125 × 312/300), for a gain of $45 ($1,170 − $1,125). The MID, however, would require an interest payment of $90. The net loss to the bank would be $45 or 1.5 percent of the deposit principal. If the index fell to 288, the bank would be holding a position worth $1,080, for a loss of $45. Since the MID would require no interest payment, the net loss would still be 1.5 percent of principal. In theory, the accumulated cost of dynamic hedging‖‖ from the first day of the MID to the day of maturity would have already amounted to the cost of a purchased option. Hence, the loss on the last day would be an additional cost due to the failure of execution.

§§This is a rise or fall of 4 percent, somewhat smaller than the magnitude of the fall in the index on Thursday, September 11, 1986.

‖‖As the previous sections show, this cost arises from the fact that the strategy of buying stocks or futures as prices rise and selling as prices fall amounts to buying "high" and selling "low." In the absence of transactions costs, these capital losses cause the cost of dynamic hedging to equal the cost of an equivalent option.

Appendix 2

The General Pricing Formula for the MID

To hedge MIDs with maturity T years and guaranteed minimum annual return r^G, the bank must explicitly or implicitly purchase index calls with the same maturity and with a strike price corresponding to the current index value, guaranteed minimum return, and upside capture or proportion of index gain. The price of such an option will be a function of the current index value S, the strike price K, the annual volatility σ, the cost-of-carry r^C, and the time to maturity T.* The function is increasing in all its arguments but the strike price. We can write the cost of one option per dollar of the deposit as

$$C(S,K,\sigma,r^C,T)/S$$

where C(.) is a standard call price formula for the case in which the strike price is

$$K = S(1 + ((1+r^G)^T - 1)/\phi)$$

*In the case of a stock index, r^C is equal to the short-term interest rate less the dividend yield. For a commodity option, r^C is the sum of the short-term interest rate and the cost of physical storage.

and ϕ is the upside capture to be offered.

The amount of options the bank can profitably hedge with will depend on the interest it would otherwise pay on funds with the same maturity (and denomination) as the MID. The MID will be priced efficiently relative to a conventional CD if the cost of the hedge in proportion to the deposit exactly equals in present value the difference between the interest cost of a conventional CD r^D and the guaranteed minimum return offered by the bank r^G. Hence the hedge expenditure per dollar of deposit should equal

$$h(r^G,r^D) = ((1+r^D)^T - (1+r^G)^T)/(1+r^D)^T.$$

The upside capture ϕ is therefore calculated as the ratio that solves

$$\phi = h(r^G,r^D)S/C(S,K,\sigma,r^C,T)$$

where K itself is a function of ϕ, S, r^G, and T. The solution can be written as $\phi(r^D,r^G,r^C,\sigma,T)$ and can be shown to be increasing in the deposit rate r^D and maturity T, decreasing in all its other arguments, and independent of the initial index value S.

Article 35

Home Equity Lending: Boon or Bane?

Home equity loans are an increasingly important source of credit for households and a growing component of bank portfolios. Commercial banks are by far the largest providers of home equity credit, with about 40 percent of all outstanding home equity loans. Between 1987 and 1988, banks' home equity loans grew by over 30 percent, from $28.9 billion to $37.5 billion. As a share of total bank assets, home equity loans grew from about one percent to over 1.3 percent. Thrifts, finance companies, and brokerage firms also engage in home equity lending.

Home equity lending is widely considered a low-risk lending activity. Like first mortgage loans, these loans are secured by housing assets, the value of which has performed well historically. Nonetheless, the rapid growth of home equity lending warrants a review of the rationale for and performance of the home equity loan market.

As discussed in this *Letter*, the home equity loan market appears to be developing conservatively. The nature of the instrument, however, makes home equity loans somewhat riskier than they may appear at first glance.

Home equity lending
A home equity loan can be structured in one of two ways. First, it can be structured as a traditional second mortgage, wherein the borrower obtains funds equal to the full loan amount immediately, and commits to a fixed repayment schedule. Alternatively, home equity borrowing can be structured as a line of credit, with check, credit card, or other easy access to the line over its life.

The home equity credit line presently is the dominant form of new home equity lending. The home equity credit line, like other "open-end" or revolving credit facilities, permits the borrower to draw advances against the line whenever needed (up to the limit of the facility). The amount of credit available at a given time depends upon the extent to which the line has

been replenished by repayment of outstanding balances.

The available data suggest that the main uses of home equity credit are to consolidate other debt (about 50 percent), finance home improvements (25 percent), and finance automobile purchases (10 percent). Financing medical expenditures and other consumer purchases account for the balance.

Home equity, taxes, and regulation
Apart from the traditional "closed-end" second mortgages that banks and thrifts have always offered, home equity lending is a relatively new line of business for financial institutions. In 1980, fewer than one percent of banking institutions offered home equity lines of credit. Today, 80 percent of commercial banks and 65 percent of thrifts offer such products.

Home Equity Loans and Home Prices 1988, By State

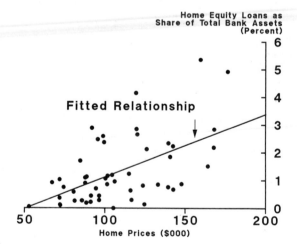

Economic and regulatory developments are responsible for the recent growth of home equity lending by banks and for the growing interest on the part of consumers. Economic forces, in particular, have been important. During the late 1970s and early 1980s, home prices rose sharply, improving the housing equity positions of many households. To the extent households have viewed this appreciation as permanent, they probably have come to consider this equity part of their stock of savings. It is natural, therefore, that the market would seek a means of mobilizing this wealth by providing a home equity credit facility. Indeed, as the chart indicates, home equity lending is most active in states were the level of home values is high.

Moreover, changes in the laws and regulations governing home equity lending facilitated the development of products that could take advantage of this stock of wealth. First, in 1982, the Truth in Lending Act was modified to remove a major impediment to home equity lending. Originally, the Act, as implemented by Federal Reserve Regulation Z, gave consumers three days to change their minds following each, separate drawdown on a line of credit secured by real estate. This stringent "right of rescission" represented a significant cost disadvantage of home equity credit facilities relative to credit card and other revolving debt lines. The 1982 law limited the right of rescission to the initial setup of the loan, thereby making home equity lines of credit more attractive to lenders.

Second, the 1982 Banking Act expanded the authority of national banks to extend flexible, home equity credit, enabling them to make real estate loans primarily on the basis of the creditworthiness and income prospects of the borrower. For federally-chartered thrifts, the Act lifted the restriction that they lend only on the security of "first lien" collateral. Both of these changes facilitated the crafting of home equity credit lines.

The 1986 and 1987 Tax Acts also have influenced the market for home equity lending. The 1986 Act phases out the deductibility of interest payments on most forms of consumer loans, making consumer debt generally more costly to households. The only exception is interest on loans secured by a taxpayer's principal or second residence, which remains deductible, although there are restrictions on the maximum principal amount of a home equity loan that qualifies for an interest deduction. The 1987 tax revisions limit the amount to the lesser of true home equity (that is, the fair market value minus acquisition debt) or $100,000. These reforms make real estate lines of credit relatively less expensive than other forms of consumer credit, and undoubtedly contribute to the strength of the home equity loan market.

Pricing home equity loans

Traditional second mortgages typically are structured like first mortgages, usually with fixed interest rates and a fully-amortizing repayment schedule. Home equity lines of credit, on the other hand, are typically adjustable-rate instruments.

The adjustable-rate feature likely is a consequence of the contingent nature of a line of credit. In essence, a line of credit embodies a series of "options" to obtain credit over the life of the line. If a fixed-rate contract were used, and interest rates rose above the contract rate, borrowers would exercise the option to borrow and profitably invest the funds in the open market at higher rates. From the standpoint of the lender, offering a fixed-rate home equity credit line, thus, is equivalent to selling long-term interest-rate "call" options.

Financial markets in general appear reluctant to offer such long-term options, perhaps because the market doubts the ability of the writer of such options (that is, the lender in the case of fixed-rate home equity lines) to perform on his obligations in an adverse economic environment. Thus, the pricing of home equity lines of credit as adjustable-rate instruments is consistent with the general rarity of pure, long-term interest rate options in the economy. Regulators also discourage lenders from writing pure options.

As with other adjustable-rate instruments, the contract rate is linked to a reference rate (often the prime rate plus about two percentage points). Home equity line rates, however, seldom have restrictive caps, implying that households (rather than banks) are bearing the entirety of interest rate risk. It can be argued that functional caps are likely to become more common as competition in home equity lending grows, since households are less able than banks to accommodate interest rate risk. Hence, as in the first lien adjustable-rate mortgage market, it is likely that capped-rate instruments ultimately will dominate pure, adjustable-rate ones in the home equity loan market.

Risk in home equity loans

One future source of risk in home equity loans, therefore, will be the interest rate risk introduced by the move towards capped-rate products. There are, however, other sources as well. A major source of risk to loans collateralized by housing, of course, is the possibility that local housing values or household purchasing power may decline, stimulating abandonment of the property and default on debt secured by the housing. Certain features of home equity loans make them particularly susceptible to such risks. First, while the adjustable-rate feature of the debt reduces the interest rate risk of the lender, the variable payment size exposes households to greater cash-flow risks than would a fixed-rate instrument, everything else being equal. This, in turn, exposes the lender to greater credit risk.

Ironically, another source of risk is the very fact that such lines employ collateral. Theory suggests that collateral reduces risk, since a general claim on a borrower is augmented by a specific claim on an asset. However, processes of "self-selection" can reverse this relationship. Namely, it is possible that borrowers who choose to pledge collateral are riskier than those who can obtain unsecured credit.

In addition to the risks inherent in self selection, there are risks introduced by the very nature of the home equity loan. They are secured by a lien that generally is junior to that of any primary mortgage debt. Thus, home equity lines of credit of a given size have less effective equity protection than first lien instruments; a decline in the value of the underlying housing results in a much greater than proportional decline in the collateral coverage of a home equity loan. This added leverage makes them correspondingly far riskier than first mortgages. Moreover, the law governing the quality or "perfection" of the lien is quite complicated, and the lien of future advances may be different from that of the initial advance since in the meantime, other events or liens may be interposed. While lenders' counsel try to craft loan agreements that avoid legal pitfalls, the effective riskiness of home equity lending likely varies somewhat with the legal environment. (There are, for example, at least 27 variations in the treatment of lien priority across states.)

This variation in contract characteristics also affects the liquidity of home equity debt. For debt to be easily pooled and sold in the secondary market, it needs to be fairly consistent in its credit- and interest rate-risk characteristics. The complexity of collateral structures, coupled with the inherently uncertain maturity of revolving credit instruments, makes home equity loan assets considerably less liquid than straight, first lien, fixed maturity debt.

Handle with care

Outstanding home equity credit, while growing rapidly, presently represents far less than 10 percent of the outstanding value of home equity, currently estimated at $3 trillion. The continued high level of home values, coupled with favorable tax treatment, likely will spur further growth in this segment of the credit market, making it a significant component of bank and thrift portfolios.

However, adverse-selection processes, legal complexities, and other features of these loans can be important sources of risk. In fact, there is some evidence that delinquency rates are higher for home equity lines than for unsecured lines. In addition, mortgage insurers tend to experience greater difficulties with adjustable-rate instruments than with fixed-rate, first lien mortgage debt. Comprehensive data on comparative rates of nonperformance and charge-offs are not presently available. It is clear, however, that continuing assessment of the risks in home equity lending is important for banks, thrifts, and their regulators.

Randall Johnston Pozdena
Assistant Vice President

Article 36

The Economics of Securitization

Without question, one of the most prominent recent features of the financial sector has been the very strong growth in securities markets transactions. These transactions take a wide variety of forms. Investors may hold security market claims on borrowers directly or buy shares in mutual funds that acquire most, if not all, of their assets in the financial markets. Alternatively, they may own securities representing an undivided interest in a pool of loans. Or, investors may hold either securities issued by banks or deposit claims on banks that own securities rather than loans.

All of these transactions are types of securitization. Securitization is a process hard to define generally. In its broadest sense, securitization is financial intermediation that involves at some stage the buying or selling of financial claims. That definition is wide enough to include the sale of loan participations among banks or packages of commercial mortgages among thrifts, and yet it excludes not only traditional bank lending but also similar activities at finance and insurance companies. A narrower definition refers to the packaging of generally illiquid assets of banks, thrifts, and other intermediaries for sale in securities form.

But perhaps the best definition of securitization is the matching up of borrowers and savers wholly or partly by way of the financial markets. Such a definition covers issuance of securities such as bonds and commercial

The author, Christine Cumming, completed this article while she was a Research Officer and Senior Economist at the Federal Reserve Bank of New York.

paper—a practice that entirely replaces traditional financial intermediation—and also sales of mortgage-backed and other asset-backed securities—transactions that rely on financial intermediaries to originate loans but use the financial markets to seek the final holders.

Securitization is different in kind from disintermediation and the difference provides some important clues to the economic forces behind securitization. To draw this distinction, it is necessary to define some terms used in this paper. *Financial intermediation* is defined very broadly as the bringing together of borrowers and savers. Banks, thrifts, and finance companies, among others, carry out *traditional financial intermediation*. These institutions make a large number of loans and fund them by issuing liabilities in their own name. *Disintermediation* refers to a displacement of traditional financial intermediation away from banks and thrifts primarily to arrangements that are similar to bank lending—loans by other financial intermediaries or direct lending between agents in the same sector (for example, trade credit)—rather than financial market transactions. In the United States, disintermediation usually took place when market interest rates rose above the ceilings set by the old Regulation Q.

Broadly, securitization breaks with traditional financial intermediation, while disintermediation tries to emulate it. Unlike securitization, disintermediation does not change the form of financial claims to any great extent. Rather, it shifts the holding of particular kinds of claims when the traditional holder is temporarily constrained by institutional features such as deposit interest rate ceilings. Securitization, by contrast, changes the form of claims, and through that change also alters the distribution of holdings among types of investors. Still, securitization and disintermediation are not entirely distinct, since both involve a shift of intermediation away from banks and thrifts.

The range of transactions that replace traditional financial intermediation today suggests that no single economic force lies behind securitization. For example, an increase in the relative cost of bank intermediation in the wholesale lending markets may explain why some firms issue more bonds and commercial paper but cannot explain why some banks are major purchasers of floating rate notes (FRNs) and Euronotes.

To identify the forces driving securitization, we break traditional financial intermediation into three key elements: (1) the agreement between borrower and intermediary, (2) the service provided by the intermediary (its value-added), and (3) the agreement between the intermediary and the investor.

In traditional bank lending, one financial claim, a loan, represents the agreement between a borrower and the bank, while a deposit represents the agreement between the bank and the investor. The service of the bank is matching up borrowers and lenders, which it can do cheaply both by reducing search costs and by realizing economies of scale in gathering and allocating funds. The bank manages risks that arise in matching up borrowers and lenders, because their preferences, and thus the instruments the bank offers them, are not identical. These risks include funding, market, and credit risk. Frequently, the bank's size gives it the capacity to pool and thus reduce risks. In addition, the bank can offer its customers payments services that enhance customers' liquidity.

The three elements of traditional financial intermediation suggest that securitization covers three separate kinds of substitutions: securities for loans, direct placement of debt claims for traditional financial intermediation, and securities for deposits. In turn, three economic forces emerge as important contributors to securitization. The first is upward pressure on the cost of bank intermediation, especially higher capital requirements not accompanied by a fall in the cost of capital at a time when transactions costs for both securities placement and risk management are falling. Second is an increase in financial risk, especially in the volatility of interest rates. Third is increased competition to relationship lenders from banks and nonbank financial institutions.

Loans versus securities

No clearcut definition distinguishes a loan from a security. The features associated with securities and not with loans are transferability, a degree of standardization and of disclosure imposed by securities laws, and often, liquidity. But the real difference between loans and securities lies not in the explicit contracts of the loan agreement and the bond but in the existence of an implicit contract between the borrower and the bank in the case of a loan and the virtual absence of such an implicit contract between the borrower and the investor in the case of a security.

A loan is essentially a private, unpublicized agreement between lender and borrower. While the loan agreement is a legally binding document, both borrower and lender understand that they can renegotiate the agreement. The loan agreement thus offers great flexibility and considerable discretion. The flexibility, discretion and durability of these arrangements is what is termed a "banking relationship." Nor does the relationship stop at a loan agreement; it also includes deposit, payment and currency services.

Consider the commercial lending relationship. There the bank can be viewed as writing options for its loan customer. Through devices such as credit lines or lending commitments, the borrower can choose the timing and the amount of a loan; the borrower can often prepay or refinance the loan with a small or even no fee. Most important, the bank makes an implicit and sometimes explicit commitment to provide funds in times when the borrower finds them difficult to obtain: when the borrower is experiencing difficulties or when liquidity has dried up. In return, the borrower may agree to allow the lender to monitor its performance over the life of the loan and agree to financial covenants restricting its behavior. While such covenants exist in bond indentures as well, they are less flexible and less meaningful.

The economics literature has tended to emphasize the importance of the bank's access to private information in distinguishing bank lending from other financial intermediation.[1] But provision of continuous access to funds in banking relationships is also crucial. In particular, the development of instruments like note issuance facilities (NIFs) and FRNs that replace bank lending underscores its importance. A NIF provides more liquidity to investors than a syndicated loan but still assures the borrower medium-term access to funds. The FRN replaces generally short-term interbank deposits with a medium-term instrument that, unlike interbank lines, cannot be cut back.

A debt security is an agreement between a borrower and lenders who are usually unspecified before the

[1]See, for example, Eugene F. Fama, "What's Different about Banks?" *Journal of Monetary Economics*, vol. 15 (1985), pp. 29-39, and Joseph E. Stiglitz, "Credit Markets and the Control of Capital," *Journal of Money, Credit and Banking*, vol. 17, no. 2 (May 1985), pp. 133-52.

terms of issue are set. No agreement is negotiated by borrower and lenders. Instead, the underwriter negotiates the terms with the borrower and attempts to find investors at somewhat more favorable terms. The security holders also have no implicit contract with the borrower. They are not expected to purchase new issues of securities or hold onto securities permanently. The terms of securities issues are seldom renegotiated and the borrower's right to prepay exists only if there is an explicit call option. The debt security's documentation may obligate the borrower to provide information to its creditors or allow a third party to monitor its performance, but the security holders are under no obligation to keep such information confidential.

These conditions do not rule out the development of a relationship in the issuance of a security. Borrowers have relationships with their investment bank insofar as the borrower provides confidential information and the investment bank counsels the borrower and supports its issues in order to assure continuous and low cost access to the financial markets. But the investment bank is not itself a source of funding nor is it a credit monitor in the same sense that a bank is. To provide these services, additional parties such as banks or rating agencies must be drawn in.

Similarly, the investor has an implicit contract with the investment bank. The investment bank may be expected to make markets in its customers' securities. In addition, securities laws require underwriters to perform "due diligence" to assure that disclosures represent the truth fairly.

The distinction drawn here between loans and securities is extreme, of course. Syndicated loans are well-publicized agreements between a borrower and a large number of banks, many of which will have no other customer relationship with the borrower. Private placement securities generally require less disclosure and also lack the liquidity associated with publicly-offered securities. Since they are placed with a small number of investors, issues can be tailor-made to investor preferences. The investors may actively monitor the creditworthiness of borrowers and manage any credit problems. Moreover, the implicit contract nature of a loan is not its only distinguishing feature. The structure of transaction costs means that securities issues are much larger in size than most loans.

Erosion of the banking relationship

One determinant of the degree to which securitization can replace traditional bank lending is the relative importance of relationship to both bank and borrower. Recently many factors have reduced the value of the banking relationship. Among these are the rise in interest rate volatility, historically high nominal interest rates in the early 1980s, asset quality problems at banks, shifts in the international flows of funds, and increased competition among banks and from other financial firms.

For banks, the sharp rise in interest-rate volatility in the late 1970s and early 1980s made the options embedded in loan agreements much more expensive. The unanticipated high level of interest rates increased both the (foregone interest) cost of reserve requirements and the effective cost of capital. As a result, the cost of holding a loan on the balance sheet in many cases exceeded the agreed lending rate, usually a base interest rate plus a spread. Thus, if the borrower exercised its right to borrow, the bank would be forced to make an unprofitable loan.

Banks responded to the higher cost of the options by withdrawing them in whole or in part where they could. In particular, they could cancel or reduce credit lines. Uncommitted lines eventually were replaced by commitments for which borrowers had to pay. These could be purchased separately from other banks that were not the traditional relationship banks. For thrifts and banks holding long-term assets that could not be called—but that exposed the institutions to much greater interest rate and prepayment risk than experienced before—selling loans grew more attractive. In extending new loans, thrifts and banks shifted from fixed-rate term lending to floating-rate loans, passing the interest rate risk to the borrower.

Interest rate volatility affected nonbank intermediaries as well. For example, life insurance companies traditionally provided implicit and explicit options in their contracts. With higher rates, however, policyholders let low-yielding policies lapse and took out low-interest policy loans in volume. The insurance companies responded by altering their liabilities to resemble those offered by depository institutions and mutual funds. To match the duration of these new liabilities more closely and to reduce their interest rate risk, life insurers have sold off part of their long-term commercial mortgage portfolio.

While banks sought to eliminate the unprofitable or risky aspects of the traditional lending relationship, the value to the bank of its other aspects has probably increased, especially as the emphasis in measuring bank performance has shifted from asset growth to rate of return on equity. Many of the nonlending services provided by banks produce fee income and are not covered by capital requirements. Customers tend to concentrate their purchases of financial services with one provider or a few. Usually the main provider is a lender. The need to offer the key service of lending pushes banks to reshape their lending activity to retain the element crucial to the borrower (access to funds) and eliminate the element unprofitable to the bank (retention on balance sheet). Thus origination of loans for sale as participations emerges as a business line.

For the borrower, the value of the banking relationship has more clearly declined for a variety of reasons. Actions such as cutting credit lines have reduced the attractiveness of banks. Legally binding commitments have replaced credit lines; NIFs and other underwritten facilities have replaced some short-term and syndicated lending; and the FRN market has replaced part of the interbank market, as even bank borrowers have tried to ensure their medium-term access to funds. In these cases, the borrower is looking for less flexibility and more certainty in the lending arrangement than under a system of bank credit lines. But the demise of the implicit contract means the demise of the distinguishing feature of a loan.

The perception that asset quality has declined at many banks and that some may be vulnerable to liquidity problems in difficult market conditions has also undermined bank credibility and the value of the banking relationship. Many of the largest, most creditworthy borrowers find that they can tap the markets at rates more favorable than those offered by most of the largest banks.

International flows of funds also affect the value of the banking relationship by changing the identity of the major lenders in the world. Traditional banking has eroded much less overseas than in the United States. In a country such as Germany, for example, banks' equity investments in major borrowers help cement the borrower-lender relationship. In addition, some foreign banks, especially Japanese banks, have acquired assets aggressively in the past few years.

But domestic borrowers may view foreign banks as less credible in a banking relationship than domestic banks for many reasons: questions regarding the lender of last resort, a history of capital controls, or even conflicts of national interest. In these cases, the borrower may prefer to use an investment bank rather than replace a domestic banking relationship with a foreign one.

Since banks chiefly provide short-term funds, corporate and other borrowers will turn away from banks when their needs call for longer-term finance. Following increased reliance on short-term debt in the latter half of the 1970s, firms turned to the long-term market in 1982 and again in 1984 through 1986, as long-term rates declined.

Finally, sharper competition among banks, including foreign banks, as well as encroachment by finance companies and thrifts on traditional bank activities such as consumer loans and commercial real estate lending, has reduced the perceived cost of severing a banking relationship. Large, high-quality borrowers now have little difficulty in finding new lenders. And the view that plenty of liquidity is around in the banking system amplifies that effect.

In particular, increased competition and a trend away from specialization by financial institutions allow borrowers to unbundle the banking relationship. By shopping for individual services such as credit lines, loans, and deposit services, the borrower can reproduce the relationship at lower cost. This kind of unbundling is separate from the unbundling of risks seen in the financial markets, which is related to the development of derivative products such as futures and options.

The weakened role of relationship is seen both in the reduced share of large U.S. banks in the prime wholesale lending market and also in the decline of loyalty among medium-size corporate customers. A recent Board survey pointed to a decline in the share of medium-size firms that bank with the institution from which they borrowed.[2]

Moreover, as the palette of services offered by nonbank financial firms grows to resemble that offered by banks, the customer views the "relationship" as more similar. The loss of uniqueness means a loss of market power. Banks can respond by bolstering their ability to offer better access to funds or they can emulate to the extent legally possible the unique product of investment banks, underwriting, by selling loans or placing commercial paper. That choice will depend on the cost of intermediation.

Bank versus market intermediation
Forms of intermediation

Almost all financial transactions are intermediated in some form. The most significant exception is the direct issuance of commercial paper, although even here the holders are often financial intermediaries. The term intermediation covers a number of functions. In its simplest form, it is brokerage: borrowers are matched with lenders for a fee. A second form of intermediation is underwriting. Borrowers are again matched with lenders, but the borrower receives a certain sum at a certain interest rate at a certain time. The underwriter therefore bears and absorbs uncertainties about the demand for the securities in return for an uncertain spread.

A third kind of intermediation is carried out by mutual funds. It involves selling shares in a pool of assets, where returns to the investor are based on the return of the portfolio of assets the fund holds. Maturities of assets and liabilities are generally matched and are

[2]Senior Loan Officer Opinion Survey, August 1986, Board of Governors of the Federal Reserve System.

either based on some agreed-upon future date when the fund will be liquidated, as in a closed-end fund, or on the preferences of the fund's investors, with assets liquidated as shareholders make withdrawals. As the fund grows in size, actual asset liquidation costs are minimized by the reasonably predictable flow of payments in and out of the fund and the continual reinvestment of part of the portfolio. Besides matching lenders with borrowers, the principal social benefit of a mutual fund is that it can offer an investor a liquid and diversified investment with a low minimum denomination.

A fourth kind of intermediation is that performed by depository institutions, insurance companies, and finance companies. Such financial firms make loans and issue liabilities against the intermediary as a whole. They absorb the interest rate and funding risk over the life of their loans. They will generally also transform maturities and absorb credit losses, and in the case of banks, thrifts, and finance companies, issue fairly liquid liabilities against rather illiquid assets.

The ability to offer a liquid liability with low credit risk against illiquid, risky assets derives from the intermediary's economies of scale, which enable it to pool risks and generate liquidity, as well as from its capital, which buffers losses. (A mutual fund makes use of these economies of scale as well.) A sizable portfolio allows diversification and thus a reduction of the variability of returns and a minimization of capital needs. Since only a fraction of depositors' liabilities will be converted to cash at any one time, cash or clearing balance needs are fairly predictable and depositors do not usually have to fear for the liquidity of their claims. The existence of a lender of last resort and the presence of deposit insurance or other forms of "safety net" arrangements provide an added layer of protection.[3]

These four types of intermediation should not be identified too closely with types of institutions, however. An investment bank that funds a large inventory of corporate and government bonds with overnight securities loans is carrying out maturity transformation. But the business purpose of an investment bank is not to bear credit risk or to fund a stock of assets, as it is for other financial intermediaries.

A simple model of bank and market intermediation

Two key questions raised by the spread of securitization are: Has the cost of maturity and liquidity transformation performed by depository institutions risen so much that it is no longer economically profitable? And has it risen sufficiently to allow the proliferation of substitute forms of intermediation? Answers to these questions require a systematic analysis of costs.

This section presents a simple model of banking and the commercial paper market, which is meant to be a representative securities market. The model views the cost of bank intermediation as the spread between lending and deposit rates needed to cover costs and earn a normal profit. The wider the spread, the greater the opportunities for securities underwriting to channel funds from investors to corporate borrowers.

A bank takes deposits from small and large investors, makes commercial and other loans, perhaps conducts nonloan fee income business, and holds capital. The depositor searches for investments that provide an attractive combination of liquidity, safety, and rate of return. Convenience and flexibility in managing other financial assets may also be important. The loan customer has a fixed borrowing need and can choose between the loan or commercial paper market. The banking and commercial paper markets are reasonably competitive, so that prices are close to marginal costs.

For a given deposit rate, the bank must earn an interest rate that will cover its marginal costs and a normal return to capital, the sum of which we will denote BSC, the cost of holding a loan on balance sheet. That cost is:

$$BSC = kE + \frac{(1-k)(R+D)}{(1-q)} + A + LL$$

where k = capital to asset ratio
E = required rate of return on equity
R = market interest rate on deposits
D = FDIC insurance premium
q = required reserve ratio
A = origination and servicing cost, expressed as a rate per dollar
LL = expected loan loss rate, net of recoveries.

For simplicity, this ignores income taxes and loan fees.

Changes in reserve and capital requirements, when the requirements are binding, will influence the spread between BSC and the deposit rate, which we denote s_b. The influence of these key variables is summarized in Table 1. Movements in the spread s_b may have a loose connection to interest rate cycles. When nominal interest rates rise, the cost of reserve requirements (foregone interest) rises. A change in the cost of capital, that is, the required rate of return determined in the stock market, will also influence s_b. The cost of capital is tied only indirectly to interest rates. As interest rates approach a cyclical peak, it seems likely that the required return would rise since returns on alternative investments will have increased. In general, the required rate of return will always be at least as high as the riskless rate of return, since the investor will view this

---

[3]Originally, commercial loans were made against short-term bills. This type of lending probably involved little maturity transformation and possibly less credit risk than commercial lending today.

as the opportunity cost of funds. But the required rate of return may at times stay high as interest rates begin to fall, because capital gains raise the return on existing long-term instruments.

At its narrowest, the spread s_b may still be large enough to allow some borrowers to finance more cheaply in the commercial paper market. As s_b widens, the commercial paper market becomes attractive to a broader group of borrowers. The cost of a commercial paper borrowing will be

$$CCP = R_{cp} + U,$$

where R_{cp} is the rate of return to the investor and U is the underwriting cost, expressed as a spread. The borrower will prefer to use the commercial paper market whenever BSC is greater than CCP. If we assume for a moment that R_{cp} is greater than R, the deposit rate, securitization will occur whenever

$$s_b > U + (R_{cp}-R).[4]$$

[4]With marginal cost pricing, the borrower pays $R_L = R + s_b$ in the loan market and $R'_L = R_{cp} + U$ in the commercial paper market. The borrower will be indifferent between them when $R_L - R'_L = 0$. That implies $R + s_b = U + R_{cp}$ or $s_b = U + (R_{cp}-R)$ at the margin.

Table 1

Factors Influencing the Spread between Loan and Deposit Interest Rates

In a competitive market, price will equal marginal cost:

$$R_L = kE + \frac{(1-k)(R-D)}{(1-q)} + A + LL$$

(The variables are those defined in the text.) The spread between the bank lending rate and the deposit rate, s_b, is:

$$s_b = kE + \frac{(1-k)(R+D)}{(1-q)} + A + LL - R.$$

In addition, we assume that the required rate of return on equity is always higher than deposit interest rates by at least a small margin. The table below summarizes the direction of change in the spread s_b when key variables increase:

Variable That Changes	Direction of Change in s_b	Comments
Deposit rate (R)	+	a rise in nominal rates raises s_b
Cost of capital (E)	+	a rise in the capital asset ratio raises s_b
Capital to asset ratio (k)	+, if $E > \frac{R+D}{1-q}$	a rise in the cost of capital raises s_b if the rate of return on equity is above the deposit rate by a sufficient margin, which will generally hold
Reserve requirements (q)	+	a rise in the reserve requirement raises s_b
Deposit insurance premium (D)	+	a rise in the deposit insurance premium raises s_b

To make a commercial paper offering attractive to investor and borrower, the marginal cost of underwriting commercial paper must be less than s_b, since the investor must earn a higher rate of return than on a bank deposit to compensate him for the somewhat higher risk and the borrower must pay a rate below the bank lending rate. If large investors at the margin require a lower rate of return on commercial paper than on bank deposits, this is an additional advantage to the commercial paper market.[5]

If there are large fixed fees involved in setting up a commercial paper program (for example, to obtain a rating), then the discounted present value of interest savings from borrowing through commercial paper must be large enough to compensate for the fixed costs. A narrow spread s_b would allow access to the commercial paper market only to large borrowers; a wider spread would allow access to many more. In other words, the borrower is likely to look at the total cost of a discrete amount of borrowing and choose the cheapest alternative.

If the spread s_b becomes sufficiently wide, more complex arrangements can link borrowers and lenders. Money market mutual funds can collect savings and purchase commercial paper. Since the fund managers will collect a fee that we can think of as a spread, hold some funds in cash at a prudential level of reserves, and earn a return to whatever capital underlies the fund (generally none), the spread s_b has to be wide enough to accommodate both the underwriting cost of the commercial paper and the cost of intermediating through the mutual fund. If we denote the mutual fund's spread as s_{mf}, then the spread is wide enough when $s_b > U + s_{mf}$ and $R_{cp}-s_{mf}$ is greater than the deposit rate available to retail investors.[6] The fairly simple structure of a mutual fund suggests that the mutual fund's spread is probably low, and certainly lower than at a bank. Some money funds charge only 50 basis points.

This framework can be generalized further to include the decision of an intermediary to sell its assets. An investor is willing to purchase a risky asset or pool of assets if the investor believes it has adequate protection against the risks assumed. If the investor is a financial institution used to assessing and bearing credit risk, it considers its own capital and its funding costs in determining the price to pay and the rate of return it

[5]Over the last ten years, top-grade commercial paper rates have sometimes been below both bank certificate of deposit (CD) rates and the London interbank offered rate (LIBOR).

[6]The spread $s_b = R_L-R$. A borrower will switch to the commercial paper market when $R_L > R_{cp} + U$. A depositor will switch to mutual funds if $R_{cp}-s_{mf} > R$, if an institutional investor, or if $R_{cp}-s_{mf} > R_D$, the retail deposit rate, if a retail investor.

earns. Most other investors, often lacking capital to absorb losses, seek to avoid nonpayment of principal by requiring greater protection from the seller: larger price discounts or a recourse provision, possibly in the form of a reserve fund. These investors also consider funding or opportunity costs.

The bank selling the asset can express the charge to income from a price discount or from setting up a reserve fund as the equivalent of a level of capital held over the life of the loan. It can compare this level with the capital it is required to hold against the loan if the loan is on its balance sheet. It can also compare the return on the asset required by investors and the bank's cost of funds.

When the amount of credit protection required by the investor is equivalent to less capital than the bank's targeted capital-asset ratio, or there are other funding cost savings, there are potential gains in selling off the asset to investors. Increases in the bank cost of capital also promote a shifting of assets to holders requiring less capital or having a lower cost of capital.

Funding and capital costs are not the only determinants of asset sales. Sales of asset pools have also grown because of the sharp reduction of costs in packaging and servicing the assets.

If the spread between the cost of holding loans and the deposit rate is loosely tied to the level of interest rates, then the share of securities in total credit extended rises as interest rates are peaking and falls as interest rates reach their trough. A certain amount of cyclicality can be observed (Chart 1).[7] Two factors work to dampen this cycle, however. First, periods of high interest rates usually coincide with periods of scarce liquidity, low private borrowing, and a shift by investors to safer, more liquid investments. Second, profitable operation of a mutual fund requires large size in order to take advantage of economies of scale inherent in many forms of financial intermediation. To gain sufficient size takes time, and the interest rate cycle in an unregulated environment may normally be too short to attain such a large scale.

These impediments to the securitization cycle have weakened in the last decade. The combination of high inflation and Regulation Q in the latter half of the 1970s created ample opportunity for money market funds to flourish. With low marginal and average costs once they reach a large size, money market funds are unlikely to

[7]Monthly and quarterly data suggest that securitization takes off just as corporate bond rates reach their peak. This pattern probably reflects both increased bank intermediation costs and the resurgence of bond demand in anticipation of capital gains. Aggregating to annual data obscures this pattern, and an inverse relationship between securitization and interest rates emerges.

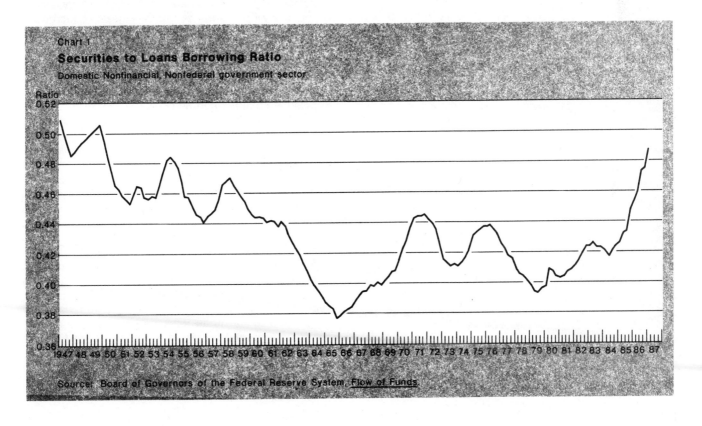

Chart 1
Securities to Loans Borrowing Ratio
Domestic Nonfinancial, Nonfederal government sector

Source: Board of Governors of the Federal Reserve System, Flow of Funds.

disappear. Their growth has expanded the market for commercial paper, which might otherwise be limited by the large minimum denomination of the instruments.

Behavior of the cost of bank intermediation

In the late 1970s, the spread s_b widened to unprecedented postwar levels and remained large (Chart 2). Since then, the spread has fallen. Under conservative assumptions, s_b was no wider in 1985-86 than it was in 1975-76. Under other assumptions, the spread since 1982 has risen beyond the 1975-78 levels (see Appendix).

In particular, the assumptions about the target level of capital at banks and the target rate of return on equity affect our perception of the importance of bank intermediation costs since 1982. The base case assumptions are that the desired bank capital-asset ratio is fairly represented by actual capital-asset ratios up to 1981 and by bank regulatory guidelines since then and that the rate of return on market equity has been constant at 15 percent over the whole period. The assumption about bank capital ratios after 1981 would seem to understate the case somewhat since most banks are targeting capital-asset ratios above the minimum required.

Under the base case assumptions, s_b averaged 85

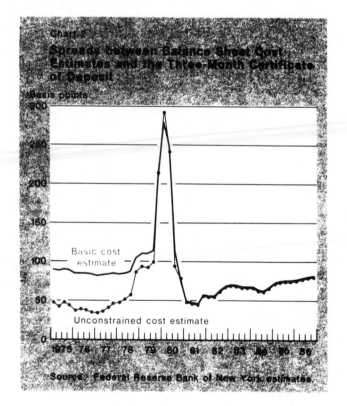

Chart 2

Spreads between Balance Sheet Cost Estimates and the Three-Month Certificate of Deposit

Basis points

Basic cost estimate

Unconstrained cost estimate

1975 76 77 78 79 80 81 82 83 84 85 86

Source: Federal Reserve Bank of New York estimates.

basis points in 1975-78, spiked in 1980-81 under the influence of the temporary imposition of marginal reserve requirements on managed liabilities, and averaged 70 basis points from 1982-85, with a rising trend. Movements in s_b have been larger than the movements in the difference between high-grade 90-day commercial paper and CD rates, which fluctuated trendlessly in a range of −10 to 10 basis points over the whole period, except for a brief dip to −20 basis points in 1978.

The base case assumptions suggest at most that bank intermediation costs remained at their high late-1970s level and thus allowed securitization to spread to new financial transactions. An argument for a cost-driven wave of securitization after 1982 needs to assume that banks were largely unconstrained by capital in the period before 1981 or that their required rate of return on capital rose after 1981. If these assumptions are plausible, the role of bank intermediation costs may be important in the latest wave of securitization.

Indeed, the rise in bank capital requirements alone cannot explain the perceived increased cost of maintaining a loan on the balance sheet. Higher capital requirements should reduce the perceived riskiness of banks and bring about a fall in the required rate of return on equity. This fall does not appear to have occurred, however, for several reasons. First, the rise in capital requirements coincided with a reassessment of the overall riskiness of banks—thus the increased capital may have prevented a larger rise. Second, banks expanded their off-balance sheet exposures even as they raised their capital, undercutting much of the effect. Third, the market for bank capital is most likely imperfect. The required rate of return may be slow to adjust to positive changes and quick to respond to potentially negative developments.[8] Fourth, the relatively high interest rates in the early 1980s no doubt put a floor under bank capital costs, preventing higher capital requirements from quickly producing a reduction in the bank cost of capital.

But the most important reason may be common to all financial firms and helps to explain the breadth of the securitization phenomenon: strong upward pressures on the cost of capital in the financial sector as a whole. Many financial firms share a tendency to fund in shorter-term markets and to hold assets that are longer-term; they tend to have some sort of negative gap. This links their returns on equity and makes their equities close substitutes in investor portfolios. In the 1980s, a broad range of financial firms have sought to raise capital: commercial banks, investment banks seeking public

[8] In particular, the required rate of return on equity may not fall if the capital requirement of the regulator is higher than that required by the market. Higher capital ratios provide a social benefit for which investors cannot be compensated.

ownership, finance companies, and a host of foreign institutions. Falling barriers to entry, especially overseas, a wave of new products, and the growth of secondary market activity have all opened up opportunities that require more financial capital. Moreover, the rate of return on investment bank equities has been much higher than on bank stocks, which puts additional pressure on banks to raise return on equity.

Indeed, as banks have lost business in the prime wholesale and in other loan markets, the loss overall has been not so much to other financial intermediaries as to institutional investors for whom capital is not really a constraint.[9] That is, as argued earlier, the loss of bank share is not a symptom of classic disintermediation.

The sustained high level of bank intermediation costs has occurred at the same time that many of the costs of transacting in the securities markets have been declining. The introduction of shelf registration through Rule 415 and the opening up of the Euromarkets significantly reduced the cost of underwriting and eased access to the markets. The growth of risk management product markets has made it easier for investment banks to hedge risks in making markets, although higher volatility may have raised those risks. Over the last 15 years, underwriting costs have fallen modestly in the commercial paper market, and more considerably in the bond markets, especially the Eurobond market. Information costs have generally fallen, so that investors are better able to evaluate borrowers. Orders are executed more rapidly.

But capital requirements are not entirely beside the point. Forms of securitization such as loan sales to foreign banks, the expansion of thrift assets where capital requirements until recently have been low (3 percent or less), and the growth of mutual funds with essentially no capital show that capital constraints matter. Even among finance companies, much of the growth has been among special purpose issuers with very thin capitalization.

As a consequence, the financial markets are intermediating a large volume of transactions. Increasingly complex chains of transactions are replacing lending by intermediaries, including mutual funds that purchase mortgage-backed bonds, high-return low-quality corporate bonds, and other securities. Ample liquidity has meant that the surge of securities issuance has not come fully at the expense of bank lending, so that overall credit has grown sharply.

[9]According to the flow of funds accounts, between 1975 and 1985 banks and thrifts lost about 7 percent of market share (measured in holdings of total financial assets), while finance companies gained 1 percent; pension funds and insurance companies, 2 percent; and mutual funds, 4 percent.

The analysis so far points to three conclusions. First, a chain of transactions that uses less capital to intermediate a financial claim than is needed to retain an asset on a bank's balance sheet can substitute for bank lending. Thus, even complex or highly illiquid assets could be securitized if the transformations needed to make them marketable (for example, credit and liquidity enhancements) and the underwriting cost involve lower capital costs and fees than bank lending.

Second, even highly profitable lines of bank lending could be sold to investors through the securities markets if the costs of packaging, underwriting, and protecting against credit losses are less than the difference between the cost of booking the loan and the cost of deposits. By selling the asset, the bank could capture some part of the profits of lending and the reduction of intermediation cost.

Third, the expectation that high spreads in traditional intermediation will persist encourages a lasting shift toward securitization. In the short run, a rise in s_b directs borrowers to the commercial paper market, increases the demand for investment banking services, and raises the rate of return on investment bank capital. If the high returns persist, capital is attracted to investment banking and rates of return begin to decline, enhancing the competitiveness of securities relative to bank lending. In the longer run, the investment bank sector is larger and the commercial bank sector is smaller. Securitization then becomes a structural feature of the financial markets.

Gaining access to the securities market

Some bank loans are not really suitable for replacement by securities. Such loans may be too small; information about the debtor may be scarce; risks assumed by the creditor may be too difficult to assess. Nevertheless, certain kinds of asset-backed securities can overcome these difficulties.

Pooling loans is one important means to reduce transactions costs and improve risk assessment. Some securities, such as mortgage-backed and auto-loan-backed issues, rely on the law of large numbers to provide more reliable statistical probabilities of events that affect the rate of return on the securities. These events include default and prepayment. Pooling implies that certain regularities of behavior can be observed among the population at large. For example, while the individual probabilities of default among all consumer borrowers at a bank may be unknown, the distribution of defaults is revealed over time and is not expected to change much. Further, aggregating a large number of loans reduces the investor's transactions cost.

The process of pooling reduces uncertainty, but in general it cannot be done without introducing new credit exposures. Most pooling arrangements lead to multiparty exposures: the investor is relying on the past and future performance of an originator, a servicer, a trustee, the "due diligence" staff at the underwriter, and the ultimate borrowers. Even if all the participants are top-quality and entail only minor credit risks, these risks accumulate.[10] Thus, the risk of multiple exposures is still greater than any single exposure.

A second method of gaining access to the market is collateralization or, more loosely, asset-backing.[11] Collateralization refers to a perfected security interest in real or financial assets that could be liquidated if the borrower defaults. Asset-backing is weaker than collateralization. The investor has no security interest in the assets but can rely on a transactions structure that removes the assets from the control of the debtor to assure repayment. Both methods substitute either the credit standing of the issuer of the underlying claims or the value of real property (or its cash flow) for the credit standing of the borrower. The substitution may be in whole or in part.

Except for first and refunding mortgage bonds, collateralized securities have never been very common in the United States. They have been common abroad, and in some domestic markets, such as Japan, they are the main form of corporate debt allowed. Recent efforts to increase the use of collateral in the United States have met with mixed success. Frequently, collateralized funding is expensive enough to compare unfavorably to other sources. For example, mortgage repurchase transactions are now generally a cheaper source of funds than collateralized commercial paper. The conservative reinvestment and prepayment assumptions of the ratings agencies account for most of the higher cost of a collateralized security. These conservative assumptions reflect real risks that are hard to quantify.

The less stringent form of asset-backing reduces this problem. In a typical asset-backed transaction, the firm originates and sells assets to a special purpose entity that is structured to be legally independent of the firm and unaffected by the firm's bankruptcy. The assets sold are generally high-quality and self-liquidating. The entity then issues a security that is backed by a letter of credit from a bank or a guarantee from an insurance company. The bank or guarantor looks to the assets to provide a cushion if the commercial paper is not paid off. In

many ways, the letter of credit resembles a performance bond since the main reason the funds generated by the receivables would not be paid over to the commercial paper holders would be if the seller/servicer failed to perform the servicing function. It may also be a way to deal with assets that are not self-liquidating.

Collateralization and asset-backing both reflect a theory of segregation of the originating firm's assets and liabilities into pools or classes. Such a theory claims to offer more security to new creditors, but it does so at the expense of the firm's existing creditors and perhaps its owners. The theory would only work if all the streams of income and expense of the firm were exactly correlated. If the income streams produced by a firm's assets are random and even somewhat uncorrelated, then the firm gains by diversification and the sum of the flows is less variable than the individual flows. Even if assets and liabilities were matched exactly and each pair packaged as an asset-backed transaction, the gains from pooling cash flows having a random component would be foregone.

A disadvantage of collateralization and asset-backing is that it may weaken the internal risk-pooling at already weak firms. The reason for pledging or isolating assets is that the overall sum of the flows is viewed as "too risky." In other words, the originating firm is not of sufficiently high credit standing to gain access to the market. The collateralized or asset-backed technique removes the higher-quality and presumably more certain income flows, weighting the firm's remaining cash flows toward more risky income. The firm can make this problem better or worse depending on how it structures the liabilities to take on interest rate risk. If asset sales or pledges sufficiently reduce its total funding risk, the firm could lower its overall risk.

In many cases, financial institutions are transforming or reducing risk by assisting in securitizing assets (for example, providing a letter of credit) and adding their own credit exposure to them. As a consequence, classes of very unrelated securities may in fact become related. For example, if bank ABC issues commercial paper, guarantees the commercial paper of XYZ, acts as paying agent for AAA's bond issue, and is trustee for auto-loan-backed securities of a major auto finance company, these securities have in common a credit exposure to bank ABC. If the "weakest link" theory is applied, as it is by rating agencies such as Standard and Poor's, a downgrading of a financial institution may lead to downgradings of securities in which the institution plays a part.

This is not to say that investors may not benefit from asset-backed securities. Such securities may offer a better risk-return trade-off than many others. But the reduction of risk—either by pooling or by segregation

---

[10]The risk of a failure of the security is the risk that any participant fails. Assuming participant failures are independent and disjoint events, the probability of default is the sum of the individual probabilities of failure.

[11]Some pools are sold through collateralized bond issues (for example, collateralized mortgage obligations) for tax reasons. Here we mean that assets of various types are pledged to back a bond issue with no reference to any pooling properties.

from the parent—cannot be achieved without introducing new credit risks, however small they may be. Failure to take account of these credit risks can lead to overpricing of securities in the markets.

If the firm uses the asset-backed market to expand its activities without expanding its balance sheet—a reason cited for some mortgage-backed and receivables-backed transactions—it may also weaken existing creditors. A firm expanding its activities does not increase the burden on its capital if the expanded activity is riskless. But activities financed by asset-backed securities are not riskless. No matter how short the time period in which assets are accumulated for packaging in securities form, some risk exists that interest rates will change and the firm will incur some loss. Unless it is hedged, more risk is borne by the existing creditors and owners of the firm. Moreover, assessing this additional risk is probably difficult.

In summary, complex transactions can replace bank lending if the costs of intermediation are low enough. But some transactions have spillover costs to existing creditors, the firm's owners, and the financial system. They may have hidden risks that are hard to analyze and price. The apparent cost of these transactions might be well below the true cost.

Deposits versus securities

The last link between investor and borrower in the traditional bank lending relationship is between the bank and the investor. Typically, savers have held claims on a bank in the form of deposits. Investors have chosen from an array of bank claims that includes subordinated debt, preferred stock, and equity, as well as deposits. But increasingly, savers and investors are replacing deposits with securities claims on banks or bypassing banks altogether. Ironically, the shift toward securities comes at a time when banks have great freedom in the type of deposit services they can offer.

The essential features of a deposit as opposed to a security of any type are the absolute absence of price risk and the low transactions costs. Certain types of deposits, such as demand and some time deposits, have a high degree of liquidity as well. Between FDIC insurance and the supervision of the banking system, bank deposits also have a very low level of credit risk.

Certificates of deposit (CDs) do not fit into this picture very neatly, since they are deposits but have many of the characteristics of securities. In particular, they can be traded over their life and therefore involve some price risk. Like other deposits, CDs have low transactions costs and the credit risk benefits of supervision.

In general, securities offer a higher rate of return and the potential for sale before maturity but carry far greater risk than bank deposits. Investors assume price, liquidity and credit risk. In well-developed, liquid markets, securities also increase flexibility in managing assets.

A number of factors have served to weaken the position of deposits as against securities. Investors have learned that some of the ostensible advantages of deposits do not in fact exist. While deposits are not subject to nominal price risk, depositors suffered heavy real losses in the highly inflationary years of the late 1970s and early 1980s. In this respect, deposits are no different from any instrument with fixed nominal value. The perception that deposits are extremely safe has probably also diminished, at least in the eyes of some large depositors. The decline in banking relationships could lead to a reduction in required bank deposits such as compensating balances held in lieu of fees for services.

But these are not the major forces that are changing the balance between deposits and securities. If they were, then new securities would probably be largely index-linked bonds or government-risk securities. Index-linked securities could provide considerable protection against inflation; government securities have no credit risk. In fact, however, the markets have taken a different direction.

Three major factors seem to be behind the stronger growth of securities demand. The first is the institutionalization of savings in the United States and other industrial countries. Savers increasingly hold claims on pension funds, insurance companies, savings plans and mutual funds—all institutional investors that manage large portfolios of assets and usually pay rates of return on liabilities related to portfolio performance. Many such holdings are favored by their tax-exempt status when provided as part of employee compensation, but these institutions also offer lower transactions costs and greater diversification than individual investors can achieve. Such institutionalization leads to the possibility of diversification and management of a portfolio of financial claims within the institution, instead of reliance on deposit-based intermediaries. Institutionalization of savings abroad, especially in Japan, is also important in a period of strong capital inflows into the United States.

Institutionalization of savings is enhanced by the growth of wealth and by investor sophistication. Indeed, the increase in investor sophistication has itself been an important reason for growing securities demand. Individual investors, motivated in part by income tax considerations and by risk/return characteristics, have shown particular interest in zero coupon bonds and equity shares.

A second factor is the development of techniques using options, futures and other hedging instruments to manage risks, especially price risks. This means that institutional investors again are less reliant on banks to achieve relatively liquid, safe portfolios; they can perform more transformation within their portfolio and hedge any resulting risks. If banks earn economic rents in providing this transformation or are inefficient in their use of capital or other resources, then the process of transformation will shift outside the banks, not just to near-banks like finance companies but also to the portfolios of investors.

The development of risk management techniques has been lopsided, however. Growing wealth and ample liquidity have given investors the wherewithal to take more risk into their portfolios. Still, no new method has been found to hedge or diversify away credit risk any more efficiently than banks have done for decades. This lies behind the paradox of the simultaneous growth of credit enhancement and development of the market for "junk" bonds, bonds with higher returns reflecting presumably higher credit risk.

Some investors are unable or unwilling to bear much credit risk. Examples are money market funds, which publish a prospectus stating that they invest only in top-quality assets so as to attract risk-averse shareholders; some institutional investors that have fiduciary responsibilities; and small retail investors. As their portfolios expand rapidly, perhaps in response to favorable tax benefits or a shift in intermediation costs, they begin to exhaust the supply of quality credits. And this problem can be made worse by a decline in the number of good names, as has occurred in the United States.

With credit enhancement, lower-quality borrowers can be made acceptable to such investors. Thus, if the demand for high-quality credits expands faster than the supply, demand for credit enhancement increases, returns to capital in the credit enhancement sector rise, and new capital is attracted, as seen in the entry of foreign banks into the letter of credit business and the incorporation of new bond insurers.

At the same time, some larger investors, including less constrained institutional investors and high net worth individuals, can manage their portfolios much like banks, holding securities of all types and using the diversification principles that banks use. Higher capital requirements reduce the efficiency of banks relative to many institutional investors, offsetting their comparative advantage in credit analysis. If other efficiencies do not counterbalance these higher capital needs, more banklike portfolios are built up outside the banking system. This expands the market for low quality assets. Junk bonds become cheaper to borrowers than a bank loan paired with a swap that fixes the interest rate.

The final type of change contributing to stronger securities demand is an apparently sharply enhanced desire for liquidity or transferability on the part of investors. When a security is compared to a deposit of equal maturity, the security offers the option of resale into a secondary market if conditions appear to be changing adversely. The deposit generally does not, although the CD is an important exception. Sometimes it is possible to borrow against a deposit or to withdraw it before maturity after paying a fee. But high penalties, highly leveraged balance sheets, or the wide spread between bank lending and deposit rates may make those alternatives unattractive. Increased volatility in interest rates—or even in the underlying creditworthiness of borrowers—makes the option to transfer a security more attractive to investors. This also helps to explain why more capital is being employed to make markets and enhance secondary market liquidity.

Developments in the last few years can account for changes in the choice between securities and deposits by savers. The wider spread for bank intermediation and the advent of new risk management techniques mean that management of banklike portfolios by investors can also substitute for the transformation performed by banks. That transformation has become more expensive for the banks because of higher capital costs. Finally, the higher volatility of interest rates experienced in recent years, along with more volatility in perceived credit quality, has enhanced the value of liquidity in the market.

Conclusion

The degree of securitization appears to depend on the relative importance of relationship in financial transactions, on the cost of traditional financial intermediation, especially bank intermediation, compared to the cost of intermediation through securities markets or private placement, and on the ability of institutional and other large investors to manage or reduce financial risks. In all three areas, changes in the last few years have hastened the development of securitization.

Relationship with borrowers and with depositors, a key aspect of commercial banking, has probably declined in value over the last few years. The response of banks and thrifts to the higher volatility of interest rates— cutting credit lines, increasing prepayment penalties, and selling assets—has resulted in contractual arrangements more easily reproduced by the market. In addition, increased competition in the financial sector has reduced both the market power of banking institutions and the cost of severing ties to banks.

The spread between deposit rates and the cost of holding loans on the balance sheet widened substantially in the late 1970s and early 1980s at the major commercial banks. By conservative measures, it has remained large or even risen above the 1975-78 levels.

The widening spread reflects the generally high level of interest rates in the early 1980s, the higher capital requirements imposed by bank regulators, and the high cost of capital. This last factor has probably contributed to higher marginal costs at all financial intermediaries and helps to explain securitization's broad base.

These higher costs allow firms specializing in underwriting and placement to capture business from traditional financial intermediaries. Underwriting securities, which has traditionally been expensive relative to bank lending, has become relatively less so. Increased competition among underwriters has lowered fees; new hedging techniques and shelf registration have reduced underwriting cost. A combination of commercial paper underwriting and mutual fund operations by money market funds can in many cases intermediate short-term commercial borrowing more cheaply than a bank.

The change in relative costs is large enough to make it attractive to shift to the market even those activities that are now profitable at banks, such as automobile financing and credit card lending. The shift occurs in part because such sales conserve on expensive capital and in part because the cost of packaging small loans has dropped so sharply. Moreover, banks can help less creditworthy borrowers tap the financial markets by backing securities issues with letters of credit. Banks still exploit their absolute advantage at credit analysis, while tying up relatively little capital.

The final major factor, the preference for securities over deposits, stems from the institutionalization of savings, improved techniques for analyzing and managing risk, and strong demand for liquidity. Institutional and retail investors are willing to assume risks that previously had been taken largely by banks and other depositories. This appetite for more complex instruments has had the perhaps unintended result of increasing the demand for credit enhancement, since no technological breakthrough in analyzing and managing most forms of credit risk, especially commercial credit risk, has been made.

Some factors have been pervasive throughout this analysis and by their nature suggest that securitization is driven by both long- and short-run forces. Increased competition from foreign banks and other intermediaries, the institutionalization of savings, growing investor sophistication, and declines in information and transactions costs in the securities markets are clearly long-run secular changes that on balance favor securitization. Other factors, such as higher volatility in financial asset prices or a higher cost of capital in the financial sector, may not be permanent and give securitization only a temporary impetus. Together, these factors have permitted the securities markets to replace traditional financial intermediation in many ways. Once established, these new intermediation methods are unlikely to disappear soon.

Christine Cumming

Appendix: Assumptions behind the Marginal Cost of Capital in Chart 2

Base Cost Assumptions

Return on equity:	15 percent assumed target rate of return on market equity
Capital/asset ratio:	Before 1981, annual weighted averages for a banking universe of 13 banks: Bank of Boston, Bank America, Bankers Trust, Chase Manhattan, Chemical Bank, Citicorp, Continental Illinois, First Chicago, Harris, J.P. Morgan, Manufacturers Hanover, Mellon, and Northern Trust; after 1981, minimum capital-asset guidelines and requirements, as recommended by the Federal Reserve System
Three-month CD rates:	Quarterly averages from Federal Reserve Bank of New York
Marginal reserve requirements:	The reserve requirement on non-personal time deposits with original maturity of 18 months or less for the largest banks, Federal Reserve Bulletin
FDIC premium:	Federal Deposit Insurance Corporation rate, including rebate

Unconstrained Cost Assumptions

Same as above, except the capital/asset ratio is assumed to be a nonbinding constraint before 1981, represented by a value of zero.

Article 37

The Prepayment Risk of Mortgage-backed Securities

By Sean Becketti

Since their creation in 1970, mortgage pass-through securities have played an increasing role in the portfolios of depository institutions. By 1988, savings and loan associations held 16 percent of their assets in mortgage-backed securities (MBSs). Commercial banks also have been increasing their share of the MBS market in recent years; they currently hold 3 percent of their assets in MBSs. Moreover, the participation of commercial banks in this market is likely to increase since mortgage pass-throughs receive favorable treatment under risk-based capital guidelines recently approved by federal regulators.

The attractions of federal agency pass-throughs for bank and S&L portfolio managers are easy to see. Most important are the federal agency guarantees, which virtually eliminate the credit

Sean Becketti is a senior economist at the Federal Reserve Bank of Kansas City. Deana VanNahmen, a research associate at the bank, provided research assistance. This article is based, in part, on research performed in collaboration with Charles S. Morris, also a senior economist at the bank.

risk of mortgage pass-throughs. In addition, an active secondary market provides high liquidity for pass-throughs. Finally, pass-through securities offer investors higher yields than comparable Treasury securities.

Despite their agency guarantees and other advantages, mortgage pass-through securities still expose investors to important risks. For one thing, the value of a mortgage pass-through is sensitive to changes in interest rates, a characteristic pass-throughs share with Treasury bonds. More important, and unlike Treasury bonds, a mortgage pass-through may be prepaid at any time. This risk of prepayment affects the interest sensitivity of mortgage pass-throughs and makes the timing of their cash flows difficult to predict.

Because of prepayment risk, mortgage-backed securities may be an unsuitable investment for many smaller depository institutions. This article examines the risks of investing in mortgage pass-through securities and highlights the role of prepayment risk. The article is divided into three sections. The first section describes the mortgage pass-through securities issued by the federal agencies and highlights the risks associated with mortgage prepayments. The second section explores the factors that determine prepayments and reports the prepayment experience of MBSs issued by the Federal National Mortgage Association (FNMA). The third section considers the practical problems prepayments pose and suggests some ways managers can reduce prepayment risk.

Mortgage pass-through securities

Mortgage pass-throughs are a relatively new security. Federal housing agencies have issued MBSs for just under 20 years.[1] Although MBSs are one of the most successful new securities of the last few decades, some of their characteristics are unfamiliar to many portfolio managers. This section describes the mortgage pass-through securities issued by the housing agencies, examines the risks of these securities, and discusses the central role played by prepayment risk.

The market for
mortgage pass-through securities

Mortgage pass-through securities are *pro rata* shares in the principal and interest payments from a pool of mortgages that underlies the securities. Between 50 and 250 basis points of the mortgage interest payments are retained by the issuing agency and the firm that originated and services the mortgages in the pool, but all other cash flows including mortgage prepayments, are ''passed-through'' to the investors. Since pass-throughs are shares in a specific pool of mortgage loans, mortgages that are prepaid are not replaced by new mortgages. Instead, the size of the mortgage pool shrinks as both prepayments and ordinary mortgage amortization reduce the balances of the mortgages in the pool.

The active secondary market for mortgage pass-throughs began in 1970 with the issue of the first MBSs by the Government National Mortgage Association (GNMA).[2] These pass-throughs were based on pools of mortgages guaranteed by the Federal Housing Administration and the Veterans Administration; that is, the individual mortgages in the pools were government-guaranteed. In 1971, the Federal Home Loan Mortgage Corporation (FHLMC) began issuing MBSs based on pools of conventional mortgages.[3] FNMA was the last of the three agencies to enter the MBS market. FNMA began issuing MBSs based both on pools of conventional mortgages and on pools of government-guaranteed mortgages in 1981.[4]

The MBS market has grown rapidly in the 18 years since the first GNMA issue. The outstanding balance of mortgage pass-throughs issued by these three agencies has grown to over $761 billion in the second quarter of 1988. From 1971 to 1988, the outstanding balance of pass-throughs has grown at an annual average rate of around 40 percent. These outstanding balances now account for almost a quarter of the total mortgage debt in the United States.[5]

---

[1] The term ''MBS'' is sometimes used to describe any mortgage-backed asset, not just mortgage pass-throughs. For the purposes of this article, only pass-throughs are included in MBSs.

[2] For a more extensive discussion of the secondary mortgage market, see Gordon H. Sellon, Jr. and Deana VanNahmen, ''The Securitization of Housing Finance,'' Federal Reserve Bank of Kansas City, *Economic Review* (July/August 1988), pp. 3-20.

[3] Conventional mortgages are mortgages that are not federally guaranteed or insured.

[4] In recent years, pass-throughs have been based on a variety of different types of mortgages, including adjustable rate mortgages. This article considers only MBSs based on pools of fixed rate mortgages, the category that accounts for the majority of mortgage pass-throughs.

[5] *Federal Reserve Bulletin*, vol. 74, No. 12 (December 1988), Table 1.54, p. A39.

Depository institutions hold a significant share of the outstanding MBSs in their portfolios. Savings and loan associations hold $212 billion of MBSs, roughly 28 percent of the amount outstanding, while commercial banks hold $85 billion of MBSs, roughly 11 percent of the amount outstanding.[6] Life insurance companies and private pension funds also hold considerable amounts of MBSs.[7]

The risks of mortgage pass-throughs

The suitability of mortgage-backed securities as an investment depends to a great extent on their risks. In looking at the risks of MBSs, a useful frame of reference is another asset of roughly similar expected maturity, such as a 10-year Treasury bond. MBSs and Treasuries can be compared on the basis of four types of risk: credit risk, liquidity risk, interest rate risk, and prepayment risk.

Credit risk, or the risk of default, is absent from both Treasury securities and MBSs. Treasury securities are backed by the full faith and credit of the U.S. government. MBSs are guaranteed by the federal agencies that issue them. These guarantees virtually eliminate the credit risk of the mortgages in the pool. In the case of MBSs issued by the Government National Mortgage Association, these guarantees carry the full faith

and credit of the United States. In other words, GNMA securities are as safe as Treasury securities. The MBSs offered by FNMA and FHLMC carry the explicit guarantee only of the issuing agency; however, these pass-throughs are considered by market participants to be default-free.[8]

Like Treasuries, MBSs have little liquidity risk. MBSs are issued in large denominations, have an active secondary market, and hence are almost as liquid as Treasury securities. As a result, depository institutions holding MBSs can easily adapt to unanticipated inflows or outflows of deposits.[9]

Holdings of both MBSs and Treasury bonds expose an institution to interest rate risk, the risk that changes in interest rates will greatly affect the market value of the asset. It is important for investors to keep in mind that pass-throughs, like Treasury bonds, are long-term investments and therefore subject to substantial interest rate risk.

Despite their similarities in other dimensions of risk, MBSs possess one important type of risk not shared by Treasury securities, prepayment

---

[6] *Federal Home Loan Bank Board News,* December 7, 1988; *Reports of Condition and Income,* Federal Reserve Board of Governors, Sept. 30, 1988; and *Federal Reserve Bulletin,* vol. 74, No. 12 (December 1988), Table 1.54, p. A39.

[7] Recent figures are difficult to find, but in June 1987 life insurance companies held $72 billion in MBSs (11 percent of the amount outstanding) and private pension funds held $33 billion (5 percent of the amount outstanding). These figures are taken from *The Mortgage Backed Securities Market: Statistical Annual 1988,* Guy D. Cecala, ed. (Probus Publishing Company, 1988), p. 17.

[8] Each agency offers a somewhat different guarantee. GNMA guarantees full and timely payment of principal and interest including prepayments and, as noted above, this guarantee carries the full faith and credit of the United States. FNMA also guarantees the full and timely payment of principal and interest including prepayments, but this guarantee is not explicitly backed by the Treasury. The FHLMC guarantees the full and timely payment of interest and the ultimate payment of principal, again without explicit Treasury backing. Judging by the market ratings of FNMA and FHLMC debt issues and by the statements of market participants, it is widely believed that FNMA and FHLMC securities issues are implicitly guaranteed by the U.S. Treasury.

[9] Note that MBSs have greater liquidity than the individual mortgages in the pool underlying the MBSs. Individual mortgages are for relatively small amounts, have little secondary market, and are extremely illiquid. Depository institutions holding mainly individual mortgages thus have greater difficulty adjusting their asset holdings up or down.

risk. Mortgage borrowers have the option to prepay their loans at any time. In contrast, the cash flows from a Treasury security are fixed. Prepayments can dramatically change the time pattern and total volume of cash flows from an MBS. For example, an increase in prepayments accelerates the return of principal payments and cuts short expected interest payments. Conversely, a decrease in prepayments slows down the payment of principal and increases the interest cash flow. Unfortunately, prepayments are difficult to predict, and this unpredictability makes it difficult to manage a portfolio that contains mortgage pass-throughs. The key to understanding MBSs is understanding the role played by prepayment risk.

The significance of prepayment risk

Prepayments make mortgage pass-throughs less attractive investments than Treasury securities in three ways. First, changes in prepayments in response to interest rate movements reduce the capital gains and increase the capital losses accruing to MBS investments. Second, prepayments accelerate the cash flows from an MBS when reinvestment opportunities for these cash flows offer low returns, and decelerate the cash flows from an MBS when reinvestment opportunities offer high returns.[10] Third, prepayments make the cash flows from an MBS unpredictable compared with the cash flows from a Treasury security.

The first of these three disadvantages—the smaller capital gains and larger capital losses of mortgage pass-throughs—reflects the borrower's option to prepay a mortgage whenever it is advantageous to do so. Just as with a Treasury security, the value of an MBS moves inversely with interest rates. However, when rates fall, some mortgage borrowers exercise their option to prepay their original mortgage and take out a new mortgage at the new, lower interest rate. These prepayments mitigate the increase in the value of the MBS by reducing the period over which MBS investors receive the original, higher mortgage interest rate. Increased prepayments cause the MBS to evaporate; they accelerate its amortization, just when the fall in interest rates increases its value.

Conversely, when interest rates rise, some mortgage borrowers remain in their homes longer than they had originally planned. In addition, home buyers may assume existing, lower-rate mortgages when possible rather than take out new mortgages. Both of these actions extend the originally anticipated term of the mortgage pass-through. In this case, reduced prepayments delay the amortization of the MBS precisely when the increase in interest rates reduces its value.

An example may be helpful in showing how much prepayments can change the interest rate sensitivity of MBSs. Consider the effect of a one percentage-point decrease in the interest rate, from 9 percent to 8 percent, on the value of a $100,000 share in a pool of newly issued, 30-year mortgages. Using published estimates of prepayment rates and discounting the cash flows from the mortgage pool by the new interest rate, it is possible to calculate the effects of this fall in rates on the market value of this hypothetical investment.[11]

---

[10] Technically, these first two disadvantages are two different aspects of a single phenomenon. The changes in prepayment rates associated with interest rate movements simultaneously alter the capital gains and losses of MBSs and alter their cash flows in ways that are disadvantageous for reinvestment. These two aspects are treated separately here to aid in understanding the effects of this single characteristic of mortgage pass-throughs.

---

[11] The effects described in this hypothetical example are calculated by applying estimated changes in prepayments and

CHART 1
The interest sensitivity of mortgage pass-throughs
(Dollar value of $100,000 share in a mortgage pool)

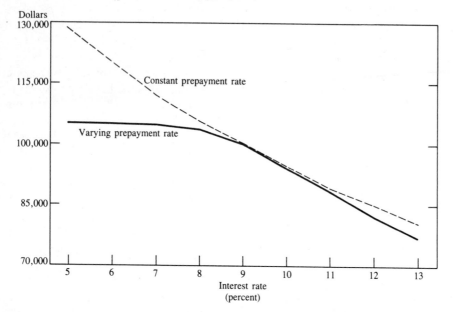

In this example, if the mortgage borrowers repaid their loans according to their original amortization schedule, allowing for a normal rate of prepayment, the fall in the interest rate would increase the value of this investment to $106,067, a 6.1 percent capital gain. However, some borrowers will take advantage of their option to prepay and will refinance their mortgages at the new lower rate. These prepayments hold the increase in value to $103,770, a 3.8 percent

capital gain. In other words, prepayments reduce the capital gain by more than a third.

Now consider the opposite case, a one percentage-point increase in the interest rate, from 9 percent to 10 percent. If the rate of prepayment did not change, the value of this investment would fall to $94,551, a 5.4 percent capital loss. However, some borrowers will be induced by the increase in mortgage rates to remain in their current homes longer than originally anticipated. The rate of prepayment will slow as a result and the MBS investment will fall in value to $94,196, a 5.8 percent capital loss. In other words, prepayments increase the capital loss by over 6 percent.

Chart 1 illustrates this same principle for a wider range of interest rate changes. The solid line represents the value of the $100,000 investment in a pool of 9 percent mortgages at various interest rates after accounting for the likely change

---

discounting the resulting cash flows by the new interest rate. The prepayment estimates used in this example are taken from Frank J. Navratil, "The Estimation of Mortgage Prepayment Rates," Research Working Paper 112 (Federal Home Loan Bank Board, April 1984), Table 3, p. 19. Many other factors influence capital gains and losses on mortgage pass-throughs, and the experience of an actual MBS investment might well differ significantly from the illustrative results reported here.

in the prepayment rate. The dashed line represents the value of the same investment if the prepayment rate remained at its original level.[12] Notice that this investment does not perform as well as it would if the prepayment rate were constant. In other words, variations in the prepayment rate limit capital gains when interest rates fall and magnify capital losses when interest rates rise.

The second disadvantage of mortgage pass-throughs relative to Treasury securities—the inopportune acceleration and deceleration of MBS cash flows—also arises from mortgage borrowers' response to changing interest rates. When rates fall, prepayments increase because some borrowers refinance. Cash flows are received earlier than anticipated and, more important, they are received when yields on new investments have fallen, that is, when yields on reinvestment are likely to be lower than the rate paid on the MBS. When rates rise, prepayments decrease. Cash flows fall off just when the yields on new investments have increased, that is, when yields are likely to be higher than the rate paid on the MBS. In contrast, the future cash flows from a Treasury security are fixed and do not respond to changes in interest rates.

The third disadvantage of mortgage pass-throughs—the unpredictability of cash flows—is *not* related to borrowers' economic incentives to exercise their prepayment option. Mortgages are prepaid for a variety of reasons, many of them having nothing to do with interest rates or economic conditions. These idiosyncratic prepayments generate unexpected cash flows for MBS investors. In addition, each prepayment alters the rest of the amortization schedule for the mortgages still in the MBS pool. These unexpected variations complicate the job of a portfolio manager trying to match the stream of cash flows from MBS investments to obligations to retire liabilities in the future.[13]

In summary, changes in prepayments in response to interest rates reduce the capital gains and increase the capital losses accruing to MBS investments. In addition, such changes in prepayments increase cash flows when yields on new investments are low and decrease cash flows when yields on new investments are high. Finally, idiosyncratic fluctuations in prepayments make MBS cash flows unpredictable, complicating the task of portfolio management.

Understanding mortgage prepayments

Prepayments are the main reason investments in mortgage pass-throughs perform differently than investments in Treasury securities. To manage their pass-through investments prudently, portfolio managers must understand the factors that influence the rate of mortgage prepayments. This section discusses the determinants of mortgage prepayments and examines the prepayment history of the mortgage pools formed by FNMA.

---

[12] Because Treasury securities are not subject to prepayment, the interest sensitivity of a comparable Treasury security would look like the dashed line, not like the solid line. Additional discussion of the differences in the interest rate sensitivities of mortgage pass-throughs and of Treasury securities can be found in Charles S. Morris and Thomas J. Merfeld, "New Methods for Savings and Loans to Hedge Interest Rate Risk," Federal Reserve Bank of Kansas City, *Economic Review* (March 1988), pp. 3-15; and Sean Becketti, "The Role of Stripped Securities in Portfolio Management," Federal Reserve Bank of Kansas City, *Economic Review* (May 1988), pp. 20-31.

---

[13] When interest rates change unexpectedly, MBS cash flows also change unexpectedly. However, prepayments change systematically with interest rates; that is, conditional on interest rate changes, prepayment changes can be anticipated to some extent. The unpredictable cash flows emphasized in this paragraph are the purely idiosyncratic fluctuations in prepayments, that is, prepayment fluctuations unrelated to any observable event.

The determinants of mortgage prepayments

Refinancing, relocation, and default are the direct causes of MBS prepayments. The factors that influence these three events, however, are the ultimate determinants of prepayments. While many different factors can influence the decisions to refinance, relocate, or default, the most important factors appear to be the *relative coupon*—the difference between the interest rate charged for new mortgages and the interest rate on the existing mortgage—and the age of the mortgage. Other idiosyncratic factors, such as the location of the home that collateralizes the mortgage, also play a role.

Direct causes of prepayments. There are three reasons for MBS prepayments: refinancing, relocation, and default. When mortgage interest rates fall, some homeowners find it to their advantage to refinance their current mortgages. These refinancings consist of taking out new mortgages at the new, lower rate and prepaying the original, higher interest rate mortgages. Since an MBS is based on a specific pool of mortgages, the new mortgages do not replace the original mortgages in the pool. The MBS investor receives the prepayments and sees the size of the MBS mortgage pool shrink. As a result, future MBS cash flows are smaller than originally anticipated.

Another reason for mortgage prepayments is relocation. When a home is sold, the home seller's mortgage is prepaid and the home buyer takes out a new mortgage. Again the MBS investor receives the prepayment and is left with a smaller mortgage pool. Relocations occur for a variety of reasons, such as job switches, changes in family size, and the like. However, home sales traditionally pick up when interest rates fall. Consequently, prepayments due both to refinancing and to relocation increase when interest rates fall and decrease when rates rise.

Another cause of prepayments is mortgage defaults. The federal housing agencies guarantee mortgage pass-throughs against default. When a mortgage borrower defaults, that mortgage is "prepaid" to MBS investors.[14] This feature of MBSs leads to increased prepayments in mortgage pools from areas with deteriorating economic conditions, particularly areas with deteriorating real estate markets. Since interest rates typically fluctuate with national economic conditions, some portion of default-induced prepayments may also be associated with movements in interest rates.

Ultimate determinants of prepayments. The relative coupon is the most important factor in the decision to refinance. If the interest rate charged for new mortgages is higher than the rate on the existing mortgage, the mortgage borrower has no reason at all to refinance. As the current mortgage rate begins to fall below the rate on the existing mortgage, the borrower would be better off with a mortgage at the new rate. However, the points and other fees charged to originate a new mortgage will outweigh modest differences in the interest rates. When the current rate falls far below the rate on the existing mortgage, the present value of the reduction in interest payments exceeds the fees paid to originate a new mortgage. Thus, refinancings increase when mortgage rates fall, and they increase more the greater the fall in mortgage rates.

The relative coupon also affects the decision to relocate. Homeowners may defer or decide against relocating when the interest rate on new mortgages is high relative to the rate on their existing mortgages. Conversely, when the mortgage rate drops, many homeowners are encour-

---

[14] Of course, someone bears the loss associated with a mortgage default. Depending on the type of mortgage and the contract between the federal agency and the mortgage servicing company, the loss may be borne by the servicer, by the MBS issuing agency, or by another agency that originally guaranteed the mortgage. In addition, the borrower may eventually repay some or all of the mortgage obligation.

aged to pay off their old mortgages and purchase a new home at the new, lower interest rate. Of course, when mortgage rates drop, the demand for homes increases because prospective home buyers find it easier to qualify for loans. This increase in demand makes it easier for homeowners to sell their current homes and relocate.

Mortgage defaults are less directly influenced by the relative coupon than are refinancings and relocations. Default occurs when the mortgage borrower is unable or unwilling to continue making mortgage payments. When economic conditions deteriorate within a region, an industry, or a nation, some mortgage borrowers find themselves without jobs and unable to meet their financial obligations. If they are unable to renegotiate their mortgages, these borrowers may be forced into default. Another kind of default occurs when home values decline unexpectedly, as they did in parts of the Southwest in recent years. In this situation, some borrowers find that the value of their homes has fallen below the value of their mortgages. In this situation, some borrowers may default on their mortgages and throw the burden of the loss in home value on the mortgage lender. The relative coupon may indirectly influence the rate of mortgage defaults, however. Interest rates typically fluctuate with national economic conditions, so defaults due to unemployment and bankruptcy may be associated with movements in interest rates. In addition, home values are affected by changes in interest rates. Therefore, defaults that result from borrowers "walking away" from their mortgage commitments may also be correlated with interest rates.

The age of a mortgage also is an important influence on the factors that directly determine prepayments. Mortgage prepayments are very low in the first few years of a mortgage pool. The prepayment rate appears to peak when the mortgages in the pool are between three and four years old. The rate of prepayment then drops a bit and remains steady until the mortgages mature. This "life cycle" of prepayments reflects, in the main, the time pattern of the incentives to relocate.

The low rate of prepayments in the first few years of a mortgage pool is due primarily to the low rate of relocation in this period.[15] It is unusual for a home buyer to move again in the first years after a home purchase. This stability is partly the effect of the transactions costs associated with relocation—mortgage points and fees, commissions to real estate agents, moving expenses, and the like. Probably a more important contributor to this stability is the time pattern of life events that influence relocation. Changes in family size, significant career advances, and the increases in wealth needed to finance the purchase of a larger home—all these occur over a period of years, not months.

These life events also help explain the peak in prepayment rates after three to four years. This span of time is long enough to allow for significant changes in a family's situation and in its demand for housing. After the peak in prepayment rates, when the prepayment rate in a mortgage pool stabilizes, the mortgages are said to be fully seasoned. The remaining households in the pool are less likely to relocate than the households that left the mortgage pool. These remaining households may have stable family sizes, long-term job attachments, or family ties to a particular area. Whatever the reason, the prepayment rate on seasoned mortgages does not change as the mortgages grow older.

Finally, idiosyncratic factors may influence the prepayment rate of a mortgage pool. For example, if the homes in a pool are located in a region where economic conditions are deteriorating,

---

[15] The rate of refinancing is also low in the first few years of a mortgage pool. In part, the low rate of refinancing reflects the amount of time it takes before mortgage rates move far enough to outweigh the costs of originating a new loan.

CHART 2

Mortgage interest rates and the average prepayment rates for two different mortgage pass-throughs

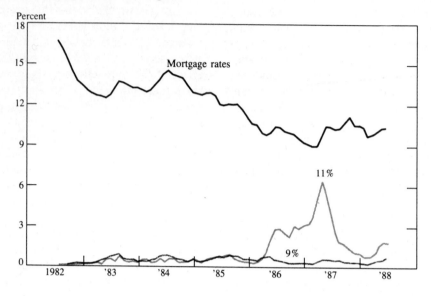

prepayments due to relocation and default may be higher for this pool than for other pools with the same relative coupons and mortgage ages. The effect of idiosyncratic factors sharply distinguishes MBSs from Treasury securities. Two "identical" MBSs, say two 9 percent FNMAs based on pools of two-year-old mortgages, will have different patterns of prepayments and, hence, different patterns of cash flows. In contrast, two Treasury securities with identical coupon rates and maturities offer investors identical cash flows.

The prepayment experience of the FNMA mortgage pass-throughs

The most important fact about prepayment rates in recent years is how rapidly they have changed. Chart 2 displays the average prepayment rates for FNMA mortgage pools with two different pass-

through rates along with the interest rate on new mortgages from July 1982 through June 1988.[16] (The pass-through rate is the interest rate paid to the pass-through investor.) The prepayment rates for both the 9 percent and the 11 percent MBSs remained fairly stable through 1985. In 1986, the prepayment rate for the FNMA 11 per-

---

16 The pass-through rate is the interest rate paid to the pass-through investor. It is analagous to the coupon rate on a Treasury bond. The weighted average interest rate on the mortgages in the pool underlying the MBS is called the weighted-average coupon and is 50 to 250 basis points higher than the pass-through rate. The data here and below on FNMA MBSs are taken from research reported in Sean Becketti and Charles S. Morris, "The Prepayment Experience of FNMA Mortgage-backed Securities," Research Working Paper (Federal Reserve Bank of Kansas City, forthcoming). This working paper is part of a larger research project on mortgage-backed securities that will also examine the experience of GNMA and FHLMC securities.

cent MBSs rose sharply as mortgage interest rates fell below 11 percent. For example, the prepayment rate of the FNMA 11s more than quadrupled from February to May of 1986, rising from a monthly rate of 0.5 percent in February to 2.1 percent in May. As mortgage rates continued to fall, the prepayment rate of the FNMA 11s continued to rise, peaking at 6.5 percent in April 1987. In contrast, the prepayment rates for the 9 percent MBSs were basically flat over this time period. This difference reflects the greater economic incentive to refinance the mortgages in the 11 percent MBS pool.

The experience of the FNMA mortgage pass-throughs provides some evidence of the effects of the relative coupon, mortgage age, and idiosyncratic factors on the rate of prepayment.

Chart 3 displays the sensitivity of prepayment rates to the relative coupon.[17] When the relative coupon is very negative (on the left side of the chart)—that is, when the rate on new mortgages is far below the rate on the existing mortgages—there is a great incentive to refinance the existing mortgages. As a result, the rate of prepayments is high, but further drops in the mortgage rate are unlikely to increase the prepayment rate; most of the borrowers who are likely to refinance their loans are already doing so.

MBSs are most exposed to prepayment risk when the relative coupon is zero or slightly negative (near the center of the the chart), that

is, when the interest rate on new mortgages is equal to or slightly below the rate on existing mortgages. For example, as shown in Chart 3, the prepayment rate on mortgages with interest rates equal to the rate on new mortgages (a relative coupon of zero) is 0.4 percent. If mortgage rates fall one percentage point (the relative coupon drops to −1.0), the prepayment rate doubles to 0.8 percent. If mortgage rates fall another point (the relative coupon drops to −2.0), the prepayment rate doubles again to 1.7 percent, and if mortgage rates fall yet another point (the relative coupon drops to −3.0), the prepayment rate climbs to 2.3 percent. Chart 3 shows that the prepayment rate hits a plateau at about 2.5 percent when the interest rate on new mortgages falls four percentage points below the existing rate; at this point, the prepayment rate is relatively insensitive to further changes in the relative coupon.

When the relative coupon is very positive (on the right side of Chart 3)—when the rate on new mortgages is far above the rate on the existing mortgages—there is no incentive to refinance the existing mortgages. As a result, the rate of prepayments is low, and further increases in the mortgage rate are unlikely to decrease the prepayment rate.

This discussion and Chart 3 highlight the fact that the rate of prepayments is relatively insensitive to moderate changes in the interest rate when the relative coupon is either very negative or positive (the left- and right-hand sides of the chart, respectively). In contrast, the rate of prepayment is highly sensitive to changes in the interest rate when the relative coupon is zero or a little negative (when the relative coupon is between zero and −4 on the chart).

Chart 4 displays the effects of mortgage age on prepayment rates. As shown in Chart 4, a mortgage pool begins its life with a very low prepayment rate. This rate rises during the next three or four years, then declines for over five

---

17 Charts 3 and 4 report the average behavior of FNMA mortgage pools for the period November 1981 through June 1988. For each chart, pools were grouped by their relative coupon rates (for Chart 3) and their ages (for Chart 4). Within each group, the average prepayment rate was calculated. These averages are the data displayed in the charts. Note that, since a particular pool's relative coupon and age change over time, each pool contributes to the average prepayment behavior for more than one relative coupon and age group. Additional details on these calculations can be found in Becketti and Morris, ''The Prepayment Experience . . . ''

CHART 3

The effect of relative coupon on the prepayment rate

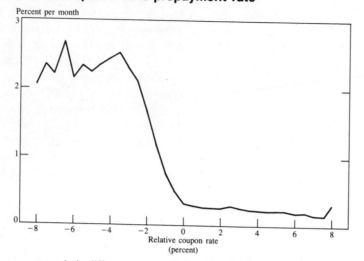

Note: The relative coupon rate is the difference between the interest rate on new mortgages and the rate on the existing mortgages in a pool. This chart displays the average relationship between prepayment rates and relative coupon rates for FNMA fixed rate, 30 year, conventional mortgage pass-throughs from November 1981 through June 1988.

Source: Becketti and Morris, "The Prepayment Experience . . ."

CHART 4

The effect of mortgage age on the prepayment rate

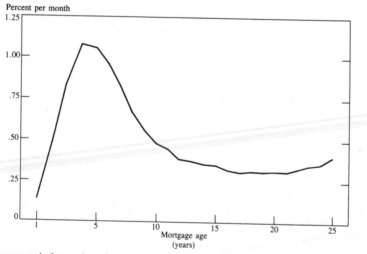

Note: The mortgage age is the number of years since the mortgages in a pool were originated. This chart displays the average relationship between prepayment rates and mortgage age for FNMA fixed rate, 30 year, conventional mortgage pass-throughs from November 1981 through June 1988.

Source: Becketti and Morris, "The Prepayment Experience . . ."

TABLE 1
Prepayment rates for five different FNMA 13s
(in percent)

Date	Pool					All FNMA 13s
	A	**B**	**C**	**D**	**E**	
1987 January	*	.0	.0	.0	5.4	6.1
February	*	13.3	.0	12.3	4.1	5.1
March	*	16.5	.0	.0	1.9	6.0
April	23.6	.0	.0	.0	8.3	6.2
May	19.8	.0	.0	.0	2.4	6.2
June	.0	.0	.0	17.7	3.8	6.2
July	.0	.0	.0	*	2.2	4.8
August	28.7	.0	.0	*	2.4	3.9
September	.0	.0	.0	*	1.4	4.4
October	.0	.0	.0	*	6.3	3.1
November	.0	.0	.0	*	.5	2.8
December	.0	.0	.0	*	2.5	2.5
1988 January	.0	.0	.0	*	.1	2.0
February	18.0	.0	.0	*	.7	1.9
March	.0	.0	.0	*	8.2	2.2
April	.0	.0	.0	20.4	.1	2.4
May	35.6	.0	.0	78.5	2.0	3.3
June	.0	.0	.0	*	5.3	3.6
Jan. 1987– June 1988	6.4	1.6	.0	6.0	3.2	4.0

Note: All pools are conventional, long-term mortgage pools.
*Less than .05.

years before stabilizing. Thus, for example, prepayments are very low in the first year of a mortgage pool's life—the average prepayment rate is only 0.1 percent per month. The rate jumps to 0.5 percent in the second year and 0.8 percent in the third. The prepayment rate peaks at 1.1 percent in the fourth year of a pool's life. The rate of prepayment then falls steadily until the tenth year when it stabilizes at just under 0.5 percent per month.

Idiosyncratic factors can generate important variations in prepayment behavior among MBSs with the same pass-through rate. Table 1 lists the prepayment rates for five different FNMA 13 percent MBS pools along with the average prepayment rate for all similar FNMA 13s for the 18 months from January 1987 through June 1988.[18] Note the diversity of behavior among these pools. For example, in May 1987, when the average prepayment rate of FNMA 13s was 6.2 percent, three of the five pools listed had no prepayments at all. The other two pools had prepayment rates of 2.4 percent and 19.8 percent. For the 18 months listed in Table 1, pools B and C appear to be "slow pay pools," pools with chronically below-average prepayments. In fact, pool C never has any prepayments. Over the same period, pools A and D appear to be "fast pay pools," pools with chronically above-average prepayments.[19]

The variety of prepayment experience listed in Table 1 suggests that portfolio managers should not assume that one MBS with a given pass-through rate will act like any other with the same pass-through rate. Each MBS has its own response to changing interest rates, and prudent investors must find ways to assess and monitor these differences if they are to anticipate prepayments accurately. This is very different from investing in Treasury securities where the absence of prepayments guarantees that one Treasury security will behave the same as any other Treasury security with the same interest rate and maturity date.

Mortgage prepayments: implications for portfolio management

Banks and S&Ls together hold roughly $300 billion in MBSs, almost 40 percent of the amount outstanding. Many observers believe banks are likely to increase their MBS investments as a result of the risk-based capital guidelines approved recently by federal regulators. Under these guidelines, banks will not have to hold as much capital against mortgage pass-throughs as they will against some other types of assets. According to the new guidelines, GNMA MBSs fall in the same risk class as Treasury securities. As a result, banks will not be required to hold any capital against GNMA MBSs.[20] FNMA and FHLMC MBSs also receive favorable treatment under the new guidelines: Banks will be required to hold only a fifth as much capital against these securities as against commercial loans.

Previous sections have shown how prepayments make mortgage pass-through securities different from Treasury securities. The large investment by insured depositories in this type of security suggests that portfolio managers should take steps to monitor and control the risks of their investments in mortgage pass-throughs. While each investor's situation is different and has its own special features, this section reviews some key points that portfolio managers should consider.

One way portfolio managers can limit exposure to prepayment risk is to monitor and control the relative coupons of their MBS holdings. As was shown in Chart 3, prepayment rates are fairly

---

[18] The pools used in Table 1 are all conventional, long-term, fixed rate FNMA pools.

[19] Table 1 does not take into account the ages of the mortgages in these five pools; however, the ages are not very different and are close to the average age of all FNMA 13s. In addition, the variations in the monthly prepayment rates are far too large to be explained by the kind of age-related changes in prepayment displayed in Chart 4.

[20] Under the new guidelines, which will be phased in over the next four years, banks will have to hold $8 of capital against every $100 of risk-weighted assets. The risk-weighted value of an asset is determined by multiplying the asset's dollar value by its risk factor. The guidelines define four categories of risk factors: 0 percent for cash and all government securities including GNMA securities; 20 percent for securities issued by such agencies as FNMA and FHLMC; 50 percent for most home mortgages and municipal revenue bonds; and 100 percent for most commercial loans and other assets. It is important to note that these risk factors are intended to reflect only the credit risk of the various assets. Guidelines for interest rate risk will be considered in future regulations.

stable for MBSs with pass-through rates that are lower than the current mortgage rate (with high relative coupons). Securities with pass-through rates higher than the current mortgage rate (low relative coupon) have high prepayment rates, but these rates are fairly stable, albeit at a high level, when the pass-through rate is a great deal higher than the current rate. MBSs with pass-through rates close to the current mortgage rate and MBSs with pass-through rates slightly higher than the current rate are the most exposed to prepayment risk, in particular, to a fall in mortgage rates. Very small changes in the current mortgage rate can have large effects on the prepayment rates of these securities. Portfolio managers may choose periodically to rebalance their MBS holdings to retain only securities whose prepayment rates are relatively insensitive to interest rate changes.[21]

Research on mortgage-backed securities has shown that there is considerable idiosyncratic prepayment risk. In other words, apparently identical mortgage pools may have dramatically different prepayment rates. The only solution to this idiosyncratic prepayment risk is diversification.

If the portfolio is a large one, a manager can reduce the idiosyncratic fluctuations in prepayments and cash flows by holding diversified blocks of MBSs within each pass-through category. For example, an investor may wish to break up a purchase of FNMA 9s across a large number of different mortgage pools. This diversification guarantees that the investor will enjoy prepayments and cash flows more similar to the average for all FNMA 9s than if the investment were concentrated in only one or a few different mortgage pools. For some MBSs, however, an investor may have to hold securities from as many as 50 to 100 different pools to be assured of adequate diversification.[22] Since only the largest, best capitalized investors are able to hold diversified portfolios of these MBSs, smaller institutions holding MBSs may expose themselves to considerable idiosyncratic prepayment risk.

Portfolio managers can, to a limited extent, reduce variations in the prepayment rate of an MBS by choosing only those securities based on pools of seasoned mortgages, that is, mortgages old enough to have a stable prepayment rate (other things being equal). The prepayment rate on younger mortgages is likely to increase for several years, then to decline for several years. Older, seasoned mortgages do not exhibit any further age-related swings in prepayments.

Finally, since MBSs expose an institution to a combination of interest rate and prepayment risk, sophisticated portfolio managers may try to manage these risks jointly through hedging operations. However, prepayments make hedging a portfolio of MBSs inherently more complicated than hedging a portfolio of other fixed rate investments.[23] In general, hedging an MBS port-

[21] Some investors may be tempted to skew their holdings toward MBSs that will perform better in a particular interest rate environment. For example, an investor who believes interest rates are likely to increase might purchase pass-throughs with a pass-through rate that is slightly higher than the current rate in the hope of benefiting from a slowdown in prepayments. Such investment strategies as these are simply bets on the future path of interest rates, and as such are inherently inappropriate strategies for depository institutions.

[22] A detailed discussion of diversifying MBS investments and estimates of the number of pools required to achieve adequate diversification can be found in Alden L. Toevs and Mark R. Hancock, "Diversifying Prepayment Risk: Techniques to Stabilize Cash Flows and Returns from Mortgage Pass-throughs," *Housing Finance Review,* vol. 7, No. 3 (Summer 1988), pp. 267-94. Note that even small investors may be able to diversify their MBS investments by holding shares in a diversified MBS mutual fund rather than by holding MBSs directly.

[23] The strategies for and problems of hedging MBSs are explained in Morris and Merfeld, "New Methods . . . "

folio requires the use of interest rate futures contracts to hedge the interest rate risk and options on interest rate futures to hedge prepayment risk. Once again, smaller institutions with limited resources to monitor and conduct hedging operations may be better off not taking on the interest rate and prepayment risk inherent in MBSs.[24]

Conclusion

The behavior of mortgage pass-throughs is a reminder that credit risk is not the only risk faced by portfolio managers. Agency guarantees virtually eliminate credit risk for MBSs. Nonetheless, an investor in pass-throughs is exposed to important risks, primarily risks associated with prepayments. As a result, MBSs are more difficult assets to manage than are Treasury securities.

There are ways for investors to manage the prepayment risks of mortgage pass-throughs. Investors can monitor the relative coupons of their MBS holdings to limit their exposure to prepayment risk. Investors can also hold large blocks of MBSs with the same pass-through rate to diversify away idiosyncratic variations in prepayments. Finally, investors can adopt hedging strategies using financial futures and options to insulate their portfolio from interest rate-induced swings in prepayments.

All of these approaches are best suited to sophisticated and well-capitalized investors. Many banks and S&Ls, particularly smaller institutions, may lack the investment experience and the capital to successfully carry out any of these strategies. Portfolio managers at these institutions may decide to avoid mortgage pass-throughs and their higher yields in favor of simpler and less risky assets. For many institutions, this may be the safest and most appropriate strategy.

---

[24] While mortgage pass-through securities are clearly riskier than Treasury securities, they are less risky than whole mortgage loans. S&Ls, which hold a large share of their assets in mortgages and mortgage-related securities, may reduce their total risk by shifting their portfolios out of whole mortgages and into MBS. Commercial banks, which historically have made relatively few mortgage loans, are likelier to increase their total risk by adding MBSs to their portfolios. For either type of institution, increasing the investment in MBSs at the expense of Treasury securities will increase the institution's riskiness.

Article 38

Off Balance Sheet Risk in Banking: The Case of Standby Letters of Credit

Barbara Bennett*

Bank regulators and other analysts worry that the recent rapid growth in standby letters of credit (SLCs) outstanding is a response to more stringent capital regulation and has increased bank risk. This analysis traces the growth of such instruments primarily to the growth of direct-finance markets in a setting of increased overall economic risk. It also finds that SLCs are at least potentially riskier than loans. Although banks may be applying higher credit evaluation standards in partial compensation, the issuance of SLCs nevertheless may warrant some form of capital-related regulation.

The off balance sheet activities of commercial banks have attracted a lot of attention lately. Regulators, securities analysts and the financial press all have voiced concerns about the rapid growth in such contingent obligations as loan commitments, financial futures and options contracts, letters of credit, and foreign exchange contracts. Although they are not recognized as assets or liabilities on bank balance sheets (hence the term, "off balance sheet activities," or OBS), these contingent claims involve interest rate, credit, and/or liquidity risks. Moreover, because they provide the opportunity for substantially greater leverage than is the case for banks' lending and investment activities, OBS have the potential to increase banks' overall risk.

Ironically, bank regulators' efforts to control risk-taking through more stringent capital regulation may be partly responsible for the growth in OBS over the last few years. Because regulatory defini-

tions of capital adequacy currently do not include OBS, banks may have an incentive to shift risk-taking towards these relatively less-regulated activities. To correct this problem, the federal bank regulatory agencies are considering ways to factor OBS exposure into their formal evaluation of a bank's capital adequacy. Consequently, regulators need to analyze the nature and degree of risk involved in each type of OBS as compared to banks' other activities.

This article examines one off balance sheet activity that has grown quite rapidly over the last several years: standby letters of credit. The first section discusses the uses for standby letters of credit and the reasons for their growth. In the second section, a framework for analyzing the risks associated with standby letters of credit is developed. Unfortunately, data limitations make impossible any definitive statements about the impact of standby letters of credit on overall bank risk. Finally, the paper concludes with some observations about the regulatory treatment of standby letters of credit.

* Economist, Federal Reserve Bank of San Francisco. Research Assistance was provided by Kimya Moghadam and Julia Santiago.

I. The Market for Standby Letters of Credit

Of all the off balance sheet activities in which U.S. banks engage, the issuance of standby letters of credit (SLCs) has attracted the most attention lately. Many observers point to the rapid growth in SLCs outstanding over the last few years as well as the prominent role such instruments played in several recent bank failures — most notably, Penn Square National Bank in 1982 — as evidence that SLCs may be increasing bank risk significantly. SLCs outstanding grew from $80.8 billion in June 1982 to $153.2 billion in June 1985 — a 90 percent increase over the period. Moreover, most of that growth occurred at the 25 largest banks, which recorded more than a $40 billion increase in SLCs outstanding.

A letter of credit (LC) is a contractual arrangement involving three parties — the "issuer" (the bank), the "account party" (the bank's customer) and the "beneficiary." Typically, the account party and the beneficiary have entered into a contract requiring the former to make payment(s) or perform some other obligation to the latter. At the same time, the account party has contracted with its bank to issue a letter of credit which, in effect, guarantees that by substituting the bank's liability for that of the account party, the account party will perform according to the terms of the original contract with the beneficiary. Initially, the bank's obligation under the LC is a contingent one because no funds are advanced to the beneficiary until that party presents the documents that are stipulated in the LC contract.

There are two types of LCs: the more traditional commercial letter of credit which generally is used to finance the shipment and storage of goods, and the standby letter of credit which is being used in connection with a growing variety of transactions, including debt issuance and construction contracts. Unlike the commercial LC, which is payable upon presentation of title to the goods that have been shipped, the SLC is payable only upon presentation of evidence of default or nonperformance on the part of the account party. As such, SLCs typically expire unused, in contrast to commercial letters of credit.

Because SLCs are payable only upon nonperformance on the part of the account party, they are a guarantee of either financial or economic performance on the underlying contract.[1] The issuer of the SLC promises to advance funds to make the beneficiary whole in the event of the account party's failure to perform according to the terms of the contract with the beneficiary. An SLC involving a financial guarantee requires the issuing bank to pay any principal or interest on debt owed the beneficiary by the account party should the latter default. According to a recent survey, just over half of banks' SLCs outstanding backs some form of debt obligation.[2] An SLC backing a construction contract, in contrast, represents a performance guarantee and requires the bank to make a payment to the beneficiary if the contractor does not complete the project satisfactorily.

By issuing an SLC, the bank is assuming the risk that normally would have been borne by the beneficiary. However, it is the account party that arranges the SLC and compensates the bank for the risk. In return for paying the bank's fee and reducing the beneficiary's risk, the account party expects to obtain a higher price for the debt issued to or the services performed for the beneficiary.

In general, the account party will choose to arrange a standby letter of credit whenever the cost of the transaction (that is, the bank's fee) is less than the value of the guarantee to the beneficiary (as measured by the premium the beneficiary is willing to pay for the account party's debt or services with the SLC backing). The size of this differential between the bank's fee and the beneficiary's willingness to pay for the guarantee depends upon two factors.

First, the value of the guarantee to the beneficiary will depend on the creditworthiness of the issuing bank as compared to that of the account party and the relative costs of obtaining information about the creditworthiness of each. An SLC issued by a bank with a poor credit rating is not likely to be worth much to the beneficiary since the probability of that bank's default on its obligation may be high. Likewise, an SLC issued by a small, unknown bank may have little value since the cost to the beneficiary of obtaining information to evaluate the bank may be greater than the cost of evaluating the account party and underwriting the risk itself.

These observations are consistent with the data presented in Tables 1 and 2, which show that most SLC issuance occurs at the largest banks and that the higher rated banks tend to do relatively more SLC business.

Second, the size of the differential will depend on the extent of the issuing bank's comparative advantage in underwriting the risk of default on the part of the account party. (Of course, the extent to which the bank's comparative advantage will be reflected in the fees the bank charges depends on the level of competition among issuers of SLCs). With respect to most beneficiaries, the issuing bank's underwriting costs are likely to be substantially lower because the bank is better able to diversify the risk associated with SLCs and because the bank enjoys certain economies in credit evaluation. For example, the marginal cost of performing an evaluation of the account party is lower for the bank than for the beneficiary because the bank frequently has an ongoing relationship with the account party; this makes the cost of obtaining information much lower for the bank.

TABLE 1

SLC Issuance by Size of Bank
(Billions of dollars)

Year-End:	1979	1980	1981	1982	1983	1984	June 1985 (Percent share)
Banks with Assets of Over $100 MM	34.1	45.7	69.9	98.3	117.4	144.3	153.2 (100)
25 Largest Banks	27.2	36.5	55.5	77.6	91.5	111.2	117.9 (77)
10 Largest Banks	24.3	32.0	47.9	65.0	77.1	92.4	96.3 (63)
15 Other Large Banks	2.9	4.5	7.6	12.6	14.4	18.8	21.6 (14)
All Other Banks	6.9	9.2	14.4	20.7	25.9	33.1	35.3 (23)

Source: Quarterly Reports of Condition

TABLE 2

SLC Issuance of 25 Largest Banks by Bank Rating*

	Dec 1982	June 1985	Percent Change
	(Billions of dollars)		
Large Banks (with assets over $50 billion)	41.6	63.1	51.7
Aaa - Aa (4 banks)	33.4	51.7	54.8
A or less (1 bank)	8.2	11.4	39.0
Medium Banks (with assets of $10-50 billion)	35.9	54.6	52.1
Aaa - Aa (11 banks)	21.9	37.4	70.8
A or less (8 banks)	14.0	17.2	22.9
Small Banks (with assets under $10 billion)	0.1	0.2	100.0
A or less (1 bank)	0.1	0.2	100.0

*Ratings of banks based on latest evaluation in *Moody's Corporate Credit Reports.*

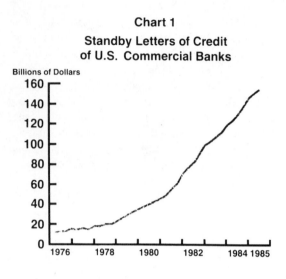

Chart 1
Standby Letters of Credit
of U.S. Commercial Banks

Billions of Dollars

The Growth of SLCs

The almost exponential growth in SLCs outstanding since the late 1970s (see Chart 1) is just one manifestation of a rapidly growing general market for guarantee-type products. In addition to the SLCs that banks offer, surety and insurance companies are now offering such guarantees as credit-risk coverages (which guarantee repayment of principal and interest on debt obligations) and asset-risk coverages, such as residual value insurance and systems performance guarantees. This expansion in the types of coverages offered has given insurance companies a rapidly growing source of premium income. Between 1980 and 1984, the insurance industry's net premiums from such surety operations[3] nearly doubled, rising from $900 million to $1.6 billion.[4] Financial guarantees offered by other, specialized providers have grown rapidly as well. Municipal bond insurance, for example, was virtually nonexistent prior to 1981, but now supports an estimated 29 percent, or $6.4 billion, of new issues of long-term municipal bonds.[5]

Two factors account for this growth in the market for financial guarantees in general, and SLCs in particular. First, the growth over the last ten to 15 years of direct-finance markets has increased the credit-risk exposure of investors who may prefer not to bear such risk. Such direct-finance markets as the commercial paper market have grown rapidly since the late 1960s because borrowers are able to obtain funds more cheaply from them than through inter-

mediaries such as banks. However, this decline in financial intermediation has also meant that the undiversified investors in such markets must bear more credit risk than if they were to invest in the deposit liabilities of commercial banks. Apparently, such an increase in credit-risk exposure is unpalatable to at least some portion of these investors because 15 percent of all dealer-placed taxable commercial paper is supported by some sort of legally binding guarantee and nearly all rated commercial paper also is backed by a bank loan commitment.[6]

The second reason that financial guarantees have grown rapidly over the last several years is that overall economic risk has increased over the same period. The rampant inflation of the late 1970s, the increased volatility of interest rates and business activity of the early 1980s, and the unexpected sharp deceleration in the rate of inflation in the middle 1980s have caused wide swings in asset prices and returns on investment. Consequently, the demand for instruments like SLCs and other guarantees that reduce the risk to the beneficiary has increased tremendously.

Banks' involvement in this market is at once an extension of their traditional lending business and, because SLCs are not funded, a significant departure from it. Like their lending business, banks' issuance of SLCs entails the underwriting of credit risk. In this area, banks enjoy certain economies of specialization that make them lower-cost issuers of financial guarantees. They can easily (that is, without cost) diversify the risk associated with SLCs. Also, banks typically have other lending and deposit relationships with their SLC customers. As a result, the marginal cost to banks of obtaining information to perform a credit evaluation for the purposes of issuing an SLC is very low. Moreover, in contrast to insurance companies, banks do not generally secure their guarantees with a formal collateral arrangement with the account party since they usually have the right to debit the account party's deposit accounts. This lack of a formal collateral arrangement makes banks' SLCs more attractive, but it also increases the bank's risk somewhat. (See the next section for a discussion of SLC risk.)

Given the enormous increase in the demand for guarantees, the fact that banks are low-cost issuers may be sufficient explanation for the rapid growth of bank-issued SLCs over the last several years. However, banks also may have an incentive to respond to this demand since they can overcome binding regulatory constraints on their lending activities by doing so. For example, at current levels of interest rates, reserve requirements add an estimated 25 to 30 basis points to banks' cost of funds, making bank credit considerably less attractive than other sources of credit.[7] Because SLCs are not funded and are therefore unaffected by reserve requirements, they represent a less costly way of assuming a given level of credit risk.

A more important regulatory constraint that undoubtedly has given banks incentive to issue SLCs is the move towards tougher capital regulation in recent years. Regulators began to express serious concern about bank capital adequacy in the late 1970s as the aggregate capital-to-assets ratio drifted to historically low levels. Then, in December 1981, the Federal Reserve Board (FRB) and the Office of the Comptroller of the Currency (OCC) issued "Capital Adequacy Guidelines" to pressure large banks into improving their capital-to-asset ratios. More formal standards for large banks were imposed in June 1983, and even more stringent standards were imposed on the industry as a whole in March 1985.

Economic theory suggests that the imposition of tighter capital regulations depresses the return on capital, causing a decline in the price of the regu-lated firm's capital unless the firm can somehow compensate either by reducing its asset base or by increasing the riskiness of its portfolio. Because nonbank competitors are not similarly regulated, a move to shrink assets will not necessarily increase the return on bank capital. Thus, in the absence of other forms of portfolio regulation, capital regulation may induce banks to take on more risk.

Much of bank portfolio regulation is crafted to prevent banks from responding to this incentive, but regulators are concerned that banks' off balance sheet activities may not be adequately covered. The current capital adequacy standards do not formally account for banks' off balance sheet exposure. Consequently, when faced with capital-related limitations on asset growth, banks may have an incentive to shift risk-taking toward SLCs and other off balance sheet activities that do not "use up" capital.

In sum, the growth in banks' SLC issuance is a reflection of an increased demand for financial guarantees both as result of increased reliance on direct-finance as a source of funds and as a result of an increase in overall risk. Banks have been willing to respond to this demand by issuing SLCs because they enjoy certain cost advantages in doing so and because regulatory constraints on their lending activities make the issuance of SLCs more attractive. The next section presents a framework for analyzing the impact of SLC growth on bank risk, as well as an evaluation of the available evidence.

II. The Risk of Standby Letters of Credit

With the deregulation of many aspects of the banking business, banks have received expanded opportunities for risk-taking. Regulators worry that increasingly risky bank practices could bankrupt the deposit insurance system, which underwrites at least a portion of any increase in bank risk. If banks did not have deposit insurance or if that insurance were priced correctly, the cost of bank liabilities and the price of shareholder equity would fully reflect any increase in bank risk. However, since all banks currently are charged the same premium for deposit insurance regardless of riskiness, and since bank regulators apparently have been reluctant to close large, troubled banks, at least large banks have an incentive to undertake more risk than they otherwise would.[8]

Consequently, bank regulators have attempted to reduce banks' opportunities (if not incentives) for risk-taking by adopting more stringent capital requirements for the industry. However, because such regulation may induce banks to try to take on more risk, bank regulators worry that the rapid growth in SLCs outstanding in recent years may be increasing overall bank risk, particularly since SLCs now equal 100 percent of aggregate bank capital. (See Chart 2.) Moreover, for the 25 largest banks, the average ratio of SLCs to capital is even higher — 165.4 percent. As a result, each of the three federal bank regulatory agencies (FRB, OCC and FDIC — Federal Deposit Insurance Corporation) recently proposed that the current capital adequacy regulation be supplemented by risk-based capital guidelines that would explicitly take into account the relative riskiness of broad categories of bank assets and certain off balance sheet items, including SLCs.[9]

Ideally, risk-based measures of capital adequacy ought to reflect the effect of a bank's SLC exposure on overall risk, taking into account the extent to which SLC risk is correlated with other risk exposures. Unfortunately, such a measure is difficult to develop given currently available data and book-value accounting conventions. Neither can the markets for bank debt and equity provide more than an approximation for this measure since the existence of deposit insurance causes these markets to under-price bank risk. As a result, bank regulators can develop only crude measures of SLC risk based on a comparison with the riskiness of banks' loan port-folios.

Loans are the logical "benchmark" for rating the riskiness of SLCs because both instruments involve credit risk. At the same time, however, a comparison of the two is impeded by some of the differences in their risk characteristics. For example, unlike loans, SLCs generally do not entail interest rate risk and liquidity risk. If the issuing bank must advance funds under the terms of the SLC contract, the interest rate on the resulting loan to the account party typically varies with market rates (plus some mark-up). Moreover, because SLCs generally do not require a commitment of the bank's funds, the risk of loss associated with meeting related cash flow obligations is very small. On the other hand, because SLCs are not funded, they provide the opportunity for a much higher degree of leverage risk than is the case for loans.

An Options Framework

Options theory can be used to evaluate the relative riskiness of loans and SLCs. However, because the development of an econometric model to evaluate these two instruments is beyond the scope of this paper (and the available data), the discussion that follows is intended only to suggest how this framework might be useful to regulators.

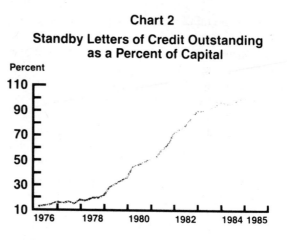

Chart 2

Standby Letters of Credit Outstanding as a Percent of Capital

Virtually any financial instrument can be model-led as an option or a series of options. In this case, because the borrower/account party can default on its obligation to the bank, a loan and an SLC both implicitly contain a put option on the assets of the borrower/account party. In other words, the bor-rower (or the account party) has the right to sell ("put") its assets to the bank at an exercise price equal to the par value of its obligation to the bank. This option will be exercised if the par value of the obligation exceeds the market value of the underly-ing assets securing the obligation.[10]

Several factors determine the risk of exercise and hence, the value of this option. First, the option's value increases with increases in the exercise price, other things equal. As the par value of the loan or SLC obligation increases, so does the bank's risk. Second, the value of this put option varies inversely with the value of the underlying assets. As the value of the underlying assets securing the obligation falls, the cost of exercising the option also falls, increasing the bank's risk. Finally, the option's value rises with increases in the riskiness of those assets (that is, variance of their price). The greater the chance that the value of the underlying assets will fall substantially, the greater is the risk to the bank.[11]

A comparison of the risk associated with SLCs and loans, then, requires an evaluation of all these dimensions of the two portfolios. Moreover, an evaluation of the impact of SLC risk on bank risk also requires an understanding of the extent to which the returns on the two portfolios are correlated. Unfortunately, data on these aspects of banks' SLC and loan portfolios are not available.

Nonetheless, it still is possible to use an options framework at least to suggest how banks' SLC issuance may be affecting bank risk. To do so, assume that the characteristics of banks' loan and SLC portfolios that are most under management control are identical. In other words, for every given SLC there is also a loan to the same customer with the same term-to-maturity and par value. The essential difference between these two portfolios, then, lies in the relative strength of their collateral arrangements. The loans, for the most part, are formally secured by the borrowers' assets, while the SLCs are not.

In an options framework, this difference amounts to a difference in the relative costs of exercising the put options contained in the loan and SLC portfolios. Because the cost of exercising the SLC-related options is lower, other things equal, the likelihood that they will be exercised is greater, making the SLC portfolio riskier than the loan portfolio. Moreover, this lower cost of exercise means that the value of the SLC portfolio is more sensitive to changes in the variance of the prices of the underlying assets (that is, changes in the financial condition of the banks' customers). For this reason as well, the SLC portfolio is riskier.

In practice, of course, banks' SLC and loan portfolios are not identical. Thus, while SLCs may be riskier than loans in this one respect, banks probably manage the other aspects of the two portfolios in a manner that mitigates some of the greater risk arising from differences in the contractual terms of the loan and SLC instruments. Specifically, the creditworthiness of banks' loan and SLC customers may be very different. Bankers have indicated that, as a matter of policy, they try to reject SLC business from customers for whom default is even a remote possibility. This is in admitted contrast to lending policy, where the standards are somewhat more relaxed.[12] (For a discussion of the other ways banks manage SLC risk, see the Appendix.)

Evidence

The rather limited data on fees and loss experience suggest that banks do, in fact, manage the risk of the two portfolios differently. First, banks' SLC fees apparently are lower than the implicit fees they charge on loans. The fees for SLCs for short-term, high quality credits range from 25 to 50 basis points and from 125 to 150 basis points or more for longer term and/or lower quality credits.[13] By contrast, the implicit loan premium for large denomination, variable rate loans is approximately 240 basis points for both short- and longer term credits.[14] This disparity in the fee structures of the two portfolios suggests that the creditworthiness of banks' SLC customers is higher than that of its loan customers.

This evidence on the relative riskiness of SLC and loan portfolios should be interpreted cautiously, however. Fees do not provide a measure of the expected return on equity. After netting out the higher administrative and other expenses associated with loans, it is likely that the expected return on and the risk of SLCs is at least as high as that for loans.

Similarly, the available evidence on the loss experience of loans and SLCs provides some evidence that the creditworthiness of banks' loan and SLC customers is different. Of course, loss experience technically does not measure credit risk because it is an *ex post* measure; however, there should be some correlation over time between risk and observed losses.

Data on SLC losses were last collected in 1978, when a special survey on SLCs was conducted by the staff of the Board of Governors.[15] That survey found that the initial default rate on SLCs averaged 2.03 percent. But because more than 98 percent was recovered, the loss rate on SLCs was extremely low — only 0.03 percent. This low figure compares very favorably to banks' loan loss rate of 0.16 percent in 1979. According to bankers in the Twelfth Federal Reserve District, the loss rate on SLCs has increased somewhat since then, but, compared to loan losses now hovering around 0.65 percent, losses on SLCs still are very low.[16] Once again, however, this evidence should not be interpreted as proof that the risk to bank capital from banks' SLC exposure is less than that from loans.

Finally, evidence from capital markets may provide some insights into the riskiness of banks' SLC portfolios. Of course, this evidence may be biased since prices will reflect the value of any perceived deposit insurance subsidy. Nonetheless, as long as investors believe that they are not fully protected against loss, they will respond to perceived increases in bank risk by demanding a higher risk premium. Consequently, an evaluation of the market's reaction to the *growth* in SLCs outstanding over time should indicate whether bank risk also has increased.

In a study of the determinants of large banks' CD rates, Goldberg and Lloyd-Davies found that the market had not penalized banks for increasing SLC exposure between 1976 and early 1982.[17] Their model explains the level of the CD rate as a function of the general level of interest rates and of various bank risk characteristics. The effect of banks' SLC exposure on CD rates is treated as having two components: a leverage risk effect (the ratio of bank capital to risky assets, including loans and SLCs) and a credit quality effect (the ratio of SLCs to risky assets — to allow for differences in the credit quality of the loan and SLC portfolios). Based on this model, they found that CD rates rose with increas-

ing leverage and fell with increases in SLCs as a proportion of total risky assets. Since these two factors tended to cancel each other, the net effect on bank risk of an increase in banks' SLC exposure apparently was negligible.

Such a result is perhaps not surprising for two reasons. First, the level of SLCs outstanding was low in relation to other risky assets and to capital for most of this period. Thus, the effects of rapid SLC growth (in percentage terms) may have been swamped by larger (absolute) increases in loan volume. Second, the regression covers a period when bank capital ratios generally were falling. Because banks were not constrained by capital regulation (at least not until the end of this period), they may have had less incentive to increase overall risk through SLC issuance. Moreover, it is significant that Goldberg and Lloyd-Davies found that, despite higher credit quality, increasing SLC exposure did not *reduce* bank risk.

III. Regulating Standby Letters of Credit

Bank regulators are concerned that the rapid growth in SLCs outstanding over the last several years is an indication that banks are attempting to take on more risk, in part, as a result of increasingly stringent capital regulation. This paper has suggested that while capital regulation may have played a modest role in the growth of SLCs, the primary reason for such growth has been an increase in the demand for financial guarantees generally. Whether this growth has increased bank risk is still open to question.

In some repects, SLCs are (potentially at least) more risky than loans, but the available evidence suggests that banks may be applying higher credit evaluation standards for SLCs than for loans to compensate for the riskier features of the SLC instrument. At the same time, however, this paper has suggested that it would be a mistake to infer from this evidence that SLCs necessarily pose less risk to capital than do loans. It is hard to believe that with the implicit subsidy to risk-taking provided by the deposit insurance system, banks actually would conduct their SLC business in a manner that entails *less* risk than lending.

Currently, bank regulators place only rather limited restrictions on banks' SLC activities. They require only that banks (1) include SLCs with loans for the purposes of calculating loan concentrations to any one borrower (the limit is 10 percent of capital) and (2) apply the same credit evaluation standards for SLCs as for loans. However, because of the greater riskiness of the SLC *instrument* as well as the greater potential for capital leverage with SLCs than with loans, some form of capital-related regulation of SLCs may be justified.

Capital adequacy regulation with respect to SLC exposure ought to do two things. First, from a bookkeeping perspective, it should ensure that institutions that are likely to experience larger losses also have a larger capital buffer to absorb those losses. Second, ideally, it should provide a structure that penalizes banks for attempting to increase overall risk through increases in SLC risk or leverage.

Accordingly, one can evaluate the risk-based capital adequacy concept that is under consideration at the federal bank regulatory agencies. Under this approach, SLCs outstanding would be added to assets for the purpose of calculating a new, risk-based capital ratio. Moreover, because it is thought that at least certain types of SLCs may entail less risk than loans, those SLCs would be accorded a lower weight in the calculation of that ratio. For example, the FRB's proposed guidelines assign a weight of 1.0 to most types of SLCs, but a weight of only 0.6 to a few types, such as performance-related SLCs.

The advantage of this basic approach is that it is easy to administer. Also, it provides a means of ensuring that as banks' SLC exposure grows, so too will their capital buffer. The disadvantage is that it treats all SLC portfolios (and all loan portfolios, for that matter) as having the same level of credit risk. Clearly, this approach will impose a higher capital cost on the banks that have higher quality SLC portfolios than is the case for banks with lower quality portfolios. As a result, the former may have an incentive to compensate for this implicit penalty by taking on more credit risk in their SLC portfolios.

To overcome this problem, the regulators could, in theory, adopt a more sophisticated measure of SLC risk along the lines of the options model outlined in this paper. Such a measure would enable regulators to take variations in the credit quality of individual portfolios into account when assigning risk weights. However, it would be difficult to administer since considerably more data on the characteristics of individual portfolios would be needed. Instead, the regulators have chosen simply to recognize the inherent weaknesses in any capital adequacy ratio and to emphasize that such ratios — even those that attempt to adjust for risk — are meant only to supplement the bank examiner's judgement. Ultimately, they argue, the bank examiner must decide whether an institution's capital is adequate based on such qualitative considerations as the quality of earnings and management and overall asset quality as measured by the level and severity of examiner-classified assets.

APPENDIX

Banks seek to manage SLC risk in several ways. First, through the fees they charge, banks require compensation in proportion to the risks they assume. Consequently, SLC fees vary with the term of the SLC and the credit rating of the account party. For short-term, high-quality credits, fees currently range from 25 to 50 basis points on the outstanding amount, while fees on longer term and lower quality credits range from 125 to 150 basis points or more.

Second, banks attempt to reduce credit risk on longer term commitments by requiring periodic (usually annual) renegotiation of the terms of the agreement. For example, SLCs backing the commercial paper of nuclear fuel trusts typically have a three-to four-year term, but are renewable each year at the bank's option. This arrangement helps protect the bank against deterioration in the credit-worthiness of the account party over the term of the SLC.

However, such arrangements are not always adequate. One large bank that issues SLCs to back industrial development bonds analyzes its risk exposure in terms of the life of the bonds (usually 20 years). It has chosen this measure instead of the life of the SLC (typically five years) because at the

expiration of the SLC, if the account party's financial condition has deteriorated such that it cannot obtain another SLC, the bondholders can declare the borrower in default under the terms of the bond identure and thus require the bank to cover any losses.* In this case, the shorter term of the SLC does not necessarily limit the bank's exposure. Likewise, a bank may be liable for the repayment of commercial paper debt if it is unwilling to renew its SLC since the bank's unwillingness most likely would result in the account party's inability to refund its debt.

Third, although SLCs frequently are unsecured, the terms of the bank's contract with the account party provide another measure of protection against loss. Typically, the bank's agreement with the account party stipulates that the bank may: 1) require the account party to deposit funds to cover any anticipated disbursements the bank must make under the SLC, 2) debit the account party's account to cover disbursements, 3) call for collateral during the term of the SLC, and 4) book any unreimbursed balance as a loan at an interest rate and on terms set by the bank.** In the event of the account party's bankruptcy, such conditions, of course, do not protect the bank against loss in the same way that a formal collateral agreement would. Under most circumstances, however, they do provide sufficient incentive for the account party to satisfy the terms of the underlying contract.

A fourth way that banks can manage the credit risk involved in SLC issuance is through portfolio diversification. (This approach, of course, cannot reduce systematic risk.) Banks that specialize in issuing certain types of SLCs — backing commercial paper issued by nuclear fuel trusts, for example — still can diversify by buying and selling participations in SLCs. By selling a participation in an SLC it has issued, a bank in effect reinsures some of the risk. If payment must be made to the beneficiary and the account party is unable to make reimbursement, the issuing bank and the bank that purchased a share of the SLC will share in the resulting losses. Under a participation arrangement, the issuing bank will be liable for the full amount of the SLC only if the participating bank were to fail. Participations of SLCs accounted for 11 percent of the $149.2 billion in SLCs outstanding as of March 1985.

Finally, in response to growing regulatory concern over banks' SLC exposure, banks are beginning to manage risk by placing limitations on SLC growth. A number of large banks have established some multiple of capital (for example, 150 percent) as a limit on the amount of their SLCs outstanding. In addition to administratively imposed limitations, the commercial paper market tends to limit SLC growth as well. Since SLC-backed commercial paper trades as an obligation of the SLC issuer, excessive SLC issuance will reduce the value of the issuing bank's guarantee as well as the price of its own commercial paper.

---

* Based on information from an informal survey of large banks in the Twelfth Federal Reserve District conducted in August 1985.

**See Lloyd-Davies' article on standby letters of credit in *Below the Bottom Line,* a staff study of the Board of Governors of the Federal Reserve System, January 1982, for a more detailed discussion of the contractual terms of the LC agreement.

FOOTNOTES

1. Historically, banking laws have prohibited banks from offering financial and performance guarantees in order to preserve the traditional separation between banking and commerce in this country. Standby letters of credit (and commercial letters of credit, for that matter) are not technically guarantees, however, since the issuing bank's obligation under an SLC is to advance funds upon presentation of certain documents regardless of whether the underlying contract between the beneficiary and the account party has been performed to both parties' satisfaction.

2. Senior Loan Officer Opinion Survey conducted by the Federal Reserve System in August 1985.

3. Insurers traditionally have issued surety bonds which are, technically, performance guarantees. Lately, they have become active issuers of financial guarantees. Revenue from these two lines of business are reported together as revenues from surety operations.

4. Eric Gelman, et al, "Insurance: Now It's a Risky Business," *Newsweek,* November 4, 1985.

5. Senior Loan Officer Opinion Survey, August 1985.

6. Senior Loan Officer Opinion Survey, August 1985.

7. This estimate is based on the opportunity cost, at current interest rates, of the 3 percent marginal reserve requirement on large CDs.

8. For a more detailed discussion of the deposit insurance system and the risk-taking incentives it creates, please see the articles by Barbara Bennett and David Pyle in the Spring 1984 issue of the Federal Reserve Bank of San Francisco's *Economic Review.*

9. The Federal Reserve Board's proposed rules on risk-based capital guidelines were set forth in *Federal Register,* January 31, 1986, p. 3976. The comment period for this proposal extends until April 25, 1986.

10. For unsecured debt and SLCs, the relevant price is the value of the bank's prorated share of the firm's assets in a bankruptcy proceeding.

11. Black and Scholes have shown that an option's value is determined by the riskiness of the underlying asset (that is, variance of return on the asset), the option's term to maturity, and the level of the risk-free interest rate, as well as the level of the exercise price and the market value of the underlying asset.

12. Based on information from an informal survey of large banks in the Twelfth Federal Reserve District conducted in August 1985.

13. *Ibid.*

14. Survey of Terms of Lending at Commercial Banks, May 1985, conducted by the Federal Reserve System.

15. Peter Lloyd-Davies, "Survey of Standby Letters of Credit," *Federal Reserve Bulletin,* December 1979, pp. 716-719.

16. August 1985 survey of large 12th District banks.

17. Michael Goldberg and Peter Lloyd-Davies, "Standby Letters of Credit: Are Banks Overextending Themselves?," *Journal of Bank Research,* Spring 1985, pp. 28-39.

REFERENCES

Board of Governors of the Federal Reserve System, "Senior Loan Officer Opinion Survey on Bank Lending Practices," August 1985.

Brenner, Lynn. "Booming Financial Guarantees Market Generates Profits and Some Questions," *American Banker,* June 24, 1985.

----------. "The Illusory World of Guarantees," *American Banker,* June 25, 1985.

----------. "Regulators Worry About Guarantees," *American Banker,* June 26, 1985.

----------. "How Much Risk is Too Much?," *American Banker,* June 28, 1985.

Comptroller of the Currency, Federal Deposit Insurance Corporation and Federal Reserve Board, *Joint News Release,* January 15, 1986.

Copeland, Thomas E. and J. Fred Weston. *Financial Theory and Corporate Policy.* Reading: Addison-Wesley Publishing Co., 2nd Edition, 1983.

"Draft of Fed Proposed Rules on Risk-Based Capital Guidelines," *Washington Financial Reports,* January 20, 1986.

Forbes, Daniel, "Financial Guarantees: Providing New Hope to Insurers," *Risk Management,* October 1984.

Gelman, Eric, et al "Insurance: Now It's a Risky Business," *Newsweek,* November 4, 1985.

Goldberg, Michael and Peter Lloyd-Davies. "Standby Letters of Credit: Are Banks Overextending Themselves?," *Journal of Bank Research,* Spring 1985.

Judd, John. "Competition Between the Commercial Paper Market and Commercial Banks," *Economic Review,* Federal Reserve Bank of San Francisco, Winter 1979.

Lloyd-Davies, Peter. "Standby Letters of Credit of Commercial Banks" in *Below the Bottom Line,* a staff study of the Board of Governors of the Federal Reserve System, January 1982.

----------. "Survey of Standby Letters of Credit," *Federal Reserve Bulletin,* December 1979.

Lyons, Lois J. "Surety Industry At a Low Point," *National Underwriter,* May 17, 1985.

Verkuil, Paul R. "Bank Solvency and Guaranty Letters of Credit," *Stanford Law Review,* May 1973.